The Healthy Woman

A Complete Guide for All Ages

U.S. Department of Health and Human Services,
Office on Women's Health

U.S. GOVERNMENT OFFICIAL EDITION NOTICE

Legal Status and Use of Seals and Logos

The seal of the U.S. Department of Health and Human Services authenticates this publication as the Official U.S. Government edition of *The Healthy Woman: A Complete Guide for All Ages*. This consumer publication serves as a reference guide for women.

Under the provisions of 42 U.S.C. 1320b-10, the unauthorized use of this seal in a publication is prohibited and subject to a civil penalty of up to $5,000 for each unauthorized copy of it that is reprinted or distributed.

The Department of Health and Human Services is the U.S. Government's principal agency for protecting the health of all Americans and providing essential human services, especially for those who are least able to help themselves.

About OWH

The Office on Women's Health within the U.S. Department of Health and Human Services promotes health equity for women and girls by educating health professionals and motivating behavior change in consumers through the dissemination of health information.

Use of ISBN

This is the Official U.S. Government edition of this publication and is herein identified to certify its authenticity. Use of the ISBN 978-0-16-077183-5 is for the U. S. Government Printing Office Official Editions only. The Superintendent of Documents of the U.S. Government Printing Office requests that any reprinted edition be labeled clearly as a copy of the authentic work with a new ISBN.

For sale by the Superintendent of Documents, U.S. Government Printing Office
Internet: bookstore.gpo.gov Phone: toll free (866) 512-1800; DC area (202) 512-1800
Fax: (202) 512-2104 Mail: Stop IDCC, Washington, DC 20402-0001

ISBN 978-0-16-077183-5

Acknowledgments

The Department would like to thank the numerous departmental scientists and staff who served as expert reviewers of this guide, representing the following agencies:

Office of the Secretary, U.S. Department of Health and Human Services

Office of Public Health and Science

Centers for Disease Control and Prevention

Health Resources and Services Administration

U.S. Food and Drug Administration

Centers for Medicaid and Medicare Services

Indian Health Service

U.S. Administration on Aging

U.S. Environmental Protection Agency

National Institutes of Health

> National Cancer Institute; National Center for Complementary and Alternative Medicine; National Heart, Lung, and Blood Institute; National Institute of Allergy and Infectious Diseases; National Institute of Arthritis and Musculoskeletal and Skin Diseases; *Eunice Kennedy Shriver* National Institute of Child Health and Human Development; National Institute on Deafness and Other Communication Disorders; National Institute of Mental Health; National Institute of Neurological Disorders and Stroke; National Institute on Aging; National Institute of Dental and Craniofacial Research; National Institute of Diabetes and Digestive and Kidney Diseases; Warren Grant Magnuson Clinical Center of the National Institutes of Health

The Department also thanks the following individual expert reviewers for their contributions:

Suganya Sockalingam, Executive Director, TeamWorks

Cathy Carothers, BLA, IBCLC, RLC, Director of Marketing, International Lactation Consultants Association

Linda Smith, BSE, FACCE, IBCLC, RLC, Director, Bright Future Lactation Centre, Ltd.

Amy Spangler, MN, RN, IBCLC, RLC, President, Amy's Baby Company

Gina Ciagne, CLC (Certified Lactation Counselor), Director, Breastfeeding and Consumer Relations, Lansinoh Laboratories, Inc.

Cheryl Scacheri, MS, CGC, Director, Genetic Counseling Program, Genomic Medicine Institute, Cleveland Clinic Lerner Research Institute

Table of Contents

The Healthy Woman: A Complete Guide for All Ages

Foreword

A few years back I was at my doctor's office, talking with the nurse, asking for some advice. She told me, "Listen to your body."

I sat there and stared at her. I understood the words but I had no idea what she was talking about. "I don't listen to my body," I joked. "I tell my body what to do!" We both laughed but I was serious.

I always felt my body was something to be pushed and prodded into shape, deprived of sleep if necessary, deprived of food if I wanted to fit into a slinky dress. But here was a nurse telling me to be kind to my body. Listen to it. Follow its lead. Let it decide—not just my brain.

It took me a long time to really get it: that my body is me. That it's the only one I have. That it won't last forever. And that, by listening to my body, I can learn how to protect it, strengthen it, and, most of all, enjoy it, delight in it.

That's what this book is all about. Straight-ahead information on the things we can do to stay healthy, tests we should get to monitor our health, how to cope with disease, and how to talk with our doctors. Simply put, how to take charge of our own health.

It's the book I wish I'd had on a sunny day in October 1999, when I sat in another doctor's office, pen and notebook in hand, and heard him tell me I had breast cancer. After years of working as a CNN correspondent, reporting on civil wars and political upheaval, I thought I was ready for the news. I would just jot the information down, do some research, find treatment, and get on with my life.

I could hardly hold the pen. My hand shook. My heart was beating out of my chest.

Later that day, a bit calmer, I began to search for information on breast cancer. Even though my doctor was very helpful and began mapping out possible treatment strategies, I knew that, ultimately, I was the one who would have to decide which options to pursue and for that I needed information. I went to the bookstore, but one look at the rows and rows of books on every conceivable aspect of health and cancer completely overwhelmed me.

On the Internet it was even more confusing. Literally hundreds of millions of hits and links to different Web sites, with no guarantee that the information you find is trustworthy. What I needed was a guide, just like this one, written and reviewed by experts who know what they are talking about.

My experience taught me so much more than the details of cancer. I learned that I had a right, a responsibility to myself, to find the best doctors I could. If I could "shop 'til you drop" for a pair of shoes, I could shop until I dropped to find the doctor I trusted, a doctor who treated me like an adult, who respected me and my opinions. I got a second opinion … and even a third opinion. I almost gave up, but you know what? The last doctor I saw was absolutely the one I had dreamed of finding, who was positive and fun and made me feel that, ultimately, I would be all right.

I was lucky because the person I loved was there with me all the way, but I also learned that, even if I weren't so lucky, I didn't have to face things alone. I joined a breast cancer support group and some of my best memories are of the six of us, all with bald heads—sporting baseball caps, bandanas, or wigs—finding ways to laugh together, even during some of our darkest days.

Finally, I learned that my nurse was right; I really should "listen to my body." If I really love myself and want to live a healthy life—physically and mentally—there are things I can do to help make that happen. Sure, I don't always want to get a mammogram and no, I don't always want to make time for physical activity. And yes, there are things I sometimes am afraid to discuss with my doctor. But I can tell you from my own experience: there is nothing more empowering than being in control of decisions about my health. And, I am happy to say, there is nothing more fabulous than being a healthy woman!

Jill Dougherty
U.S. Affairs Editor
CNN International

Taking Charge of Your Health

Have you ever walked out of your doctor's office after a visit confused about what she or he just told you? If your answer is yes, you are not alone. Health issues can be complex and hard to understand.

At the same time, it seems that we are being asked to do more and more to improve our health. There are almost daily news reports about advice on eating certain foods or exercising to prevent certain diseases. Keeping track of all this information can seem overwhelming. And the sometimes conflicting advice clouds our understanding even more. Plus, if you have a family, you are likely making health choices not only for yourself, but also for them!

Although the matter of health can be challenging, there are ways to make it easier. To start, it is important to learn about the things you can and can't control.

Understanding risk factors: Learning what you can and can't control

Part of learning how to take charge of your health involves understanding your risk factors for different diseases. Risk factors are things in your life that increase your chances of getting a certain disease.

Some risk factors are beyond your control. You may be born with them or exposed to them through no fault of your own. Risk factors that you have little or no control over include your:

- family history of a disease
- sex

- ancestry
- age
- health—having one health problem may raise your risk of having another (for instance, having diabetes increases your chances of getting heart disease)

Risk factors you can control include:

- what you eat
- how much physical activity you get
- whether you use tobacco
- how much alcohol you drink
- whether you use illegal drugs
- whether you use your seatbelt

In fact, it has been estimated that almost 35 percent of all U.S. early deaths in 2000 could have been avoided by changing just three behaviors:

- stopping smoking

- eating a healthy diet (for example, eating more fruits and vegetables and less red meat)
- getting more physical activity

Having more than one risk factor

You can have one risk factor for a disease or you can have many. The more risk factors you have, the more likely you are to get the disease.

One doctor has suggested thinking of multiple risk factors for a disease in terms of your chances of breaking a leg when leaving a building.* If you're a healthy person and don't have any risk factors for, say, heart disease, it's like leaving the building on the ground floor. In this case, your chances of breaking a leg are small.

But let's say you have one risk factor for heart disease: diabetes. Now it's like leaving the building by jumping from the second floor. Your chances of breaking a leg are now greater. If you also have another risk factor, such as high blood pressure, it's like jumping from the third floor. If you also smoke tobacco, now you're jumping from the fourth floor.

To lower your risks, all you have to do is come down the stairs. In the case of heart disease, that means taking steps such as quitting smoking and controlling your blood pressure through healthy eating, physical activity, and taking medications.

Inheriting risk—your family health history

Rarely, you can inherit a mutated gene that alone causes you to get a disease. Genes control chemical reactions in our bodies. If you inherit a faulty gene, your body may not be able to carry out an important chemical reaction. For instance, a faulty gene may make your blood unable to clot. This problem is at the root of a rare bleeding disorder.

More often, you can inherit genes from one or both of your parents that put you at higher risk of certain diseases. But having a gene for a certain disease does not mean you will get it. There are many unknown factors that may raise or lower your chances of getting the disease.

You can't change your genes, but you can change behaviors that affect your health, such as smoking, inactivity, and poor eating habits. People with a family health history of chronic disease may have the most to gain from making lifestyle changes. In many cases, making these changes can reduce your risk of disease even if the disease runs in your family.

Another change you can make is to have screening tests, such as mammograms and colorectal cancer screening. These screening tests help detect disease early. People who have a family health history of a chronic disease may benefit the most from screening tests that look for risk factors or early signs of disease. Finding disease early, before symptoms appear, can mean better health in the long run.

How do I find out my disease risks?

It is important to talk to your doctor or nurse about your individual health risks, even if you have to bring it up yourself. And it's important for your doctor to know not just about your health, but your family health history as well. Come to health care visits armed with information about you, your children, siblings, parents, grandparents, aunts and uncles, and nieces and nephews, including:

- major medical conditions and causes of death
- age of disease onset and age at death
- ethnic background
- general lifestyle information like heavy drinking and smoking

Your doctor or health professional will assess your risk of disease based on your family health history and other risk factors. He or she may also recommend things you can do to help prevent disease, such as getting more physical activity, changing your diet, or using screening tests to detect disease early.

Web sites also can help you calculate your risks of getting certain diseases, some of which are listed on page 426 of the Appendix. **These online tools should never replace the information from or advice of a doctor or nurse.**

How this book can help you
In this book, we discuss the risk factors for major diseases that affect women—both those that you can control and those you can't. If it is possible to control a risk factor to lower your chances of getting a disease, we will tell you how. We will also discuss diseases for which causes and risk factors are not yet understood.

This book also explains:

- what happens to your body with certain diseases

- tips for handling many diseases and health conditions
- how to stay healthy during key phases of your life, such as during pregnancy and menopause
- how to communicate with doctors and nurses
- the screenings, tests, and immunizations women need
- where to find more health information that you can trust

In each chapter, besides important health tips, you will also find personal stories from women across the country. You may find that some of their experiences are similar to what you may be going through. Hopefully, these stories will show you that you are not alone.

How this book can help you help your family
As you learn about diseases that affect women, you will learn how to improve your family's health as well. Diseases such as heart disease, cancer, and stroke can, of course, affect men as well as women. Steps you can take to reduce your chances of getting these diseases can also apply to the men in your life. And because heart disease may start as early as childhood due to poor eating habits and lack of physical activity, your efforts may help your children lead longer and healthier lives.

What you do today counts—for you and your loved ones. Take charge of your health! ∎

*Edwards A. Communicating risks through analogies. *BMJ*. 2003;327:749.

Heart Disease

We used to think of heart disease as a man's problem. Now we know that it is the number one killer of women, just as it is of men. Yet women are more likely than men to be both underdiagnosed and undertreated. Fortunately, you have the power to impact your heart health in many ways! Commit to a healthy lifestyle that includes heart-healthy eating, regular physical activity, and not smoking. Understand the warning signs of a heart attack, because they can be different for women than for men. Let your doctor be your partner in helping you. And no matter how old you are, take action to protect your heart.

A woman's disease

Many women may not be aware that they are at risk of heart disease. Many doctors also make the mistake of thinking that heart disease strikes men more often than women. In fact, some research shows that doctors are more likely to diagnose and treat heart disease in a man than a woman, even if the two have the same symptoms.

Another problem is that until about 15 years ago, women were often not included in heart disease research. We assumed that the results of research involving men applied to women as well. Now we know this is not the case.

Still, we have learned a lot about heart disease in women—how to find out if you have the disease, how to treat it, and, most important, how to prevent it.

Coronary artery disease (CAD)

When people talk about heart disease, they usually mean coronary artery disease (CAD). It is the most common type of heart disease. With CAD, plaque builds up on the walls of the arteries that

How Your Heart Works

Your heart is a fist-sized muscle in the middle of your chest. An electrical system regulates its pumping action. With each heartbeat, blood is pumped through a large network of blood vessels. The blood supplies oxygen and nutrients to all the cells. It also picks up carbon dioxide and waste products from the cells. Arteries are the blood vessels that carry oxygen-rich blood away from the heart to all the parts of the body. The coronary arteries supply fresh blood to the heart itself, so it can work. Blood vessels that return blood from the body to the heart are called veins (vayns).

The heart has four chambers. The two upper chambers are called atria (AY-tree-uh). The two lower chambers are called ventricles. A system of inlet and outlet valves works to keep the blood flowing in the right direction.

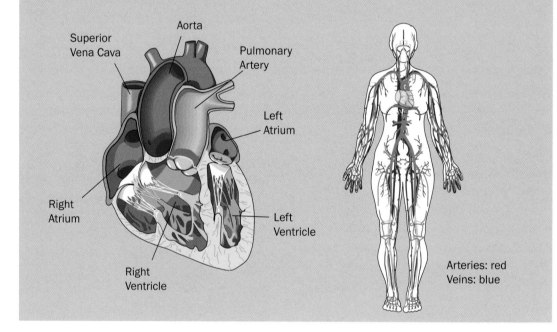

Superior Vena Cava
Aorta
Pulmonary Artery
Left Atrium
Right Atrium
Left Ventricle
Right Ventricle
Arteries: red
Veins: blue

carry blood to the heart. Over time, this buildup causes the arteries to narrow and harden, called atherosclerosis (a-thuh-roh-skluh-ROH-suhss). When this happens, the heart does not get all the blood it needs. This can lead to:

- **Angina** (an-JEYE-nuh)—chest pain or discomfort that happens when the heart doesn't get enough blood.

- **Heart attack**—happens when a clot mostly or completely blocks blood

flow to the heart muscle. Without blood the heart will start to die. If a person survives a heart attack, the injured area of the heart muscle is replaced by scar tissue. This weakens the pumping action of the heart.

Although there are different types of heart disease, the main type discussed here is coronary artery disease.

Heart Attack: Warning Signs

Many people think a heart attack is sudden and intense, like a "movie" heart attack, where a person clutches his or her chest and falls over.

The truth is that many heart attacks start slowly, as a mild pain or discomfort. If you feel such a symptom, you may not be sure what's wrong. Your symptoms may even come and go. Even those who have had a heart attack may not recognize their symptoms, because the next attack can have entirely different ones.

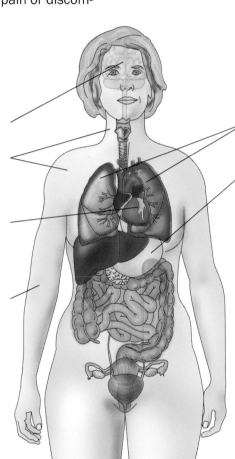

Head
Lightheadedness

Arm(s), Back, Jaw, Neck, Between Shoulders
Pain, discomfort, numbness

Chest
Pain, pressure, fullness or squeezing (lasts more than a few minutes or comes and goes)

Skin
Cold sweat

Lungs
Trouble breathing (shortness of breath)

Stomach
Upset stomach, urge to throw up

Other Signs
In addition, some women may feel very tired, sometimes for days or weeks before a heart attack occurs. Women may also have heartburn, a cough, or heart flutters or lose their appetite.

If you think that you are having a heart attack, you must act quickly to prevent disability or death. **Wait no more than a few minutes—5 at most—before calling 911.** Treatments for opening clogged arteries work best when given within the first hour after a heart attack starts.

Women are more likely than men to die of a heart attack. One reason is that women often have less-common heart attack symptoms, which might be misdiagnosed by a woman or even her doctor. If you think you're having a heart attack, don't let anyone tell you that you're overreacting or to wait and see. Get emergency help right away. Ask for tests that can show if you are having a heart attack. It's better to be safe than sorry.

Who is at risk of getting heart disease?

Risk factors are conditions or habits that make you more likely to develop heart disease. The more risk factors you have, the greater your chances of getting heart disease. Some risk factors, such as your age or family history, cannot be changed. But many risk factors can be changed by making simple changes in the way you live.

Risk factors that you can change

Abnormal blood cholesterol and triglyceride levels

Cholesterol (koh-LESS-tur-ol) and triglycerides (treye-GLIH-suh-ryds) are types of fat found in your blood and other parts of the body. They are carried in the blood by lipoproteins (lip-uh-PROH-teens). Your body needs small amounts of these substances to work well. But too much can lead to plaque buildup on your artery walls. In fact, plaque is made up mostly of unused cholesterol.

A blood test will help measure your levels of:

- **Low-density lipoprotein (LDL) or "bad" cholesterol**—High levels lead to buildup of cholesterol in arteries.

> **Unique to Women**
> - Low HDL cholesterol is more dangerous than having high LDL cholesterol.
> - High triglycerides combined with low HDL cholesterol can mean a very high risk of heart disease.

Risk factors that you can change (pages 18–25):
- Abnormal blood cholesterol and triglyceride levels
- High blood pressure
- Cigarette smoking
- Diabetes
- Being overweight or obese
- Metabolic syndrome
- Lack of physical activity
- Heavy alcohol use
- Sleep apnea

Risk factors that you cannot change (page 26):
- Age (55 years and older for women)
- Family history of early heart disease

Other possible risk factors (pages 26–28):
- Depression, anxiety, and stress
- Lower income
- Not enough sleep

- **High-density lipoprotein (HDL) or "good" cholesterol**—High levels are good. HDL cholesterol travels from other parts of your body to your liver, where it is processed to be removed from the body. This lowers the total cholesterol level in the body.
- **Total cholesterol**—LDL cholesterol plus HDL cholesterol
- **Triglycerides**

Ask your doctor for the results of your blood test and find out your risk in the table below. These numbers help measure your chances of getting heart disease. Nearly half of U.S. women are at borderline high or high risk of heart disease.

Some people have a tendency toward high cholesterol. But most cases of high cholesterol and triglyceride levels are from eating unhealthy foods, not exercising, and other lifestyle choices. In many cases, adopting a heart-healthy lifestyle can lower total cholesterol, LDL cholesterol, and triglyceride levels. In addition, moderate physical activity for at least 30 minutes on 5 or more days of the week can raise your HDL cholesterol levels. This can help reduce your heart disease risk.

If lifestyle changes do not bring your cholesterol and triglyceride levels back to normal, your doctor may prescribe one or more of these types of medicines:

- statins
- bile acid resins (REZ-ins)

Cholesterol and Triglyceride Levels and Heart Disease Risk

Cholesterol and triglyceride levels are measured in milligrams (mg) per deciliter (dL) of blood.

Total Cholesterol Level	Risk Group
Less than 200 mg/dL	Desirable
200–239 mg/dL	Borderline high
240 mg/dL and above	High

LDL Cholesterol Level	Risk Group
Less than 100 mg/dL	Optimal (ideal)
100–129 mg/dL	Near optimal/above optimal
130–159 mg/dL	Borderline high
160–189 mg/dL	High
190 mg/dL and above	Very high

HDL Cholesterol Level	Risk Group
Less than 40 mg/dL	High
60 mg/dL and above	Somewhat protective

Triglyceride Levels	Risk Group
Less than 150 mg/dL	Desirable
150–199 mg/dL	Borderline high
200 mg/dL and above	High

- fibrates
- cholesterol absorption inhibitors

High blood pressure (hypertension)

Blood pressure is the force your blood makes against the walls of your arteries. Your blood pressure is highest when your heart pumps blood into your arteries. This is called systolic (siss-TOL-ihk) pressure. It is lowest between beats, when the heart relaxes. This is called diastolic (deye-uh-STOL-ihk) pressure.

Your blood pressure varies throughout the day. But if your blood pressure stays above normal most of the time, then you have high blood pressure, or hypertension. If your blood pressure is borderline high, then you have prehypertension. This means that you don't have high blood pressure now but are likely to develop it in the future.

High blood pressure is called the "silent killer" because you can have no symptoms. But years of high blood pressure can damage artery walls, causing atherosclerosis and heart disease. High blood pressure is a common problem among women, especially African American women.

If you have hypertension or prehypertension, you may be able to lower your blood pressure by:

- losing weight if you are overweight or obese
- getting 30 minutes of moderate-intensity physical activity on most days of the week
- limiting alcohol to one drink per day
- quitting smoking if you smoke
- eating foods that are good for your heart
- reducing stress

If lifestyle changes do not lower your blood pressure back to normal, your doctor may prescribe medicine. Some types commonly used to treat hypertension include:

- diuretics (deye-yoo-RET-ihks)
- beta blockers
- calcium channel blockers
- angiotensin (an-jee-oh-TEN-suhn) converting enzyme (ACE) inhibitors
- angiotensin II receptor blockers (ARBs)

If you have hypertension or prehypertension, you should also know that you may be at increased risk of developing type 2 diabetes (see Diabetes section on page 21). You should get tested for type 2 dia-

Blood Pressure Categories

	Systolic (mmHg)*	Diastolic (mmHg)*
Normal	Less than 120	Less than 80
Prehypertension	120–139	80–89
Hypertension	140 or higher	90 or higher

*mmHg means millimeters of mercury.

betes if your blood pressure readings:

- are too high
- are borderline high
- have been steadily increasing for the last several years but are still in the normal range

Cigarette smoking

The more you smoke, the higher your risk of heart disease. In fact, about half of all heart attacks in women are due to smoking. What's more, if you smoke and also take birth control pills, you are at high risk of heart disease.

If you are among the nearly 1 in 5 women in the United States who smokes, now is the time to quit. Talk to

your doctor if you need help. There are medicines that can help you quit. Counseling and support groups can also be helpful.

Diabetes

Diabetes is a disease in which blood glucose (sugar) levels are too high. Type 2 diabetes—the most common type— usually begins after the age of 40, often in people who are overweight or obese. Uncontrolled diabetes can damage artery walls, leading to atherosclerosis and heart disease. In fact, uncontrolled diabetes raises a woman's risk of heart disease more than it does for a man. Also, women with diabetes do not recover as well from a heart attack as men with diabetes do.

If you have type 2 diabetes and are overweight or obese, you might be able to lower your blood glucose levels back to normal by losing weight. If this doesn't work, your doctor might give you medicines or insulin, a hormone that lowers blood glucose levels.

For more information on type 2 diabetes, see the *Type 2 Diabetes* chapter on page 69.

Being overweight or obese

The more overweight you are, the higher your risk of heart disease—even if you have no other risk factors. Being overweight or obese also raises your chances of developing diabetes, high blood pressure, and high blood cholesterol.

Being overweight or obese is common among women in the United States, especially among African American and Hispanic women.

How do you know if you are overweight or obese? Use the chart below to find your height and weight. The point at which the two meet is your body mass index (BMI).

BMI	Normal weight						Overweight					Obese			
	19	20	21	22	23	24	25	26	27	28	29	30	35	40	45
Height	Weight (lb.)														
4'7"	82	86	90	95	99	103	108	112	116	120	125	129	151	172	194
4'8"	85	89	94	98	103	107	112	116	120	125	129	134	156	178	201
4'9"	88	92	97	102	106	111	116	120	125	129	134	139	162	185	208
4'10"	91	96	100	105	110	115	119	124	129	134	138	143	167	191	215
4'11"	94	99	104	109	114	119	124	128	133	138	143	148	173	198	222
5'0"	97	102	107	112	118	123	128	133	138	143	148	153	179	204	230
5'1"	100	106	111	116	122	127	132	137	143	148	153	158	185	211	238
5'2"	104	109	115	120	126	131	136	142	147	153	158	164	191	218	246
5'3"	107	113	118	124	130	135	141	146	152	158	163	169	197	225	254
5'4"	110	116	122	128	134	140	145	151	157	163	169	174	204	232	262
5'5"	114	120	126	132	138	144	150	156	162	168	174	180	210	240	270
5'6"	118	124	130	136	142	148	155	161	167	173	179	186	216	247	278
5'7"	121	127	134	140	146	153	159	166	172	178	185	191	223	255	287
5'8"	125	131	138	144	151	158	164	171	177	184	190	197	230	262	295
5'9"	128	135	142	149	155	162	169	176	182	189	196	203	236	270	304
5'10"	132	139	146	153	160	167	174	181	188	195	202	207	243	278	313
5'11"	136	143	150	157	165	172	179	186	193	200	208	215	250	286	322
6'0"	140	147	154	162	169	177	184	191	199	206	213	221	258	294	331
6'1"	144	151	159	166	174	182	189	197	204	212	219	227	265	302	340
6'2"	148	155	163	171	179	186	194	202	210	218	225	233	272	311	350
6'3"	152	160	168	176	184	192	200	208	216	224	232	240	279	319	359
6'4"	156	164	172	180	189	197	205	213	221	230	238	246	287	328	369
6'5"	160	169	177	186	194	202	211	219	228	236	245	253	295	337	380
6'6"	164	173	182	190	199	208	216	225	234	242	251	260	303	346	390
6'7"	169	178	186	195	204	213	222	231	240	249	251	266	311	355	400

BMI calculators can be found at some of the Web sites listed at the end of this chapter.

Once you have found your BMI, check it against the ranges below:

Normal weight: BMI = 18.5–24.9

Overweight: BMI = 25–29.9

Obese: BMI = 30 or higher

For women, a waist size of more than 35 inches also increases heart disease risk. This is because fat located in the abdomen increases atherosclerosis more than fat located in other areas, such as the hips.

If you are overweight, obese, or your waist size is more than 35 inches, losing weight can help prevent health problems like heart disease and diabetes. Work with your doctor to create a weight-loss plan that stresses heart-healthy foods and regular physical activity.

Metabolic syndrome

Having metabolic (met-uh-BOL-ihk) syndrome doubles your risk of getting heart disease or having a stroke. You have it if you have any 3 of these 5 risk factors:

- waist measurement of more than 35 inches

- triglyceride level more than 150 mg/dL

- HDL cholesterol level less than 50 mg/dL

- systolic blood pressure greater than or equal to 130 mmHg or diastolic blood pressure greater than or equal to 85 mmHg

- blood glucose level after fasting for at least 8 hours of greater than 110 mg/dL

Taking steps to eliminate these risk factors will improve your heart and, overall, health.

Lack of physical activity

Lack of physical activity increases your heart disease risk, even if you have no other risk factors for heart disease. It also increases your chances of developing high blood pressure and diabetes and of being overweight or obese. If finding time to be physically active seems like an impossible challenge, take heart. As little as 30 minutes of moderate-intensity physical activity on most, if not all, days of the week helps protect your heart. You can even split this time into three segments of at least 10 minutes each.

Drinking alcohol

Heavy drinking causes many heart-related problems. More than 3 drinks per day can raise blood pressure and triglyceride levels. Too much alcohol also can damage the heart muscle, leading to heart failure. Overall, people who drink heavily on a regular basis have more heart problems than either moderate drinkers or nondrinkers.

However, moderate drinkers are less likely to develop heart disease than people who don't drink any alcohol or who drink too much. Red wine drinkers in particular seem to be protected to some degree against heart disease. Red wine contains flavonoids (FLAY-vuh-noidz), which are thought to prevent plaque buildup. Red grapes, berries, apples, and broccoli also contain flavonoids.

Drinking more than one drink per day increases the risks of certain cancers, including breast cancer. And if you are pregnant, planning to become pregnant, or have another health condition that could make alcohol use harmful, you should not drink.

Alcohol

If you drink alcohol, drink no more than one drink per day. One drink is counted as:

- 5 ounces of wine
- 12 ounces of beer
- 1½ ounces of 80-proof hard liquor

With the help of your doctor, decide whether moderate drinking to lower heart attack risk outweighs the possible increased risk of breast cancer or other medical problems. If you do decide to drink alcohol, remember that moderation is the key.

Sleep apnea

Has anyone ever told you that you snore? Loud snoring can be a sign of sleep apnea (AP-nee-uh), a sleep disorder that can raise your chances of having a heart attack. With obstructive sleep apnea—the most common type—the tissue in the back of the throat relaxes and blocks airflow to your lungs. This lowers the oxygen level in your blood, which makes your heart work harder and often leads to high blood pressure. Also, these repeated pauses in breathing cause fragmented sleep, which results in daytime sleepiness.

Women are more likely to develop obstructive sleep apnea after menopause.

Heart-Healthy Eating

Eating a healthy diet is a powerful way to impact your heart health. It can lower and possibly eliminate many key risk factors for heart disease, including:

- high cholesterol and triglyceride levels
- high blood pressure
- diabetes
- obesity and overweight

When striving to eat heart healthy, a special eating plan called the DASH eating plan can help guide your food choices. It also will help lower your blood pressure if it is too high. DASH stands for Dietary Approaches to Stop Hypertension. The DASH eating plan:

- stresses low-cholesterol foods that are good for your heart, such as fruits and vegetables; whole-grain breads and other foods; low-fat (1 percent) or fat-free milk and dairy products; nuts, seeds, and beans; and moderate amounts of skinless poultry and fish*
- is rich in magnesium, potassium, calcium, protein, and fiber
- is low in saturated fat, *trans* fat, and total fat
- limits red meat, sweets, and sugary drinks

*Oily fish like salmon, herring, and tuna contain omega-3 fatty acids, which have been shown to reduce your risk of dying of heart disease. Also, taking omega-3 fatty

Other things that may increase the risk of obstructive sleep apnea are:

- being overweight or obese
- smoking
- using alcohol or sleeping pills
- a family history of sleep apnea

If you think that you have sleep apnea, talk with your doctor. Your doctor might suggest a sleep test to see how severe your sleep apnea is. Mild cases often can be helped by lifestyle changes, such as losing weight and not drinking alcohol before bed. If you have severe obstructive sleep apnea or another type, your doctor may suggest other treatments, such as using a machine that props open your airway during sleep or having surgery.

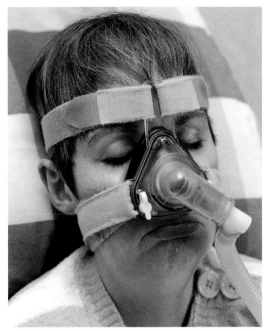

A SPECIAL DEVICE HELPS PEOPLE WITH SLEEP APNEA BREATHE FREELY AND SLEEP SOUNDLY.

acids in capsule form might help women with heart disease or high triglyceride levels. If you have these problems, ask your doctor if you should take omega-3 supplements.

If you need to lower your blood pressure, eating less sodium also might help. Sodium is found in table salt and processed foods, such as canned soups, snacks, and deli meats. Many grocery stores sell salt substitutes that provide the flavor of salt without the sodium.

Another eating plan, called the Therapeutic Lifestyle Changes (TLC) eating plan, is designed for people whose LDL cholesterol levels are too high. The TLC eating plan will help to reduce your LDL cholesterol and lower your chances of developing heart disease. If you already have heart disease, it will lessen your chances of a heart attack and other heart-related problems. On the TLC eating plan, you should eat as follows:

- Less than 7 percent of the day's total calories from saturated fat. Lowering saturated fat is the most important dietary change for reducing blood cholesterol.
- Less than 200 mg of dietary cholesterol a day.
- No more than 25 to 35 percent of daily calories from total fat (includes saturated fat calories).
- Just enough calories to reach or maintain a healthy weight. (Ask your doctor or registered dietitian what is a reasonable calorie level for you.)

For more information on heart-healthy eating, see the *Nutrition* chapter on page 317.

Risk factors that you cannot change

Age

Women develop heart disease about 10 to 15 years later than men. This is because until you reach menopause, your ovaries make the hormone estrogen, which protects against plaque buildup. But once you reach menopause, your ovaries stop making estrogen and your risk of developing heart disease goes up. By age 70, women have about the same chances of developing heart disease as same-aged men.

Even apart from the increased risk brought on by menopause, getting older is a risk factor for heart disease in women. With age, arteries stiffen and thicken. Also, systolic blood pressure often goes up. These and other changes contribute to plaque buildup in artery walls.

Family history of early heart disease

Women with a father or brother who developed heart disease before age 55 are more likely to develop heart disease. Women with a mother or sister who developed heart disease before age 65 are also more likely to develop the disease. These trends suggest that you can inherit genes that increase your risk of heart disease. Still, young women with a family history appear to be less aware of

Other conditions such as chronic kidney failure can raise your risk of heart disease. Discuss your health and your risk with your doctor. This information will help your doctor decide how best to care for you.

their risks and less careful about living a heart-healthy lifestyle than men with a family history.

Other possible risk factors

Depression, anxiety, and stress

Negative emotions— such as depression, anxiety, and anger—have all been shown to increase your chances of developing or dying of heart disease. We don't know why this is so. Perhaps being depressed, anxious, or angry leads to behaviors that put your heart health at risk, such as smoking, drinking, and eating high-fat foods. It is also possible that negative emotions affect the body in ways that trigger atherosclerosis or blood clot formation within arteries.

Stress also appears to be linked to heart health in some way. Here are some examples:

- **Work stress.** Feelings that you have little control over what happens to you at work or that you are not being rewarded enough for the work that you do have been linked to getting heart disease.

- **Stress at home.** If you are caring for a disabled or ill spouse, the stress of this role may raise your risk of heart attack.

- **Combined stress.** Being stressed both at work and at home has been shown to increase your chances of having a heart attack or severe angina more than either type of stress by itself.

- **Low social support.** People with few friends or family to help them deal with stress are more likely to develop heart disease.

If you're unhappy with your life or feel distressed in some way, talk to your doctor. Although we don't know if treating emotional problems or reducing stress can lower your chances of getting heart disease, doing so can boost your emotional health and overall well-being.

For more information on managing stress, see the *Mental Health* chapter on page 207.

Lower income

Research shows that lower income adults have an increased risk of heart disease. Also, children born into lower income families are more likely to have heart disease in adulthood. There are many possible reasons for this link. For instance, low-income adults are less likely to be physically active and eat a heart-healthy diet, and they are more likely to smoke.

It can be difficult to eat a heart-healthy diet in lower income neighborhoods. Many of these neighborhoods lack a grocery store that sells fresh fruits and vegetables. Or if they do, these items may be too costly. People in some of these neighborhoods have dealt with these problems by forming food co-ops that buy fresh fruits and vegetables in bulk and then sell them at low prices.

Also, it can be difficult to be physically active in neighborhoods that are unsafe. Some communities have dealt with this problem by creating physical activity programs at local recreation centers or churches. Contact your local parks department and churches to see if any such programs exist in your community.

Not enough sleep

Most adults need 7 to 9 hours of sleep to feel well rested during the day. Your heart needs a good night's sleep too. Sleeping 5 hours or less each night doubles the risk of high blood pressure for people between the ages of 32 and 59. One reason for this may be that feeling cranky, tired, and stressed due to lack of sleep makes it harder to follow a heart-

healthy lifestyle. Try these tips to get the good quality sleep your heart needs:

- Go to bed and wake up at the same time each day (even weekends).

- Engage in a relaxing activity before bed, such as reading or taking a bath.

- Make sure your bedroom is dark, quiet, and cool.

- Use your bed for sleep and sex only.

- Don't eat or become physically active for several hours before sleep.

- Avoid alcohol, caffeine, and nicotine close to bedtime.

Can menopausal hormone therapy prevent heart disease?

Some research has shown that women who start estrogen or certain types of hormone therapy around the time of menopause are less likely to get heart disease. But a very large study by the U.S. National Institutes of Health (NIH) had different results. The NIH research found that:

- Estrogen alone didn't affect the risk of a heart attack. Estrogen did increase the risk of stroke. Estrogen also increased the risk of blood clots in the legs.

- Estrogen plus progestin may have slightly increased the risk of a heart attack. Progestin is a man-made form of the female hormone progesterone (proh-JESS-tuh-rohn). Estrogen plus progestin raised the risk of stroke and blood clots in the legs and lungs.

Researchers continue to study this issue. The age at which menopausal hormone therapy is started may be the key to whether this therapy reduces your chanc-es of getting heart disease. Most of the women in the NIH study did not start menopausal hormone therapy until after the age of 60, yet menopause happens for most women after the age of 45. Some experts think that many of the women in the NIH study may have already developed atherosclerosis because of many years in which their estrogen levels were low. This would explain why estrogen did not protect against heart disease in the study.

More research on younger women may support the use of some kind of menopausal hormone therapy to prevent heart disease. And more research will be needed to ensure that the benefits of such a therapy outweigh its risks.

For now, the safest option for menopausal hormone therapy is to stick with the lowest dose for the shortest time to treat menopausal symptoms or prevent osteoporosis (OSS-tee-oh-puh-ROH-suhss), but not to prevent heart disease. For more information on menopausal hormone therapy, see the *Healthy Aging* chapter on page 221.

Can antioxidant or folic acid supplements prevent heart disease?

Antioxidants (an-tee-OKS-uh-duhnts), such as beta carotene and vitamins A, C, and E, and folate are substances found naturally in many foods. They can also be taken as dietary supplements, either in pill form or added to food. Some early research suggested that taking antioxidant supplements might prevent atherosclerosis. But more recent research has not found this to be the case. The best way to get your antioxidants is by eating fruits, vegetables, whole-grain products, and nuts.

As with antioxidants, some early research suggested that taking folic acid supplements might reduce the risk of heart disease. But more recent research has not found this to be the case. Currently, the American Heart Association does not recommend that women use folic acid supplements to prevent heart disease. Even so, you need some folic acid in your diet to help your body make blood cells. Folic acid also is very important for women who are or plan to become pregnant.

Questions to Ask Your Doctor or Nurse

Getting answers to these questions will give you vital information about your heart health and what you can do to improve it. You may want to bring this list with you to your visit with your doctor or nurse.

1. What is my risk of heart disease?
2. What is my blood pressure? What does it mean for me, and what do I need to do about it?
3. What are my cholesterol numbers? (These include total cholesterol, LDL or "bad" cholesterol, HDL or "good" cholesterol, and triglycerides.) What do they mean for me, and what do I need to do about them?
4. What are my "body mass index" and waist measurement? Do they indicate that I need to lose weight for my health?
5. What is my blood glucose level, and does it mean I'm at risk of diabetes?
6. What other screening tests for heart disease do I need? How often should I return for checkups for my heart health?
7. What can you do to help me quit smoking?
8. How much physical activity do I need to help protect my heart?
9. What is a heart-healthy eating plan for me? Should I see a registered dietitian or qualified nutritionist to learn more about healthy eating?
10. How can I tell if I'm having a heart attack?

Diagnosing heart disease

If your doctor suspects that you have heart disease, there are a number of tests that she can perform to find out for sure. You may get just one test or more than one. It's normal to feel worried or anxious before having tests. Tell your doctor if your fears are keeping you from getting the tests you need.

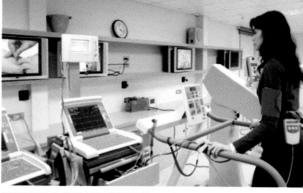

SOME TESTS, SUCH AS ELECTROCARDIOGRAPHY AND ECHOCARDIOGRAPHY, ARE DONE WHILE EXERCISING TO SEE HOW THE HEART PERFORMS UNDER STRESS.

Test	What it tells your doctor
Electrocardiography (ih-lek-troh-kar-dee-OG-ruh-fee), or ECG or EKG	Shows how well your heart performs under the stress of physical activity using electrodes placed on the body
Perfusion imaging	A safe, radioactive substance is injected into the blood and viewed with a special camera to look for blockage in your coronary artery or damage to your heart muscle due to a heart attack
Echocardiography (ek-oh-kar-dee-OG-ruh-fee)	Sound waves create a moving picture of your heart as it beats, which can show if your heart is damaged or not getting enough blood
Coronary angiography (an-jee-OG-ruh-fee)	Detects problems in blood flow in a coronary artery using x-ray and a dye that is injected into the blood
Blood tests	Show if you've had a heart attack by detecting substances that are released into the blood when the heart muscle is damaged
Computed tomography (tuh-MOG-ruh-fee) (CT)	Uses x-ray to show plaque buildup and to detect early stages of atherosclerosis
Computed tomography angiography	Uses x-ray to produce three-dimensional pictures of the heart and its coronary arteries to detect blockages
Gated single photon (FOH-ton) emission computed tomography, or gated SPECT	A safe, radioactive substance is injected into the blood and viewed with a special camera to look for problems with blood flow to the heart, heart damage, or problems pumping blood throughout the body

Treating heart disease

If you have heart disease, it is extremely important to control it. You can help to do this by:

- eating a heart-healthy diet
- quitting smoking if you smoke
- getting regular physical activity
- losing weight if you are overweight or obese
- reducing stress
- taking medicines as directed by your doctor

For more information on healthy eating, see the *Nutrition* chapter on page 317. For more information on physical activity, see the *Fitness* chapter on page 337.

Medicines

Along with making lifestyle changes, you may need medicines to help control your heart disease. These medicines can include:

- cholesterol-lowering medicines
- beta blockers, calcium channel blockers, or ACE inhibitors to lower blood pressure and lighten the workload for the heart

At times, other medicines may be needed:

- Antiplatelet medicines stop blood cells called platelets from clumping together and forming clots.
- Anticoagulants stop clots from forming in your arteries and blocking blood flow.
- Nitrates, such as nitroglycerin (neye-truh-GLISS-ur-uhn), widen the coronary arteries, which helps lessen chest pain.
- Thrombolytic (throm-buh-LIT-ihk) agents break up blood clots that form during a heart attack. The sooner these drugs are given to someone having a heart attack, the better they are at preventing heart damage.

Special procedures or surgery

If lifestyle changes and medicines do not improve your heart disease symptoms, your doctor may suggest special procedures or surgery. These include:

- **Angioplasty** (AN-jee-uh-plass-tee). This procedure is usually done right away if coronary angiography shows problems in blood flow in a coronary artery. A thin tube with a balloon at one end is threaded into a coronary artery that has narrowed because of plaque buildup. Once in place, the balloon is inflated to push the plaque against the artery wall. This opens the artery more so that blood can flow freely.
- **Stent.** A stent is a mesh tube used to hold open a narrowed or weakened artery. It is put in place during an angioplasty. Some stents are coated with a medicine to keep arteries from narrowing or becoming blocked again. Not all people who have angioplasty need a stent.
- **Coronary artery bypass surgery.** In this procedure, a short piece of vein or artery from another part of your

Aspirin

One well-known antiplatelet medicine is aspirin. In fact, aspirin is given right away to anyone suspected of having a heart attack. Your doctor may also suggest that you take aspirin every day if you are at risk of heart disease. If you are younger than 65 years and are at low risk of heart disease, your doctor will probably not suggest that you take aspirin.

Aspirin may not be good for some women because it can cause side effects. These include bleeding in the stomach, intestines, and brain. If you're thinking about using aspirin to treat or prevent heart problems, talk with your doctor first.

body is used to reroute blood around a blockage in a coronary artery. This restores blood flow to the heart.

Other types of heart disease

Other types of heart disease that affect many women include heart failure and arrhythmias (uh-RITH-mee-uhz). These can result from coronary artery disease or other problems.

Heart failure

Heart failure happens when the heart can't pump enough blood throughout the body. Heart failure doesn't mean that your heart has stopped or is about to stop working. It means that your heart can't fill with enough blood or pump with enough force, or both.

Heart failure develops over time as the pumping action of the heart grows weaker.

It's more common in people older than 65 years. Coronary artery disease, high blood pressure, and diabetes are leading causes.

Heart failure can affect the left side, the right side, or both sides of the heart. Most cases involve the left side, in which the heart can't pump enough blood to the rest of the body. As a result, blood and fluid back up in the lungs and you feel short of breath.

When the right side of the heart is affected, blood backs up in the body, causing swelling, mainly in the lower legs and ankles. If both sides of the heart are failing, which is often the case, you also feel tired and weak because not enough blood is flowing to your muscles.

Heart failure usually can't be cured. Treatment often involves making lifestyle changes and taking medicines. If you have severe heart failure, you may need a mechanical heart pump or a heart transplant.

Arrhythmia

An arrhythmia is a problem with the speed or rhythm of the heartbeat caused by a disorder in the heart's electrical system. There are many types of arrhythmias. Most are harmless, but some can be serious or even life threatening.

The most common type of serious arrhythmia is atrial fibrillation (fib-ruh-LAY-shuhn), or AF. With AF, the walls of the atria quiver very fast (called fibrillation) instead of beating normally. As a result, blood isn't pumped into the ventricles as it should, and it pools in the atria. This can cause blood clots to form in the atria. If a clot breaks off, it might get stuck in a blood vessel and cut off blood supply to the brain. This is a type of stroke. People with AF sometimes take blood thinners to prevent clots and medicines to slow the heart rate.

Arrhythmias that start in the ventricles can be very dangerous. With ventricular fibrillations (v-fib), blood is not pumped out to the body. If the heart stops pumping entirely, the condition is known as sudden cardiac arrest. In a sudden cardiac arrest, a person will faint within seconds and die within minutes if not treated quickly.

Cardiac Arrest

A sudden cardiac arrest is not the same as a heart attack. In a heart attack, the heart usually does not suddenly stop beating. But sudden cardiac arrest may happen during recovery from a heart attack.

Sudden cardiac arrest requires immediate treatment with a defibrillator (dee-FIB-ruh-lay-tur), a device that sends an electrical shock to the heart to restore normal rhythm.

If you suspect that someone is in sudden cardiac arrest, call 911 immediately. With every minute of delay in providing defibrillation, the chances of surviving sudden cardiac arrest drop rapidly.

Living with heart disease

If you are taking medicines or have undergone special procedures or surgery to treat coronary artery disease, you still need to stick with those healthy lifestyle changes to keep plaque from clogging up your arteries again. Follow your doctor's advice on what foods to eat, how to ease back into a physical activity routine if you have had surgery, and how to reduce stress. And if you smoke, it is vital that you quit.

Taking care of your emotional health is also important. People with heart disease are often depressed, especially those who have had a heart attack. If you have heart disease and find yourself feeling depressed or "blue," talk with your doctor about ways to get help.

Treating depression may do more than just help you feel better emotionally. If you have had a heart attack, antidepressants may lower your chances of having a second heart attack or dying of heart disease. So don't wait to seek help if you are feeling down.

Good news about heart health

More women are becoming aware that they are at risk of heart disease, which is the crucial first step. Even better, more women are also taking heart-healthy action.

If you haven't already joined this growing trend of heart-savvy women, now is the time to start. Urge your children and other family members to join you in your efforts to lower heart disease risk. Living heart healthy takes effort. But the rewards can mean a healthier, longer life for you and your loved ones. ∎

One Woman's Story

On a Wednesday I told my doctor that my right hand had been numb for about a month. He agreed that it sounded like carpal tunnel syndrome. But he also suggested I have an electrocardiogram (ECG or EKG), which turned out to be abnormal. On hearing this, I figured it was due to rushing and not eating breakfast or lunch.

The next day I stayed home from work. I couldn't say exactly why—just that I felt extra sensitive and couldn't imagine being around a lot of people. The same thing happened on Friday. I left my laptop open at work with unfinished spreadsheets neatly displayed. I left personal letters, without stamps, waiting to be mailed. This was not at all like me.

After an errand, I could no longer dismiss the feelings of radiating pain—heartbeats of pain. My chest felt heavy. It felt like a pair of really big hands was squeezing my chest, like an elephant's enormous feet were pressing outward on my chest. When my husband came home I told him my back and chest hurt and that I needed to go to the hospital.

Blood tests at the hospital showed that I had not had a heart attack, and the cardiologist said, "You're young and a woman. I think it's probably acid reflux, and women have abnormal EKGs. Let's schedule a stress/echo test this week. Since it's the weekend, you'll feel better at home."

I didn't believe for one minute that I had acid reflux. But did I say anything? No. But it's easy to feel stupid against someone in a position of authority.

> **We must make ourselves our number one cause and, as with me, be given another chance at life.**

As it turns out, much worse back pain sent me back to the hospital. I had an angiogram, and the next day I signed papers for open-heart surgery or another angiography with stent deployment. My life was forever changed that day, the day I was told I had coronary artery disease—premature heart disease, which I inherited from my father, who died young.

My mission is to send a warning to women. We must make ourselves our number one cause and, as with me, be given another chance at life. You are your own best advocate and you deserve to be heard.

Lois

La Habra, California

For More Information...

Office on Women's Health, HHS
200 Independence Ave SW, Room 712E
Washington, DC 20201
Web site: www.womenshealth.gov/heart
www.womenshealth.gov/faq/heartdis.htm
Phone number: (800) 994-9662,
(888) 220-5446 TDD

**National Heart, Lung, and Blood Institute
Health Information Center, NIH**
PO Box 30105
Bethesda, MD 20824-0105
Web site: www.nhlbi.nih.gov
www.hearttruth.gov
Phone number: (301) 592-8573,
(240) 629-3255 TTY

Office of Women's Health, FDA
5600 Fishers Ln
Rockville, MD 20857
Web site: www.fda.gov/womens
Phone number: (888) 463-6332

WISEWOMAN – Well-Integrated Screening and Evaluation for Women Across the Nation, CDC
4770 Buford Hwy NE, MS K-77
Atlanta, GA 30341-3717
Web site: www.cdc.gov/wisewoman
Phone number: (800) 232-4636,
(888) 232–6348 TTY

American Heart Association
7272 Greenville Ave
Dallas, TX 75231
Web site: www.americanheart.org
Phone number: (800) 242-8721

Sister to Sister
4701 Willard Ave, Suite 223
Chevy Chase, MD 20815
Web site: www.sistertosister.org

Texas Heart Institute Heart Information Center
PO Box 20345
Houston, TX 77225-0345
Web site: www.texasheartinstitute.org/HIC
Phone number: (800) 292-2221

Stroke

If you are having a stroke, you need to be taken to the hospital right away. Thankfully, there are stroke treatments that can increase your chances of walking away from an attack with few or no disabilities. But you have to get these treatments within 3 hours from the start of your symptoms for them to work. Be aware of the signs of stroke so you can help yourself or someone else get vital treatment.

What is a stroke?

A stroke occurs when part of your brain doesn't get the blood that it needs. A stroke is sometimes called a "brain attack." This is because, like a heart attack, a stroke involves the loss of blood flow, leading to the death of cells. In fact, without blood, your brain cells start to die within minutes.

There are two types of stroke:

- **Ischemic (ih-SKEE-mik) stroke—** When a blood vessel bringing blood to the brain becomes blocked. For instance, a blood clot may form within

What are the symptoms of a stroke?

A stroke happens fast. The most common signs of a stroke are sudden:

- numbness or weakness of the face, arm, or leg, especially on one side of the body
- trouble seeing in one or both eyes
- trouble walking, dizziness, or loss of balance or coordination
- confusion or trouble speaking or understanding
- severe headache with no known cause

If you have any of these symptoms or see anyone with these symptoms, call 911 right away. Every minute counts!

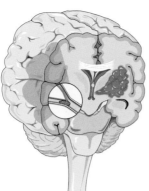

ISCHEMIC STROKE

What is a "mini-stroke"?

If you have signs of a stroke that don't last long, you've had what is called a transient ischemic attack (TIA), or "mini-stroke." TIAs typically last from 5 to 15 minutes, with no lasting symptoms. They are often caused by a blood clot getting stuck in a brain artery for a short time but then breaking up, allowing the blood to flow freely again. If your symptoms last longer than 24 hours, then you've had a major stroke rather than a TIA.

> If you're having stroke symptoms, there's no way of knowing whether you're having a TIA or a major stroke. You should still call 911 as soon as possible.

Even a "mini-stroke" is considered a stroke and needs treatment. A TIA is often a sign that you may have a major stroke in the near future—perhaps in the next few days. Your doctor may prescribe medicines or surgery that may help you

the heart or an artery in the neck. The clot is carried by the blood to the brain, where it gets stuck in a smaller artery. There, it cuts off blood flow to a part of the brain. About 80 percent of strokes are ischemic strokes.

- **Hemorrhagic (hem-ur-RAJ-ihk) stroke**—When a blood vessel in or on the surface of the brain breaks open. As a result, blood flows into the wrong areas. This blood, which would normally supply brain cells with oxygen and nutrients, can no longer get to these cells. Also, this blood in the wrong areas puts pressure on nearby brain cells. For both of these reasons, brain cells die. In an intracerebral (ihn-truh-suh-REE-bruhl) hemorrhage, the blood flows into the brain itself. In a subarachnoid (suhb-uh-RAK-noid) hemorrhage, the blood flows into a thin space outside the brain but still inside the skull. About 20 percent of strokes are hemorrhagic strokes.

If you're having a stroke, you may not be able to call 911. In fact, you may not even be able to move or talk! In most stroke cases, it's a family member, coworker, or other bystander who calls 911. That's why everyone should become familiar with the signs of a stroke.

avoid having a major stroke that could cause lasting damage.

Your doctor may give you aspirin or some other drug to reduce blood clotting. Your doctor may also recommend a type of surgery called carotid endarterectomy (kuh-ROT-ihd en-dar-tuh-REK-tuh-mee). In this procedure, the carotid artery in the neck is opened up and plaque is removed from the artery walls. This allows the blood to flow more freely in the artery and reduces the chances of a clot forming.

Another way to open a clogged carotid artery is to insert a stent. A stent is a tiny, slender metal-mesh tube that can be expanded to keep an artery open. A stent placed in a carotid artery is very similar to a stent placed in an artery in the heart for treating coronary artery disease. (See page 31 of the *Heart Disease* chapter for more information on stents.)

Who is at risk of having a stroke?

Although anyone can have a stroke, some people are at higher risk than others. You have no control over some risk factors for stroke, such as your age or sex. But there are many risk factors that you can change or control, such as high blood pressure or cigarette smoking.

Stroke and heart disease share many of the same risk factors. The good news is that 80 percent of strokes can be prevented by changing or controlling certain risk factors.

Stroke risk factors that you cannot change

Previous stroke. Having had a previous stroke is the biggest risk factor for having another stroke.

Age. For every decade after the age of 55, your stroke risk doubles.

Sex. If you consider all ages, men are more likely to have strokes than women. But between the ages of 45 and 64, women are more likely to have strokes than men. This is probably because blood pressure and cholesterol (koh-LESS-tur-ol) levels rise more quickly in women than men during this period. High blood pressure and poor cholesterol levels are both risk factors for stroke.

Menopause. The risk of stroke increases after menopause.

Race. African Americans are more likely to have a stroke than other people. This is partly because African Americans are more likely to have certain risk factors, such as high blood pressure and diabetes.

Stroke family history. If stroke runs in your family, it may be because your family carries genes that increase your chances of having a stroke. An example would be genes that increase your chances of forming a blood clot. Or it may be that your family has a lifestyle that increases your chances of having a stroke. For example, your family may eat a diet high in saturated fat.

Stroke risk factors that you can change

High blood pressure. High blood pressure is the biggest risk factor for stroke. In fact, it increases your chances of having a stroke 4 to 6 times.

For information on risk factors for heart disease, see the *Heart Disease* chapter on page 15.

Heart disease. The second biggest risk factor for stroke is heart disease, especially a disease called atrial fibrillation (fib-ruh-LAY-shuhn). In atrial fibrillation, the upper chambers of the heart beat faster and more irregularly than the rest of the heart. As a result, blood doesn't flow

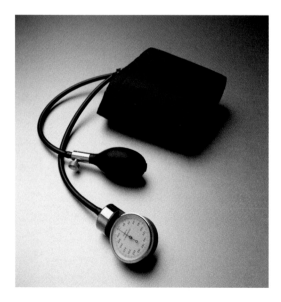

through these chambers correctly and can clot. A clot may then dislodge and travel up to the brain, where it can cause an ischemic stroke.

Blood cholesterol levels. High LDL (bad) cholesterol and low HDL (good) cholesterol levels increase your risk of stroke. They do this by causing the build-up of plaque.

Plaque and Atherosclerosis

Plaque is a fatty substance that builds up in the walls of arteries. Plaque is made up largely of cholesterol and fat. The narrowing and hardening of arteries caused by plaque buildup is called atherosclerosis (a-thuh-roh-skluh-ROH-suhss).

Cigarette smoking. Cigarette smoking has been linked to plaque buildup in the carotid artery. Other ways that cigarette smoking increases your stroke risk include:

- The nicotine in cigarettes raises blood pressure.
- Carbon monoxide from smoking reduces the amount of oxygen your blood can carry to the brain.
- Cigarette smoke makes your blood thicker and more likely to clot.

Your doctor can recommend programs and medications that may help you quit smoking.

Obesity. Postmenopausal women with a waist size larger than 35 inches and a high triglyceride (treye-GLIH-suh-ryd), or blood fat, level have 5 times the risk of having a stroke.

Diabetes. Diabetes is a disease in which the blood glucose, or sugar, level becomes too high. Diabetes damages blood vessels throughout the body, including the brain. As a result, diabetes triples the risk of stroke. If the blood glucose level is high at the time of a stroke, brain damage is usually more severe than if the level is normal. Treating diabetes can delay the onset of blood vessel changes that increase stroke risk.

For information on treating diabetes, see the *Type 2 Diabetes* chapter on page 69.

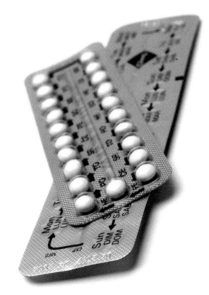

Heavy alcohol use, illegal drug use. For women, more than one alcoholic drink per day raises stroke risk. Cocaine use is a common cause of hemorrhagic stroke in young people. Long-term marijuana smoking may also be a risk factor for stroke.

Pregnancy. On rare occasions, pregnancy can cause stroke, especially in the first few months after delivery. Pregnancy increases blood pressure, and clots are more easily formed.

Birth control pills or patch. Taking birth control pills or using the birth control patch is generally safe for young, healthy women. With the pill, stroke risk is greater for women who also smoke cigarettes or who have migraines with aura (extreme headaches with a visual disturbance).

With the patch, the stroke risk is greater for women who also smoke cigarettes. Research has not yet shown whether women who have migraines with aura also have an increased risk of stroke when using the patch. If you get this type of headache, tell your doctor when discussing your birth control options.

For an important warning on birth control pills and the patch and stroke and heart attack risks, see page 164 of the *Reproductive Health* chapter. For information on migraine headaches, see page 357 of the *Pain* chapter.

Menopausal hormone therapy. Menopausal hormone therapy can increase stroke risk. If you use menopausal hormone therapy, you should take it at the lowest possible dose and for the shortest amount of time. Work with your doctor to come up with a plan that works best for you.

For information on menopausal hormone therapy and the risks of stroke and heart attack, see page 28 of the *Heart Disease* chapter.

Brain aneurysm. An aneurysm (AN-yuh-riz-uhm) is a bulge that forms at a weak spot in an artery wall. Because most brain aneurysms look like a berry hanging from a vine, they are often called "berry" aneurysms. Most aneurysms occur in arteries on the brain's surface. You can have a brain aneurysm for years and not have any symptoms. But sometimes the aneurysm bursts, and blood flows into the space outside the brain. The result is a subarachnoid hemorrhage, a type of hemorrhagic stroke. (See page 38 for more information.)

Symptoms of aneurysm may include:

- pain above and behind the eye
- numbness or weakness on one side of the face
- problems seeing (such as double vision)

Call your doctor if you have these symptoms. Large aneurysms can often be treated to prevent them from bursting.

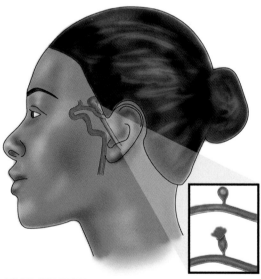

BRAIN ANEURYSM

Preventing stroke

At some point, 39 percent of women in the United States will develop heart disease, stroke, or other diseases involving narrowing or hardening of the arteries. It is important for all women to pay attention to their risk factors for these diseases. The most important things you can do to reduce your chances of stroke are:

- Treat high blood pressure.
- Don't smoke cigarettes.
- Maintain an active lifestyle.

If you have high blood pressure, you may be able to lower it by:

- losing weight if you are overweight or obese
- getting 30 minutes of moderate-intensity physical activity on most days of the week
- limiting alcohol to one drink per day
- eating foods that are good for your heart
- reducing stress

Your doctor may prescribe medicines to lower your blood pressure. It is important to take them as prescribed and not stop them unless directed by your doctor.

Some research suggests that healthy women older than age 65 may reduce their stroke risk by taking 80 mg aspirin, or baby aspirin, daily. Aspirin makes blood clots less likely, which reduces the risk of an ischemic stroke. But aspirin can have serious side effects, such as bleeding in your stomach or intestines. If you're thinking about taking aspirin, talk with your doctor first.

Choosing a hospital

The hospital you go to can matter a great deal. You have a better chance of having a good outcome if you are taken to a certified stroke center at a hospital with the staff, equipment, and experience needed to treat stroke quickly and correctly.

Stroke Centers

To find a certified stroke center near you, see the Web sites of the Joint Commission on the Accreditation of Healthcare Organizations and the National Stroke Association, listed in the resource section on page 48.

As of August 2007, the following states have developed or are in the process of developing their own regulations for certifying hospitals as stroke centers:

- Florida
- Maryland
- Massachusetts
- New Jersey
- New York
- Texas

If you live in these states, call your state health department to find out if there is a state-certified stroke center near you.

Find the nearest certified stroke center, and share the name and address with your family or caregivers. Tell them that if you have a stroke, you want to be taken to that hospital. Even if you live in a rural area, you might be able to be taken to a certified stroke center by helicopter.

How is a stroke diagnosed?

Once you get to the hospital, the following things will happen quickly:

- A doctor or nurse will ask you or your companion about your symptoms and when they began.

- You will be asked to perform several physical and mental tasks to see what parts of your brain might be affected by the stroke.

- You will be given various tests to rule out other possible causes of your symptoms.

If your doctor decides that you may have had a stroke, the next step will be to use one or more brain imaging techniques to see where the stroke is located. The two main techniques are computed tomography (tuh-MOG-ruh-fee) (CT) scan and magnetic resonance imaging (MRI). A CT scan is more commonly used because it is faster and more readily available in most hospitals.

How is a stroke treated?

If your brain scan shows that you've had an ischemic stroke, you may be given a shot of tissue plasminogen (plaz-MIN-uh-juhn) activator, or t-PA, into one of your veins. This drug travels in the blood to the brain and breaks up the clot. t-PA must be given within 3 hours from the time your stroke started for it to work properly and safely. In fact, the sooner t-PA is given, the better it works. That's why it's important for you to get to the hospital as quickly as possible.

A new therapy for ischemic strokes is the Mechanical Embolus Removal for Cerebral Ischemia (MERCI) system. This involves threading a thin wire through your blood vessels and into the artery in the brain that is blocked by a clot. The wire is used to pull the clot out of the body. The MERCI system can be used for up to 8 hours after the start of an ischemic stroke.

There are fewer treatments for intracerebral hemorrhages (bleeding into the brain) than for ischemic strokes. Usually, little can be done to stop the bleeding. But treatment usually involves trying to reduce pressure within the skull caused by bleeding with drugs or surgery. Research suggests that a new drug, called activated factor VII, can slow the bleeding if given within 4 hours of when it started. But this drug is still being tested and is not yet available for use in hospitals.

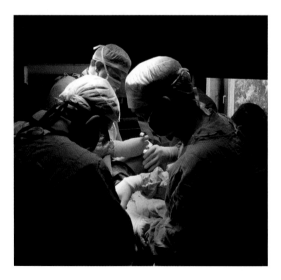

If you have a subarachnoid hemorrhage because of a burst aneurysm, brain surgery will be needed to stop the bleeding from the aneurysm.

Stroke Treatment Research

Much progress in stroke treatment has been made over the past decade. And many new treatments are in the final stages of testing and likely to be available for widespread use in the next few years. Not long ago, doctors considered stroke an untreatable disease, but no more. The future of stroke treatment is looking brighter.

Effects of a stroke

After a stroke, you may have problems caused by damage to parts of your brain. What problems you have depend on which parts of your brain were damaged. Some of the problems that you may have after a stroke include:

- **Movement.** You may have problems moving an arm, a leg, a part of your face, or the entire side of your body. You may also have problems swallowing.

- **Sensations.** You may lose the ability to feel touch, pain, temperature, or position. Or you may experience pain or odd sensations of tingling or prickling.

- **Language.** You may have problems speaking, writing, or understanding spoken or written words.

- **Thinking and memory.** You may have a short attention span or have trouble remembering something you just learned. Or you may lose the ability to plan and carry out steps in a complex task.

of your abilities. Also, there seems to be no time limit for recovering. Research shows that some people who have had a stroke may keep recovering for years after the stroke.

There are many different types of therapies used to help stroke patients lead independent lives.

- Physical therapy helps you relearn simple movements, such as walking, sitting, standing, and lying down.

- Occupational therapy helps you relearn everyday activities, such as eating, drinking, dressing, and going to the bathroom.

- Speech therapy helps you relearn how to speak and use language. Speech therapists can also help if you're having trouble swallowing.

- Psychotherapy helps you deal with your emotional problems. Depression, for instance, can be treated with a combination of medicines and counseling.

- **Emotions.** The most common emotional problem faced by stroke survivors is depression. If you have depression, it's important that you get treatment (see below for information on treating depression). Another common problem among stroke survivors is pseudobulbar (soo-doh-BUHL-bar) affect. If you have this condition, you might laugh or cry at inappropriate times. For instance, you might laugh at a sad story or cry for no reason. Because a person with pseudobulbar affect may cry uncontrollably, the condition is often mistaken for depression.

Therapies for stroke recovery

In the first several months after a stroke, some of the abilities that you lost may return on their own, but others may not. The good news is that there are therapies that can help you recover functions or learn new ways of doing things. The more you work at these therapies, the more likely you will be to recover many

Research is leading to exciting new techniques to help stroke survivors. For instance, experts are developing robotic braces that fit over one or more joints and help you relearn movements.

Most stroke survivors find that regaining lost abilities is hard work. It is normal to feel tired and discouraged at times because things that used to be easy are now difficult. The important thing is to notice the progress you make and take pride in each achievement.

How family members can help

If you are a family member of a stroke survivor, here are some things you can do:

- Support your loved one's efforts to help make decisions about their therapies.

- Encourage them to be as independent as possible.

- Strive to be compassionate, patient, positive, tolerant, and respectful.

- Visit and talk with your loved one. Do things together, such as playing cards or a board game.

- Participate in education offered for stroke survivors and their families.

- Ask physical and occupational therapists how to outfit your home for the stroke survivor. For instance, you may need to install grab bars in the bathroom to help your loved one use the toilet, tub, or shower.

- If your loved one has trouble speaking or understanding speech, ask the speech therapist how you can help.

- To prevent bedsores, make sure your loved one does not sit or lie in the same position for long periods of time.

- Take care of yourself by eating well, getting enough rest, and taking time to do things that you enjoy.

Perhaps most important, remember that caring family and friends can be a key factor in helping stroke survivors recover. ■

One Woman's Story

I was 5 months pregnant and 36 years old at the time, casually talking on the phone when suddenly my right side became paralyzed and I lost my ability to speak. I began crawling on my hands and knees, motioning to my older daughter for help. Ten-year-old Chelsea knew I was in serious trouble and called 911 right away.

When I arrived at the hospital, I was paralyzed on the right side of my body and could not talk. My husband described me as being "in a vegetative state," and the doctors discussed nursing home placement. I remained in the hospital for five days and was then transferred to another facility for rehabilitation.

I was determined to regain function, and soon I was doing exercises to strengthen my hand and arms. I had to learn how to change a baby diaper and bathe a baby using only one hand. I progressed to walking just three days after being discharged home and by the seventh day, I had regained my speech.

As an African American woman, I was also at a higher risk for stroke.

I had thought I was in good health. Yet prior to getting pregnant, I sought an evaluation from my doctor for some frightening symptoms: my right arm would become numb for a short period of time or I would experience "pins and needles." Sometimes I would have vision changes. Sometimes I could not speak. But these symptoms would last only a short time before everything would return to normal. I now know that I had been experiencing TIAs, which often serve as warning signs for an impending stroke. My original doctor did not order testing, and I was forced to change doctors to get the care I needed. My new doctor's tests all came back negative and I received the OK to get pregnant.

I learned that while stroke is uncommon in pregnancy, it does happen. I also had high blood pressure during the pregnancy, which is a risk factor for stroke. As an African American woman, I was also at a higher risk for stroke.

My baby is fine. I have a healthy son. I can once again care for my family. After my recovery, my mission became to raise awareness of stroke symptoms, not just as a survivor and mom, but as Mrs. New Jersey 2002—winner of the state beauty pageant!

Cynthia
New Jersey

This story is provided courtesy of the Women's Heart Foundation.

For More Information...

Office on Women's Health, HHS
200 Independence Ave SW, Room 712E
Washington, DC 20201
Web site: www.womenshealth.gov/heart
www.womenshealth.gov/faq/stroke.htm
Phone number: (800) 994-9662,
(888) 220-5446 TDD

**National Heart, Lung, and Blood Institute
Health Information Center, NIH**
PO Box 30105
Bethesda, MD 20824-0105
Web site: www.nhlbi.nih.gov
www.hearttruth.gov
Phone number: (301) 592-8573,
(240) 629-3255 TTY

**National Institute of Neurological
Disorders and Stroke, NIH**
PO Box 5801
Bethesda, MD 20824
Web site: www.ninds.nih.gov
Phone number: (800) 352-9424,
(301) 468-5981 TTY

American Stroke Association
7272 Greenville Ave
Dallas, TX 75231
Web site: www.strokeassociation.org
Phone number: (888) 478-7653

The Internet Stroke Center
Washington University School of Medicine
Department of Neurology
660 S Euclid, Box 8111
St Louis, MO 63110
Web site: www.strokecenter.org

National Stroke Association
9707 E Easter Ln, Building B
Centennial, CO 80112
Web site: www.stroke.org
Phone number: (800) 787-6537

To find a stroke center near you, visit:

The Joint Commission
www.qualitycheck.org

Cancer

Cancer is one of the most common causes of death in American women. But thanks to improved cancer screening and treatment, you have a better chance of beating cancer than ever before. About 66 percent of people diagnosed with cancer between 1996 and 2002 survived for at least 5 years. As the science of cancer detection and treatment continues to advance, even more people will survive cancer in the future.

What is cancer?

Cancer is a disease in which abnormal cells grow, divide, and spread, often forming a mass called a tumor. Although any abnormal growth is a tumor, some tumors are benign (bih-NYN) (not cancer) and some are malignant (muh-LIG-nuhnt) (cancer). Cancers may invade nearby tissues and metastasize (muh-TASS-tuh-syz), or spread to other parts of the body. Cancer can develop in almost any part of the body. In two types of cancer, leukemia (loo-KEE-mee-uh) and lymphoma (lim-FOH-muh), tumors do not form. Instead, cancer cells spread throughout the blood and the immune system, respectively.

Even if you haven't been diagnosed with cancer, it is important to know that there are steps you can take to:

- reduce your chances of getting cancer

- detect cancer early

- make sure you get the treatment you need

What causes cancer?

A number of factors may affect your cancer risk—your chances of developing cancer in your lifetime. Your family history, personal history, and environment all play a part. Some risk factors are beyond your control, such as age and family history. But you can change some aspects of your behavior or environment to reduce your risk. Keep in mind that most women with these risk factors will never have cancer.

Body Parts That Can Be Affected by Cancer

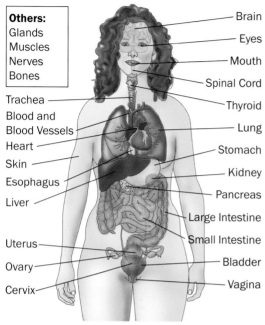

Others:
Glands
Muscles
Nerves
Bones

Trachea
Blood and
Blood Vessels
Heart
Skin
Esophagus
Liver
Uterus
Ovary
Cervix

Brain
Eyes
Mouth
Spinal Cord
Thyroid
Lung
Stomach
Kidney
Pancreas
Large Intestine
Small Intestine
Bladder
Vagina

Genetic Mutations

Changes to a cell's DNA, called genetic mutations, may cause the cell to become cancerous. Most of the mutations that cause cancer are caused by the environment, behavior (such as smoking cigarettes), or chance. But some cancer-causing mutations are inherited. For more information about genetics and health, see page 408 of the Appendix.

Age

Age is the most important risk factor for cancer. Most cancers—77 percent—occur in persons who are 55 years old or older. For this reason, you will need more tests and checkups to detect early signs of cancer as you get older.

Inherited risk

Inherited genetic mutations, on their own, cause very few cancers. Several common types of cancer tend to run in families. These include breast cancer, ovarian cancer, colon cancer, melanoma (me-luh-NOH-muh), and lung cancer. However, environment and behavior also affect the development of these cancers.

If you have a family history of a certain type of cancer, it does not mean that you will develop that disease. Talk to your doctor about cancer in your family. You may need to take steps to reduce your risk or be screened more often or at an earlier age.

Tobacco use

Tobacco use is one of the leading causes of cancer. It increases the risk of cancers of the lung, larynx, mouth, nose, pharynx, esophagus, pancreas, kidney, bladder, liver, cervix, and stomach. Tobacco use causes 30 percent of all cancer deaths and 87 percent of lung cancer deaths in the United States.

Smoking not only causes cancer in smokers, but also may raise the risk of lung cancer for nonsmokers who breathe in secondhand smoke.

You can reduce your risk of lung cancer and other cancers by not smoking or using other tobacco products. You should also avoid secondhand smoke. If you currently smoke, quitting can lower your risk of cancer.

For more information on the benefits of quitting smoking, see the *Respiratory Health* chapter on page 279.

Breast and Ovarian Cancer: Inherited Risk Factors

Women with a family history of breast or ovarian cancer may inherit mutated genes that increase their risk of developing these diseases. Mutations of the *BRCA1* or *BRCA2* genes are most strongly linked to these cancers, but other genes also play a role. Inherited mutated genes cause only about 5 to 10 percent of breast and ovarian cancers. And even women who inherit these mutated genes may not develop cancer.

If you have a family history of breast or ovarian cancer, talk to your doctor. Genetic counseling can help you decide if testing for BRCA mutations might be helpful. If you do test positive, your doctor may suggest:

- additional screening tests
- taking tamoxifen or an aromatase inhibitor, a drug that reduces breast cancer risk
- surgery to remove the breasts or ovaries to prevent cancer

For more information about genetics and health, see page 408 of the Appendix.

Excessive alcohol intake

Drinking alcohol is a risk factor in cancers of the mouth, pharynx, esophagus, larynx, and liver. It may increase your risk of breast, colon, and rectal cancers. When drinking alcohol is combined with tobacco use, the risks of mouth, pharyngeal, and esophageal cancers are further increased. However, low or moderate alcohol intake may lower your risk of heart disease.

You can reduce your risk by avoiding drinking alcohol to excess. If you drink alcohol, do it in moderation.

Ultraviolet (UV) rays

The sun's UV rays cause most skin cancers. The amount of UV rays in sunlight depends on the time of day, season, and location. There are more UV rays at midday, during the summer months, and at locations close to the equator. However, you may be exposed whenever you are outdoors during the day—even on cloudy days. Water and snow, which reflect sunlight back toward your skin, can also increase your UV exposure.

You can reduce your risk by protecting your skin from UV rays.

- Avoid sun exposure between 10 AM and 4 PM, when the sun's rays are the most damaging.
- Wear protective clothing and a hat that shades your face.
- Avoid artificial UV rays from tanning beds or sunlamps.
- If you plan to spend time outside, apply sunscreen 30 to 60 minutes before you go out.

- Apply a broad-spectrum sunscreen with a sun protective factor (SPF) of at least 15. Reapply it after sweating or bathing.

Some medications

The female hormones estrogen and progesterone (proh-JESS-tuh-rohn) affect the growth and development of certain cancers. Drugs that contain these female hormones affect cancer risk.

Menopausal hormone therapy (MHT) relieves the symptoms of menopause and may prevent osteoporosis (OSS-tee-oh-puh-ROH-suhss). There are two types of MHT. Both types affect cancer risk:

- Estrogen-only MHT increases the risk of endometrial cancer and ovarian cancer. Progestin is added to MHT to reduce endometrial cancer risk.

- Combined MHT, which contains estrogen and progesterone or progestin, increases the risk of breast cancer. But it lowers the risk of colon cancer.

Birth control pills also contain female hormones. The pill lowers the risk of endometrial and ovarian cancers. But it may increase the risk of cervical, liver, and breast cancers. Today, birth control pills contain lower hormone levels than in the past. So the effects of the pill on cancer risk may be reduced.

Drugs used to suppress the immune system during an organ transplant may also lead to cancer, especially lymphoma. Chemotherapy drugs, used to treat many types of cancer, may cause leukemia. Cancer survivors are at higher risk of this disease.

You can learn more by talking to your doctor about the benefits and risks of these medications.

Substances in the home, workplace, and the environment

Some chemicals, particles, metals, radioactive materials, and other substances can increase your risk of developing cancer.

- **Radon** is a radioactive gas. It can build up in underground spaces, such as basements, if there is not enough airflow.

- **Asbestos** is a fibrous material that was widely used in building insulation until 1980.

- **Secondhand smoke** includes smoke from burning cigarettes and exhaled smoke.

- **Air pollution** is caused by substances and fine particles released into the air. Sources may include motor vehicles, power plants that burn fossil fuels, and factories.

Chemicals and metals in pesticides, solvents (paint thinners, grease removers, and dry cleaning chemicals), and other substances may increase cancer risk.

Workers in agriculture, mining, manufacturing, and other industries may be exposed to carcinogens more often and at higher concentrations. Therefore, they may have an even greater cancer risk.

You can reduce your risk by avoiding or reducing your exposure to cancer-causing substances at home and at work.

Infections

Some infections may increase your risk of developing cancer.

- **Human papillomavirus (HPV)** is the most common sexually transmitted infection in the United States. HPV is the primary cause of most cervical cancers. There is a new HPV vaccine available for girls and young women. This vaccine and regular screening can reduce infections and cancer risk. (See page 134 of the *Sexually Transmitted Infections* chapter for more information.)

- **Hepatitis B and hepatitis C viruses** may be transmitted by injected drug use, intimate sexual contact, or contact with infected blood. Infection may lead to liver cancer. These viruses are more common in Asia than in the United States. Because of this, Asian American women who have recently

Ten Most Common Cancers in American Women*	Ten Cancers Responsible for the Most Deaths Among American Women*
Breast cancer	Lung cancer
Lung cancer	Breast cancer
Colon and rectal cancers	Colon and rectal cancers
Endometrial cancer	Pancreatic cancer
Non-Hodgkin lymphoma	Ovarian cancer
Melanoma (skin cancer)	Non-Hodgkin lymphoma
Ovarian cancer	Leukemia
Thyroid cancer	Endometrial cancer
Pancreatic cancer	Brain tumors
Leukemia	Myeloma

*2000–2004

Cancer

immigrated have a higher risk of infection and liver cancer.

- *Helicobacter pylori* (*H. pylori*) **bacteria** cause a common stomach infection that increases the risk of developing stomach cancer. *H. pylori* is more common in developing countries than in the United States. Recent immigrants from Asia or Latin America have a greater chance of infection and risk for stomach cancer.

You can reduce your risk by taking steps to prevent infection when possible. Vaccines are available for HPV and the hepatitis B virus. If you think you may be at high risk for any of these infections, talk to your doctor about tests and treatments.

Types of cancer

The following chart lists some common types of cancer in women, along with their risk factors and symptoms. Some of these symptoms can be caused by conditions other than cancer. Even if you have these symptoms, you may not have cancer.

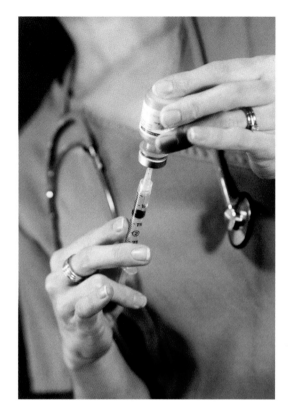

Cancers Affecting Women: Risk Factors and Symptoms	
Brain tumors	
Risk factors*	• Age • Family history
Symptoms†	• Severe headaches • Nausea • Problems with speech, vision, or hearing • Loss of balance • Changes in mood or personality • Memory loss • Seizures • Numbness in extremities

Cancers Affecting Women: Risk Factors and Symptoms

Breast cancer

Risk factors*	• Age
	• Family history
	• High breast tissue density
	• Hyperplasia (an increase in number of cells in the breast; detected by a biopsy)
	• X-ray exposure, particularly at young ages or high doses
	• Early onset of menstruation and/or late menopause
	• Never having children
	• Having first child after age 30
	• Use of birth control pills (within 10 years of stopping use, risk returns to normal)
	• Overweight or obesity after menopause
	• Use of menopausal hormone therapy containing both estrogen and progestin
	• Excessive alcohol consumption
	• Inherited mutations of *BRCA1* and *BRCA2* genes
Symptoms†	• Abnormalities (may be detected by a mammogram‡)
	• A lump in the breast (may be detected by a mammogram‡)
	• Changes in the breast (See page 160 of the *Reproductive Health* chapter for more information.)

Cervical cancer

Risk factors*	• Human papillomavirus (HPV); a vaccine can now prevent infection with strains of the virus responsible for most cervical cancers; condoms also offer partial protection
Symptoms†	• Abnormal cells (can be detected by Pap test‡)
	• Abnormal vaginal bleeding

Colon and rectal cancers

Risk factors*	• Age
	• Family history
	• History of inflammatory bowel disease
	• Obesity
	• Smoking
	• Excessive alcohol consumption
	• Inherited genetic mutations
Symptoms†	• Polyps or tumors (can be detected by screening tests‡)
	• Blood in stool (may be detected by screening tests‡)
	• Changes in bowel habits
	• Pain or cramping

Cancers Affecting Women: Risk Factors and Symptoms

Endometrial cancer

Risk factors*	• Use of estrogen-only menopausal therapy (in women with an intact uterus) • Early onset of menstruation and/or late menopause • Never having children • Obesity
Symptoms†	• Abnormal uterine bleeding, especially after menopause

Leukemia

Risk factors*	• Exposure to benzene or ionizing radiation • Cancer radiation treatment • Down syndrome and some other genetic abnormalities • Retrovirus human T-cell leukemia/lymphoma virus-1 (HTLV-1)
Symptoms†	• Fatigue • Paleness • Weight loss • Repeated infections • Fever • Easy bruising • Nosebleeds

Liver cancer

Risk factors*	• Age • Family history • Hepatitis B or hepatitis C infection • Cirrhosis (sur-ROH-suhss) • Exposure to a toxic substance, aflatoxin, in mold that grows in nuts, seeds, and legumes
Symptoms†	• Abdominal pain on the right side • Abdominal swelling • Weight loss • Loss of appetite • Fatigue • Nausea • Jaundice • Fever

Cancers Affecting Women: Risk Factors and Symptoms

Lung cancer

Risk factors*	• Smoking • Exposure to airborne carcinogens such as asbestos, radon, secondhand smoke, some chemicals and metals, and air pollution
Symptoms†	• Cough that does not go away • Cough that produces blood • Chest pain • Repeated pneumonia (noo-MOH-nyuh) or bronchitis

Lymphoma (Hodgkin and non-Hodgkin lymphomas)

Risk factors*	• Reduced immune function due to autoimmune (aw-toh-ih-MYOON) disorders • Infection with HIV, retrovirus human T-cell leukemia/lymphoma virus-1 (HTLV-1), or hepatitis C • Family history • Workplace exposures to herbicides and other chemicals • Medications that reduce immune function for organ transplant
Symptoms†	• Swollen lymph nodes • Night sweats • Fatigue • Weight loss • Fever

Myeloma (cancer of plasma cells in blood)

Risk factors*	• Age • History of a condition called monoclonal gammopathy of undetermined significance (MGUS)
Symptoms	• Pain in or broken bones of the back and spine • Fatigue • Thirst • Repeated infections or fevers

Oral cavity and pharyngeal cancers

Risk factors*	• Tobacco use (including cigarettes, cigars, pipes, and smokeless tobacco products) • Excessive alcohol consumption
Symptoms†	• Sores that bleed and/or do not heal • Lumps or thickening • Ear pain • A mass on the neck • Cough that produces blood • Red or white patch that does not go away • Difficulties chewing or swallowing

Cancers Affecting Women: Risk Factors and Symptoms

Ovarian cancer

Risk factors*	• Age • Use of estrogen-only menopausal hormone therapy • Overweight and obesity • Personal or family history of breast cancer • Mutations of *BRCA1* and *BRCA2* genes • Personal or family history of hereditary nonpolypsis colon cancer (HNPCC)
Symptoms†	• Bloating • Pelvic or abdominal pain • Difficulty eating or feeling full quickly • Digestive problems • Urinary problems (urgency or frequency) • Fatigue • Back pain • Abnormal vaginal bleeding

Pancreatic cancer

Risk factors*	• Smoking • Chronic pancreatitis (PAN-kree-uh-TYT-uhss) • Diabetes • Cirrhosis • Obesity
Symptoms†	• Weight loss • Abdominal discomfort • Jaundice

Skin cancer (melanoma, basal cell, and squamous cell cancers)

Risk factors*	• Personal or family history of skin cancer • Many moles or large moles • Sunburning easily • Natural blonde or red hair • Personal history of major sunburns and use of tanning booths • Workplace exposure to certain substances
Symptoms†	• Changes in the skin, such as a new growth, change in an existing growth, or sores that do not heal

Cancers Affecting Women: Risk Factors and Symptoms

Thyroid cancer

Risk factors*	• Age
	• Family history
	• Exposure to radiation or x-rays, especially at young ages
	• Diet lacking iodine
	• Workplace exposure to certain substances
Symptoms†	• Lump at the front of the neck
	• Swollen lymph nodes
	• Difficulty swallowing, speaking, or breathing
	• Throat or neck pain

*The factors listed have been shown to increase the risk of developing cancer. These factors are not listed in any particular order. Many people without any risk factors may develop cancer, whereas most people who are at risk will never have the disease.

†Some of these symptoms are common and may be caused by conditions other than cancer. Most women who experience these symptoms do not have cancer.

‡Screening tests may detect some cancers, or conditions that may lead to cancer, before you notice any symptoms. See below for more information about cancer screening.

These cancers can affect women from diverse racial or ethnic groups differently. Recent studies have shown that African American women are more likely to develop aggressive types of breast cancer. Cancers of the stomach, liver, and cervix are caused by infections. These infections are more common in Latin America and Asia. Therefore, rates of these cancers are higher among women who have emigrated from these regions. For more information on cancers caused by infection, see pages 55 and 56.

Finding out if you have cancer

Cancer symptoms

At first, cancer may not produce any symptoms. As a tumor grows, you may feel discomfort or pain at the tumor site, abnormal bleeding, fatigue, and weight loss. Other symptoms may depend on the location of the cancer. (See chart starting on page 56 for symptoms of several common types of cancer.)

Cancer screening

Depending on your age and risk factors, you should be screened for some cancers. This is important even if you feel healthy. Screening can allow your doctor to find and remove abnormal cells before they turn into cancer. These tests can also detect cancer early, before you feel any symptoms.

Screening is not recommended for all women or for all types of cancer. Screening tests are not completely accurate, and they can have harms. Talk to your doctor about the benefits and harms of commonly used screening tests. Tests may produce false-positive results, meaning they may show you have cancer when you don't. This can cause worry and unneeded medical procedures. Tests may also produce false-negative results that miss cancer. Your doctor will need to do more tests to confirm the results. Your primary care doctor may also refer you to an oncologist for more tests. An oncologist is a doctor who specializes in cancer.

The chart below lists the screenings recommended for women with average risk for some common cancers. If you think you may have higher than average risk, talk to your doctor about your risk factors. You may need additional tests. (See pages 418–421 of the Appendix for more information.)

Breast cancer

You should be screened for breast cancer on the following schedule:

- In your 20s and 30s, you should have a clinical breast exam every 3 years. After you turn 40, you should have a clinical breast exam every year.
- Starting at age 40, you should have mammograms (an x-ray examination of the breasts) every 1 to 2 years.
- At any age, you should be familiar with the normal feel and appearance of your breasts. Report any changes to your doctor right way.

Discuss breast cancer risk with your doctor. If you are at higher risk, you may need mammograms at an earlier age. You may also need more frequent exams or additional tests.

Cervical cancer

Beginning 3 years after the start of sexual activity or at age 21, you should have a Pap test each year. A Pap test is a microscopic examination of cells taken from the cervix. After three normal tests, you only need to be tested every 3 years. If you are older than age 65 and have had three normal tests, you may choose to stop being testing. If you have had your cervix removed as part of a hysterectomy, you do not need to be screened (unless the hysterectomy was performed to treat cancer).

Colorectal cancer

Beginning at age 50, you should be screened for colorectal cancer on one of the following schedules.

- You may have a fecal occult blood test (FOBT) (a test that checks for blood in the stool) once each year.
- Flexible sigmoidoscopy (examination of the lower colon) may be performed once every 5 years.
- FOBT each year may be combined with flexible sigmoidoscopy once every 5 years.
- You may have a colonoscopy (examination of the colon) every 10 years.
- Computed tomography (tuh-MOG-ruh-fee) (CT) scans of the colon ("virtual colonoscopy") are used at some medical centers for screening.

Talk to your doctor about which type of testing is best for you. If you are at high risk of colon cancer, your doctor may recommend additional testing.

Diagnosis

Once a tumor is found, your doctor will collect a tissue sample. This procedure is called a biopsy. Your doctor will examine the tissue to find out whether it is cancer. More tests may be needed to determine the cancer's stage or how advanced it is. The stage is based on the location and

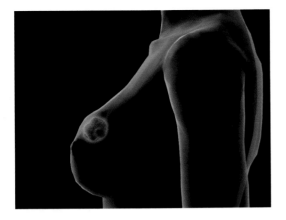

size of a tumor and whether the cancer has spread. At earlier stages, cancer is easier to treat.

Cancer treatment

After diagnosing and staging the cancer, your doctor will discuss cancer treatment with you. Treatments may include measures aimed at curing the cancer and therapies that ease symptoms and improve quality of life. Depending on the type of cancer and its stage, doctors may recommend one or more of the treatments below.

- **Surgery** alone may be able to remove the cancer if it has not spread beyond the tissues where it began. Surgery may also be combined with other treatments.

- **Chemotherapy**, or chemo, uses drugs to destroy cancer cells. It may cure cancer, prevent it from growing or spreading, or relieve symptoms. Chemo may also harm healthy cells. This causes side effects such as fatigue, nausea, hair loss, weight loss, and anemia (uh-NEE-mee-uh).

- **Radiation therapy** targets cancer cells with a type of energy called ionizing radiation. It may destroy a tumor or shrink it, and it may harm healthy cells near the area being treated.

- **Biological therapy** stimulates the body's immune system to fight the cancer. It may also ease the side effects of other cancer treatments.

- **Hormone therapy** may be used to treat breast, ovarian, and endometrial cancers. Female hormones help these cancers grow. Hormone therapy reduces or blocks the effect of these hormones.

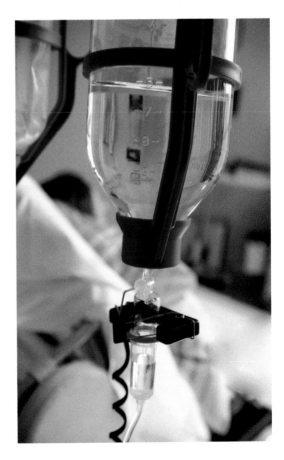

- **Complementary or alternative medicines** are treatments that are not part of standard medical care. These treatments include herbal medicines, massage therapy, acupuncture, meditation, and others. These practices or medicines are called "complementary" when they are used along with standard care. When they are used in place of standard treatments, they are called "alternative." You may find complementary medicine helpful for relieving cancer symptoms. It may also help with the side effects of other treatments. Talk to your doctor before trying complementary or alternative medicine. Your doctor can make sure it will not interfere with other treatments.

For more information, see the *Complementary and Alternative Medicine* chapter on page 367.

Scientists are working to improve existing treatments to target cancer cells without damaging healthy cells. New types of treatment include gene therapy (changing the genetic material in cells) and vaccines. These treatments may be used to treat some cancers in the future.

Fertility

Depending on the site of your cancer and type of treatments, cancer may affect your ability to have children. Before you start cancer treatments, discuss your concerns with your doctor. Some treatments may make it difficult or impossible for you to have children. You may wish to consider procedures that protect fertility before treatment. Options may include:

- freezing embryos, eggs, or ovarian tissue

- moving ovaries to another part of the body to protect them from radiation

- surgeries that remove cancer but do not cause infertility

If you decide to become pregnant after cancer treatment, talk to your doctor or a doctor who specializes in fertility issues or reproductive problems. You may have special health risks or problems conceiving. You may also wish to consider whether your cancer is likely to come back.

What you can do to feel better

Coping with fatigue and pain

Fatigue—feeling weak or tired—is one of the most common symptoms of cancer. It can have a big effect on your quality of life, day-to-day activities, work life, and relationships. Many people with cancer experience pain, either from the cancer itself or from cancer treatments. It is important to talk to your doctor about these and any other symptoms or side effects you experience. There are treatments that can help you feel better.

Taking care of your emotions

Cancer and cancer treatment can affect your emotional well-being in many ways. For example, you may feel shock, anger, or fear when you learn you have cancer. Cancer may change your sense of yourself and your future. And the disease or treatments may alter your appearance, abilities, and body image. These and other factors can lead to depression, which affects one-third to one-half of all women diagnosed with cancer.

It's important to take care of your emotions after a cancer diagnosis. You may find it helpful to seek additional support.

- Join a cancer support group where you can discuss your feelings with others who share your experience.

- Talk to your doctor if you are feeling depressed or anxious. There are medications that may help.

- Seek counseling or therapy to help cope with your emotions.

- Seek support from your family and friends.

- Talk with a spiritual advisor or religious leader.

Surviving cancer

Thanks to improved screening and treatment, more and more women are surviving longer after a cancer diagnosis. Cancer may affect your health, emotions, work, and relationships long after your treatment ends. As a cancer survivor, you need to continue to take care of your physical and emotional health.

- Talk to your doctor about any symptoms you have, such as pain, fatigue, or depression.

- Set up a schedule for follow-up care with your doctor. At follow-up appointments, your doctor can address any side effects of treatment and check to see if the cancer has returned or spread.

- Talk to your health care team about a wellness plan that can improve your health and may reduce the chances that your cancer will return.

- Take care of your emotions and seek support when you need it. ■

One Woman's Story

I have been a nurse for more than three decades and am currently working as a home health nurse and a professor. Cancer is not who I am—it's what is happening to me.

Early in October 2006, I felt pain in my upper left breast and noticed a lump. My doctor ordered a mammogram and an ultrasound, and then a biopsy. I was horrified when the biopsy revealed that it was, in fact, cancerous. After careful consideration, I elected to have a bilateral mastectomy because of the high possibility of reoccurrence in my right breast. A plastic surgeon performed the reconstruction at the same time. I am grateful for such cutting-edge treatment, and I am thankful to the federal government for mandating that insurance companies cover 100 percent of reconstructive breast surgery.

When I found out I had cancer, I was initially in denial—devastated and numb. Two previous biopsies I had were negative; I was the picture of health and was rarely sick. It turns out the hardest thing about being diagnosed with breast cancer was breaking the news to my family.

> **My body may be beaten and tired, but I am not defeated.**

Now, even though I pretend to be fine, I still have moments of uncertainty. Every day is truly a miracle for me. The hair loss has been hard, and the chemotherapy leaves me tired and drained. The taste in my mouth is probably the worst. My favorite food, enchiladas, don't taste right. I still maintain a healthy diet because I know it's in my best interest.

Surviving cancer has been challenging, to say the least, but a good outlook helps. So does having a strong support team at work and at home. My body may be beaten and tired, but I am not defeated. Cancer doesn't define me and I will not let it win. I am a survivor; through cancer I have learned not to take things, people, situations, and life for granted. Every day is precious, and I must give it my best and be a testimony for others who may be facing breast cancer this very day.

Bettie

Las Cruces, New Mexico

For More Information...

Office on Women's Health, HHS
200 Independence Ave SW, Room 712E
Washington, DC 20201
Web site: www.womenshealth.gov/
breastcancer
www.womenshealth.gov/quitsmoking
www.womenshealth.gov/faq/bsefaq.htm
www.womenshealth.gov/faq/pap.htm
Phone number: (800) 994-9662,
(888) 220-5446 TDD

**National Breast and Cervical Cancer
Early Detection Program, CDC**
4770 Buford Hwy NE, MS K-64
Atlanta, GA 30341-3717
Web site: www.cdc.gov/cancer/nbccedp
Phone number: (800) 232-4636,
(888) 232-6348 TTY

National Cancer Institute, NIH
6116 Executive Blvd, Room 3036A
Bethesda, MD 20892-8322
Web site: www.cancer.gov
Phone number: (800) 422-6237,
(800) 332-8615 TTY

**National Center for Complementary and
Alternative Medicine, NIH**
PO Box 7923
Gaithersburg, MD 20898
Web site: www.nccam.nih.gov
Phone number: (888) 644-6226,
(866) 464-3615 TTY

American Cancer Society
250 Williams St
Atlanta, GA 30303
Web site: www.cancer.org
Phone number: (800) 227-2345,
(866) 228-4327 TTY

American Institute for Cancer Research
1759 R St NW
Washington, DC 20009
Web site: www.aicr.org
Phone number: (800) 843-8114

CancerCare
275 Seventh Ave, Floor 22
New York, NY 10001
Web site: www.cancercare.org
Phone number: (800) 813-4673

Fertile Hope
65 Broadway, Suite 603
New York, NY 10006
Web site: www.fertilehope.org
Phone number: (888) 994-4673

Gynecologic Cancer Foundation
230 W Monroe, Suite 2528
Chicago, IL 60606
Web site: www.thegcf.org
Phone number: (800) 444-4441

Lance Armstrong Foundation
PO Box 161150
Austin, TX 78716-1150
Web site: www.livestrong.org
Phone number: (866) 467-7205

National Ovarian Cancer Coalition
500 NE Spanish River Blvd, Suite 8
Boca Raton, FL 33431
Web site: www.ovarian.org
Phone number: (888) 682-7426

Susan G. Komen for the Cure
5005 LBJ Freeway, Suite 250
Dallas, TX 75244
Web site: www.komen.org
Phone number: (877) 465-6636

Type 2 Diabetes

About 9.7 million women in the United States have diabetes. Most women and men diagnosed with diabetes have type 2 diabetes. Type 2 diabetes used to be called adult-onset diabetes. But now we know that people can develop type 2 diabetes at any age—even during childhood or adolescence.

The good news is that doctors know a lot about managing diabetes. You can lead a long and healthy life with diabetes. Getting treatment and taking care of yourself can help prevent health problems. In fact, your doctor will want you to take an active part in your diabetes care.

What is diabetes?

Diabetes is a disorder of metabolism—the way your body uses digested food for growth and energy. Much of the food you eat is broken down into glucose, the form of sugar in the blood. Glucose is the main source of fuel for your body.

After digestion, glucose enters your bloodstream. Then glucose goes to your body's cells to be used for energy. For glucose to enter into your cells, insulin must be present. Insulin is a hormone produced by your pancreas (PAN-kree-uhss), a large gland behind your stomach.

When you eat, your pancreas automatically produces the right amount of insulin to move glucose from your blood into your cells. But if you have type 2 diabe-

tes, your body's system for producing energy doesn't work correctly. One or both of the following things can happen:

- Your cells don't respond properly to your own insulin, a condition called insulin resistance.

- Your pancreas makes little or no insulin.

As a result, glucose builds up in your blood and passes out of your body in your urine. Your body loses its main source of fuel, even though your blood contains large amounts of glucose.

You could have type 2 diabetes and not know it. In fact, sometimes type 2 diabetes has no warning signs at all.

- Of the 1.3 million women aged 18 to 44 years with diabetes, one-half million don't know they have it.

- Of the 4 million women aged 65 years and older with diabetes, 1 million don't know they have it.

Another form of diabetes, type 1 diabetes, formerly called juvenile diabetes or insulin-dependent diabetes, is usually first diagnosed in children, teenagers, or young adults. In type 1 diabetes, cells in the pancreas no longer make insulin because the body's immune system has attacked and destroyed them. People with type 1 diabetes must take insulin by injection or with an insulin pump.

Know your risk of type 2 diabetes

The following factors put you at risk for type 2 diabetes. Some of these factors are not under your control. But you can control a number of the risk factors and lower your chances of getting type 2 diabetes. To learn your risk of type 2 diabetes, place a check mark beside each item that applies to you. Then show this list to your doctor and ask whether you should be tested for diabetes.

Risk factors you can't control

❏ I am age 45 or older.

❏ My family background is African American, American Indian/Alaska Native, Hispanic, Asian American, or Pacific Islander.*

❏ I have had gestational (jess-TAY-shuhn-uhl) diabetes, or I gave birth to a baby weighing more than 9 pounds. (See page 71 for gestational diabetes information.)

❏ I have a parent, brother, or sister with diabetes.

❏ I have polycystic ovary syndrome, also called PCOS.

❏ I have had blood vessel problems affecting my heart, brain, or legs.

Risk factors you can control

❏ I am overweight. (See page 22 of the *Heart Disease* chapter for the Body Mass Index chart.)

❏ I am fairly inactive. I exercise fewer than three times a week.

❏ My blood pressure is 140/90 mmHg or higher, or I have been told that I have high blood pressure.

❏ My cholesterol (koh-LESS-tur-ol) levels are not normal. My HDL (good) cholesterol is below 35 mg/dL, and/or my triglyceride (treye-GLIH-suh-ryd) level is above 250 mg/dL.

❏ I have been told that I have higher than normal blood glucose levels, also called pre-diabetes, impaired glucose tolerance, or impaired fasting glucose.

❏ The skin around my neck or in my armpits looks dark, thick, and velvety, a skin condition associated with insulin resistance called acanthosis nigricans (ak-an-THOH-suhss NIG-ruh-kanz).

❏ I have blood vessel problems affecting my heart, brain, or legs.

If you're an African American, Hispanic, American Indian/Alaska Native, Asian American, or Pacific Islander woman, you're more than twice as likely as a Caucasian woman to get type 2 diabetes.

What is gestational diabetes?

Gestational diabetes is a type of diabetes that first develops during pregnancy and usually disappears on delivery. It increases the mother's risk of developing diabetes later in life. For more information on how it is diagnosed and treated, see the *Pregnancy* chapter on page 169.

What is metabolic (met-uh-BOL-ihk) syndrome?

Metabolic syndrome is a group of conditions that increases your risk of developing type 2 diabetes, heart disease, or a stroke. If you have any three of the following five conditions, you have metabolic syndrome, also called insulin resistance syndrome:

• a large waistline: 35 inches or more

• high triglyceride levels: 150 mg/dL or higher

• low HDL cholesterol levels: below 50 mg/dL

• high blood pressure levels: 130/85 mmHg or higher

• above-normal fasting blood glucose levels: 100 mg/dL or higher

Preventing or delaying type 2 diabetes

A major research study has shown that type 2 diabetes can be prevented or delayed in people at high risk of diabetes, including women with a history of gestational diabetes. People who participated in the study

• lowered their intake of fat and calories

• exercised about 30 minutes a day, 5 days a week

These efforts resulted in a modest weight loss and prevented or delayed diabetes. If you are at risk of diabetes, making these same lifestyle changes to help prevent or delay diabetes is important.

Warning signs of type 2 diabetes

You might have no warning signs at all. Or you might have these signs:

- increased thirst
- increased hunger
- fatigue
- increased urination, especially at night
- weight loss
- blurred vision
- sores that don't heal
- tingling or numb feet or hands

Diagnosing type 2 diabetes

Your doctor can use any of the following ways to diagnose type 2 diabetes:

- A fasting plasma glucose test measures your blood glucose level after you have gone at least 8 hours without eating. Experts recommend this test for diagnosis.

- An oral glucose tolerance test measures your blood glucose level after you have gone at least 8 hours without eating and 2 hours after you drink a glucose-containing beverage.

- In a random plasma glucose test, your doctor checks your blood glucose level at any time of the day without regard to when you last ate. Your doctor will also ask about signs and symptoms of diabetes.

If the results of any of these tests show you have diabetes, your doctor will confirm the results by testing you again on a different day.

Health effects of type 2 diabetes

Over time, high blood glucose levels can lead to serious health problems with your eyes, kidneys, nervous system, feet, skin, teeth, and gums. But the most serious problems, especially for women with diabetes, are problems with the heart and blood vessels. Such problems can lead to heart disease, heart attacks, and strokes. Diabetes is a more common cause of heart disease in women than in men. When heart disease occurs in women with diabetes, the damage can be worse than it is in men with diabetes. The good news is that you can prevent or delay serious problems by taking care of your health.

Body Parts That Can Be Affected by Type 2 Diabetes

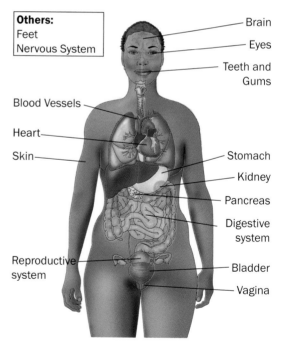

Others:
Feet
Nervous System

Brain
Eyes
Teeth and Gums
Blood Vessels
Heart
Skin
Stomach
Kidney
Pancreas
Digestive system
Reproductive system
Bladder
Vagina

TYPE 2 DIABETES CAN AFFECT MANY PARTS OF YOUR BODY, BUT YOU CAN DO A LOT TO TAKE CARE OF YOURSELF AND PREVENT HEALTH PROBLEMS.

Fasting* Blood Glucose Numbers (mg/dL) and What They Mean

Blood glucose numbers	What they mean
From 70 to 99	Normal
From 100 to 125	Pre-diabetes, also called impaired fasting glucose
126 and above on more than one test	Diabetes

*Note: Fasting means not eating or drinking for at least 8 hours.

What Women With Type 2 Diabetes Need to Know

Urinary tract infections	• You might have an increased risk of urinary tract infections. (See the *Urologic and Kidney Health* chapter on page 251.)
Bladder problems	• You might have an increased risk of urinary incontinence. (See the *Urologic and Kidney Health* chapter on page 251.)
Fungus or yeast infections	• If you are overweight and have high blood glucose levels, you might be at increased risk of fungus or yeast infections. These infections can occur in the vagina and genital area, under the breasts, or under skin folds.
Menstrual cycle	• Changes in your hormone levels before, during, and after your menstrual cycle can affect your blood glucose levels. Talk with your doctor about how to adjust your medicines and meal plan to keep your blood glucose levels on target.
Birth control	• Talk with your doctor about which birth control method would be best for you. (See the *Reproductive Health* chapter on page 153.)
Sexual dysfunction	• You might experience decreased sexual desire, trouble becoming aroused or having an orgasm, or pain during intercourse.
Pregnancy	• Meet with your doctor several months before you try to get pregnant. Your doctor can help you make a plan for getting your blood glucose on target before conception. • Keeping your blood glucose as close to normal as possible before you get pregnant and during your pregnancy is the most important thing you can do to stay healthy and have a healthy baby. (See the *Pregnancy* chapter on page 169.)
Breastfeeding	• Breastfeeding is highly recommended for the babies of women with diabetes. (See the *Breastfeeding* chapter on page 187.)
Menopause	• As you start to go into menopause, swings in hormone levels can lead to swings in blood glucose levels. • Changes in hormone levels with menopause can lead to lower blood glucose levels. You might need lower doses of your diabetes medicine. (See the *Healthy Aging* chapter on page 221.)

How to prevent or delay heart disease and other health problems

You can lower your chances of having heart disease and other health problems by managing the ABCs of diabetes.

Goals for the ABCs of Diabetes	
A is for the A1C blood glucose test. The result shows your average blood glucose level for the past 2 to 3 months.	• Aim for lower than 7 percent. • Your doctor may ask you to aim for lower than 6 percent. **Ask your doctor what goal is best for you.** **Write your goal here: _____.**
B is for Blood pressure.	• Aim for lower than 130/80 mmHg.
C is for Cholesterol.	• Aim for: LDL cholesterol: lower than 100 mg/dL HDL cholesterol: higher than 50 mg/dL Triglycerides: lower than 150 mg/dL

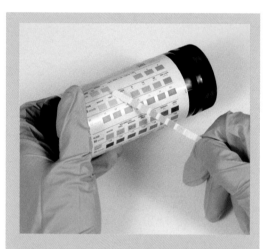

Questions to Ask Your Doctor About Your A1C Test Result

- What was the result of my latest A1C test?

- What does the result mean in terms of my risk of long-term health problems?

- What can I do to lower my risk of long-term health problems?

Managing diabetes

Taking care of diabetes requires a team approach involving you, your doctor, a diabetes educator, a nurse, a dietitian, other health care providers, and other specialists as needed. You are an important part of the team because you will be making the decisions about your food, physical activity, and other important parts of your daily diabetes care.

Treatments for Type 2 Diabetes

Meal planning	• Ask for a personalized meal plan, tailored to your daily routine, from a registered dietitian. • Your dietitian can show you how to include your favorite foods in your meal plan. • Choosing sensible serving sizes will help keep your blood glucose levels on target. • If you want to lose weight, your dietitian can design a meal plan to help you reach your goal. • If you choose to drink alcoholic beverages, talk with your doctor about personalized guidelines. In general, most women with diabetes should limit themselves to one drink a day or less.
Physical activity	• Before you start an exercise program, ask your doctor what kinds of physical activity would be best for you. • Moderate aerobic physical activity, at least 3 days a week, can help you reach your target blood glucose levels and your body weight goal, and lower your risk of heart and blood vessel disease. • Resistance exercise, three times a week, is also recommended for women with type 2 diabetes.
Medicines	• There are three types of diabetes medicines: pills, insulin (taken by injection or with an insulin pump), and other injectable medicines. • You might need a combination of medicines to control your blood glucose levels. • You also might need medicines for other medical conditions, such as high blood pressure or high cholesterol. Talk with your doctor about birth control methods. • Ask your doctor whether you should take aspirin every day to prevent a heart attack or a stroke.

All about your blood glucose levels

Keeping blood glucose levels on target day to day will help you feel better and help delay or prevent long-term health problems. You can check your own blood glucose levels using a blood glucose meter. Your doctor or diabetes educator can show you how to use a meter. Goals for most women are shown below.

er you get to your goals, the more you will lower your risk of health problems. Every step helps.

Blood glucose levels rise and fall many times during the day and night. The chart on the next page can help you understand why. Remember—sometimes you won't be able to explain why your blood glucose is up or down.

Blood Glucose Targets for Most Women With Diabetes

When	Target levels
Before meals	70 to 130 mg/dL
1 to 2 hours after the start of a meal	Less than 180 mg/dL

No one expects you to reach your blood glucose targets all the time. But the clos-

What Factors Make Blood Glucose Levels Rise or Fall?	
Reasons blood glucose levels rise	• Eating a meal or a snack
	• Eating more food or more carbohydrates than usual
	• Being physically inactive
	• Having an infection, surgery, injury, or being ill
	• Being under stress
	• Having changes in hormone levels, such as during certain times in your menstrual cycle
	• Taking certain medicines (side effects)
	• Taking too little diabetes medicine or not taking your diabetes medicine
Reasons blood glucose levels fall	• Missing or delaying a meal or a snack
	• Eating less food or fewer carbohydrates than usual
	• Being physically active
	• Drinking alcoholic beverages, especially on an empty stomach
	• Having changes in hormone levels, such as during menopause
	• Taking certain medicines (side effects)
	• Taking too much diabetes medicine

Low blood glucose

Low blood glucose, also called hypogly-cemia (heye-poh-gleye-SEE-mee-uh), happens when your blood glucose is too low to provide enough energy for your body's activities. Low blood glucose can make you feel shaky, nervous, sweaty, dizzy, or confused.

Low blood glucose can occur

- as a side effect of diabetes medicines that lower blood glucose levels

- if you miss or delay a meal

- if you eat less than usual

- if you're more active than usual

Eating or drinking something with car-bohydrates, such as glucose tablets or fruit juice, can bring your blood glucose level back to normal. Ask your doctor how to handle low blood glucose.

Keeping track of your health

You and your health care team will work together to keep track of your health. During your office visits, you'll review your blood glucose records, talk about your medicines, meal plans, a physi-cal activity routine, and other concerns. You can use the following reminder list of diabetes checkups and discuss other things to do to make sure you get the best diabetes care.

Diabetes Checkups

- **A1C test.** Have this blood glucose test at least twice a year. Your result will tell you what your average blood glucose level was for the past 2 to 3 months.

- **Blood pressure.** Have your blood pressure checked every time you visit your doctor.

- **Blood fat (lipid) lab tests.** Get a blood test at least once a year to check your cholesterol and other blood fats. These test results will help you plan how to prevent heart disease, heart attack, and stroke.

- **Kidney function tests.** Get a urine test once a year to check for protein. Get a blood test at least once a year to measure the amount of creatinine (kree-AT-uh-neen). The results of these tests will tell you how well your kidneys are working.

- **Dilated eye exam.** See an eye care professional once a year for a complete eye exam.

- **Dental exam.** See your dentist twice a year for a cleaning and checkup.

- **Foot exam.** Ask your health care provider to check your feet at least once a year to make sure your foot nerves and your blood circulation are OK.

- **Flu shot.** Get a flu shot each year.

- **Pneumonia (noo-MOH-nyuh) vaccine.** Get a pneumonia vaccination. If you're older than 64 and your vaccine was more than 5 years ago, get another one.

Be sure to ask your doctor or diabetes educator if you have questions about what to do during these special times:

When you're ill. Illness can raise blood glucose levels. Your doctor may suggest you check your blood glucose levels more often at these times. Ask your doctor for other special instructions about taking your diabetes medicines when you're ill.

When you travel. When you travel, always carry the following with you:

- your diabetes medicines

- your diabetes supplies for checking your blood glucose

- food for snacks, a meal, and for treating low blood glucose

Never put your diabetes medicines or supplies in your checked baggage.

When you change time zones. If you'll be changing time zones, meet with your doctor or diabetes educator several weeks ahead of time to learn how to adjust your diabetes medicines, especially if you take insulin.

When you take a long car trip. If you take diabetes medicines that can cause low blood glucose, check your blood glucose before you drive to make sure it's in the normal range. Stop and check your blood glucose every 2 hours. If your blood glucose is low, eat or drink something. Low blood glucose can be dangerous when you're driving because you can pass out.

Diabetes and your emotions

Sometimes having a chronic disease like type 2 diabetes leads to emotional upset. You might feel angry, afraid, guilty, or overwhelmed. It's normal to feel this way. Perhaps you're the one in your family who takes care of everyone else. Maybe you worry about how you'll have time to take care of yourself.

Depression, a serious medical condition that's more than feeling sad (see the *Mental Health* chapter on page 207), is common in women with diabetes. Depression can get in the way of taking care of yourself. If you're depressed, talk with your doctor. Treatment can help.

You can learn how to cope with having diabetes, manage stress, and find support. Share your concerns with your doctor.

Some women enjoy going to support groups where they can talk with others who have diabetes. Or you can get help from family and friends.

Paying for Diabetes Care

If you're worried about the cost of your diabetes care and need financial assistance, ask your doctor for help in finding resources. Medicare helps pay for diabetes equipment, supplies, and other services. Call (800) MEDICARE for more information.

Living well with type 2 diabetes

You can learn how to live a full and active life with diabetes. Taking care of yourself can help delay or prevent diabetes-related health problems. Your health care team can provide care and guidance during all of the stages of your life. ∎

One Woman's Story

In 2007, I was on top of the world for a change with respect to my health. With a new focus on health once I hit age 40 and knowledge of my family history of high blood pressure, cancer, and diabetes, I knew I needed to make some life changes. I didn't want to struggle with those same health problems. I paid attention to what I was eating and was physically active four to five times a week. I was even able to stop taking my blood pressure medicine. I thought things were going great.

Then at my annual physical, the doctor ran some blood tests and scheduled me to come back in a few days. I went back, expecting to get an all-clear. The last thing I expected to hear was that I now have type 2 diabetes. I was in complete shock! I said to the doctor, "What? That can't be right. I've been doing all the right things." I went into shutdown mode mentally. The words just kept echoing in my head. The doctor kept talking as if this was not a life-changing statement, and there was no sense of concern on her part. I was given a monitor and told I could use it or not and wasn't given very much more information except to stay away from potatoes, rice, and starches. She never mentioned working with a dietitian, following a healthy lifestyle regimen, or finding support groups. I left the office feeling like I had been punched in the stomach. I called my mom, who also has type 2 diabetes, and she was a great help to me. She told me to get on the Internet and seek out support groups in my area that would be able to help me navigate life with diabetes.

> **I called my mom, who also has type 2 diabetes, and she was a great help to me.**

I am fortunate that I am able to control my diabetes with a personalized eating plan and physical activity. I do not have to take insulin at this point. It has been a long journey, but I am moving through this transition in a positive direction with a positive outlook. And I am taking much-needed steps to find a new doctor to help me continue to control my diabetes—someone who can inform me and support me in my efforts.

Sandra
Las Vegas, Nevada

For More Information...

Office on Women's Health, HHS
200 Independence Ave SW, Room 712E
Washington, DC 20201
Web site: www.womenshealth.gov/faq/
diabetes.htm
Phone number: (800) 994-9662,
(888) 220-5446 TDD

Division of Diabetes Translation, CDC
4770 Buford Highway NE, MS K-10
Atlanta, GA 30341-3717
Web site: www.cdc.gov/diabetes
Phone number: (800) 232-4636,
(888) 232-6348 TTY

National Diabetes Education Program, NIH
1 Diabetes Way
Bethesda, MD 20814–9692
Web site: www.ndep.nih.gov
Phone number: (888) 693-6337

National Diabetes Information Clearinghouse, NIH
1 Information Way
Bethesda, MD 20892-3560
Web site: www.diabetes.niddk.nih.gov
Phone number: (800) 860-8747

Office of Women's Health, FDA
5600 Fishers Ln
Rockville, MD 20857
Web site: www.fda.gov/womens
www.fda.gov/womens/taketimetocare/
diabetes
Phone number: (888) 463-6332

American Association of Diabetes Educators
200 W Madison St, Suite 800
Chicago, IL 60606
Web site: www.diabeteseducator.org
Phone number: (800) 832-6874 to find a
diabetes educator

American Diabetes Association
1701 N Beauregard St
Alexandria, VA 22311
Web site: www.diabetes.org
Phone number: (800) 342-2383

American Dietetic Association
120 S Riverside Plaza, Suite 2000
Chicago, IL 60606–6995
Web site: www.eatright.org
Phone number: (800) 877-1600 ext.5000

Autoimmune Diseases

If you have an autoimmune (aw-toh-ih-MYOON) disease, your experience may have been frustrating and confusing. It can be hard to describe the often debilitating symptoms many people endure. And the medical community is still learning about these diseases, which affect mostly women. To date, there are no cures.

The good news is that there are treatments available to manage tough symptoms and you can feel better. At the same time, experts are working toward better treatments and perhaps even a way to prevent these diseases someday.

What are autoimmune diseases?

The immune system is a complex network of special cells and organs that defends the body from "foreign" invaders. These invaders can be germs, viruses, and other foreign things called antigens (AN-tih-juhnz).

At the core of the immune system is the ability to distinguish between self and nonself: what's you and what's foreign. A flaw can make the body unable to tell the difference between self and nonself. When this happens, the body makes autoantibodies (AW-toh-AN-teye-bah-deez) that attack normal cells by mistake. At the same time, special cells called regulatory T cells fail to do their job of keeping the immune system in line. The result is a misguided attack on your own body. This causes the damage we know as an autoimmune disease.

Body Parts That Can Be Affected by Autoimmune Diseases

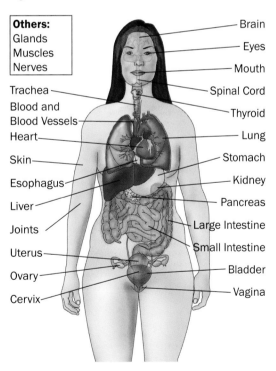

Others:
Glands
Muscles
Nerves

Trachea
Blood and Blood Vessels
Heart
Skin
Esophagus
Liver
Joints
Uterus
Ovary
Cervix

Brain
Eyes
Mouth
Spinal Cord
Thyroid
Lung
Stomach
Kidney
Pancreas
Large Intestine
Small Intestine
Bladder
Vagina

The more than 80 different autoimmune diseases are each defined by the kind of damage involved and the body part(s) affected. The blood, skin, eyes, nerves, and heart are just some of the body parts that can be involved.

Who is at risk of getting autoimmune diseases?

Individually, autoimmune diseases are rare. Together, they are a leading cause of disability and death. The number of people with autoimmune diseases is growing, but it is unclear why. It is also unclear why certain people are at greater risk of getting these diseases. To learn more, experts are studying patients to see what they may have in common.

Women of childbearing age. Of the more than 23.5 million people with autoimmune diseases, most are women. As a group, these diseases are a leading cause of death among young and middle-aged women. Often, they strike during childbearing years when women are likely juggling multiple roles as mothers, caregivers, employees, friends, community members, and much more. Dealing with an autoimmune disease can be a trying experience on top of an already busy life.

Hormones are thought to play an important role because some autoimmune diseases "act" differently during pregnancy, menstruation, and menopause. Hormone changes at these times can cause symptoms to either get worse or better, depending on the disease. For instance, rheumatoid arthritis (ROO-muh-toid ar-THREYE-tuhss) improves during pregnancy, whereas systemic

lupus erythematosus (LOO-puhss ur-ih-thee-muh-TOH-suhss), known as lupus, worsens. Pregnancy is also known to trigger thyroiditis (theye-roi-DEYE-tiss) after the baby is born. Yet the question about whether female hormones *cause* these diseases is yet to be answered.

People with a family history. Heredity plays an important role. Some diseases run in families, such as lupus, multiple sclerosis (MUHL-tip-uhl sklur-OH-suhss), and vitiligo (vit-uhl-EYE-goh). It is also common for different members of one family to have different types of autoimmune diseases.

For instance:

- A woman may have rheumatoid arthritis.
- Her mother may have Hashimoto's (hah-shee-MOH-tohz) disease.
- Her grandmother may have type 1 diabetes.

To understand this family link, experts need to identify the genes that make people more likely to get certain autoimmune diseases. The good news is that some progress has been made, often by studying families with multiple members who have autoimmune diseases. In the past few years, more has been learned about the genetic basis of rheumatoid arthritis, vitiligo, lupus, psoriasis (suh-REYE-uh-suhss), and others.

> For more information on genes and genetic counseling, see pages 408 and 409 of the Appendix.

People who are around certain things in the environment. Many things may cause or intensify certain diseases:

- The ultraviolet rays in sunlight can make the symptoms of lupus worse.

- Being around industrial solvents may increase the risk of developing scleroderma (sklair-oh-DUR-muh) or lupus.

- Dietary iodine may be responsible for an increase in the number of people who have thyroiditis.

- Research has linked infections caused by a variety of bacteria and viruses that have been linked to many immune diseases, including multiple sclerosis, type 1 diabetes, rheumatoid arthritis, lupus, and others. Sex hormones may further boost the immune system's overreaction to infections in women who are already at risk for these diseases. This could help explain why these diseases are more common in women.

Although these links have been seen, experts don't yet know if avoiding infections and sunlight can stop an autoimmune disease from happening. And other possible triggers, such as some metals, need to be studied more.

People with certain ethnic backgrounds. Experts are not yet sure why, but some ethnic groups seem to be at greater risk of certain diseases.

- Type 1 diabetes is more common in white people.

- Lupus is three times more common in African American women. Lupus is also more common in Hispanic, Asian, and American Indian women. The disease is more severe for African American and Hispanic people, who also develop symptoms at a younger age.

Common Links Among People With Autoimmune Diseases

- women of childbearing age
- people with a family history
- people who are around certain things in the environment
- people of certain ethnic backgrounds

- Choctaw Native Americans have higher rates of scleroderma. African Americans, Hispanics, and Native Americans may also have more severe forms of the disease.

These differences may be due to a genetic link. Exposure to similar things in the environment may also explain why certain communities are affected more than others.

Genes + Environment

Inheriting certain genes can raise your risk of getting an autoimmune disease, but it may be an event or exposure to something outside of your body that actually triggers it.

The role of environmental exposures in the absence of a genetic link is still unclear. In the case of heart disease, we know you can lower your risk by eating less saturated fat, exercising, and taking other heart-healthy steps. We don't yet know if the things you do—or don't do—can raise or lower your risk of autoimmune diseases on their own.

Types of autoimmune diseases

Some autoimmune diseases are life threatening. Nearly all of these diseases are debilitating and require lifelong medical care. Although each is unique, these diseases in general have much in common. Many of them share hallmark symptoms, such as fatigue, dizziness, and low-grade fever. Many also go through remissions, when symptoms go away, and "active" disease stages, when symptoms flare.

The autoimmune diseases discussed in the following chart are more common in women than in men.

Types of Autoimmune Diseases

Disease	Body part(s) involved	Who gets it?	Symptoms	Tests to find out if you have it (See page 91 for a blood test glossary.)
Antiphospholipid (an-teye-FOSS-foh-lip-ihd) **antibody syndrome (aPL)** A disease that causes problems in the inner lining of blood vessels resulting in blood clots in arteries or veins. *Also called sticky blood syndrome*	Clots can develop in the brain, the veins of the legs and lungs, or in the placenta of pregnant women.	More common in women	• Blood clots in veins or arteries • Multiple miscarriages • Lacy, net-like red rash on the wrists and knees	• Blood test • The disease is suspected if you have a history of blood clots or multiple miscarriages.

Types of Autoimmune Diseases

Disease	Body part(s) involved	Who gets it?	Symptoms	Tests to find out if you have it (See page 91 for a blood test glossary.)
Graves' disease A disease that causes the thyroid gland to make too much thyroid hormone. *Also called diffuse thyrotoxic goiter or overactive thyroid*	Thyroid gland	Women older than 20, although it may occur at any age and may also affect men	• Insomnia (not being able to sleep) • Irritability • Weight loss • Heat sensitivity • Sweating • Fine brittle hair • Muscle weakness • Light menstrual periods • Bulging eyes • Shaky hands You may have no symptoms.	Blood test for thyroid-stimulating hormone (TSH)
Hashimoto's thyroiditis Inflammation of the thyroid gland that stops it from making enough thyroid hormones. It is the most common thyroid disease in the United States. *Also called autoimmune thyroiditis, chronic thyroiditis, or underactive thyroid*	Thyroid gland	• Middle-aged women • People with a family history	• Fatigue • Weakness • Weight gain • Sensitivity to cold • Muscle aches and stiff joints • Facial swelling • Constipation	Blood test for thyroid-stimulating hormone (TSH)
Multiple sclerosis A disease in which the immune system attacks the protective coating, called myelin, around the nerves. The damage affects the brain and spinal cord, causing muscle weakness, loss of coordination, and vision and speech problems.	Central nervous system (brain and spinal cord)	• More common in women than men • Most common between ages 20 and 40, but can strike at any age	• Weakness and trouble with coordination, balance, seeing, speaking, and walking • Paralysis • Tremors • Numbness and a tingling feeling in the arms, legs, hands, and feet • Symptoms vary because the location and extent of each attack vary.	• An exam of your body • An exam of your brain, spinal cord, and nerves (a neurological exam) • X-ray tests • Other tests on the brain and spinal cord fluid

Types of Autoimmune Diseases

Disease	Body part(s) involved	Who gets it?	Symptoms	Tests to find out if you have it (See page 91 for a blood test glossary.)
Myasthenia gravis (MG) (meye-uhss-THEEN-ee-uh GRAV-uhss) A disease in which the immune system attacks the nerves and muscles, causing weakness and problems with seeing, chewing, walking, and talking.	Muscles throughout the body and the thymus gland, which is in the chest	• Can affect people at any age • Most common in young women and older men	• Double vision, trouble keeping a steady gaze, and drooping eyelids • Trouble swallowing, with frequent gagging or choking (called a *crisis*) • Weakness or paralysis • Muscles that work better after rest • Drooping head • Trouble climbing stairs or lifting things • Trouble talking	• Physical and neurologic exams • Blood test • Injection of a drug that briefly improves muscle strength in people with MG • Nerve stimulation tests that can show impaired nerve-to-muscle communication in people with MG • Tests to measure breathing strength
Rheumatoid arthritis A disease in which the immune system attacks the lining of the joints throughout the body.	Joints, lungs, heart, and other organs	Usually occurs in people between ages 25 and 55	• Joint pain, stiffness, swelling, and malformation • Reduced movement and function May have: • Fatigue • Fever • Weight loss • Eye inflammation • Anemia (uh-NEE-mee-uh)	• An exam of your body • X-rays of the joints • Blood test to detect anemia, the antibody rheumatoid factor (RF), and citrulline antibodies (CCP). (Some people with RF never get this disease. Others who have this disease do not have this antibody.) • Test of the fluid in the joints may be needed

Types of Autoimmune Diseases

Disease	Body part(s) involved	Who gets it?	Symptoms	Tests to find out if you have it (See page 91 for a blood test glossary.)
Scleroderma A disease causing abnormal growth of connective tissue in the skin and blood vessels. In more severe forms, this tissue can build up internally, leading in some cases to organ failure.	Skin and possibly the kidneys, lungs, heart, and gastrointestinal tract	• People 30 to 50 years old, more often women • People around silica dust and polyvinyl chloride may be at risk	• Fingers and toes that turn white, red, or blue in response to heat and cold (called Raynaud phenomenon) • Pain, stiffness, and swelling of fingers and joints • Thickening of the skin • Skin that looks shiny on the hands and forearm • Tight and mask-like facial skin • Sores on the fingers or toes • Trouble swallowing • Weight loss • Diarrhea or constipation • Shortness of breath	• Exam of the skin for tightness, thickening, and hardening • Blood tests • Urine test • Chest x-ray • Lung function test • Skin biopsy
Sjögren's syndrome (SHOH-grins) A disease in which the immune system targets the glands that make moisture, such as tears and saliva, leading to dryness of the eyes, mouth, and other body tissues.	Mucous membranes, such as the eyes and mouth	Most common in women 40 to 50 years old	• Dry eyes or eyes that itch • Dryness of the mouth, which can cause sores • Trouble swallowing • Loss of sense of taste • Severe dental cavities • Hoarseness • Fatigue • Joint swelling or pain • Swollen glands • Cloudy eyes	• Blood tests • Biopsy of the salivary gland • A test to see if you make enough tears • An eye test using a special dye

Types of Autoimmune Diseases

Disease	Body part(s) involved	Who gets it?	Symptoms	Tests to find out if you have it (See page 91 for a blood test glossary.)
Systemic lupus erythematosus A disease that can damage the joints, skin, kidneys, and other parts of the body. *Also called SLE or lupus*	Skin, joints, lungs, kidneys, brain, lungs, and heart	Mostly young women	• Fever • Weight loss • Hair loss • Mouth ulcers (sores) • Extreme fatigue • "Butterfly" rash across the nose and cheeks • Rashes on other parts of the body • Painful or swollen joints and muscle pain • Sensitivity to the sun	• An exam of your body • Urine test • Blood test

Other autoimmune diseases include Addison's disease, vitiligo, type 1 diabetes, and celiac (SEE-lee-ak) disease. You are more likely to get a second autoimmune disease if you already have one. For instance, people with Addison's disease often have type 1 diabetes.

Getting diagnosed

You may not have a clear pattern of symptoms at first. You may not have the same pain or problem every time. Some diseases may also not have any symptoms until they have advanced. And most of these diseases lack the diagnostic "checklist" that helps doctors identify them early. Many tests and exams may be needed to make a diagnosis.

The following steps will help your doctor diagnose your disease:

- **Medical history.** The doctor will ask about your symptoms and how long you have had them. Your symptoms may not point to one disease. But they can be a starting point for your doctor. Tell your doctor if you have a family member with autoimmune disease.

- **Physical exam.** Your doctor will check for signs such as swollen joints or lymph nodes, or skin that looks off color.

- **Medical tests.** No one test will show that you have an autoimmune disease. But doctors may find clues in a blood sample. (See page 91 for information on blood tests.)

Digestive Diseases

There are some autoimmune diseases that affect the digestive system that are more common in women. For more information on Crohn's disease, autoimmune hepatitis, primary biliary cirrhosis (BIL-ee-air-ee sur-ROH-suhss), and ulcerative colitis, see the *Digestive Health* chapter on page 265.

What type of blood tests may be done?

Antinuclear antibody or ANA (also known as fluorescent antinuclear antibody):
This test detects autoantibodies. The presence of ANA can be a marker or sign of several autoimmune diseases. ANA is most commonly seen in lupus.

Rheumatoid factor (RF):
This test detects and measures RF, an autoantibody that can mean you have rheumatoid arthritis, Sjögren's syndrome, or other autoimmune diseases. Some people have RF without any disease.

C-reactive protein (CRP):
C-reactive protein is a substance made by the liver that can be found in the blood. A high level of this substance can mean there is inflammation in the body. This test can help diagnose inflammatory bowel disease, rheumatoid arthritis, lupus, and other diseases.

Erythrocyte sedimentation rate (ESR):
This test is used to measure inflammation. It can't tell exactly where the inflammation is, so it is used along with other tests.

Citrulline antibody (CCP or anti-CCP):
This fairly new test detects citrulline antibodies, thought to be made by the immune system during inflammation. CCP can be useful in diagnosing rheumatoid arthritis early, especially in people who have symptoms but do not have RF (see RF test above).

Some people may be able to get a diagnosis quickly. For others, the process is much slower. Some people may be told they have something autoimmune related, but they are unable to get a precise label for their symptoms. Others find they can't get a diagnosis at all and spend years searching for answers. Still others find it difficult to get a *correct* diagnosis. Sadly, many patients have been told that their symptoms were stress related or in their heads. The hope is that increased awareness and research efforts will improve this experience. In the meantime, there are steps you can take to help make things easier.

What you can do:

- Write down your family's health history and share it with your doctor. Include all of the health problems your parents, siblings, grandparents, and cousins (if possible) have had.

- Write down all of the symptoms you have had and share the list with your doctor. Some symptoms may not seem related, but they may be after all. Put the symptoms that bother you the most at the top of your list.

- Seek out referrals to good doctors, starting with a specialist who deals with your most major symptom. Check with family members, friends, and health care professionals in your community for recommendations.

- Ask about your doctor's experience with autoimmune diseases. The more patients he or she has treated, the better.

- Get a second, third, or fourth opinion if need be. If a doctor doesn't take your symptoms seriously or refers you to a psychologist, find another doctor. You know how you are feeling and you are your own best advocate. Be sure to check on your insurance first to find out if it covers your visits.

Reproductive health

In the past, women with autoimmune diseases were told not to have children. This advice has changed with better treatments and understanding. Many health risks can be lowered by not getting pregnant during active stages of disease, when symptoms flare. Health risks can also be lowered by taking medicine that your doctor says is safe to take while pregnant. There may still be some risks for both the mother and baby, depending on the disease and how severe it is.

But women with autoimmune diseases can safely have children. And, although symptoms may be worse during pregnancy for some women, others may find that their symptoms improve.

Before Pregnancy

It is important to talk to your doctor before trying to get pregnant. Along with your regular doctor(s), you may also need care from a maternal-fetal-medicine specialist. This type of doctor cares for women with health problems that may affect pregnancy.

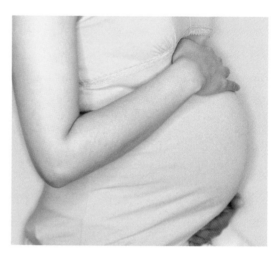

How Autoimmune Diseases Affect Pregnancy	
Disease	**What you should know about pregnancy**
Antiphospholipid antibody syndrome (aPL)	Pregnancy poses serious risks for both mother and baby. These risks include stroke, blood clots, high blood pressure, and repeated miscarriage. For the baby, there is a risk of stillbirth or fetal death, poor growth in the womb, and preterm birth. Pregnant women with aPL often need more frequent prenatal care visits.
	It is not clear whether this disease gets worse or better during pregnancy.
Hashimoto's thyroiditis	Also called painless thyroiditis or hypothyroidism, some women get this disease while pregnant. It causes thyroid problems in women after the baby is born. These problems are often not permanent. Many times, women have postpartum depression at the same time.

How Autoimmune Diseases Affect Pregnancy

Disease	What you should know about pregnancy
Lupus	Pregnant women with lupus must be closely watched to help prevent problems such as preterm birth and stillbirth. Treatment may be needed during pregnancy to control your disease.
	Symptoms tend to worsen during the second half of pregnancy and after the baby is born. Yet this will not make the outcome of the disease worse for you. A long period of remission before getting pregnant can lower your chances of a flare-up during pregnancy.
	Rarely, babies born to women with lupus have neonatal lupus. This is not the same thing as lupus in adults. Babies with neonatal lupus can have a rash and, sometimes, a problem with their heartbeat. This problem is treatable. Babies with neonatal lupus have only a small chance of having lupus later in life.
Graves' disease	Also called hyperthyroidism, Graves' disease can lead to preterm birth and low birth weight. Women may be at risk of high blood pressure during pregnancy.
	Pregnancy does not appear to make the disease worse. Some women may have trouble getting pregnant. Pregnant women must have their thyroid levels watched throughout pregnancy. There are certain drugs that may cause birth defects and should not be used.
Rheumatoid arthritis	Symptoms generally improve during pregnancy, often allowing women to take less medicine. Symptoms usually flare up after the baby is born.
Scleroderma	It may be best to wait to get pregnant for some time after the disease is diagnosed. It is important to talk to a doctor about timing. It is not clear if having this disease makes it harder for women to get pregnant, but some drugs can cause infertility.
	Pregnant women will need to have their blood pressure watched carefully. Skin problems common to patients with scleroderma do not pose extra problems during pregnancy. The disease may be more active following delivery.
Multiple sclerosis (MS)	Symptoms tend to improve during pregnancy. Pregnancy does not appear to make the disease worse. Women who don't yet know they have MS may be more likely to start having symptoms during pregnancy.
	Having MS may make it hard for women to carry a pregnancy. Muscle weakness, coordination problems, and fatigue may make falls more likely. If in a wheelchair, women may have more urinary tract infections. Labor may also be more difficult, but there are things doctors can do to help.
Myasthenia gravis (MG)	Symptoms that lead to trouble breathing—a crisis—may happen during pregnancy. For some women, though, the disease may go into remission.
	There are some risks for pregnant women with MG, such as greater chances of preterm labor. It is also possible that the medicine used to treat MG may cause contractions. MG crises are also more likely to happen during labor.
	Pregnancy does not make the outcome of the disease worse for women.
Sjögren's syndrome	Many women first get this disease after childbearing age. Pregnancy-related problems tend to be tied to lupus or aPL, which patients with Sjögren's often also have.

Experts have long suspected the hormone estrogen to be a lupus trigger, leading them to warn against the use of birth control pills. Yet research has shown birth control pills to be safe in women with lupus.

Infertility

Some women with autoimmune diseases may have trouble getting pregnant. There are a few reasons behind this challenge:

- Type 1 diabetes, lupus, and hypothyroidism (Hashimoto's thyroiditis) are linked to a higher risk of early menopause or premature ovarian failure (POF). Women with POF stop menstruating before age 40, lack estrogen, and are infertile.

- Infertility is also caused by autoimmune oophoritis (oo-for-EYE-tuhss). With this disease, the body attacks its own cells that release reproductive hormones. This causes ovarian failure.

- Some treatments may cause infertility. Chemotherapy drugs, used to treat severe cases of lupus, can cause fertility to decline early.

Let your doctor know if you are having trouble getting pregnant. There are tests that can be done to see if your autoimmune disease is the root of the problem. Your doctor can also tell you if fertility treatments are an option for you.

Breastfeeding Safety

After pregnancy, it is important to talk to your doctor about the safety of your medications during breastfeeding.

Other health issues

Fatigue can be a big problem for people who have autoimmune diseases. And some people may also have chronic fatigue syndrome (CFS) or fibromyalgia (feye-broh-meye-AL-juh) (FM) at the same time. Although these two conditions may share similar symptoms, they are not autoimmune diseases. CFS can cause you to have trouble concentrating, feel weak and very tired, and have muscle pain.

FM causes widespread body pain. People with FM also feel tired and have low energy. FM mainly occurs in women of childbearing age.

For more information on chronic fatigue syndrome and fibromyalgia, see the *Pain* chapter on page 351.

People with some autoimmune diseases can also be at greater risk of atherosclerosis (a-thuh-roh-skluh-ROH-suhss) and osteoporosis (OSS-tee-oh-puh-ROH-suhss). Atherosclerosis is the hardening and narrowing of the arteries. This problem can lead to heart disease. It is not clear why people with autoimmune diseases are at greater risk for this problem. People with osteoporosis have low bone mass and weak bones. This disease leads to increased risk of fractures of the hip, spine, and wrist. Some treatments taken over time can cause osteoporosis. Routine care can help you spot and manage these health problems.

For more information on atherosclerosis, see the *Heart Disease* chapter on page 15. For more information on osteoporosis, see the *Healthy Aging* chapter on page 221.

Managing your disease

Having an autoimmune disease can cause debilitating symptoms, loss of organ function, reduced productivity at work, and high medical expenses. At the same time, it does not have to stop you from living your life. For many people, the disease does not define them. Rather, it is yet another challenge they can successfully manage. And there are many ways to cope with the different ways in which these diseases can affect your life.

- **How you look and your self-esteem.** Depending on your disease, you may have discolored or damaged skin or hair loss. Your joints may look different. Such problems can't always be prevented. But their effects can be reduced with treatment. Cosmetics, for example, can hide a skin rash. Surgery can correct a malformed joint.

- **Caring for yourself.** Painful joints or weak muscles can make it hard to do simple tasks. You may have trouble climbing stairs, making your bed, or brushing your hair. If doing daily tasks is hard, talk with a physical therapist. The therapist can teach you exercises to improve strength and function. An occupational therapist can show you new ways to do things or tools to make tasks easier.

- **Family relationships.** Family members may not understand why you don't have energy to do things you used to do. They may even think you are just being lazy. But they may also be overly concerned and eager to help you. They may not let you do the things you can do. They may even give up their own interests to be with you. Share what you learn about your disease with your family. Involve them in counseling or a support group. It may help them better understand the disease and how they can help.

- **Sexual relations.** Damage to glands that produce moisture can lead to vaginal dryness. This makes intercourse painful. Pain, weakness, or stiff joints may make it hard for you to move the way you once did. You may be unsure of how you look. Or you may be afraid that your partner will no longer find you attractive. With communication, good medical care, and perhaps counseling, many of these issues can be overcome.

Dealing with doctors

If you have an autoimmune disease, you will likely need to see different health care professionals to treat varied health problems. For instance, patients with lupus may see a rheumatologist to treat the main disease, a nephrologist to treat kidney problems, and a dermatologist for skin problems. This can make getting care tough, especially if insurance coverage is lacking.

It can also be hard if you don't have one doctor in charge of managing your overall care. Without this point person, it may be harder to deal with multiple specialists who don't communicate well with one another. Ask if there is a way to designate one doctor to take the lead. It will also help to partner with your doctors early to learn how to deal with the long-term effects of your disease.

Treatments

How people fare varies with the specific disease. Most autoimmune diseases are chronic or ongoing, but many can be controlled with treatment. There are many types of treatment available, some of which treat more than one disease. Your treatment depends on the type of disease, how severe it is, and its symptoms. Treatments can do the following:

- **Relieve symptoms.** Relieving symptoms may be as simple as taking a drug for pain relief. It may also be as involved as having surgery.

- **Preserve organ function.** Treatment may be needed to prevent organ damage. Examples include drugs to control an inflamed kidney in people with lupus and insulin injections to regulate blood sugar in people with diabetes. These treatments don't stop the disease. But they can save organ function. They can also help people live with disease complications.

- **Target disease mechanisms.** Some drugs may also be used to target how the disease works. In other words, they can suppress the immune system. These drugs include chemotherapy, at lower doses than used for treating cancer. A fairly new class of drugs called anti-TNF medications blocks inflammation in people with various forms of autoimmune arthritis and psoriasis. These drugs can lessen pain and improve quality of life for many people.

Specialists Who Treat Autoimmune Diseases

A **rheumatologist** treats arthritis and other rheumatic diseases, such as scleroderma and lupus.

An **endocrinologist** treats gland and hormone problems, such as diabetes and thyroid disease.

A **neurologist** treats nerve problems, such as multiple sclerosis and myasthenia gravis.

A **hematologist** treats diseases that affect the blood, such as pernicious anemia and autoimmune hemolytic anemia.

A **gastroenterologist** treats problems with the digestive system, such as Crohn's disease and ulcerative colitis.

A **dermatologist** treats problems of the skin, hair, and nails caused by diseases such as psoriasis, lupus, and alopecia areata (AL-uh-PEE-shuh AR-ee-AYT-uh).

A **nephrologist** treats kidney problems, such as inflamed kidneys caused by lupus.

A **physical therapist** helps patients with stiffness, weakness, and restricted body movement with proper levels of physical activity.

An **occupational therapist** helps patients improve their ability to perform daily activities, despite pain or other health problems. Special equipment and devices are used to help make things easier at work and at home.

A **speech therapist** helps people with speech problems from illnesses such as multiple sclerosis.

New treatments may be on the horizon. Experts are studying new drugs that prevent the immune system from attacking healthy body parts. These may prove helpful for treating a number of autoimmune diseases.

What you can do to feel better

Outside of treatments, there are things you can do to help yourself feel better.

- Eat a healthy diet, including balanced meals.
- Get regular physical activity. But be careful not to overdo it, and talk with your doctor first about physical activity plans. A gradual and gentle physical activity program often works well for people with long-lasting muscle and joint pain. Some types of yoga or tai chi exercises may also be helpful.

For more information on healthy eating, see the *Nutrition* chapter on page 317. For more information on physical activity, see the *Fitness* chapter on page 337.

- Try to lower your stress. Stress and anxiety can cause symptoms to flare up with some autoimmune diseases. So finding ways to relax can help manage a cycle of stress and flare-ups. Try using relaxation techniques, such as meditation. Other coping methods include:

- pacing yourself and your activities
- joining a support group
- talking with a professional counselor

Above all, be patient with yourself. Autoimmune diseases can be a big challenge, but not an impossible one. Care is better today than ever before, and continued improvement is likely. The extensive research taking place holds much promise for better ways to diagnose and treat these diseases. ■

Watch Your Symptoms

Your doctor may not prescribe a treatment. If your symptoms are mild, the risks of treatment may be worse than the symptoms. But you should watch for signs that your disease is progressing.

- Visit your doctor regularly so that you can catch changes before they lead to serious damage.
- Tell your doctor if your symptoms are flaring up.
- Talk to your doctor before starting any alternative treatments, such as natural supplements.

One Woman's Story

As a 55-year-old female with diagnosed lupus since 1990, I have many stories to tell: the difficulty in obtaining a diagnosis, the problem with having good treatment options, the anxiety of introducing the disease to both my professional and social communities. I wondered if this disease would change my life goals.

There is also the problem of carrying a disease that does not provide real clues to those who witness the struggle. No one *sees* the fatigue, the joint pain, the internal damage. Therefore, you can't be too sick. The other side of the coin is that I didn't want to be known as the women *with* lupus. I wanted to be known as the incredible woman with loads of positive characteristics and personality who *has* lupus!

Thankfully, I have found support in many ways and realized the importance of women in women's lives. There are the wonderful women friends who attempt to understand and commit to befriending the disease as well as the person. I have also been fortunate to find a female nurse practitioner who researches and studies ways to assist in dealing with the disease and its challenges.

> # No one *sees* the fatigue, the joint pain, the internal damage.

And support groups are so important—not only for those who confront medical challenges, but because the support of each other as human beings allows us to feel loved, accepted, supported, and respected. An autoimmune disease can forever alter your self-image, the path you walk, and the journey you have painted for yourself. Once the diagnosis is made, the challenges accepted, and the choices identified, you can repaint your journey. Be an artist who accepts the challenge and is determined to continue the adventure, despite the bumps and curves in the path!

Linda

Cody, Wyoming

For More Information...

Office on Women's Health, HHS
200 Independence Ave SW, Room 712E
Washington, DC 20201
Web site: www.womenshealth.gov/faq/
autoimmune.htm
Phone number: (800) 994-9662,
(888) 220-5446 TDD

National Institute of Allergy and Infectious Diseases, NIH
6610 Rockledge Dr, MSC 6612
Bethesda, MD 20892-6612
Web site: www.niaid.nih.gov
Phone number: (866) 284-4107,
(800) 877-8339 TDD

National Institute of Arthritis and Musculoskeletal and Skin Diseases Information Clearinghouse, NIH
1 AMS Circle
Bethesda, MD 20892-3675
Web site: www.niams.nih.gov
Phone number: (877) 226-4267,
(301) 565-2966 TTY

National Institute of Neurological Disorders and Stroke, NIH
PO Box 5801
Bethesda, MD 20824
Web site: www.ninds.nih.gov
Phone number: (800) 352-9424,
(301) 468-5981 TTY

American Autoimmune Related Diseases Association
22100 Gratiot Ave
East Detroit, MI 48021-2227
Web site: www.aarda.org
Phone number: (800) 598-4668 Literature requests, (586) 776-3900 Patient information

American College of Rheumatology
1800 Century Pl, Suite 250
Atlanta, GA 30345-4300
Web site: www.rheumatology.org
Phone number: (404) 633-3777

American Thyroid Association
6066 Leesburg Pike, Suite 550
Falls Church, VA 22041
Web site: www.thyroid.org
Phone number: (800) 849-7643

APS Foundation of America
PO Box 801
LaCrosse, WI 54602-0801
Web site: www.apsfa.org

Arthritis Foundation
PO Box 7669
Atlanta, GA 30357-0669
Web site: www.arthritis.org
Phone number: (800) 283-7800

Lupus Foundation of America
2000 L St NW, Suite 710
Washington, DC 20036
Web site: www.lupus.org
Phone number: (800) 558-0121
Information request line

Myasthenia Gravis Foundation of America
1821 University Ave W, Suite S256
St. Paul, MN 55104
Web site: www.myasthenia.org
Phone number: (800) 541-5454

National Graves' Disease Foundation
PO Box 1969
Brevard, NC 28712
Web site: www.ngdf.org
Phone number: (877) 643-3123

For More Information...

National Multiple Sclerosis Society
733 Third Ave
New York, NY 10017-3288
Web site: www.nationalmssociety.org
Phone number: (800) 344-4867

Scleroderma Foundation
300 Rosewood Dr, Suite 105
Danvers, MA 01923
Web site: www.scleroderma.org
Phone number: (800) 722-4673

Sjögren's Syndrome Foundation
6707 Democracy Blvd, Suite 325
Bethesda, MD 20817
Web site: www.sjogrens.org
Phone number: (800) 475-6473

Blood Disorders

Blood is essential for life. It carries oxygen and nutrients to every part of the body. Blood also fights infections and heals injuries. Therefore, disorders of the blood can have a great effect on your health.

You can protect your health by understanding the symptoms of common blood disorders. If you think you may have one of these conditions, talk to your doctor. With early diagnosis and the right treatment, many women with blood disorders are able to live full and healthy lives.

What is blood?

Blood is made up of several types of cells and proteins:

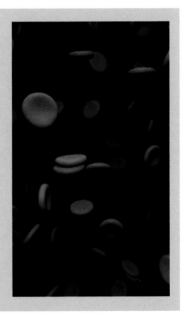

- **Red blood cells** carry oxygen from the lungs to cells throughout the body.
- **White blood cells** help fight infections.
- **Platelets** help form clots to stop bleeding.
- **Plasma**, the liquid part of blood, contains many types of proteins. These include proteins that help the blood to clot and proteins that protect the body from viruses and infection. Plasma also contains substances such as dissolved salts, sugars, and hormones.

Blood cells are produced by the soft tissue inside your bones, called bone marrow. Your body produces hundreds of billions of new blood cells each day.

Blood disorders

Blood disorders are diseases that affect one or more parts of the blood. The symptoms depend on the part of the blood affected:

- Bleeding disorders prevent the blood from forming clots, which stop bleeding after an injury. (See pages 106 and 107 for more information on different bleeding disorders.)

- Clotting disorders cause blood to clot too easily, creating a condition called thrombophilia (throm-boh-FIL-ee-uh). (See page 109 for more information.)

- Anemia (uh-NEE-mee-uh) is a condition in which the blood has too few healthy red blood cells. (See page 109 for more information.)

- Disorders of the bone marrow, such as leukemia (loo-KEE-mee-uh), may affect the production of blood cells. (See page 58 of the *Cancer* chapter for more information.)

Causes of blood disorders

Many blood disorders are inherited. If you have a history of a blood disorder in your family, you might have a higher risk of developing the disorder yourself or carrying the gene for the disorder. Blood disorders may also be caused by:

- other diseases or conditions

- the side effects of medications

- a lack of certain nutrients in your diet

Blood disorders can be acute or chronic. Acute blood disorders occur suddenly and last a short time. For example, rapid or excessive blood loss may cause acute anemia. Once the bleeding is stopped and blood levels return to normal, the anemia is cured.

A chronic blood disorder is a disorder that develops slowly or lasts a long time. Many chronic disorders, such as sickle

What is coagulation?

Coagulation (koh-ag-yuh-LAY-shuhn)—or clotting—stops bleeding after a blood vessel is injured. There are three steps in this process:

1. The blood vessel narrows, slowing the flow of blood.

2. The platelets begin to "stick" to the site of the injury and form a clot.

3. Clotting factors in the blood help to build the clot and keep it in place. After the bleeding stops, the blood vessel starts to heal, and the clot begins to break down.

Bleeding disorders can disrupt any part of this process.

cell anemia, cannot be cured. But the symptoms can be treated.

It is important to have blood disorders diagnosed and treated as early as possible. Proper treatment can relieve symptoms and prevent complications.

Bleeding disorders

If you have a bleeding disorder, your blood may not clot normally. The chart on pages 106 and 107 describes several common bleeding disorders that affect women.

Causes of bleeding disorders

Some bleeding disorders are inherited, including von Willebrand disease (vWD) and hemophilia (hee-muh-FIL-ee-uh). If there is a history of bleeding problems in your family, talk to your doctor. You may need to be tested.

Other factors that prevent or slow clotting include:

- certain types of drugs—including aspirin, nonsteroidal anti-inflammatory drugs (NSAIDs), antibiotics, and chemotherapy drugs
- a lack of vitamin K
- other disorders, including autoimmune (aw-toh-ih-MYOON) diseases, bone marrow disorders, leukemia, thyroid disease, Cushing syndrome, and liver and renal diseases

Symptoms of bleeding disorders

Bleeding disorders often cause unusual bleeding of the female reproductive system. You may have heavy menstrual bleeding. If you have a reproductive disorder that causes bleeding, such as endometriosis (EN-doh-MEE-tree-OH-suhss), a bleeding disorder can make your symptoms worse. (See page 158 of the *Reproductive Health* chapter for more information.)

Other symptoms of bleeding disorders are:

- bleeding or bruising easily
- bleeding too much or for a long time
- nosebleeds

Getting diagnosed

Mild bleeding disorders often go undiagnosed. Because women normally bleed with menstruation and childbirth, it may be hard for you or your doctor to recognize abnormal bleeding.

Discuss your symptoms with your doctor. You may need to be tested for a bleeding disorder if you:

- have heavy menstrual bleeding
- have a history of bleeding disorders in your family

Pregnancy

Pregnancy boosts levels of proteins that help the blood to clot. This may help control bleeding. However, levels of these clotting proteins will still be lower than normal. If you have a bleeding disorder, you may be at risk for problems during pregnancy such as:

- miscarriage or stillbirth
- bleeding during pregnancy
- heavy bleeding after childbirth

These are symptoms that your menstrual bleeding might be heavier than normal:

- soaking through a pad or tampon every hour for 2 to 3 hours in a row
- blood clots more than 1 inch in diameter
- anemia (See page 109 for more information.)

You may need to consult a hematologist, a specialist in blood disorders, for additional blood tests. Tests for one of the most common disorders, vWD, may be uncertain. You may need repeated testing to find out if you have vWD.

Treating bleeding disorders

Inherited bleeding disorders cannot be cured. But treatments can:

- relieve symptoms
- prevent dangerous bleeding during or after surgery or dental work
- prevent complications during and after pregnancy

The treatments below can reduce blood loss. Your treatment plan will depend on the type of bleeding disorder you have and your symptoms.

- Birth control pills may help reduce menstrual bleeding.
- Desmopressin acetate (dess-moh-PRESS-uhn A-suh-tayt) is a drug that can control menstrual bleeding and prevent excessive bleeding during and after surgery or dental work.

- Antifibrinolytics (an-teye-FEYE-bruhn-uhl-IHT-ihks) are drugs that keep clots from breaking down. They can help reduce menstrual bleeding, nosebleeds, and excess bleeding from surgery or dental work.
- Clotting factor concentrates—medicines that provide extra factors to help blood clot—may improve symptoms when other treatments don't work.

Heavy menstrual bleeding can interfere with your personal and professional life. If the treatments above don't help control this symptom, there are surgeries that can permanently stop menstruation. However, these surgeries will cause you to be unable to get pregnant.

Talk to your doctor about the risks and benefits of treatments. You may need to try several treatments to find out what works best for you.

Common Bleeding Disorders in Women

von Willebrand Disease (vWD)

Causes	vWD is the most common inherited bleeding disorder. It is caused by deficiencies or defects in von Willebrand Factor (vWF). vWF is a substance in the blood that helps clots to form.
Symptoms	• Heavy bleeding during periods (the most common symptom) • Bruising easily • Prolonged or excessive bleeding after dental work or surgery • Excessive postpartum bleeding
Diagnosis	• Blood tests can measure vWF activity in your blood. • Hormones and medications affect vWF levels, making diagnosis difficult. • If you have symptoms but your blood tests are negative for vWD, you may need to be tested again.
Treatments	vWD cannot be cured, but the following treatments may relieve your symptoms: • Birth control pills • Desmopressin acetate • Antifibrinolytics • Clotting factor concentrates • Surgery to stop menstruation

The Healthy Woman: A Complete Guide for All Ages

Common Bleeding Disorders in Women

Hemophilia Carrier Status

Causes	Hemophilia is caused by an inherited genetic mutation on the X chromosome. If men inherit this trait, they have hemophilia, a severe bleeding disorder. Women who inherit this mutation are carriers of the disease—they do not have hemophilia, but they may pass the disease on to their children.
Symptoms	Most hemophilia carriers do not have symptoms. Some women have mild bleeding symptoms, such as: • Heavy bleeding during periods • Prolonged or excessive bleeding after dental work, surgery, serious injury, or childbirth
Diagnosis	If you have a family history of hemophilia, genetic testing can determine whether you are a carrier.
Treatments	Hemophilia cannot be cured. The following treatments can stop or prevent excessive bleeding: • Birth control pills • Desmopressin acetate • Antifibrinolytics • Clotting factor replacement Scientists are studying gene therapy, which may treat, or even cure, hemophilia in the future.

Thrombocytopenia

Causes	Thrombocytopenia (throm-buh-syt-uh-PEE-nee-uh) is a condition in which there are too few platelets in the blood. It is caused by medications and by other diseases, including: • Anemia • Leukemia • HIV • Disorders such as Gaucher's disease that cause the spleen to become enlarged and trap platelets • Disorders in which platelets break down too quickly
Symptoms	• Bruising easily • Heavy bleeding during periods • Bleeding under the skin and bleeding of the gums and digestive tract
Diagnosis	Blood tests can detect low platelet levels. Additional testing may be needed to find the cause.
Treatments	The underlying cause must be treated.

Clotting disorders

If you have a clotting disorder, your blood may clot too easily. This condition is called thrombophilia (throm-boh-FIL-ee-uh). It may cause blood clots to form in veins and sometimes in arteries. These clots can move through the bloodstream and block small blood vessels.

Causes of thrombophilia

Thrombophilia may be inherited or acquired. Common causes include gene

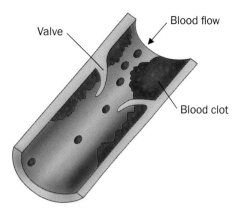

Valve

Blood flow

Blood clot

mutations, protein deficiencies, and certain autoimmune disorders.

If you have thrombophilia, some conditions or drugs can increase your risk of clotting:

- heart failure
- obesity, which puts pressure on veins
- pregnancy
- using the birth control pill or menopausal hormonal therapy

Your risk can also be raised by sitting or lying in one position for a long time, such as during recovery from surgery or sitting still during a long flight.

Symptoms of thrombophilia

The main symptom is clotting in veins or arteries. Clots may cause swelling, pain, or redness.

Thrombophilia may cause blood clots to form in veins deep inside the leg. This is called deep vein thrombosis (throm-BOH-suhss), commonly known as DVT. These clots can break loose and block blood vessels in the lung. This is called a pulmonary embolism (PE). Symptoms of PE are shortness of breath or sharp chest pains, especially when you inhale. Because the clot stops the flow of blood,

PE can damage lung tissue and even cause death.

Thrombophilia is a common disorder, affecting about 1 in every 5 Americans. Many people with thrombophilia never develop clots. Because pregnancy and medications that contain hormones increase the risk of blood clots, women are at higher risk for clotting than men.

Getting diagnosed

If you have a personal or family history of blood clots, DVT, or PE, talk to your doctor about whether you should be tested for thrombophilia. You should also talk to your doctor before using the birth control pill, birth control patch, or menopausal hormone therapy. Finding out whether you have the disorder can help you get the proper treatment.

Treating thrombophilia

Inherited thrombophilia cannot be cured. However, blood-thinning drugs prevent excessive clotting. You may need these drugs only when you are at high risk of clots—during pregnancy, for instance. Some women need to take these drugs throughout their lives.

Common Clotting Disorders in Women

Thrombophilia

Causes	Inherited conditions that cause thrombophilia include: • Mutated genes, such as Factor V Leiden (LAY-din) mutation and prothrombin (proh-THROM-bin) 20210 mutation • A lack of certain blood proteins, including protein C, protein S, and antithrombin • Hyperhomocysteinemia (heye-pur-hoh-moh-siss-tuh-NEE-mee-uh), an increase in an amino acid in the blood caused by a mutation in the *MTHFR* gene Scientists are still studying how genes contribute to thrombophilia. This research may help to improve diagnosis and treatment. Thrombophilia may be caused by some autoimmune disorders (see the *Autoimmune Diseases* chapter on page 83 for more information about these diseases): • Antiphospholipid (an-teye-FOSS-foh-lip-ihd) antibody syndrome • Systemic lupus erythematosus (LOO-puhss ur-ih-thee-muh-TOH-suhss)
Symptoms	• Blood clots in veins or arteries, such as deep vein thrombosis • Pulmonary embolism
Diagnosis	Blood tests can diagnose thrombophilia and determine its cause.
Treatments	• Blood thinning drugs heparin and warfarin can prevent future clots. • Some women need to take blood thinners only when they are at high risk of a clot. • Some women may need continuous treatment.

Disseminated Intravascular Coagulation (DIC)

Causes	DIC is a type of acquired thrombophilia. Excessive clotting depletes platelets and clotting factors. DIC may be caused by: • Severe infections • Cancer • Pregnancy complications, such as placental abruption (the breaking away of the placenta from the womb) or a dead fetus that remains in the womb This clotting removes platelets and clotting factors from the blood, causing uncontrolled bleeding.
Symptoms	• Blood clots throughout the bloodstream • Excessive bleeding
Diagnosis	Blood tests
Treatments	The cause of DIC must be treated. Platelets and clotting factors are administered to control bleeding.

Anemia

Anemia is caused by a lack of healthy red blood cells. It is a common disorder, affecting more than 3 million Americans. Women, especially women of childbearing age, are more likely to have anemia than men. This is because women lose blood during menstruation and childbirth.

Causes of anemia

There are many different types of anemia and a variety of causes, including:

• major blood loss

- lack of iron, vitamin B^{12}, folic acid, or vitamin C
- diseases that damage bone marrow
- inherited disorders that cause defects in red blood cells
- disorders that cause your immune system to attack red blood cells

Symptoms of anemia

Anemia is a condition in which the number of healthy red blood cells in your blood is lower than normal. This lowers oxygen levels in the blood. If you have mild anemia, you may not have symptoms, or you may have symptoms only when you are physically active.

What is sickle cell disease?

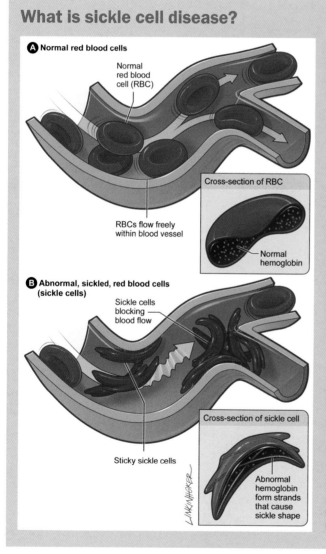

A Normal red blood cells

Normal red blood cell (RBC)

Cross-section of RBC

RBCs flow freely within blood vessel

Normal hemoglobin

B Abnormal, sickled, red blood cells (sickle cells)

Sickle cells blocking blood flow

Cross-section of sickle cell

Sticky sickle cells

Abnormal hemoglobin form strands that cause sickle shape

Sickle cell disease is an inherited blood disorder. It causes red blood cells to be crescent-shaped instead of round. These sickle cells break down more quickly than normal cells, causing anemia. Sickle cells may also block blood vessels, a condition called a sickle cell crisis. Crises cause pain and complications such as stroke, infections, and organ damage.

If you inherit two sickle cell genes, one from each parent, you will have sickle cell disease. If you inherit only one gene, you will have the sickle cell trait. Although women with sickle cell trait may not have any symptoms, they can pass the trait on to their children.

People whose ancestors are from sub-Saharan Africa have the greatest risk of the disease.

ILLUSTRATION USED WITH PERMISSION FROM THE NATIONAL HEART, LUNG, AND BLOOD INSTITUTE, NATIONAL INSTITUTES OF HEALTH, U.S. DEPARTMENT OF HEALTH AND HUMAN SERVICES. ILLUSTRATION: MICHAEL LINKINHOKER, LINK STUDIO, LLC.

Symptoms include fatigue, dizziness, and shortness of breath.

Getting diagnosed

If you experience these symptoms, talk to your doctor. Blood tests can find out whether you have anemia. Additional tests may be needed to find the cause.

Treating anemia

Your treatment will depend on the type of anemia you have. In some cases, treating the cause will cure anemia. Inherited forms of anemia, such as sickle cell disease, cannot be cured, but treatments can relieve the symptoms and prevent complications. Scientists are studying new medicines and treatments such as gene

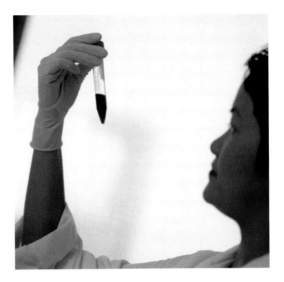

therapy and bone marrow transplants. These may provide even better treatments for anemia in the future.

Types of Anemia

Acute blood loss anemia

Causes	Blood loss may be caused by: • Injury • Surgery • Childbirth • Heavy menstrual bleeding • Bleeding from the digestive or urinary tracts
Symptoms	• Fatigue • Dizziness • Shortness of breath • Pale skin • Cold hands and feet • Chest pain
Diagnosis	• Blood tests are used to diagnose anemia. • Physical exams and other tests may be needed to find the cause of the blood loss.
Treatment	• If your anemia is caused by internal bleeding, surgery may be needed to stop the blood loss. • Lost blood may be replaced with a blood transfusion.

Types of Anemia

Iron deficiency anemia

Causes	You may have low iron because of: • Blood loss • Lack of iron in your diet • Problems absorbing the iron in your diet
Symptoms	• Fatigue • Dizziness • Shortness of breath • Pale skin • Cold hands and feet • Chest pain • A condition called pica, in which you crave nonfood items (ice, dirt, or paint, for example) • Restless leg syndrome
Diagnosis	• Blood tests can diagnose anemia. • A physical exam and other tests may be needed to determine the cause. • Because iron deficiency anemia is very common during pregnancy, pregnant women should be tested.

Treatment	Iron deficiency anemia may be treated (and even prevented) by:
	
	• Taking iron supplements, as directed by your doctor
	
	• Eating iron-rich foods, such as:
	    • meat (especially red meat)
	    • eggs
	    • iron-fortified grains and cereals
	    • beans and nuts
	    • dried fruit
	    • dark green, leafy vegetables
	
	• Eating foods that contain vitamin C, folate, and vitamin B_{12}, which help your body absorb iron

Types of Anemia

Sickle cell disease

Causes	Sickle cell disease is an inherited disorder that affects red blood cells. • Red blood cells are crescent-shaped, instead of round. • Sickle cells die more quickly than normal cells, causing anemia. • Sickle cells may block blood vessels, leading to painful crises and organ damage.
Symptoms	• Fatigue • Pale skin • Jaundice • Shortness of breath • Sickle cell crises (caused by blocked blood vessels)
Diagnosis	• Blood tests can determine whether you have sickle cell disease or the sickle cell trait.
Treatment	Treatments include: • Hydroxyurea (heye-DRAHK-see-yoo-REE-uh), a drug that can prevent sickle cell crises • Flu shots and vaccinations to prevent infection • Pain medications To prevent crises: • Get regular checkups. • Avoid conditions that may trigger a crisis, such as stress and dehydration. • Maintain a healthy lifestyle.

Thalassemia

Causes	Thalassemia (thal-uh-SEE-mee-uh) is a group of inherited blood disorders that cause defective red blood cells and anemia. These disorders are most common among people from Africa, the Middle East, Southeast Asia, Southern China, and the Mediterranean.
Symptoms	Anemia symptoms may be mild to severe, depending on the type of thalassemia.
Diagnosis	Blood and genetic tests are used to diagnose the disease.
Treatment	• Blood transfusions supply healthy red blood cells. • Iron chelation (kee-LAY-shuhn) therapy may be needed to remove iron, which builds up after repeated blood transfusions.

Bone marrow disorders

Some disorders damage bone marrow, where blood cells are produced. This may increase or decrease the number of healthy cells in your blood, causing excessive bleeding or clotting, anemia, or increased fevers and infections.

Myeloproliferative (MEYE-uh-loh-pruh-LIF-uh-ruh-tiv) diseases and myelodysplastic (MEYE-uh-loh-diss-PLASS-tik) syndromes are bone marrow disorders that are most common among older adults.

- Myeloproliferative diseases cause too many blood cells to be produced. These cells may be red blood cells, white blood cells, or platelets.

- Myelodysplastic syndromes reduce the number of healthy blood cells. You may have too few red blood cells, white blood cells, or platelets.

These disorders may turn into leukemia, a cancer that affects the bone marrow. (See page 58 of the *Cancer* chapter for more information.)

Fertility and pregnancy

Many blood disorders cause complications during pregnancy. You may also worry about passing these disorders on to your children. Getting diagnosed before you conceive can help you protect your health and the health of your children. The following chart describes common fertility and pregnancy issues that women with blood disorders may face.

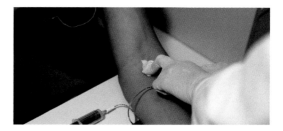

Blood Disorders, Fertility, and Pregnancy

Bleeding disorders

Fertility issues	• Treatments for heavy menstrual bleeding can interfere with fertility. The effects of the birth control pill are temporary. Surgeries to prevent menstruation, such as hysterectomy or endometrial ablation (destruction of the lining of the uterus), result in permanent sterility. If you plan to become pregnant, ask your doctor about other treatment options.
	• Women with a family history of hemophilia may worry about passing the disease on to their children. It is important to get tested before you conceive.
	• If you are a hemophilia carrier, genetic counseling can help you understand your risks and your options.
Pregnancy issues	• Because pregnancy increases certain clotting proteins in the blood, you may have fewer symptoms during pregnancy.
	• Women with some types of bleeding disorders have a higher risk of:
	• miscarriage and stillbirth
	• bleeding during pregnancy
	• excessive bleeding after childbirth
	• Talk to your doctor about treatments to prevent these complications.

Blood Disorders, Fertility, and Pregnancy

Thrombophilia

Pregnancy issues	Blood clots more easily during pregnancy. Therefore, women with thrombophilia are at even greater risk of developing clots in blood vessels. Thrombophilia also increases the risk of: • miscarriages • stillbirth • placental abruption (detachment of the placenta) Pregnant women should be tested for thrombophilia if they have had: • A blood clot • Family members who have experienced blood clots before the age of 50 • The pregnancy complications listed above Treatment with blood thinning drugs such as heparin can help prevent dangerous blood clots and pregnancy complications.

Anemia

Fertility issues	• Women who have sickle cell disease or thalassemia—or who carry the genes for these disorders—may worry about passing the diseases on to their children. • Genetic counseling and testing can help you understand your risks and options.
Pregnancy issues	• Talk to your doctor about whether you need to take iron supplements, change your diet to prevent or treat anemia, or both. • Women need more iron during pregnancy. Therefore, iron deficiency anemia is common, affecting about half of all pregnant women. • You should be tested for anemia during pregnancy, even if you do not have any symptoms.

Living with blood disorders

Blood disorders do not have to interfere with your day-to-day activities, work, or quality of life.

- **Get diagnosed.** If you have a family or personal history of blood disorders or symptoms, talk to your doctor. You may need to be tested.

- **Get the treatment you need.** Although many blood disorders cannot be cured, treatments can relieve your symptoms and help you feel better.

- **Take care of your health.** For some disorders, there are steps you can take to prevent symptoms and dangerous complications.

- **Take care of your emotions.** You may have symptoms, such as heavy menstrual bleeding or fatigue, that affect your life on a daily basis. You may also face fears about your own health or the health of your children. Counseling can help you cope with your disorder and make informed choices about your health. ■

One Woman's Story

In the summer of 2003, my marriage began to unravel, and by December my husband had moved out of our home. In January I began to feel tired and listless, leading my doctor to diagnose me with depression. Agreeing that I had enough to be depressed about, I began taking antidepressants. I realized immediately that depression was not my problem; the antidepressants were making me feel even worse.

For weeks I went to the doctor, spent my lunch hours resting in my car, and was barely able to work. I depended on my coworkers to do most of my work. Finally, one of my coworkers confronted me in tears, worried about me. Out of desperation, and in tears myself, I called a friend who is a physician, although not mine. She took blood samples and found that I was very anemic. She gave me a prescription for iron tablets and asked to see me again in a week. At the end of the week I had not improved at all. In fact, my hemoglobin was dangerously low. At that point she called my doctor, explained the situation, and asked her to admit me to the hospital. Reluctantly, my doctor admitted me, and I spent a week having tests and getting blood transfusions. At the end of the hospital stay we knew I was bleeding somewhere internally—we just didn't know where.

> **Anemia can be a sign of a variety of health issues, and I am so glad we were able to get to the root cause of mine.**

I had my medical records moved to my friend's office and she continued to search for a solution to my bleeding problem. Finally, after I had consulted with an oncologist and received several doses of iron intravenously, it was discovered that I have spots on my intestines that seep blood. The good news was that I could manage the condition. If I never take aspirin, keep a close watch on my hemoglobin, and get transfusions of iron when my hemoglobin is low, I am fine.

My experience shows that you have to trust your instincts and not be afraid to switch doctors to find the answers you need. Anemia can be a sign of a variety of health issues, and I am so glad we were able to get to the root cause of mine.

Jackee
Burlington, North Carolina

For More Information...

Office on Women's Health, HHS
200 Independence Ave SW, Room 712E
Washington, DC 20201
Web site: www.womenshealth.gov/faq/
bleed.htm
Phone number: (800) 994-9662,
(888) 220-5446 TDD

Division of Blood Disorders, CDC
1600 Clifton Rd
Atlanta, GA 30333
Web site: www.cdc.gov/ncbddd/hbd
Phone number: (800) 232-4636,
(888) 232-6348 TTY

**National Heart, Lung, and Blood Institute
Information Center, NIH**
PO Box 30105
Bethesda, MD 20824-0105
Web site: www.nhlbi.nih.gov
Phone number: (301) 592-8573,
(240) 629-3255 TTY

**National Hematologic Diseases
Information Service, NIH**
7 Information Way
Bethesda, MD 20892–3571
Web site: www.hematologic.niddk.nih.gov
Phone number: (888) 828–0877

American Society of Hematology
1900 M St NW, Suite 200
Washington, DC 20036
Web site: www.hematology.org

Cooley's Anemia Foundation
330 Seventh Ave, Suite 900
New York, NY 10001
Web site: www.thalassemia.org
Phone number: (800) 522-7222

Iron Disorders Institute
2722 Wade Hampton Blvd, Suite A
Greenville, SC 29615
Web site: www.irondisorders.org
Phone number: (888) 565-4766

National Anemia Action Council
555 E Wells St, Suite 1100
Milwaukee, WI 53202
Web site: www.anemia.org

National Hemophilia Foundation
116 W 32nd St, 11th Floor
New York, NY 10001
Web site: www.hemophilia.org
www.projectredflag.org
Phone number: (800) 424-2634

**Sickle Cell Disease Association of
America**
231 E Baltimore St, Suite 800
Baltimore, MD 21202
Web site: www.sicklecelldisease.org
Phone number: (800) 421-8453

Sexually Transmitted Infections

You probably have heard of sexually transmitted infections (STIs)—also called sexually transmitted diseases, or STDs. But if you are like many women, you might not know that much about how STIs could impact your health. You might not think you need to worry about STIs. Yet STIs are a major public health concern in the United States, where an estimated 19 million new infections occur each year. STIs affect people of all backgrounds and economic levels. And women have more frequent and more serious complications from STIs than men. Thankfully, most STIs are preventable. Taking a few protective steps can lower your risk of getting an STI.

What is a sexually transmitted infection (STI)?

A sexually transmitted infection (STI) is an infection you can get by having intimate sexual contact with someone who already has the infection. STIs can be caused by viruses, bacteria, and parasites. Many STIs have mild or no symptoms. So you can have an STI and not even know it. Most STIs can be found by simple tests, but routine testing is not widespread. So many cases of STIs go undiagnosed and untreated, which can lead to serious health problems—particularly for women.

One partner can expose you to many diseases. You are at risk of getting all of the STIs that your partner's past and present partners have had.

YOU

STIs are easily passed through intimate sexual contact

STIs are spread during vaginal or anal intercourse, oral sex, and genital touching. It is possible to get some STIs without having intercourse. Here are some other reasons STIs spread so easily:

- You can't tell if a person has an STI by the way he or she looks.

- Talking about sex is awkward for some people. They may not bring up safe sex or STIs with their partners.

- Many STIs have no or only mild symptoms. So many people don't know that they have an STI or that they are putting their partners at risk.

- If you have unprotected sex, you may be exposed to the STIs that your partner's past and present partners have had. This is true even if you have been sexually active with only one person.

- Myths and false beliefs about STIs put people at risk of getting and passing on STIs.

TRUE statements about STIs:

You CAN get an STI without having intercourse.

You CANNOT get HIV from sitting on toilet seats.

Birth control pills DO NOT protect from STIs.

STIs: Dangerous to women

Both men and women get STIs. But women have more frequent and more serious complications from STIs than men. Overall, untreated STIs can cause cancer, infertility, pregnancy problems, and other health problems in women. Women also need to be concerned about STIs for these reasons:

- Mild symptoms can be mistaken for "nothing" or something else, such as a urinary tract infection or vaginal yeast infection.

- A woman's ability to protect herself from STIs depends on whether she is able to get her partner to use a condom. Women who don't feel they can choose to use a condom are at greater risk of getting STIs because they may feel forced to take part in unsafe sexual practices. This is true for women in relationships and for women who are victims of sexual assault.

- Some STIs increase a woman's risk of getting HIV/AIDS and other STIs because they irritate the vagina. Some cause open sores. This makes it easier for semen or vaginal fluid carrying HIV or other STIs to get inside a woman's body.

- Having prior STIs raises a woman's risk of future STIs. The reasons for this are complex and include biological, behavioral, and social issues.

- Silent and harmful STIs, such as chlamydia, affect young women at higher rates.

- Women of color have STIs at higher rates than other women. In 2005, the rate of reported chlamydia was 7 times greater in black women and almost 5 times greater in American Indian/Alaska Native women than in white women. These differences might reflect limited access to quality health care, higher rates of poverty, and other health issues among these women.

Will I get an STI?

The answer depends on whether you take steps to reduce your risks. Keep in mind that more than half of Americans will have an STI at some point in their lifetime.

Learning more: Types of STIs

More than 25 infections are known to be passed through sexual contact. The STIs discussed here are among the most common and dangerous to women.

Types of STIs			
Bacterial vaginosis (BV)	**How you get it**	**Symptoms**	**How to find out if you have it**
BV is the most common vaginal infection in women of childbearing age. With BV, the normal balance of bacteria in the vagina is changed so that there are more "harmful" bacteria and fewer "good" bacteria. Antibiotics are used to treat and cure BV.	Not much is known about how women get BV. Any woman can get BV. But BV rarely occurs in women who have never had vaginal sex. Having BV can increase a woman's risk of getting an STI, including HIV. These things put you more at risk for BV: • Having a new or many sex partners • Douching • Using an intrauterine device (IUD) for birth control • Not using a condom	You cannot get BV from such objects as toilet seats, bedding, or swimming pools. Most women have no symptoms. Women with symptoms may have: • Vaginal itching • Pain when urinating • Discharge with a fishy odor	Your doctor will test a sample of fluid from your vagina. Your doctor also may be able to see signs of BV, like a grayish-white discharge, during an exam.
Chlamydia	**How you get it**	**Symptoms**	**How to find out if you have it**
Chlamydia is the most frequently reported STI caused by bacteria. It is a "silent" disease because 75 percent of infected women and at least half of infected men have no symptoms. Severe complications can result from untreated chlamydia. Antibiotics are used to treat and cure chlamydia.	Women and men can get chlamydia by having vaginal, anal, or oral sex with an infected person. An infected mother can also pass chlamydia to her baby during childbirth.	Most women have no symptoms. If symptoms do occur, they usually appear within 1 to 3 weeks of exposure. Symptoms, if any, include: • Abnormal vaginal discharge • "Burning" when passing urine • Bleeding between periods • Lower abdominal pain • Low back pain • Nausea • Fever • Pain during sex	Your doctor can tell if you have chlamydia by testing your urine or by testing a swab sample taken from the infected site, such as the cervix.

The Healthy Woman: A Complete Guide for All Ages

Types of STIs

Genital herpes	How you get it	Symptoms	How to find out if you have it
Genital herpes is caused by the herpes simplex viruses type 1 (HSV-1) and type 2 (HSV-2). Most genital herpes is caused by HSV-2. About 1 in 4 women in the United States have had HSV-2 infection. The virus will stay in the body forever. But outbreaks, for people who have them, tend to be less severe and occur less often over time. Also, antiviral therapy can shorten outbreaks and make them less severe, or keep them from happening.	Genital herpes is spread through genital-to-genital or genital-to-oral contact. It spreads most easily when an infected person has open sores. But you also can get herpes from an infected person who has no symptoms. You do not need to have intercourse to get herpes. You cannot get herpes from objects such as toilet seats, bathtubs, or towels.	Most people have mild or no symptoms. For people who have "outbreaks," the symptoms are clear: • Small red bumps, blisters, or open sores show up where the virus entered the body, such as the penis, vagina, or mouth • Vaginal discharge • Fever • Headache • Muscle aches • Pain when passing urine • Itching, burning, or swollen glands in the genital area • Pain in legs, buttocks, or genital area • Symptoms may go away and then come back. Sores heal after 2 to 4 weeks. Your doctor can tell you if you have genital herpes by looking at the sores and by taking a sample from the sore for lab testing.	It can be hard to tell if you have herpes without symptoms. Blood tests can help detect herpes when there are no symptoms or between outbreaks.

Types of STIs

Gonorrhea	How you get it	Symptoms	How to find out if you have it
Gonorrhea is caused by a type of bacteria that thrives in warm, moist areas of the reproductive tract. It also can grow in the mouth, throat, eyes, and anus. Most women who have gonorrhea have *no symptoms*. Untreated gonorrhea can lead to serious health problems. Antibiotics are used to cure gonorrhea. But gonorrhea has become more and more resistant to antibiotics, which means the drugs do not work as well or at all. Still, it's important to get tested and treated by a doctor.	You can get gonorrhea through contact with an infected vagina, penis, anus, or mouth. It is spread through semen and vaginal fluid during unprotected sexual contact with a person who has it. Touching infected sex organs, and then touching your eyes can cause an eye infection. An infected pregnant woman can pass gonorrhea to her baby during vaginal delivery. You cannot get gonorrhea from shaking hands or sitting on toilet seats.	Most women have *no symptoms*. When a woman does have symptoms, they most often appear within 10 days of becoming infected. Symptoms can include: • Pain or burning while passing urine • Yellowish and sometimes bloody vaginal discharge • Bleeding between periods • Pain during sex • Heavy bleeding during periods These signs can be mistaken for a urinary tract infection or another vaginal infection. Gonorrhea that affects the anus might cause discharge, soreness, bleeding, itching, or painful bowel movements. Infections in the throat could cause a sore throat. With eye infection, symptoms may include redness, itching, or discharge from the eye.	Your doctor can tell if you have gonorrhea by testing your urine or by testing a swab sample taken from the infected site, such as the cervix.

The Healthy Woman: A Complete Guide for All Ages

Types of STIs

Hepatitis B	How you get it	Symptoms	How to find out if you have it
Hepatitis B (HBV) is one type of viral hepatitis. With hepatitis, the liver does not work well. In most people, HBV gets better on its own. Long-lasting hepatitis (chronic) can lead to scarring of the liver, liver failure, and liver cancer. Chronic HBV can be suppressed with some antiviral drugs. But these drugs don't work for all people. *Vaccines are available for hepatitis A and B.*	HBV is spread by exposure to an infected person's blood. This can happen by having vaginal, anal, or oral sex with someone who is infected. It also can be passed from an infected mother to her baby during vaginal childbirth or through sharing needles with an infected person. You also can get HBV by sharing personal items, such as razors or toothbrushes, with an infected person. You cannot get hepatits through casual contact, such as shaking hands, hugging, or kissing.	Some people with viral hepatitis have no signs of infection. Others might have: • Low-grade fever • Headache • Muscle aches • Tiredness • Loss of appetite • Nausea • Vomiting • Diarrhea • Dark-colored urine and pale bowel movements • Jaundice	Your doctor can tell if you have viral hepatitis through blood tests and a medical exam.

HIV/AIDS

For complete information, see the *HIV/AIDS* chapter on page 139.

Pubic lice	How you get it	Symptoms	How to find out if you have it
Also called "crabs," pubic lice are parasites found in the genital area on pubic hair and sometimes on other coarse body hairs. Pubic lice are common. They are different from head lice. Special shampoos and medicines are used to kill pubic lice.	Pubic lice usually are spread through sexual contact. Intercourse does not need to occur. Rarely, pubic lice are spread through contact with an infected person's sheets, towels, or clothes. Pubic lice CANNOT be spread by sitting on a toilet seat. Animals do not get or spread pubic lice.	Symptoms of pubic lice include: • Itching in the genital area • Visible nits (lice eggs) or crawling lice (which look like crabs when viewed with a magnifying glass)	Doctors can tell if a person has pubic lice by looking closely at the pubic hair for nits or young or adult lice.

Types of STIs

Human papillomavirus (HPV) and genital warts	How you get it	Symptoms	How to find out if you have it
There are more than 100 types of HPV, 30 of which are passed through sexual contact. The types of HPV that infect the genital area are called genital HPV. HPV is very common. Most sexually active people will have it at some point in their lives. Some types of genital HPV are "high risk," which means they put a woman at greater risk of getting cervical cancer. "High risk" does not have to do with the risk of getting HPV. Low-risk types of HPV do not cause cervical cancer. But low-risk types of HPV may cause genital warts. *There is no treatment or cure for HPV. But a new HPV vaccine protects women against some HPV types that cause cancer or warts. (See page 134 for more information.)*	Genital HPV is passed by skin-to-skin and genital contact, mainly during vaginal and anal intercourse. It might also be possible to pass it during oral sex.	HPV usually has no symptoms. Both low-risk and high-risk types of HPV can cause growths on the cervix and vagina. These often are invisible. Low-risk types of HPV can cause genital warts. Warts can form weeks, months, or years after sexual contact with a person who has genital HPV. They can grow inside and around the outside of the vagina, on the vulva and cervix, groin, and in or around the anus. Warts can be raised or flat, alone or in groups, small or large, and sometimes they are shaped like a cauliflower. High-risk types of HPV may cause cervical changes that, if not treated, may progress into cervical cancer.	A Pap test can find changes on the cervix that are caused by HPV infection. Women who have had the HPV vaccine still need to have a regular Pap test. An HPV test, which is a DNA test that detects high-risk types of HPV, may be done for women who are older than 30 or for women who are younger than 30 who have abnormal Pap test results. An abnormal Pap test result does not mean for sure that a woman has HPV or cervical cancer. Follow-up tests are needed to confirm any diagnosis. Having genital warts is another way a doctor can tell if a person has an HPV infection.

The Healthy Woman: A Complete Guide for All Ages

Types of STIs

Syphilis	How you get it	Symptoms	How to find out if you have it
Syphilis is caused by a type of bacteria. It progresses in stages. Without treatment, the infection will continue to progress, possibly leading to death. Syphilis can be cured with an antibiotic. Penicillin is the preferred drug to treat syphilis at all stages. Doctors can use other medicines for people who cannot take penicillin.	Syphilis is spread during vaginal, anal, or oral sex through contact with an open sore or contact with a skin rash of an infected person. The bacteria can enter the body through the penis, anus, vagina, mouth, or through broken skin. It can be spread during the first two stages of the disease. An infected pregnant woman also can pass syphilis to her baby during pregnancy and childbirth. Syphilis is not spread by contact with toilet seats, doorknobs, swimming pools, hot tubs, bathtubs, shared clothing, or shared food and drinks.	In the primary stage, a single, painless sore appears about 10 to 90 days after infection. It can appear in the genital area, tongue, lips, or other parts of the body. The sore will heal with or without treatment. The secondary stage starts 3 to 6 weeks after the sore appears. Symptoms can include: • Skin rash with rough, red or reddish-brown spots both on the hands and feet that usually does not itch and clears on its own • Fever • Sore throat and swollen glands • Patchy hair loss • Headaches and muscle aches • Weight loss • Tiredness In the latent stage, symptoms go away, but can come back. When symptoms come back, the infection can be passed to others. People without treatment may or may not move to the late stage. In the late stage, the infection spreads and can cause damage throughout the body. Some people may die.	A doctor can tell if a person has syphilis in a number of ways: • Recognizing the signs and symptoms and confirming with tests • Looking at the fluid from a sore or swollen lymph node under a microscope • Testing the patient's blood in the lab

Types of STIs

Trichomoniasis	How you get it	Symptoms	How to find out if you have it
This infection, also called "trich," is caused by a parasite. It usually is passed through sexual contact. But it also can be picked up from contact with damp, moist objects. Antibiotics are used to treat and cure trichomoniasis.	The parasite can be passed though penis-in-vagina intercourse or vulva-to-vulva contact with an infected partner. Women can get the disease from infected men or women. It also can be passed if the genital area comes in contact with damp towels, wet clothing, toilet seats, or other moist objects where the parasites are present.	Many women do not have symptoms. Symptoms, which usually appear 5 to 28 days after exposure, can include: • Yellow, green, or gray vaginal discharge (often foamy) with a strong odor • Discomfort during sex or when passing urine • Itching and discomfort in the genital area • Lower stomach pain (rarely)	A doctor will do a pelvic exam and lab test to tell if a person has trichomoniasis. The doctor sometimes can see small, red sores inside the vagina or on the cervix. The doctor also will take a fluid sample from the vagina and look for the parasite under a microscope or send the sample to a lab for testing, or use other lab tests.

> **If you have any symptoms of an STI, stop having sex and contact your doctor right away.**

Treating STIs

The treatment depends on the type of STI. For some STIs, treatment may involve using medicine or getting a shot. For STIs that cannot be cured, like genital herpes, treatment can ease symptoms. During treatment, follow all of your doctor's orders and avoid sex during treatment or an outbreak. And be sure to finish all the medicine your doctor gives you, even if your symptoms go away. With most STIs, your sexual partner(s) should be treated, too. This can keep you from getting the STI again or your partner from passing it to other people. Remember, the sooner an STI is found, the easier it is to treat and the less likely you will have health complications.

How untreated STIs can affect your health

You might be too shy to talk to your doctor about your risk of STIs or any symptoms you might be having. But not talking to your doctor could be far worse than any embarrassment you might feel. Untreated STIs can cause severe health problems for women, such as pelvic inflammatory disease, infertility, ectopic pregnancy, widespread infection to other parts of the body, cancer, organ damage, and even death.

STIs and pregnancy

STIs can cause many of the same health problems for pregnant women as for women who are not pregnant. Moreover, STIs during pregnancy can cause early labor, cause the water to break early, and cause infection in the uterus after the birth. STIs also can cause problems for the unborn baby. Some STIs can cross the placenta and infect the baby while

What is pelvic inflammatory disease (PID)?

Pelvic inflammatory disease, or PID, is a broad term used to describe an infection of a woman's pelvic organs. Many types of bacteria can cause PID. Often, PID is a complication of untreated STIs—mainly chlamydia and gonorrhea. Damage from PID can cause a woman to become infertile (not able to become pregnant). In fact, about 1 in every 5 women with PID becomes infertile. PID also can cause chronic pelvic pain and ectopic pregnancy (pregnancy in the fallopian tube, which can be life threatening). It can be hard to tell if a woman has PID because there are no specific tests for PID and she might have mild or no symptoms. Women who have symptoms might have:

- pain in the lower belly area
- fever
- unusual vaginal discharge, which may smell bad
- pain during sex
- bleeding between periods
- pain during pelvic exam

A doctor will ask about symptoms and can perform a pelvic exam and tests to tell if a woman has PID. Once found, PID can be cured with antibiotics. But any damage already done to a woman's reproductive organs before treatment cannot be reversed. So early treatment of PID is important. A woman should see her doctor right away if she thinks she might have an STI or PID.

it is in the uterus. Others can be passed from a pregnant woman to the baby during delivery. The harmful effects to babies range from low birth weight, to chronic liver disease, to stillbirth. Some of these problems can be prevented if the mother has routine prenatal care, which includes screening tests for STIs at various points during the pregnancy. Other problems can be treated if the infection is found at birth or within a few days after birth.

STIs and breastfeeding mothers

Some STIs can be passed to your baby through breastfeeding. And some medicines used to treat STIs can pass to your baby through your breast milk. Talk to your doctor about whether you should breastfeed if you have an STI. (See page 199 of the *Breastfeeding* chapter for more information.)

How to protect yourself from STIs

Even though STIs pass easily from person to person, there are steps you can take to lower your risk of getting an STI. The following steps work best when used together—no single strategy can protect you from every single type of STI.

- **Don't have sex.** The surest way to avoid getting any STI is to practice abstinence, which means not having vaginal, oral, or anal sex. Keep in mind that some STIs, such as genital herpes, can be spread without having intercourse.

- **Be faithful.** Having sex with one uninfected partner who only has sex with you will keep you safe from STIs. Both partners must be faithful *all the time* to avoid STI exposure. This means that you have sex only with each other and no one else. The fewer sex partners you have, the lower your risk of being exposed to an STI.

- **Use condoms correctly and EVERY time you have sex.** Use condoms for all types of sexual contact, even if penetration does not take place. Condoms work by keeping blood, a man's semen, and a woman's vaginal fluid—all of which can carry STIs—from passing from one person to another. Use protection from the very beginning to

How to Use Condoms Correctly

Both male and female condoms are highly protective when used correctly. But don't use them both at the same time! They do not stay in place when used together. Read the instructions and practice a few times before using condoms for the first time. Also, follow these guidelines:

Male condom

Use male condoms made of latex, or polyurethane if you or your partner is allergic to latex. "Natural" or "lambskin" condoms don't protect against STIs. Use male condoms for vaginal, anal, or oral sex.

- Keep male condoms in a cool, dry place. Storing condoms where it can get hot, such as in the car or your wallet, can cause them to break or tear.

- Check the wrapper for tears and to make sure the condom is not too old to use. Carefully open the wrapper—don't use your teeth or fingernails. Make sure the condom looks okay to use. Don't use a condom that's gummy, brittle, discolored, or has even a tiny hole.

- Put on the condom as soon as the penis is erect, but before it touches the vagina, mouth, or anus.

- Use only lubricants made with water (such as, K-Y Jelly™, Astroglide™, AquaLube™, glycerine). Oil-based lubricants, such as Vaseline™, can weaken the condom. The lubricant is put on the outside of the condom. It helps to keep the condom from tearing. Don't regularly use lubricants with spermicide called nonoxynol-9 (N-9), which might make it easier for an STI—including HIV—to get into your body.

the very end of each sex act, and with every sex partner. And be prepared: Don't rely on your partner to have protection.

- **Know that certain birth control methods—and other methods—don't protect against STIs.** Birth control methods including the pill, shots, implants, intrauterine devices (IUDs), diaphragms, and spermicides will not protect you from STIs. They only can help keep you from getting pregnant.

Still, many women who use these forms of birth control don't use condoms. If you use one of these birth control methods, make sure to also use a condom with every sex act. Also, don't use contraceptives that contain the spermicide nonoxynol-9 (N-9). N-9 can irritate the vagina, which might make it easier for an STI—including HIV—to get into your body. Keep in mind that women who are unable to become pregnant can get STIs.

- After sex, pull out the penis while it is still erect, holding the condom firmly at the base of the penis so it does not slip off.
- Use a new condom if you want to have sex again or in a different way.

Female condom

The female condom (Reality™) is made of the plastic polyurethane. It has a ring on each end. The inside ring holds the condom in place inside the vagina. The outer ring stays outside the vagina so it covers the labia. Use female condoms for vaginal sex if your partner can't or won't use a male condom.

- Check the wrapper for tears and to make sure the condom is not too old to use. Open the wrapper carefully—don't use your teeth or fingernails. Make sure the condom looks okay to use.
- Put the condom into the vagina up to 8 hours before having sex, but before the penis touches the vagina. The condom cannot disappear inside your body.
- It is okay to use water or oil-based lubricants. The lubricant is put on the inside and outside of the condom.
- After sex, remove the condom before standing up. Grasp the outside ring and twist the condom to trap in fluid and gently remove.
- Use a new condom if you want to have sex again or in a different way.

You might have heard of other ways to keep from getting STIs—such as washing genitals before sex, passing urine after sex, douching after sex, or washing the genital area with vinegar after sex. These methods DO NOT prevent the spread of STIs.

- **Talk with your sex partner(s) about using condoms before having sex.** This way, you can set the ground rules and avoid misunderstandings during a moment of passion. Hopefully, you and your partner will agree to use condoms all the time. But know this: You can control their use by making it clear that you will not have any type of sex at any time without a condom. Remember, it's your body, and it's up to you to make sure you are protected.

- **Don't assume you're at low risk for STIs if you have sex only with women.** Some common STIs are spread easily by skin-to-skin contact. Also, most women who have sex with women have had sex with men, too. So a woman can get an STI from a male partner, and then pass it to a female partner.

- **Don't abuse drugs or alcohol. Heavy drinking and drug use can put you at greater risk of STIs.** Drinking too much and using drugs are linked to sexual risk-taking, such as having sex with more than one partner and not using condoms. Drug users who share needles risk exposure to blood-borne infections that also can be passed sexually, such as HIV and hepatitis B. Drinking too much alcohol or using drugs puts you at risk of sexual assault and possible exposure to an STI.

- **Get tested for STIs.** If either you or your partner has had other sexual partners in the past, get tested for STIs before becoming sexually active. Don't wait for your doctor to ask you about getting tested—ask your doctor! Many tests for STIs can be done at the same time as your regular pelvic exam.

- **Have regular checkups and pelvic exams—even if you think you're healthy.** During the checkup, your doctor will ask you a lot of questions about your lifestyle, including your sex life. This might seem too personal to share. But answering honestly is the only way your doctor is sure to give you the care you need. Your doctor might also do a Pap test to check for signs of cancer in your cervix. Ask your doctor how often you need a Pap test. Also, ask your doctor if the HPV vaccine is right for you. (See page 134 for more information.)

After diagnosis: What to do if you have an STI

Finding out that you have an STI might be difficult to face, especially if the source of your STI is an unfaithful partner or if it cannot be cured. For many, coping with the emotional side of having an STI is more difficult than managing the physical effects. But once you know what you are up against, you can start treatment right away and take steps to keep you and your partner(s) healthy.

Let partners know

Although you might not want to tell anybody about your STI, informing *all* your sexual partner(s) is the only way to stop the STI from getting passed to others or possibly reinfecting you. If your partner has other partners, they should be notified too. There are a few ways to do this:

1. Tell your partner(s) yourself and urge your partner(s) to get treated for the STI. For gonorrhea or chlamydial infection, you might be able to give your partner the needed medicine without him seeing a doctor. This is called expedited partner therapy (EPT). EPT is a last-resort option for partner(s) who won't or can't see a doctor. EPT is not possible in all states. If your partner is unwilling to seek treatment, ask your doctor if EPT is possible where you live.

2. Ask your doctor or the clinic where you were diagnosed to notify your sexual partner(s) anonymously. That means they won't disclose your name.

3. Tell your main partner, but ask that your medical provider inform all other or past partners.

4. Ask your doctor for help if you fear that notifying your partner(s) might lead to a violent or abusive reaction.

Follow treatment orders

Different STIs are treated differently. Follow your doctor's orders and finish any medicine you are given to cure or manage the infection. Even if your symptoms go away, you still need to finish all the medicine. Your doctor also will instruct you to not have sex until you and your partner(s) have finished treatment and until symptoms, such as sores, have completely cleared. You might also need to get a follow-up test after treatment to make sure the infection is cured. Doing these things is the only way to be sure your STI is treated and won't be passed to other people.

Be responsible sexually

Whether you are in a long-term relationship or involved with somebody new, it's up to you to act responsibly when it comes to your and your partner's(s') sexual health. This means:

- talking honestly about your having an STI, so that your current or fu-

Frequently Asked Questions About the HPV Vaccine

I've never heard of the HPV vaccine. What is it?

Many women don't know about the HPV vaccine and question whether it is something they need. That's because the HPV vaccine came out in 2006. It is the first vaccine to prevent cervical cancer and other diseases caused by certain types of genital human papillomavirus (HPV). The vaccine protects women against four HPV types, which together cause 70 percent of cervical cancers and 90 percent of genital warts. It does not treat existing HPV infections. The vaccine is given through a series of three shots over a 6-month period. Getting the vaccine is important, because more than half of sexually active women and men are infected with HPV at some point in their lives.

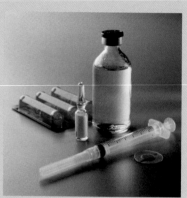

Who should get this vaccine?

It is recommended for 11- to 12-year-old girls, and it can be given to girls as young as 9—an age when most girls are not yet sexually active. It is also recommended for 13- to 26-year-old females who have not yet received or completed the vaccine series.

How long does vaccine protection last?

So far, we know that protection from HPV lasts at least 5 years in women who have been vaccinated.

I'm older than 26. Why isn't the vaccine recommended for me—or for men?

So far, the vaccine has been widely tested only in 9- to 26-year-old females. Research is just beginning to look at whether the vaccine also is safe and effective in women older than 26. Researchers also are working to find out if the vaccine will prevent HPV in men and boys.

I'm pregnant. Should I get the HPV vaccine?

Pregnant women should not get the HPV vaccine until after the baby is born. There is not enough research to know how the vaccine might affect pregnant women and their unborn babies.

After I get the HPV vaccine, do I still need to be screened for cervical cancer?

Yes. There are three reasons why. First, the vaccine does not protect against all HPV types that cause cancer. Second, women who don't get all the vaccine doses (or at the right time) might not be fully protected. Third, women may not fully benefit from the vaccine if they got it after acquiring one or more of the four HPV types.

ture partner(s) can make an informed choice whether or not to be intimate with you

- abstaining from sexual contact during treatment or when you have symptoms, such as warts or sores

Take care of your emotions

If you recently found out that you have an STI, you might feel like you're the only one or that you're now "different" from other people. You might feel embarrassed, a sense of "dirtiness," shame, or guilt. These feelings might keep you from wanting to seek treatment or telling your partner(s). You also might worry about getting better or that an STI will keep you from having a long-lasting romantic relationship in the future. Rest assured that these feelings are normal at first and will lessen over time. The following tips might also help you to adjust to the diagnosis:

- Learning the facts about the STI will help put your situation in perspective and give you a sense of greater control over your health and well-being.

- Talking to a trusted friend or loved one will ease stress.

- Connecting with a support group can help you to feel less alone and to see how others have dealt with similar situations in a positive way.

Keep in mind that stigma is behind many of the negative feelings that surround STIs. If you are living with an STI, try not to become a victim of stigma yourself. The more you know about STIs, the better control you will have over your sexual health. At the same time, knowing more can make it easier to talk about STIs with a loved one. ■

One Woman's Story

At the start of my sophomore year, I couldn't have been more prepared to take on the year. I spent the summer interning and training for a race with my sister. I felt accomplished and healthy. But my first test of the year changed everything.

My yearly Pap showed abnormal cells, so we ran an HPV test, which confirmed that I have human papillomavirus (HPV). The next step was to see a gynecologist and have a colposcopy.

I was sure I would die from cervical cancer. If not, stress would do me in. I spent hours with the nurse practitioner, getting medical leave for doctor's appointments, worrying about how to cover the cost of procedures and doctor's visits, and coping with possibly spreading HPV to my boyfriend.

At some point, my sister sent a card with a few encouraging words. "Don't let three letters define you," she wrote. Her words helped me through the most difficult parts. Telling my mom I wasn't sure how I got HPV was extremely hard. I was disappointed in myself, and it felt even worse that my mom might be too. Telling friends, who used to know everything about me, that I had a doctor's appointment without elaborating or talking with my boyfriend about how HPV impacts him were the most challenging moments in those relationships.

Don't let three letters define you.

This year I've had two Pap tests, two colposcopies, and an undying sense of guilt for bringing this on my family and boyfriend. I feel guilty because I knew how to prevent STIs. I can only be reassured knowing that when cell changes are monitored, cervical cancer is rare. I can't go back and change the past, but I can prevent this from getting worse. I choose what defines me, and this is not it.

Kathleen
Toms River, New Jersey

For More Information...

Office on Women's Health, HHS
200 Independence Ave SW, Room 712E
Washington, DC 20201
Web site: www.womenshealth.gov/faq/
stdsgen.htm
Phone number: (800) 994-9662,
(888) 220-5446 TDD

Division of STD Prevention, CDC
1600 Clifton Rd NE
Atlanta, GA 30333
Web site: www.cdc.gov/std
Phone number: (800) 232-4636,
(888) 232-6348 TTY

American College of Obstetricians and Gynecologists
409 12th St SW, PO Box 96920
Washington, DC 20090-6920
Web site: www.acog.org
Phone number: (202) 863-2518 Resource
Center

American Social Health Association
PO Box 13827
Research Triangle Park, NC 27709
Web site: www.ashastd.org
Phone number: (800) 227-8922 STI
Hotline

CDC National Prevention Information Network
PO Box 6003
Rockville, MD 20849-6003
Web site: www.cdcnpin.org
Phone number: (800) 458-5231

Planned Parenthood Federation of America
434 W 33rd St
New York, NY 10001
Web site: www.plannedparenthood.org
Phone number: (800) 230-7526

HIV/AIDS

No matter how young or old you are, if you have sex or inject illegal drugs, you should be concerned about becoming infected with human immunodeficiency (IH-myoo-noh-dih-FISH-uhn-see) virus, or HIV. HIV causes acquired immunodeficiency syndrome (AIDS), a disease that weakens your body's ability to fight infections and certain cancers.

The good news is that there are ways to prevent and treat HIV/AIDS. And if you are infected, there are treatments that can help you stay healthy for a long time.

The difference between HIV and AIDS

HIV is a type of virus. When you are infected with a virus, it first invades a few cells in the body and makes many copies of itself. The new viruses then leave these cells and seek out more cells to invade. Viruses often kill the cells they invade.

HIV invades cells of the immune system, which protects the body from disease. HIV primarily invades immune cells called CD4 positive (CD4$^+$) T cells. These cells tell other immune cells when they are needed to fight a specific infection.

Usually, a healthy, uninfected person has about 1000 CD4$^+$ T cells per microliter (millionth of a liter) of blood. This is known as your CD4 count. If you become HIV-infected, your CD4 count may stay normal for several years. This is because your body is able to replace the CD4$^+$ T cells that HIV destroys, at least for a while.

Without treatment, your CD4 count will eventually drop. When it drops below 200, you have developed AIDS. You can also develop AIDS if your CD4 count is above 200 and you have certain infections or cancers.

AIDS rates among women

Women are increasingly affected by AIDS. In 1985, less than 5 percent of new AIDS cases in the United States were among women and girls aged 13 years and older. By 2005, it was nearly 27 percent.

African American and Hispanic women have higher rates of new AIDS cases. Together, these two groups represent 24 percent of all U.S. women. But in 2005 they accounted for 82 percent of new AIDS cases in women.

Older women also get AIDS. Most women with AIDS are diagnosed between the ages of 15 and 39. But in 2005, 9 percent of new AIDS cases in women occurred in those older than 45.

How HIV is spread

Having sex

The main way to get HIV is through sexual activity. This is because HIV in an infected man is present in his semen. HIV in an infected woman is present in her vaginal fluid.

- **Vaginal sex.** During vaginal sex, HIV is more likely to be spread from a man to a woman than from a woman to a man. This is because the vaginal lining is exposed to semen for a longer period of time than the opening of the man's penis is exposed to vaginal fluid.

- **Anal sex.** Anal sex with an HIV-infected man is even riskier than vaginal sex. This is because the lining in

Prevention Tips

- **Abstinence,** which means not having sex of any kind. Abstinence is the only way to be sure that you won't become HIV-infected from having sex.

- **Use condoms.** If you do have sex, you should use a male or female condom every time. For information on condoms, see the *Sexually Transmitted Infections* chapter on page 119. If you have a casual sexual encounter, you should always use a condom. If you are in a long-term relationship, you and your partner should get tested regularly for HIV and other sexually transmitted infections (STIs). (See pages 142–144  for information on HIV testing.) If you both remain disease-free and have sex with only each other, then the risk of getting HIV from sex is low. If your partner gets violent when you ask him to use a condom, see the *Violence Against Women* chapter on page 235 for tips on dealing with domestic violence.

- **Use dental dams.** These are small square pieces of latex that are sometimes used by dentists. They can also be used to help reduce your risk of getting HIV and other STIs during oral-vaginal or oral-anal sex. The partner performing oral sex holds the dam against the vulva or anus of the partner. Women who have sex with women should also use dental dams.

the rectum is thinner and more likely to be torn during sex than is the vaginal lining.

- **Oral sex.** Becoming infected with HIV through oral sex is rare but does occur.

Injection drug use

The next most common way that HIV is spread is by sharing items used in injection drug use, such as injection needles and syringes. Some drug users think that they can avoid becoming HIV-infected if they don't inject into a vein. Instead, they inject just under the skin's surface or into a muscle. These types of injections can also spread HIV.

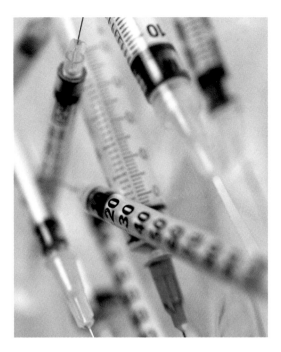

- **Get treated for any STIs.** Having an STI, particularly herpes simplex virus, increases your chances of becoming HIV-infected during sex. If your partner has an STI in addition to HIV, that also increases your risk for HIV infection. If you have an STI, you should also get tested for HIV. (See pages 142–144 for information on HIV testing.)

- **Get treated for vaginal infections.** These also increase your chances of becoming HIV-infected during sex. For information on vaginal infections, see the *Reproductive Health* chapter on page 153.

- **Avoid inserting into your vagina objects** or sex toys that have not been cleaned with soap and water. This also applies to women who have sex with women.

- **Avoid douching.** Vaginal douching increases your risk of developing a vaginal infection.

- **Avoid using:**
  - **vaginal deodorants or vaginal cleansers**
  - **substances to dry or tighten the vagina**
  - **alcohol or drugs** when you're having sex, because you're more likely to take risks when you're drunk or under the influence of drugs

Also, you shouldn't confuse preventing pregnancy with preventing HIV infection. Taking the pill, using an intrauterine device (IUD) or diaphragm, or having your "tubes tied"—all of which are used for preventing pregnancy—will not prevent HIV infection.

Spread of HIV from mother to child

HIV can be spread from an infected mother to her fetus during pregnancy or delivery. Also, HIV from an infected mother can be spread to her baby through breastfeeding. The spread of HIV from mother to infant has been greatly reduced by:

- giving the mother anti-HIV drugs during pregnancy, labor, and delivery

- giving the newborn baby an anti-HIV drug for 6 weeks after birth

- giving the mother good prenatal care

- avoiding procedures during pregnancy or delivery that expose the baby to the mother's blood or vaginal secretions

- delivering the baby by cesarean section (in cases in which treatment with anti-HIV drugs is not able to reduce the HIV level in the mother's blood to a "safe" level for vaginal delivery)

- feeding the baby formula rather than breastfeeding

Blood transfusion

Because U.S. blood banks test donated blood for HIV, getting infected with HIV through a blood transfusion is very unlikely.

Ways that HIV is not spread

HIV is not spread through:

- kissing

- sharing of food utensils, towels and bedding, telephones, or toilet seats

- swimming pools

- hugging or handshakes

- being around someone with HIV

- biting insects such as mosquitoes or bedbugs

Get tested for HIV

By the end of 2003, more than a million people in the United States were living with HIV or AIDS. Of these people, about 25 percent were unaware that they were infected. Many new HIV infections are caused by people who are unaware that they have the virus. Experts estimate that somewhere between 54 and 70 percent of new HIV infections that occur through sexual activity happen because of having sex with someone who is unaware that they are HIV-infected. Getting tested is crucial to helping stop the spread of HIV.

If you have been infected with HIV, the earlier you know, the better. It's important that your infection be detected early so that you can start treatment. Taking anti-HIV drugs early in the infection may prevent you from developing AIDS. Also, once you know your HIV status, you can take the proper steps to protect your sexual partners.

Types of HIV tests

- **Antibody tests** detect the presence of anti-HIV antibodies in body fluids. Antibodies are substances produced by the immune system to try to fight germs such as HIV. Antibodies against HIV generally can be detected between 2 weeks and 3 months after infection. Most tests detect these antibodies in the blood, but some can detect them in saliva or urine.

When you get tested for HIV, your doctor or nurse will first give you a screening test. Some of these tests provide results within 20 minutes. If you test positive with the screening test, then you will need to get a second type of test to confirm that you are infected. With this more sensitive test, you have to return after a few days or weeks to get the results.

A home HIV antibody test, called "The Home Access HIV-1 Test System," is also available. It can be found in most drugstores. With this test, you mail a blood sample to a lab. Results are provided over the phone by a counselor. If you use the home test, you do not have to supply your name. Instead, the laboratory assigns a personal identification number to your sample. If you test positive with the home test, your counselor will give you a referral to a doctor or medical clinic where you can get a second test to confirm whether you are infected.

- **Tests for HIV genetic material.** Instead of detecting antibodies against HIV, these tests detect parts of HIV itself. As such, they measure your "viral load," which is the number of HIV copies per milliliter of blood. Tests of HIV genetic material are useful:

  - in the period between when you're infected and when your body starts producing anti-HIV antibodies

  - if the results of standard antibody tests are unclear

  - in testing for HIV in a newborn baby whose mother is infected

  - in helping your doctor see if your treatments for HIV infection are working

Preventing HIV After Exposure

Some research shows that if you have been exposed to HIV, you may be able to prevent HIV infection if you:

- start taking anti-HIV drugs within 3 days of your exposure
- continue taking the drugs for 28 days

If you think that the blood or genital fluids of someone you know or suspect to have HIV has entered your body, see a doctor as soon as possible.

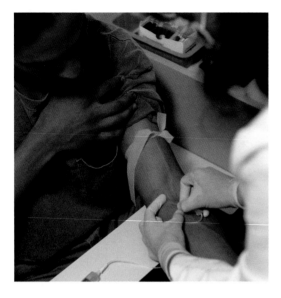

How often should you get tested?

Everyone aged 13 to 64 years should be tested routinely for HIV infection. How often you should get tested depends on your HIV risks.

- You and your partner should get tested before starting a new sexual relationship.

- Pregnant women should be tested as early as possible during pregnancy.

People at High Risk

- injection drug users and their sex partners

- people who exchange sex for money or illicit drugs

- sex partners of HIV-infected persons

- people who have had any new sex partners since their most recent HIV test

- people whose sex partners have had any new sex partners since their most recent HIV test

Where can you get tested?

To find an HIV testing site near you, visit the National HIV Testing Resources Web site or call the CDC National Prevention Information Network listed in the resource section on page 151. You can also get tested at your doctor's office or local public health clinic.

Testing should be repeated in the third trimester for women known to be at high risk for HIV.

- If you are at high risk for HIV infection, you should be tested at least once a year.

- You should also get tested if you:
  - have tuberculosis (too-bur-kyuh-LOH-suhss) (TB) (a common disease among AIDS patients)
  - are being treated for an STI
  - have early symptoms of HIV infection (see "Symptoms of HIV infection and AIDS" below)

If you do not fit any of the categories listed above, talk with your doctor about how often you should get tested for HIV.

Symptoms of HIV infection and AIDS

Early symptoms of HIV infection

About half of people with HIV develop flu-like symptoms about 3 to 6 weeks after becoming infected. These symptoms include:

- fever
- feeling tired
- rash

- headache
- enlarged lymph nodes
- sore throat
- upset stomach
- night sweats
- stiff neck
- open sores in the mouth

Because these symptoms are not specific for HIV infection, doctors may sometimes make the wrong diagnosis. If you have these symptoms and have been behaving in ways that put you at risk for HIV infection, be sure to tell your doctor or get tested for HIV.

After the initial infection, you may have no symptoms. This may last a few months or it may last more than 10 years. During this time, HIV is making many copies of itself. It is also infecting and killing cells of your immune system. As your viral load goes up, your CD4 count goes down. Starting treatment early can:

- slow the spread of HIV in your body
- slow the destruction of your immune system
- delay the onset of AIDS-related infections and cancers

Opportunistic infections and cancers

If you don't get treatment for HIV infection, you will probably get one or more opportunistic infections. They are called opportunistic because the germs that cause these infections take advantage of the opportunity provided by your weakened immune system. You may also get certain types of cancer.

AIDS-Related Diseases

Disease	What it is	What you need to know
Pneumocystis pneumonia (noo-muh-SISS-tuhss noo-MOH-nyuh), or PCP	A lung disease	Symptoms include: - Shortness of breath when you are physically active - A cough that does not produce phlegm (a "dry" cough)
Candidiasis (kan-dih-DEYE-uh-suhss)	A type of fungal infection	Candidiasis causes different symptoms, depending on the site of infection. Thrush is candidiasis inside the mouth. Thrush causes white curdlike patches on the tongue, roof of the mouth, and lips. Vaginal candidiasis, or vaginal yeast infection, may cause: - Vaginal itch or soreness - A thick vaginal discharge that looks like cottage cheese - Pain or discomfort while having sex

AIDS-Related Diseases

Disease	What it is	What you need to know
Toxoplasmosis (tok-soh-plaz-MOH-suhss)	A parasitic infection that can damage your brain	You can avoid toxoplasmosis by: • Cooking meat until it is no longer pink in the center • Avoiding contact with cat feces. Ask someone who is not HIV-infected and is not pregnant to change the litter box daily. If you must clean the box yourself, wear gloves and wash your hands well with soap and water right after changing the litter.
Cytomegalovirus retinitis (SEYE-toh-MEG-uh-loh-VEYE-ruhss ret-uhn-EYE-tuhss)	An inflammation in the back of your eye that can cause vision loss	To avoid becoming infected with cytomegalovirus: • Wash your hands frequently and thoroughly • Use condoms
Tuberculosis	A disease that most often affects the lungs	Symptoms include: • Pain in the chest • Coughing up blood or phlegm from deep inside the lungs
Cervical cancer	Caused by infection with certain types of human papillomavirus (See the *Sexually Transmitted Infections* chapter on page 119.)	HIV-infected women should get regular Pap tests to check for precancerous cells. How often they should get tested depends on test results.
Lymphomas (lim-FOH-muhz)	Cancers of the immune system	See your doctor if you have any of the following problems: • Weight loss or fever for no known reason • Night sweats • Painless, swollen lymph nodes in the neck, chest, underarm, or groin • A feeling of fullness below the ribs

Treatment for HIV/AIDS

Drugs that are used to treat HIV/AIDS are known as antiretroviral (an-teye-RE-troh-veye-ruhl) drugs. Different antiretroviral drugs block HIV at different stages of the infection.

If you are HIV-infected, your doctor may give you a combination of antiretroviral drugs. Some combinations of antiretroviral drugs are known as "highly active antiretroviral therapy," or HAART. If you take the drugs as directed, HAART can reduce your viral load. This allows your immune system to recover and protect your body from infections.

It is common practice to say that HAART may be able to suppress HIV to "undetectable" levels. This means that most HIV tests cannot detect the virus. Some people make the mistake of thinking that "undetectable" means that they no longer have HIV. But the virus is still in their body and they can still infect other people. So far, no drug combination has been able to totally get rid of the virus.

AIDS Drug Assistance Programs

AIDS Drug Assistance Programs (ADAPs) provide antiretroviral drugs to low-income people with HIV/AIDS who:

- don't have health insurance, or
- have private health insurance that doesn't pay for antiretroviral drugs

For information on the ADAP program in your state, contact your state health department.

Some people have trouble taking antiretroviral drugs as directed because of side effects such as:

- nausea and vomiting
- skin rashes
- feeling tired or weak

If you get serious side effects, your doctor may switch you to other drugs. But it's important not to stop taking the drugs on your own. If you go on and off the drugs, the HIV in your body may develop a resistance to the drugs. When that happens, the drugs may no longer be able to suppress the virus.

If you have an opportunistic infection, your doctor can give you various antimicrobial (an-teye-meye-KROH-bee-uhl) drugs. These will help your body fight the infection. Your doctor may also give you vaccines to prevent you from getting other diseases, such as hepatitis or measles.

Tips for Staying Healthy Longer

There are many things you can do to stay healthy. Here are a few:

- Follow your doctor's instructions. If your doctor prescribes medicine for you, take it just the way he or she tells you to. Taking only some of your medicine gives your HIV infection more chance to fight back.

- If you get sick from your medicine, call your doctor for advice. Do not make changes to your medicine on your own or because of advice from friends.

- If you smoke or use drugs not prescribed by your doctor, quit.

- Eat healthy foods. This will help keep you strong, keep your energy and weight up, and help your body protect itself.

- Be physically active on a regular basis.

- Get enough sleep and rest.

Psychosocial issues

For many women, being told that they are HIV-infected or have AIDS adds to the many other serious problems they have to deal with, such as:

- unemployment
- low income
- depression
- sexual assault

Dealing with HIV infection on top of all of your other problems can seem overwhelming. A good place to start is to work with a case manager. A case manager is a health professional who can help you manage your care and connect you with programs that can help with:

- medical care
- mental health treatment
- treatment for drug and alcohol abuse
- job options or learning new job skills
- housing

- food
- domestic violence shelters
- child care

To find a case manager:

- Ask your doctor or nurse.
- Call your city, county, or state health department.
- Call your local AIDS organization.

Another problem faced by people with HIV/AIDS is the stigma associated with the disease. People with HIV/AIDS are often rejected by their families, loved ones, and communities because they feel that AIDS is a shameful disease. Women with HIV/AIDS can deal with HIV stigma by:

- joining HIV/AIDS support groups
- becoming HIV/AIDS patient advocates
- becoming HIV educators or public speakers

Research on HIV/AIDS

Many researchers around the world are working to find new ways to prevent and treat HIV/AIDS. Researchers are working to develop:

- **vaccines** that could prevent or treat HIV/AIDS
- **new drugs** that:
  - target HIV at different stages at which it is reproducing itself
  - could be given to high-risk people to prevent them from becoming HIV-infected
  - treat opportunistic infections
- **topical microbicides** (meye-KROH-buh-sydz). These are creams or gels that:
  - women could apply in their vagina or rectum before having sex
  - would help protect people from HIV and other STIs
  - would be non-irritating, inexpensive, and not easily detectable by their sex partner

If you would like to help with HIV/AIDS research, consider volunteering for a clinical trial. A clinical trial is a research study in which a new drug, vaccine, or other product is tested in people after having been shown to be safe and effective in animals. AIDS clinical trials need women to volunteer, whether they test positive or negative for HIV.

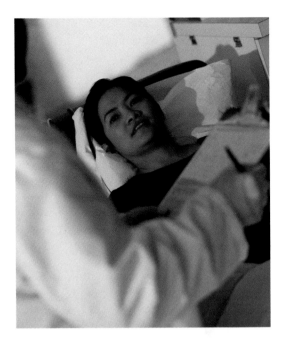

For information on volunteering for an AIDS clinical trial, see the AIDS.gov and AIDSinfo contact information listed in the resource section on page 151.

Much progress has been made in treating HIV/AIDS since the disease first surfaced in the early 1980s. In fact, many people are living full lives with the help of treatment advances and support from family and friends. And with continued support from researchers and advocates around the world, a cure just may be possible. ■

One Woman's Story

When my mother was diagnosed in the late '80s, AIDS was still considered a "gay" disease. She was a single woman with two young children who didn't use drugs and wasn't a gay man, so how did she end up with this disease? My mother had no time to worry about the past. She had to figure out how to live for the future. Rather than burden others or shame herself, she kept her HIV status a secret from her family for over 10 years. She only shared this information with her doctors and partners.

My mother decided to tell her family that she was HIV positive in 1998. I couldn't believe what was happening. She is the smartest woman I know, my best friend, the wind beneath my wings. How could she have this disease that has killed millions? Was she going to die, too?

My mother said that she was afraid of what her family and friends would think of her. She didn't want to lose them. But what would they say except, "You are my sister/daughter/aunt/best friend, and I love you." Back then, the stereotypes attached to HIV were still considered truths. Even though the black community was strongly affected by this epidemic, it was still uneducated and misinformed about the disease. Who was to say that our family was any different?

I know firsthand that HIV/AIDS is not a death sentence.

In 2003, my mother started to feel more secure and was ready to talk about it. She began speaking to small groups and even did a radio interview. So when she was asked to participate in a special episode of the UPN show "Girlfriends," she proudly said yes. On May 12, 2003, the rest of our family and the world found out that my mother, Julaun Lewis, was living with HIV. During her appearance, she was beautiful, strong, and, most important, forever free of the burden of this secret. I had never been more proud of both her and my family. Like we'd hoped, everyone had the same response: "We love you and always will."

The key to stopping this disease is education and acceptance. Once we as a community educate ourselves about the disease, and our own personal status, we will open our hearts and minds and finally accept how HIV/AIDS has affected our community. I know firsthand that HIV/AIDS is not a death sentence. People with it can live long, full, and healthy lives. We need to move past stereotypes so that no one will have to keep being HIV-positive a secret.

Jeneane

Los Angeles, California

Taken from *Not in My Family: AIDS in the African-American Community* (Agate).

For More Information...

Office on Women's Health, HHS
200 Independence Ave SW, Room 712E
Washington, DC 20201
Web site: www.womenshealth.gov/hiv
Phone number: (800) 994-9662,
(888) 220-5446 TDD

AIDS.gov, HHS
200 Independence Ave SW
Washington, DC 20201
Web site: www.aids.gov

AIDSinfo, NIH
PO Box 6303
Rockville, MD 20849-6303
Web site: www.aidsinfo.nih.gov
Phone number: (800) 448-0440,
(888) 480-3739 TTY

Divisions of HIV/AIDS Prevention, CDC
1600 Clifton Rd NE
Atlanta, GA 30333
Web site: www.cdc.gov/hiv
Phone number: (800) 232-4636,
(888) 232-6348 TTY

HIV/AIDS Bureau, HRSA
5600 Fishers Ln
Rockville, MD 20857
Web site: www.hab.hrsa.gov
Phone number: (888) 275-4772

National HIV Testing Resources, CDC
PO Box 6003
Rockville, MD 20849-6003
Web site: www.hivtest.org
Phone number: (800) 458-5231

National Institute of Allergy and Infectious Diseases, NIH
6610 Rockledge Drive, MSC 6612
Bethesda, MD 20892-6612
Web site: www.niaid.nih.gov/
healthscience/healthtopics/HIVAIDS
Phone number: (866) 284-4107,
(800) 877-8339

Office of Special Health Issues, FDA
5600 Fishers Ln
Rockville, MD 20857
Web site: www.fda.gov/oashi/aids/
hiv.html
Phone number: (888) 463-6332

HIV and AIDS Medicines to Help You
www.fda.gov/womens/medicinecharts/
hiv.html

AIDS InfoNet
PO Box 810
Arroyo Seco, NM 87514
Web site: www.aidsinfonet.org

The Body
250 W 57th St
New York, NY 10107
Web site: www.thebody.com

CDC National Prevention Information Network
PO Box 6003
Rockville, MD 20849-6003
Web site: www.cdcnpin.org
Phone number: (800) 458-5231

Project Inform
1375 Mission St
San Francisco, CA 94103-2621
Web site: www.projectinform.org
Phone number: (800) 822-7422

Reproductive Health

A healthy reproductive system makes the miracle of life possible. Taking good care of your reproductive health is important because problems with this system can make it hard or impossible for you to become pregnant. Reproductive health problems also can be harmful to your overall health and emotional well-being and can make it hard to enjoy a sexual relationship. Fortunately, many reproductive health problems can be prevented or corrected if you take good care of your body and see your doctor for regular checkups and screenings.

Caring for your reproductive health involves:

- Learning how your reproductive system works and what is normal for you. Knowing these things will help you to tell if you need to see a doctor.

- Keeping away from substances and chemicals that can harm your reproductive health and ability to produce healthy children.

- Seeing your doctor for routine checkups and screenings. This way, problems can be found early, so they can be treated or kept from getting worse.

- Protecting yourself from sexually transmitted infections (STIs), which are very common and easily spread. They can damage reproductive organs and make it hard to get pregnant or cause problems during pregnancy.

- Incorporating family planning.

Your reproductive system

A woman has reproductive organs both inside and outside her body. All the organs play a role in the reproductive process, which includes:

- menstrual cycle—a woman's monthly cycle, which includes getting your period
- conception—when a woman's egg is fertilized by a man's sperm
- pregnancy
- childbirth

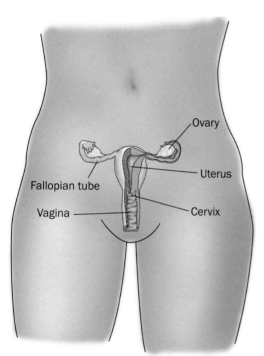

Here are the major reproductive organs and what they do:

Ovaries—These two small glands contain eggs (ova) and make hormones. One of the ovaries releases an egg about once a month as part of the menstrual cycle. This is called ovulation.

Fallopian tube—When an egg is released, it travels through the fallopian tube to the uterus. You will get pregnant if you have sex with a man, and his sperm fertilizes the egg on its way to your uterus.

Uterus—The uterus, or womb, is a hollow, pear-shaped organ. The tissue that lines the uterus is called the endometrium. If a fertilized egg attaches itself to the lining of the uterus, it may continue to develop into a fetus. The uterus expands as the fetus grows. The muscular walls of the uterus help to push the mature fetus out during birth. If pregnancy does not occur, the egg is shed along with the blood and tissue that lines the uterus. This is menstruation, also called getting your period.

Cervix—This narrow entryway connects the vagina and uterus. The cervix is flexible so that it can expand to let a baby pass through during birth.

Reproductive health topics found elsewhere in this book:

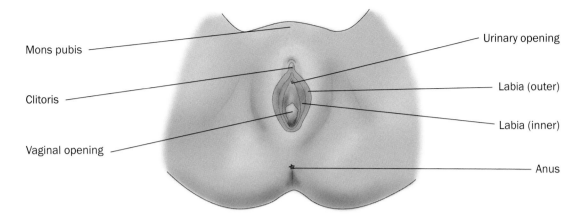

Mons pubis

Clitoris

Vaginal opening

Urinary opening

Labia (outer)

Labia (inner)

Anus

Vagina—Also called the birth canal, the vagina stretches during childbirth.

The external female genital organ is the vulva. The vulva has five parts: mons pubis, labia, clitoris, urinary opening, and vaginal opening.

Caring for Your Vulva

The vulva does not need special care. But there are a few things you can do to stay comfortable and prevent infections:

- Do not douche. Douching may make a woman more prone to vaginal infections and make it harder to get pregnant for women who want to.

- Wear only cotton underpants and avoid tight-fitting pants and pantyhose.

- Use a personal lubricant for intercourse if the vagina is dry or more lubrication is needed. Frequent use of lubricants that contain the spermicide nonoxynol-9 (N-9) can irritate the vulva and vagina and might increase the risk of infections, including HIV.

- Use a mirror to check your vulva once a month. If you notice any signs of problems, such as swelling, changes in color, or change in your usual discharge, contact your doctor.

Know your period

Chemicals a woman's body makes called hormones rise and fall during the month and make the menstrual cycle happen. Keep track of your menstrual cycle with a menstrual diary or calendar, so you can know what's normal for you. Make a note of the day your period starts and ends in your calendar and if your bleeding is heavier or lighter than usual. Most cycles are about 28 days long. Your period might not be the same every month. Also make a note of changes in your

mood or body during your cycle. Some women have mild pain on one side of their abdomen during ovulation. You might also notice these symptoms in the days leading up to your period:

- cramping, bloating, and sore breasts
- food cravings
- mood swings and irritability
- headaches and fatigue

Women whose symptoms are severe may have premenstrual syndrome (PMS). Let your doctor know if you have trouble coping with the symptoms of your period, especially mood swings.

Regular periods: A sign of good health

Sometimes women have problems with their menstrual cycle. These are some common menstrual problems:

- Abnormal uterine bleeding includes very heavy or long-lasting periods (menorrhagia) (MEN-uh-RAY-jee-uh) or irregular bleeding. Uterine fibroids (FY-broidz) are the most common cause of menorrhagia in adult women. Young teenage girls often have longer cycles until their reproductive system is fully mature. Also, periods may become irregular as you near menopause.

- Amenorrhea (ay-men-uh-REE-uh) occurs when a young woman hasn't started menstruating by age 16, or when a woman who used to have a regular period stops menstruating for at least 3 months. The most common cause is pregnancy. But amenorrhea can be a symptom of a disorder, such as polycystic ovary syndrome, prema-

ture ovarian failure, or thyroid problems. It is also a sign of a less common but serious condition called female athlete triad, which affects a woman's menstrual cycle, eating habits, and bone health. Competitive athletes and women who engage in a great deal of physical activity are at risk of this disorder.

- Dysmenorrhea (diss-men-uh-REE-uh) is severe pain during a woman's period. The natural production of a hormone called prostaglandin (PROSS-tuh-GLAN-duhn) can cause intense cramping. It is a problem found mainly in girls and young women. In women in their 20s, 30s, and 40s, a condition such as uterine fibroids or endometriosis (EN-doh-MEE-tree-OH-suhss) may cause painful periods.

- Premature ovarian failure (POF) is when a woman's ovaries stop working normally before she is 40. POF is not the same as early menopause. Some women with POF still get a period

When to Get Help for Problem Periods

Problem periods often are a symptom of another condition, which may or may not need treatment. See your doctor if:

- you have not started menstruating by the age of 16
- your period suddenly stops
- you are bleeding for more days than usual
- you are bleeding much more than usual
- your periods become irregular after having had regular, monthly cycles
- your period occurs more often than every 21 days or less often than every 45 days
- you suddenly feel very sick while or after using tampons, experiencing symptoms such as high fever, headache, throwing up, rash, or feeling faint
- you bleed between periods (more than just a few drops)
- you have severe pain during your period
- you have severe emotional or physical symptoms in the days before your period

now and then. But getting pregnant is hard for women with POF. Women with POF also are more likely to develop certain conditions, including osteoporosis (OSS-tee-oh-puh-ROH-suhss), low thyroid function, and an autoimmune (aw-toh-ih-MYOON) disease called Addison's disease. (See page 83 of the *Autoimmune Diseases* chapter for more information.) No treatment will restore ovary function. But some symptoms of POF and the risk of bone loss can be helped by hormone therapy. The cause of POF is not known. But it appears to run in some families. POF also occurs in some women who carry the mutated gene that causes Fragile X syndrome. Women with POF should talk to their doctors about being tested to see if

they are a carrier of this mutated gene. (See page 408 of the Appendix for information on genetic testing.)

- Premature menopause is when a woman's period stops completely before she is 40. This can occur naturally or because of medical treatment or surgery. Early menopause puts a woman at greater risk of heart disease and osteoporosis, but there are treatment options to lower these risks.

Reproductive and gynecologic health

There are many conditions and disorders that can affect the organs in a woman's abdominal and pelvic areas. We don't know what causes many reproductive health problems. But there are ways to manage symptoms or make them go away, such as with medicine, surgery, physical therapy, or lifestyle changes. The specific problem, your symptoms, your age, and your desire to have children are factors that often guide treatment choices.

Disorder	Signs to look for
Endometrial hyperplasia (EN-doh-MEE-tree-uhl HEYE-pur-PLAY-zhee-uh) occurs when the lining of the uterus grows too thick. It is not cancer. But if the cells of the lining become abnormal, it can lead to cancer of the uterus.	Abnormal bleeding is the most common sign.
Endometriosis occurs when tissue that's like the uterine lining grows outside the uterus. It is very common, mainly affecting women in their 30s and 40s. It is one of the top three causes of infertility. Assisted reproductive technology (ART) helps many women with endometriosis become pregnant. (See the *Pregnancy* chapter on page 169 for more information on treating infertility.)	Pelvic pain is the main symptom. Other types of pain include very painful periods; chronic pain in the belly, lower back, and pelvis; pain during sex; and pain during bowel movements or while passing urine. Difficulty becoming pregnant is another sign. Symptoms often improve after menopause.
Ovarian cysts are fluid-filled sacs in the ovaries. In most cases, a cyst is completely normal: It does no harm and goes away by itself. Most women have them at some point in their lives. Often, a woman finds out about a cyst when she has a pelvic exam. Cysts are rarely cancerous in women younger than 50. See also, polycystic ovary syndrome.	Cysts may not cause any symptoms. Some cysts may cause pain, discomfort, and irregular periods—but not always. If you have cysts, watch for changes or acute symptoms. Call your doctor right away if you have: • Sudden, severe pain in your pelvis or abdomen • Pain with fever or throwing up
Painful sexual intercourse (dyspareunia) (DISS-puh-ROO-nee-uh) can cause distress for a woman and her partner. Some causes of pain are: • Vaginal dryness • Infections • Vaginismus—spasms of the muscles around the vagina • Uterine fibroids • Scar tissue • Past experiences, negative attitudes about sex, or fear of pain also can play a role	Pain during sex can have many forms. Some women have pain outside the vagina, such as with vulvodynia. Some women feel like "something is being bumped into" when the penis is inside the vagina. You might feel pain every time you have sex or only now and then. It might be hard for women who have pain during sex to become aroused, even if they don't have pain all the time.
Pelvic floor problems occur when tissues that support the pelvic organs weaken or are damaged. This can happen because of pregnancy, childbirth, weight gain, surgery, and normal aging. In uterine prolapse, the uterus drops into the vagina. In some cases this causes the cervix to come out through the vaginal opening. In vaginal prolapse, the top of the vagina loses support and can drop through the vaginal opening.	You might notice a feeling of heaviness or pressure as if something is "falling" out of the vagina. It might also be hard to empty your bladder completely. You might also get frequent urinary tract infections. Sometimes, urinary and anal incontinence are signs of pelvic support problems. Kegel exercises can make your pelvic muscles stronger. (See page 256 of the *Urologic and Kidney Health* chapter for more information.)

The Healthy Woman: A Complete Guide for All Ages

Disorder	Signs to look for
Pelvic pain can have a number of causes. Often, it is a symptom of another condition, or infection. Sometimes, the reason for pelvic pain is not found. Pain that lasts a long time can disrupt a woman's quality of life and lead to depression.	Pain comes in many forms. Acute pain lasts a short time. Chronic pelvic pain lasts for more than 6 months and does not improve with treatment. Describing your pain will help your doctor find out the cause. A pain diary is a good way to keep track of your pain.
Polycystic ovary syndrome (PCOS) is a hormone imbalance problem, which can interfere with normal ovulation. This can lead to irregular periods and multiple cysts on the ovaries. PCOS is the most common cause of female infertility. Women with PCOS also are at higher risk of diabetes, high blood pressure, metabolic syndrome, heart disease, and perhaps fibroids and depression.	Signs of PCOS include: • Irregular, infrequent periods • Obesity • Excess hair growth on the face, chest, stomach, thumbs, or toes • Acne • Trouble becoming pregnant
Uterine fibroids are tumors or lumps that grow within the wall of the uterus. They are not cancer. Fibroids may grow as a single tumor or in clusters. A single fibroid can be 1 inch or less in size or grow to 8 inches across or more. Fibroids are very common, affecting at least one-quarter of all women. African American women and women who are overweight are at greater risk. Women who have given birth are at lower risk.	Some women don't have any symptoms. But fibroids can cause: • Heavy bleeding or painful periods • Bleeding between periods • Feeling "full" in the lower abdomen • Frequent need to pass urine • Pain during sex • Lower back pain • Infertility, more than one miscarriage, or early labor Most women with fibroids are able to become pregnant. Often, fibroids stop growing or shrink after menopause.
Vaginitis is when the vagina is inflamed. It can happen for these reasons: • Vaginal yeast infection—an overgrowth of fungus, such as candida, which is normally present in the vagina • Bacterial vaginosis—an overgrowth of certain kinds of bacteria that are normally present in the vagina • Sexually transmitted infections • Allergy to douches, soaps, feminine sprays, spermicides, etc	Vaginitis may not always have symptoms. When it does, you might notice these signs: • Burning • Itching • Redness or puffiness • Abnormal discharge with a "fishy" odor or change in the way it normally looks. Yeast infections often cause cottage cheese–like discharge.
Vulvodynia is chronic pain and discomfort of the vulva. It can make it hard to sit comfortably, be active, or enjoy a sexual relationship. Over time, coping with pain can lower self-esteem and lead to depression.	You might feel burning, stinging, rawness, or aching even though the vulva might look normal. Pain might be felt all over the vulva or in a single spot. Pain can be constant or come and go. You might feel pain only after touch or pressure, such as from using tampons, having sex, or riding a bike.

Hysterectomy

Hysterectomy is surgery to remove the uterus. It is the second most common surgery among women in the United States. Some reasons a woman might need a hysterectomy include:

- uterine fibroids
- endometriosis
- uterine prolapse
- cancer
- abnormal uterine bleeding

In some cases, women have other treatment options, such as new medicines or procedures. These alternatives might offer lower risk and quicker recovery time. But they might have drawbacks, too. With your doctor, discuss all the treatment options that might help your problem. Consider getting a second opinion to help you make a wise choice.

Breast health

Breast health is important to a woman's sexual health, overall health, and breast-feeding. Your breasts will change at different times of your life. You might notice lumpiness or tenderness during your period. Your breasts might get bigger during pregnancy. As you get older, the milk-producing tissue of your breasts turns into soft, fatty tissue, which might feel different to you. It's important to know the way your breasts normally feel and look so you can tell your doctor if you notice changes. A change can be a sign of a problem, including breast cancer. Although not all lumps or breast changes mean you have cancer or a prob-

lem, any change in breast tissue should be checked by a doctor. Ask your doctor how you can do a self-exam. Checking your breasts once a month, a few days after your period ends, can alert you to these reasons to call your doctor:

- a hard lump or knot in or near the breast or in your underarm
- dimpling, puckering, or ridges of the skin on the breast
- a change in the size or shape of your breast
- clear or bloody fluid that leaks out of the nipple
- itchy, scaly sore or rash on the nipple
- unusual swelling, warmth, or redness

You should also get a clinical breast exam as part of your regular checkup. This is done by your doctor. Women age 40 and older should have screening mammograms every 1 to 2 years. It is an x-ray of the breast. Ask your doctor how often you need one. A mammogram along with a clinical breast exam is the best way to find breast cancer. (See page 62 of the *Cancer* chapter for more information.)

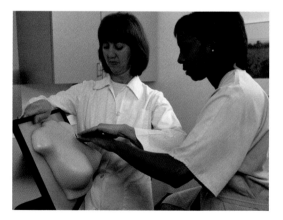

Preventing unintended pregnancy

About one-half of all pregnancies in the United States are unintended. Not having sex or using a safe and effective birth control method (contraception) is the best way to avoid pregnancy. Use this chart to learn about birth control methods, and talk to your doctor to find one that's right for you.

Method	How you get it	Failure rate* (Number of pregnancies expected per 100 women) *Methods range in effectiveness from light (most effective) to dark (least effective).*	Some side effects and risks**
Sterilization surgery for women	One-time procedure, which is permanent	Less than 1	Pain Bleeding Complications from surgery Ectopic (tubal) pregnancy
Sterilization implant for women	One-time procedure, which is permanent	Less than 1	Pain Ectopic (tubal) pregnancy
Sterilization surgery for men (vasectomy)	One-time procedure, which is permanent	Less than 1	Pain Bleeding Complications from surgery
Implantable rod	One-time procedure, which lasts up to 3 years	Less than 1 This method might not work as well for women who are overweight or obese.	Acne Weight gain Cysts of the ovaries Mood changes Depression Hair loss Headache Upset stomach Dizziness Sore breasts Changes in period Lower interest in sex
Intrauterine device (IUD)	One-time procedure, which can stay in place for 5 to 10 years	Less than 1	Cramps Bleeding between periods Pelvic inflammatory disease Infertility Tear or hole in the uterus

Method	How you get it	Failure rate* (Number of pregnancies expected per 100 women) *Methods range in effectiveness from light (most effective) to dark (least effective).*	Some side effects and risks**
Shot/injection	Your doctor gives you one shot every 3 months	Less than 1	Bleeding between periods Weight gain Sore breasts Headaches Bone loss with long-term use
Oral contraceptives (combination pill, or "the pill")	Prescription	5 Being overweight may increase the chance of getting pregnant while using birth control pills.	Dizziness Upset stomach Changes in your period Changes in mood Weight gain High blood pressure Blood clots Heart attack Stroke New vision problems
Oral contraceptives (continuous/ extended use, or "no-period pill")	Prescription	5 Being overweight may increase the chance of getting pregnant while using birth control pills.	Same as combination pill Spotting or bleeding between periods Hard to know if pregnant
Oral contraceptives (progestin-only pill, or "mini-pill")	Prescription	5 Being overweight may increase the chance of getting pregnant while using birth control pills.	Spotting or bleeding between periods Weight gain Sore breasts
Skin patch	Prescription	5 The patch may be less effective in women weighing more than 198 pounds.	Similar to those for the combination pill Greater exposure to estrogen than with other methods
Vaginal ring	Prescription	5	Similar to those for the combination pill Swelling of the vagina Irritation Vaginal discharge
Male condom	Over the counter	11–16	Allergic reaction

The Healthy Woman: A Complete Guide for All Ages

Method	How you get it	Failure rate* (Number of pregnancies expected per 100 women) *Methods range in effectiveness from light (most effective) to dark (least effective).*	Some side effects and risks**
Diaphragm with spermicide	Prescription	15	Irritation Allergic reactions Urinary tract infection Toxic shock if left in too long
Sponge with spermicide	Over the counter	16–32	Irritation Allergic reactions Hard time removing Toxic shock if left in too long
Cervical cap with spermicide	Prescription	17–23	Irritation Allergic reactions Abnormal Pap smear Toxic shock if left in too long
Female condom	Over the counter	20	Irritation Allergic reactions
Natural family planning	Ask your doctor or natural family planning instructor for information	25	None
Spermicide alone	Over the counter	30 Spermicides can offer added pregnancy protection if used with another barrier method, such as a condom.	Irritation Allergic reactions Urinary tract infection
Emergency contraception—if your primary method of birth control fails. It should not be used as a regular birth control method.			
Emergency contraception ("morning-after pill")	Over the counter for adults. Girls younger than 18 need a prescription.	15 It must be used within 72 hours of unprotected sex.	Upset stomach Vomiting Stomach pain Fatigue Headache

*Failure rates depend on whether a birth control method is used correctly and consistently. Your chances of getting pregnant are lowest if birth control always is used correctly and every time you have sex.

**Only condoms can protect against most sexually transmitted infections (STIs). The male latex condom offers the best protection against STIs if used correctly and all the time.

See your doctor regularly, even if you're feeling fine

Talk to your doctor about how often you need to schedule a general checkup and specific screenings or tests. This will depend on your age, risk factors, symptoms, and other issues. Here are guidelines for some of the exams, screenings, and vaccines you might need.

- **Human papillomavirus (HPV) vaccine**—It is recommended that girls 11 and 12 years of age get the HPV vaccine. Also, girls and women 13 through 26 years of age should get the vaccine if they did not get it when they were younger.

For more information on the HPV vaccine, see page 134 of the *Sexually Transmitted Infections* chapter.

- **Mammogram**—Women age 40 and older should have screening mammograms every 1 to 2 years.

- **Pap test and pelvic exam**—Women should have a Pap test at least once every 3 years, beginning about 3 years after they begin to have sexual intercourse, but no later than age 21. Women who have had the HPV vaccine still need to have Pap tests.

- **Sexually transmitted infection (STI) screening**—New partners should get tested for common STIs, including HIV, before becoming sexually active.

For information on testing, see pages 122–128 of the *Sexually Transmitted Infections* chapter.

By taking steps to prevent problems and seeing your doctor for regular checkups, you can feel good knowing you're doing all you can to take care of your reproductive health at all stages of life. ■

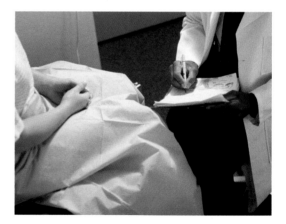

One Woman's Story

I have long suffered from cramps, excessive bleeding, feeling bloated, and frequent urination. I thought that it was normal and did not complain to my parents. During my first trip to the OB-GYN, I learned that I had a uterine fibroid the size of a small gumball. My doctor suggested we monitor its growth but not take action. Consequently, each month I continued to deal with the same problems.

During the birth of my daughter, a nurse suggested that I have the fibroid removed after I was back on my feet. I did have to use the bathroom even more frequently while pregnant, but I didn't blame it on the fibroid. With all of the excitement of having a new baby in the house, I forgot about addressing my problem. Also, my OB-GYN recommended we leave it alone because it would shrink as I aged.

A move led to a new doctor who told me that the fibroid was about the size of an egg, but that we would continue to monitor the size. I was concerned that it had grown so significantly. The problems that I experienced continued to get worse over time, and it became increasingly more difficult to get my job done because of frequent trips to the ladies' room. I was embarrassed to fly on an airplane because I did not want to disturb the people who sat in my row on the plane. Each month I had to take a couple of days off from work because of severe pain. I was very physically active, but I did not see any reduction in the size of my abdominal area.

> **Each month I had to take a couple of days off from work because of severe pain.**

Finally, I decided to seek advice from an OB-GYN surgeon, who explained my options. We discussed laser technology to shrink the fibroid and a hysterectomy, although I was not prepared to experience menopause. After much consideration and discussions with my spouse, I determined that the best option for me was a myomectomy—surgical removal of the fibroid. My hope was to minimize the changes to my body.

The surgery was successful, and I learned that there were actually three fibroids connected to one another. Afterward, I no longer experienced excessive bleeding, cramps, bloating, or frequent urination. I recommend that every woman with these symptoms schedule regular checkups and talk about her options with her doctor. You may not have to suffer!

Cordelia
Chicago, Illinois

For More Information...

Office on Women's Health, HHS
200 Independence Ave SW, Room 712E
Washington, DC 20201
Web site: www.womenshealth.gov/faq/
menstru.htm
www.womenshealth.gov/faq/ovarian_
cysts.htm
Phone number: (800) 994-9662,
(888) 220-5446 TDD

Center for the Evaluation of Risks to Human Reproduction, NIH
PO Box 12233
Research Triangle Park, NC 27709
Web site: http://cerhr.niehs.nih.gov
Phone number: (919) 541-3455

Division of Reproductive Health, CDC
4770 Buford Hwy NE, MS K-20
Atlanta, GA 30341-3717
Web site: www.cdc.gov/reproductivehealth

***Eunice Kennedy Shriver* National Institute of Child Health and Human Development, NIH**
PO Box 3006
Rockville, MD 20847
Web site: www.nichd.nih.gov
Phone number: (800) 370-2943,
(888) 320-6942 TTY

Office of Women's Health, FDA
5600 Fishers Ln
Rockville, MD 20857
Web site: www.fda.gov/womens
Phone number: (888) 463-6332

American College of Obstetricians and Gynecologists
409 12th St SW, PO Box 96920
Washington, DC 20090-6920
Web site: www.acog.org
Phone number: (202) 863-2518 Resource Center

American Society for Reproductive Medicine
1209 Montgomery Hwy
Birmingham, AL 35216-2809
Web site: www.asrm.org

Association of Reproductive Health Professionals
2401 Pennsylvania Ave NW, Suite 350
Washington, DC 20037
Web site: www.arhp.org
Phone number: (202) 466-3825

Endometriosis Association
8585 N 76th Place
Milwaukee, WI 53223
Web site: www.endometriosisassn.org

Planned Parenthood Federation of America
434 W 33rd St
New York, NY 10001
Web site: www.plannedparenthood.org
Phone number: (800) 230-7526

Polycystic Ovarian Syndrome Association
PO Box 3403
Englewood, CO 80111
Web site: www.pcosupport.org

Pregnancy

If you are pregnant or even just thinking about it, now is the time to begin caring for your unborn baby. Doing so involves caring for your own health both before and during pregnancy. It also involves learning about important pregnancy topics and milestones. Taking these steps will help you to have a safe pregnancy and healthy baby. Also, knowing what to expect will help to ease any worries you might have so you can enjoy this exciting time.

Your health before pregnancy

The chances of having a safe pregnancy and healthy baby are best when pregnancy is planned. This way, you can take action early on to prevent health problems that might affect you or your baby later. If you are sexually active, talk to your doctor about your preconception health. Be sure to discuss your partner's health, too. Ask your doctor about:

- Family planning and birth control.
- Taking folic acid.
- Vaccines you may need.
- Managing health problems such as diabetes, high blood pressure, thyroid disease, obesity, depression, eating disorders, and asthma. Find out how

pregnancy may affect, or be affected by, health problems you have.

- Tests for hepatitis, HIV, and other sexually transmitted infections (STIs).
- Medicines you use, including over-the-counter, herbal, and prescription drugs and supplements.

Preconception Health

This is a woman's health before she becomes pregnant. It means knowing how health problems and risk factors could affect a woman or her baby if she becomes pregnant.

Unplanned Pregnancy

If you have an unplanned pregnancy, start taking care of yourself right away. You will feel good knowing that you are doing all you can to care for your unborn baby.

- Ways to improve your overall health, such as reaching a healthy weight, making healthy food choices, being physically active, caring for your teeth and gums, quitting smoking, and avoiding alcohol.

- How to avoid illness. Some infections, like cytomegalovirus (SEYE-toh-MEG-uh-loh-VEYE-ruhss), can cause birth defects.

- Health problems that run in your family, such as phenylketonuria (fee-nuhl-kee-toh-NUR-ee-uh) (PKU) or sickle cell anemia (uh-NEE-mee-uh). (See page 408 of the Appendix for more information about genetic testing and working with a genetic counselor.)

- Problems you have had with prior pregnancies.

Becoming pregnant

You are most likely to become pregnant if you have sex just before or just after ovulation. Most women ovulate between day 11 and day 21 of their menstrual cycle. Count day one as the first day of your last normal period. Most couples who are trying are able to conceive within 1 year. If you think you might be pregnant, you can take a home pregnancy test 1 to 2 weeks after a missed period. Your doctor can confirm pregnancy with a blood test and pelvic exam.

For at least 3 months *before* and *throughout* your pregnancy:

- **Get 400 micrograms of folic acid daily** to lower the risk of certain birth defects, including spina bifida. Folic acid pills are best. You can also take a multivitamin that contains at least 400 micrograms of folic acid or eat foods with folic acid.

- **Stop alcohol, tobacco, and drug use,** which can harm your baby. Only use medicines your doctor says are okay.

- **Eat healthy foods** like fruits, vegetables, whole grains, calcium-rich foods, and lean meats.

- **Drink extra fluids, especially water.**

- **Try to control stress and keep active.** Set limits and get plenty of sleep. Talk with your doctor about safe ways for you to stay fit during pregnancy.

- **Avoid exposure to unsafe substances,** including lead, mercury, arsenic, cadmium, pesticides, solvents, some household chemicals, and cat and rodent feces. Exposure to some toxins and substances that carry infection can harm your unborn baby or increase the risk of miscarriage, preterm birth, and other pregnancy problems. To be safe, check product labels for warnings and ask your doctor how you can protect yourself from unsafe substances found in your workplace or home.

For more information on your reproductive system, see the *Reproductive
Health* chapter on page 153.

Infertility

Some women want children but either
can't conceive or keep miscarrying. This
is called infertility. Both women and
men can have fertility problems. Many
things can affect fertility, including stress,
smoking, STIs, and other health problems. Also, the older a woman becomes,
the harder it is for her to get pregnant.
Talk to your doctor if you have not been
able to conceive after 1 year of trying, or
after 6 months if you are 35 or older.

Happily, doctors are able to help many
infertile couples go on to have babies.
Treatment can include:

- lifestyle changes, such as reducing
  stress

- medicine, such as those to help women
  ovulate

- surgery to repair reproductive organs

- assisted reproductive technology, such
  as in vitro fertilization

Infertility can be stressful, tiring, and expensive. Many couples find that support
groups or counseling can help them to
cope.

Prenatal care

Medical checkups help keep you and
your baby healthy during pregnancy. At
your first visit your doctor will perform
a full physical exam, take your blood for
lab work, and calculate your due date.

Typically, routine checkups occur:

- once each month for weeks 4 through
  28

- twice a month for weeks 25 through 36

- weekly for weeks 36 to birth

At each visit, your doctor will check your
blood pressure and weight. Once you
begin to show, your doctor will measure your abdomen to check your baby's
growth.

You also will have some routine tests.
Some tests are suggested for all women,
such as blood work to check for anemia,
your blood type, HIV, and other factors.
Most women have a glucose challenge
screening at 26 to 28 weeks or earlier
to check risk of gestational (jess-TAY-
shuhn-uhl) diabetes. (See page 180 for
more information.) Before delivery, your

Ectopic (ek-TOP-ihk) Pregnancy

This happens when a fertilized egg
implants outside the uterus, usually
in the fallopian tube. It is a medical
emergency. Get medical care right
away if you have these signs:

- abdominal pain

- shoulder pain

- vaginal bleeding

- feeling dizzy or faint

With ectopic pregnancy, the egg cannot develop. Drugs or surgery are used
to remove the ectopic tissue so that
your organs are not damaged. Many
women who have had ectopic pregnancies go on to have healthy pregnancies later.

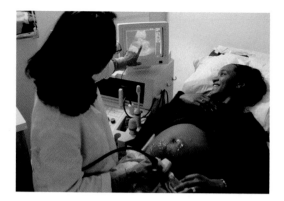

- your age
- your personal or family health history
- your ethnic background
- the results of routine tests you have had

Some tests are screening tests. These detect risks for or signs of *possible* health problems in you or your baby. One common example is an ultrasound. This tool allows your doctor to view your baby's organ and body systems through the use of sound waves. Based on screening test results, your doctor might suggest diagnostic tests. Diagnostic tests confirm or rule out health problems in you or your baby. Genetic disorders and certain birth

doctor also will test you for group B strep, harmful bacteria that your doctor can treat to prevent passing them to your baby during labor.

Other tests might be offered based on:

Stages of Pregnancy

Pregnancy lasts about 40 weeks, counting from the first day of your last normal period. The weeks are grouped into three "trimesters" (TREYE-mess-turs).*

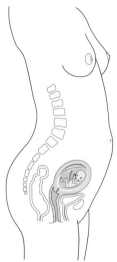

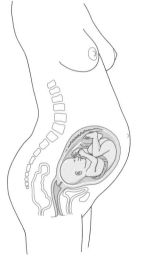

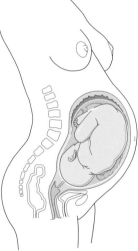

First trimester (week 1–week 12)—All the major organs are formed. The eyes and ears are in position. If you push on your abdomen, your baby moves. At week 12 your baby is about 3 inches long and weighs less than an ounce.

Second trimester (week 13–week 28)—Essential organs begin to function. Fingers, toes, eyelashes, and eyebrows develop. Your baby can suck his or her thumb. At week 24, your baby is about 1½ pounds and 12 inches long.

Third trimester (week 29–week 40)—Kicks become more frequent. Your baby gains about half a pound per week. You might notice the baby "dropping," or moving lower in your abdomen.

*According to the American College of Obstetricians and Gynecologists.

defects are examples of health problems that might be confirmed or ruled out with diagnostic tests while you are pregnant. An amniocentesis (AM-nee-oh-sen-TEE-suhss) is an example of a diagnostic test.

Talk to your doctor if you don't understand or are concerned about any tests suggested for you. Your doctor also can explain what your test results mean and possible next steps if a problem is found. Keep in mind that women who get early and regular prenatal care have healthier pregnancies and babies.

High-risk pregnancies

Pregnancies with greater chance of complications are called "high-risk." But this doesn't mean there will be problems. The following factors may increase the risk of problems during pregnancy:

- being very young or older than 35
- overweight or underweight
- problems in previous pregnancy
- health conditions (high blood pressure, diabetes, or HIV)
- being pregnant with twins or other multiples

Health problems also may develop during a pregnancy, which make it high-risk. Women with high-risk pregnancies need prenatal care more often and sometimes from a specially trained doctor.

Eating for two

Eat a variety of healthy foods and drink plenty of water during pregnancy. Pregnant women need more protein, iron, calcium, folic acid, and fluids than at other times. Ask your doctor about:

- How much weight you need to gain and your calorie needs. This will depend on your pre-pregnancy weight.
- Taking prenatal vitamins.
- Whether drinking caffeine is okay for you. Small amounts of caffeine (about one 12-ounce cup of coffee) appear to be safe during pregnancy. But the effects of too much caffeine are unclear.

Also, talk with your doctor about special diet needs:

- **Diabetes**—Review your meal plan and insulin needs with your doctor. High blood glucose can be harmful to your baby. (See page 69 of the *Diabetes* chapter for information on diabetes.)
- **Lactose intolerance**—Find out about low-lactose or reduced-lactose products and calcium supplements.
- **Vegetarian**—Ensure that you are eating enough protein, iron, vitamin B^{12}, and vitamin D.
- **PKU**—Keep good control of phenylalanine levels in your diet.

You can learn more about what kinds and how much food you should eat while pregnant at the MyPyramid for Pregnancy and Breastfeeding Web site listed in the resource section on page 185.

Keep You and Your Baby Safe From Food-Borne Illness

Health concern	How to lower risk
Listeria (lih-STEER-ee-uh) This harmful bacteria found in some refrigerated and ready-to-eat foods can cause early delivery or miscarriage.	Do not eat: • Hot dogs or deli meats unless steaming hot • Refrigerated meat spreads • Unpasteurized milk • Store-made salads, such as chicken, egg, or tuna salad • Unpasteurized soft cheeses, such as unpasteurized feta, Brie, queso blanco, queso fresco, and blue cheeses
Toxoplasmosis (TOK-soh-plaz-MOH-suhss) Caused by a parasite, this infection can be passed to your unborn baby and cause hearing loss, blindness, or mental retardation.	• Wash hands with soap after touching soil or raw meat. • Cook meat completely. • Wash cooking utensils with hot soapy water. • Wash produce before eating. • Don't clean cats' litter boxes.
Mercury Too much of this metal found in some fish can harm your baby's nervous system.	• Do not eat shark, swordfish, king mackerel, or tilefish. • Eat only 6 ounces per week of white (albacore) tuna.

Being active

For most pregnant women, physical activity is safe. However, first check with your doctor and avoid:

- being hit in the abdomen—NO kickboxing, soccer, or basketball
- falling—NO horseback riding, downhill skiing, or other sports that risk falling or require good balance
- scuba diving

Is it safe to wear a seatbelt while pregnant?

Yes—you should always wear a seatbelt. The lap strap should go under your belly, across your hips. The shoulder strap should go between your breasts and to the side of your belly. Make sure it fits snugly.

Having sex

Unless your doctor tells you otherwise, sex is safe. Call your doctor if sex causes pain, vaginal bleeding, or fluid leakage. You may find that your interest in sex changes during pregnancy. Talk to your partner about other positions if the way you usually have sex is awkward or no longer feels good.

Understanding body changes

Body changes differ for each woman and may differ for each pregnancy. Many physical and emotional changes are normal. Still, tell your doctor about any changes you have—they may signal problems.

Body Changes During Pregnancy

Change		What might help
Body aches	• Back, abdomen, groin, and thigh pain	• Lie down. • Rest. • Apply heat.
Breast changes	• Heavy and tender breasts • Leaking breast "pre-milk"	• Wear a maternity bra with good support. • Put pads in bra to absorb leakage.
Constipation	• Hard, dry stool • Fewer than 3 bowel movements per week • Painful bowel movements	• Drink 8 to 10 glasses of water daily. • Don't drink caffeine. • Eat fiber-rich foods. • Try mild physical activity.
Digestive problems	• Nausea and vomiting, called "morning sickness," but often occurring at other times of day • Bloating • Indigestion • Heartburn	• Eat 6 to 8 small meals—eat slowly. • Don't eat greasy or fried foods. • Eat dry toast, saltines, or dry cereals. • Drink club soda between, but not with, meals. • Take small sips of milk or eat ice chips. *Call your doctor if you have flu-like symptoms, which may signal a more serious condition.*
Dizziness	• Feeling faint or dizzy	• Stand up slowly. • Avoid standing for too long. • Don't skip meals. • Lie on your left side. • Wear loose clothing. *Call your doctor if you feel faint and have vaginal bleeding or abdominal pain.*
Fatigue, sleep problems	• Tiredness, fatigue • Restless sleep • Trouble falling or staying asleep	• Lie on your left side. • Use pillows for support, such as behind your back, tucked between your knees, and under your tummy. • Practice good sleep habits. (See pages 27–28 for more information.) • Go to bed a little earlier. • Nap if you are not able to get enough sleep at night. • Drink needed fluids earlier in the day, so you can drink less in the hours before bed.

Body Changes During Pregnancy

Change		What might help
Hemorrhoids (HEM-roids)	• Itchiness around anus • Swelling of veins around anus	• Drink lots of fluids. • Eat fiber-rich foods. • Try not to strain with bowel movements.
Itching	• Itchiness in abdomen, palms, and soles	• Use gentle soaps and moisturizing creams. If symptoms don't improve after a week, talk to your doctor. • Avoid hot showers and baths. • Avoid itchy fabrics.
Leg cramps	• Sudden spasms in legs or feet	• Gently stretch muscles. • Try mild physical activity. • For sudden cramps, flex your foot forward. • Ask your doctor about calcium supplements.
Nasal problems	• Nosebleeds • Stuffiness	• Blow your nose gently. • Drink fluids and use a cool mist humidifier. *Call your doctor if bleeds are frequent and do not stop in a few minutes.*
Numb or tingling hands	• Feeling of swelling, tingling, and numbness in fingers and hands, called carpal tunnel syndrome	• Take frequent breaks to rest hands. • Ask your doctor about fitting you for a splint to keep wrists straight.
Stretch marks, skin changes	• Pink, red, or brown streaks on thighs, buttocks, abdomen, and breasts • Darker colored nipples • Line on skin running from belly button to pubic hairline • Patches of darker skin, usually over the cheeks, forehead, nose, or upper lip. Patches often match on both sides of face.	• Be patient—stretch marks and other changes usually fade after delivery.
Swelling (edema)	• Puffiness in face, hands, or ankles	• Drink 8 to 10 glasses of fluids daily. • Don't drink caffeine or eat salty foods. • Rest and elevate your feet. • Ask your doctor about support hose. *Call your doctor if your hands or feet swell suddenly or you rapidly gain weight—it may be preeclampsia. (See page 179 for more information on preeclampsia.)*

Body Changes During Pregnancy

Change		What might help
Urinary frequency and leaking	• More frequent need to urinate • Leaking of urine when sneezing, coughing, or laughing	• Take frequent bathroom breaks. • Drink plenty of fluids to avoid dehydration. • Do Kegel exercises to tone pelvic muscles. (See page 256 of the *Urologic and Kidney Health* chapter for information on how to do Kegel exercises.) *Call your doctor if you experience burning along with frequency of urination—it may be an infection.*
Varicose veins	• Twisted or bulging veins raised above the skin's surface, usually on the legs	• Avoid tight knee-highs. • Sit with your legs and feet raised.

Mothers of Multiples

Moms of twins and other multiples have more severe body changes:

• rapid weight gain in first trimester

• intense nausea and vomiting

• extreme breast tenderness

There also is a greater risk of early delivery, low birth weight, and pre-eclampsia. More frequent prenatal visits help to monitor the health of mother and babies.

Complications of pregnancy

Complications of pregnancy are health problems that occur during pregnancy. They can involve the mother's health, the baby's health, or both. Whether a complication is common or rare, there are ways to manage problems that come up during pregnancy. Talk to your doctor if you have symptoms described in the following chart or if you're not feeling like yourself. Seek medical attention if you suspect the baby is moving less or you have:

• severe headaches or abdominal cramps

• bleeding or fluid leaking from your vagina

• severe and sudden swelling

• nausea or vomiting that doesn't ease

• blurred vision or dizziness

• fever

Pregnancy Complications

Problem	Symptoms	Treatments
Anemia Lower than normal number of healthy red blood cells	• Feel tired or weak • Look pale • Feel faint • Shortness of breath	• Take iron and folic acid supplements. • Monitor iron levels.
Depression Extreme sadness during pregnancy or after birth (postpartum) (See page 215 for more information.)	• Intense sadness • Helplessness and irritability • Appetite changes • Thoughts of harming self or baby *Tell your doctor about any symptoms of depression. Seek medical attention right away if you have thoughts of harming yourself or your baby.*	• Therapy • Support groups • Medication
Fetal problems Unborn baby has health issue, such as poor growth or heart problems.	• Baby moving less • Baby is smaller than normal for gestational age • Fewer than 10 kicks per day after 26 weeks • Some problems have no symptoms, but are found with prenatal tests	• Monitor baby's health more closely until delivered. • Special care until the baby is delivered. • Early delivery may be required.
Gestational diabetes Too high blood sugar levels during pregnancy (See page 180 for more information.)	• Usually, there are no symptoms. Sometimes, extreme thirst, hunger, or fatigue • Tests show high blood sugar levels	Control blood sugar levels through: • Healthy meal plan from your doctor • Medication (if needed)
Hepatitis B Viral infection that can be passed to baby	There may be no symptoms. Symptoms can include: • Nausea, vomiting, and diarrhea • Dark urine and pale bowel movements • Whites of eyes or skin look yellow	Lab tests can find out if a mother is a carrier of hepatitis B. • First dose of hepatitis B vaccine plus HBIG shot given to baby at birth • Second dose of hepatitis B vaccine given to baby at 1–2 months old • Third dose of hepatitis B vaccine given to baby at 6 months old (but not before)
High blood pressure (pregnancy related) High blood pressure that starts after 20 weeks of pregnancy and goes away after birth	• High blood pressure without other signs and symptoms of preeclampsia	• Closely monitor health of mother and baby to make sure high blood pressure is not preeclampsia. (See below to learn more about preeclampsia.)

Pregnancy Complications

Problem	Symptoms	Treatments
Hyperemesis gravidarum (HEYE-pur-EM-ih-suhss grav-uh-DAR-uhm) Severe, persistent nausea and vomiting during pregnancy—more extreme than "morning sickness"	• Nausea that does not go away • Vomiting several times every day • Weight loss • Reduced appetite • Dehydration • Feeling faint or fainting	• Dry foods and fluids if can keep down • Sometimes, medication to ease nausea • In extreme cases, hospitalization for IV fluids and medicines
Miscarriage Pregnancy loss from natural causes before 20 weeks. As many as 20 percent of pregnancies end in miscarriage. Often, miscarriage occurs before a woman even knows she is pregnant.	Signs of a miscarriage can include: • Vaginal spotting or bleeding* • Cramping or abdominal pain • Fluid or tissue passing from the vagina *Spotting early in pregnancy doesn't mean miscarriage is certain. Still, contact your doctor right away if you have any bleeding.*	• In most cases, miscarriage cannot be prevented. • Sometimes, treatment is needed to remove any remaining pregnancy tissue in the uterus. • Counseling can help with emotional healing.
Parvovirus B19 (fifth disease) Viral infection that can harm baby	• Low-grade fever • Tiredness • Rash on face, trunk, and limbs • Painful and swollen joints	• Rest • Special care, as needed
Placental abruption Placenta separated from uterine wall	• Vaginal bleeding • Cramping, abdominal pain, and uterine tenderness	• Bed rest • Special care
Placenta previa Placenta covers part or entire opening of cervix inside of the uterus	• Painless vaginal bleeding during second or third trimester • For some, no symptoms	• Bed rest • May require hospital care and c-section
Preeclampsia (pree-ee-CLAMP-see-uh) A condition starting after 20 weeks of pregnancy that causes high blood pressure and problems with the kidneys and other organs. Also called toxemia.	• High blood pressure • Swelling of hands and face • Too much protein in urine • Stomach pain • Blurred vision • Dizziness • Headaches	• Deliver baby if near term. • If too early to deliver baby, medications and bed rest to lower blood pressure; sometimes must stay in hospital until safe to deliver baby. • Monitor health of mother and unborn baby. • Medicine to prevent mother from having seizures.
Preterm labor Going into labor before 37 weeks of pregnancy.	• Increased vaginal discharge • Pelvic pressure and cramping • Back pain radiating to the abdomen • Contractions	• Stopping labor with medicine • Bed rest • Early delivery (Giving birth before 37 weeks is called "preterm birth.")

Pregnancy Complications

Problem	Symptoms	Treatments
Urinary tract infection (UTI) Bacterial infection in urinary tract	• Pain or burning when urinating • Frequent urination • Pelvis, back, stomach, or side pain • Shaking, chills, fever, sweats	• Antibiotics
Uterine fibroids Noncancerous tumors that grow within the wall of the uterus	Some women have no symptoms. But uterine fibroids can cause: • Pain • Bleeding • Feeling "full" in lower abdomen	• Rest. • Monitor for miscarriage and premature or breech birth. • C-section delivery, if blocking birth canal.

Gestational Diabetes

If you have gestational diabetes, pregnancy is causing your blood sugar level to be too high. With your doctor's help, you can keep your blood sugar well controlled. Poorly controlled diabetes can increase the risk of:

• preeclampsia

• early delivery

• c-section

• having a big baby, which can complicate delivery

• baby born with low blood sugar, breathing problems, and jaundice

Gestational diabetes usually goes away after delivery. But you are at higher risk of developing type 2 diabetes later in life. A healthy lifestyle can lower this risk. If you want to get pregnant again, have a blood sugar test up to 3 months before becoming pregnant to make sure your blood sugar levels are normal. High blood sugar early in pregnancy increases the risk of birth defects.

Getting ready for your newborn

Becoming a parent is both a joy and a responsibility. Look for a baby book that tells how to prepare and care for a newborn. Your doctor's office might also have free patient booklets with this information. Also, take these steps to prepare:

• Make sure smoke and carbon monoxide detectors are working.

• Take childbirth, parenting, and CPR classes.

• Select a doctor for your baby.

• Buy a car seat and crib with mattress.

• Childproof your home.

In the United States, the preterm birth rate has been on the rise since 1990. About 1 in 8 babies is born early. Researchers are trying to find out why and how to prevent preterm birth.

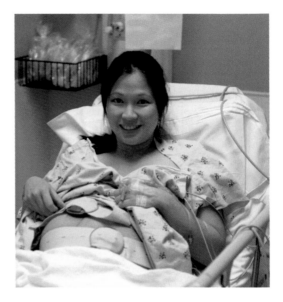

Preparing for delivery

Labor and delivery will be less stressful if you plan ahead. To get ready:

- Decide where you will deliver. Most women deliver in a hospital or birthing center. Contact your health plan to learn your options. Visit the facility beforehand—note directions, parking, and where to check in.

- Find out how to reach the doctor when you are in labor.

- Ask your doctor about what to expect during labor. If you are worried about pain, ask about ways to manage pain during labor. Some women do fine with natural childbirth. Others are helped by epidural or pain medicines.

- Discuss how to care for your newborn, including deciding about breastfeeding or bottle-feeding, and circumcision if you have a boy. (See page 187 for more information.)

- Pack a bag with your health insurance card, bras and nursing pads, nursing pillows, sleeping clothes, toiletries, and going-home outfits for you and your baby.

Signs of labor

Call your doctor right away if you have any of these signs of labor:

- contractions becoming stronger at regular and increasingly shorter intervals

- lower back pain and constant cramping

- water breaking

- bloody mucus discharge

Labor occurs in three stages. How labor progresses and how long it lasts are different for every woman. The first stage begins with the onset of labor and ends when the cervix is fully opened (dilated).

Many women spend the early part of labor at home. Your doctor will tell you when to go to the hospital or birthing center. The second stage involves pushing and delivery of your baby. Pushing is hard work, and a support person can really help keep you focused. The third stage involves delivery of the placenta (afterbirth). Once the placenta is delivered, you can rest and enjoy your newborn.

Types of deliveries

The baby's position and your and your baby's health will determine how you will deliver your baby. You and your doctor will discuss the best options for you. Some terms used during labor and delivery include:

- **Vaginal birth**—as the head appears, the doctor guides the baby through the birth canal. Your doctor may make a small cut, called episiotomy (uh-peez-ee-OT-oh-mee), near the canal.

- **Cesarean section** (c-section)—surgery to deliver the baby. The doctor removes the baby by making a cut in the abdomen and uterus. The surgery is relatively safe for mother and baby. Still, it is major surgery and carries risks. It also takes longer to recover from a c-section than from vaginal birth.

- **Induced labor**—medicines, or other methods, are used to jump-start the birth process.

- **Assisted birth**—your doctor uses forceps or suction to deliver the baby.

- **Breech presentation**—the baby's feet or buttocks are in position to deliver first. The doctor may try to turn the baby or suggest a c-section.

Did my water break?

It's not always easy to know. If your water breaks, it could be a gush or a slow trickle of amniotic (AM-nee-OT-ihk) fluid. Let your doctor know the time your water breaks and any color or odor. Also, call your doctor if you think your water broke, but are not sure. Often a woman will go into labor soon after her water breaks. When this doesn't happen, her doctor may want to induce (bring about) labor. This is because once your water breaks, your risk of getting an infection goes up as labor is delayed.

Your newborn

Most newborns weigh between 5 pounds 8 ounces and 9 pounds 2 ounces. Doctors will examine your baby right away, checking temperature, weight, length, and head size. Your baby will have several other health tests before leaving the hospital.

Before you go home, ask your baby's doctor how to spot problems with your baby's health. Also, pick up your doctor's records or discharge summary, as well as your baby's health records to give to your baby's doctor. Schedule your baby's first doctor's visit. During this visit, discuss vaccines.

Recovering from birth

It takes time for your body to go back to the way it was before pregnancy. During your recovery, you may have:

- Vaginal discharge called lochia (LOH-kee-uh). It is the tissue and blood that lined your uterus during pregnancy. It is heavy and bright red at first, becom-

The Healthy Woman: A Complete Guide for All Ages

ing lighter in flow and color until it goes away after a few weeks.

- Cramping and constipation.
- Swelling in legs and feet.
- Tender breasts that may leak milk.

Your doctor will check your recovery at your postpartum visit, about 6 weeks after birth. Ask about resuming normal activities, as well as eating and fitness plans

At Home: When to Call the Doctor

Once home, look out for signs of problems that might need a doctor's care. Call your doctor if you have:

- unexplained fever
- more vaginal bleeding or you soak more than one pad an hour
- more redness and swelling or pus from a c-section or episiotomy
- new pain or swelling in legs
- hot-to-the-touch, very red, and sore breasts or nipples that are cracked and bleeding
- vaginal discharge that smells bad
- pain with urinating or sudden urge to urinate
- more pain in the vaginal area
- flu-like symptoms, chest pain, or vomiting
- feelings of depression
- thoughts of harming yourself or your baby

to return to a healthy weight. Also ask your doctor about having sex and birth control. Your period could return in 6 to 8 weeks, or sooner if you do not breastfeed. If you breastfeed, your period might not resume for many months. Still, using reliable birth control is the best way to prevent pregnancy until you want to have another baby.

Many women also feel sadness called "baby blues" after having a baby. These feelings usually go away quickly. But if sadness lasts more than 2 weeks, go see your doctor. Don't wait until your postpartum visit to do so.

Keep in mind that adjusting to a new baby takes time, and your daily routines will change. Talk to your partner about sharing household and family duties. Ask for and accept help from family and friends. Caring for yourself—both physically and emotionally—will help you more fully enjoy your new baby and the rewards of motherhood. ■

One Woman's Story

At the start of my last trimester, my glucose screening test indicated that I might have gestational diabetes. Shortly thereafter, a glucose tolerance test showed definitively that I had it. I wasn't too surprised, as my mother had gestational diabetes during all four of her pregnancies. Nevertheless, I felt comforted by my nurse-midwife's explanation that my gestational diabetes could be controlled and it did not mean that I currently had type 2 diabetes. But I am at risk for type 2 diabetes in the future, so eating right and keeping fit will be especially important as I get older.

Soon, I made plans to meet with a dietitian at a local medical center who explained the personal eating plan to which I should adhere in order to control the gestational diabetes without medication. If the eating plan alone didn't work, I would have medication prescribed to me. I was given a monitor to test my blood sugar level.

After the first week, my blood sugar level was not being maintained as needed with the eating plan alone, so I was prescribed a dosage of insulin that would keep my blood sugar at a safe level while not harming the baby. Even with the insulin, I needed to follow the same personal eating plan and see my nurse-midwife weekly to monitor my health. Together, these steps meant a healthy pregnancy after all. I was able to maintain a healthy weight gain. And my son was born after a relatively easy labor and delivery at just under 8 pounds—a nice, healthy weight.

At times it was challenging to stick to my eating plan—especially when I wanted to down a whole quart of ice cream—but I am extremely pleased with how everything turned out! I even learned a lot about disciplining myself to eat healthier!

...my mother had gestational diabetes during all four of her pregnancies.

Ji

Gaithersburg, Maryland

For More Information...

Office on Women's Health, HHS
200 Independence Ave SW, Room 712E
Washington, DC 20201
Web site: www.womenshealth.gov/
pregnancy
Phone number: (800) 994-9662,
(888) 220-5446 TDD

U.S. Department of Agriculture
3101 Park Center Dr, Room 1034
Alexandria, VA 22302-1594
Web site: www.mypyramid.gov/
mypyramidmoms
Phone number: (888) 779-7264

**National Center on Birth Defects and
Developmental Disabilities, CDC**
1600 Clifton Rd
Atlanta, GA 30333
Web site: www.cdc.gov/ncbddd
Phone number: (800) 232-4636,
(888) 232-6348 TTY

***Eunice Kennedy Shriver* National
Institute of Child Health and Human
Development, NIH**
PO Box 3006
Rockville, MD 20847
Web site: www.nichd.nih.gov
Phone number: (800) 370-2943,
(888) 320-6942 TTY

Office of Women's Health, FDA
5600 Fishers Ln
Rockville, MD 20857
Web site: www.fda.gov/womens
Phone number: (888) 463-6332

American College of Nurse Midwives
8403 Colesville Rd, Suite 1550
Silver Spring, MD 20910
Web site: www.mymidwife.org

**American College of Obstetricians and
Gynecologists**
409 12th St SW, PO Box 96920
Washington, DC 20090-6920
Web site: www.acog.org
Phone number: (202) 863-2518 Resource
Center

American Pregnancy Association
1425 Greenway Dr, Suite 440
Irving, TX 75038
Web site: www.americanpregnancy.org
Phone number: (800) 672-2296

**American Society for Reproductive
Medicine**
1209 Montgomery Highway
Birmingham, AL 35216-2809
Web site: www.asrm.org

Lamaze International
2025 M St NW, Suite 800
Washington, DC 20036-3309
Web site: www.lamaze.org
Phone number: (800) 368-4404

March of Dimes
1275 Mamaroneck Ave
White Plains, NY 10605
Web site: www.marchofdimes.com

Postpartum Support International
Web site: www.postpartum.net
Phone number: (800) 944-4773

**RESOLVE: The National Infertility
Association**
8405 Greensboro Dr, Suite 800
McLean, VA 22102-5120
Web site: www.resolve.org

Breastfeeding

As a mother, one of the best things that only you can do for your baby is to breastfeed. Breastfeeding is more than a lifestyle choice—it is an important health choice, and any amount of time that you can do it will help both you and your baby. Enjoy the special bond with your baby as he or she stares into your eyes and warmly nuzzles against your skin while breastfeeding—it's an amazing feeling!

Breastfeeding is best

It is best to give your baby only breast milk for the first 6 months of life. This means not giving your baby any other food or drink—not even water—during this time. Drops of liquid vitamins, minerals, and medicines are, of course, fine, as advised by your baby's doctor. It is even better if you can breastfeed for your baby's first year or longer, for as long as you both wish. Solid iron-rich foods, such as iron-fortified cereals and pureed vegetables and meats, can be started when your baby is around 6 months old. Before that time, a baby's stomach cannot digest them properly. Solids do not replace breastfeeding. Breast milk stays the baby's main source of nutrients during the first year. Beyond one year, breast milk can still be an important part of your child's diet.

Breastfeeding is normal and healthy for infants and moms. Breast milk has disease-fighting cells called antibodies that help protect infants from germs, illness, and even sudden infant death syndrome (SIDS).

Breast milk is different from infant formula

- Colostrum (koh-LOSS-truhm), the thick, yellow first breast milk that you make during pregnancy and just after birth, will give your baby the best start at life. It is known as "liquid gold." It is rich in nutrients and antibodies to protect your baby as he or she first enters the world. Although your baby gets only a small amount of colostrum at each feeding, it matches the amount his or her tiny stomach can hold. A

Breastfeeding Is Linked to a Lower Risk of These Health Problems	
In infants:	**In mothers:**
• Ear infections	• Type 2 diabetes
• Stomach viruses	• Breast cancer
• Respiratory infections	• Ovarian cancer
• Atopic dermatitis (ay-TOP-ihk DUR-muh-TEYE-tuhss)	• Postpartum depression
• Asthma (in young children)	
• Obesity	
• Type 1 and type 2 diabetes	
• Childhood leukemia (loo-KEE-mee-uh)	
• Sudden infant death syndrome (SIDS)	
• Necrotizing enterocolitis (NE-kroh-teye-zeeng en-tur-oh-koh-LEYE-tuhss), a disease that affects the gastrointestinal tract in preterm infants	

Studies are still looking at the effects of breastfeeding on osteoporosis (OSS-tee-oh-puh-ROH-suhss) and weight loss after birth.

newborn stomach is only the size of a large marble at first! Colostrum is exactly what a new baby needs at first.

• Your milk changes over time to meet your baby's needs. Your breast milk that begins to be made by the third to fifth day after birth has just the right amount of fat, sugar, water, and protein that is needed for your baby's growth. It will be a thinner type of milk, but just as full of all of the nutrients and antibodies for your baby.

• Infant formula cannot match the exact chemical makeup of human milk, especially the cells, hormones, and antibodies that fight disease.

• For most babies, breast milk is easier to digest than formula. It takes time for their stomachs to adjust to digesting proteins in formula because they are made from cow's milk.

How the breast makes milk

There are special cells inside your breasts that make milk. These cells are called alveoli (al-VEE-uh-leye). When your breasts become fuller and more tender during pregnancy, this is a sign that the alveoli are getting ready to work. Some women do not feel these changes in their breasts and some women experience breast changes after their baby is born. If you have a question about your breast changes, you can ask your health care provider or a lactation consultant.

The alveoli make milk in response to the hormone prolactin, which rises when the baby suckles. Another hormone, oxytocin (oks-ee-TOH-suhn), causes these small muscles around the cells to contract and move the milk through a series of small tubes called milk ducts. The milk ducts are located underneath the nipple and areola (air-ee-OH-luh), which is the darker skin that circles your nipple.

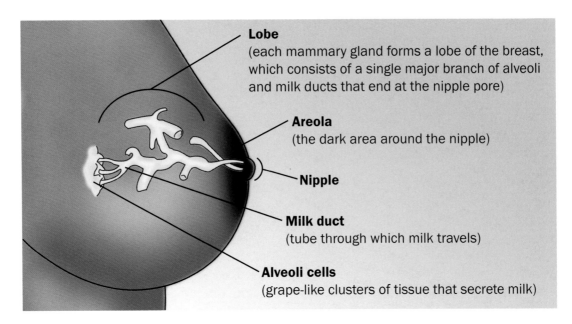

Lobe
(each mammary gland forms a lobe of the breast, which consists of a single major branch of alveoli and milk ducts that end at the nipple pore)

Areola
(the dark area around the nipple)

Nipple

Milk duct
(tube through which milk travels)

Alveoli cells
(grape-like clusters of tissue that secrete milk)

Babies knows how to latch and feed

Did you know that an alert, healthy newborn infant can latch on to the mother's breast with little or no help? Babies are born knowing how to find the breast and suckle all by themselves. All they need is a chance to practice. The more milk your baby removes from the breasts, the more milk you will make. Immediately after birth, ask the hospital to delay unnecessary procedures, if possible, and to allow you and your partner some quiet time to snuggle with your baby during the first hour or two.

Learning to "dance"

Learning to breastfeed is like learning to dance. It is best to wait until you and your baby are calm.

- Hold your baby, wearing only a diaper, skin-to-your-skin up against your bare chest and upright with his or her head under your chin. Your baby will be comfortable in that cozy valley between your breasts. You can ask your partner or a nurse to place a blanket across your baby's back and bring your bedcovers over you both. Your skin temperature will rise to warm your baby.

- Softly talk to your baby and massage him or her with gentle strokes.

- When awake, your baby will move his or her head back and forth, looking

USED WITH PERMISSION BY SONJA, JANNA AND THE INTERNATIONAL LACTATION CONSULTANT ASSOCIATION.

and feeling for the breast with his or her mouth and lips. Your baby might even look up at you and make eye contact. This is an important time for your baby to learn that you are his or her mother, so enjoy this special time by talking or singing softly to your baby.

- Support his or her neck and shoulders with one hand and hips with the other as he or she twists and turns in an effort to find your breast.

As your baby looks for your breast

- Support your baby with your arms so that you both are comfortable.

- Allow your breast to hang naturally and, when your baby feels it with his or her cheek, he or she will open his or her mouth wide and reach it up and over the nipple.

- Your baby's head should be tilted back slightly to make it easy to suck and swallow. With his or her head back and mouth open, the tongue is naturally down and ready for the breast to go on top of it.

- You will see that, at first, your baby's nose is lined up opposite your nipple. As his or her chin presses into your breast, his or her wide, open mouth will get a large mouthful of breast for a deep latch.

- Allow your baby's arms to hug your breast.

- Do not put your hands on your baby's head. As it tilts back, you can support your baby's upper back and shoulders with the palm of your hand and pull your baby in close.

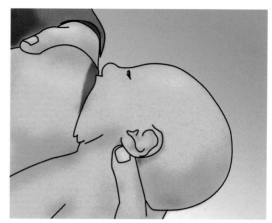

EXAMPLE OF A GOOD LATCH

Signs of a good latch

- How it feels is more important than how it looks. The latch feels comfortable to you, without hurting or pinching.

- Your baby's chest is against your body and he or she does not have to turn his or her head while drinking.

- You see little or no areola, depending on the size of your areola and the size of your baby's mouth. If areola is showing, you will see more above your baby's lip and less below.

- When your baby is positioned well, his or her mouth will be filled with breast.

- The tongue is cupped under the breast, although you might not see it.

- You hear or see your baby swallow. Some babies swallow so quietly, a pause in their breathing may be the only sign of swallowing.

- You see the baby's ears "wiggle" slightly.

- Your baby's lips turn out like fish lips, not in. You may not even be able to see the bottom lip.

- Your baby's chin touches your breast.

Ask for help if you need it!

Once you have started to breastfeed, keep trying! There are many people who can support you in your effort to give your baby the best start. Some may already have been helping you during your pregnancy and birth.

International Board Certified Lactation Consultant (IBCLC) – also called a "lactation consultant," this person is a credentialed health care professional with the highest level of knowledge and skill in breastfeeding support. IBCLCs help mothers to breastfeed comfortably by helping with positioning, latch, and a wide range of breastfeeding concerns. Ask your hospital or birthing center for the name of a lactation consultant who can help you. You also can contact the International Lactation Consultant Association, which has a lactation consultant directory. (See page 205 for contact information).

Breastfeeding Peer Counselor or Educator – a breastfeeding counselor who can teach others about the benefits of breastfeeding and help women with basic breastfeeding challenges and questions. A "peer" means a person has breastfed her own baby and is available to help other mothers. You can find a peer counselor with the Women, Infants and Children (WIC) Program or mother-to-mother support group meetings from the La Leche League resources at the end of this chapter, or call the National Breastfeeding Helpline. Some breastfeeding educators have letters after their names like CLC (Certified Lactation Counselor) or CBE (Certified Breastfeeding Educator). These are not the same as IBCLCs but still can be quite helpful.

Doula (DOO-la) – a woman who is professionally trained and experienced in giving social support to birthing families during pregnancy, labor, and birth and at home during the first few days or weeks after birth. Doulas help women physically and emotionally, and those who are trained in breastfeeding can help you be more successful with breastfeeding after birth.

Pediatrician – a medical doctor who focuses on treating babies, children, and teens.

OB/GYN or obstetrician/gynecologist – a medical doctor who focuses on treating women's reproductive health issues before, during, and after pregnancy.

Certified Nurse-Midwife – a health professional who provides care to women during pregnancy, labor, and birth. Midwives can also provide breastfeeding advice.

Practice makes perfect

- During the early days and weeks during breastfeeding, you and your baby are both learning how to breastfeed. Take your time and be patient. Breastfeed as often and as long as your baby wants. Soon you will both be experts!

- As your baby gets older, you will be able to hold your baby close to you at

Call the National Breastfeeding Helpline at (800) 994-9662 to talk to a trained peer counselor for answers to common questions and problems.

your breast with his or her mouth at your nipple and your baby will latch on easily.

- What works well for one feeding might not work well at the next. Try different positions until you find one that works for both of you.

Problems latching

If your baby is having trouble latching, you can gently stroke your baby's lips with your nipple until he or she opens his or her mouth really wide and keeps it open. Then you can pull your baby close so that the chin and lower jaw moves into your breast first to take a large mouthful of breast.

Get help if you are having trouble. (See page 191 for a list of people who can help you.)

Tips for Making Breastfeeding Work

1. Breastfeed early and often. Breastfeed as soon as possible after birth, within the first hour of life. If you had a vaginal birth you can hold your baby and breastfeed right away. If you had a c-section or general anesthesia after the birth for a surgery, tell your doctor and nurse that you want to breastfeed as soon as you are both in the recovery room.

2. Breastfeed at least 8 to 12 times every 24 hours to make plenty of milk for your baby.

3. Keep your baby in your hospital room with you (also called "rooming in") so you can see your baby's first signs of being hungry. When babies are hungry they become more alert and active, may put their hands or fists to their mouths, make sucking motions with their mouth, or turn their heads looking for the breast. Crying is a late sign of hunger.

4. Make sure you are both comfortable and follow your baby's lead after he or she is latched well onto the underside of the breast, not just the nipple. Some babies take both breasts at each feeding, while others only take one breast at a feeding. Help your baby finish the first breast, as long as he or she is still sucking and swallowing. Your baby will let go of the breast when he or she is finished, and often falls asleep. Offer the other breast if he or she seems to want more. Let your baby decide when to stop nursing.

5. Keep your baby close to you. Remember that your baby is not used to this new world and needs to be held very close to his or her mother. Being skin-to-skin with you helps babies cry less, and stabilizes the baby's heart and breathing rates.

6. Avoid using pacifiers, bottles, and supplements of infant formula in the first few weeks unless there is a medical reason to. It's best just to breastfeed to get the milk process running smoothly and to keep your baby from getting confused while he or she is learning to breastfeed.

Breastfeeding holds

Some moms find that the following positions are also helpful ways to get comfortable and support their babies in finding a good latch. You also can use pillows under your arms, elbows, neck, or back to give you added comfort and support.

1. **Cradle Hold** – an easy, common hold that is comfortable for most mothers and babies. Hold your baby with his or her head on your forearm and his or her whole body facing yours.

2. **Cross Cradle or Transitional Hold** – useful for premature babies or babies with a weak suck because it gives extra head support and may help babies stay latched. Hold your baby along the opposite arm from the breast you are using. Support your baby's head with the palm of your hand at the base of his or her neck.

3. **Clutch or "Football" Hold** – useful for mothers with large breasts, flat or inverted nipples, overactive let-down, or who had a c-section. It is also helpful for babies who prefer to be more upright. This hold allows you to better see and control your baby's head and keeps the baby away from a c-section incision. Hold your baby at your side, lying on his or her back, with his or her head at the level of your nipple. Support baby's head with the palm of your hand at the base of the head.

4. **Side-Lying Position** – useful for mothers who had a c-section or to help any mother get some extra rest or sleep while the baby breastfeeds. This hold allows you to rest or sleep while your baby nurses. Lie on your side with your baby facing you. Pull your baby close so your baby faces your body.

What if...

You have pain? Many moms report that breasts can be tender at first until both they and their baby find comfortable breastfeeding positions and a good latch. Once you have done this, breastfeeding should be comfortable. If it hurts, your baby may be sucking on only the nipple. Gently break your baby's suction to your breast by placing a clean finger in the corner of your baby's mouth and try again. Your nipple also should not look flat or compressed when it comes out of your baby's mouth. It should look round and long, or the same shape as it was before the feeding.

You or your baby are frustrated? Take a short break and hold your baby in an upright position. Consider holding him or her skin-to-your-skin. Talk, sing, or provide your finger for sucking for comfort. Try to breastfeed again in a little while.

Your baby has a weak suck, or makes only tiny suckling movements? Break your baby's suction and try again. He or she may not have a deep enough latch to remove the milk from your breast. Talk with a lactation consultant if your baby's suck feels weak or if you are not sure he or she is getting a good feeding of milk. Your baby might have a health problem that is causing the weak suck.

You have other concerns? Contact a lactation consultant or your doctor for help.

Making plenty of milk

Your breasts will easily make and supply milk directly in response to your baby's needs. The more often and effectively a baby breastfeeds, the more milk will be made. Babies are trying to double their weight in a few short months, and their tummies are small, so they need many feedings to grow and to be healthy.

- You can expect at least 8 to 12 feedings in a 24-hour day

- In the first few days after birth, your baby will likely want to breastfeed about every hour or two in the daytime, and a couple of times at night during which your baby can have one longer sleep stretch.

- Babies develop their own feeding schedules. Some babies feed every hour for 2-6 hours and then sleep for a longer period, and others will breastfeed every 2-3 hours day and night. Follow your baby's cues for when he or she is ready to eat.

How to know baby gets enough milk

Many babies, but not all, lose a small amount of weight in the first days after birth. Your baby's health care provider will check his or her weight at your first visit after you leave the hospital. Make sure to visit your baby's health care provider within 3 to 5 days after birth and then again at 2 to 3 weeks of age for checkups. You also can tell if your baby is getting plenty of milk by keeping track of the number of wet diapers and diapers with bowel movements.

> **Most mothers can make plenty of milk for their baby. If you think you are having a milk supply problem, talk to a lactation conultant.**

Minimum Number of Wet Diapers and Bowel Movements in a Baby's First Week (It Is Fine if Your Baby Has More)			
Baby's age (1 day = 24 hours)	# of wet diapers	# of bowel movements	Color & texture of bowel movements
Day 1 (first 24 hours after birth)	1	The first one usually occurs within 8 hours after birth	Thick, tarry, and black
Day 2	2	3	Thick, tarry, and black
Day 3	5–6	3	Looser, greenish to yellow
Day 4	6 or more	3	Yellow, soft and watery
Day 5	6 or more	3	Loose, seedy yellow color
Day 6	6 or more	3	Loose, seedy yellow color
Day 7	6 or more	3	Larger amounts of loose, seedy yellow color

Some babies will switch to less frequent but large bowel movements at about 6 weeks of age.

Common Concerns and Solutions

Most breastfeeding concerns can be prevented, and, if an issue arises, there are many ways to treat it right away by calling on a lactation consultant or other health care provider. Getting plenty of rest and fluids, reducing stress, and eating a healthy diet will also help you feel better and be able to cope with any early challenges you might face after your baby is born.

Other signs that your baby is getting plenty of milk are:

- Baby is mostly content and gaining weight steadily after the first week of age. From birth to 3 months, typical weight gain is 2/3 to 1 ounce each day.

- Baby is passing clear or pale yellow urine, not deep yellow or orange. Baby has at least three stools every 24 hours after day 1.

- Baby alternates short sleeping periods with wakeful, alert periods. Baby is satisfied and content after feedings.

- Your breasts feel softer after you feed your baby.

Consult your baby's health care provider if you are concerned about your baby's weight gain.

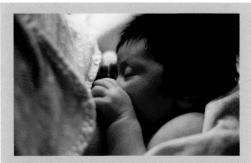

Ways to Wake Your Baby to Breastfeed

In the early weeks after birth, you should wake your baby to feed if 4 hours have passed since the beginning of the last feeding. You can:

- Remove any blankets.
- Change your baby's diaper.
- Place your baby skin-to-skin.
- Massage your baby's back, abdomen, arms, and legs.

Babies With Special Needs

Some babies have health problems that make it more challenging to breastfeed. You can stay firm with your choice to breastfeed and get help from a lactation consultant. Breast milk and early breastfeeding are still best for both the health of you and your baby, especially if your baby is premature or sick. Even if your baby can't breastfeed directly from you, it's best to express or pump your milk and give it to your baby with a cup or bottle. Be sure to continue lots of skin-to-skin contact with your baby.

Some of the most common health problems at birth are:

- being born early, or being premature
- Down syndrome
- heart defect
- jaundice
- cleft lip or palate
- tongue-tied
- needing to be in the intensive care unit

Pumping and hand expression

If you must be away from your baby, it will be important to remove milk during the times your baby normally would feed to make sure you will continue to make enough milk for him or her. Milk can be removed through a breast pump or by hand. When pumping or hand expressing milk, you can help your milk to start flowing by having a picture of your baby, a baby blanket, or other piece of your baby's clothing that has your baby's scent on it close by. You also can apply a warm, but not hot, moist compress to the breast, gently massage the breasts, or sit quietly and think of a relaxing setting. It is best to wash your hands before pumping your breast milk and to make sure the area where you are pumping is also clean. After each pumping, you can refrigerate your milk, place it in a cooler or insulated cooler pack, or freeze it in small (2 to 3 ounce) batches for the baby to be fed later. You can keep germs from getting into the milk by washing your pumping equipment with soap and water and letting it air dry.

Human Milk Banks

If you can't breastfeed and still want to give your baby human milk, the best place to go is to a milk bank that can dispense donor human milk to you if you have a prescription from your doctor. Many steps are taken to ensure the milk is safe. Go to the **Human Milk Banking Association of North America (HMBANA)** resource listed in the resource section on page 205.

Ways to Express Your Milk

Type	How it works	What's involved	Average cost
Hand expression	You use your hand to massage and compress your breast to remove milk.	Requires practice, skill, and co-ordination. Gets easier with practice; can be as fast as pumping. Good if you are seldom away from baby or need an option that is always with you.	Free, unless you need help from a breastfeeding professional who charges for her services.
Manual pump	You use your hand and wrist to operate a hand-held device to pump the milk.	Requires practice, skill, and coordination. Useful for occasional pumping if you are away from baby once in a while.	$30 to $50
Automatic, hospital-grade pump	Runs on battery or plugs into an electrical outlet.	Easy to use. Can pump one breast at a time or both breasts at the same time. Double pumping may collect more milk in less time, so it is helpful if you are going back to work or school full-time. Need places to clean and store the equipment between uses.	$150 to $250 or more

Going back to work

Breastfeeding keeps you connected to your baby, even when you are away at work, and your baby will continue to receive the best nutrition possible.

- After you have your baby, arrange with your employer to take as much time off as you can, because it will help you and your baby get into a good breastfeeding routine and help you make plenty of milk.

- If you can't breastfeed your baby directly during your work breaks, plan to leave your expressed or pumped milk for your baby. The milk can be given to your baby by the caregiver with a bottle or cup. Some babies don't like bottles; they prefer to breastfeed. So be patient and give your baby time to learn this new way of feeding. Babies may better learn other ways of feeding from their dad or another family member.

- You can help your baby practice bottle-feeding by giving him or her a bottle occasionally after he or she is around 4 weeks old and well used to breastfeeding. During these practice times, offer just a small amount (an ounce or two) of milk once a day.

- Talk with your employer about breastfeeding, such as why breastfeeding is important, why pumping is necessary, and how you plan to fit pumping into your workday, such as during lunch or other breaks. You could suggest making up work time for time spent pumping milk. If your day care is close to your job, try to arrange to go there to breastfeed your baby during work time.

- Request a clean and private area where you can pump your milk, preferably some place other than the bathroom. You also need a place to wash your hands and your pump parts.

- You can start pumping and storing your milk before you go back to work so that you have lots of milk stored and ready for the first week when you are away from your baby. It is helpful to copy your baby's feeding schedule when coming up with your pumping schedule. Pumping patterns are affected by your breast size and milk storage capacity, so pay attention to your breasts. When they start to feel full, pump until your milk stops spraying and then for a few more minutes each time. Don't wait until they are very full and swollen. Expect each breast to make about 1 ounce of milk every hour.

- Some states have laws that say employers have to allow you to breastfeed at your job, set up a space for you to breastfeed, and/or allow paid or unpaid time for breastfeeding or pumping.

To see if your state has a breastfeeding law for employers check on the La Leche League International Web site listed in the resource section on page 205. Even if your state does not have breastfeeding laws, most employers support breastfeeding employees when they explain their needs.

Breastfeeding in Public

The federal government and many states have laws that allow women to breastfeed anyplace they are usually allowed to be. If you still feel uncomfortable breastfeeding in public you can:

- Wear clothes that allow easy access to your breasts, such as tops that pull up from the waist.

- Breastfeed your baby in a sling. Slings or other soft infant carriers are especially helpful for traveling—making it easier and in keeping your baby comforted and close to you.

- Slip into a women's lounge or dressing room to breastfeed.

It's usually helpful to breastfeed your baby before he or she becomes fussy so that you have time to get into a comfortable place or position to feed.

Common Q&As

If I have small breasts or very large breasts, can I still breastfeed? Of course! Breast size is not related to the ability to produce milk for a baby. Breast size is due to the amount of fatty tissue in the breast and the milk storage capacity of your breast. Small breasts make plenty of milk; they just do not store a lot of milk. Therefore, babies will breastfeed often from a mother with smaller breasts. Large breasts make plenty of milk too.

Can I still breastfeed if I had breast surgery? How much milk you can produce depends on how your surgery was done and where your incisions are, and the reasons for your surgery. Women who have had incisions in the fold under the breasts are less likely to have problems making milk than women who have had incisions around or across the areola, which can cut into milk ducts and nerves. Women who have had breast implants usually breastfeed successfully. If you ever had surgery on your breasts for any reason, talk with a lactation consultant. If you are planning breast surgery, talk with your surgeon about ways he or she can preserve as much of the breast tissue and milk ducts as possible.

Can I breastfeed if I become ill? Yes! Most common illnesses, such as colds, flu, or diarrhea, can't be passed through breast milk, and your milk will have antibodies in it to help protect your baby from getting the same sickness.

Can I take medicines while breastfeeding? Although almost all medicines pass into your milk in small amounts, most medicines have no effect on the baby and are compatible with continuing to breastfeed. The list of medicines that you should not take while breastfeeding is very short. Discuss any medicines you are taking with your doctor and also ask before you start taking new medicines, including prescription and over-the-counter drugs, vitamins, and dietary or herbal supplements. For some women with chronic health problems, stopping a medicine can be more dangerous than the effects it will have on the breastfed baby. The American Academy of Pediatrics has more detailed information on this topic. See page 430 for contact information.

Do I need a special diet while breastfeeding? Women often try to improve their diets while they are pregnant. Staying with this improved diet after your baby is born will help you stay healthy, which will help your mood and energy level. You can eat the same number of calories that you ate before becoming pregnant, which helps weight loss after birth. But every mother's needs are unique. There are no special foods you should avoid and no special foods that will help you make more milk.

If you follow a vegan diet or one that does not include any forms of animal protein, you or your baby might not get enough vitamin B^{12} in your bodies. In a baby, this can cause symptoms such as loss of appetite, slow motor development, being very tired, weak muscles, vomiting, and problems with the blood. You can protect your and your baby's health by taking vitamin B^{12} supplements while breastfeeding.

All mothers should drink enough fluids to stay well hydrated for their own health. But fluid intake does not affect the amount of milk you are making. Always drink when you are thirsty. If your urine is dark yellow you should drink more fluids. Excessive caffeine intake (more than five 5-ounce cups of coffee or caffeinated soft drinks per day) can cause the baby to be fussy and not able to sleep well, but moderate caffeine intake (fewer than five 5-ounce cups) usually doesn't cause a problem for most breastfeeding babies.

You also should avoid drinking large quantities of alcohol. If you have an occasional drink of alcohol, you should wait for about 2 hours to pass before breastfeeding. Also, many babies don't like the taste of your milk after you have had an occasional drink and will breastfeed more when the alcohol is out of your system.

For more information on healthy eating, see the *Nutrition* chapter on page 317 and the MyPyramid Web site listed in the resource section on page 205.

Can my baby be allergic to my milk?
Research shows that a mother's milk is affected only slightly by the food in her diet. Breastfeeding mothers can eat whatever they have eaten during their lifetimes and do not need to avoid certain foods. Babies love the flavors of foods that come through in your milk. Sometimes a baby may be sensitive to something you eat, such as dairy products like milk and cheese. Symptoms in your baby of an allergy or sensitivity to something in your diet include some or all of these:

- green stools with mucus (MYOO-kuhss), diarrhea, vomiting

- rash, eczema (EG-zuh-muh), dermatitis, hives, dry skin

- fussiness during and/or after feedings

- crying for long periods without being able to feel consoled

- sudden waking with discomfort

- wheezing, coughing

Babies who are highly sensitive usually react to the food the mother eats within minutes or within 4 to 24 hours afterward. These signs do not mean the baby is allergic to your milk itself, only to something you are eating. If you stop eating whatever is bothering your baby or eat less of it, the problem usually goes away on its own. You also can talk with your baby's doctor about his or her symptoms. If your baby ever has problems breathing, call 911 or go to your nearest emergency room.

Will physical activity affect my breast milk? Regular physical activity helps you stay healthy, feel better, and have more energy. It does not affect the quality or quantity of your breast milk or your baby's growth. If your breasts are large or heavy, it may help to wear a comfortable support bra or sports bra during physical activity. (See page 346 of the *Fitness* chapter for more information.)

Do I have to restrict my sex life while breastfeeding? No. But, if you are having vaginal dryness, you can try more foreplay and water-based lubricants. You can feed your baby or express some milk before lovemaking so your breasts will be more comfortable and less likely to leak. During sex, you also can put pressure on the nipple when it lets down, or have a towel handy to catch the milk.

Do I still need birth control if I am breastfeeding? Breastfeeding can delay the return of normal ovulation and menstrual cycles. But, like other forms of birth control, breastfeeding is not a sure way to prevent pregnancy. You should talk with your doctor or nurse about birth control choices that are compatible with breastfeeding, including the lactational amenorrhea (ay-men-uh-REE-uh) method (LAM).

Can I breastfeed if I smoke? If you smoke tobacco, it is best for you and your baby if you try to quit as soon as possible. If you can't quit, though, it is still better to breastfeed, since your baby is at higher risk of having respiratory problems and SIDS. Breastfeeding lowers the risk of both of these health problems in your baby. Be sure to smoke away from your baby and change clothes to keep your baby away from the secondhand smoke on your clothing.

I heard that breast milk can have toxins in it from my environment. Is it still safe for my baby? Breast milk remains the best way to feed and nurture young infants and children. The advantages of breastfeeding far outweigh any possible risks from environmental pollutants. Infant formula is usually not a better choice because the formula itself, the water it is mixed with, and/or the bottles or nipples used to give it to the baby can be contaminated with bacteria or chemicals.

For more information on your health and the environment, see page 400.

Will my baby get enough vitamin D if I breastfeed? All infants and children, including those who are exclusively breastfed and those who are fed formula, should have at least 200 International Units (IU) of vitamin D per day, starting during the first 2 months of life, to help them build strong bones. New research suggests that the mother should be getting 200 to 400 IU of vitamin D per day to ensure plenty of vitamin D in her milk and for her own health. You can buy vitamin D supplements for infants at a drug store or grocery store. Sunlight can be a major source of vitamin D, but it is hard to measure how much sunlight your baby gets. Ask your doctor and your baby's doctor about vitamin D.

Does my breastfed baby need vaccines? Is it safe for me to get a vaccine when I'm breastfeeding? Yes. Vaccines are still important to your baby's health. Follow the schedule your doctor gives you and, if you miss any, check with him or her about getting back on track. Most nursing mothers may also receive vaccines. Breastfeeding does not affect the vaccine and vaccines are not harmful to breast milk. Breastfeeding during or after the vaccines are given can help with pain relief and soothing an upset baby.

What should I do if my baby bites me? A baby can't bite and breastfeed at the same time, although many older babies will try! If your baby starts to clamp down, you can put your finger in his or her mouth and take him or her off of your breast with a firm, "No." If your baby continues to bite you, you can try a few things:

- Stop the feeding immediately so the baby is not tempted to get another reaction from you. Don't laugh. This is part of your baby's learning limits.

- Offer a teething toy, or a snack or drink from a cup instead.

- Put your baby down for a moment to show that biting brings a negative consequence. You can then pick him or her up again to give comfort.

I just found out that I'm pregnant. Can I still breastfeed my toddler? Breastfeeding during your next pregnancy is not a risk to either the breastfeeding toddler or to the new developing baby. If you are having some problems in your pregnancy, such as uterine pain or bleeding, a history of preterm labor, or problems gaining weight during pregnancy, your doctor may advise you to wean. Some women also choose to wean at this time because they have nipple soreness caused by pregnancy hormones, are nauseous, or find that their growing stomachs make breastfeeding uncomfortable. Your toddler also may decide to wean on his or her own because of changes in the amount and flavor of your milk. He or she will need additional food and drink because you will likely make less milk during pregnancy.

If you keep nursing your toddler after your baby is born, you can feed your newborn first to ensure he or she gets the colostrum. Once your milk production increases a few days after birth you can decide how to best meet everyone's needs, especially the new baby's needs for you and your milk. You may want to ask your partner to help you by taking care of one child while you are breastfeeding. Also, you will need more fluids, healthy foods, and rest because you are taking care of yourself and two small children.

Breastfeeding is a unique experience and every mother has the potential to succeed and make it a wonderful experience. Whether you are a new or expecting mom, or a partner or family member of one, the information and resources here can help you. ∎

One Woman's Story

When Julian was born, I knew I wanted to breastfeed. And like many other new moms, I assumed it would go smoothly and that I would have fountains of milk for my sweet boy. But we didn't have the blissful start I had imagined.

He latched for the first time, and after a few breastfeeding sessions, I was the proud owner of bruised, sore nipples and was terrified the pain would just continue. While in the hospital, I saw two lactation consultants to help me with Julian's positioning, but he continued to have an "inefficient latch," which kept him from getting enough milk, slowed down my milk production, and left me with sore nipples. Another challenge I faced was having Julian away from me to be under "bili lights" to be treated for jaundice, so he received formula as a supplement. This undermined my confidence and hampered my milk production even more. So it was not surprising when we brought our bundle of joy home that, despite what seemed to be nearly endless nursing sessions, Julian still wasn't getting enough milk and wouldn't stop crying. I was crushed when we had to give him the bottle of formula sent home from the hospital. I felt betrayed by my body and like a total failure as a mother.

> **Before I returned to work, we were able to phase out the formula supplementation.**

The good news is that we got effective help. Our pediatrician referred us to a great lactation consultant whose "hands-on" approach helped to improve Julian's latch and rebuild my milk supply. Before I returned to work, we were able to phase out the formula supplementation. It took long, hard work, but we got there. Then, while working full time, I was able to pump enough milk to give Julian breast milk nearly all the time, using only one bottle of formula each day.

I proudly breastfed my son for 32 months and strongly feel that a child can benefit from breast milk no matter how much you can give him or her. I learned that what makes you a successful mom doesn't have anything to do with your breast milk supply and everything to do with always trying your best.

Ann

Washington, D.C.

For More Information...

Office on Women's Health, HHS
200 Independence Ave SW, Room 712E
Washington, DC 20201
Web site: www.womenshealth.gov/
breastfeeding
National Breastfeeding Helpline:
(800) 994-9662, (888) 220-5446 TDD

U.S. Department of Agriculture
3101 Park Center Dr
Alexandria, VA 22302-1594
Center for Nutrition Policy and Promotion
Web site: www.mypyramid.gov/
mypyramidmoms
Phone number: (888) 779-7264

The Special Supplemental Nutrition
Program for Women, Infants, and Children
Web site: www.fns.usda.gov/wic
Phone number: (703) 305-2746

Division of Nutrition, Physical Activity, and Obesity, CDC
4770 Buford Highway NE, MS K-24
Atlanta, GA 30341-3717
Web site: www.cdc.gov/breastfeeding
Phone number: (800) 232-4636,
(888) 232-6348 TTY

Food and Drug Administration
5600 Fishers Ln
Rockville, MD 20857
Breast Pump Information: www.fda.gov/
cdrh/breastpumps
Infant Formula Information:
www.cfsan.fda.gov/~dms/inf-toc.html
Phone number: (888) 463-6332

American College of Nurse-Midwives
8403 Colesville Rd, Suite 1550
Silver Spring, MD 20910
Breastfeeding Information:
www.gotmom.org
Web site: www.mymidwife.org

American College of Obstetricians and Gynecologists
409 12th St SW, PO Box 96920
Washington, DC 20090-6920
Web site: www.acog.org
Phone number: (202) 863-2518 Resource
Center

Human Milk Banking Association of North America
1500 Sunday Dr, Suite 102
Raleigh, NC 27607
Web site: www.hmbana.org

International Lactation Consultant Association
1500 Sunday Dr, Suite 102
Raleigh, NC 27607
Web site: www.ilca.org
Phone number: (919) 861-5577

La Leche League International
PO Box 4079
Schaumburg, IL 60168-4079
Web site: www.llli.org
Breastfeeding and the Law: www.llli.org/
Law/LawUS.html
Phone number: (800) 525-3243,
(847) 592-7570 TTY

Mental Health

A healthy mind is as important as a healthy body to your overall well-being. Good mental health helps you feel good about yourself, connect with others, find meaning in life, and thrive at home, work, and play. Good mental health doesn't mean you will never be sad, insecure, or worried. But good mental health can help you keep problems in perspective.

Some factors that influence mental health are out of our control, such as our genes and some life events. But many are not. Just like physical activity and eating right help to keep your body healthy, you can make lifestyle choices to help keep emotionally healthy, too.

What is mental health?

Mental health is how we think, feel, and act as we cope with life. It helps determine how we handle stress, relate to others, and make choices. Your mental health is shaped by the interplay of many forces. These include:

- brain chemicals
- culture
- environment
- genes
- hormones
- illness
- life events
- personality
- reproductive cycle
- society

Mental health exists on a spectrum. At one end are feelings, thoughts, and behaviors that allow you to thrive. At the other are feelings, thoughts, and behaviors that disrupt life and cause distress. Your point on the spectrum will change from moment to moment as the forces that shape your mental health change. You might not notice small changes in your mental health. But the big changes are easy to see and feel, such as the highs you might feel after reaching a personal goal or the lows after losing a job.

Your personal journey through life is unique. But there are predictable stages of a woman's life cycle, from girlhood to older adulthood. At some points, a woman's mental health may be more at risk of problems, such as after having a baby or in the years just before menopause. But with each stage comes a capacity for strength and growth, too.

Stress matters

We feel stressed when the demands of life and our skills and resources for coping are out of balance. We have short-term and long-term stress. Missing the bus or arguing with a spouse can cause short-term stress. Single parenting or financial hardship can lead to long-term stress. Even some of our happiest times can be stressful, like during the holidays or having a baby. Some of the most common stressful life events include:

- death of a spouse
- death of a close family member
- divorce
- losing your job
- major personal illness or injury
- marital separation
- marriage
- pregnancy
- retirement
- spending time in jail

Social conditions such as living in poverty and dealing with racism can expose people to ongoing stress. So can discrimination or harassment at work. Stress caused by trauma, intimate partner violence, or an abusive or troubled home life during childhood can have potent and long-lasting effects on a woman's mental health. In fact, childhood sexual abuse, which is more frequent among girls, may have effects that last into adulthood—ranging from depression and anxiety to posttraumatic stress disorder (PTSD).

More familiar to many women is day-to-day stress. Stress that builds up can take a toll on your physical and mental health. Did you know that you are more likely to catch a cold during times of high stress? Long-term stress can put you at risk of more serious health problems, like depression or hypertension. Or make health problems you already have worse.

At the same time, not all stress is bad. Just enough stress keeps you focused and helps you to perform your best, such as the stress you might feel before speaking in front of a group of people. It also can prompt you to change a situation for the better, such as leaving a dead-end job. But any stress can affect your health. Pay attention to your body for signs that stress is building up. And try these tips to keep stress in check:

- Take time each day to relax and unwind, even if only for a few minutes.
- Aim for 7 to 9 hours of sleep every night.
- Eat healthy foods, which give you energy.
- Make time for physical activity, which relieves tension and boosts mood.
- Talk to friends and loved ones. They are good listeners and might offer a different way of seeing things.

Signs of Role Strain and Stress

Juggling multiple roles is a fact of life for most women today. Sometimes, our roles as wives, partners, mothers, workers, and caregivers can feel like they are competing for our time and energy. Role strain and stress can happen easily if you take on too much, set standards that are too high, and/or don't get the support you need. But life roles can enhance and support each other, too. Research suggests that multiple roles are better for you than having just one. Look out for these signs that you are spreading yourself too thin:

- anxiety
- depression
- feeling you don't have control, or a need for too much control
- forgetfulness
- headaches
- lack of energy
- lack of focus
- low morale
- not being able to get things done
- poor self-esteem
- short temper
- trouble sleeping
- upset stomach
- withdrawal

appears to have a strong effect on mood and mental health. But the exact process is still unclear. We do know that depression rates for girls go up suddenly at puberty—the time when a girl's period begins. Mood changes right after having a baby can range from mild, short-lived "blues," which last 2 weeks or less, to major depression, which lasts longer than 2 weeks. Some women report an increase in depressive symptoms in the years before menopause.

Even though hormones are powerful, keep in mind that many factors contribute to mood. A woman's normal hormone rhythms are only one piece of the puzzle.

- Make time to do things you enjoy and that fulfill you.

- Set limits. Be realistic about what you can handle at work and in your personal life. Talk to your boss if work demands are too big to handle alone. If you feel overburdened, ask family and friends for help and say "no" to requests for your time and energy. Women often put the needs of others before their own.

Hormone rhythms and mood

Hormones are your body's chemical messengers. They affect many different processes in your body. The menstrual cycle is one example. Hormones rise and fall during the month and make the menstrual cycle happen. Many women notice physical and mood changes in the week or two before their period. We know that hormones have an effect on the brain chemistry that controls feelings and mood. In particular, estrogen

Taking care of your mental health

When you take care of your body, you likely strive to eat right, stay active, and take care to look your best. Your mental health needs similar care. In fact, to be healthy overall, you need to take care of both your body and mind—the two are closely connected. If you neglect caring for one, the other will suffer. These ideas will help you to care for both mind and body:

- **Build self-esteem.** Good self-esteem is linked to mental well-being, happiness, and success in many areas of life. It protects mental health during tough times. One way to build self-esteem is to value who you are and what you do. This is hard to do if you judge yourself by other people's standards or rely on others to make you feel good about yourself. Instead, accept the qualities—both strengths and weaknesses—that make you unique

- **Set realistic standards and goals.**
Take pride in your achievements, both
small and big. Positive thinking also
boosts self-esteem. This comes naturally to some people. But it's a skill you
can learn, too. Many people are lifted
up by their spirituality. It can shape
beliefs and values and be a source of
comfort in hard times. It can be good
to tune out the outside world and connect with the spirit within you.

- **Find value and purpose in life.** People who pursue goals based on their
own values and dreams enjoy stronger mental well-being. Think about
your values and dreams. What makes
you happy? What do you care deeply
about? What are you good at? If you
could change one thing in the world,
what would it be? What do you dream
about? How do you want your friends
and family to remember you? Use your
answers to set short-term and long-
terms goals for yourself. Keep your
goals realistic. Review them every once
in a while, and make changes as your
values and priorities change.

- **Learn healthy ways to cope with hard
times.** How do you react to stress,
change, or hardship? Do you see set-
backs as failures or merely bumps in
the road? Do you avoid problems or
look for solutions? Do you obsess
about issues without taking action
to resolve them? If your style needs
improving, take heart: Positive coping styles and traits can be learned
with some effort. If you have trouble
improving thinking patterns on your
own, a mental health professional can
help. You might also benefit from life-

skills classes. For example, parenting
classes can prepare new mothers for
what to expect. Being informed helps
people to understand, control, and
deal with situations that are new and
stressful.

Do I have a problem with alcohol?

Many women drink alcohol to cope
with stress. But some women drink too
much. Alcohol abuse and addiction
cause stress in a job and family. Answer these questions to help find out if
you might have a problem:

1. Have you ever felt you should cut
   down on your drinking?

2. Have people criticized your drinking?

3. Have you ever felt bad or guilty
   about your drinking?

4. Have you ever had a drink first thing
   in the morning to steady your nerves
   or to get rid of a hangover?

Talk with your doctor about your drinking if you answered "yes" to one or
more questions. Even if you answered
"no" to all the questions, talk to your
doctor if drinking is causing you problems with your job, relationships,
health, work, or the law.

- **Build healthy relationships.** We need healthy relationships to grow, thrive, and sustain us in hard times. They also protect from loneliness and isolation, which can lead to depression. Surround yourself with people who encourage and support you. You might draw strength from your ethnic or cultural community. Relationships that cause you to feel neglected, shameful, disrespected, or afraid are not healthy. Keep in mind that just as you need people, you are needed by others. Reach out and connect.

What is mental illness?

Mental illness is a collective term for a wide range of mental disorders. Mental disorders are medical conditions that disrupt how a person thinks, feels, and/or acts, resulting in distress and/or impaired functioning. Mental illness can be disabling, making it hard to meet and keep friends, hold a job, manage everyday tasks, or enjoy life. Mental illness is very common—affecting about 1 in 4 U.S. adults each year. Some mental disorders are more common in women. It's not your fault if you have mental illness. These disorders are real diseases that cannot be wished or willed away. Fortunately, recovery is possible from most mental disorders.

Causes of mental illness

Most mental disorders do not have a precise cause. Rather, cause lies in a mix of the same forces that shape mental health. We do know that biology plays a key role in the development of mental disorders, as it does with all health and illness. For example, PTSD can develop after a person is exposed to a very stressful or terrifying event. Yet not everyone who experiences trauma gets PTSD. For those who do, other factors must make them more vulnerable to PTSD. We do know that women are more likely to develop PTSD than men. We also know a link exists between some physical diseases and mental illnesses, such as between heart disease and depression. The relation between mental illness and other diseases is an area of abundant research.

Sometimes, mental illness can be a symptom of another disease. For example, depression can be a symptom of an underactive thyroid or overactive thyroid. When thyroid problems are treated, the depressive symptoms go away.

Faces of mental illness

Mental illness can affect people of any age, race, ethnicity, sex, income, or background. Certain groups of people have higher rates of reported mental illness. Rates of mental illness are much higher among the homeless, the incarcerated, and people living in poverty. African Americans are overrepresented in these vulnerable groups of people. And African Americans with mental health needs are much less likely to seek or receive professional help. American Indians and Alaska Natives have limited access to help and appear to have much higher rates of depression, including suicide. Asian Americans have been stereotyped as "mentally healthier." But studies show rates of mental illness similar to those of other Americans. Hispanic American youths are at much greater risk of poor mental health than white youths.

Women and mental illness

Being a woman puts you at greater risk of certain mental disorders, including depression, some anxiety disorders, and eating disorders. Some mental disorders show up differently in women and men. An example is attention-deficit/

hyperactivity disorder (ADHD), which can cause similar problems for both males and females. Yet different symptoms appear to be one reason ADHD is often not recognized in girls and women. Also, it's not unusual for people to have more than one mental disorder at the same time. About 15 percent of all adults who have a mental disorder in 1 year also have problems with drugs or alcohol, which makes treatment harder.

Anxiety disorders are the most common mental illness. They affect about 40 million American adults each year. For these people, feelings of fear, uncertainty, and anxiety do not go away and get worse over time. They may have chest pains or nightmares. They may even be afraid to leave home. Most anxiety disorders are treatable. Anxiety disorders include:

- generalized anxiety disorder (GAD)
- obsessive-compulsive disorder (OCD)
- panic disorder
- PTSD
- social anxiety disorder
- specific phobias

Mood disorders affect mood, energy level, and ability to function. More than 20 million American adults have a mood disorder. With depression, feelings of sadness and hopelessness do not go away. Severe depression can lead to thoughts of death or suicide. Most depressive disorders respond well to treatment. People with bipolar disorder have extreme mood swings, sometimes with normal mood in between. It is a lifelong condition that must be carefully managed. Mood disorders include:

- major depressive disorder
- dysthymia (diss-THEYE-mee-uh)—mild, chronic depression
- premenstrual dysphoric (diss-FOR-ihk) disorder (PMDD)—a severe form of premenstrual syndrome (PMS)
- postpartum depression (See page 215 for more information.)
- bipolar disorder
- seasonal affective disorder (SAD)—depressed mood triggered by the change in seasons, usually in the fall and winter

Eating disorders involve serious problems in eating behavior, plus extreme concern for body shape or weight. Women are much more likely than men to have eating disorders. They usually start in the teenage years, but some women seek treatment for the first time in midlife. Getting help early is important. Eating disorders can cause heart and kidney problems and even death. The main types of eating disorders are:

- **anorexia nervosa**—an intense fear of getting fat that causes you to not eat, even though you become too thin
- **bulimia nervosa**—involves bouts of overeating followed by purging, such as by throwing up
- **binge eating**—out-of-control eating

Body dysmorphic disorder (BDD) occurs when a person is overly concerned about an imagined defect in appearance. BDD is not an eating disorder. But it may be present with an eating disorder, as well as an anxiety disorder or depression.

Substance abuse and addiction can occur with other mental disorders or be a stand-alone problem, which causes problems at work and in relationships. Also, people often use alcohol and drugs to cope with life problems. This use can lead to abuse and addiction. Drug and alcohol addiction is a serious, long-lasting problem. There are no easy cures. But it's possible to overcome addiction with treatment.

Schizophrenia is a chronic, severe, and disabling mental disorder. People who have it may hear voices, see things that aren't there, or think that others are reading or controlling their minds. They have trouble thinking logically and expressing emotion. In women, symptoms usually start in the mid-20s to early 30s. Medicines can help many of the symptoms, but it can take many tries to find the right drug. With treatment, many people improve enough to have a good quality of life.

Pregnancy and Depression

Depression is common during and after pregnancy. Pregnant women with depression can have a hard time caring for themselves. This can hurt the unborn baby. And depression that is not controlled during pregnancy triples the risk of postpartum depression (see below). You might not know you have depression because some normal pregnancy changes cause similar symptoms. So it's important to let your doctor know about any mood changes you might be having while you're pregnant.

After childbirth, many women get the "baby blues"—feeling sad, weepy, and overwhelmed for a few days. But some women develop postpartum depression, a serious but treatable condition that needs a doctor's help. Postpartum depression can happen anytime within the first year of birth. In rare cases, a woman might have a severe form called postpartum psychosis. Some women don't tell anyone about their symptoms because they feel embarrassed or guilty for having these feelings at a time when they think they should be happy. Don't let this happen to you! Postpartum depression can make it hard to take care of your new baby. Infants of mothers with postpartum depression can have delays in learning how to talk. They can have problems with emotional bonding. They also might have problems with behavior, lower activity levels, sleep problems, and distress. **Call your doctor if:**

- Your baby blues don't go away after 2 weeks.
- Depressive symptoms get more and more intense.
- Strong feelings of sadness or anger come on 1 or 2 months after delivery.
- It is hard for you to perform tasks at work or at home.
- You cannot care for yourself or your baby.
- You have thoughts of harming your baby or yourself.

Keep in mind that there are ways to treat depression during and after pregnancy. Seek help if you find yourself feeling depressed at any time.

If you are taking medicine for depression and become pregnant, do not stop without talking to your doctor. Not using medicine that you need may be more harmful to you and your baby than using the medicine.

Personality disorders are long-term patterns of thoughts and behaviors that cause serious problems with relationships and work. People with personality disorders have a hard time dealing with everyday stresses and problems. They often have stormy relationships with other people. Borderline personality disorder (BPD) is one of 10 types of personality disorders. It has been defined as affecting mostly young women. People with BPD have problems controlling emotion. Many, but not all, people with BPD were abused or neglected as young children.

Alzheimer's disease is not a mental illness. For more information on Alzheimer's disease, see the *Healthy Aging* chapter on page 221.

How to know when you need help

Mental illness can be mild or severe. Even though mental illness is widespread, only about 1 in 17 Americans with mental illness is severely debilitated as a result. Many people with mild forms of mental illness might not seek help, even though their quality of life is suffering. If emotional problems interfere with daily living, you should talk to your doctor. Keep in mind that professional help might benefit you in rough times, even if you do not have a diagnosable condition.

Stigma: A barrier to treatment and recovery

Stigma, negative ideas linked to mental illness, is the biggest barrier to getting better. Many people don't seek help for mental health problems because they are ashamed, even though treatment is available. One reason stigma persists is because mental illness is still widely misunderstood. Here are some common myths about mental illness:

- Mental illness is not a real illness, like cancer or heart disease.
- Mental illness is caused by emotional or personal weakness.
- Children don't get mental illness.
- People with mental illness are violent.
- People with mental illness can will it away if they really want to.

Your culture also can influence whether you think it's okay to seek help. Seeking help and drawing support from loved ones who understand is the only way to get better. Don't let stigma stand in the way of getting help!

Where to go for help

There are many types of mental health professionals. They include:

- certified alcohol and drug abuse counselors
- clinical social workers
- faith-based counselors
- licensed professional counselors
- marital and family therapists
- mental health counselors
- nurse psychotherapists

Feeling hopeless?

If you are feeling hopeless or thinking about death or suicide, get help right away! Call this toll-free number: (800) 273-TALK (8255). You will reach the National Suicide Prevention Lifeline. This service is available to anyone, 24 hours a day, every day of the year. With help, it's possible to feel good again.

- psychiatrists
- psychologists

A good place to start looking for help is the doctor who normally cares for you. Your doctor can suggest mental health professionals based on the nature of your problem. If you do not have a regular doctor, contact a community mental health center near you. These centers can help you find a doctor or mental health counselor, even if you cannot afford to pay for care. If you don't feel comfortable with the professional you choose, it's okay to contact somebody else. Feeling comfortable with the doctor or counselor helping you is important to getting better.

Treating mental illness

Today, many treatment options can help people with mental health problems and illness. Thanks to improved understanding of the brain and biology, new medicines are making it possible for people with serious disorders to work and enjoy a fulfilling life. Talking face-to-face with a mental health professional is another important tool for treating mental health problems. This is called psychotherapy. Some types are:

- behavioral therapy—seeks to change destructive behavior

- cognitive therapy—seeks to change or get rid of destructive thought patterns
- family therapy—involves every family member in the discussion and solving of problems
- group therapy—helps a small group of people with similar problems through use of a facilitator
- movement/art/music therapy—helps people to express emotions
- psychoanalysis—seeks to understand how past experiences influence mental health

Treating a mental health problem often involves more than one type of therapy, such as using medicine and behavior therapy. A problem might be helped with only a few sessions of counseling. Or treatment might last years. With severe mental illness, treatment in a hospital or outpatient clinic sometimes is necessary. Let your health care provider know if you don't begin to feel better after starting treatment. Keep in mind that recovery can take time.

Recovery is a journey

The sooner a mental disorder is discovered, the better the chance for full recovery. Unlike most disabling physical illnesses, mental illness often begins early in life. Also, there is no lab test to tell if you have a problem that needs help. For these reasons, it's important to talk with your doctor about any concerns you might be having as soon as possible. This way, if you do have a mental health problem or illness, you can start treatment early and begin a journey toward feeling good again. ■

One Woman's Story

On the day I came home from the hospital with my beautiful baby daughter, my world began to disintegrate. I was hit with intense nausea, vomiting, diarrhea, dehydration, and fainting. Breastfeeding my baby was out of the question. Every time I held her to my breast, I had to quickly lay her back down so I could run to the bathroom.

During the first 3 months of my daughter's life, I was hospitalized twice, separated for a week at a time from her and my 16-month-old son. I was transformed from a very healthy, vibrant, and physically active 30-year-old to someone unable to perform even the simplest everyday tasks. I was devastated. I was a failure as a mom and couldn't even get out of bed. I wanted to die.

During my second hospital stay, a nurse gently suggested that I might have postpartum depression. I was stunned. How could the horrible gastrointestinal symptoms I was experiencing be caused by depression? I could understand how I could be depressed because of the sickness I was suffering, but not the other way around. And I had never heard of postpartum depression. But I took her suggestion to heart and quickly sought a diagnosis, information, and help.

> **How could the horrible gastrointestinal symptoms I was experiencing be caused by depression?**

I started taking an antidepressant and soon felt nearly like my former self, able to take care of my babies and function around the house. I also immediately began seeing a psychologist and after about a year of therapy, I got my life back. And not only that, I went on to have another beautiful baby girl a few years later, armed with the knowledge I needed in case postpartum depression struck again.

When I look back on that horrible time, I cringe, knowing that there are still new mothers out there who are dealing with the exact same thing. There is so much that needs to be done to spread awareness of perinatal mood disorders. I never hesitate to share my story with anyone who will listen. If I am able to reach out and help even one new mother, then what I went through will have been worth it.

Kristin
Chandler, Arizona

For More Information...

Office on Women's Health, HHS
200 Independence Ave SW, Room 712E
Washington, DC 20201
Web site: www.womenshealth.gov/mh
Phone number: (800) 994-9662,
(888) 220-5446 TDD

National Center for Posttraumatic Stress Disorder, VA
Web site: www.ncptsd.va.gov
Phone number: (802) 296-6300

National Institute of Mental Health, NIH
6001 Executive Blvd, Room 8184, MSC 9663
Bethesda, MD 20892-9663
Web site: www.nimh.nih.gov
Phone number: (866) 615-6464,
(866) 415-8051 TTY

National Mental Health Information Center, SAMHSA
PO Box 42557
Washington, DC 20015
Web site: http://mentalhealth.samhsa.gov
Phone number: (800) 789-2647,
(866) 889-2647 TDD

American Psychiatric Association
1000 Wilson Blvd, Suite 1825
Arlington, VA 22209
Web site: www.healthyminds.org
Phone number: (888) 357-7924

American Psychological Association
750 First St NE
Washington, DC 20002-4242
Web site: www.apa.org
www.apahelpcenter.org

Anxiety Disorders Association of America
8730 Georgia Ave, Suite 600
Silver Spring, MD 20910
Web site: www.adaa.org

Mental Health America
2000 N Beauregard St, 6th Floor
Alexandria, VA 22311
Web site: www.mentalhealthamerica.net
Phone number: (800) 969-6642,
(800) 433-5959 TTY

National Alliance on Mental Illness
Colonial Place Three
2107 Wilson Blvd, Suite 300
Arlington, VA 22201-3042
Web site: www.nami.org
Phone number: (800) 950-6264

National Center for Girls and Women with AD/HD
3268 Arcadia Pl NW
Washington, DC 20015
Web site: www.ncgiadd.org
Phone number: (888) 238-8588

National Eating Disorders Association
603 Stewart St, Suite 803
Seattle, WA 98101
Web site: www.nationaleatingdisorders.org
Phone number: (800) 931-2237

National Suicide Prevention Lifeline
Web site: www.suicidepreventionlifeline.org
Phone number: (800) 273-8255,
(800) 799-4889 TTY

Postpartum Support International
Web site: www.postpartum.net
Phone number: (800) 944-4773

Healthy Aging

Facing aging is not a new concept. But our views on older age are changing. Experts on aging now know that poor health and loss of independence are not a natural and normal part of getting older. And there are many steps that you can take now to help maintain your health, vitality, and independence throughout your golden years.

You're never too old to live healthy

Adopting healthy behaviors—even later in life—can help prevent, delay, and control disease. In fact, research has shown that a healthy lifestyle matters more than your genes in helping you to avoid poor health as you age. A healthy lifestyle can protect you from frailty, too. Preventing health problems also saves money. The cost of providing health care for an older American is 3 to 5 times greater than the cost for someone younger than 65. So why wait? Take these steps to boost your physical health and self-esteem:

- **Get moving!** By age 75, about 1 in 2 women does not engage in any physical activity. But physical activity can help people of all ages—even those with serious health problems. For instance, muscle-building physical activity can help people with heart failure in ways that medicine cannot. Talk to your doctor about safe ways for you to become active.

- **Eat healthy food.** Nutrient-rich foods are vital to our health as we age. If shopping for or preparing good food

is hard for you, contact your local Area Agency on Aging (the number is in the phone book) or Eldercare locator (see the resources listed in the resource section on page 233). You may be able to enjoy free or low-cost meals for older people at a community center, church, or school or have meals delivered to your home.

- **Quit smoking.** If you have smoked for many years, you might think it's too late for you to quit—that the damage is done. But quitting has immediate health benefits even for lifelong smokers and people with smoking-related diseases. For instance, smokers have twice the risk of dying of heart disease as nonsmokers. But this risk begins to drop after quitting. After 15 years of not smoking, past smokers' risk of heart disease is similar to those who have never smoked.

- **See your doctor regularly for health screenings and vaccines.** Tell your doctor about any health changes you notice. Also, tell your doctor if you feel sad, lonely, or like you don't have the energy or interest in doing things you once enjoyed. (See page 416 in the Appendix for screening and immunization guidelines.)

- **Be safe when drinking alcohol.** The body responds differently to alcohol with age. Even a small amount can impair judgment, coordination, and reaction time. And many medicines do not mix well with alcohol. Talk to your doctor about your alcohol use and the medicines you are taking.

- **Stay connected.** You can protect yourself from isolation and depression by interacting with others. Get involved with a volunteer, hobby, or special interest group. Local senior centers offer social programs. Your local Area Agency on Aging can help you connect with outreach programs if you are homebound.

Consumer Alert—Don't Be a Victim of Health Scams

Living with chronic health problems can be hard. You might be willing to try just about anything to feel better—including unproven remedies that promise a quick or painless cure. Be smart and talk to your doctor before buying a product that sounds too good to be true. Quacks— people who sell unproven remedies— target older people. Those who fall victim to their scams waste money and put their health at risk.

Normal age-related decline affects most of our body's organs and systems. How and when this happens is different for each of us. It depends on many factors, including our genes, lifestyle, and health history.

"Normal" Aging

Brain	Brain structure changes with age, the effects of which are unclear. Healthy older people might notice some mild changes, such as needing new information repeated or more time to learn something new.
Heart and arteries	The heart muscle thickens, and arteries tend to stiffen with age. This makes it harder for the heart to pump oxygen-rich blood throughout the body. It also becomes harder for the body to take out the oxygen from blood.
Lungs	The amount of air the lungs can breathe in and out can decrease with age, causing shortness of breath while working hard or during brisk activities.
Kidneys	Over time, the kidneys don't work as well at removing waste from the blood.
Bladder	With age, the bladder cannot hold as much urine.
Body fat	Levels of body fat stay about the same from middle age until late life, when body weight tends to decline. Older people tend to lose both muscle and body fat. Fat also shifts from just beneath the skin to deeper organs.
Skin	The skin thins and loses elasticity as it ages, leading to wrinkles and sags. Loss of sweat and oil glands can lead to dry and flaky skin. Spots appear on sun-damaged skin.
Hair	Hair often grays and becomes brittle. Some women also notice hair loss or thinning.
Muscles	Without physical activity, muscle mass declines up to 22 percent in women between age 30 and 70, affecting strength, flexibility, and balance.
Bones	Bone mineral is removed and replaced throughout life. Beginning in the 40s, bone may be lost faster than it can be replaced. Bone loss speeds up even more after menopause. Over time, bones can weaken and become brittle.
Eyes	In midlife, it can become harder to focus on close-up items, such as a book. From 50 on, glare tends to interfere more with vision, and seeing in low-light and detecting moving objects become more and more difficult. Seeing detail can become a challenge in the 70s.
Ears	Higher pitched sounds become more difficult to hear with age. Understanding speech, especially if there is background noise, can be a problem, even for older adults with good hearing.
Reproductive system	Menopause marks the end of a woman's reproductive years. She no longer has periods and she cannot become pregnant.
Hormones	Hormones are chemical messengers that control the function of many organs and tissues. As we age, our bodies make less of certain hormones, such as estrogen and growth hormone, and more of others, such as parathyroid hormone (PHT). Estrogen and PHT affect bone health. Researchers are studying the effect of this change on aging.
Immune system	The organs and cells of the immune system work throughout the body to protect it from infection. With age, these cells become less active, making the body less able to defend against bacteria and viruses. Researchers think that this system might play an important role in the aging process.

Important health topics for aging women

Menopause

Menopause marks the end of a woman's reproductive years. You have reached menopause when a full year has passed without having a period. This happens for most women after age 45. Some women are hardly aware of the changes occurring as they near menopause. Some are bothered by hot flashes, night sweats, and vaginal dryness. You might notice other changes too, such as mood changes and memory problems. We don't always know if changes are related to menopause, aging, or both. For most women, some discomforts related to menopause, such as hot flashes, may go away 3 to 5 years after reaching menopause. Other symptoms, such as vaginal dryness, may not go away.

Many women are able to cope with mild menopause discomforts. Try these tips:

- **Hot flashes**
  - Wear fabrics that breathe, and dress in layers.
  - Drink something cold when a hot flash starts.
  - Keep track of when hot flashes happen so you can avoid triggers.
- **Night sweats**
  - Keep your bedroom cool or use a fan.
  - Wear breathable nightclothes.
- **Vaginal dryness and discomfort**
  - Water-based lubricants or estrogen creams or tablets can help restore moisture and tissue health when dryness is caused by reduced estrogen.

Taking hormones, called menopausal hormone therapy (MHT), can be good at relieving moderate to severe symptoms and preventing bone loss. But MHT has some serious risks, especially if used for a long time. Talk to your doctor about the benefits and risks of MHT. If you decide to try MHT, use the lowest dose that helps for the shortest time you need it.

Keep in mind that menopause is a normal part of a woman's life—not a disease. But it can affect your health in some important ways. Lower levels of estrogen increase your risk of bone disease in the postmenopausal years. Heart disease risk also increases after menopause. You might wonder if MHT can help. But recent studies suggest that women should not use MHT to protect against heart disease. (See page 28 of the *Heart Disease* chapter for more information.) And other drugs can help bone loss. You also can take steps to lower your risks for these health problems. (See the section "Bone health" that follows.)

Hysterectomy

Some types of surgery can bring on early menopause. A woman who has her uterus removed (hysterectomy) and/or both ovaries removed will stop having periods. But if her ovaries are left in place, she could still have symptoms of menopause in her 40s and 50s. If both ovaries are removed, symptoms of menopause can begin right away, regardless of age.

Bone health

Men and women lose bone as they grow older. But women need to give bone health their full attention, even more so than men. Women have smaller bones than men. But also, they lose bone faster than men do because of hormonal changes that occur during the menopause transition and after menopause. Over time bone loss can lead to osteoporosis (OSS-tee-oh-puh-ROH-suhss), which makes your bones weak and more likely to break. Of the 10 million Americans with osteoporosis, 80 percent are women. Osteoporosis affects all people, including women of color. But those at greatest risk are:

- Caucasian women
- thin, small-boned women
- women with a family history of bone breaks because of weak bones or who have broken a bone as an adult
- women who smoke
- women who use certain medicines for a long time, such as those used to treat asthma, lupus, and seizures

Your bone health matters because your risk of falling goes up as you get older. About 1 in 4 women age 50 and older falls each year. Broken bones that result from falls are frequently caused by osteoporosis or low bone mass. A broken bone—commonly of the hip, spine, or wrist—is often how a woman finds out she has osteoporosis.

Don't let a broken bone be your wake-up call. Talk to your doctor about your risk of osteoporosis and whether you need a bone density test. This test can tell how strong your bones are and if you have a higher chance for breaks. You should get a bone density test if you are age 65 or older or if you are between ages 60 and 64, weigh less than 154 pounds, and don't take estrogen. Also, take these steps to help keep your bones strong and prevent bone loss:

- Eat foods rich in calcium and vitamin D. Both are needed to build bone and keep bones strong. Adults age 50 and older need 1200 mg of calcium and 400 to 600 IU or more of vitamin D[3] daily. Supplements can help if you cannot get the amount you need from the foods you eat.

- Engage in weight-bearing physical activity 3 to 4 times a week to make bones stronger. Examples include walking, jogging, tennis, and dancing.

- Don't smoke, and use alcohol only in moderation. Smoking is a risk factor for osteoporosis. Heavy drinking is linked to lower bone density and high risk of bone breaks.

Preventing Falls

Falls are the most common cause of injury and injury-related death among older adults. Falls that result in serious injury, like a broken bone, can threaten your physical health and independence. Even if you don't get hurt from a fall, a fear of falling again can keep you from doing things you want or need to do. This can result in isolation and depression. There are many reasons older people fall more. But hazards around you are the leading cause of falls. Many times, these falls could have been avoided. Here are some steps you can take to lower your risk of falling:

- Get regular physical activity to improve strength and balance.

- Ask your doctor to review the medicines you are using to check for side effects and interactions that might make you dizzy or sleepy.

- Have your eyesight checked by an eye doctor every 1 or 2 years.

- Make your home safer: Install handrails and grab bars, secure throw rugs, improve lighting, remove clutter you can trip over, keep items you use daily within easy reach, and wear supportive shoes both inside and outside.

For women at high risk of bone disease, many medicines can help slow bone loss and reduce the risk of bone breaks. Short-term use of estrogen (menopausal hormone therapy, or MHT) can relieve symptoms of menopause and prevent bone loss. But long-term estrogen use has serious risks. If used, MHT should be used for the shortest time possible. Currently, no "natural" products, such as phytoestrogens (feye-toh-ESS-truh-juhnz), are recommended to prevent osteoporosis. If you are at high risk, talk to your doctor about your options.

Brain health

Many women want to live a long life, but worry about memory loss or becoming "senile." Our brain health—or cognitive health—involves the functions we need for everyday activities. These include thinking, learning, memory, judgment, planning, talking, and perception. Some people think that losing these functions is a normal part of aging. But this is not true. Most older adults do not have the marked decline in mental function that so many of us fear.

Still, declines that are not related to normal aging are a distressing reality for many older people and their families. These can range from mild cognitive impairment (MCI) to severe dementia (dih-MEN-chuh). People with MCI have a slight mental decline, such as memory loss, that is worse than that expected for their age. But it does not interfere with the ability to care for oneself. Some experts think MCI, mainly involving memory, might be an early sign of Alzheimer's disease (AD).

Dementia is a group of symptoms that are caused by changes in brain function. AD and stroke are the most common causes of dementia in older people. People with severe dementia are not able to think or remember well enough to take care of themselves. They might not have control of their emotions. Their personalities might change. They sometimes see things that are not there.

AD develops over time, and more women have it than men. One reason for this is that women live longer than men, and the risk of AD goes up greatly with age. In fact, nearly 1 in 2 people older than 85 have AD. More and more people are expected to develop AD in the future be-

Tips for Mental Fitness

Taking these steps might help maintain mental fitness:

- Lower high cholesterol (koh-LESS-tur-ol) levels.
- Lower high blood pressure.
- Maintain a healthy weight.
- Control diabetes.
- Don't smoke.
- Engage in regular physical activity.
- Take part in social activities.
- Stay connected with friends and family.
- Read, do puzzles, play games, or learn something new to keep your brain active.

Minority Women's Health

Chronic disease hits older minority women the hardest, in part because they are in poorer health, have less access to health services, and have lower health literacy. The reasons for these disparities are complex. Many minority women face huge social, economic, and cultural barriers to protecting their health.

cause of longer life spans and our aging population. How to best care for people with AD and support their caregivers are areas of intense public health interest.

We don't know what causes AD, how to prevent it, or how to make it better. Beyond age, family history of AD and having a lower level of education are other risk factors for AD. Research also strongly suggests a link between poor heart health and cognitive decline. It also suggests that a healthy lifestyle can help to maintain mental function. This is important because older adults with cognitive decline are at higher risk of getting dementia later in life.

Common health concerns of older women

Today, people are living longer than ever before. As a result many women will have health concerns that are more common in old age. This can include chronic diseases, as well as conditions that are more bothersome than harmful to your health.

Almost 8 in 10 people older than 65 have at least one chronic condition. If you have one, you can help yourself to keep active and independent by learning about your condition, adopting healthy habits, and seeing the doctor regularly.

Chronic Health Conditions Common in Older Age		
Chronic condition	**Did you know?**	**Where to learn more**
Asthma	Many people get asthma for the first time as an older adult.	*Respiratory Health* chapter, page 279
Cancer	Breast, lung, and colorectal cancers are most common in women, and risk goes up with age.	*Cancer* chapter, page 51
Chronic obstructive pulmonary disease (COPD)	Smoking is the main cause of COPD, which is the fourth leading cause of death in the United States and world.	*Respiratory Health* chapter, page 279
Depression	Twice as many older women as men have depression, often along with other chronic illnesses common in later life, such as heart disease and cancer. Widows are at increased risk of depression.	*Mental Health* chapter, page 207
Diabetes	The risk of diabetes increases with age. Diabetes that is not controlled can hurt your eyes, heart, and kidneys. It also is linked with depression.	*Type 2 Diabetes* chapter, page 69
Epilepsy (E-puh-LEP-see)	Many older adults don't realize that epilepsy is as likely to begin in older age as in young children. Having a seizure can be scary, but epilepsy can be treated.	
Gum disease	Many older people did not grow up with drinking water with fluoride or fluoride toothpastes, which protect teeth. This has caused many to have gum and other oral diseases, which can lead to tooth loss.	*Oral Health* chapter, page 293
Heart disease	Heart disease is the number one killer of women. But most heart attacks in women may be preventable.	*Heart Disease* chapter, page 15
High blood pressure	After menopause your risk of high blood pressure goes up, even if you had normal blood pressure most of your life. High blood pressure is called the "silent killer" because there are no symptoms.	*Heart Disease* chapter, page 15
HIV	More and more older women are finding out they have HIV. One reason is that women who no longer worry about getting pregnant may be less likely to use a condom and to practice safe sex.	*HIV/AIDS* chapter, page 139

Chronic Health Conditions Common in Older Age

Chronic condition	Did you know?	Where to learn more
Incontinence	Urinary incontinence is common among older women, but it is not a normal part of aging. Treatment can help most women.	*Urologic and Kidney Health* chapter, page 251
Pain	Poorly controlled pain can lead to depression. Back pain can make it hard to get around and enjoy life. Also, daily back pain might be associated with a higher risk of heart disease.	*Pain* chapter, page 351
Stroke	More women die of stroke than men. People who survive stroke often need a caregiver.	*Stroke* chapter, page 37

Not all people struggle with the health concerns in the chart that follows, but many older people do. Talk to your doctor about symptoms that bother or concern you.

Other Common Health Concerns

Concern	What you can do	When to see your doctor
Arthritis Age-related arthritis, called osteoarthritis (OSS-tee-oh-ar-THREYE-tuhss), occurs when the tissue that cushions the ends of the bones within joints wears away.	• Get plenty of rest. • Get physical activity to reduce stiffness. • Wear supportive shoes. • Use gadgets to help you do things such as open jars and turn doorknobs. • Try medicines to reduce pain and swelling.	Call your doctor if one or more of these symptoms last more than 2 weeks: • Lasting joint pain • Joint swelling • Joint stiffness • Tenderness or pain when touching a joint • Problems using or moving a joint normally • Warmth or redness in a joint
Balance problems Disturbances in the inner ear, other health problems, and some medicines can cause a balance problem—a reason many older people fall.	• Eat a low-salt, heart-healthy diet. • Get physical activity to improve strength and balance. • Avoid alcohol and caffeine. • Don't stand up too quickly or change direction suddenly. • Ask your doctor to review the medicines you are using.	Call your doctor if you: • Feel unsteady • Feel like you or your surroundings are spinning or moving • Feel like you are falling • Lose your balance and fall • Ever feel disoriented • Feel like you might faint • Have blurred vision
Dry skin and itching Dry skin and itching—mainly on lower legs, elbows, and forearms—is a common complaint of older people.	• Use moisturizers—mainly creams and ointments. • Bathe less often and use mild soaps and warm—not hot—water. • Drink plenty of water. • Stay out of the sun, and protect your skin with sunscreen. • Don't smoke, which dries out skin.	See your doctor if: • Your dry skin does not improve with self-care • Your dry skin affects your sleep • You have sores that do not heal • You notice a change on the skin, such as a new growth or a mole that looks different

Other Common Health Concerns

Concern	What you can do	When to see your doctor
Eye problems Many people notice changes in vision as they age. Other common eye complaints include having too many tears, dry eyes, or eyelid problems.	• Have your eyes checked every 1 to 2 years by an eye-care professional. An eye exam is the only way to find out about some eye diseases. • Ask your doctor if you are at high risk of eye disease. • Wear sunglasses to protect your eyes from harmful UV rays.	Call your doctor if you have: • Eye pain • Fluid coming out of your eye • Double vision • Redness • Swelling of your eye or eyelid Call your doctor **right away** if: • You suddenly cannot see or everything looks dim • You see flashes of light
Flu and pneumonia (noo-MOH-nyuh) The flu—short for "influenza"—can make you very sick, especially if you have health problems like heart disease or diabetes. Older people who get the flu are more likely to also get another infection, such as pneumonia.	• People age 50 and older should get a flu vaccine every year. • All people 65 and older should get a one-time-only pneumonia vaccine. • Clean your hands often. • Avoid touching your eyes, nose, or mouth. • Stay away from people who are sick.	Call your doctor if you have these symptoms, even if you got the flu shot: • Fever • Headache • Aches and pains • Extreme tiredness and weakness • Chest discomfort or cough • Stuffy nose, sneezing, sore throat (less common)
Hearing loss Hearing problems come in many forms and have many causes. Ignoring a hearing problem can lead to depression.	• Have your hearing checked every 3 years. • Review the medicines you are using with your doctor. • Wear earplugs or earmuffs to protect your hearing from loud noise.	See your doctor if: • People you talk to seem to mumble • You have to strain to understand what others are saying • Others say you play the TV or radio too loudly • You cannot hear the doorbell or phone ring • You have trouble hearing in crowded or noisy rooms • You have dizziness, pain, or ringing in your ears
Shingles Shingles is a painful skin rash caused by the chicken pox virus. As you get older, the virus may come back as shingles.	• Most people 60 and older should get the one-time-only herpes zoster vaccine, which can prevent shingles. Some people with specific health conditions should not get it. Your doctor can tell you if it's okay for you.	Call your doctor right away if: • You feel burning or shooting pain and tingling or itching, usually on one side of the body or face • You have a rash or blisters appear on the side of the trunk or face

Other Common Health Concerns

Concern	What you can do	When to see your doctor
Sexual problems Many women remain sexually active in older age. But about one-half of them report at least one bothersome sexual problem.	• Try over-the-counter lubricants to relieve vaginal dryness. • If you have more than one partner or are divorced or widowed and have started a new sexual relationship, have your partner wear a condom to protect against sexually transmitted infections (STIs).	See your doctor if: • You have problems that make it hard for you to enjoy an active sex life • You have pain during sex
Sleep problems Older women still need between 7 and 9 hours of sleep each night to stay healthy and alert. But sleep problems are more common with age.	• Try to avoid daytime napping, which can keep you from getting a restful night's sleep. • Practice good sleep habits. (See page 28 in the *Heart Disease* chapter for more information.) • Avoid alcohol and caffeine before bedtime.	Talk to your doctor if: • You have trouble falling and staying asleep • You wake up many times during the night • You don't feel well-rested on wakening or feel sleepy during the day • You feel tingling or crawling in your legs that disrupts your sleep

Planning ahead

Life changes can happen quickly and without warning. To avoid making important decisions in haste or under stress, it's best to plan ahead. Some issues you should discuss with loved ones include:

- **Your health and health care.** Discuss your health insurance and health care options, including long-term care.

- **Where to live.** Think about health conditions you have that might affect your independence as you age. Talk to your family about your wishes, should you need help from a caregiver.

- **End-of-life issues.** Make sure your will is up to date, and advance directives are in place. Advance directives are instructions that direct a person's medical care should she become unable to do so herself. You might also want to give someone you trust the power to act in your place, should you be too sick to do so. Make sure your important papers are organized and in one place, and let family members know where to find them.

Living a healthy lifestyle, becoming informed, and planning ahead are steps you can take now to help make your golden years among the best of your life. ∎

One Woman's Story

I was born 65 years ago into a hardworking, Midwestern, German immigrant, meat-and-potatoes family. I grew up mowing the lawn, shoveling snow, tilling the garden, hanging out laundry, picking fruit in orchards that my father had painstakingly nurtured, and bagging and carrying groceries at the small grocery store my parents owned. It wasn't until I chose a more sedate career as a college faculty member that "physical activity" became a yes-or-no decision.

I'm blessed with good health and see keeping fit as an opportunity to enjoy the wonders that surround me, wherever they may be. So over the years, my husband and I have hiked some of the most beautiful trails in the Oregon Cascades and the German Alps, fished in pure Wyoming mountain streams, biked scenic trails in nearly a dozen states, and tried in vain to ski as well as our kids. In my 40s and 50s, I ran local road races and would still be doing so if the cartilage in my right knee hadn't worn away. Instead, today I go to a gym 5 days a week to get my physical activity.

> **I make sure to also get the other regular screening tests and exams that I need for my age.**

Regrettably, my family history can't be denied—the same stock that gave me physical strength and spiritual and emotional optimism also brings a genetic history of heart problems that claimed the lives of most of my family members before the age of 70.

So my doctor and I are watching my blood pressure readings, cholesterol numbers, and triglyceride levels. I make sure to also get the other regular screening tests and exams that I need for my age. We also focus on healthy food choices that are high in nutrients. The meat on our table is leaner, the chicken is skinless, the fish is broiled or baked, we choose a wide variety of vegetables, and our bread is now whole wheat. But we don't always forget about the pie—we just make sure apples are in it!

Ruth

Cumberland, Maryland

For More Information...

Office on Women's Health, HHS
200 Independence Ave SW, Room 712E
Washington, DC 20201
Web site: www.womenshealth.gov/ow
Phone number: (800) 994-9662,
(888) 220-5446 TDD

Administration on Aging, HHS
1 Massachusetts Ave
Washington, DC 20201
Web site: www.aoa.gov
www.eldercare.gov
www.longtermcare.gov
Eldercare Locator: (800) 677-1116

Centers for Medicare and Medicaid Services, HHS
7500 Security Blvd
Baltimore, MD 21244
Web site: www.cms.hhs.gov
www.medicare.gov
Phone number: (800) 633-4227,
(877) 486-2048 TTY

Healthy Aging Program, CDC
4770 Buford Highway NE, MS K-51
Atlanta, GA 30341-3717
Web site: www.cdc.gov/aging

National Institute of Neurological Disorders and Stroke, NIH
PO Box 5801
Bethesda, MD 20824
Web site: www.ninds.nih.gov
Phone number: (800) 352-9424,
(301) 468-5981 TTY

National Institute on Aging, NIH
Building 31, Room 5C27
31 Center Dr, MSC 2292
Bethesda, MD 20892
Web site: www.nia.nih.gov
Phone number: (800) 222-2225

Osteoporosis and Related Bone Diseases National Resource Center, NIH
2 AMS Circle
Bethesda, MD 20892-3676
Web site: www.niams.nih.gov/Health_Info/Bone
Phone number: (800) 624-2663

AARP
601 E St NW
Washington, DC 20049
Web site: www.aarp.org
Phone number: (888) 687-2277

The AGS Foundation for Health in Aging
350 Fifth Ave, Suite 801
New York, NY 10118
Web site: www.healthinaging.org

Alzheimer's Association
225 N Michigan Ave, Fl 17
Chicago, IL 60601-7633
Web site: www.alz.org
Phone number: (800) 272-3900,
(866) 403-3073 TDD

American College of Obstetricians and Gynecologists
409 12th St SW, PO Box 96920
Washington, DC 20090-6920
Web site: www.acog.org
Phone number: (202) 863-2518 Resource Center

The North American Menopause Society
5900 Landerbrook Dr, Suite 390
Mayfield Heights, OH 44124
Web site: www.menopause.org
Phone number: (800) 774-5342

Violence Against Women

Women of all ages and backgrounds are at risk of many different types of violence. In fact, millions of women in this country have experienced violence. Violence greatly affects the lives and health of women: the impact can last for years—even a lifetime. But there are places to turn for help, ways to protect yourself, and hope for healing and a better future.

Women at risk

Women and girls of all ages, races, cultures, religions, education levels, and sexual orientations can experience violence. Based on reported cases, U.S. women most at risk of violence are:

- American Indians/Alaskan Natives
- African Americans
- Hispanics
- girls younger than 18
- women and girls living in poverty

The impact of violence

Experiencing violence can greatly impact how you feel about yourself, relationships, and the world around you. It can affect your physical and mental health. And it can change your behavior and daily life.

No one has the right to hurt you or make you feel afraid. Do not let feelings of fear, shame, or guilt stop you from seeking help. You are not at fault, and you do not need to hide what has happened. Many people and groups are willing to help you.

Forms of Violence

Many terms are used to describe violence against women:

- Intimate partner violence
- Domestic violence
- Spouse or partner abuse
- Wife beating
- Rape, marital rape, date rape
- Family violence
- Sexual abuse, sexual violence, sexual assault
- Molestation
- Beating, battering
- Homicide, femicide
- Dating violence, dating abuse, teen dating violence
- Indecent exposure
- Voyeurism
- Stalking
- Harassment
- Human trafficking
- Genital mutilation
- Exploitation
- Forced prostitution
- Forced pornography

Effects of Violence on Women

Mental health	Women hurt by violence may have:
	• Depression
	• Low self-esteem, loss of confidence
	• Posttraumatic stress disorder (PTSD)
	• Guilt or shame
	• Shock and disbelief
	• Anxiety and panic attacks
	• Emotional numbness
	• Anger
	• Self-hate or self-blame
	• General sense of fear
	• Fear of men, being alone, going out in public, intimacy, or anything that may trigger memories of the violence
	• Suicidal thoughts
	• Sense of being worthless or without hope

The Healthy Woman: A Complete Guide for All Ages

Effects of Violence on Women

Behavior	Common actions after experiencing violence are: • Thoughts or acts of suicide or self-injury • Risky sexual behaviors, such as unprotected sex • Alcohol or drug abuse • Eating disorders • Avoiding doctor visits or making unnecessary doctor visits
Physical health	Common physical injuries and health problems from violence include: • Increased risk of sexually transmitted infections (STIs) and HIV, which can lead to pelvic inflammatory disease and a higher risk of cervical cancer • Unwanted pregnancies, or rapid, repeat pregnancies • Miscarriages and other reproductive problems • Vaginal bleeding or pelvic pain • Injuries such as bruises, cuts, broken bones, or internal damage • Back or neck pain • Chronic pain syndrome • Trouble sleeping and nightmares • High blood pressure or chest pain • Arthritis • High stress and lowered immune system • Central nervous system problems, such as headaches, seizures, or nerve damage • Respiratory problems, such as asthma and shortness of breath • Digestive problems, such as stomach ulcers and nausea
Economic	Common financial struggles due to violence are: • Loss of income from missed work or a partner who withholds money • Medical bills • Legal fees • Rent or moving costs of new housing • Extra child care and protection costs
Social	Common social issues due to violence include: • Stigma and discrimination • Trouble getting medical, social, and legal services • Strained relationships with friends and family • Social isolation (from family, friends, and others who could help)

Impact on children

Violence against women can also impact children. About 50 percent of men who assault their wives also physically abuse their children. Also, women who are abused are more likely to abuse their children. And children can be injured during violence between their parents.

Studies show children who witness or experience violence at home may have long-term physical, emotional, and social problems. They are also more likely to experience or commit violence in the future. Protect your children by getting help for yourself.

Common forms of violence

Although women often fear being attacked or hurt by a stranger, they are at greatest risk of violence from people they know:

- About 25 to 30 percent of women are physically or sexually abused by a romantic partner.

- One in 6 women reports being raped or sexually assaulted in her lifetime. And nearly 70 percent are attacked by someone they know. (Research has shown that most women do not report their rapes to police, so the actual number of women raped may be much higher.)

- Around 1 million women are stalked each year, most often by someone they know, such as an ex-husband, ex-boyfriend, or peer.

This chapter focuses on three types of common violence against women:

- intimate partner violence
- sexual violence
- stalking

Intimate partner violence (IPV)

IPV can be a one-time event or a pattern of physical, sexual, or psychological harm by a current or former partner or spouse. It happens in both heterosexual and same-sex couples. And it can happen in nonsexual relationships. Teen dating violence has many of the same risk factors, warning signs, and effects as IPV.

The Healthy Woman: A Complete Guide for All Ages

Forms of IPV	
Physical violence or threats	Your partner may: • Hurt or threaten you, possibly with a weapon • Become violent after alcohol or drug use • Destroy your things
Sexual abuse or threats	Your partner may: • Force you to have sex or be sexual in other ways • Threaten to rape or hurt you sexually
Psychological/emotional abuse	IPV often starts with emotional abuse, then leads to physical violence. Your partner may: • Control who you spend time with, where you go, and what you do • Trace your phone calls • Insult you and get angry about small things • Accuse you of cheating • Make fun of you • Control how you spend your money or refuse to give you money • Act jealous when you spend time with friends • Blame you for his or her violence • Use your children to manipulate you • Follow you when you go out • Try to make you afraid

IPV is never okay, even if it only happens once in a while. It can be hard to admit you are in an abusive relationship or find a way out. But if your partner is hurting you, it is time to get help.

Many abused women stay with their partner out of fear or because they do not see a way out. Others stay because they love their partner and believe he or she will change. But the longer the abuse goes on, the more damage it can cause. Whether you decide to leave your partner or stay, make a safety plan in case IPV happens again. (See page 241 for "Planning Ahead.")

If you leave, plan ahead for legal, medical, and emotional support, because IPV can escalate even after leaving a partner.

You may even need help from police and women's shelters. They can help you find ways to protect yourself and your children.

- If you are in immediate danger, call 911.
- For 24-hour help and support, call the National Domestic Violence Hotline toll-free number listed in the resource section on page 249.

Preventing IPV

Help prevent IPV in your own life by seeking and building healthy relationships. Below are some signs of healthy and unhealthy relationships.

IPV and Pregnancy

IPV can affect the health of the mother and unborn baby. Abuse from a partner may begin, or increase, during pregnancy and can lead to:

- low-birth-weight babies and other health risks
- death of unborn and newborn babies
- homicide, which is the second leading cause of traumatic death for pregnant women and mothers with newborns

Signs of a healthy relationship	Signs of an unhealthy relationship
• Respect for each other	• Disrespect
• Honesty	• Blaming and lying
• Trust and support	• Mistrust and jealousy
• Able to compromise	• Put-downs, insults, name calling
• Shared decision making	• One partner controls decision making
• You are able to be yourself	• "Need" to be with partner; cannot be without the other
• Time spent together and apart	• Fear of partner's temper or actions
• Good communication	• Partner pressures or forces other to be sexual
• Peaceful solutions to conflict	• Fights get out of control
• Anger control	• Feeling worthless or bad about yourself
• Self-confidence and happiness	• Feeling unsafe with your partner
• Feeling safe with partner, even when he or she is upset	

Early warning signs of IPV

If your partner displays one or more of the early signs below, get help early to prevent future IPV. If you start dating someone who displays warning signs, think twice about getting involved.

Does your partner or person you date:

- Get jealous when you spend time with other people?
- Act possessive?
- Have low self-esteem?
- Act aggressive?
- Create conflict, use put-downs, or argue a lot?
- Mistreat animals?
- Abuse drugs or alcohol?
- Have poor relationships with others?
- React badly to stress?
- Have extreme emotional highs and lows?

- Have a quick temper and lots of anger?
- Punch walls or throw things when angry?
- Need to be in control of the relationship?
- Have a history of bad relationships?

Highest risks of IPV

You cannot always predict whether your partner will become violent. But studies show some traits increase the risk of someone becoming violent with their partner. These traits include:

- abusing drugs or alcohol
- thinking violence in a relationship is all right
- strict beliefs about traditional gender roles
- having a lot of anger or hostility
- a history of partner abuse
- depression
- career or life stress, such as not having a job
- having been a victim of, or exposed to, violence as a child

Planning Ahead

If you are being abused, create a safety plan. Contact the National Domestic Violence Hotline for help.

A few ways to prepare are to:

- Plan all possible escape routes from your home.
- Know your partner's "red flags"; leave the house if you sense your partner will become violent.
- Avoid fights in rooms without access to a door or where weapons are kept.
- Find a safe place to go if you are in danger—family, friends, a shelter.
- Get a court protective order.
- Memorize emergency numbers.
- Have money available—cash kept with a friend, a separate savings account, a credit card.
- Teach your children not to get in the middle of a fight between you and your partner.
- Have a cell phone or calling card handy; do not use your home phone or cell phone to call for help if your partner can trace the numbers.
- Create a signal to use with friends and family to alert them to danger.
- Have access to important items such as extra car keys, a driver's license, social security number, checkbook, address book or a list of important numbers, health insurance card, passport, immigration papers, copies of birth certificates for you and your children, school and medical records, and children's favorite toys.
- Keep copies of important papers and items (including a change of clothes) with a trusted friend or relative.

Leaving an abusive partner takes courage, support, and planning. But it is possible. For your safety and the safety of your children, talk about your options with an IPV counselor before you leave. If the IPV is mild or has just started, get professional help before it gets worse. If you choose to stay with your partner, the abuse may get worse over time—even if you get help. So have a safety plan ready.

You cannot change your partner by loving him or her more, by changing yourself, or by hoping he or she will change if you wait it out. Your partner needs to get help, but even that may not stop the abuse. A relationship should not leave you feeling scared, depressed, hopeless, worthless, or in danger. You deserve to be safe and treated well. If the abuse continues, help is just a phone call away.

Sexual violence

Sexual violence is *all* completed or attempted sexual contact or behavior that happens without your clear, voluntary consent. No one has the right to make you be sexual, including your partner. Sexual violence can shatter a woman's life in an instant. And it can take years to emotionally heal from the experience.

Sexual violence includes:

- Improper and unwanted touching, kissing, fondling, and groping.

- Sexual assault, such as rape or attempted rape (vaginal, oral, or anal). This includes sex when the victim is drunk, unconscious, or unable to give willing consent. It also includes unwanted sex with a partner, spouse, or date.

- Verbal, visual, or other noncontact sexual actions that force a person to join in unwanted sexual contact or attention. This includes flashing of sexual

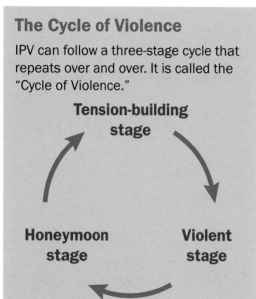

The Cycle of Violence

IPV can follow a three-stage cycle that repeats over and over. It is called the "Cycle of Violence."

Tension-building stage

Honeymoon stage

Violent stage

1. **Tension-building stage:** Tension builds over time and may include "minor" incidents such as pushing or threats. To delay movement to stage two the victim may act passive, "stay out of the way," and avoid making the partner upset.

2. **Violent stage:** Tension explodes, resulting in severe abuse.

3. **Honeymoon stage:** The abuser apologizes, promises to stop the abuse, and often is very loving for a while. The abuser may feel sorry about the abuse, promise to stop and get help, and show regret and extra kindness. The victim then feels loved and believes the violence will end. The cycle then repeats.

In time, the honeymoon stage may get shorter, and the tension-building and violent stages longer.

Elder Abuse

Elder abuse is doing something, or failing to do something, that causes harm or risks harm to a vulnerable older adult. Nearly 90 percent of the abusers are family members, most often adult children or spouses. Elder abuse also happens in places such as nursing homes and hospitals. Among the elderly, women ages 80 and older are at highest risk for being abused or neglected.

Elder abuse includes:

- physical, sexual, or emotional abuse
- financial abuse such as taking or misusing an elderly person's money or property, or tricking her into spending or investing money
- ignoring or abandoning an elderly person under your care

If you think an elderly person you know is being abused, please tell someone. Call your local adult protective services, long-term care ombudsman, or the police.

If you are being abused, you can:

- Tell someone you trust, such as a doctor or friend.
- Call the U.S. Administration on Aging's Eldercare Locator toll-free number listed in the resource section on page 249 to find a local agency that can help.
- Contact your state or local adult protective services (APS).

body parts, being shown pornography, and verbal or written sexual harassment.

Sexual violence can happen anywhere—on a date, at a party, at work, at home, or in public. The attacker may be a stranger or someone you know, such as a partner, family member, or peer. In fact, in 8 of 10 rape cases, the victims know their rapist.

Survivors may feel shame or guilt. But you are never at fault—even if you didn't fight back or say no because of fear or shock. You are *never* to blame for someone else's violence.

If you are a survivor of sexual violence, professional help and support groups are available. Even if the abuse or assault is from childhood, it may still deeply af-

fect you. You are not alone, and you do not need to hide what happened. Silence only gives the abuser more power. Help stop sexual violence by healing yourself, speaking out, and supporting other survivors.

Sexual Violence: Risk Factors

Risk factors for experiencing sexual violence	• Young age—more than half of all rapes occur before age 18 • Drug or alcohol abuse • Having experienced past sexual violence • Living in poverty • Having risky sex, such as unprotected sex, sex with many partners, and/or sex at a young age
Risk factors for becoming sexually violent	• Alcohol and drug abuse • Fantasies about forced sex (rape) • Impulsive and antisocial behavior • Preference for impersonal sex • Hostility toward women • Extreme male stereotyped behaviors • Sexual and physical abuse as a child • Witnessed family violence as a child

Getting help after a sexual assault

Take steps right away if you've been assaulted:

• Get away from the attacker and find a safe place as fast as you can. Call 911 and report the crime.

• Call a friend or family member you trust. Or call a crisis center or a hotline, such as the National Sexual Assault Hotline toll-free number listed in the resource section on page 249.

• Do not wash, comb, or clean any part of your body. Do not change clothes if possible, so the hospital staff can collect evidence. Do not touch or change anything at the crime scene.

• Go to your nearest hospital emergency room right away. You need to be examined and treated for injuries.

• Ask if the hospital has a Sexual Assault Nurse Examiner (SANE) who can perform your exam and provide emotional support. She will collect evidence using a rape kit to find fibers, hairs, saliva, semen, or clothing the attacker may have left behind.

• You will be screened for sexually transmitted infections, offered counseling, or given other treatment.

- Most hospitals will offer emergency contraception pills to help prevent pregnancy. If it is not offered, you can request it.
- The hospital staff can call the police and contact a rape crisis center counselor.

Ways to protect yourself

To reduce your risk of sexual violence:

- Trust your feelings. If you feel in danger, you probably are and need to get away.
- Notice what and who is around you. Know where you are going and stay in well-lit areas. Park your car in well-lit areas.
- After getting in your car, drive away. Do not sit in your car to look at items you bought or make phone calls.
- If you are in danger, blow a whistle, or yell "FIRE" instead of "help" or "rape."
- Never leave a social event with someone you just met or do not know well.
- Never walk or jog alone at night or in secluded areas.
- Meet new dates in public places. Be careful when meeting people from Internet dating sites. Tell a friend where you are going and who you are going out with.
- Never drink anything that has been out of your sight, or that you did not see being poured from a new bottle. Date rape drugs are odorless and tasteless.
- Avoid parties where a lot of alcohol may be served, such as fraternity events. Control your drinking at events.
- Keep your car and home doors locked. Lock home windows. Install home security.
- Go out in groups and have friends watch out for each other.
- Offer help to other women who may be in danger.

Stalking

Stalking is a pattern of repeated, unwanted attention, harassment, or contact that directly or indirectly communicates a threat or scares a person.

Stalkers may:

- follow or wait for you in certain places
- appear at your home or work
- sit outside your home
- make harassing phone calls
- leave written messages or objects

Cyberstalking

Cyberstalking is use of the Internet, e-mail, or other forms of online communications to stalk another person. It can include:

- harassment or threats in chat rooms
- e-mail, instant messages (IM), or text message threats and harassment
- improper messages on a message board or in a guest book
- tracing your computer and Internet use
- obscene or improper e-mail messages or photo attachments
- sending electronic viruses
- someone pretending to be you in a chat room

If you are cyberstalked:

- Log off right away and stay off-line for at least 24 hours.
- Send the person a clear, written warning to stop harassing you and to never contact you again.
- If the harassment continues, do not respond to anything the person writes. It gives them a sense of power and can increase the stalking.

- damage or steal your things
- harass you through the Internet, e-mail, or chat rooms
- use a hidden camera to watch you
- use computer software and hardware tools to track and harass you
- send gifts or love letters
- call all the time

Stalking is illegal, yet 1 in 12 women will be stalked in their lifetimes. It is a crime that can be hard to prove, harder to stop, and difficult to get others to take seriously. Yet 76 percent of women killed by their intimate partners were first stalked by them.

Most victims are stalked for about 1.8 years. These women often feel helpless, anxious, and depressed. They often have nightmares; feel out of control; have trouble sleeping, eating, and concentrating; and live with constant fear. Stalking can also cause financial problems if fear or depression keeps a woman from going to work.

Steps to take if you are being stalked:

- Trust your instincts. If you are, or think you may be, in danger, find a safe place to go, such as a police station, fire station, or public area.
- Plan in advance what you will do if you are in danger.
- If you cannot get out of danger, but can get to a phone, call 911.
- Get a restraining order. If the order does not stop the stalker, call a violence hotline for advice (toll-free numbers are listed in the resource section on page 249.)

- Change your online identity and all of the information in your IM or chat profile.
- Change your e-mail address and Internet service provider (ISP).
- For e-mail stalking, contact the person's ISP and file a complaint.
- Keep all e-mails or log files from the stalker for evidence.

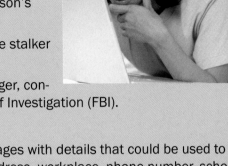

- If you think you are in physical danger, contact the police or Federal Bureau of Investigation (FBI).

Be safe online:
- Never post online profiles or messages with details that could be used to identify or locate you (such as age, sex, address, workplace, phone number, school, teams you play on, or places you hang out).
- Do not post photos on a site that can be accessed by the public, such as in a MySpace profile, online dating profile, chat group, or blog.
- Do not tell anyone your online ID or passwords.

- Take threats seriously. File a complaint with the police. If they cannot help, call a violence hotline for advice. Until the stalkers do something they can be arrested for, police can only talk to them.

- Collect evidence for police. Record every incident. Include the time, date, and other important information.

- Keep videotapes, audiotapes, answering machine/voicemail messages, e-mail messages, photos of the person outside your home or workplace, property damage, and any letters or e-mail.

- Cut off all contact with the stalker.

- Carry a cell phone at all times.

- Secure your home with alarms and motion-sensitive lights.

- Keep your garage and car locked. Check around you before getting in the car. Get a locking gas cap. Know safe locations you can drive to if being followed, and stay in the car and blow your horn to get attention when you stop.

- Get help. Tell police, your employer, and family, friends, and neighbors about the stalking.

Violence against women is a serious threat to health and well-being. Yet you can take important steps to reduce your risk of violence. If you have experienced violence, there are people who can help you heal emotionally and safely move on with your life. The first step is to ask for help. If you or someone you know is experiencing violence, contact the resources listed in "For more information" or talk with someone you trust. No one deserves to be hurt.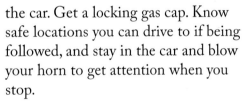

One Woman's Story

When I started a new job in a different state, it was hard for me to meet new people and make friends. I became very lonely, so I turned to the Internet for help. I discovered that through online dating sites, I could easily find men willing to meet me and buy me drinks. I enjoyed the company and attention; each time I met a new person was exciting, and it made me feel attractive, sexy. I became addicted to that feeling. While at first I was cautious about meeting them in person, I later became less concerned about my own personal safety. I ignored the horror stories I heard about women disappearing or being murdered by someone they met on the Internet. All I wanted was that next time when I would get dressed up, go out with someone new, and feel on top of the world. I was blessedly lucky—at first.

I met Joe online (his name has been changed), and even though he lived 2 hours away, we arranged to meet at a halfway point. I missed all the warning signs from the start. He had me meet him at a gas station where we left his car and took mine. We went to a club, and I drank too much to drive home safely. He said he would pay for a hotel and promised he would not try anything sexual. I trusted him. He did not keep his promise, no matter how many times I said STOP. I should

Don't let anything come before your personal safety.

have screamed at the top of my lungs. I should have kicked him. I should have left and never looked back. But all I kept thinking was, "This only happens to people I hear about in the news, not me. Maybe this is my fault. Did I bring this upon myself?" I should have kicked and screamed and MADE him stop. But I didn't want to make a scene. I didn't want to drive home drunk. I didn't want to strand him there with his car halfway across town. I lay there and cried. He asked what was wrong and I told him, "You RAPED me." He denied it and made me feel like an idiot. I never reported him.

The next morning I cursed myself all the way home for being so stupid. It took a lot of time and therapy to realize that, although it was stupid to put myself in such a dangerous situation, what happened to me was not my fault. Even now it's hard to believe that. The point of this story is not to scare anyone out of online dating. Years later I signed up for online dating again—my sense of personal safety and self-esteem intact—and I met the man of my dreams. The important thing to remember is this: don't let anything come before your personal safety. And don't be afraid to scream like crazy and cause a scene. You are worth it.

Lisa

San Diego, California

For More Information...

Office on Women's Health, HHS
200 Independence Ave SW, Room 712E
Washington, DC 20201
Web site: www.womenshealth.gov/
violence
Phone number: (800) 994-9662,
(888) 220-5446 TDD

Administration on Aging, HHS
1 Massachusetts Ave
Washington, DC 20201
Web site: www.eldercare.gov
Eldercare Locator: (800) 677-1116

National Center on Elder Abuse, AOA
c/o Center for Community Research and
Services
University of Delaware
297 Graham Hall
Newark, DE 19716
Web site: www.ncea.aoa.gov
Phone number: (302) 831-3525 for
information on elder abuse,
(800) 677-1116 to find help in your state

**Office for Victims of Crime Resource
Center, DOJ**
PO Box 6000
Rockville, MD 20849-6000
Web site: www.ojp.usdoj.gov/ovc/ovcres
Phone number: (800) 851-3420

**National Center for Victims of Crime and
the Stalking Resource Center**
2000 M St NW, Suite 480
Washington, DC 20036
Web site: www.ncvc.org
Phone number: (800) 394-2255,
(800) 211-7996 TTY/TDD

National Domestic Violence Hotline
PO Box 161810
Austin, TX 78716
Web site: www.ndvh.org
Phone number: (800) 799-7233,
(800) 787-3224 TTY

National Teen Dating Abuse Hotline
Web site: www.loveisrespect.org
Phone number: (866) 331-9474,
(866) 331-8453 TTY

**Rape, Abuse and Incest National
Network and the National Sexual Assault
Hotline**
2000 L St NW, Suite 406
Washington, DC 20036
Web site: www.rainn.org
Phone number: (800) 656-4673

Urologic and Kidney Health

Do you ever leak urine when you sneeze or cough? Have you ever had a urinary tract infection or kidney stone? Do you need to urinate dozens of times a day? Are you at risk of kidney disease? If you answer yes to any of these questions, you are not alone. Urologic and kidney problems are common in women. They can impact your daily life, physical activity, pregnancy, sexual relations, social life, and future health. But most conditions can be treated and, in some cases, cured.

How a woman's urinary system works

The urinary system is made up of two kidneys, two ureters, the bladder, two sphincter muscles, and the urethra.

- **Kidneys:** Fist-sized, bean-shaped organs that produce urine. They are near the middle of your back, right below your rib cage.

- **Ureters** (YOOR-uh-turz): Thin tubes that take urine from your kidneys to your bladder.

- **Bladder:** A balloon-shaped organ that stores urine.

- **Sphincter** (SFEENK-tur) **muscles**: Round muscles that open and close to let fluid pass in or out of an organ. They keep your bladder closed until it is time to urinate.

- **Urethra** (yoo-REE-thruh): A tube that carries urine out of your body.

The organs, tubes, and muscles in this system all work together to create, store, and move urine out of the body.

What does "urologic" mean?

"Urologic" refers to the field of urology. Urology deals with the urinary system, also called the urinary tract.

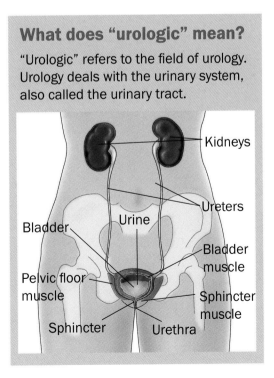

Labels: Kidneys, Ureters, Urine, Bladder, Bladder muscle, Pelvic floor muscle, Sphincter muscle, Sphincter, Urethra

Signs of urologic problems

Common symptoms of urologic problems include:

- pain or "burning" when you urinate
- bladder control problems such as leaking urine, dribbling urine after going to the bathroom, and having frequent or intense urges to urinate
- bloody urine
- cloudy, dark, or strong-smelling urine
- a change in your urine color
- having a weak stream of urine
- long-term pressure or pain in your pelvis or lower abdomen
- long-term pain in the back or sides

What to do about urologic or kidney problems

See a doctor right away. You may feel awkward talking about urologic problems, but don't ignore them. Symptoms may worsen over time if the problem isn't treated. See your primary doctor, a urologist, a urogynecologist, or a nephrologist for help. A urologist is an expert in urine and bladder problems. A urogynecologist is an expert in women's urine and bladder issues. A nephrologist is a kidney specialist.

The doctor will ask about your health history and perform a physical exam to look for problems or abnormalities in your urinary tract. After the exam, medical tests may be ordered.

Common urologic and kidney conditions in women

The most common urologic conditions among women are:

Keeping a Bladder Diary

If one of your symptoms is loss of bladder control, start a bladder diary and share it with your doctor. The details can help your doctor make the right diagnosis. In a bladder diary, you track the following by the hour:

- how much you drink
- what you drink
- how many times you urinate
- how much you urinate
- urine leakage or strong urges to urinate
- what you were doing when you had a leak or a strong urge (such as physical activity, laughing, or sitting)

- urinary tract infections
- urinary incontinence

Also common are:

- interstitial cystitis/painful bladder syndrome
- urinary stones
- urinary system cancers

The most serious kidney condition is chronic kidney disease.

Urinary tract infections

Nearly 53 percent of women will have at least one urinary tract infection (UTI) at some point in life. UTIs are serious and often painful. But most are simple to treat. You need to see your doctor for treatment.

Understanding UTIs

What is a UTI?	An infection in the urinary tract
Causes	Most are caused by bacteria that enter the tract through the urethra.
Risk factors	• Being sexually active • Previous UTIs • Being pregnant • Being postmenopausal • Using a tube (catheter) in the bladder • Having a kidney stone • Having a weak immune system • Using a diaphragm or spermicide for birth control
Symptoms	• A "burning" or pain when you urinate • Pain in your back, sides, or lower belly • Frequent or intense urges to urinate • Trouble urinating • Passing only small amounts of urine • Bloody urine • Dark, cloudy, or strong-smelling urine • Chills or fever
Diagnosis	• **Urine tests:** A clean urine sample is tested for signs of infection and the kind of bacteria causing any infection. For UTIs that come back, the doctor may use: • **Images of the urinary tract:** x-rays, ultrasound, or a computed tomography (tuh-MOG-ruh-fee) (CT) scan • **A cystoscopy** (siss-TOSS-kuh-pee)**:** a thin tube with lenses and a light used to look inside the bladder
Treatment	• Most are treated with antibiotics. • Drink plenty of water to help the antibiotics clear your body of bacteria.
Prevention	• Drink plenty of water each day (6–8 glasses). • Urinate when you feel the urge. • Use underpants or pads designed to collect urine instead of an inserted catheter. • After using the bathroom, always wipe front to back. • Urinate after having sex. • Avoid using spermicides or diaphragms if they cause you to have UTIs. • Avoid feminine hygiene products such as deodorant sprays, douches, and powders.
Impact on pregnancy	• If you are pregnant and think you have a UTI, see a doctor right away. A UTI can lead to premature delivery and other health risks. • Not all antibiotics can be taken during pregnancy. Your doctor will select the right treatment for you.

Urinary incontinence

Women of all ages have bladder control problems. These problems are called urinary incontinence (UI).

UI is the most common urologic issue among women:

- Between ages 18 and 44, about 24 percent of women have UI.
- More than 13 million Americans experience UI.
- Women are twice as likely to have UI as men.

For many women, UI is minor. For others, it affects their whole lives. Severe UI can lead to infections, skin problems, and sleep disruption. Women with UI might

also avoid social events, feel depressed, avoid having sex, stop traveling, and reduce physical activities.

One survey showed that most women live with UI symptoms for 6.5 years before getting help. Don't wait. Most UI can be improved, and sometimes cured.

Understanding UI

Types of UI and their causes	**Stress:** Slight urine leakage during physical movement. It often happens when you are physically active, sneeze, laugh, cough, or lift something heavy.
	It is caused by weak pelvic floor muscles (which support the bladder). Physical changes resulting from pregnancy, childbirth, and menopause often cause stress on these muscles. A cystocele (SISS-toh-seel), rectocele (REK-toh-seel), or fibroids (FEYE-broidz) can also lead to UI.
	• Cystocele occurs when the wall between the vagina and bladder weakens and the bladder sags into the vagina.
	• Rectocele occurs when the front wall of the rectum bulges into the vagina.
	• Fibroids are noncancerous tumors that grow in the muscle wall of the uterus.
	Stress UI is more common in Caucasian women than African American or Hispanic women.
	Urge, sometimes called overactive bladder: Frequent, strong, and sudden urges to urinate, even when the bladder isn't full. It can cause you to leak a lot of urine without warning, such as during sleep. Causes include overactive bladder muscles and damage to bladder nerves and bladder muscles.
	Functional: When someone has a problem thinking, moving, or communicating, which prevents them from reaching a toilet or from knowing when the bladder is full. Problems can include spinal cord injuries, being immobile, wheelchair use, or Alzheimer's disease.
	Overflow: Urine leakage due to a full bladder. It is caused when the bladder doesn't fully empty. It is rare in women.
	Mixed: A mix of types—most often stress and urge.
	Transient: UI that comes and goes because of a temporary problem.

Understanding UI

Diagnosis	Ways your doctor may diagnose UI: **Medical history and symptoms:** Your bladder diary will come in handy at this point. **A physical exam.** **Urodynamic** (YOOR-oh-deye-NAM-ihk) **tests:** They measure how much urine your bladder can hold and release. **Stress test:** You cough strongly and the doctor looks for urine loss. **Urine tests:** Urine is checked with a microscope for signs of infection and the type of bacteria that may be present. **Cystoscopy:** A thin tube with a camera on it is put in the urethra to see inside the urethra and bladder. **Ultrasound:** Sound waves make images of your urinary tract.
Treatment	Your treatment will depend on which type of UI you have. Treatment may include some or all of these options: **Pelvic muscle exercises:** Used to strengthen pelvic floor muscles, including Kegel exercises. (See page 256 for information on how to do Kegel exercises.) **Bladder retraining:** Used to increase bladder control. You track the times when you leak or urinate, then plan in advance when you will go to the bathroom. You gradually increase the time between urinating. **Medicines:** Some help relax or tighten sphincter muscles; some help stop bladder contractions. **Electrical stimulation:** Small doses of electric pulses can make pelvic muscles stronger. These pulses can be given through the vagina or by using patches on the skin. **Pessary** (PESS-uh-ree): A removable device put in the vagina to help support vaginal walls and pelvic muscles. **Implants/Injections:** Substances that add bulk to tissues around the urethra to help close it and stop UI. **Implanted devices:** A device is placed in the lower back to send mild electrical pulses to the nerves. **Surgery:** If the bladder droops into the vagina (cystocele), it can be pulled back into place with surgery. **Biofeedback:** Bladder training that uses electronic devices to help you learn to control the bladder muscles. **Catheter:** A tube put into the urethra to drain urine. It is used when the bladder can't empty due to physical or nerve damage. **Weight loss:** Helps with some cases of UI. **Diet changes:** Certain foods and drinks may increase your need to urinate, such as coffee, alcohol, and caffeinated drinks. **If you smoke, quit:** It can irritate the bladder, make UI worse, and lead to chronic coughing. **Absorbent underwear or bulky pads:** Used to catch leaking urine.

How to Do Kegel Exercises

This simple exercise helps make your pelvic floor muscles stronger.

First, find the right muscles. Your doctor, nurse, or physical therapist can help make sure you are doing the exercises the right way.

1. Try to stop the flow of urine when you are sitting on the toilet. If you can do it, you are using the right muscles.

2. Imagine that you are trying to stop passing gas. Squeeze the muscles you would use. If you sense a "pulling" feeling, those are the right muscles for pelvic exercises.

3. Lie down and put your finger inside your vagina. Squeeze as if you were trying to stop urine from coming out. If you feel tightness on your finger, you are squeezing the right muscles.

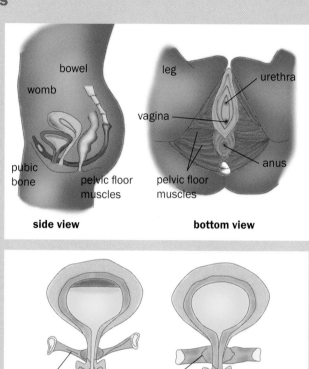

Don't squeeze other muscles at the same time. Be careful not to tighten your stomach, legs, or other muscles or it can put more pressure on your bladder control muscles.

Repeat, but don't overdo it. Find a quiet spot to practice. Lie on the floor. Pull in the pelvic muscles and hold for a count of 3. Then relax for a count of 3. Work up to 10 to 15 repeats each time you exercise.

Do your pelvic exercises at least three times a day. Use three positions for the best results: lying down, sitting, and standing.

Be patient. It may take 3 to 6 weeks to notice any change in bladder control.

Understanding Cystocele

Cystocele (SISS-toh-seel) is also called fallen bladder. It occurs when the wall between the bladder and the vagina weakens and allows the bladder to droop into the vagina. Some studies have shown African American women to have the lowest risk of cystocele and Hispanic women to have the highest.

Common causes of cystocele are:

- childbirth: Labor and delivery can weaken the muscles and ligaments that support and hold the vagina in place.
- strain from lifting heavy objects
- constipation and straining with bowel movements
- lack of estrogen after menopause that weakens vaginal and bladder muscles
- being overweight or obese
- heavy, long-term coughing

Interstitial cystitis/painful bladder syndrome

Interstitial cystitis (IN-tur-STISH-uhl siss-TEYE-tiss) (IC) is a condition that causes frequent discomfort or pain in the bladder and pelvic region. Symptoms vary from case to case and even in the same woman. You may feel mild discomfort, pressure, tenderness, or intense pain in the bladder and pelvic area. The pain level may change as the bladder fills with urine or as it empties. Women's symptoms often get worse during their periods. It is also called painful bladder syndrome (PBS).

IC/PBS can severely impact daily life and lead to feelings of depression and frustration. It can cause a woman to urinate up to 60 times a day. The urge to urinate can be sudden and intense. It may feel also as if you have a full bladder most of the time, which is painful and uncomfortable.

Women with IC/PBS may want to be near a bathroom at all times. They may avoid travel and social activities. They may avoid sex because it causes pain or they worry about having to urinate often. Some women with IC/PBS have fewer symptoms during pregnancy. Others have more symptoms. Research has not shown that IC/PBS affects fertility or the health of a fetus.

Currently, around 1.2 million American women are estimated to have IC/PBS.

Understanding IC/PBS

Causes	The cause(s) of IC/PBS is still unknown. Research is ongoing.
Symptoms	• Urinary frequency • Urinary urgency • Long-term pain, pressure, or discomfort in the bladder and pelvis • Pain when having sex • Ulcers in the walls of the bladder
Diagnosis	Opinions still differ about how and when IC/PBS can be diagnosed. Getting the right diagnosis can take years, because no single test can be used to diagnose IC/PBS. Your doctor will rule out other problems and diseases using: • **Physical exam** • **Urine tests** to rule out infection and other health problems • **Cystoscopy** with **hydrodistension** (HEYE-droh-diss-ten-shuhn) slows stretching of the bladder with liquid. This relieves symptoms in some women. • **Bladder biopsy** Many other ways to diagnose IC/PBS are being studied.
Treatment	So far there is no cure for IC/PBS. Current treatment aims to reduce symptoms, lower pain levels, and improve quality of life. Many treatments can be used at once. Treatments include: • **Bladder instillations.** The bladder is filled with water or medicine. It can help stretch the bladder and may help lessen pain. • **Certain medicines** • **Over-the-counter** pain killers and acid reducers • **Nerve stimulation** with electric pulses. It helps reduce pelvic pain in some women. • **Bladder training** to better control when you urinate • **Pelvic floor physical therapy** to make pelvic floor muscles stronger • **Surgery**, which is the last resort. Options include making the bladder larger, removing the bladder, putting electrodes into the body for permanent nerve stimulation, and burning or cutting out any ulcers. Dozens of new treatments are being researched.
Coping with IC	• Keep a bladder diary. Avoid foods or drinks that seem to increase your symptoms (such as acidic fruits, spicy foods, tomatoes, and coffee). • Learn gentle stretching exercises. • Get emotional support if you need it. (See the resource section on page 263.) • Learn stress reduction techniques. • If you smoke, quit. • Learn bladder training methods to reduce how often you need to empty your bladder.

Urinary stones

Urinary stones may form in the kidneys, bladder, or ureters. Kidney stones are the most common type. About 5 percent of women will have had at least one stone by age 70.

Understanding Urinary Stones	
What is a urinary stone?	A urinary stone is a hard mass created from substances in urine.
Causes	The four main types of stones and their causes are: • **Calcium:** These are the most common stones. They come from excess calcium in the body. They are made of calcium and oxalate (OKS-uh-layt). • **Struvite** (STROO-vyt): These may come from having an infection, such as UTI. • **Uric** (YOOR-ihk) **acid**: These are less common. They most often stem from chemotherapy, a high-protein diet, or an inheritable disorder. • **Cystine** (SISS-teen): These are rare. They are caused by a hereditary disease.
Risk factors	Your chance of getting a stone is higher if you: • Do not drink enough water and other fluids • Have had a stone before • Have certain diseases that can lead to stones, such as renal tubular acidosis (ASS-uh-DOH-suhss) and irritable bowel syndrome • Take certain medicines • Eat a high-protein diet • Are in your 50s Stones are more common in Caucasian women than in African American women.
Symptoms	• Long-term pain in your back, side, or groin • Blood in the urine • Fever and chills • Urine that smells bad or looks cloudy • "Burning" when you urinate • Vomiting (when combined with the other symptoms above)
Diagnosis	• CT scan • X-rays • Ultrasound • Intravenous pyelogram (IHN-truh-VEE-nuhss PEYE-el-oh-GRAM) (IVP): x-rays where dye is put in the body to better see the kidneys
Treatment	• Drink 2–3 quarts of water in 24 hours. The stone may move on its own with enough fluid. For stones that persist, treatment options include: • Shock waves used to break up the stone, called lithotripsy (LITH-oh-TRIP-see) • A small tool with a camera put on it—a ureteroscope (yoo-REE-tur-oh-skohp)—can be put through the urethra and bladder and into the ureter to remove the stone. • Tunnel surgery, where a tunnel is made through the back to the kidney to take out the stone.

Urologic and Kidney Health

Understanding Urinary Stones

Prevention of future stones	To find out what kind of stone you had and prevent future stones: • Your stone will be tested. • Your blood will be tested. • A 24-hour urine sample will be tested. Prevention tips depend on the type of stone you have. Options include: • Drink enough water to produce 2 or more quarts of urine a day—about 12 full glasses of water. • Drink fluid with lots of citrate (such as lemonade). • For a uric acid stone, eat a low-protein diet. • For a calcium stone, eat fewer foods with oxalate (such as chocolate, coffee, nuts, cola, and spinach). • For a calcium stone, avoid calcium pills, but eat enough foods that have calcium naturally to keep your bones healthy. • Take certain medicine prescribed by your doctor.

Kidney disorders

Chronic kidney disease

Many kidney disorders exist, and the most serious is chronic kidney disease (CKD). CKD is the permanent loss of kidney function.

If you are at risk of, or have, CKD, take steps to prevent or slow down kidney failure. After all, 26 million Americans—1 in 8 American adults—already have CKD, and millions more are at increased risk of developing it.

Understanding CKD

What is CKD?	CKD is a slow and, most often, permanent loss of kidney function. Over time—months to years—CKD may lead to total kidney failure.
Causes	CKD may come from a physical injury or disease that damages the kidneys, such as polycystic kidney disease. Damaged kidneys do not remove wastes and extra water from the blood in the way they should. Diabetes and high blood pressure are the most common causes of CKD. In fact, diabetes leads to 45 percent of new cases.
Risk factors	• A family history of CKD • Heart disease • Being African American, American Indian, or Hispanic
Symptoms	Early CKD has no symptoms. If you are at risk, ask your doctor about being tested for CKD.
Diagnosis	• **Blood test:** A glomerular filtration rate (GFR) test measures how fast your kidneys filter wastes from blood. The rate is based on the level of creatinine (kree-AT-uh-neen). A high level of creatinine is a sign of CKD. • **Urine test:** The amount of protein in the urine is tested. High levels of protein are a sign of CKD. • **Blood pressure:** High blood pressure can lead to, or be a sign of, CKD.

Understanding CKD

Treatment	There is no cure for CKD. But your doctor will help you manage your CKD to try to avoid kidney failure. If the kidneys fail, you will need medical help to live. The two methods for the treatment of kidney failure are: • **Dialysis:** The process of cleaning wastes from the blood with special equipment. • **Kidney transplant:** A donated kidney is put in your body. You will need to take medicine to keep your body from rejecting the new kidney.
Other health issues	CKD increases your chances of having: • **Anemia** (uh-NEE-mee-uh): Lower than normal number of healthy red blood cells. • **Acidosis:** When blood acid levels are too high. • **Cardiovascular disease:** Leads to heart attack and stroke. • **Bone problems:** CKD can lead to bone mineral imbalance, causing weak bones.
Prevention	If you are at risk of CKD or if you have CKD and would like to keep it from progressing to kidney failure: • Control your blood glucose (sugar) level if you have diabetes. • Lower your blood pressure if it is too high. Try to keep it below 140/90 mmHg. If you already have CKD, try to keep it below 130/80 mmHg. • If you have CKD, eat less protein and work with a dietitian to make sure you have a healthy diet. • Take prescribed drugs, such as those for diabetes and high blood pressure.

Urologic Problems and Sexual Relations

If you have a urologic problem, it can affect how you feel about yourself and your desire to have sex. It can also impact your sex drive and physical comfort level. But urologic problems don't need to mean the end of sexual relations.

Talk with your doctor about physical concerns and treatments. There are ways to help make sex more comfortable if you have pain. If you feel anxious or depressed, you can talk with a mental health professional or a support group of other women with the same issues. Knowing you aren't alone and that other women with urologic problems have fulfilling sexual relationships may bring you hope and give you the courage to talk with your partner.

With time and an understanding partner, sex can remain an enjoyable part of your life.

Your urologic and kidney health

Although urologic and kidney problems are common in women, much can be done to treat them and improve your life. Recognizing symptoms and risks is the first step to resolving any problems. If you think you have a urologic problem, or are at risk of chronic kidney disease, contact your doctor for treatment. ■

One Woman's Story

After success at four Winter Olympic Games, I hung up my skates to become a motivational speaker and a member of the U.S. Speed Skating Board of Directors, as well as a wife and mother of two.

Like many new mothers, I had no idea that pregnancy could bring about a potentially embarrassing condition: stress urinary incontinence (SUI), the leaking of urine during daily activities. After giving birth to my son, I was so excited to have the chance to run again—until I got about a block away from my house and realized my shorts were soaked. I didn't understand why this had happened to me.

I was upset and embarrassed, and I did not tell my doctor or my family what was happening to me. Instead, I tried to cope by wearing dark shorts, using feminine pads, and limiting my fluid intake.

After one year of fighting this condition by myself, I shared it with my doctor, who said that my pelvic muscles supporting the bladder and urethra became damaged or weakened during childbirth. As a result, my urethra lost its seal and allowed urine to escape with any movement from the diaphragm that put stress on the bladder, such as coughing, sneezing, laughing, or exercising.

I tried different therapies, including Kegel exercises, weights, and electrical stimulation, to strengthen my pelvic muscles, but nothing

> ## I had no idea that pregnancy could bring about a potentially embarrassing condition...

worked. After the birth of my second child and a consultation with my doctor, I decided to undergo a minimally invasive procedure to treat my SUI that involves the insertion of a "sling" made of a special synthetic mesh tape to hold up the urethra.

After the procedure, I returned home, and within a day or two was back to most of my daily activities. I resumed morning runs, and now one of my favorite activities is jumping on the trampoline in the backyard with my two children. My family has noticed a difference in my attitude.

My experience is similar to many women who have given birth, which is why I want to encourage women to talk to their doctors so they can treat and beat SUI like I did. It's not something you have to learn to cope with. SUI is treatable. And while surgery was the answer for me, there are several other treatment options available to women. The important thing is to talk to your doctor about these options rather than suffer in silence.

Bonnie Blair, winner of five gold medals and a bronze for speed skating at the 1984, 1988, 1992, and 1994 Winter Olympic Games.

The Healthy Woman: A Complete Guide for All Ages

For More Information...

Office on Women's Health, HHS
200 Independence Ave SW, Room 712E
Washington, DC 20201
Web site: www.womenshealth.gov/faq/
urinary.htm
www.womenshealth.gov/faq/Easyread/
uti-etr.htm
Phone number: (800) 994-9662,
(888) 220-5446 TDD

National Kidney and Urologic Diseases Information Clearinghouse, NIH
3 Information Way
Bethesda, MD 20892-3580
Web site: www.kidney.niddk.nih.gov
Phone number: (800) 891-5390

American Association of Kidney Patients
3505 E Frontage Rd, Suite 315
Tampa, FL 33607
Web site: www.aakp.org
Phone number: (800) 749-2257

American Kidney Fund
6110 Executive Blvd, Suite 1010
Rockville, MD 20852
Web site: www.kidneyfund.org
Phone number: (800) 638-8299

American Physical Therapy Association
1111 N Fairfax St
Alexandria, VA 22314-1488
Web site: www.apta.org
Phone number: (800) 999-2782

American Urogynecologic Society
2025 M St NW, Suite 800
Washington, DC 20036
Web site: www.augs.org

American Urological Association Foundation
1000 Corporate Blvd
Linthicum, MD 21090
Web site: www.urologyhealth.org
Phone number: (866) 746-4282

Interstitial Cystitis Association
110 N Washington St, Suite 340
Rockville, MD 20850
Web site: www.ichelp.org
Phone number: (800) 435-7422

The National Association for Continence
PO Box 1019
Charleston, SC 29402-1019
Web site: www.nafc.org
Phone number: (800) 252-3337

National Kidney Foundation
30 E 33rd St
New York, NY 10016
Web site: www.kidney.org
Phone number: (800) 622-9010

Polycystic Kidney Disease Foundation
9221 Ward Parkway, Suite 400
Kansas City, MO 64114-3367
Web site: www.pkdcure.org
Phone number: (800) 753-2873

Digestive Health

Everyone has digestive problems from time to time—an upset stomach, gas, heartburn, constipation, or diarrhea. Many digestive problems may be uncomfortable or embarrassing, but they are not serious and don't last long. Others can be controlled with simple changes in your diet. But sometimes even common digestive symptoms can be signs of a more serious problem. Knowing when you should talk to your doctor can help you take care of your digestive health.

Digestive System

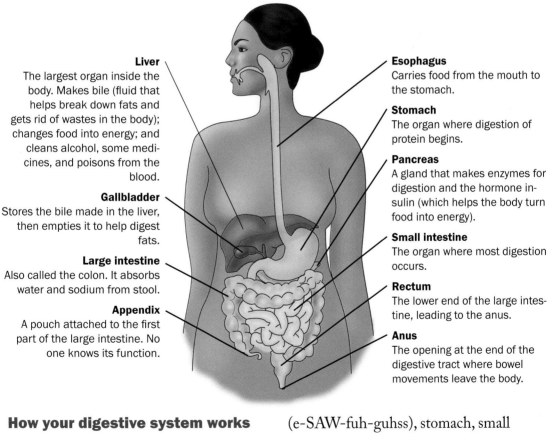

Liver
The largest organ inside the body. Makes bile (fluid that helps break down fats and gets rid of wastes in the body); changes food into energy; and cleans alcohol, some medicines, and poisons from the blood.

Gallbladder
Stores the bile made in the liver, then empties it to help digest fats.

Large intestine
Also called the colon. It absorbs water and sodium from stool.

Appendix
A pouch attached to the first part of the large intestine. No one knows its function.

Esophagus
Carries food from the mouth to the stomach.

Stomach
The organ where digestion of protein begins.

Pancreas
A gland that makes enzymes for digestion and the hormone insulin (which helps the body turn food into energy).

Small intestine
The organ where most digestion occurs.

Rectum
The lower end of the large intestine, leading to the anus.

Anus
The opening at the end of the digestive tract where bowel movements leave the body.

How your digestive system works

The digestive tract is a series of hollow organs—the mouth, esophagus (e-SAW-fuh-guhss), stomach, small intestine, large intestine (colon), rectum, and anus—through which food and liquids pass and are absorbed or eliminated. Along the way, two solid digestive organs, the liver and the pancreas, add digestive juices. These juices help break down food into nutrients that can be absorbed by the body. Another organ, the gallbladder, stores bile between meals. Bile is the digestive juice produced by the liver that helps digest fats. At mealtime, the gallbladder empties bile into the small intestine.

Most nutrients in digested food are absorbed through the walls of the small intestine and travel through the bloodstream to other parts of the body. There, they are used to build and nourish cells and provide energy. Waste products, including the undigested parts of food known as fiber, leave the body through a bowel movement.

Common signs of a digestive system problem

Common digestive complaints such as nausea, vomiting, bloating, gas, heartburn, diarrhea, and constipation can be temporary. They can be caused by:

- certain types of food
- food contaminated with harmful bacteria
- flu or other short-term illness
- menstruation
- pregnancy

But sometimes these symptoms are signs of a more serious digestive disease or other health problem such as colon cancer or ovarian cancer. (See pages 57 and 60 of the *Cancer* chapter for more information.)

Digestive problems that affect women

Some digestive problems, such as irritable bowel syndrome and gallstones, are more common in women than men. Others occur equally in both sexes, but affect women in unique ways. For example, women with inflammatory bowel disease may have irregular menstrual periods. Some women with celiac (SEE-lee-ak) disease experience infertility or miscarriage. And heartburn caused by gastroesophageal (GASS-troh-uh-SOF-uh-JEE-uhl) reflux is common in pregnancy.

Common Digestive Problems in Pregnancy	
Problem	**What you can do**
Nausea and vomiting	• Avoid smells that bother you. • Eat smaller, more frequent meals. • Eat crackers before getting out of bed in the morning.
Heartburn	• Eat smaller, more frequent meals. • Avoid lying down after eating. • Ask your doctor what kind of antacid you can take.
Constipation	• Eat more fiber. • Drink plenty of water. • Take a daily walk.

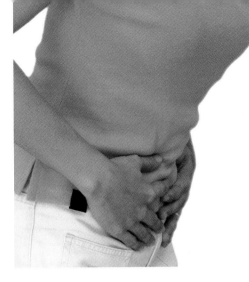

Irritable bowel syndrome

Irritable bowel syndrome (IBS) is not a disease but a syndrome, meaning a group of symptoms. People with IBS most often have abdominal pain, bloating, and discomfort. Some people have constipation—infrequent bowel movements with hard, dry, or difficult-to-pass stools. Other people with IBS have diarrhea—frequent loose, watery stools. Still others go back and forth between constipation and diarrhea. Symptoms may go away for a few months, then return. Or symptoms may be constant and get worse over time.

IBS does not damage the intestines. Instead, it affects the way the digestive tract functions, and so is called a "functional disorder." The exact cause is unknown, but in people with IBS, the colon seems to be extra sensitive to certain foods and stress. Normally, women are more sensitive to irritants in the digestive tract than men. This may help explain why IBS is more common in women. Hormones may play a role as well. Symptoms often become worse just before or at the start of a woman's period.

Having IBS can disrupt your everyday life. Pain that comes on without warning and the need for frequent bathroom trips can get in the way of social activities and work. You may be embarrassed, frustrated, or anxious about the lack of control over your symptoms. IBS might cause problems in your sex life, such as painful intercourse or loss of interest in sex. These stressful feelings in turn can make symptoms worse.

You can often control mild symptoms by making changes to your diet and lifestyle. Fiber supplements or over-the-counter medicines to control diarrhea may help. Prescription drugs are sometimes used to treat women with severe IBS, but some may have serious side effects. Researchers are studying new drugs and other approaches to relieve symptoms of IBS.

Coping With IBS

Learning to cope with IBS can help you live a more normal life and control your symptoms. Try these steps to manage your IBS.

- Find a supportive doctor who has experience with IBS.

- Learn your triggers. Large meals may make symptoms worse. So can certain foods and drinks such as chocolate, milk products, caffeinated drinks, and alcohol.

- Get support from your friends and family or join a support group.

- Plan ahead when going out; know where the public restrooms are.

- Try to reduce stress through regular physical activity, relaxation techniques such as meditation, or talking with a professional counselor.

Gallstones

Gallstones form when elements in bile harden into small, pebble-like pieces in the gallbladder. Most gallstones are made mainly of hardened cholesterol (koh-LESS-tur-ol). If liquid bile contains too much cholesterol, or the gallbladder doesn't empty completely or often enough, gallstones can form.

Women are twice as likely as men to have gallstones. Estrogen, a female hormone, raises cholesterol levels in the bile and slows gallbladder movement. The effect is even greater in pregnancy as estrogen levels rise. This helps explain why many women develop gallstones when pregnant or after having a baby. Likewise, if you take birth control pills or menopausal hormone therapy, you have a greater chance of developing gallstones.

You are also more likely to have gallstones if you:

- have a family history of gallstones
- are overweight
- eat a high-fat, high-cholesterol diet
- have lost a lot of weight quickly
- are older than 60
- are American Indian or Mexican American
- take cholesterol-lowering drugs
- have diabetes

Sometime gallstones have no symptoms and don't need treatment. But if gallstones move into the ducts that carry bile from the gallbladder or liver to the small intestine, they can cause a gallbladder "attack." An attack brings steady pain in the right upper abdomen, under the right shoulder, or between the shoulder blades. Although attacks often pass as the gallstones move forward, sometimes a stone can become lodged in a bile duct. A blocked duct can cause severe damage or infection.

Warning Signs of a Blocked Bile Duct

If you have any of these symptoms of a blocked bile duct, see your doctor right away:

- pain lasting more than 5 hours
- nausea and vomiting
- fever
- yellowish skin or eyes
- clay-colored stool

Here are some step you can take to help prevent gallstones.

- Maintain a healthy weight.
- If you need to lose weight, do it slowly—no more than ½ to 2 pounds a week.
- Eat a low-fat, low-cholesterol diet.

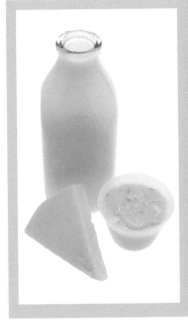

Can't drink milk? You may have lactose intolerance.

Lactose intolerance is a common digestive disorder. It means your body can't digest lactose, the sugar found in milk products. After eating foods with lactose, you may have nausea, cramps, bloating, gas, or diarrhea. Lactose intolerance is not serious but can be quite uncomfortable. You can easily control it by changing your diet.

You may not have to give up milk products entirely. Some people with lactose intolerance can eat yogurt or aged cheeses, like cheddar and Swiss, with no problem. Lactose-reduced milk is widely available. And taking supplements that contain lactase—the enzyme that breaks down lactose in the intestines—can help you digest dairy foods. You can find lactase supplements at most grocery and drug stores.

Gastroesophageal reflux disease (GERD)

If you have ever felt food or fluid rise from your stomach into your throat, then you know what gastroesophageal reflux (GER) feels like. You may know it as acid reflux or acid indigestion. GER occurs when the ring of muscle between the lower part of the esophagus and the stomach opens at the wrong time. This muscle, called the lower esophageal sphincter (e-SOF-uh-JEE-uhl SFEENK-tur), opens when you swallow to let food pass into the stomach, then closes again. In GER, the sphincter relaxes when it shouldn't and allows stomach contents to flow back into the esophagus.

If you have GER more than twice a week, you may have gastroesophageal reflux disease (GERD). The main symptom of GERD is frequent heartburn—a burning sensation in your chest or throat. But some adults and most children with GERD don't have heartburn. Instead,

they may have a dry cough, asthma symptoms, or trouble swallowing.

It's not always clear why some people get GERD, but a hiatal hernia may be one factor. In this condition, the upper part of the stomach protrudes into the chest through the diaphragm—the muscle wall that separates the abdomen from

Complications of GERD

Over time, untreated GERD can damage the lining of the esophagus. This damage can cause bleeding or ulcers. Scar tissue can narrow the esophagus and make it hard to swallow. Some people develop abnormal cells in the lining of the esophagus, called Barrett's esophagus. This condition affects more men than women and usually occurs in people older than 60. Rarely, Barrett's esophagus can progress to cancer of the esophagus.

Keeping Your Digestive System Healthy

- Don't smoke.
- Maintain a healthy weight.
- Eat a balanced diet.
- Get regular physical activity.
- Learn how to reduce stress.

the chest. When this happens, it's easier for stomach contents to rise into the esophagus.

Being overweight puts extra pressure on the stomach and diaphragm, making acid reflux more likely. So does pregnancy. What's more, the pregnancy hormone progesterone (proh-JESS-tuh-rohn) can contribute to GERD. Progesterone relaxes many of your muscles, including the lower esophageal sphincter.

Smoking can make symptoms worse. So can some foods, such as citrus fruits, chocolate, caffeinated drinks, and fatty or fried foods.

Making changes in your lifestyle may help ease the symptoms of GERD.

- If you smoke, stop.
- Avoid foods and drinks that worsen symptoms.
- Lose weight if you are overweight.
- Eat small, frequent meals.
- Wear loose-fitting clothes.
- Avoid lying down for 3 hours after a meal.
- Raise the head of your bed 6 to 8 inches by putting wood blocks under the bedposts. Just using extra pillows will not help.

Autoimmune disorders

Some digestive diseases are autoimmune (aw-toh-ih-MYOON) disorders. (See the *Autoimmune Diseases* chapter on page 83 for more information.) These disorders oc-

Hepatitis A, B, and C: Preventable Liver Diseases

Hepatitis is inflammation, or swelling, of the liver. It can be caused by the hepatitis A, B, or C viruses. Hepatitis A spreads through food or water contaminated by the feces of an infected person. You can get hepatitis B through contact with infected blood, semen, or other body fluids. The virus can also pass from mother to child during childbirth. Hepatitis C is spread mainly through contact with infected blood.

Hepatitis A can cause flu-like symptoms and usually resolves on its own in a few weeks. But the hepatitis B and C viruses can cause chronic, or long-term, infection. Chronic hepatitis can lead to cirrhosis (sur-ROH-suhss), when scar tissue builds up in the liver and replaces healthy tissue.

Good hygiene, avoiding tap water when traveling to developing countries, and a vaccine all protect against hepatitis A. The hepatitis B vaccine protects people who may be exposed to the virus. There is no vaccine for hepatitis C. The only way to prevent the disease is to avoid sharing drug needles or toothbrushes, razors, and other personal items with an infected person.

cur when the body's immune system mistakenly attacks different parts of the body. Autoimmune digestive diseases include:

- inflammatory bowel disease
- celiac disease
- autoimmune hepatitis
- primary biliary cirrhosis

Inflammatory bowel disease

Inflammatory bowel disease (IBD) is chronic inflammation of the digestive tract. The most common forms of IBD are Crohn's (krohnz) disease and ulcerative colitis (UHL-sur-uh-tiv koh-LEYE-tuhss). Crohn's disease can affect any part of the digestive tract, causing swelling that extends deep into the lining of the affected organ. It most often affects the lower part of the small intestine. Ulcerative colitis affects the colon or rectum, where sores called ulcers form on the top layer of the intestinal lining.

Most people with IBD have abdominal pain and diarrhea, which may be bloody.

Other people have rectal bleeding, fever, or weight loss. IBD can also cause problems in other parts of the body. Some people develop swelling in the eye, arthritis, liver disease, skin rashes, or kidney stones.

In people with Crohn's disease, swelling and scar tissue can thicken the wall of the intestine and create a blockage. Ulcers can tunnel through the wall into nearby organs such as the bladder or vagina. The tunnels, called fistulas, can become infected and may need surgery.

No one knows for sure what causes IBD, but researchers think it may be an abnormal immune response to bacteria that live in the intestines. Heredity may play a role, because it tends to run in families. IBD is more common among people of Jewish heritage. Stress or diet alone does not cause IBD, but both can trigger symptoms. IBD occurs most often during the reproductive years.

IBD and Pregnancy

It's best to get pregnant when your IBD is not active (in remission). Women with IBD usually don't have more trouble getting pregnant than other women. But if you have had a certain type of surgery to treat IBD, you may find it harder to get pregnant. Also, women with active IBD are more likely to miscarry or have preterm or low-birth-weight babies. If you are pregnant, work closely with your doctors throughout pregnancy to keep your disease under control. Many of the drugs used to treat IBD are safe for the developing fetus.

IBD can affect your life in other ways. Some women with IBD have discomfort or pain during sex. This may be a result of surgery or the disease itself. Fatigue, poor body image, or fear of passing gas or stool can also interfere with your sex life. Even though it may be embarrassing, be sure to tell your doctor if you are having sexual problems. Painful sex could be a sign that your disease is getting worse. And talking with your doctor, a counselor, or a support group may help you find ways to address emotional issues.

Currently, IBD cannot be prevented. But you can make some lifestyle changes that can ease your symptoms.

- Learn what foods trigger your symptoms and avoid them.

- Eat a nutritious diet.

- Try to reduce stress through physical activity, meditation, or counseling.

Researchers are studying many new treatments for IBD. These include new drugs, supplements of "good" bacteria that help keep your intestines healthy, and other ways to reduce the body's immune response.

Celiac disease

People who have celiac disease (also known as celiac sprue) can't tolerate gluten, a protein found in wheat, rye, and barley. Gluten is even in some medicines. When people with celiac disease eat foods or use products that have gluten in them, the immune system responds by damaging the lining of the small intestine. This damage interferes with the body's ability to absorb nutrients from

food. As a result, a person with celiac disease becomes malnourished, no matter how much food she eats.

Celiac disease runs in families. Sometimes the disease is triggered—or becomes active for the first time—after surgery, pregnancy, childbirth, a viral infection, or severe emotional stress.

Celiac disease affects people differently. Symptoms may occur in the digestive system or in other parts of the body. For example, one person might have diarrhea and abdominal pain, whereas another person may be irritable or depressed. Some people have no symptoms.

Because malnutrition affects many parts of the body, the impact of celiac disease goes beyond the digestive system. Celiac disease can lead to anemia (uh-NEE-mee-uh) or the bone-thinning disease osteoporosis (OSS-tee-oh-puh-ROH-suhss). Women with celiac disease may face infertility or miscarriage.

The only treatment for celiac disease is to follow a gluten-free diet. If you have celiac disease, work with your doctor or a dietitian to develop a gluten-free diet plan. A dietitian can help you learn how to read ingredient lists and identify foods that contain gluten. These skills will help you make the right choices at the grocery store and when eating out.

The chart below lists examples of foods you can eat and foods you should avoid if you have celiac disease.

Gluten-Free Diet Examples

Gluten-free grains and starches	• Amaranth • Arrowroot • Buckwheat • Cassava • Corn • Flax • Indian rice grass	• Job's tears • Legumes • Millet • Nuts • Potatoes • Quinoa • Rice	• Sago • Seeds • Soy • Sorghum • Tapioca • Wild rice • Yucca

Foods to avoid	• Barley
	• Rye
	• Triticale (a cross between wheat and rye)
		• Wheat, including:
		  • einkorn
		  • emmer
		  • spelt
		  • kamut
			• wheat starch
			• wheat bran
			• wheat germ
			• cracked wheat
			• hydrolyzed wheat protein

Other terms for wheat	• Bromated flour • Durum flour • Enriched flour • Farina	• Graham flour • Phosphated flour • Plain flour	• Self-rising flour • Semolina • White flour

© American Dietetic Association. Adapted with permission.

Autoimmune Liver Diseases

Autoimmune hepatitis and primary biliary cirrhosis (BIL-ee-air-ee sur-ROH-suhss) are rare liver diseases that affect mainly women. In autoimmune hepatitis, the body's immune system attacks and damages liver cells. In primary biliary cirrhosis, the bile ducts are slowly destroyed. Both diseases can lead to cirrhosis. Symptoms include fatigue, itchy skin, and yellowing skin and eyes. Autoimmune hepatitis can also cause joint pain and abdominal discomfort. Dry eyes and mouth are common in primary biliary cirrhosis.

If caught early, autoimmune hepatitis can usually be controlled with drugs that suppress, or slow down, an overactive immune system. This helps keep the immune system from attacking and damaging liver cells. Treatment for primary biliary cirrhosis is aimed at slowing the progress of the disease and relieving symptoms. In both conditions, a liver transplant may be needed if liver damage is severe.

Diagnosis and Treatment of Digestive Disorders

Irritable bowel syndrome

Symptoms	• Cramping • Abdominal pain or discomfort • Bloating • Constipation • Diarrhea
Diagnosis	• Review of symptoms • Diagnostic tests to rule out other gastrointestinal problems
Treatment	• No cure, but symptoms can be treated • Dietary changes • Medications (over-the-counter and prescription) • Stress management

Gallstones

Symptoms	• Pain in right upper abdomen, under right shoulder, or between shoulder blades • Nausea and vomiting • Fever • Yellowish skin or eyes • Clay-colored stool
Diagnosis	• Ultrasound • Sometimes other tests, such as a computed tomography (tuh-MOG-ruh-fee) (CT) scan or an endoscopic procedure that uses a long, flexible tube with a camera inserted down the throat, through the stomach, and into the small intestine to detect problems in the nearby gallbladder and bile ducts
Treatment	• Gallbladder removal • Stone removal with an endoscope • Sometimes drugs to dissolve gallstones

GERD

Symptoms	• Frequent heartburn (in adults) • Sometimes dry cough, asthma symptoms, or trouble swallowing
Diagnosis	• Review of symptoms • Diagnostic tests such as x-rays or endoscopic procedure to look for abnormalities if symptoms don't respond to lifestyle changes or medication
Treatment	• Lifestyle changes • Medications (over-the-counter and prescription) • Surgery to strengthen the sphincter or repair a hiatal hernia

The Healthy Woman: A Complete Guide for All Ages

Diagnosis and Treatment of Digestive Disorders

Inflammatory bowel disease

Symptoms	• Abdominal pain
	• Diarrhea, which may be bloody
	• Less common symptoms
	   • rectal bleeding
	   • weight loss
	   • fever
	   • fatigue
	   • mouth ulcers (in Crohn's disease)
	   • painful or difficult bowel movements (in ulcerative colitis)

Diagnosis	• Blood tests • Stool sample • Colonoscopy (KOH-luhn-OSS-kuh-pee) or sigmoidoscopy (SIG-moi-DOSS-kuh-pee), using a long, flexible tube with a camera that is inserted through the rectum into the intestine • Barium x-rays
Treatment	• Medication • Surgery

Celiac disease

Symptoms	• Abdominal bloating and pain • Diarrhea or constipation • Weight loss or weight gain • Fatigue • Missed menstrual periods • Itchy skin rash called dermatitis herpetiformis (DUR-muh-TEYE-tuhss hur-PET-uh-FOR-muhss)
Diagnosis	• Blood tests • Small intestine biopsy
Treatment	• Gluten-free diet

Digestive problems can range from mild to severe. You can overcome many problems by making simple lifestyle changes—watch what you eat, maintain a healthy weight, learn to deal with stress, and if you smoke, quit. Other digestive problems require medication or even surgery. New treatments for IBS, IBD, and even celiac disease are on the horizon. If you are concerned about your digestive health, work with your doctor to find the solution that's right for you. ■

One Woman's Story

I was fresh out of graduate school, working at my first job, living in my first house with a new dog, and serving as a bridesmaid in a horrible wedding. I didn't have time for health problems. But a constant dull pain and trouble "going" in the morning, combined with mucus, blood, and more pain, proved me wrong and sent me to a gastroenterologist.

My grandfather's death from colon cancer weighed at the back of my mind, but luckily I wasn't at that point. The doctor quickly and easily diagnosed me with ulcerative colitis and scheduled a colonoscopy. After the pain of the disease and the less-than-pleasant diagnostic procedure, the first steroid treatment made me feel like a million bucks! I had a surge of energy and endurance that encouraged my obsession with physical activity. The aftereffects were not so pleasant, though. I puffed up with chipmunk cheeks, lost 30 to 40 percent of my hair, and broke out in a rash. A sulfa drug was the next treatment, but my reactions were no better: extreme sensitivity to the sun and flu-like symptoms, which did nothing to help me maintain my physical activity. Eventually, I found that 12 tablets a day of yet another medicine would barely keep the issue under control. Not wanting to be dependant on 12 pills a day forever, I did my own research on healthy eating for people diagnosed with irritable bowel syndrome, colitis, ulcers, and other digestive issues.

> **...listening to my body, not following a specific diet, was best.**

I soon found that eliminating or eating more of any one type of food didn't help, and that listening to my body, not following a specific diet, was best. I got to know what foods my body needed and which to avoid. For me, I found it helpful to avoid fruit after noon and fluids with meals and to make sure I have carbohydrates at every meal.

I also changed my physical activity routine. While I still enjoy intense workouts like cycling, running, or hiking, yoga has really helped me be more in tune with how outside experiences affect me and also how foods affect me. Now that I am in control of my disease, I hope I will be able to work with my doctor to eliminate medication slowly and replace it with alternative methods of eating well and practicing yoga.

Susan

Denver, Pennsylvania

For More Information...

Office on Women's Health, HHS
200 Independence Ave SW, Room 712E
Washington, DC 20201
Web site: www.womenshealth.gov/faq/
ibd.htm
www.womenshealth.gov/faq/ibs.htm
Phone number: (800) 994-9662,
(888) 220-5446 TDD

**National Digestive Diseases Information
Clearinghouse, NIH**
2 Information Way
Bethesda, MD 20892-3570
Web site: www.digestive.niddk.nih.gov
Phone number: (800) 891-5389

American College of Gastroenterology
PO Box 342260
Bethesda, MD 20827-2260
Web site: www.acg.gi.org/patients

**American Gastroenterological
Association**
4930 Del Ray Ave
Bethesda, MD 20814
Web site: www.gastro.org/patient

American Liver Foundation
75 Maiden Ln, Suite 603
New York, NY 10038
Web site: www.liverfoundation.org
Phone number: (800) 465-4837

**Crohn's and Colitis Foundation of
America**
386 Park Ave S, 17th floor
New York, NY 10016
Web site: www.ccfa.org
Phone number: (888) 964-8872

**International Foundation for Functional
Gastrointestinal Disorders**
PO Box 170864
Milwaukee, WI 53217-8076
Web site: www.iffgd.org,
www.aboutibs.org,
www.aboutgimotility.org
Phone number: (888) 964-2001

**National Foundation for Celiac
Awareness**
PO Box 544
Ambler, PA 19002-0544
Web site: www.celiaccentral.org
Phone number: (215) 325-1306

Respiratory Health

If you have had a cold or suffered from allergies, you know what it feels like to have trouble breathing. For women with respiratory diseases such as asthma, breathing troubles can become a permanent, rather than temporary, problem. If you have a respiratory disease, the right medical treatment—and learning how to manage your condition—can help you breathe easier.

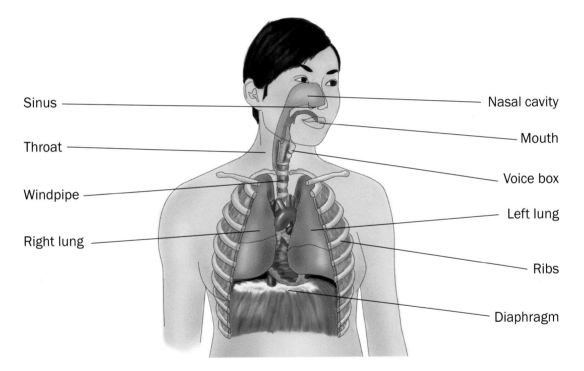

Sinus — Nasal cavity

Throat — Mouth

Windpipe — Voice box

Right lung — Left lung

— Ribs

— Diaphragm

How the respiratory system works

Your respiratory system is made up of your nose, sinuses, mouth, throat, voice box, windpipe, lungs, diaphragm, and blood vessels. Breathing is the process of inhaling and exhaling. When you inhale, you bring oxygen-rich air into your body.

When you exhale, you release carbon dioxide into the air from your body.

You breathe about 25,000 times during a normal day. If you are healthy, this process is easy. But for the millions of women with chronic, or long-term, respiratory diseases, breathing is not that simple.

Symptoms of respiratory disease

Because respiratory diseases affect your lungs, symptoms are related to how well you can breathe. In the early stages of respiratory disease, you might just feel tired. Other symptoms include:

- feeling short of breath, especially during physical activity or activities such as climbing stairs or carrying groceries

- feeling as though you cannot get enough air

- a cough that won't go away

- coughing up blood or mucus (MYOO-kuhss), a thick, sticky substance, making it hard for air to get in and out of the lungs

- uncomfortable or painful breathing

- a feeling of tightness in the chest

- wheezing, or a squeaky sound when you breathe

Your symptoms depend on your illness—how advanced it is—and your overall health. For instance, having another chronic illness or being overweight could make your symptoms worse.

How respiratory disease is diagnosed

A doctor will identify the cause of your breathing problems based on your symptoms, medical history—including your family history—and a checkup. Several tests can also help diagnose respiratory illness. You might get one or more of the following tests, depending on your condition and the test results:

- **Pulmonary function tests.** These are a series of tests that measure how well your lungs take in and release air and how well they transfer oxygen into the blood.

- **Blood gases test.** This test measures how much oxygen and carbon dioxide are in your blood. If the results of this test are not normal, it may mean your body is not getting enough oxygen or is not getting rid of enough carbon dioxide.

- **Bronchoscopy** (brong-KOSS-kuh-pee). This test allows your doctor to see your airways using a tube passed through your mouth or nose into your lungs.

- **Chest x-ray.** A chest x-ray lets your doctor see your lungs. It takes pictures of your heart, lungs, airways, blood vessels, and bones in your spine and chest. A chest x-ray is the most commonly performed diagnostic x-ray exam.

- **Computed tomography** (tuh-MOG-ruh-fee) **(CT) scan of the chest.** Your doctor might perform a CT scan of your chest if a mass or tumor is suspected or to look for bleeding or fluid in your lungs or other areas.

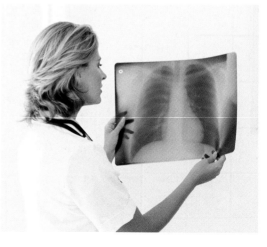

- **Electrocardiography** (ih-lek-troh-kar-dee-OG-ruh-fee) **(ECG or EKG).** This test checks to see if heart disease is causing your symptoms. An ECG measures how fast and steadily your heart beats, whether there is heart damage, and the effects of drugs or devices that regulate the heart, such as a pacemaker.

Common respiratory diseases in women

The most common respiratory diseases in women are asthma; chronic obstructive pulmonary disease (COPD), which includes chronic bronchitis (brong-KEYE-tuhss) and emphysema (em-fuh-ZEE-muh); and lung cancer.

Asthma

Asthma is a chronic disease that makes the airways leading to the lungs very sensitive and swollen, making it hard to breathe. Viruses, mold, pollen, dust, air pollution, animal dander, smoke, cold weather, stress, and some medicines can cause the airways to swell. Things that cause airways to swell and asthma to flare up are called triggers.

An asthma attack can happen quickly. It can be mild or very serious. In a severe asthma attack, the airways can close so much that your body's main organs do not get enough oxygen. People can die of severe asthma attacks.

Physical activity can trigger a problem called exercise-induced asthma. Asthma

Rare Lung Diseases

Several rare lung diseases that also affect women include:

Lymphangeiomyomatosis (lim-fan-jee-oh-meye-oh-muh-TOH-suhss): In this disease, known as LAM, an unusual type of cell grows out of control in the lungs and other parts of the body. This slowly blocks airways and destroys normal lung tissue. LAM primarily affects women in their mid-40s.

Sarcoidosis (sar-coi-DOH-suhss): This disease disproportionately affects African American women between the ages of 20 and 40, as well as people in this age group of Asian, German, Irish, Puerto Rican, and Scandinavian descent. It causes tiny lumps of cells to grow in the lungs. These lumps affect how the lungs work.

Cystic fibrosis (SISS-tik feye-BROH-suhss): In cystic fibrosis, a mutated gene causes mucus in the body to become thick and sticky. The mucus builds up in the lungs, blocking airways. Repeated lung infections from a buildup of bacteria can seriously damage the lungs.

Pulmonary arterial hypertension: This disease causes continuous high blood pressure in the pulmonary arteries, or the blood vessels that carry oxygen-poor blood from the heart to the small blood vessels in the lungs. It can be inherited or occur for no known reason. The disease also may result from another condition, such as heart disease or chronic lung disease. Twice as many cases of the inherited form of the disease occur in women, most often in their 30s.

Airway in Person with Asthma

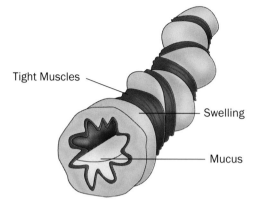

Tight Muscles

Swelling

Mucus

Normal Airway

Muscle

Lining

symptoms are usually triggered by cold, dry air during physical activity. For some women, symptoms such as coughing, wheezing, and shortness of breath can occur within minutes of beginning physical activity and get worse afterward. Other women have symptoms only once they finish exercising.

Although the exact cause of asthma is unknown, you are more likely to have the disease if it runs in your family. Asthma is also closely linked to allergies. Although asthma affects women of all ages, the disease is more likely to start in childhood.

Women are more likely than men to have asthma. More than 12.6 million women in the United States had the disease in 2005, compared with 8.7 million men. The number of women—especially young women—in the United States with asthma is growing.

Asthma: Differences between men and women

Studies have shown that asthma can affect men and women differently, and medical researchers want to know more about why this is the case.

Scientists are studying how changing hormone levels in women might cause or affect asthma. One study found that men with asthma were less likely than women to report severe and frequent symptoms and limits on their activity. Another study found that female hormones may contribute to adult women getting asthma.

Asthma treatments

Asthma can't be cured, but you can work with your doctor or nurse to treat, manage, and control your illness. Most asthma medicines open the airways to your lungs and reduce swelling. These include:

- **Corticosteroids** (KORT-ih-koh-STAIR-oidz). These medicines can prevent and decrease swelling in the airways and reduce the amount of mucus you have. They are available in pill or inhaled form and are often taken over a long period of time.

- **Bronchodilators** (brong-koh-DEYE-lay-turs). These fast-acting medicines prevent or stop an asthma attack once it has started. Two common, inhaled, fast-acting medicines are albuterol (al-

BYOO-tur-ol) and pirbuterol (pur-BYOO-tur-ol). They can relieve symptoms in minutes by quickly relaxing tightened muscles around the airways. Long-acting bronchodilators, which are often combined with antiswelling medicines, help relieve asthma symptoms over time.

Other ways of controlling asthma require that you change or manage your behavior, such as avoiding secondhand smoke, stopping your own tobacco use, limiting your contact with triggers, and managing other health problems that could affect your asthma, such as stress and sleep apnea (AP-nee-uh), a disorder caused by repeated interrupted breathing during sleep. (See page 287 for more information on managing respiratory disease triggers.)

Asthma and pregnancy

Asthma can be one of the most serious medical conditions to interfere with pregnancy, so it is very important to manage your symptoms if you become pregnant. Uncontrolled asthma during pregnancy can increase the risk of pre-eclampsia (pree-ee-CLAMP-see-uh), a condition that could lead to seizures in the mother or baby; preterm birth; low birth weight; and even infant death. The most likely time for a pregnant woman to have asthma-related problems is in the late second or early third trimester. Asthma is hardly ever a problem at delivery. Continuing your asthma medicines and controlling triggers will help prevent an attack and help ensure your baby gets enough oxygen.

Inhaled medicines are less likely to be passed on to the baby than medicines you take by mouth, but you should speak with your doctor or nurse about the best way to control your asthma while you are pregnant. You also should ask about getting a flu shot, because the flu can be serious for pregnant women with asthma.

Pregnant women with other conditions that can make asthma worse, such as allergic rhinitis (reye-NEYE-tuhss), sinusitis (SEYE-nyoo-SEYE-tuhss), and gastroesophageal (GASS-troh-uh-SOF-uh-JEE-uhl) reflux (GER), should bring those to the attention of a doctor or nurse. These illnesses often get worse during pregnancy.

For more information about GER, see the *Digestive Health* chapter on page 265.

Chronic obstructive pulmonary disease (COPD)

COPD is a lung disease that has two forms: emphysema and chronic bronchitis. Many people with COPD have both forms.

COPD is the fourth leading cause of death in the United States and throughout the world. More than 12 million people in the United States have COPD and another 12 million may have the disease and not know it.

Emphysema

Emphysema is a chronic disease that weakens lung tissue and destroys the walls between the air sacs, or alveoli (al-VEE-uh-leye). Because oxygen passes into the blood through these sacs, emphysema reduces the amount of oxygen in the blood. In 2005, 1.5 million women and 2.1 million men had emphysema. The most common cause of emphysema is smoking.

Chronic bronchitis

Smoking is also the most common cause of chronic bronchitis, which is a swelling of the bronchial tubes. The swollen tubes produce a buildup of mucus. About 5.3 million women and 2.8 million men had chronic bronchitis in 2005.

Emphysema: Differences between men and women

A 2007 study found notable differences between men and women who had severe emphysema. Even though the women in the study hadn't smoked as long as the men, they had more trouble with breathing and physical activity. They also reported feeling more depressed and scored lower on a test measuring overall mental health.

COPD treatments

Like asthma, COPD cannot be cured. But you can slow the disease down by not smoking and avoiding secondhand smoke. If you smoke, quitting will reduce future damage to your lungs.

Medicines to help you feel better if you have COPD are similar to those for asthma: inhaled corticosteroids and bronchodilators. Your doctor also might prescribe medicines called antibiotics if

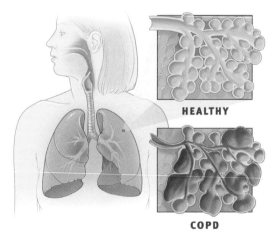

HEALTHY

COPD

ILLUSTRATION USED WITH PERMISSION FROM THE NATIONAL HEART, LUNG, AND BLOOD INSTITUTE.

your lungs are infected. Other treatments include:

- **Supplemental oxygen.** Getting extra oxygen some or all of the time, depending on how bad your illness is, can help you breathe better. Extra oxygen, which you inhale through a mask or tube connected to an oxygen tank, can help you sleep better, stay more alert during the day, and live longer.

- **Pulmonary rehabilitation.** A pulmonary rehabilitation program teaches you how to control your disease by being physically active, eating right, setting goals, managing your symptoms, and getting proper medical care. A team of health care providers will work together to create a program just for you.

Lung cancer

Lung cancer kills more women in the United States than any other kind of cancer. Lung cancer causes unhealthy cells in the lungs to divide and spread. These cells invade nearby tissue and spread to other parts of the body.

In 2003, lung cancer accounted for more deaths than breast cancer, prostate cancer, and colon cancer combined. During that year, 105,508 men and 84,789 women got lung cancer, and 89,906 men and 68,084 women died of it.

Although nonsmokers do get lung cancer, smoking leads to 87 percent of all lung cancer cases.

For more information on lung cancer, see the *Cancer* chapter on page 51.

Lung cancer: Differences between men and women

Researchers are studying the effects of hormones, such as estrogen, on the development of lung cancer in nonsmoking women and on drug treatments for cancer. A 2006 study reported that women who were recently diagnosed with lung cancer had lungs that functioned normally. These patients also had better results on lung tests than men who were recently diagnosed. The study also found that many more men than women with lung cancer also developed COPD.

Studies have shown that women with lung cancer respond better than men to some types of therapy and that women with lung cancer live longer than men with the disease.

Lung cancer treatments

Treatment for lung cancer includes surgery, radiation treatment, and chemotherapy (drug treatment) or a combination of these.

Respiratory Diseases, Symptoms, Tests, and Treatment	
Asthma	
Symptoms	• Coughing • Wheezing • Chest tightness • Trouble breathing
Tests	• Spirometry (spuh-ROM-uh-tree)—measures how much air you can blow out of your lungs and how quickly • Allergy and sinus • Chest x-ray • Electrocardiography
Treatment	• Corticosteroids • Fast-acting and long-term control bronchodilators • Managing your disease, such as controlling triggers and using a peak flow meter to check how your lungs are working. A peak flow meter measures how fast you blow air into it.
COPD	
Symptoms	• Coughing • Producing mucus • Shortness of breath, especially with physical activity • Wheezing • Chest tightness
Tests	• Spirometry • Bronchodilator reversibility—repeats a spirometry test, adding a bronchodilator medicine to measure how the medicine affects your breathing; the bronchodilators relax muscles around the airways to make it easier to breathe. • Diffusion capacity testing—measures how well your lungs transfer oxygen from the air into your blood • Chest x-ray • Blood gases test
Treatment	• Corticosteroids • Bronchodilators • Antibiotics • Pulmonary rehabilitation • Supplemental oxygen

Respiratory Diseases, Symptoms, Tests, and Treatment

Lung cancer

Symptoms	• Coughing that gets worse or does not go away
	• Trouble breathing
	• Constant chest pain
	• Coughing up blood
	• Hoarse voice
	• Feeling very tired all the time
	• Lung infections, such as pneumonia (noo-MOH-nyuh)
	• Losing weight
Tests	• Blood tests
	• Chest x-ray
	• CT scan
Treatment	• Surgery
	• Radiation
	• Chemotherapy

Sleep Apnea

Sleep apnea, or sleep-disordered breathing, is a common breathing disorder that can be very serious. Sleep apnea causes breathing to stop or become very shallow for 10 to 20 seconds or longer many times throughout the night. One of 50 middle-aged women has sleep apnea. It is more common in African Americans, Hispanics, and Pacific Islanders than in Caucasians. A doctor can recommend changes in daily activities or treatments for sleep apnea.

How to decrease respiratory disease triggers

Reducing your contact with triggers that can make your breathing problems worse is a must for managing your illness. Here are some things you can do:

- **Quit smoking.** The best thing you can do for your overall health is quit. Also avoid secondhand smoke—only smoke-free environments will ensure your safety from tobacco chemicals that irritate your lungs.

- **Avoid breathing chemicals.** Stay away from strong cleaning or chemical agents whenever possible or wear a mask and use them in well-aired

Feel Great: Quit Smoking

15 years after quitting
- Your risk of heart disease is now the same as someone who doesn't smoke.

20 minutes after quitting
- Your heart rate drops.

10 years after quitting
- Your risk of dying of lung cancer is half that of a smoker's.
- Your risk of cancer of the mouth, throat, esophagus, bladder, kidney, and pancreas also decreases.

12 hours after quitting
- The carbon monoxide (a gas that can be toxic) in your blood drops to normal.

2 weeks to 3 months after quitting
- Your heart attack risk begins to drop.
- Your lungs are working better.

5 years after quitting
- Your risk of having a stroke is the same as someone who doesn't smoke.

1 year after quitting
- Your risk of heart disease is half that of a smoker's.

1 to 9 months after quitting
- Coughing, sinus congestion, fatigue, and shortness of breath decrease.
- Your lungs start to function better, lowering your risk of lung infections.

spaces. Avoid dust, dry-cleaning and cosmetic chemicals, asbestos, coal dust, soot, paint and chemicals used in construction, and wood and furniture refinishing products.

- **Plan outdoor time carefully.** Avoid being outdoors as much as possible during allergy season—spring and fall. Keep your house and car windows closed, and wash your clothes and vacuum once you come inside.

- **Watch when and where you get physical activity.** Try to walk or be physically active early in the morning or later in the evening (before and after rush hour traffic). Fewer cars on the roads will help you avoid car fumes. Consider finding an area to be physically active that is less crowded but not so empty as to be unsafe.

Another option is to be physically active indoors. Fitness equipment and

indoor tracks, tennis, basketball, volleyball, and racquetball courts allow you to exercise without going outside. Being indoors also helps you control the air temperature so you can avoid cold, dry air.

If you have exercise-induced asthma, you might start to have trouble breathing within 5 to 20 minutes after physical activity. Warming up with short bursts of activity might help relieve your asthma symptoms. Physical activity that involves only short bursts of activity or activity that you stop and start again, such as walking, volleyball, basketball, gymnastics, or baseball, tend to be better for people with exercise-induced asthma. Swimming is also good because you are breathing warm, moist air instead of cold, dry air. You can get medicine to take several minutes to an hour before you begin physical activity to prevent an asthma attack.

- **Manage stress and prevent panic attacks.** Panic attacks brought on by stress can cause trouble breathing. Prevent panic attacks by managing stress: lighten your load, learn to say no, share tasks with coworkers or family members, make time for yourself, get enough sleep, and manage your time better. (See pages 208–210 of the *Mental Health* chapter for more information about stress.)

- **Prevent the flu and pneumonia by getting vaccinated.** Influenza, or the flu, and pneumonia are respiratory infections that can cause serious problems in people with respiratory diseases. Getting flu and pneumonia shots can greatly reduce your risk of these problems.

Asthma, COPD, and lung cancer are the most common respiratory diseases in women. If you have any of these diseases and smoke, quit now. With the help of your doctor, you can learn to manage the symptoms of asthma and COPD and improve your quality of life. If you have lung cancer, appropriate treatment, especially when started early, can prolong life. ■

One Woman's Story

It was a typical August day in Michigan, hot and humid. I sat in our basement family room watching my three kids play and wondering if I could somehow pull it together to walk upstairs and make dinner. My chest felt tightly wrapped up, and I was so tired. Somehow the cooler air in the basement seemed to relieve some of the pressure in my chest. When my husband came home, I would go sit in his air-conditioned car, and slowly the pressure would ease.

I decided it was time to see our family doctor. We had lived in Michigan for only 4 years, but I found I was extremely tired in the late summers and felt like I was breathing underwater. I always blamed it on the humidity from living near Lake Michigan, but the tests my doctor sent me for proved otherwise.

"You have asthma," he told me. "You're kidding! How could I get asthma at my age?" I responded. He smiled and shook his head. "You have two children with asthma. Why would you be shocked that you have it? It runs in families."

I was surprised at the diagnosis. Although my older daughter had been diagnosed with asthma after being hospitalized and my son diagnosed the following year, it never occurred to me that the symptoms I was experiencing were the same ones my children lived with on a regular basis. My heart went out to them as I thought about how terrifying it is when they struggle to take each breath.

...my personal Asthma Action Plan to help me keep asthma under control

I started educating myself about allergies and asthma with an eye toward myself as the patient. I learned to avoid irritants that triggered my asthma. I tested positive for allergies to mold, dust mites, and grasses and took action to control my environment. I also see my doctor annually, monitor my lung function with a peak flow meter, and step up my medications per my personal Asthma Action Plan to help me keep asthma under control.

Ongoing education about asthma and allergies and working with my doctor provide the tools I need to stay in control of asthma rather than letting asthma control me. It's been 18 years since my diagnosis, and I can count the number of times when asthma has gotten in my way.

Sandra
Butler, New Jersey

For More Information...

Office on Women's Health, HHS
200 Independence Ave SW, Room 712E
Washington, DC 20201
Web site: www.womenshealth.gov/
quitsmoking
www.womenshealth.gov/faq/lung_
disease.htm
Phone number: (800) 994-9662,
(888) 220-5446 TDD

**Centers for Disease Control and
Prevention**
1600 Clifton Rd
Atlanta, GA 30333
Web site: www.cdc.gov
Phone number: (800) 232-4636,
(888) 232-6348

National Cancer Institute, NIH
6116 Executive Blvd, Room 3036A
Bethesda, MD 20892-8322
Web site: www.cancer.gov
Phone number: (800) 422-6237,
(800) 332-8615 TTY

**National Heart, Lung, and Blood Institute
Information Center, NIH**
PO Box 30105
Bethesda, MD 20824-0105
Web site: www.nhlbi.nih.gov
www.hearttruth.gov
Phone number: (301) 592-8573,
(240) 629-3255 TTY

**National Institute of Allergy and
Infectious Diseases, NIH**
6610 Rockledge Dr, MSC 6612
Bethesda, MD 20892–6612
Web site: www.niaid.nih.gov
Phone number: (866) 284-4107,
(800) 877-8339 TDD

Office of Women's Health, FDA
5600 Fishers Ln
Rockville, MD 20857
Web site: www.fda.gov/womens
Phone number: (888) 463-6332

**Allergy and Asthma Network Mothers of
Asthmatics**
2751 Prosperity Ave, Suite 150
Fairfax, VA 22031
Web site: www.aanma.org
Phone number: (800) 878-4403

**American Academy of Allergy, Asthma,
and Immunology**
555 E Wells St, Suite 1100
Milwaukee, WI 53202-3823
Web site: www.aaaai.org

**American Association for Respiratory
Care**
9425 N MacArthur Blvd, Suite 100
Irving, TX 75063-4706
Web site: www.aarc.org
www.yourlunghealth.org

American College of Chest Physicians
3300 Dundee Rd
Northbrook, IL 60062–2348
Web site: www.chestnet.org/patients/
guides

American Lung Association
61 Broadway, 6th Floor
New York, NY 10006
Web site: www.lungusa.org
Phone number: (800) 548-8252

COPD Foundation
2937 SW 27th St, Suite 302
Miami, FL 33133
Web site: www.copdfoundation.org
Phone number: (866) 316-2673

Oral Health

Oral refers to the mouth, which includes the teeth, gums, and supporting tissues. And having a healthy mouth means more than just having nice-looking teeth—your whole mouth needs care. It is also important to be aware that many serious diseases, such as diabetes, HIV, and some eating disorders, can cause oral health problems. Regular oral exams will help manage any problems and maintain good oral health. There is also a lot you can do on your own to protect and preserve your oral health.

Steps to a healthy mouth

Use good oral hygiene

- Drink fluoridated water.

- Brush your teeth at least twice each day with fluoride tooth- paste. Look for the American Dental Association's (ADA) Seal of Acceptance.

- Floss daily.

- Gently brush all sides of your teeth with a soft bristled brush and toothpaste. Circular and short back-and-forth strokes work best.

- Take time to brush along the gum line. Brush your tongue lightly.

- Change your toothbrush when the bristles spread out, or at least every 3 months.

- If you wear dentures, remove them at night and clean them before putting them back in.

Choose a healthy lifestyle

- Don't use tobacco. It raises your risk of getting gum disease, oral and throat cancers, and oral fungal infections.

- Limit alcohol use. Heavy alcohol use raises your risk of oral and throat cancers.

- Using alcohol and tobacco together raise your risk of oral cancer even more than using one alone.

- Eat a well-balanced diet and healthy snacks.

- Limit soft drinks. Even diet sodas contain acid that can erode tooth enamel.

Have regular checkups

Have an oral exam once or twice a year. Your dentist may recommend more or fewer visits depending on your oral health. At most routine visits, you will be treated by the dentist and a dental hygienist. A thorough checkup includes:

- A health history and oral exam of your teeth and gums. You will be examined for changes, problems, signs of oral cancer or other diseases, and overall oral health.

- Teeth cleaning and polishing to remove hardened plaque and stains.

- X-rays of the teeth and mouth to look for cavities, injury, and problems below the gumline. How often you need x-rays depends on your health, age, disease risk, and symptoms. Radiation risk is very low.

See your dentist right away if:

- Your gums bleed often.

- You see red or white patches on the gums, tongue, or floor of the mouth that last more than 1 to 2 weeks.

- You have mouth or jaw pain that does not go away.

- You have mouth sores that do not heal within 2 weeks.

- You have problems swallowing or chewing.

Types of Oral Health Care Providers

Dentists: Specialists in the care of the teeth, gums, and mouth. Dentists who specialize in children are pediatric dentists.

Dental hygienists: Members of the dental staff who clean gums and teeth and teach patients how to maintain good oral health.

Dental specialists: Many dentists have advanced training in certain areas. Your general dentist may refer you to one of these specialists for more advanced treatments:

- **Periodontists:** Dentists who treat gum disease and place dental implants.

- **Oral surgeons:** Dentists who operate on the mouth and supporting tissues.

- **Orthodontists:** Dentists who straighten teeth and align jaws.

- **Endodontists:** Dentists who perform root canals.

- **Prosthodontists:** Dentists trained in restoring and replacing teeth.

Your teeth, decay, and cavities

Teeth vary in size, shape, and location in the jaws. Teeth start to form under the gums well before you are born. Most people are born with 20 primary (baby) teeth. These teeth start to push through the gums at around 5 to 6 months of age. All 20 baby teeth usually erupt by about age 2. Baby teeth are then lost as early as age 6 and are usually all gone by age 13. Permanent teeth then fill in. By age 21 most people have 32 permanent teeth—28 if wisdom teeth are removed.

Everyone is at risk of tooth decay, or cavities (CAV-ih-teez). Tooth decay is one of the most common oral health problems.

Bacteria that naturally live in your mouth use sugar in food to make acids. Over time, these acids destroy the outside layer of your teeth, causing holes

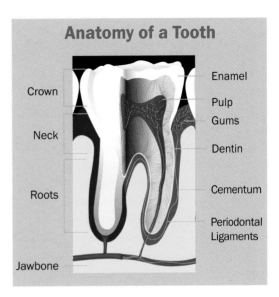

Anatomy of a Tooth

Crown
Neck
Roots
Jawbone

Enamel
Pulp
Gums
Dentin
Cementum
Periodontal Ligaments

and other tooth damage. There are ways to help prevent tooth decay. Your dentist may use:

- **Fluoride** (FLOR-eyed) – A mineral that helps prevent tooth decay. Studies show fluoride to be safe, and only small amounts are needed for good oral health. The level of fluoride in drinking water varies, so use fluoride toothpaste. Many mouth rinses, gels, and supplements also contain fluoride.

  Depending on your risk of tooth decay, dentists will sometimes put fluoride on your teeth during dental visits.

- **Sealants** (SEE-luhnts) – Clear, plastic coatings put mainly on the chewing surfaces of the back teeth to prevent tooth decay.

Dentists can also treat cavities by "filling" them. Some materials used to fill cavities include, but are not limited to:

- dental amalgam (uh-MAL-guhm) (silver), made of liquid mercury and a powder made of metals and tooth-colored plastic composite materials. Studies have shown amalgams to be safe.

- composite (white)
- gold
- ceramics
- porcelain

Gum diseases

Gum diseases are infections caused by bacteria in the mouth, along with mucus and other particles that form a sticky plaque on the teeth.

Gingivitis (jin-juh-VEYE-tuhss) is a mild form of gum disease that causes gums to become red and swollen and to bleed easily. It can be caused by plaque buildup. Plaque that is not removed hardens and forms "tartar." The longer plaque and tartar are on teeth, the more harm they do. Gingivitis can most often be reversed with daily brushing and flossing and with regular cleanings at the dentist's office. Gingivitis does not cause loss of bone or tissue surrounding the teeth.

When gingivitis is not treated, it may advance to periodontitis (pair-ee-oh-don-TEYE-tuhss). Then the gums pull away from the teeth and form infected "pockets." You also may lose supporting bone. Left untreated, teeth loosen over time and must be removed.

You are at higher risk of gum disease if you smoke or have diabetes or HIV.

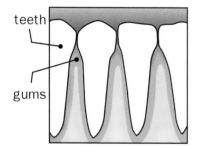

Normal, healthy gums
Healthy gums and bone anchor teeth firmly in place.

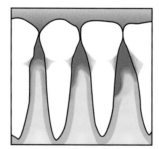

Periodontitis
Unremoved plaque hardens into calculus (tartar). As plaque and tartar continue to build, the gums pull away from the teeth and pockets form between the teeth and gums. Bone supporting the teeth may become infected and start to weaken.

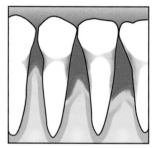

Advanced periodontitis
The gums recede further, destroying more bone and the ligament around the tooth. Teeth may become loose and need to be removed.

Oral Cancer

Oral cancer can affect any part of the mouth. People who smoke or chew tobacco are at higher risk. Alcohol use along with smoking greatly raises risk. Yet more than 25 percent of oral cancers affect nonsmokers.

Warning signs include:

- A sore that bleeds easily or does not heal.
- A color change in the mouth.
- A lump, rough spot, or other change.
- Pain, tenderness, or numbness anywhere in the mouth or on the lips.
- Trouble chewing, swallowing, speaking, or moving the jaw or tongue.
- A change in the way your teeth fit together. Your dentist should check for signs of oral cancer at each dental exam.

Early detection is important for the prevention and treatment of oral cancer.

Other Common Oral Health Problems

Burning mouth

What it is	A burning feeling in the mouth or tongue.
Causes	The cause is unknown. Most common in postmenopausal women, the condition may be linked to: • Hormones • Dry mouth • Taste problems • Nutritional deficiencies • Use of ACE inhibitors (blood pressure medicines)
Treatment	Treatment depends on the cause—if it can be determined—and may include: • Menopausal hormone therapy • Vitamin supplements • Pain medicines or other medicines

Canker sores (aphthous ulcers)

What it is	Small, open ulcers in the mouth. They are white with a red border.
Causes	The cause is unknown, but immune system problems may be one cause. A cut inside your mouth can also cause a canker sore to develop. Fatigue, stress, trauma, or allergies can trigger canker sores. Some women get canker sores during menstruation. And women are more likely than men to have canker sores that recur. People with celiac disease or Crohn's disease also are more likely to develop canker sores.
Treatment	Sores heal by themselves in 1 to 3 weeks. See your dentist if you get a large sore (larger than a half inch) because you may need medicine. Also see your dentist if you get canker sores often. To ease pain: • Avoid hot, spicy foods • Use mild mouthwashes or salt water • Try over-the-counter coatings or pain medicines

Other Common Oral Health Problems

Cold sores—herpes simplex virus type 1 (HSV-1)

What it is	Small, painful blisters caused by herpes simplex virus type 1 (HSV-1).
Causes	A contagious viral infection. Changes in hormone levels during menstruation may trigger cold sores.
Treatment	Over-the-counter medicines to relieve pain while sores heal, which takes about 7 to 10 days. If you get frequent cold sores, talk with your doctor or dentist about antiviral drugs to reduce healing time and the number of new sores.

Halitosis (hal-lih-TOH-suhss)

What it is	Bad-smelling breath
Causes	• Poor oral hygiene • Some foods • Dentures • Gum disease • Dry mouth • Tobacco use • Respiratory, digestive, or other health problems • Some medicines
Treatment	• Brush and floss at least twice a day • Brush your tongue or use a tongue scraper • Eat more fruits and vegetables • Treat gum disease • Avoid tobacco • See your dentist for help Mouthwashes only mask breath odor for a few hours. If you always need mouthwash to hide bad breath, see your dentist.

Osteonecrosis (OSS-tee-oh-nuh-croh-suhss)

What it is	When bone becomes infected and dies. It can happen around the teeth or in the jaws.
Causes	Cancer and cancer treatments, infection, some medicines.
Treatment	Treatment may include surgery to remove bone.

Taste disorders

What it is	• Loss of some or all of your sense of taste • A change in what tastes good and bad
Causes	The many causes include: • Colds • Sinus problems • Head or nerve injury • Some medicines • Lack of proper nutrition • Oral cancer • Tobacco use • Radiation treatment • Aging
Treatment	If you notice a lasting change (more than 2 weeks, or after you stop using tobacco) in how you taste food and drink, see your health provider.

Other Common Oral Health Problems

Thrush, or oral candidiasis (kan-dih-DEYE-uh-suhss)

What it is	A fungal infection in the mouth or throat. It can cause white patches in the mouth with red tissue underneath that may bleed when the white patches are wiped off.
Causes	Often caused by overgrowth of the fungus Candida, which lives in your mouth naturally. You are at greater risk if your resistance to infection is low, you make very little saliva, or you take antibiotics.
Treatment	Antifungal mouthwash or lozenges. You may need stronger medicine if the infection spreads or your immune system is weak. If your infection is from having a weak immune system, your doctor or dentist may have you take antifungal medicine on a regular basis.

Xerostomia (ZEER-oh-STOH-mee-uh) (dry mouth)

What it is	Not having enough saliva in your mouth.
Causes	Salivary glands do not make enough saliva. Dry mouth is more common in women than men and may be a: • Side effect of medicines or medical treatment • Health problem such as saliva and salivary gland disorders, Sjögren's (SHO-grins) syndrome, or rheumatoid arthritis (ROO-muh-toid ar-THREYE-tuhss) (For more information, see the *Autoimmune Diseases* chapter on page 83.) • Blockage of a salivary gland
Treatment	• Medicines that stimulate the salivary glands • Artificial saliva • Changes in medicines or health treatments • Tobacco and alcohol avoidance • Dietary changes, such as avoiding spicy and salty foods, sipping water often, and using sugarless candy or gum • Nighttime humidifier See your oral health provider if the above treatments do not lessen your symptoms.

Other problems

What is it	Oral health problems from other health conditions or treatments
Causes	Many health issues can lead to oral heal problems. Three common causes are: **Chemotherapy** for any cancer treatment can cause temporary dry mouth, painful mouth sores, and cracked, peeling lips. **Radiation treatment** to the head and neck can cause permanent dry mouth, tooth decay, painful mouth sores, and cracked peeling lips. **HIV/AIDS** can lead to many oral health problems, such as fungal and viral infections, lesions on the lips and tongue, warts, and white patches on the tongue.
Treatment	To maintain oral health, have regular dental and medical visits, use all prescribed medicines, and use good oral hygiene. See an oral health provider *before* you start cancer treatment.

Joint or muscle problems such as temporomandibular joint dysfunction (TMJ) can also cause oral or facial pain. For more information on TMJ, see page 358 of the *Pain* chapter.

Tooth arrangement and tooth loss

There are a variety of treatments for tooth arrangement problems and tooth loss:

- **Orthodontics:** Braces can fix crooked teeth, overbites, underbites, jaw-joint problems, and jaw position.

- **Dental bridges:** A dental bridge is a way to replace missing teeth. Healthy teeth are capped to hold the bridge in the mouth.

- **Dental implants:** If you lose a permanent tooth, it can also be replaced with an implant. Implants are small posts put into your upper or lower jaw bone to hold a replacement tooth or set of teeth.

- **Dentures:** If you lose all your teeth, dentures will be made to replace them. They are removable and can look quite natural. If you lose some of your teeth, a partial denture can made to replace them.

Pregnancy and oral health

Before you become pregnant, it is best to have dental checkups every 6 months to keep your mouth in the best health possible before your pregnancy.

If you are pregnant and have not had regular checkups, consider the following:

- Have a complete oral exam early in your pregnancy. Because you are pregnant, you might not receive routine x-rays. But if you must have x-rays for a dental problem requiring treatment, the health risk to your unborn baby is small.

- Dental treatment during pregnancy is safe. The best time for treatment is between the 14th and 20th weeks.

During the last months of pregnancy, you might be uncomfortable sitting in a dental chair.

- Do not avoid necessary dental treatments—you may risk your and your baby's health.

- Your dentist may need to avoid giving you certain medicines that could affect your baby, such as the antibiotic tetracycline.

- Use good oral hygiene to control your risk of gum diseases. Pregnant women may have changes in taste and develop red, swollen gums that bleed easily. This condition is called pregnancy gingivitis. It can be caused by both poor oral hygiene and higher hormone levels during pregnancy. Until recently, it was thought that having gum disease could raise your risk of having a low-birth-weight baby. Researchers have not been able to confirm this link, but some research is still under way to learn more.

After you give birth, maintain good oral hygiene to protect your baby's oral health. Bacteria that cause cavities can transfer from you to your child by a kiss on the mouth, letting your baby put her fingers in your mouth, tasting food on your baby's spoon, or testing the temperature of a baby bottle with your mouth.

Common cosmetic issues

- **Teeth whitening:** Options vary in price and effectiveness. Talk with your dentist before using them to figure out what is best for you. Whitening your teeth does not make them healthier.

- **Tongue studs:** Jewelry worn in your tongue after it is pierced. Tongue studs put you at risk of chipped teeth, nerve and gum damage, and infections. If you decide to get a tongue stud, talk with your dentist and have the piercing done by a medical professional.

Dental Work: Antibiotics and Your Heart

According to the American Heart Association, most people with heart problems do not need short-term antibiotics before dental treatments. Antibiotics may be used before certain dental treatments to help prevent infective endocarditis—infection of the heart's inner lining or valves—if you have:

- artificial heart valves
- a history of infective endocarditis
- certain serious congenital heart conditions
- a cardiac transplant that develops a problem in a heart valve

If you have questions, discuss them with your oral health provider.

Low-Cost Dental Services

Clinical trials	Oral health clinical trials (research studies) may provide limited free or low-cost dental treatment. To see if you qualify for any current studies, contact the National Institute of Dental and Craniofacial Research. Contacts are listed in the resource section on page 303.
Dental schools	Most schools let dental students treat patients at reduced costs. For a full list of dental schools, see the American Dental Association listed in the resource section on page 303.
Community health centers	To find community health centers that provide free or low-cost dental care, call (888) ASK-HRSA (888-275-4772) or visit the HRSA Information Center at www.hrsa.gov/pc.
State and local resources	Call your local or state health department to find out about financial assistance programs.
Centers for Medicare and Medicaid Services	For information about low-cost health insurance, call (877) 267-2323.

Good oral hygiene and regular dental checkups are vital to a healthy mouth. If you have problems or questions about oral health, see your dentist. For information about oral health issues, see the resources at the end of this chapter. A healthy mouth can keep you smiling for a lifetime. ■

One Woman's Story

Almost everyone has heard of "early detection." But what do you think of when you hear these words? Do you picture a woman having a mammogram or remind yourself to schedule your next Pap test? We may be familiar with screening for breast and cervical cancers, but this is not yet the case for oral cancer. We need to become more aware of oral cancer so that we can prevent this deadly disease before it begins.

Oral cancer is as common as leukemia...

Oral cancer often follows changes in your mouth that look like white or red patches or spots. Your dentist should identify such changes, test them, and remove those that have the potential to become cancerous or are early cancer growths. Early detection is critical to improving survival rates. Right now, fewer than half the people diagnosed with oral cancer are able to survive more than 5 years after the disease is first found. Oral cancer is as common as leukemia and claims more lives than either melanoma or cervical cancer. Risk factors include the use of tobacco or alcohol or both, but up to 25 percent of oral cancer patients have no known risk factors. For women, the incidence of oral cancer has increased, mainly due to smoking.

Regular dental exams are important and should also involve an examination of the head and neck to check for oral cancer. This involves looking at the hard and soft tissues of the mouth to detect abnormal color change or growths and feeling lymph nodes of the head and neck to detect abnormal swelling. Dentists and dental hygienists are taught to carry out this full exam for all their patients as part of the routine 6-month dental checkup.

I'm a dentist, and I make sure to get a complete dental exam and cleaning every 6 months. It's become so routine for me that I don't pay attention once I've hopped into the dental chair. I assume the dental team will ensure that my mouth is healthy.

But sure enough, one appointment I had with a very popular dentist in a well-established practice came and went without any effort by the dentist or hygienist to check for oral cancer. I was surprised and disappointed. How many of his patients were leaving their appointment without realizing an important part of their dental exam was missing? How many oral cancers were being missed?

I realize that dental exams aren't routine for everyone, but everyone should know what they are entitled to expect during one. Oral cancer can happen to anyone, so make sure you know your risk and get checked—early detection saves lives!

Mary, Dentist and Patient
Boston, Massachusetts

For More Information...

Office on Women's Health, HHS
200 Independence Ave SW, Room 712E
Washington, DC 20201
Web site: www.womenshealth.gov/faq/
oral_health.htm
Phone number: (800) 994-9662,
(888) 220-5446 TDD

Division of Oral Health, CDC
4770 Buford Highway NE, MS F-10
Atlanta, GA 30341
Web site: www.cdc.gov/oralhealth
Phone number: (800) 232-4636,
(888) 232-6348 TTY

**National Oral Health Information
Clearinghouse, NIH**
1 NOHIC Way
Bethesda, MD 20892-3500
Web site: www.nidcr.nih.gov
Phone number: (301) 402-7364

Academy of General Dentistry
211 E Chicago Ave, Ste 900
Chicago, IL 60611-1999
Web site: www.agd.org/public

American Academy of Periodontology
737 N Michigan Ave, Suite 800
Chicago, IL 60611-6660
Web site: www.perio.org

American Association of Orthodontists
401 N Lindbergh Blvd
St Louis, MO 63141-7816
Web site: www.braces.org

American Dental Association
211 East Chicago Ave
Chicago, IL 60611-2678
Web site: www.ada.org

Skin and Hair Health

How our skin and hair look is important to many of us. At the same time, your skin and hair are organs that do special jobs that support life. Skin protects your inside organs from injury, bacteria, and viruses. Your skin, hair, and sweat glands help control body temperature. Body hair also alerts you to heat and touch. You can take steps to keep your skin and hair healthy. You can also look to your skin and hair for clues to your overall health. And, as a bonus, good skin and hair care will help you to feel your best, too.

Caring for your skin and hair

Good skin and hair care involves:

- eating a variety of healthy foods rich in vitamins and nutrients
- keeping physically active
- managing stress
- practicing sun safety
- limiting alcohol
- not using tobacco and other recreational drugs
- drinking plenty of water

Unhealthy behaviors can take a toll on skin and hair. For instance, habits like smoking and sunbathing dry out skin and cause wrinkles.

Caring for your skin

Follow this simple skin care routine to keep your skin healthy and radiant:

- Bathe in warm—not hot—water using mild cleansers that don't irritate. Wash gently—don't scrub.

- Keep skin from drying out by drinking plenty of water and using gentle moisturizers, lotions, or creams.

- Practice sun safety to prevent skin cancer. Sun exposure puts you at greater risk of skin cancer, whatever your skin color or ethnicity. To protect your skin:

  - Limit exposure to the midday sun (10 AM-4 PM).

  - Wear protective clothing, such as wide-brimmed hats and long sleeves.

  - Use sunscreen with a sun protection factor (SPF) of 15 or higher and with both UVA and UVB protection.

  - Avoid sunlamps and tanning booths.

- Check your skin for sun damage. Tell your doctor about changes on the skin, such as a new growth, a sore that

Age Spots

Years of sun exposure can cause flat, brown spots called "liver" or age spots to appear on your face, hands, arms, back, and feet. They are not harmful. But if the look of age spots bothers you, ask your doctor about skin-lightening creams, laser therapy, and cryotherapy (freezing). Use sunscreen to prevent more age spots.

doesn't heal, or a change in an old growth. Ask your doctor how often you should have a clinical skin exam to check for signs of skin cancer. (See pages 53 and 54 of the *Cancer* chapter for more information.)

- Ask your doctor if the medicines you are taking can affect your skin. For instance, blood thinners and aspirin can cause you to bruise more easily. Some antibiotics and vitamins make skin sunburn more easily.

Skin and hair: Clues to overall health

Healthy skin and hair are signs of good overall health. Some skin and hair changes can signal a health problem. For instance, a "butterfly" rash on your face can be a sign of lupus. Distinct rashes appear with some viruses, such as the measles and chicken pox. An allergic reaction can cause hives, redness, and itching. Diabetes and thyroid disease can cause hair loss. Knowing how your skin and hair normally look and feel will help you notice changes to ask your doctor about.

Nail Health

Healthy fingernails and toenails are smooth, with an even color. Keep your nails clean, dry, and trimmed to prevent ingrown nails. If you wear artificial (fake) nails, check around the base and sides of the nails for redness, pain, and infection. Bacteria and fungus can grow between the artificial nail and your natural nail. Tell your doctor if you notice nail changes, which also could be the result of health problems, such as diabetes or heart disease.

Common skin complaints

Sensitive skin

Women with sensitive skin may have itching, burning, stinging, or tightness after using products such as soaps or makeup. Women of color are more prone to sensitive skin. Look for products made for sensitive skin. Talk with your doctor if these products don't help.

Pimples (acne)

Pimples form when hair follicles under your skin clog up. Although most common in the teen years, many women get pimples into their 50s. Acne also is common during pregnancy and menopause, when hormones are changing. Medicines, such as birth control pills, can also lead to breakouts.

The cause of acne is unclear. We do know that dirt, stress, and foods do not cause acne. But stress and certain foods, such as chocolate or greasy foods, can make acne worse. Acne also appears to run in some families.

To care for acne, use mild soaps, avoid touching your skin, and wear oil-free makeup. Your doctor may also suggest an acne medicine. If so, ask about the side effects. Do not take isotretinoin (eye-soh-trih-TIN-oh-in) (Accutane®) if you are pregnant or trying to get pregnant—it can hurt your baby.

Dry skin

Skin can dry out and become rough, scaly, and itchy for a number of reasons. Dry skin (xerosis, zih-ROH-suhss) can be caused by:

- dry air
- overuse of soaps, antiperspirants, and perfumes

- not drinking enough water
- stress
- smoking
- the sun

Doctors report a higher rate of dry skin in African Americans. Try the skin care routine on pages 305 and 306. If dry skin does not improve, talk to your doctor. Sometimes, dry skin signals a health problem, such as diabetes or kidney disease.

Cellulite

Cellulite is fat that collects just below the surface of your skin, giving it a dimpled look. Women of all sizes can get it. Once formed, you cannot get rid of cellulite. No amount of weight loss, exercise, or massage reduces cellulite. Spa wraps, creams, and vitamins also do not help. Liposuction can make it look even worse. To prevent cellulite, try eating well, being active, and not smoking.

Stretch marks

Rapid growth and weight gain, such as with puberty and pregnancy, can stretch your skin, leaving pink, red, or brown streaks on your breasts, stomach, hips, buttocks, or thighs. Medicines, such as cortisones, and health problems, like diabetes or Cushing's syndrome, also can cause stretch marks. Creams that claim to prevent stretch marks are of little value. Yet stretch marks often fade over time.

Skin and Scalp Conditions

Condition	Symptoms	Possible treatments
Athlete's foot Fungal infection	• Red, itchy, and cracked skin on the toes • Thick, yellow, and crumbly toenails	• Antifungal cream • Wash feet daily, wear clean socks, and do not walk barefoot
Burns Tissue damage caused by heat, sunlight, electricity, chemicals, or radiation	• Swelling, blistering, and scarring • Damage to outer layer of skin, which can extend into body tissues • If serious, shock and even death	• Antibiotics • Hospital care may be needed • Deep burns with tissue damage may require skin grafts
Cellulitis Bacterial infection	• Hot, painful, or tender skin • Tight, glossy look to skin • Sudden rash on face or legs	• Antibiotic cream • Clean area with soap and water • Call your doctor if symptoms worsen
Cold sores Fever blisters caused by herpes simplex virus	• Tingling, itching, or burning on mouth, gums, or lips • Small, painful blisters filled with fluid *May spread by kissing or touching, or sharing razors, towels, or dishes*	• Medicine to rub on sores • Medicine taken by mouth • Wash sores with soap and water • Ice sores to reduce pain • Without treatment, sores usually heal in 2 weeks
Corns and calluses Skin layers that thicken because of too much rubbing or pressure on the same spot	• Thick and hardened skin, which may be flaky and dry • Usually on hands or feet	• Wear shoes that fit • Wear gloves during weight lifting, gardening, and other activities that cause pressure • Use a pumice stone to gently rub off dead skin

Skin and Scalp Conditions

Condition	Symptoms	Possible treatments
Dandruff Chronic scalp disorder usually caused by an overgrowth of fungus normally found on the scalp	• Itchy, scaly scalp • Flakes of dead skin on scalp and shoulders	• Over-the-counter and prescription shampoos • Manage stress • Don't use styling products
Eczema (EG-zuh-muh) Chronic skin condition; also called atopic dermatitis (ay-TOP-ihk DUR-muh-TEYE-tuhss)	• Dry and itchy skin • Rashes on the face, inside the elbows, behind the knees, and on the hands and feet • Sometimes, redness, swelling, cracking, crusting, and sores that seep clear fluid	• Special skin care routine • Avoid triggers, like perfumes, smoke, and stress • Medicine • Light treatment
Head lice Insects that live on your head	• Itchy scalp or tickling feeling in your hair *Spreads through head-to-head contact and by touching personal items like hats, scarves, and combs*	• Medicine applied to the scalp • Wash clothing, combs, bedding, and other personal items
Impetigo (im-puh-TEE-goh) Skin infection caused by bacteria, usually staph or strep	• Tiny, itchy blisters on face, arms, or legs • Thick, light-brown scabs *May spread through personal contact, or by sharing towels, razors, or clothing*	• Antibacterial cream • Medicines taken by mouth • Wash with antibacterial soap several times a day, gently remove scabs • Use clean washcloth and towel each time you wash
Pigment disorders Darker or lighter area of skin; called a "birthmark" if present at birth	• Skin with too much or too little pigment (color) • Usually on elbows, knuckles, and knees • Bronze color on soles and palms	• Creams to lighten the skin • Cosmetics to mask area • Avoid direct sun and use sunscreen
Psoriasis (suh-REYE-uh-suhss) An autoimmune (aw-toh-ih-MYOON) disease	• Thick red patches, covered with scales, usually appearing on head, elbows, and knees • Itching and pain, which can make it hard to sleep, walk, and care for yourself	• Medicine • Light treatment
Rosacea (roh-ZAY-shuh) Chronic skin condition; more common after menopause	• Redness and flushness on the face, mainly in adults with fair skin • Small red lines under the skin, bumps on the skin, and inflamed eyes	• Green-tinted makeup to hide redness • Medicines • Laser surgery
Scabies Infection caused by a type of insect called a mite laying eggs beneath your skin	• Mark that looks like a pencil line • Itchy bites or sores on hands and feet • Pimples on your abdomen *May spread by sharing clothing and bedding*	• Creams to rub on infected area • Medicines taken by mouth • Cool baths and calamine lotion • Wash clothing and bedding to reduce spreading

Skin and Scalp Conditions

Condition	Symptoms	Possible treatments
Shingles Painful skin rash caused by the chicken pox virus	• Rash of raised dots or red blisters • Small fluid-filled blisters with scabs • Shooting pain on one side of your body *Most people 60 and older should get the one-time-only herpes zoster vaccine, which can prevent shingles. Ask your doctor if you can get it.*	• Medicines to reduce pain and other symptoms
Vitiligo (vit-ihl-EYE-goh) An autoimmune disease (See page 84 of the *Autoimmune Diseases* chapter for more information.)	• White patches on areas exposed to the sun, or on armpits, genitals, and rectum • Hair turns gray early • Loss of color inside your mouth	• Steroid creams to rub on patches • Medicines taken by mouth • Light therapy • Cosmetics or tattoos to cover patches • Counseling to cope with changes in appearance

Caring for your hair

Your hair is one of the first things that others notice about you. The shape and structure of your hair depend on your race. For instance, African hair is typically flat with tight curls. Asian hair is typically round and thick. Caucasian hair may be fine and straight or thick and wavy. Natural oils from hair glands also affect the look and feel of your hair.

Basic hair care involves a healthy lifestyle and proper care. Wash oily hair daily and limit how much you touch your hair. For dry hair, keep blow-drying time short and avoid overstyling, which can lead to dryness and breakage. Protecting your hair from wind, sun, and chlorine in water also will help to keep it from drying out and breaking.

If you color or relax your hair, carefully read the product label. Hair dyes and relaxers can harm both your skin and hair. Talk with your doctor if your skin or scalp swells or gets itchy after using any hair product. Even natural products, such as henna dye, can cause an allergic reaction.

Hair disorders

Living with a hair disorder can be hard, especially in a culture that views hair as a feature of beauty. To cope, try to value yourself for who you are—not by how you look. Also, play up your best features, which can boost self-esteem. Many women with hair disorders also find that talking to others with the same problem is helpful.

Hair loss

It's normal to shed about 100 hairs each day as old hairs are replaced by new ones. But some women have hair loss—called alopecia (AL-uh-PEE-shuh). Hair loss can happen for many reasons:

- Female-pattern baldness causes hair to thin, but rarely leads to total baldness. It tends to run in families.

- Alopecia areata (AR-ee-AYT-uh) is an autoimmune disease that causes patchy hair loss on the scalp, face, or other areas of your body.

- Hormone changes during and after pregnancy.

- Underlying health problems, such as polycystic ovary syndrome (PCOS) or thyroid disease.

- Certain medicines, such as birth control pills or those to treat cancer, arthritis, depression, or heart problems.

- Extreme stress, such as from a major illness.

- Hairstyles that twist or pull hair.

Whether or not hair will grow back depends on the cause of hair loss. Some medicines can help speed up the growth of new hair. If hair loss is permanent, you can try hair weaving or changing your hairstyle. Or talk with your doctor about other options, such as a hair transplant.

Hirsutism

When dark, thick hair grows on a woman's face, chest, belly, or back, the condition is called hirsutism (HUR-suh-TIZ-uhm). Health problems and family genes can cause high levels of male hormones, which can result in hirsutism. If you are overweight, try losing weight, which reduces male hormone levels. Consider methods for removal of unwanted hair. (See page 312 for more information.) Also, ask your doctor about medicines to slow or reduce hair growth.

Polycystic Ovary Syndrome (PCOS)

Women with polycystic ovary syndrome (PCOS) make too many male hormones. This can cause male-pattern balding or thinning hair and/or hirsutism. (See page 159 of the *Reproductive Health* chapter for more information on PCOS.)

Trichotillomania

People with trichotillomania (TRIH-koh-TIL-uh-MAY-nee-uh) have a strong urge to pull out their hair, which leads to visible hair loss. Some people with this hair-pulling disorder also pluck their eyebrows, eyelashes, and body hair. Hair pulling gives people with this disorder a sense of relief or pleasure. But it also is a source of distress and shame. Behavioral therapy and medicines can help a person stop hair pulling.

Cosmetic practices

Makeup

Good skin care is the foundation of beauty. But many women enjoy using makeup (cosmetics) too. If you use makeup, follow these tips:

- Read the labels for product content and safety information.
- Wash your hands before applying makeup.
- Throw out products if the color changes or they get an odor.

- Throw out mascara after 3 months.
- Keep product containers tightly closed when not in use.
- Don't share your makeup.
- Call your doctor if a product causes skin changes like itching and rash—you may be having an allergic reaction.

Tattoos and permanent makeup

Tattoos are colored inks inserted under your skin. Permanent makeup is a tattoo made to look like eyebrow, lip, and eye liner. If you like tattoos, keep these health risks in mind: Needles that are not properly cleaned can pass infections—even HIV—from person to person. Allergic reactions to tattoo ink are rare but can happen. Also, poorly applied tattoos can be costly to remove. Temporary tattoos and other skin-staining products, including henna dyes, can cause allergic reactions. Henna is approved by the U.S. Food and Drug Administration (FDA) only for use as a hair dye.

Hair removal

Cultural norms often affect a woman's choice to remove body hair. Many women shave their legs and underarms. Wet hair first, then shave in the direction that your hair grows. Chemicals called depilatories dissolve unwanted hair. Depilatories can irritate, so always test on a small area of skin before using. Never use chemicals around your eyes or on broken skin. For laser, epilator (electrolysis), waxing, sugaring, or threading treatments, find a licensed technician. Serious side effects of hair removal can include swelling, blistering, scarring, and infection.

Cosmetic Procedures and Surgery

Some women choose to have cosmetic procedures to improve appearance and self-esteem. But the decision to have a cosmetic procedure should not be made lightly. If you are thinking about having a cosmetic procedure, ask your doctor:

- How is the procedure done?
- Am I good candidate for the procedure?
- How does my health history affect my risk of problems?
- What results and side effects can I expect?
- What are the risks?
- When can I restart normal activities?
- How much will the procedure cost? (Cosmetic procedures usually are not covered by insurance.)
- What is your training and experience?
- Can you provide references from patients you have treated?

Body piercing

Before piercing—poking a hole and inserting jewelry in—any part of your body, learn about the health risks. Piercings in your tongue, cheeks, and lips may cause gum disease. Infection is common in mouth and nose piercings, so talk with your doctor about signs of infection as well as allergies. Also ask if your shots, especially hepatitis and tetanus, are up to date. And make sure the shop follows safety and sanitary steps as set by the law.

Beauty tips to live by

Skin or hair care products claiming to reduce wrinkles or enhance shine are tempting to try. But keep in mind, the best beauty tips are free and up to you to follow. Living a healthy lifestyle and practicing sun safety can have you radiating beauty from both outside and within. ■

One Woman's Story

My first bald spots appeared when I was 22 years old. A dermatologist gave me several cortisone shots, but he never said that I had a condition. He attributed my hair loss to stress. The shots worked; my hair grew back and I went on with my life. He didn't say it, but I left his office with the impression that I was "cured."

I wasn't. I had to go back for more cortisone shots, but he still didn't give me a name for what I had. The bald spots would happen more frequently and take longer to fill in, if they filled in at all. I would get some regrowth, but it was sparse, thin, very fine, and sometimes gray. It also did not stay. I finally went to another dermatologist who told me I probably had alopecia areata and that it was not serious.

Alopecia is an autoimmune disorder that causes hair follicles to become inactive. While alopecia is physically benign, the psychological effects can be devastating and debilitating. It can strike swiftly and without warning; or it can happen over a period of years, changing constantly.

Don't let alopecia stop your life.

Over the years, I have seen several dermatologists who used different treatments with little success. Then I met a doctor who told me, "It's only hair. Get over it." His comment sent me into a deeper depression.

Then I met a compassionate, but honest, dermatologist. After she took my history and waited for me to stop crying, she explained alopecia to me in a way that I could understand. She explained that the pattern of hair loss indicates the probability of regrowth. Since my hair loss began around the perimeter of my head and was worse in the back of my head, the probability of it growing back was very slim. Even though this was not good news, it made sense. It gave me something to work with, allowed me to move on.

I used to think, "Why did this have to happen to me?" The answer is "Why not?" Once I stopped whining and started to count my blessings, alopecia did not seem that bad in the larger scheme of things. I'm not saying I would not like to have my hair, eyebrows, and eyelashes back. I am saying that I'm still all right without them.

Don't let alopecia stop your life. Go to a support group. It gets easier knowing you are not alone. I don't intend to get over it, but I do intend to deal with it and support other alopecians.

Cassandra
Columbia, Maryland

For More Information...

Office on Women's Health, HHS
200 Independence Ave SW, Room 712E
Washington, DC 20201
Web site: www.womenshealth.gov/faq/
cosmetics.htm
www.womenshealth.gov/faq/varicose.htm
Phone number: (800) 994-9662,
(888) 220-5446 TDD

National Institute of Arthritis and Musculoskeletal and Skin Diseases Information Clearinghouse, NIH
1 AMS Circle
Bethesda, MD 20892-3675
Web site: www.niams.nih.gov
Phone number: (877) 226-4267,
(301) 565–2966 TTY

Office of Women's Health, FDA
5600 Fishers Ln
Rockville, MD 20857
Web site: www.fda.gov/womens
Phone number: (888) 463-6332

American Academy of Dermatology
PO Box 4014
Schaumburg, IL 60618-4014
Web site: www.aad.org/public
www.skincarephysicians.com
Phone number: (888) 462-3376

American Academy of Family Physicians
PO Box 11210
Shawnee Mission, KS 66207-1210
Web site: www.familydoctor.org

American Society for Dermatologic Surgery
5550 Meadowbrook Dr, Suite 120
Rolling Meadows, IL 60008
Web site: www.asds.net

American Society of Plastic Surgeons
444 E Algonquin Rd
Arlington Heights, IL 60005
Web site: www.plasticsurgery.org

National Eczema Association
4460 Redwood Highway, Suite 16D
San Rafael, CA 94903-1953
Web site: www.nationaleczema.org
Phone number: (800) 818-7546

National Psoriasis Foundation
6600 SW 92nd Ave, Suite 300
Portland, OR 97223-7195
Web site: www.psoriasis.org
Phone number: (800) 723-9166

National Rosacea Society
800 S Northwest Highway, Suite 200
Barrington, IL 60010
Web site: www.rosacea.org
Phone number: (888) 662-5874

Phoenix Society for Burn Survivors
1835 R W Berends Dr SW
Grand Rapids, MI 49519-4955
Web site: www.phoenix-society.org

Nutrition

Life can be hectic, and sometimes it's hard to take the time to make healthy food choices. But making wise food choices—along with regular physical activity—can offer big benefits, now and in the future. Good nutrition may help you lower your risk of some chronic diseases, have healthy pregnancies and healthy babies, and reach and stay at a healthy body weight. Healthy eating habits can help you feel your best—today and every day.

Healthy eating plan

You might feel confused by all the conflicting information you hear about what to eat. But, in reality, a healthy eating plan can help you make wise food choices. A healthy eating plan includes:

- fruits and vegetables
- whole grains
- fat-free or low-fat versions of milk, cheese, yogurt, and other milk products
- lean meats, poultry, fish, dry beans and peas, eggs, and nuts

What should you limit? Your healthy eating plan should be low in:

- saturated fat
- *trans* fat
- cholesterol (koh-LESS-tur-ol)
- salt (sodium)
- added sugars
- alcohol

If you're a vegetarian, you can still have a healthy eating plan, even if you avoid some foods.

Women and Nutrition

Women have special nutritional needs throughout life. For more information on folic acid, vitamin D, iron, and calcium—some of the vitamins and minerals you need to be healthy—see pages 325 and 326.

Healthy eating also means there's a balance between the number of calories you eat and the number of calories you burn. Your body burns calories two ways:

- through daily routine activities and body functions, such as sitting, moving around, breathing, and digesting

- with physical activity, such as walking, biking, or other forms of exercise

Getting personalized recommendations about eating

Where can you turn for reliable information, tailored to your needs? Here are two options.

- You can use the MyPyramid food guidance system, a system developed by the U.S. Department of Agriculture (USDA) to help Americans make healthy food choices. The guidelines in this chapter are based on this system. On the MyPyramid Web site, you can get a food plan based on your age, weight, height, sex, and activity level. The plan will show you what kinds and how much food to eat each day. The MyPyramid Web site also has worksheets and helpful hints.

- You can see a registered dietitian for a personalized nutrition plan. Your doctor can provide a referral. Or you can contact the American Dietetic Association for the name of a dietitian near you.

What is a calorie?

A calorie is a measure of the energy used by the body and of the energy that food supplies to the body.

Carbohydrates, proteins, fats, and alcohol all have calories. Your caloric needs are determined by your age, your size, how physically active you are, whether you are pregnant or breastfeeding, and other special conditions. Your caloric needs also depend on whether you want to lose or gain weight or keep your weight where it is.

Web sites and phone numbers for MyPyramid and the American Dietetic Association are listed in the resource section on page 335.

Tips for making wise food choices

Here are some tips to get you started on making wise food choices. For more detailed information, check out MyPyramid online or see *A Healthier You*, published by the U.S. Department of Health and Human Services, also available online.

A Healthier You: Free Book About Nutrition With Recipes

Want to learn how to make smart food and fitness choices for good health? Based on the 2005 Dietary Guidelines for Americans, *A Healthier You* can show you how. It also includes recipes and tips for eating out. See the Web site listed on page 335, under U.S. Department of Health and Human Services, to view the book online and order print copies.

Grains

Make sure at least half of your grain choices are whole grain. Examples of grain foods are cereals, breads, crackers, and pasta. Check the list of ingredients. Look for grain foods that list "whole" or "whole grain" as the first ingredient, such as whole wheat flour in bread. Whole grains haven't lost any fiber or nutrients from processing. They help meet your nutrient needs, as do foods made from enriched grains.

Vegetables

Choose a variety of vegetables, including:

- dark green vegetables, such as broccoli, kale, and collard greens
- orange vegetables, such as carrots, sweet potatoes, and pumpkin
- dry beans and peas, such as pinto beans, kidney beans, black beans, garbanzo beans, split peas, and lentils

What are nutrients?

Nutrients are substances found in food that nourish your body. Carbohydrates, proteins, and fats are all nutrients. Vitamins and minerals are also nutrients.

It's best to get nutrients from foods instead of vitamin and mineral supplements. That's because foods provide a number of other substances that keep you healthy. But sometimes you might need to take a supplement, such as when you're pregnant.

Nutrition

Fruits

For most of your fruit servings, choose a variety of fruits (without added sugars) in various forms, such as fresh, frozen, canned, or dried. For example, try fresh apples, frozen blueberries, canned peaches, or dried apricots. Look for canned fruit packed in water or 100 percent fruit juice, instead of syrup. Go easy on fruit juice because it lacks fiber. If you do have fruit juice, make sure it's 100 percent fruit juice.

Milk, cheese, and yogurt

- Choose low-fat or fat-free milk, cheese, and yogurt.

- If you have lactose intolerance, you can still get calcium from reduced-lactose milk, other milk products, and non-dairy sources of calcium. Many people with lactose intolerance can eat small amounts of milk, cheese, yogurt, and other milk products without discomfort. Or you can take the enzyme lactase in the form of pills or liquid drops before you eat dairy products.

- If you can't or don't consume milk, cheese, or yogurt, choose other sources of calcium, such as calcium-fortified soy drinks, calcium-fortified tofu, collard greens, or fortified ready-to-eat cereals.

Meat, beans, and other foods high in protein

- Choose low-fat or lean meats and poultry, such as chicken without the skin, or top round (a lean cut of beef).

- Prepare meat, fish, and poultry using low-fat cooking methods, such as baking, broiling, or grilling.

- Vary your protein choices. Try fish, beans, peas, nuts, and seeds. For example, try making a main dish without meat for dinner, such as pasta with beans, at least once a week.

The Healthy Woman: A Complete Guide for All Ages

Fats

- Everyone needs some fat as part of a healthful diet. Fats should provide about 20 to 35 percent of your daily calories. Even though some fats are heart-healthy, they are still high in calories. Limit serving sizes of all fats.

- Choose heart-healthy fats: foods with monounsaturated fats and polyunsaturated fatty acids, such as salmon or corn oil. (See page 324 for more examples.) Most of the fat you eat should come from vegetable oils, nuts, and fish. For example, cook with canola oil. Snack on nuts. Have fish for dinner.

- Limit how often you have heart-harmful fats: foods with saturated fat, *trans* fat, and cholesterol, such as bacon, whole milk, and foods with hydrogenated or partially hydrogenated fats. (See page 325 for more examples.) Limit how often you have fats that are solid at room temperature and the foods that contain them, such as fatty cuts of meat. If you eat foods with heart-harmful fats, limit how much you eat of them.

Salt (sodium)

Limit your sodium to less than 2300 milligrams each day. Choose foods with little sodium. Fruits, vegetables, dry beans and peas, and fresh meat, poultry, and fish are naturally low in sodium. You can also check the Nutrition Facts label on food packages. (Food labels use the word "sodium" instead of salt.) Many processed foods are high in sodium. Try to cut back on how much salt you add while you cook and at the table.

Added sugars

Limit the amount of foods and drinks you consume with added sugars, such as cakes, cookies, regular soft drinks, and candy. Check the Nutrition Facts label to find added sugars. (See page 328 for a list of names of added sugars.) Added sugars will be shown in the list of ingredients. The Nutrition Facts label lists the total sugars content. However, the total includes naturally occurring sugar, such as the sugar in fruit, plus added sugar.

How to start changing the way you eat

Sometimes it's hard to change habits. But making a change step by step can help.

- Choose one small change you'd like to make.

- Make your idea as specific and realistic as possible. For example, instead of saying, "I will eat more high-fiber food," say, "I will have an orange three days a week for breakfast."

- Decide on when you will make this change, choosing a short period of time. For example, set a goal for this week.

- Write down your plan, using the guide on the following page.

- When your idea has become a regular habit, choose something new to try.

Use the questions on the next page to make your plan for change.

My Plan for Changing the Way I Eat

What I'll do: _____

_____

_____

Example: I'll have fruit for my evening snack instead of potato chips.

When (or how often) I'll do it: _____

_____

_____

Example: I'll do that every night before I go to bed.

What I'll need to get ready: _____

_____

_____

Example: I'll buy some apples.

What might interfere with my plan: _____

_____

_____

Example: Having potato chips in the house.

How I'll overcome my barriers: _____

_____

_____

Example: I'll stop buying potato chips this week.

When I'll start my plan: _____

Example: I'll start on Monday and try it for 1 week.

How I'll reward myself (with a non-food reward): _____

_____

_____

Example: I'll go to the movies each week if I meet my goal.

The Healthy Woman: A Complete Guide for All Ages

Ideas for improving your food choices

Start with one of these ideas to improve your food choices this week. Or maybe you already have your own idea.

Instead of...	Try...
Whole milk	Low-fat (1%) milk or fat-free (skim) milk
Sour cream	Plain yogurt, low-fat or non-fat
White bread or flour tortillas	Whole wheat bread or whole wheat tortillas
Bacon	Canadian bacon or lean ham
Regular ground beef (25% fat)	Extra-lean ground beef (5% fat)
Regular ice cream	Low-fat frozen yogurt
Fried chicken	Roasted chicken without the skin

Your quick reference to the basics of nutrition

Here's a summary of the basics about nutrition. You can use this chart to learn what each nutrient does and where to find it. For more information about how much to have of each nutrient, talk with your doctor or dietitian.

Carbohydrates

Type	What you need to know	sources
	• Carbohydrates are part of a healthful diet. They supply energy to your body.	• Fruits • Vegetables • Grains • Milk and yogurt • Dry beans and peas
Fiber	• Fiber may lower your risk of heart disease and helps your digestive system run smoothly.	• Fruits • Vegetables • Whole grains • Dry beans and peas
Sugars	• Some sugars occur naturally in foods that are important in a healthy diet.	• Fruits • Milk
Added sugars	• Some foods and drinks are sweetened with added sugars and syrups. (See page 328 for a list of names of added sugars.) • Added sugars provide calories, and no additional nutrients. • Choosing foods and drinks with little added sugars may help you reduce calories and help with weight control.	• Regular soft drinks • Candy • Cakes, cookies, and pies • Fruit drinks • Ice cream • Sweetened yogurt and sweetened grains such as sweetened cereals (These foods provide nutrients but may not be the best choices because of extra calories from added sugars.)

Protein

What you need to know	Sources
• Protein plays an important role in many body structures and functions.	• Meat • Poultry • Fish and shellfish • Eggs • Nuts • Peanut butter • Seeds • Dry beans and peas • Tofu • Soybeans • Vegetarian burgers

Fats

Heart-Healthy Fats—Unsaturated Fats (Best for Your Heart)

Type of fat	What you need to know	Sources
Monounsaturated fat	• It can lower your blood cholesterol level.	• Nuts • Canola oil • Olive oil • High oleic safflower oil ("High oleic" means the oil has a high percentage of monounsaturated fatty acids.) • Sunflower oil
Polyunsaturated omega-3 fatty acids (a type of polyunsaturated fat)	• They help your body work well. If you already have heart disease, they may protect your heart.	• Walnuts • Flaxseed • Salmon • Trout • Herring • Soybean oil • Canola oil
Polyunsaturated omega-6 fatty acids (a type of polyunsaturated fat)	• They help your body work well (when they replace saturated fat).	• Corn oil • Soybean oil • Safflower oil

Fats

Heart-Harmful Fats (Worst for Your Heart)

Type of fat	What you need to know	Sources
Saturated fat	• It can increase your blood fat levels. This can raise your heart disease risk.	• Bacon • Butter • Coconut • Whole milk products • Lard • Fatty cuts of meat • Palm oil
Trans fats, also called *trans* fatty acids	• They can increase your blood fat levels. This can raise your heart disease risk.	• Foods made with partially hydrogenated or hydrogenated oils • Foods in which *trans* fats occur naturally, such as butter, milk products, cheese, beef, and lamb
Cholesterol	• It can increase your blood fat levels. This can raise your heart disease risk.	• High-fat milk products, such as cheese, ice cream, and whole milk • Egg yolks • Liver • Meat • Poultry

Vitamins

Name	What you need to know	Sources*
Folic acid (folate)	• It helps make and maintain new cells and can help lower the risk of some birth defects. (For more information, see the *Pregnancy* chapter on page 169.)	• Fortified foods, such as enriched breads, cereals, and pasta • Dry beans and peas • Spinach, collard greens, and other leafy green vegetables • Orange juice
Vitamin A	• It's important for your vision. It also helps your body fight infections.	• Carrot juice • Sweet potatoes • Carrots • Spinach • Collards

Vitamins

Name	What you need to know	Sources*
Vitamin C	• It helps with repair of your body.	• Guavas • Red sweet peppers • Oranges • Orange juice • Green peppers • Grapefruit juice
Vitamin D	• It helps your body create and maintain strong bones.	• Sunshine. Your body can make vitamin D after your skin is exposed to sunlight without sunscreen for 10 to 15 minutes twice a week. But be sure to use sunscreen after your 15 minutes of exposure and at all other times. Eat foods with vitamin D throughout the year. • Salmon • Shrimp • Milk fortified with vitamin D (Most milk is fortified.)

*Food sources in this chart are listed in order of the amount of a nutrient they provide in a typical serving—from high to low. See *A Healthier You* for more sources. See page 335 to find out how to get *A Healthier You*.

Minerals

Name	What you need to know	Sources*
Calcium	• It helps build strong bones and teeth.	Dairy sources: • Plain yogurt, non-fat • Cheese • Fruit yogurt, low-fat • Fat-free (skim) milk Non-dairy sources: • Fortified ready-to-eat cereals • Calcium-fortified soy drinks • Calcium-fortified tofu • Collards
Iron	• It plays an important part in many basic body functions, such as taking oxygen to cells. • Vitamin C–rich foods help your body absorb iron from non-animal foods, such as fortified cereals.	• Beef, bottom round • Fortified ready-to-eat cereals (Check the label for amounts.) • Fortified instant cooked cereals • Soybeans • Lentils • Spinach

The Healthy Woman: A Complete Guide for All Ages

Minerals

Name	What you need to know	Sources*
Potassium	• It helps all cells work properly. It also helps build muscles and plays a part in growth.	• Sweet potatoes • Potatoes, baked • Tomato puree • Halibut • Bananas • Spinach • Oranges

*Food sources in this chart are listed in order of the amount of a nutrient they provide in a typical serving—from high to low. See *A Healthier You* for more sources. See page 335 to find out how to get *A Healthier You*.

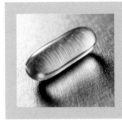

Taking Vitamin and Mineral Supplements

If you take vitamin and mineral supplements, talk to your health care provider about what you're taking. Ask whether taking supplements is right for you. Sometimes dietary supplements can interact with your medicines or affect your health in unwanted ways.

Salt (Sodium)

What you need to know	Recommendation
• Most people eat too much sodium. • Reducing the amount of sodium in your diet can help lower your blood pressure. • Meeting your potassium requirement (4700 milligrams each day) by eating foods rich in potassium can also help lower blood pressure. • Talk with your doctor about how much sodium you should consume each day.	• Limit yourself to less than 2300 milligrams of sodium (about 1 teaspoon of salt) each day. • People with high blood pressure, African Americans, and middle-aged and older adults should aim to have no more than 1500 milligrams of sodium each day. They should also make sure they have 4700 milligrams of potassium each day by eating foods with potassium. • You can limit sodium by cutting down on how much salt you add to food while cooking and at the table and watching out for sodium-containing foods. Check the Nutrition Facts labels and make sure your choices don't exceed 100 percent of the daily value for sodium.

Alcoholic Beverages

What you need to know	Recommendation
• Alcoholic beverages have calories but few nutrients. • Avoid alcoholic beverages if you're pregnant, breastfeeding, or if you're of childbearing age and might become pregnant.	• If you choose to drink alcoholic beverages, limit yourself to no more than one drink each day. One drink is equal to 12 fluid ounces of beer, 5 fluid ounces of wine, or 1.5 fluid ounces of 80-proof distilled spirits.

Using the Nutrition Facts label

Information on the Nutrition Facts food label can help you make wise food choices.

- Check the serving size. Use it as a guide to compare products and make better choices. The serving size information tells you how many servings are in one package.

Nutrition Facts

Serving Size 1 cup (228g)
Servings Per Container 2

Amount Per Serving

Calories 250	Calories from Fat 110

	% Daily Value*
Total Fat 12g	18%
Saturated Fat 3g	15%
Trans Fat 3g	
Cholesterol 470mg	10%
Sodium 470mg	20%
Potassium 700mg	20%
Total Carbohydrate 31g	10%
Dietary Fiber 0g	0%
Sugars 5g	
Protein 5g	
Vitamin A	4%
Vitamin C	2%
Calcium	20%
Iron	4%

* Percent Daily Values are based on a 2,000 calorie diet. Your daily values may be higher or lower depending on your calorie needs:

	Calories:	2,000	2,500
Total Fat	Less than	65g	80g
Sat Fat	Less than	20g	25g
Cholesterol	Less than	300mg	300mg
Sodium	Less than	2,400mg	2,400mg
Total Carbohydrate		300g	375g
Dietary Fiber		25g	30g

- Look at the calories per serving. You can use the information about calories to compare foods.

- Check the list of ingredients. Ingredients are listed in order by weight.

  - If you're trying to avoid foods with a lot of added sugar, limit foods that list added sugars as the first few ingredients. Other names for added sugars include brown sugar, corn sweetener, corn syrup, dextrose, fructose, fruit juice concentrates, glucose, high fructose corn syrup, honey, invert sugar, lactose, maltose, malt syrup, molasses, raw sugar, sucrose, and syrup.

  - If you're trying to increase your fiber intake, choose foods with a whole grain, such as whole wheat, listed as the first ingredient. Other whole grains are whole oats, oatmeal, whole-grain corn, popcorn, brown rice, whole rye, whole-grain barley, wild rice, buckwheat, triticale, bulgur (cracked wheat), millet, quinoa, and sorghum. You can also increase your fiber intake by eating more vegetables, fruits, beans, and nuts.

Comparing foods using the percent (%) Daily Value

The % Daily Value column (see the purple area in the example label) can help you compare packaged foods. Use this quick guide to the numbers:

- 5% or less is low.

- 20% or more is high.

For a healthy diet, you want to **get enough** of these nutrients (see the green area in the example label):

- potassium
- fiber
- vitamins A and C
- calcium
- iron

For example, if a **cereal** has a daily value of **20% for fiber**, it's **high** in fiber. That means it's a **wise** choice for fiber.

For a healthy diet, you want to **limit** these (see the gold area in the example label):

- total fat
- saturated fat
- *trans* fat
- cholesterol
- sodium

You also want to limit added sugars for a healthy diet. Make sure that added sugars are not among the first few items in the list of ingredients.

For example, **fat-free milk** has a daily value of **1% for cholesterol**, meaning it's **low** in cholesterol. That means it's a **wise** choice if you're limiting your intake of cholesterol. Fat-free milk is also low in total fat, saturated fat, and *trans* fat, meaning it's a wise choice if you're limiting all of these fats.

Reaching and staying at a healthy weight

To reach and stay at a healthy weight, you need both healthful eating and physical activity. These two strategies work well together.

For information on physical activity, see the *Fitness* chapter on page 337.

Many American women are overweight. Being overweight or obese may increase your risk of heart disease, high blood pressure, type 2 diabetes, and other conditions. You can keep from gaining weight by balancing the number of calories you eat and drink with the number of calories you burn with physical activity and body functions. To lose weight, you need to use more calories than you eat and drink.

How do you know whether you're overweight? One way is to check the Body Mass Index chart. (See page 22 of the *Heart Disease* chapter.)

Choosing sensible portions can help you control your weight. You can estimate serving sizes of your food using everyday items. See the guide below.

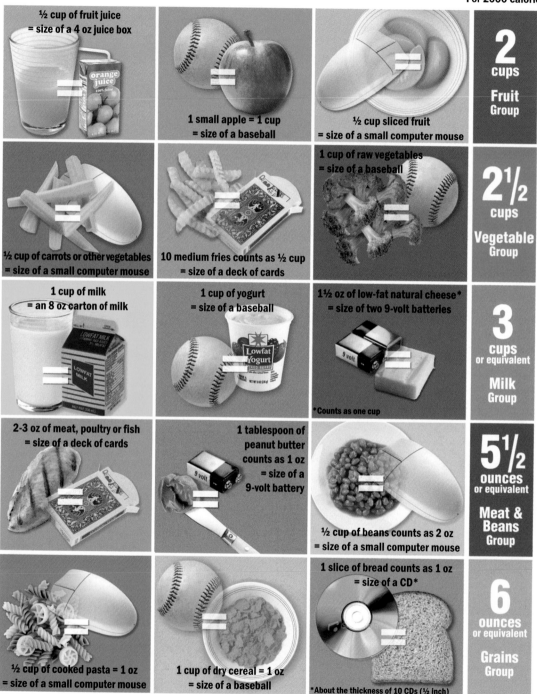

Amount of foods
For 2000 calories

½ cup of fruit juice = size of a 4 oz juice box

1 small apple = 1 cup = size of a baseball

½ cup sliced fruit = size of a small computer mouse

2 cups Fruit Group

½ cup of carrots or other vegetables = size of a small computer mouse

10 medium fries counts as ½ cup = size of a deck of cards

1 cup of raw vegetables = size of a baseball

2½ cups Vegetable Group

1 cup of milk = an 8 oz carton of milk

1 cup of yogurt = size of a baseball

1½ oz of low-fat natural cheese* = size of two 9-volt batteries

*Counts as one cup

3 cups or equivalent Milk Group

2-3 oz of meat, poultry or fish = size of a deck of cards

1 tablespoon of peanut butter counts as 1 oz = size of a 9-volt battery

½ cup of beans counts as 2 oz = size of a small computer mouse

5½ ounces or equivalent Meat & Beans Group

½ cup of cooked pasta = 1 oz = size of a small computer mouse

1 cup of dry cereal = 1 oz = size of a baseball

1 slice of bread counts as 1 oz = size of a CD*

*About the thickness of 10 CDs (½ inch)

6 ounces or equivalent Grains Group

ADAPTED FROM U.S. DEPARTMENT OF AGRICULTURE, TEAM NUTRITION. USDA DOES NOT ENDORSE ANY PRODUCTS, SERVICES, OR ORGANIZATIONS. PROVIDED BY WOMENSHEALTH.GOV.

The Healthy Woman: A Complete Guide for All Ages

Making wise food choices when you're away from home

We all eat many meals and snacks while we're on the run. These tips can help you stay on track.

When	Tips
Snacks	Try these healthier choices: • Fruit • A small handful of nuts • Baby carrots and cherry tomatoes • Whole-grain crackers with low-fat cheese • Low-fat or fat-free yogurt • Fat-free frozen yogurt • Low-fat, lower sodium crackers • Lower fat cookies such as graham crackers or fig bars
Lunches	Make sandwiches with: • Low-fat cheese or fat-free cheese • 95 to 97 percent fat-free lunch meats • Chicken or turkey without the skin • Water-packed tuna • Lettuce leaves, tomato slices, cucumber slices, and other vegetables • Whole-grain breads, rolls, or tortillas • Reduced-calorie margarine or mayonnaise • Mustard

When	Tips
Lunches	Bring or buy healthy main-dish salads with: • A variety of vegetables—not just lettuce • Lower fat, lower sodium high-protein food, such as grilled chicken or turkey, water-packed tuna, or low-fat cheese • Lemon juice, herb vinegar, or reduced-calorie salad dressing • Whole-grain crackers or whole-grain bread on the side
	Bring frozen meals—choose ones lower in fat and sodium—and add a salad or some fruit, plus low-fat milk.
Eating out	In any restaurant: • Ask for salad dressing, gravy, or sauce on the side and use sparingly. • Choose main dishes that are broiled, baked, roasted, or grilled, instead of deep-fried or pan-fried. • Don't be afraid to make special requests, such as asking that something be cooked with less fat.
	When ordering a sandwich: • Add lettuce and tomato. • Ask for whole wheat or rye bread. • Choose mustard instead of mayonnaise.
	At Chinese restaurants: • Have brown rice instead of white rice. • Order a side dish of steamed broccoli.
	At fast-food places: • Order smaller burgers. • Have grilled chicken. • Choose water or low-fat milk instead of regular soda.
	At pizza places: • Ask for vegetable toppings, such as mushrooms or peppers, rather than meat toppings. • Get whole wheat crust. • Request half the cheese. • Eat a salad with low-fat dressing in place of a slice of pizza.

Research in nutrition today

Scientists are researching what types of diets are best for preventing and controlling disease. For example, one study is examining the effect of the typical American diet on the risk of heart disease in African American and Caucasian women. In another project, scientists are trying to find the best treatment for osteoporosis (OSS-tee-oh-puh-ROH-suhss) in older women. Much research is also devoted to the prevention and control of obesity, a major problem in the United States.

Taking the time to make wise food choices—it's up to you

It's never too late to make changes in how you eat. Small changes can make a big difference. Think about what you are willing to do. When you're ready to make a change, decide on a plan and give it a try.

If your plan doesn't work, it doesn't mean you've failed. Instead, it means you might need to try something different. Keep in mind that you'll do a lot for your health, day to day and in the long run, if you make wise food choices most of the time. ■

One Woman's Story

My story of successful weight loss and fitness began in 2003 at age 46. A wife and mother of two teenage girls, I felt myself beginning to age. A frank, life-changing conversation with an older nurse at my annual physical set the course for change. She painted a grim picture of my future, with chronic health problems like arthritis and diabetes, if I didn't change my ways. Tired and obese, with high cholesterol, indigestion, body aches, and a slowed metabolism already a part of my life, I realized she was right, and it scared me into action.

Out of fear came commitment and determination to do everything possible to achieve good health. The challenge was to be successful after a lifetime of poor eating habits and failed diets. Success came this time, not because I started an elaborate physical activity program or went on a special diet, but because I focused on behavior. I started a simple routine that was easy to remember and could be done at home. It combined elements of everything I had learned about good nutrition, physical activity, and healthy weight loss over the years.

...I am in better health now than I was at 25!

For starters, I walked briskly every day for an hour and made wiser food choices at dinner. I focused on fruits, vegetables, whole grains, low-fat dairy products, and lean meat. At the same time, I chose foods lower in saturated fat and *trans* fat, cholesterol, added sugars, and salt. I made the same wiser food choices at the store, including choosing healthier snacks for my family. I made my health a top priority and stayed committed, and my family supported me. They were willing to cook and do whatever it took to help me accomplish my goal.

Four years later, I continue to work hard on my health every day and follow the new routine I set up. I lost and have kept off 50 pounds, dropped 68 points from my cholesterol numbers, and no longer have any of the health problems that I did before. In fact, I am in better health now than I was at 25! My friends and family are amazed at the results, and I feel wonderful. I've found that good eating and physical activity habits are contagious, as my family and close friends are now in better health, too.

For me, less was more in finally finding a way to achieve and maintain good health. I didn't need to join a gym or enroll in an expensive weight loss program to be successful. Instead of dwelling on pounds lost or calories eaten, I focused on making specific lifestyle changes. I will always be thankful to the nurse who cared enough to warn me and share her own experiences. I will never forget her. She may have saved my life.

Bev

Cary, North Carolina

For More Information...

Office on Women's Health, HHS
200 Independence Ave SW, Room 712E
Washington, DC 20201
Web site: www.womenshealth.gov/
FitnessNutrition
Phone number: (800) 994-9662,
(888) 220-5446 TDD

**Center for Food Safety and Applied
Nutrition, FDA**
5100 Paint Branch Parkway
College Park, MD 20740-3835
Web site: www.cfsan.fda.gov
Phone number: (888) 723-3366

U.S. Department of Agriculture
1400 Independence Ave SW
Washington, DC 20250
Web site: www.usda.gov
www.mypyramid.gov
www.nutrition.gov

**U.S. Department of Health and Human
Services**
200 Independence Ave, SW
Washington, DC 20201
Web site: www.healthierus.gov
www.smallstep.gov
www.health.gov/dietaryguidelines

To order *A Healthier You*, call (866)
512-1800 or visit http://bookstore.
gpo.gov/collections/healthier_you.jsp

**Division of Nutrition, Physical Activity
and Obesity, CDC**
4770 Buford Highway NE, MS K-24
Atlanta, GA 30341-3717
Web site: www.cdc.gov/nccdphp/dnpa
Phone number: (800) 232-4636,
(888) 232-6348 TTY

**Food and Nutrition Information Center,
USDA**
National Agricultural Library
10301 Baltimore Ave, Room 105
Beltsville, MD 20705
Web site: http://fnic.nal.usda.gov
Phone number: (301) 504-5414

Office of Dietary Supplements, NIH
6100 Executive Blvd, Room 3B01, MSC
7517
Bethesda, MD 20892-7517
Web site: www.ods.od.nih.gov

Weight-Control Information Network, NIH
1 WIN Way
Bethesda, MD 20892-3665
Web site: www.win.niddk.nih.gov
Phone number: (877) 946-4627

American Dietetic Association
120 S Riverside Plaza, Suite 2000
Chicago, IL 60606-6995
Web site: www.eatright.org
Phone number: (800) 877-1600 ext.5000

Fitness

You have probably heard by now that physical activity is good for you. It helps you manage your body weight and prevent gradual weight gain. This may reduce your risk of certain health problems. Yet with all the benefits of being physically active, maybe you haven't *quite* gotten around to starting a regular activity routine.

If you are having trouble becoming physically active, you are not alone. In fact, only 48 percent of U.S. adults get the minimum recommended level of physical activity each week. What you should know is that regular physical activity may help prevent heart disease, as well as breast and colon cancers, stroke, type 2 diabetes, and osteoporosis. All you need to get started is a good pair of walking shoes.

What is healthy physical activity?

When some people think of physical activity, they think of playing sports or working out at a gym. If you don't like doing those sorts of things, then the whole idea of being physically active may not be appealing.

But being physically active doesn't have to mean playing basketball, doing push-ups, or jogging. Activities that require as much or more effort as 10 minutes of brisk walking count as healthy physical activity. For instance, if you manage a household and spend much of your day running up and down stairs, vacuuming floors, and chasing after toddlers, you may be getting plenty of healthy physical activity at home. If you work at a job that involves a lot of walking or lifting, you

may be getting plenty of healthy physical activity at work.

One type of physical activity is aerobic activity, in which you move large muscles

in your arms, legs, and hips over and over again. During aerobic activity, you breathe faster and more deeply and your heart beats faster.

If your breathing and heart rate increase to a moderate degree, your activity is considered moderate intensity. Put another way, moderate-intensity physical activity is any activity that burns 3.5 to 7 calories per minute. An example would be walking on a level surface at a brisk pace (about 3 to 4 miles per hour).

If your breathing increases so much that it is difficult to carry on a conversation, your activity is considered vigorous intensity. Vigorous-intensity activity is any activity that burns more than 7 calories per minute. An example would be jogging.

Below are some moderate and vigorous physical activities that you might consider.

Moderate and Vigorous Physical Activities

	Moderate activities	Vigorous activities
Leisure activities	Walking, ballroom dancing, leisurely bicycling, roller skating, canoeing	Jogging, bicycling fast or uphill, jumping rope, swimming continuous laps
Sports	Golfing, softball, badminton, downhill skiing	Singles tennis, beach volleyball on sand, basketball, soccer, cross-country skiing
Home activities	Pushing a power lawn mower, gardening, raking the lawn, moderate housework	Pushing a hand mower, heavy or rapid shoveling (more than 10 pounds per minute), carrying items weighing 25 pounds or more up a flight of stairs
Occupational activity	Maid service, waiting tables, feeding or grooming farm animals, manually milking cows, picking fruits or vegetables, walking while carrying a mailbag	Teaching an aerobic dance class, heavy farm work

How much physical activity do I need?

To reduce the risk of chronic disease, adults should engage in:

- moderate-intensity physical activity for 30 minutes or more on 5 or more days of the week, OR
- vigorous-intensity physical activity for 20 minutes or more on 3 or more days of the week

This physical activity should be in addition to your routine activities of daily living, such as cooking or spending a few minutes walking from the parking lot to your office.

If you are older than 65, you should still engage in regular physical activity. Doing so will:

- help you keep your strength so that you can stay independent
- improve your balance so that you are less likely to fall and break bones

- help prevent or delay some of the diseases linked with aging, such as osteoporosis (OSS-tee-oh-puh-ROH-suhss)
- help prevent constipation
- help you sleep better at night

If you have not been physically active for a long time, you may need to start slowly and then work your way up as you become more fit. For example, if you do not feel up to walking for 30 minutes, try walking for 10 minutes. Then increase your walking time by 5 minutes each week until you reach 30 minutes.

If walking at a speed of 3 to 4 miles per hour is too fast for you, it's okay to walk at a slower pace. As long as you are breathing hard, it's considered moderate intensity. A good rule of thumb is to pay attention to how hard it is for you to talk while being active. If you can talk without any trouble at all, you are not working hard enough. If you can't talk at all, you're working too hard.

Other ways to be active

As mentioned, one form of physical activity is aerobic activity. There are also three other types of physical activity:

- strength-training activities
- stretching activities
- balance activities

To be physically fit, adults should do a combination of aerobic, strength-training, and stretching activities. In addition to these three, older adults should also do balance activities.

Strength-training activities

Strength-training activities increase the strength and endurance of your muscles. Examples of strength-training activities include working out with weight machines and free weights.

You do not need to invest in a gym membership or buy expensive home gym equipment to do strength-training activities. Hand, wrist, and ankle weights are less costly options. Also, homemade weights, such as plastic soft drink bottles filled with sand or water, may work just as well. You can also use your own body weight, doing activities such as push-ups, pull-ups, and sit-ups. You could also buy a resistance band at a sporting-goods store. It looks like a giant rubber band, and stretching it helps build muscle.

In each strength-training session, you should do 8 to 10 different activities using the different muscle groups throughout your body, such as the muscles in your abdomen, chest, arms, and legs. Repeat each activity 8 to 12 times, using a weight or resistance that will make you feel tired. When you do strength-training activities, slowly increase the amount of weight or resistance that you use. Also, allow 1 day in between sessions to avoid excess strain on your muscles and joints.

Don't hold your breath during strength-training activities. That could cause changes in your blood pressure. It may seem strange at first, but you should breathe out as you lift something, and breathe in as you relax.

Below is a strength-training activity that you can do at home, and all that you need is a chair and some pillows. It's called the "Chair Stand," and it strengthens muscles in your abdomen and thighs. It also helps improve your balance.

1. Place pillows on the back of a chair.
2. Sit toward the front of the chair, knees bent, feet flat on the floor.
3. Lean back on the pillows in a half-reclining position. Keep your back and shoulders straight throughout the activity.
4. Raise your upper body forward until sitting upright, using your hands as little as possible (or not at all, if you can). Your back should no longer lean against the pillows.
5. Slowly stand up, using your hands as little as possible.
6. Slowly sit back down. Pause.
7. Repeat 8 to 15 times.

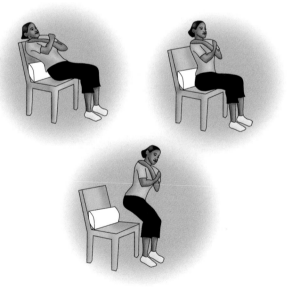

Stretching activities

Stretching can help you be more flexible, allowing more freedom of movement. Moving more freely will make it easier for you to reach down to tie your shoes or look over your shoulder when you back the car out of your driveway.

You should do stretching activities after your muscles are warmed up—for example, after strength training. Stretching your muscles before they are warmed up may cause injury. Also, stretching should never cause pain, especially joint pain. If you feel pain when you stretch, you are stretching too far.

Below is an example of an activity that stretches the muscles in the front of your thighs:

1. Lie on your side on the floor. Your hips should be lined up so that one is directly above the other one.

2. Rest your head on a pillow.

3. Bend the knee that is on top.

4. Reach back and grab the heel of that leg.

5. Gently pull that leg until the front of your thigh stretches.

6. Hold this position for 10 to 30 seconds.

7. Reverse position and repeat.

8. Repeat 3 to 5 times on each side.

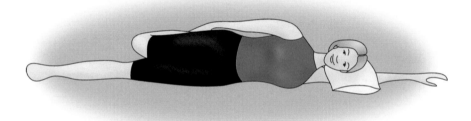

Balance activities

As you get older, your risk of falling due to losing your balance increases. To prevent falling injuries, you should do activities to maintain or improve your balance. Below are two balance activities that you can do almost anytime, anywhere, and as often as you like, as long as you have something sturdy nearby to hold onto if you become unsteady.

- Walk heel-to-toe. Position your heel just in front of the toes of the opposite foot each time you take a step.

- Stand on one foot (for example, while waiting in line at the grocery store or at the bus stop). Alternate feet.

Physical activity and health problems

More and more, research is suggesting that physical activity can help prevent or even help treat certain health problems.

Overweight and obesity

Being overweight or obese is a common struggle in the United States: Sixty-two percent of U.S. women older than 20 are overweight or obese. Being overweight or obese increases your chances of getting many diseases, including:

- coronary artery disease
- type 2 diabetes
- stroke
- cancer of the colon, breast, endometrium, thyroid, esophagus, kidney, gallbladder, and pancreas

When you're overweight or obese, extra fat is deposited in many places in your body. The body fat that is most dangerous to your health is visceral (VISS-ur-uhl) fat, which surrounds your stomach, intestines, and other internal organs. Having too much visceral fat increases your risk of heart disease, diabetes, and other diseases. It tends to increase in women after menopause. The good news is that becoming physically active can help overweight postmenopausal women reduce the amount of visceral, as well as total, fat.

Coronary artery disease (heart disease)

Physical activity can help reduce your risk of heart disease. It doesn't have to be vigorous activity. Moderate physical activity for at least 30 minutes on 5 or more days of the week can help reduce your heart disease risk by:

- increasing HDL (good) cholesterol (koh-LESS-tur-ol)
- lowering blood pressure
- helping you maintain your weight (in addition to eating healthy foods and limiting how much you eat)
- improving the fitness of your heart

Although your risk of getting heart disease goes up after menopause, you should not wait until menopause to start becoming active. Research suggests that women who have high LDL (bad) cholesterol levels and other heart disease risk factors before menopause may be more prone to artery problems after menopause. So the sooner you get moving, the better.

For more information on coronary artery disease, see the *Heart Disease* chapter on page 15.

Stroke

As is the case with coronary artery disease, the risk of stroke increases as women age. The most common type of stroke results when a blood clot blocks an artery carrying blood from the heart to the brain. Some research has shown that physical activity, including brisk walking, can lower women's chances of having this type of stroke. Research has also shown that women who had been inactive but became active in middle or older age had a lower stroke risk than those who stayed inactive. So it is never too late to start lowering your risk of stroke.

For more information on stroke, see the *Stroke* chapter on page 37.

Type 2 diabetes

Physical activity can help people who have type 2 diabetes, as well as people who have pre-diabetes—higher than normal blood sugar levels that often lead to type 2 diabetes. In fact, research suggests that lifestyle changes—such as getting more physical activity, eating a healthier diet, and losing excess weight—are at least as effective as drug therapy for delaying type 2 diabetes.

If you already have type 2 diabetes, physical activity can help keep your blood sugar levels at a normal level. One research study showed that people with type 2 diabetes were able to lower their blood sugar levels with either aerobic activities or strength-training activities. People who did both activities were able to lower their blood sugar levels even more.

For more information on type 2 diabetes and pre-diabetes, see the *Type 2 Diabetes* chapter on page 69.

Cancer

Research suggests that physical activity may reduce your risk of breast and colon cancers. Some experts think that one of the ways that physical activity may reduce your cancer risk is by reducing body fat. Fat may help cause cancer by releasing substances, including hormones such as estrogen and insulin, that may promote cancer cell growth.

Research also suggests that physical activity can help if you already have cancer. Although chemotherapy or radiation treatment can make you feel too tired for much physical activity, even some physical activity may:

- help you feel less tired, anxious, and depressed

- reduce pain

- help your immune system recover from chemotherapy

For patients with breast cancer receiving chemotherapy, physical activity may also:

- reduce hot flashes and sweats
- prevent muscle loss and inappropriate weight gain

For patients with cancer in general, once treatment is finished and the cancer is gone, staying active may help:

- prevent your cancer from returning
- reduce your chances of dying of cancer

If you are being treated for cancer or have recovered from an attack of cancer, be sure to talk with your doctor before starting any physical activity routine.

For more information on cancer, see the *Cancer* chapter on page 51.

Osteoporosis

Research suggests that physical activity may help prevent osteoporosis, a disease that weakens bones. To help prevent osteoporosis, you should do weight-bearing activities. These are activities in which your body works against gravity. Jogging, walking, stair climbing, and dancing are all weight-bearing activities because you are holding up your body against the force of gravity. Weight lifting, or strength training, is another type of weight-bearing activity. In contrast, swimming is an example of an activity that is not weight bearing because the water is helping to hold up your body.

Engaging in weight-bearing activities helps reduce your risk of osteoporosis by:

- helping you grow healthy bones during your teenage years
- helping you maintain healthy bones in adulthood
- reducing your rate of bone loss during aging

For more information on osteoporosis, see page 225 of the *Healthy Aging* chapter.

Arthritis

Research suggests that physical activity can reduce your chances of getting osteoarthritis (OSS-tee-oh-ar-THREYE-tuhss). More common in women after 55 years of age, this type of arthritis causes pain most often in the hip, knee, spine, and finger joints.

For more information on osteoarthritis, see page 229 of the *Healthy Aging* chapter and page 360 of the *Pain* chapter.

Does physical activity have positive effects on the mind?

Depression and anxiety

Research suggests that regular physical activity:

- reduces feelings of mild to moderate depression and anxiety

- improves mood

- increases feelings of well-being

Physical activity is not a cure for depression or anxiety. But it may help you manage your symptoms by:

- giving you a sense of success, which can boost your confidence

- helping you meet other people

- taking your mind off your problems

Also, physical activity may help you feel better by:

- increasing the level of substances in the brain that improve your mood

- reducing levels of stress hormones

Research suggests that, for some people, physical activity can work as well as an antidepressant in treating major depression. But if you are now taking an antidepressant, do not stop taking it on your own. You should discuss with your doctor how physical activity might fit into your overall treatment plan before making any changes.

For more information on major depression and anxiety disorders, see the *Mental Health* chapter on page 207.

Quitting smoking

As every smoker knows, quitting smoking can be hard to do. Every year, many smokers try to quit but only a few succeed. One research study suggests that vigorous physical activity can help women quit smoking, even women who have been heavy smokers for many years. As an added bonus, vigorous physical activity can also help you gain less weight after you quit.

It is not known for sure how vigorous physical activity might help you quit smoking. One way it might help is by reducing stress, which might reduce your urge to smoke.

Cognitive decline during aging

As we age, we sometimes forget things. Maybe we no longer think as quickly as we used to. Experts call this "cognitive decline," where "cognitive" refers to thinking, learning, and memory, as opposed to emotions.

It was once thought that cognitive decline was a normal part of aging. But

research now suggests that staying physically active as you get older may slow cognitive decline, at least for a while. Some experts think that physical activity may slow cognitive decline in part by increasing blood flow to the brain. In addition, physical activity may even help new brain cells grow.

Physical activity during and after pregnancy

Health experts say that most pregnant women should get 30 minutes or more of moderate physical activity each day. Such activity offers many benefits. It can:

- lessen some of the discomforts of pregnancy

- give you more energy and make you feel better

- improve your posture

- increase your chances of an early recovery after delivery

Moderate activity during pregnancy may also reduce your risk of:

- preeclampsia (pree-ee-KLAMP-see-uh), a condition that involves high blood pressure and other problems during pregnancy

- depression

Physical activity during and after pregnancy can also help keep you from gaining too much weight. Women who gain too much weight during pregnancy and do not take it off afterward are more likely to be obese 8 to 10 years later.

When you are being active during pregnancy, do not push yourself to the point of exhaustion. If you cannot talk easily while you're active, you may be overdo-

ing it. Also, avoid being physically active during very hot weather. And be sure to drink plenty of water so that you do not become dehydrated.

Pregnancy

Check with your doctor before becoming active to ensure the safety of you and your baby. Your doctor may ask you to avoid some or all physical activity if you have certain medical conditions or complications involving your pregnancy.

For information on preeclampsia, see page 179 of the *Pregnancy* chapter.

Physical activity and menopausal symptoms

Menopause affects every woman differently. Common symptoms of menopause include:

- hot flashes (feelings of warmth)

- trouble sleeping through the night

- mood swings, feeling crabby, crying spells

If you have hot flashes, physical activity is probably not going to reduce them. But research suggests that being physically active may offer other benefits, such as:

- improved sleep quality
- fewer feelings of nervousness, anxiety, and depression

Physical activity tips

With all the things that you have to do each day, finding the time and motivation to get moving can be challenging. Here are some suggestions for ways to get started:

- If you do not have 30 minutes in one stretch to set aside for moderate physical activities, try being active in three 10-minute periods throughout the day.
- Join a sports team. For example, you may work for a company that has a baseball team that you could join.
- Join a hiking or running club.
- Use stairs instead of the elevator.
- Walk or bike to work or to the store.
- Be physically active at lunch with co-workers, family, or friends.
- Take a break at work to stretch or take a quick walk.
- Go dancing with your partner or friends.
- Plan active vacations rather than only driving trips.
- Wear a pedometer (a small tool worn on your belt that counts the number of steps you take). Try to walk 10,000 steps each day.
- While watching TV, use a stationary bicycle or treadmill. Another idea is to work out with hand weights.
- Spend time in active play with your kids. While you're at it, you could also teach your kids about the health benefits of physical activity. Children and adolescents should be engaging in at least 60 minutes of moderate-intensity physical activity on most, and preferably all, days of the week.
- If you are having trouble finding the time or motivation to be physically active, figure out what is holding you back and then brainstorm with family and friends about ways to overcome these barriers.

Perhaps the most important tip, though, is to find physical activities that you enjoy. You are more likely to keep physically active if you are having fun. ■

Safety Tips

While you are being physically active, be sure to keep safety in mind. We have already mentioned some safety tips, such as starting slow if you have not been physically active for a long time. Below are a few more safety tips:

- Use safety equipment. For example, wear a helmet for bike riding or the right shoes for walking or jogging.
- Drink plenty of fluids when you are physically active, even if you are not thirsty.
- Always bend forward from the hips, not the waist. If you keep your back straight, you're probably bending the right way. If your back "humps," that's probably wrong.

One Woman's Story

After turning 40, I realized that I was at my highest weight ever and my blood pressure was borderline high. Since I have a strong family history of heart disease, I knew that I needed to take action.

I started by walking on the treadmill. After losing the first few pounds, I really liked the feeling of getting healthy, so I started to add to my home gym. The first addition was a set of dumbbells and a bench purchased at a yard sale. I had absolutely no clue how to use them, so I read countless books and researched on the Internet. I wanted to learn everything I could about physical activity and fitness.

I'll admit that there were days when I wanted to give up. I was working out on my own, but it would have been very helpful to have someone to keep me motivated. However, I didn't quit, and after 24 weeks I managed to lose 48 pounds! I loved physical activity and challenging myself, and I also loved the fact that I felt better at 40 than I did when I was 20.

> ## For many people, having that helping hand can make the difference between success and failure.

For Christmas, my husband gave me a gift certificate for time with a personal trainer. Working out with a trainer helped me realize how important it could be to have someone there to count on for inspiration and support. For many people, having that helping hand can make the difference between success and failure.

I knew then that I wanted to be a trainer myself. I began by training family and friends; after great success, I became certified through the American Council on Exercise. I wanted to help people take control of their health and maybe learn something about themselves along the way. I truly want all my clients to succeed. I want them to have the feeling I had when I reached my goal—a feeling of accomplishment and well-being that comes from making healthy choices.

I eventually opened a private studio. I want to help the people who might not want to go to a conventional gym for one reason or another, but want the guidance and structure needed to be successful with their specific goals. I have improved my quality of life and want to help others do the same.

Colleen

Oakdale, Pennsylvania

For More Information...

Office on Women's Health, HHS
200 Independence Ave SW, Room 712E
Washington, DC 20201
Web site: www.womenshealth.gov/
FitnessNutrition
Phone number: (800) 994-9662,
(888) 220-5446 TDD

U.S. Department of Health and Human Services
200 Independence Ave, SW
Washington, DC 20201
Web site: www.healthierus.gov
www.smallstep.gov

Division of Nutrition, Physical Activity and Obesity, CDC
4770 Buford Highway NE, MS K-24
Atlanta, GA 30341-3717
Web site: www.cdc.gov/nccdphp/dnpa
Phone number: (800) 232-4636,
(888) 232-6348 TTY

The President's Challenge
501 N Morton, Suite 203
Bloomington, IN 47404
Web site: www.presidentschallenge.org
Phone number: (800) 258-8146

The President's Council on Physical Fitness and Sports
Department W
200 Independence Ave SW, Room 738-H
Washington, DC 20201-0004
Web site: www.fitness.gov
Phone number: (202) 690-9000

Weight-Control Information Network, NIH
1 WIN Way
Bethesda, MD 20892-3665
Web site: www.win.niddk.nih.gov
Phone number: (877) 946-4627

National Center on Physical Activity and Disability
1640 W Roosevelt Rd
Chicago, IL 60608-6904
Web site: www.ncpad.org
Phone number: (800) 900-8086 voice and TTY

Women's Sports Foundation
1899 Hempstead Turnpike, Suite 400
East Meadow, NY 11554
Web site:
www.womenssportsfoundation.org

Pain

Are you in a lot of pain every day? Have you had doctors tell you that "it's all in your head" or "it's just nerves"? If so, you're not alone. Pain is often undertreated in women. The good news is that there are different ways to explain your pain so that you can get the help you need. There are also many things you can do to manage your pain and feel better.

The truth about pain

Pain is a regular, if unwelcome, reality for many women, perhaps even more than it is for men. Most women have pain with menstruation at some point in their lives, and childbirth can be painful. Some common disorders of the female reproductive tract are painful. Also, painful autoimmune (aw-toh-ih-MYOON) diseases are much more common in women. To cope with their pain, women tend to use more approaches than men, such as learning about their condition, turning to others for support, and finding ways to relax more and manage stress.

Still, it can be hard for a woman to get help for her pain. Some doctors are less likely to give women painkillers because they think that women overstate the amount of pain they feel. Studies have shown that given the same amount of pain, men are less likely to report it than women. Men might feel they need to "tough it out." But this doesn't mean that the pain women are reporting isn't real.

Chronic pain

Women are more likely to have chronic pain conditions. Pain is chronic if it lasts more than 3 months. Chronic pain can sometimes last years or even decades. Sometimes, pain is caused by injury or disease. In such cases lab tests show definite signs of injury or disease in an organ or other body part. In other chronic pain conditions, the pain can't be traced to any specific disease or injury. The exact cause of the pain is unknown. In these cases, the chronic pain is the disease.

Whatever its cause, chronic pain can interfere with all aspects of your life. It can:

- make it difficult to work and interact with family and friends
- make you feel irritable and depressed
- make it hard to sleep
- make you lose interest in food and sex
- make you less inclined to get physical activity (as a result, you may gain weight, which can make some chronic pain problems worse)
- lead to dependency on narcotic pain-killers or alcohol as a way of coping with chronic pain
- cause you to have the burden of many doctor bills that come from trying to treat it

Chronic pain is different from acute pain, which is pain that lasts less than 3 months. Acute pain, such as pain from a cut, is closely linked to an injury, infection, or inflammation. Inflammation is the body's response to injury or irritation, signaled by pain, swelling, redness, and heat. When the cause of the acute pain goes away, so does the pain.

Getting diagnosed

The first step in treating your pain is a diagnosis. During your first visit, your doctor will ask you questions about:

- when your pain started
- location of your pain
- how your pain feels (for instance, does it feel like a sharp stabbing pain, a steady burning, or a dull ache?)
- what makes your pain better or worse
- how the pain affects your activities of daily living (for instance, bathing, dressing, and eating)
- all of the medicines that you have ever used to treat your pain (both those that were prescribed by a doctor and those that you bought over the counter)
- any side effects you may have from these medicines

The doctor may also ask you questions to find out if you are depressed. Being depressed is quite common among patients with chronic pain. For some patients, though, the depression comes first. The chronic pain may be caused by or be part

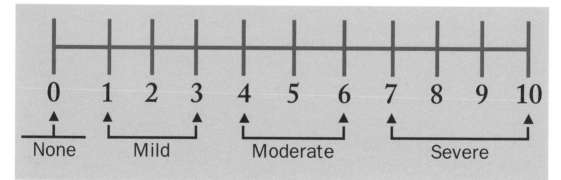

YOUR DOCTOR MAY SHOW YOU A PAIN INTENSITY SCALE, SUCH AS THIS NUMERIC RATING SCALE, AND ASK YOU TO RATE YOUR PAIN ON A SCALE FROM 0 TO 10.

of the depression. In fact, many people who are depressed complain about pain problems, such as frequent headaches, back pain, or stomach pain, rather than depression. The only way your doctor can find out and treat your real problem is for you to answer your doctor's questions honestly.

Managing your pain

Treatments for pain include:

- medicines
- physical therapies
- psychological and behavioral therapies
- complementary and alternative therapies
- surgery

To get a treatment plan involving a variety of approaches, you may want to try a pain clinic. These clinics have a team of therapists, including:

- doctors
- psychologists
- physical therapists
- complementary and alternative therapists (such as acupuncturists or massage therapists)

Together, the team will put together a pain management plan for you, often involving a combination of different treatments. If you do not have a pain clinic where you live, ask your doctor for referrals to therapists near you.

Because everyone is different, a treatment that works for one patient may not work for others. You may have to try a variety of treatments before you find one or more that work for you.

Medicines

Medicines that reduce pain are called analgesics (an-uhl-GEE-ziks). They block the pain signals carried by nerves but do not cure the problem that is causing the pain. When an analgesic wears off, the pain often returns.

Nonsteroidal anti-inflammatory drugs

Nonsteroidal anti-inflammatory drugs (NSAIDs) are a class of analgesics. They reduce pain and also reduce fever and inflammation. Common ones include:

- aspirin
- ibuprofen
- naproxen

When used once in a while, these drugs cause few side effects. But long-term use can irritate the stomach and intestines. NSAIDs other than aspirin also may increase the risk of heart attacks and stroke. Some of the NSAIDs may cause liver or kidney disease as well.

Acetaminophen

Acetaminophen (uh-see-tuh-MIN-uh-fuhn) works in much the same way as NSAIDs but doesn't reduce inflammation.

Acetaminophen is less likely to bother the stomach than NSAIDs. But taking too high a dose of acetaminophen can damage your liver, especially if you drink a lot of alcohol.

Opioids

Opioids (OH-pee-oids), or narcotics, are the most powerful pain medicines. Opioids commonly prescribed include morphine, methadone (METH-uh-dohn), and oxycodone (OKS-ih-KOH-duhn).

Opioid side effects include:

- nausea

- vomiting

- feeling drowsy

- difficulty having a bowel movement

If you take an opioid drug for more than a week or two (and, for some people, as little as a few days), you can become physically dependent on the drug. This means that you will have withdrawal symptoms when you stop taking the drug. Withdrawal symptoms include nervousness, diarrhea, and tremor, or shaking. Physical dependence on opioids is a normal response to taking the drugs and not something to be overly concerned about. Physical dependence is not the same as addiction.

Addiction to opioids means that you crave opioid drugs and feel driven to take them for reasons other than easing your pain. You spend a lot of time finding and taking the drugs and neglect your family, job, and other responsibilities. You may buy the drugs illegally and get into trouble with the law.

When taken properly, the chances of becoming addicted to opioids are low. But many doctors and patients are overly concerned about the risk of opioid addiction. As a result, patients are sometimes not given high enough doses of opioids and suffer pain needlessly.

Early research suggests that women's pain responds better than men's to a class of opioids called kappa opioids. This suggests that male and female brains handle pain signals in different ways. It also suggests that kappa opioids might

Serious Side Effects of Methadone

Women are more likely than men to have serious side effects with methadone use. Call 911 or go to the nearest emergency room if you are taking methadone and get one or more of these symptoms:

- rapid, irregular pulse

- sensation of feeling the heart beat

- light-headedness or dizziness

- fainting

- shortness of breath

- chest discomfort or pain

be an option for women in pain who do not respond well to typical opioids. More research is needed in this area.

Researchers are also working on developing opioid medicines that hopefully will not be addictive and will have fewer side effects. Some of these are showing promise in research on animals. But none are yet available for use in humans.

Antidepressants and anticonvulsants
Some medicines used to treat depression can treat some painful conditions, including migraine and tension headaches. In a way, this is not surprising, because we know that the part of the brain where pain is processed is also involved in depression.

Other medicines that can been used for treating certain types of pain are anticonvulsants. These medicines were developed to treat epilepsy. But they are sometimes useful for treating painful conditions caused by damage to the nervous system.

Other therapies for pain

Your therapists may suggest nondrug treatments instead of or along with taking medicines. Not only do women use more nondrug therapies than men, women are more likely to respond well to them.

Physical therapy

Many patients with chronic pain move as little as possible, thinking that physical activity will harm them. In fact, the opposite is true. When you get out of shape, your pain may become worse. If you have a chronic pain problem, a physical therapist can help you find a physical activity program that is gentle, moderate, and right for you. You should follow the program, even if you feel some pain during physical activity. In this case, the pain does not mean that you are harming your body.

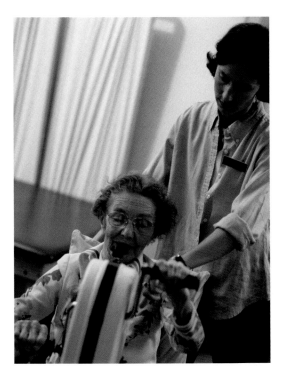

Types of physical therapy that may help your pain include:

- heat treatment—hot water baths, heating pads, high-frequency sound waves to produce gentle heat deep in your tissues

- cold treatment—ice packs, ice baths, ice massage

- gentle stretching

- muscle-strengthening physical activities

- massage—applying pressure to specific points on the body

- vibration therapy—a probe is applied to a part of your body with moderate pressure and vibrated several thousand times per second

Nerve stimulation therapies

These therapies involve the use of low electrical currents and/or fine needles that are placed in specific parts of the body. Acupuncture is one example. These therapies seem to interfere with the sending of pain signals to the brain. They may also cause the body to release natural painkillers, called endorphins.

Psychological and behavioral therapies

Therapies that help you relax or change your thinking patterns can sometimes help you cope with pain. Examples of these therapies include:

- **cognitive therapy**—helps you to gain control over your pain by teaching you to recognize and change emotions that can make pain worse, such as anxiety, anger, and sadness

- **progressive muscle relaxation**—tensing and then relaxing muscles helps to ease muscle tension that may be adding to your pain

- **deep breathing exercises**—helps you to relax

- **guided imagery**—imagining a pleasant scene takes your mind off your pain

- **biofeedback**—electronic equipment tells you about your muscle tension, skin temperature, and other body functions, so you can learn to control these functions and reduce your pain

Pain can make depression worse, and depression can make your pain worse. So if you are in pain and also are depressed, you need to treat depression and pain at the same time.

Chronic pain disorders

Many chronic pain disorders common among women have no known cause. To diagnose your pain, your doctor will need to rule out other possible causes. This might take a long time. Once your pain is diagnosed, you can explore your treatment options with your doctor. Symptoms of some common disorders and their treatments can be found in this table.

Tension headache	
Symptoms	• Tight band of pain around head • Tense muscles in back and neck • Often occur at times of high stress • Often go along with depression
Treatment	• Relaxation—taking a break from what you're doing and resting in bed • Biofeedback • Analgesics (usually NSAIDs) • Antidepressants • Stress management

Migraine headache	
Symptoms	• Throbbing pain that usually starts on one side of your head and then spreads • Light, sound, and physical activity can make pain worse • Nausea and vomiting • Aura (jagged, shimmering, or flashing lights or a blind spot with flickering edges) about 1 hour before the migraine begins • Tingling, balance problems, weakness in an arm or leg, problems talking • Sometimes goes along with depression
Treatment	• Avoiding migraine triggers • Medicines called triptans are good at stopping a migraine from progressing if taken when it is just beginning. (In very rare cases, triptans have caused heart attacks and death in healthy young women.) • Other over-the-counter and prescription medicines to provide pain relief or prevent migraines • Medicines to help nausea and vomiting • Biofeedback; relaxation training

Tracking Your Migraines

Migraine attacks often are brought on by triggers. Common triggers include:

- lack of food or sleep
- menstruation-related hormone changes
- stress and anxiety
- foods, such as chocolate, red wine, or aged cheese
- food additives, such as MSG (monosodium glutamate) or nitrates

Keeping a headache diary can help you to pinpoint any triggers you might have. You might be able to prevent future migraines by avoiding these triggers.

Headache Diary

Date: _____

Pain location and type: _____

Other symptoms (aura, nausea, etc.): _____

Number of days into your menstrual cycle (Day 1 is the first day of your period.): _____

What was I doing when the migraine started?_____

Possible triggers: _____

A sudden, severe headache could be a sign of a stroke. For more information, see the *Stroke* chapter on page 37.

Temporomandibular (TEM-puh-roh-man-DIB-yuh-lur) joint disorders (TMJ)

Symptoms	• Pain in the chewing muscles or temporomandibular joint(s), which connects your lower jaw to the bones on the side of your head
	• Clicking, popping, or grating sounds in the joint when you open or close your mouth
	• Limited movement or locking of the jaw
	• Pain in the face or neck
Treatment	• Eating soft foods
	• Massaging painful muscles
	• Moist heat or cold packs on the face
	• Relaxation techniques
	• NSAIDs or muscle relaxants
	• Reducing stress

Complex regional pain syndrome

Symptoms	• Burning pain that often starts after an injury to a muscle, nerve, or other tissue
	• Pain worsens over time even though injury has healed
	• Pain spreads, often affecting an entire arm, leg, hand, or foot
	• Affected area might also have:
	• changes in skin temperature and color
	• changes in nail and hair growth patterns
	• sweating
	• swelling
Treatment	Treatment is aimed at relieving symptoms. Therapies include:
	• Physical therapy
	• Psychotherapy
	• Medicines, including antidepressants, opioids, and analgesics applied to the skin
	• Injecting a drug that blocks the nerves thought to play a role in causing the pain

Chronic fatigue syndrome

Symptoms	• Long-lasting fatigue that doesn't get better with rest
	• Flu-like symptoms, headache, sore throat, muscle and joint aches, and fever
Treatment	• NSAIDs for the fever, headache, and body pain
	• Antidepressants to improve sleep and mood
	• Moderate physical activity
	• Cognitive therapy to help you keep a positive outlook

Fibromyalgia (feye-broh-meye-AL-juh)	
Symptoms	Main symptoms: • Pain felt all over the body • Tenderness or pain in at least 11 of 18 "tender points," specific spots on the neck, shoulders, back, hips, arms, and legs Other symptoms: • Fatigue • Trouble sleeping • Morning stiffness
	## Fibromyalgia Tender Points
Treatment	• Pregabalin (pre-GAB-uh-lin) and other anticonvulsant medicines • Sleeping longer and better by changing bedtime and sleep habits or using medicines to help you sleep • Low-impact physical activity, such as walking or swimming • Reducing stress • Massage

If you have pain in your chest, this could be a sign of angina (an-JEYE-nuh) or a heart attack. For more information, see the *Heart Disease* chapter on page 15.

Osteoarthritis (OSS-tee-oh-ar-THREYE-tuhss)	
Symptoms	• Pain and swelling in joints • Limited joint motion • Might be able to hear the sound of grinding bones
Treatment	• NSAIDs to reduce pain and swelling • Opioids • Moderate physical activity, such as swimming • Heat and cold treatments • Surgery to repair or replace damaged joints • Weight control
Carpal tunnel syndrome	
Symptoms	Symptoms begin gradually, starting with: • Numb or tingling sensation in first 3 fingers Over time, you might feel: • Burning, aching feeling in these fingers • Painful numbness in your palm • Shooting pain from your wrist into the forearm or fingers • Trouble moving your fingers
Treatment	• Wearing a splint to keep your wrist from bending • NSAIDs to reduce pain and swelling • Surgery

Injury-related pain

If you have experienced a serious injury, such as a bone fracture or severe bleeding, consult a doctor as soon as possible. Also, consult a doctor if you have received a blow to your head that causes you to have one or more of the following:

• blurred vision

• slurred speech

• loss of memory

• loss of consciousness

If you have a minor injury, such as a sprained ankle, you can often treat the problem yourself with the classic RICE treatment:

• **R (rest).** Reduce or stop using the injured area for at least 48 hours. This will minimize bleeding and swelling.

• **I (ice).** Put an ice pack on the injured area for 10 minutes and then remove

it for 10 minutes. Keep this up for at least an hour and then repeat for as long as swelling and bruising continue.

- **C (compression).** Gently compress, or squeeze, the injured area with an elastic bandage. Don't wrap the area so tightly that you cut off blood flow.

- **E (elevate).** Keep the injured area raised above the level of the heart to help decrease swelling. Use a pillow to prop up an injured arm or leg.

If RICE treatment does not help your injury, be sure to see a doctor.

Why do women have more pain disorders?

Scientists don't know why women get more chronic pain disorders than men. But they have some theories:

Women may be more sensitive to pain.

In one research study, scientists looked at the pain responses of newborn babies. When nurses pricked their heels to get blood for a lab test, girl babies showed more pain on their faces than boy babies. This suggests that females may be more sensitive to pain than males right from birth.

In research studies with adults that look at normal pain responses, women usually report more pain than men. Women also have more sensitive pain reflexes. For instance, women pull their leg up sooner than men when increasingly greater electric shocks are applied to a nerve in the foot.

Research has shown that women become more sensitive to pain after repeated ex-

posure to painful stimuli than do men. Some think that a lifetime of painful experiences, such as painful periods, may make a woman's nervous system more sensitive to pain. As a result, sensations that normally would not be felt as painful are in some women. This might explain disorders such as fibromyalgia, in which pain is felt all over the body.

Female sex hormones may help cause pain disorders.

Pain disorders seem to be related to sex hormone levels in many women. For instance, after puberty, when sex hormone levels rise, girls start to have more migraines than boys. But other painful conditions, such as joint pain, don't become more common in women until after menopause, when sex hormone levels drop. It's not clear yet which hormones affect pain and, if they do, how they affect pain.

If you're in pain

No matter why women have more painful disorders than men, the fact is that they do. If you're in pain and you're not getting the help you need from your doctor, feel free to switch doctors. If your health plan doesn't allow you to switch doctors or you live in an area where there aren't any other doctors, then you need to speak up for yourself to get the treatment you need.

No woman should be told that her pain isn't real or not severe enough for treatment. You deserve to live your life as pain-free as possible. ■

Other disorders involving pain are discussed throughout the book:

Disorder	Chapter
Irritable bowel syndrome	Digestive Health
Interstitial cystitis	Urologic and Kidney Health
Lupus	Autoimmune Diseases
Multiple sclerosis	Autoimmune Diseases
Scleroderma	Autoimmune Diseases
Rheumatoid arthritis	Autoimmune Diseases
Painful reproductive disorders, including vulvodynia, endometriosis, and uterine fibroids	Reproductive Health

One Woman's Story

In 1996, I accepted a position as the transportation planning manager for the City of Alexandria, Virginia. Living and working in the Washington, DC, area was a dream I had held dear for many years.

Most of my life I had suffered with migraine headaches, often going to the emergency room for treatment. My headaches became worse, and I found myself struggling to keep up the pace. The doctors I consulted gave me a variety of reasons for my pain, from allergies to the pollution to a lung infection. After a year, I realized I had to make a change to improve my health, and I left my dream job for a rural area without pollution.

The doctors I consulted gave me a variety of reasons for my pain...

The next few years I struggled not only with fatigue, but widespread pain, stiffness, and noticeable cognitive issues. I finally had to move back to my home in Shreveport, Louisiana. After spending three months in bed, I was diagnosed with fibromyalgia in January 2001. I was barely able to get up for meal preparation and necessary household duties. Obviously, I was no longer able to work.

It took years of navigating the insurance issues and multiple therapies before I found a doctor whose eyes did not glaze over when I mentioned fibromyalgia. He believed the symptoms of fibromyalgia were real, and he even conducted research to help his patients.

Since 2004 I have been taking a medicine that has lessened my pain levels and diminished the fatigue to a point that I have a quality lifestyle. I also now understand what is happening to my body to cause the many symptoms caused by fibromyalgia.

Berenda

Shreveport, Louisiana

For More Information...

Office on Women's Health, HHS
200 Independence Ave SW, Room 712E
Washington, DC 20201
Web site: www.womenshealth.gov/faq/
carpal.htm
www.womenshealth.gov/faq/migraine.htm
Phone number: (800) 994-9662,
(888) 220-5446 TDD

**National Institute of Arthritis and
Musculoskeletal and Skin Diseases,
Information Clearinghouse, NIH**
1 AMS Circle
Bethesda, MD 20892-3675
Web site: www.niams.nih.gov
Phone number: (877) 226-4267,
(301) 565–2966 TTY

**National Institute of Neurological
Disorders and Stroke, NIH**
PO Box 5801
Bethesda, MD 20824
Web site: www.ninds.nih.gov
Phone number: (800) 352-9424,
(301) 468-5981 TTY

NIH Pain Consortium
Bethesda, MD 20892
Web site: http://painconsortium.nih.gov/
pain_index.html

American Chronic Pain Association
PO Box 850
Rocklin, CA 95677
Web site: www.theacpa.org
Phone number: (800) 533-3231

American Pain Foundation
201 North Charles St, Suite 710
Baltimore, MD 21201-4111
Web site: www.painfoundation.org
Phone number: (888) 615-7246

**The Chronic Fatigue and Immune
Dysfunction Syndrome Association of
America**
PO Box 220398
Charlotte, NC 28222-0398
Web site: www.cfids.org

Fibromyalgia Network
PO Box 31750
Tucson, AZ 85751-1750
Web site: www.fmnetnews.com
Phone number: (800) 853-2929

National Headache Foundation
820 N Orleans, Suite 217
Chicago, IL 60610
Web site: www.headaches.org
Phone number: (888) 643-5552

National Pain Foundation
300 E Hampden Ave, Suite 100
Englewood, CO 80113
Web site: www.nationalpainfoundation.org

Complementary and Alternative Medicine

Perhaps you have seen a bottle of an herbal medicine in the drugstore and wondered if it might help get rid of your cold. Or you have thought about going to a chiropractor (KEYE-ruh-PRAK-tur) to treat your back pain. If so, you are not alone. Every year, millions of Americans try some form of complementary and alternative medicine—practices and products that are different from those normally used by your family doctor.

But you may wonder: Do these treatments work? Am I wasting my money? Most important, are they safe? Health experts are still trying to answer these questions. More research will hopefully shed light on the real benefits and risks of these alternative treatments.

What is complementary and alternative medicine?

The treatments used by most doctors are considered conventional medicine. Complementary and alternative medicine (CAM) consists of a group of health care practices and products that are considered out of the mainstream.

An "out-of-the-mainstream" treatment is considered complementary if you use it *along with* conventional medicine. An example would be using acupuncture along with painkilling drugs to reduce labor pains. A treatment is considered

alternative if you use it *instead of* conventional medicine. An example would be using acupuncture as your only treatment for headache.

This chapter will help you learn about the major CAM treatments and how they might benefit you. Also, just as important, it will tell you about the risks of certain CAM treatments and what to watch out for.

Who uses CAM?

Research shows that 40 percent of women in the United States use some form of CAM. If you include prayer for health reasons and taking large doses of vitamins as types of CAM, that number rises to 69 percent. CAM is used more by:

* women

* people with more education

* people who live in or near cities

Why do people use CAM?

People try CAM for a variety of reasons, including:

* Conventional medicine has not helped solve their medical problem.

* They believe that products derived from nature are healthier and safer than prescription drugs, even though they may not be.

* They like the holistic approach taken by CAM therapists. A holistic approach involves paying attention to all of a client's needs to help her regain and maintain her health. These include not just physical but also emotional, social, and spiritual needs.

Although something can be said for all of these reasons, you should be aware of some of the downsides of using CAM treatments, such as:

* No CAM treatment has been proven to work beyond a shadow of a doubt.

* Some CAM products, although derived from plants, can cause health problems. For instance, ephedra, a Chinese herbal product, was being sold in the United States to help people lose weight and to enhance athletic performance. Because ephedra increased the risk of heart problems and stroke, the U.S. Food and Drug Administration (FDA) banned the sale of ephedra.

* Some CAM products interfere with how prescription drugs work. For instance, St. John's wort, which some people take to treat depression, can

interfere with the actions of drugs for treating HIV, cancer, and other diseases. It may also reduce the effectiveness of birth control pills.

- Some herbal products, such as black cohosh, are unsafe to use during pregnancy. The safety of many other herbal products, either during pregnancy or breastfeeding, has not been studied.

- Some people might use an unproven CAM treatment that may not work or may carry risks, instead of a conventional treatment that is known to be effective.

If you choose to try a CAM treatment, be sure to discuss it first with your doctor. Your doctor should know whether the therapy may be helpful and is safe to try along with your current treatments. Some people don't mention their use of CAM treatments to their doctor because they think that their doctor will have negative feelings about CAM. If you are in this situation and would like to try a CAM treatment, perhaps you may want to find a doctor that you feel more comfortable talking to about this.

CAM Treatment Categories

- CAM treatments found in nature
- energy medicine
- therapies that adjust the body
- mind-body medicine
- whole medical systems

CAM treatments found in nature

Some CAM treatments use substances found in nature, such as herbs, vitamins, and minerals. The idea that natural substances might be used as medicines is not new. Practically since the beginning of time, people have used parts of plants and animals to treat diseases. In fact, some conventional drugs come from nature. For instance, aspirin is derived from a substance found in the bark of the willow tree.

Some CAM products are sold as dietary supplements. These are products taken by mouth that are intended to supplement, or add to, the diet. They come in many forms, including tablets, teas, and powders.

Label Regulations

The FDA regulates dietary supplements as foods rather than drugs. The laws about putting foods (including supplements) on the market are less strict than the laws for drugs. For instance, a manufacturer does not have to prove that a supplement is useful for treating any health problem before it is sold.

Some dietary supplements have been shown not to contain what was listed on the label. In some cases, pills did not contain as much of the supplement as the label said they did, or they contained more. In other cases, supplements were found to be contaminated with toxins, bacteria, or other substances. To address these problems, the FDA has issued new regulations requiring that:

- a dietary supplement contains what its label says it contains and in the dose listed on the label

- supplements are not contaminated

The new regulations took effect in August 2007 and will be phased in over 3 years.

Below are some CAM products found in nature that have been tried for various diseases and medical conditions:

Black cohosh and other plant products for treating menopausal symptoms

Black cohosh is often used for treating hot flashes and other menopausal symptoms. Research has generally shown that black cohosh by itself has little to no effect on menopausal symptoms. But one research study found that black cohosh combined with St. John's wort was somewhat effective in treating these symptoms.

Research studies have followed women taking black cohosh for only 6 months or less, so it's not known if the herb is safe to take for periods longer than 6 months. Black cohosh has been linked to a few cases of hepatitis (inflammation of the liver), but it is not clear whether it caused the problem.

Other plant products that have been used for treating menopausal symptoms include:

- **Red clover.** Research has not shown red clover to be effective in reducing hot flashes.

- **Dong quai** (doong kweye). Research has not shown dong quai to be effective in reducing hot flashes. It also contains substances that may cause cancer.

- **Ginseng.** Research has shown that ginseng might help menopausal symptoms such as insomnia, depression, and feeling tired. But it does not seem to reduce hot flashes.

- **Kava.** Kava may decrease anxiety but does not seem to reduce hot flashes. The FDA has issued a warning about kava because it can damage the liver.

- **Soy.** Research on the effects of soy on hot flashes has produced mixed results. When taken as a food or dietary supplement for short periods of time, soy appears to have few if any serious side effects. But taking soy extracts for several years may cause thickening of the uterine lining. This can cause abnormal vaginal bleeding.

Cranberry

We normally think of cranberry as a food. But research suggests that cranberry can also be used for its health benefits. Cranberry—in the form of juice or tablets—may be able to prevent urinary tract infections in women. Cranberries contain a substance that prevents bacteria from sticking to cell walls in the urinary tract.

Echinacea

Echinacea (EK-ih-NAY-shuh) is commonly used to prevent or treat colds, flu, and other infections that affect breathing. Research suggests that echinacea is not effective in preventing or treating colds in adults. One research study showed that echinacea was not effective in treating colds and similar infections in children but reduced the chances that the children would develop them again later.

ECHINACEA FLOWER, ALSO CALLED PURPLE CONEFLOWER

FRESH GINGER

Ginger

Research suggests that ginger can relieve the nausea and vomiting of pregnancy. Researchers studied pregnant women who were given about 1 gram of ginger per day, which is about the amount commonly used in cooking. They took the ginger for up to 3 weeks. No serious side effects occurred using ginger in these amounts and for this length of time. But some herbal medicine textbooks caution against using larger amounts of ginger. If you are pregnant and considering using ginger, discuss it with your doctor.

Energy medicine

Some CAM therapies involve using different types of energy to treat illness. Some of these therapies use energies that everyone agrees exist, such as the energy field surrounding magnets. Other therapies claim to use a "life energy," which may or may not exist.

Magnetic therapy

Magnets have been used at least since the time of the ancient Egyptians to treat medical problems. The magnets that we are most familiar with are static magnets. These are usually made of iron or steel, and their magnetic fields are static, meaning that they do not change. Refrigerator magnets are a type of weak static magnet.

Static magnets have been used to treat painful conditions, such as painful menstruation. Typically, magnets are placed directly on the skin or into products that come into contact with the body, such as bandages.

Research studies on the use of static magnets to relieve pain have produced mixed results. Some experts say that research studies that have shown pain relief have used stronger magnets than those that have not shown pain relief.

Another type of magnet is the electromagnet. Electromagnets consist of an iron core surrounded by a wire coil. When electricity flows through the coil, the iron core produces a magnetic field. When the electricity is turned off, the magnetic field goes away. In general, research studies using electromagnetic therapy to reduce pain have produced more positive results than those using static magnets.

"Life energy" therapies

The idea that a special type of "life energy" flows through people's bodies is common among cultures around the world. For instance, the ancient Chinese called

it qi (chee), whereas ancient Hindus called it prana (PRAH-nuh). Also common is the idea that certain "healers" can treat illnesses by passing their life energy into others. They do this by holding their hands on or near a person's body. In Japan, this is known as Reiki (RAY-kee). In Western cultures, it's called therapeutic touch, laying on of hands, or polarity therapy. Some researchers have claimed to detect a unique form of energy given off by healers. But the findings of these research studies are controversial.

In research studies, energy healing seemed to:

- reduce pain in conditions involving muscles, bones, and joints
- help women receiving radiation treatment for cancer feel more energetic and less pain

In other research, energy healing did not seem to be effective. These research studies showed that energy healing:

- had no effect on the nerve pain that can occur in diabetes
- had no useful effect in people recovering from a stroke

Therapies that adjust the body

Some CAM practices involve handling, pressing, or moving parts of the body. Examples include:

- chiropractic
- osteopathy (OSS-tee-OP-uh-thee)
- massage

Chiropractic

Chiropractors believe that the body has a natural healing ability that is controlled by the nervous system. They also believe that if the bones in the spine are not sitting on top of each other correctly, they put pressure on nerves along the spine. This can disrupt the flow of nerve signals to parts of the body. If a body part does not receive its normal supply of nerve signals, it becomes diseased, according to this theory.

To make the spinal bones line up straight, chiropractors make one or more "adjustments." A chiropractic adjustment involves applying a sudden controlled force to a joint.

Research suggests that chiropractic adjustments may offer short-term relief for low back pain. However, most cases of short-term low back pain get better in several weeks no matter what treatment is used.

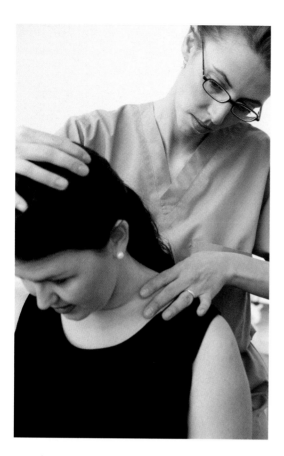

work with parts of the body to relieve muscle tension and help joints move more smoothly. Techniques include:

- thrust technique, in which the osteopath applies a brief rapid force to a joint, often causing a "popping" noise
- muscle energy, in which the osteopath directs you to move into a certain position while providing a specific amount of resistance against the movement
- myofascial (MEYE-oh-FASH-ee-uhl) release, in which the osteopath gently applies force to a tense body area

Osteopaths receive training in conventional medicine as well as osteopathic medicine. Because of this, osteopaths can prescribe drugs and perform surgery.

Research suggests that osteopathic manipulations may be useful for treating low back pain.

Chiropractic adjustments for low back pain are generally safe. But there have been cases of stroke following neck adjustments because of the tearing of arteries leading to the brain. There has also been concern that some chiropractors overuse x-rays, which may increase your risk of cancer.

Osteopathy

Osteopaths believe that the bones and muscles of the body need to be positioned properly so that blood and other body fluids flow as they should. This is thought to help ensure health. An osteopath will first feel the patient's body to find tense muscles and joints that do not move well. They then manipulate or

Massage

Massage therapists press, rub, or move muscles and other soft tissues of the body. Most people use massage to reduce muscle soreness and tension and relieve stress and anxiety.

Research suggests that massage therapy may be useful in treating various conditions, including:

- fibromyalgia (feye-broh-meye-AL-jee-uh)
- osteoarthritis (OSS-tee-oh-ar-THREYE-tuhss) of the knee
- anxiety

Also, research has shown that preterm infants who receive daily massage treatments gain more weight per day and show fewer stress behaviors than those who do not receive these treatments.

Mind-body medicine

Perhaps you have noticed that your mood can affect whether or not you get sick. If you feel well, you are less likely to get sick. If you feel bad, you are more likely to get sick. In fact, research has shown that mood can affect your health. For instance, in one research study, people who were energetic, happy, and relaxed were less likely to develop a cold even though they were infected with a cold virus than were people who were sad, tense, and angry.

Mind-body medicine is a branch of CAM that seeks to understand how your mind and body affect each other. Mind-body therapies attempt to use this information to improve your health. Two examples of mind-body therapies are biofeedback and hypnosis.

Biofeedback

Biofeedback allows people to control things about their body that they ordinarily would not be able to control. These include heart rate, skin temperature, and muscle tension. During a biofeedback

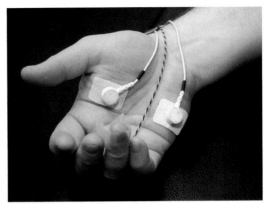

SENSORS USED IN BIOFEEDBACK

session, therapists apply electrical sensors to parts of a client's body. These sensors measure something about the body that would be useful to control. For instance, someone who gets tension headaches because of increased muscle tension in the head would have sensors on the head to detect muscle tension. When the muscles become more tense, this is made known to the client by a beeping sound or a flashing light. The client learns to turn off the sound or light by relaxing head muscles. This helps get rid of the headache.

Biofeedback has been shown to be helpful in treating a variety of medical conditions, including:

- high blood pressure
- hot flashes
- irregular heartbeats

Hypnosis

Hypnotists try to produce a mental state in which you are more open to suggestions. To hypnotize someone, a therapist will first get them to relax and concentrate on an object. Then the therapist will tell them something such as, "You will not feel pain when you give birth."

Research has shown that hypnosis can be useful for:

- reducing labor pain
- reducing anxiety before medical or dental procedures
- treating tension headaches

Not everyone can be hypnotized. Research suggests that people who can become absorbed in activities such as reading, listening to music, or daydreaming have a greater ability to be hypnotized.

Whole medical systems

Whole medical systems are health care methods that have evolved separately from conventional Western medicine. Each medical system involves several therapies that are often used in combination.

Traditional Chinese medicine

Traditional Chinese medicine includes:

- acupuncture, a treatment that involves inserting thin needles into specific points on the skin

- moxibustion (MOKS-ee-BUHSS-chuhn), the burning of the herb moxa (MOKS-uh) (also known as mugwort) at an acupuncture point to stimulate the point with heat
- Chinese herbal medicines

The part of traditional Chinese medicine that has been studied the most in terms of its health effects is acupuncture. Acupuncture was developed in China more than 2000 years ago. According to ancient Chinese beliefs, disease is due to a blockage in the flow of qi energy through the body. Inserting needles into acupuncture points unblocks qi to restore health, according to this theory. Modern scientists think that acupuncture may work by causing the release of natural painkillers in the brain.

Research has shown that acupuncture may be useful for reducing:

- pain after dental procedures
- severe vomiting that can occur during pregnancy
- labor pain
- pain in osteoarthritis of the knee

The Healthy Woman: A Complete Guide for All Ages

Also, research suggests that acupuncture plus moxibustion may cause a breech baby to move to the head-down position, which allows for a normal vaginal birth. Before birth, most babies are in this head-down position in the mother's uterus. But sometimes the part of the baby that is down near the vagina is the buttocks or the feet. When a baby is in one of these positions before birth, it's called a breech baby. Doctors often deliver breech babies by cesarean section.

Compared with acupuncture, less research has been done on the health effects of Chinese herbal medicines. But drugs for treating malaria have been developed from one Chinese herbal medicine.

Ayurveda

Ayurveda (AH-yur-VAY-duh) is one of the world's oldest systems of medicine. It started in India more than 5000 years ago. Ayurveda involves many different treatments, including:

- herbal medicines

- meditation
- yoga (a system of exercises designed to help you gain control of your body and mind)

Research on Ayurvedic treatments is still in the early stages. But a number of Ayurvedic herbs and spices are showing promise in treating various diseases. For instance, tumeric, a spice that is often used in Ayurvedic treatments, contains a substance that may help treat Alzheimer's disease.

Homeopathy

Homeopathy (HOH-mee-OP-uh-thee) is a medical system developed in Germany in the early 1800s. It is based on the idea that drugs that produce symptoms similar to those of a disease can help cure that disease. Homeopathic products contain these drugs in very small doses dissolved in water or alcohol.

Homeopathic products have been tried for many health issues, including menopausal hot flashes and premenstrual syndrome. A few research studies have shown homeopathic products to work for some conditions. But many experts question these results because homeo-

Warning

Some Chinese and Ayurvedic herbal medicines have been found to contain toxic metals and other harmful substances. Some Chinese herbal medicines have also been found to contain prescription drugs that were not listed on the label. Before taking any Chinese or Ayurvedic herbal medicines, you should talk to your doctor. For information about new FDA regulations to address problems with dietary supplements, which includes these medicines, see page 370.

pathic products contain such small doses of the active drug. More research is needed before homeopathy can be considered useful for any medical condition.

Tips on selecting a CAM therapist

Selecting a CAM therapist is much like selecting a conventional doctor. You want someone you feel comfortable with and who will help you with your health concerns. Below are some tips for choosing a CAM therapist:

- Talk with your primary care doctor about your interest in trying a CAM therapy. Discuss possible benefits and risks of the therapy. Ask if the therapy might interfere with your conventional treatments. Also, ask your doctor to recommend someone who practices the type of therapy that you are interested in.

- Some large medical centers have CAM therapists on staff. Check to see if there is such a center near you.

- Contact a national association for the therapy that you are interested in and ask for a list of certified therapists in your area. To find CAM associations, ask your local librarian for directories that you can look in.

- Some states have agencies that regulate and license certain types of CAM therapists. The agency may be able to provide you with a list of therapists who meet their standards.

- Find out if your health insurance company will cover your visit to a CAM therapist. Most CAM therapies are not covered by insurance.

- After you choose a CAM therapist, go to your first visit with a list of questions that you want answered. Also, be prepared to discuss your health history and the other treatments that you are receiving.

A final word

Be sure to mention any CAM therapies that you are considering trying with your primary care doctor. Your doctor will be able to tell you about the possible benefits and risks of the treatment. Also, when it comes to CAM therapies, it is probably best to steer a middle course. Keep an open mind but, at the same time, be skeptical. ■

One Woman's Story

I have found massage therapy to be a very valuable complementary therapy. As a single mother, raising four children, I have over the years worked through periods of extreme stress. This overload of stress has contributed to severe headaches and shoulder and back pain. I have found that getting a good massage is the single most effective intervention to reduce stress and relieve the muscle tension resulting from too many hours in front of a computer.

Massage therapy has been a safe and effective complementary therapy for me.

Several years ago, while sitting at a red light in my car, I was struck from behind and suffered a whiplash injury to my neck. I suffered terribly for months with pain, and none of the typical treatments provided relief. Not content to spend my evenings doped up on painkillers and muscle relaxers and unable to participate in my children's lives, I visited my massage therapist, who also was trained in cranialsacral therapy, which involves adjusting bones in the head and spine. After just a few sessions of cranialsacral therapy and massage, the pain from the whiplash injury went away and has never returned.

Massage therapy has been a safe and effective complementary therapy for me. If we all had biweekly massages, perhaps we as a nation would be healthier!

Sarah

Olney, Maryland

For More Information...

National Center for Complementary and Alternative Medicine Clearinghouse, NIH
PO Box 7923
Gaithersburg, MD 20898
Web site: www.nccam.nih.gov
Phone number: (888) 644-6226,
(866) 464-3615 TTY

Office of Cancer Complementary and Alternative Medicine, NIH
6116 Executive Blvd, Suite 609,
MSC 8339
Bethesda, MD 20892
Web site: www.cancer.gov/cam
Phone number: (800) 422-6237

Office of Dietary Supplements, NIH
6100 Executive Blvd, Room 3B01,
MSC 7517
Bethesda, MD 20892-7517
Web site: www.ods.od.nih.gov

American Academy of Medical Acupuncture
4929 Wilshire Blvd, Suite 428
Los Angeles, CA 90010
Web site: www.medicalacupuncture.org

American Chiropractic Association
1701 Clarendon Blvd
Arlington, VA 22209
Web site: www.acatoday.org

American Holistic Medical Association
1 Eagle Valley Ct, Suite 201
Broadview, OH 44147
Web site: www.holisticmedicine.org

American Massage Therapy Association
500 Davis St, Suite 900
Evanston, IL 60201-4695
Web site: www.amtamassage.org
Phone number: (877) 905-2700

American Osteopathic Association
142 East Ontario St
Chicago, IL 60611
Web site: www.osteopathic.org
Phone number: (800) 621-1773

American Society of Clinical Hypnosis
140 N Bloomingdale Rd
Bloomingdale, IL 60108
Web site: www.asch.net

Association for Applied Psychophysiology and Biofeedback
10200 W 44th Ave, Suite 304
Wheat Ridge, CO 80033
Web site: www.aapb.org

Appendix

Additional Health Information and Tips

Know Your Body

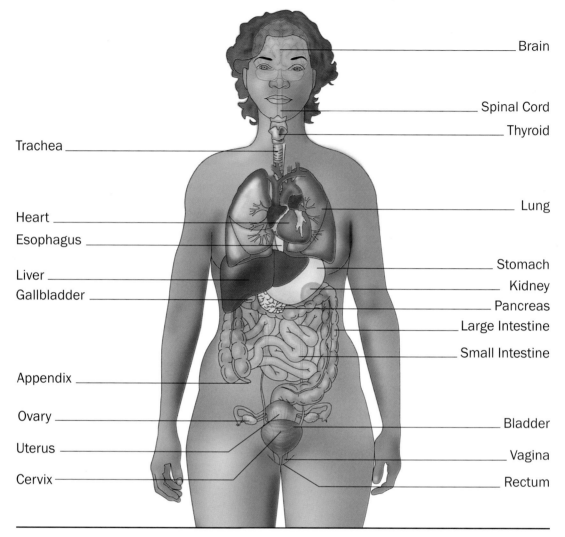

Brain

Spinal Cord

Thyroid

Trachea

Lung

Heart

Esophagus

Liver

Gallbladder

Stomach

Kidney

Pancreas

Large Intestine

Small Intestine

Appendix

Ovary

Bladder

Uterus

Vagina

Cervix

Rectum

Women's Body Systems

Cardiovascular and Circulatory

Digestive (gastrointestinal)

Endocrine

Nervous (neurologic) and Skeletal

Reproductive

Respiratory

Urinary (renal)

See the systems diagrams on pages 387-390

Know Your Body

Cardiovascular and Circulatory Systems

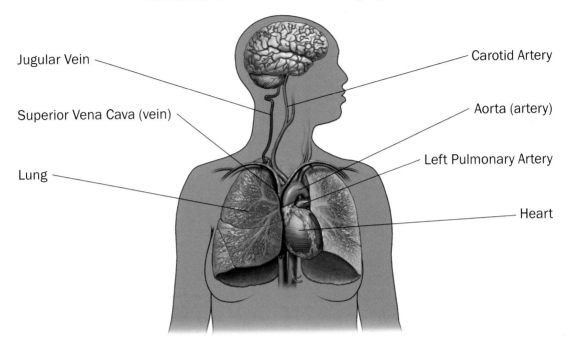

Jugular Vein

Carotid Artery

Superior Vena Cava (vein)

Aorta (artery)

Left Pulmonary Artery

Lung

Heart

Digestive (gastrointestinal) System

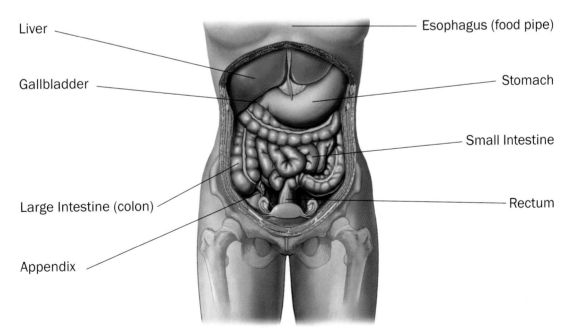

Liver

Esophagus (food pipe)

Gallbladder

Stomach

Small Intestine

Large Intestine (colon)

Rectum

Appendix

Know Your Body

Endocrine System

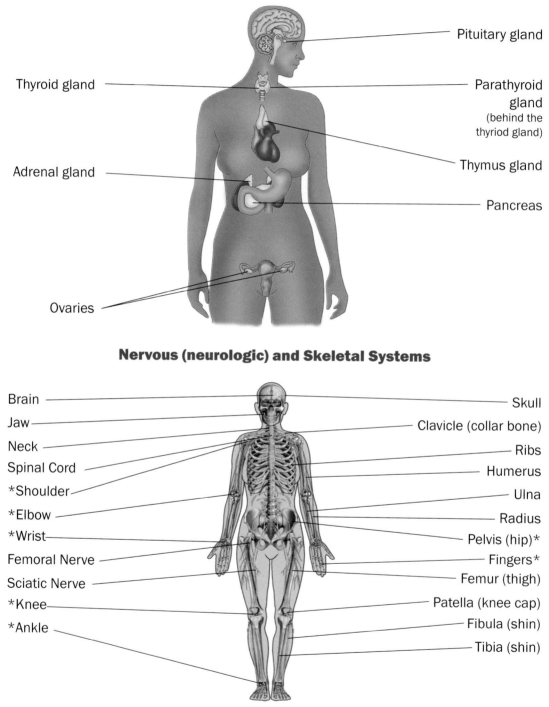

Pituitary gland

Thyroid gland

Parathyroid gland
(behind the thyriod gland)

Thymus gland

Adrenal gland

Pancreas

Ovaries

Nervous (neurologic) and Skeletal Systems

Brain

Jaw

Neck

Spinal Cord

*Shoulder

*Elbow

*Wrist

Femoral Nerve

Sciatic Nerve

*Knee

*Ankle

Skull

Clavicle (collar bone)

Ribs

Humerus

Ulna

Radius

Pelvis (hip)*

Fingers*

Femur (thigh)

Patella (knee cap)

Fibula (shin)

Tibia (shin)

*Major joints where arthritis or joint disease can occur.

The Healthy Woman: A Complete Guide for All Ages

Know Your Body

Reproductive System

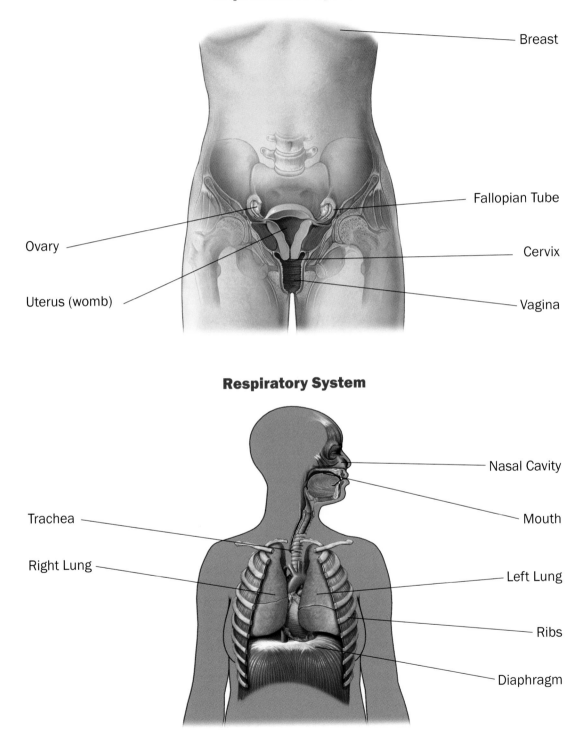

- Breast
- Fallopian Tube
- Ovary
- Cervix
- Uterus (womb)
- Vagina

Respiratory System

- Nasal Cavity
- Trachea
- Mouth
- Right Lung
- Left Lung
- Ribs
- Diaphragm

Know Your Body

Urinary (renal) System

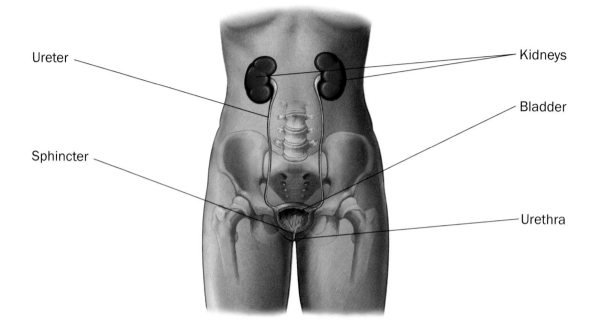

Ureter

Kidneys

Bladder

Sphincter

Urethra

HOW TO
Talk to Your Doctor or Nurse

Waiting in your doctor's office can make you feel nervous, impatient, or even scared. You might worry about what's wrong with you. You might feel annoyed because you're not getting other things done. Then when you see your doctor or nurse, the visit seems to be so short. You might have only a few minutes to explain your symptoms and concerns. Later that day, you might remember something you forgot to ask. You wonder if your question and its answer matter. Knowing how to talk to your doctor, nurse, or other members of your health care team will help you get the information you need.

Tips: What to do

- **List your questions and concerns.** Before your appointment, make a list of what you want to ask. When you're in the waiting room, review your list and organize your thoughts. You can share the list with your doctor or nurse.

- **Describe your symptoms.** Say when these problems started. Say how they make you feel. If you know, say what sets them off or triggers them. Say what you've done to feel better.

- **Give your doctor a list of your medications.** Tell what prescription drugs and over-the-counter medicines, vitamins, herbal products, and other supplements you're taking.

- **Be honest about your diet, physical activity, smoking, alcohol or drug use, and sexual history.** Not sharing information with your doctor or nurse can be harmful!

- **Describe any allergies to drugs, foods, pollen, or other things.** Don't forget to mention if you are being treated by other doctors, including mental health professionals.

- **Talk about sensitive topics.** Your doctor or nurse has probably heard it before! Don't leave something out because you're worried about taking up too much time. Be sure to talk about all of your concerns before you leave. If you don't understand the answers your doctor gives you, ask again.

- **Ask questions about any tests and your test results.** Get instructions on what you need to do to get ready for the test(s). Ask if there are any dangers or side effects. Ask how you can learn the test results. Ask how long it will take to get the results.

- **Ask questions about your condition or illness.** When your illness is diagnosed, ask your doctor how you can learn more about it. What caused it? Is it permanent? What can you do to help yourself feel better? How can it be treated?

- **Tell your doctor or nurse if you are pregnant or intend to become preg-**

The Healthy Woman: A Complete Guide for All Ages

nant. Some medicines may not be suitable for you. Other medicines should be used with caution if you are pregnant or about to become pregnant.

- **Ask your doctor about any treatments he or she recommends.** Be sure to ask about all of your options for treatment. Ask how long the treatment will last. Ask if it has any side effects. Ask how much it will cost. Ask if it is covered by your health insurance.

- **Ask your doctor about any medicines he or she prescribes for you.** Make sure you understand how to take your medicine. What should you do if you miss a dose? Are there any foods, drugs, or activities you should avoid when taking the medicine? Is there a generic brand of the drug you can use? You can also ask your pharmacist if a generic drug is available for your medication.

- **Ask more questions if you don't understand something.** If you're not clear about what your doctor or nurse is asking you to do or why, ask to have it explained again.

- **Bring a family member or trusted friend with you.** That person can take notes, offer moral support, and help you remember what was discussed. You can have that person ask questions, too!

- **Call before your visit to tell them if you have special needs.** If you don't speak or understand English well, the office may need to find an interpreter. If you have a disability, ask if they can accommodate you. ∎

HOW TO
Get a Second Opinion

Even though doctors may get similar medical training, they can have their own opinions and thoughts about how to practice medicine. They can have different ideas about how to diagnose and treat conditions or diseases. Some doctors take a more conservative, or traditional, approach to treating their patients. Other doctors are more aggressive and use the newest tests and therapies. It seems like we learn about new advances in medicine almost every day.

Many doctors specialize in one area of medicine, such as cardiology or obstetrics or psychiatry. Not every doctor can be skilled in using all the latest technology. Getting a second opinion from a different doctor might give you a fresh perspective and new information. It could provide you with new options for treating your condition. Then you can make more informed choices. If you get similar opinions from two doctors, you can also talk with a third doctor.

Tips: What to do

- **Ask your doctor for a recommendation.** Ask for the name of another doctor or specialist, so you can get a second opinion. Don't worry about hurting your doctor's feelings. Most doctors welcome a second opinion, especially when surgery or long-term treatment is involved.

- **Ask someone you trust for a recommendation.** If you don't feel comfortable asking your doctor for a referral, then call another doctor you trust. You can also call university teaching hospitals and medical societies in your area for the names of doctors. Some of this information is also available on the Internet.

- **Check with your health insurance provider.** Call your insurance company before you get a second opinion. Ask if they will pay for this office visit.

Many health insurance providers do. Ask if there are any special procedures you or your primary care doctor needs to follow.

- **Ask to have medical records sent to the second doctor.** Ask your primary care doctor to send your medical records to the new doctor. You need to give written permission to your current doctor to send any records or test results to a new doctor. You can also ask for a copy of your own medical records for your files. Your new doctor can then examine these records before your office visit.

- **Learn as much as you can.** Ask your doctor for information you can read.

Go to a local library. Search the Internet. Find a teaching hospital or university that has medical libraries open to the public. The information you find can be hard to understand, or just confusing. Make a list of your questions, and bring it with you when you see your new doctor.

- **Do not rely on the Internet or a telephone conversation.** When you get a second opinion, you need to be seen by a doctor. That doctor will perform a physical examination and perhaps other tests. The doctor will also thoroughly review your medical records, ask you questions, and address your concerns. ■

HOW TO
Be Prepared for Emergencies

When disaster strikes, you may not have much time to act. To help protect loved ones, take simple steps now to prepare your family for sudden emergencies or other disasters.

Three basic steps for disaster or emergency preparedness

1. **KNOW** what natural or other disasters could occur in your area and how to prepare for them. Learn about local evacuation routes, so that you know how to leave an area quickly. The Federal Emergency Management Agency offers information on preparedness at www.fema.gov.

2. **PLAN** out on paper the steps you should take during an emergency and give family members a copy. Talk about potential disasters or emergencies and how to respond to each. Choose a meeting place, other than your home, for family members to gather in case you can't go home. Make sure you choose an "emergency check-in" contact person and teach your children the phone number for this person.

3. **PACK** emergency supplies in your home to meet your needs for 3 days. Always keep all your important documentation together, in one place, in case you have to "grab and go" during an evacuation.

Need to evacuate? Have a kit ready that includes:

- identification for yourself and your children, such as birth certificates and social security cards

- important personal papers, such as health insurance identification cards, immigration papers, and children's school records

- funds in the form of cash, traveler's checks, credit cards, and checkbook

- keys to the house, car, and safety deposit box or post office box

- ways to communicate, including a calling card, cell phone and extra battery, and the emergency check-in number for family members to call

- prescription medications, including written prescription orders, and supplies such as contact lens cleaner and feminine hygiene products

Essential items for disaster preparedness

Relief workers will most likely be on the scene after a disaster, but they cannot reach everyone immediately. Gather the supplies below in case you have to stay where you are.

Water. Keep at least a 3-day supply of water for each person, stored in plastic containers. Each person needs 1 gallon of water each day.

Food. Store at least a 3-day supply of nonperishable food such as canned meat, beans, vegetables, fruit and juices; peanut butter or other high-energy food; and unsalted crackers. Keep a nonelectric can opener handy. If you have pets, stock up on canned pet food.

Infant care. Store baby formula and water to prepare it if a child is not breastfed. If you need to evacuate quickly, bring towels or sheets to carry a baby instead of a bulky stroller.

Other supplies. Make sure you have large plastic bags that seal for water-proofing important papers, a battery-powered flashlight and radio with extra batteries, and a first aid kit.

Breastfeeding during an emergency

When an emergency occurs, breastfeeding saves lives.

- Breastfeeding protects babies from the risks of a contaminated water supply.

- Breastfeeding helps protect against respiratory illnesses and diarrhea—diseases that can be fatal in populations displaced by disaster.

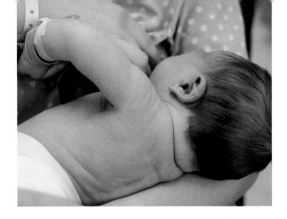

The basics of breastfeeding during an emergency are much the same as they are in normal times. Continuing to breast-feed whenever the baby seems hungry maintains a mother's milk supply and is calming to both mother and baby. Visit www.lalecheleague.org for information on how to breastfeed in an emergency, even if you have been giving your baby formula. (See the *Breastfeeding* chapter on page 187 for more information.)

Food and water safety during an emergency

Food may not be safe to eat during and after an emergency. Water may not be safe to drink, clean with, or bathe in after an emergency such as a hurricane or flood because it can become contaminated with bacteria, sewage, agricultural or industrial waste, chemicals, and other substances that can cause illness or death. The Centers for Disease Control and Prevention has information about keeping your food and water safe at www.bt.cdc.gov/disasters/foodwater.

Staying safe from violence during an emergency

After disasters, women are at greater risk of sexual assault or other violence. Visit www.womenshealth.gov/violence for safety tips. ■

HOW TO
Read Drug Labels

Medicines, or drugs, come as either prescription or over the counter (OTC). Prescription drugs are used under a doctor's care. OTC drugs can be bought and used without a doctor's prescription, and you buy them at a drugstore or grocery store. When using any kind of drug, it's really important to read the drug label for instructions. Not following the instructions can hurt your health. Read the label each time you use a new bottle of a drug, just in case there have been changes to it since the last time you used it. See the drug label below and on the next page to know what to look for. If you read the label and still have questions, call your doctor, nurse, or pharmacist for help. ■

Prescription Drug Label

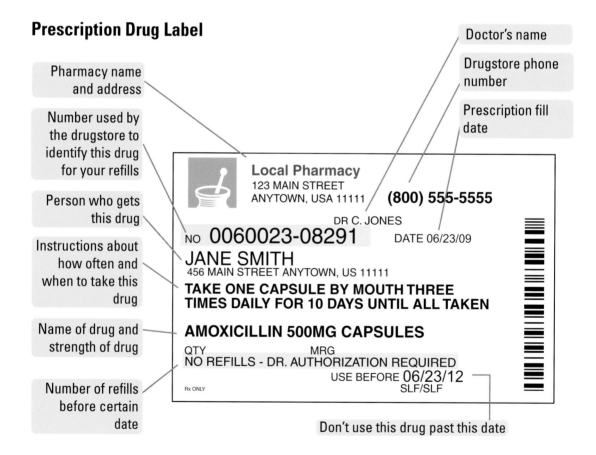

Doctor's name

Drugstore phone number

Prescription fill date

Pharmacy name and address

Number used by the drugstore to identify this drug for your refills

Person who gets this drug

Instructions about how often and when to take this drug

Name of drug and strength of drug

Number of refills before certain date

Local Pharmacy
123 MAIN STREET
ANYTOWN, USA 11111   **(800) 555-5555**
DR C. JONES
NO **0060023-08291**   DATE 06/23/09
JANE SMITH
456 MAIN STREET ANYTOWN, US 11111
TAKE ONE CAPSULE BY MOUTH THREE TIMES DAILY FOR 10 DAYS UNTIL ALL TAKEN

AMOXICILLIN 500MG CAPSULES
QTY   MRG
NO REFILLS - DR. AUTHORIZATION REQUIRED
USE BEFORE **06/23/12**
Rx ONLY   SLF/SLF

Don't use this drug past this date

Over-the-Counter (OTC) Medicine Label

Therapeutic substance in drug

Product type

Symptoms or diseases the drug treats

When not to use this drug, when to stop taking it, when to see a doctor, and possible side effects

Read carefully: how much to take, how often to take it, and when to stop taking it

More information on how to store the drug

Other things in the drug, such as colors or flavorings

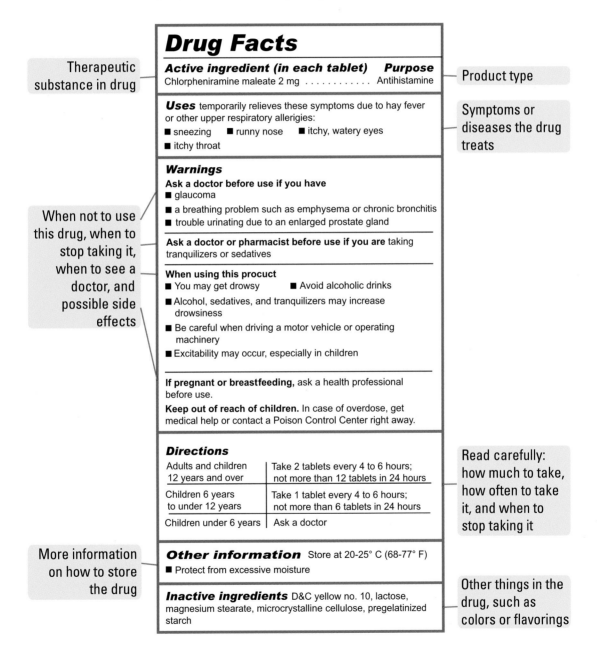

Drug Facts

Active ingredient (in each tablet)   **Purpose**
Chlorpheniramine maleate 2 mg . . . .   Antihistamine

Uses temporarily relieves these symptoms due to hay fever or other upper respiratory allergies:
■ sneezing   ■ runny nose   ■ itchy, watery eyes
■ itchy throat

Warnings
Ask a doctor before use if you have
■ glaucoma
■ a breathing problem such as emphysema or chronic bronchitis
■ trouble urinating due to an enlarged prostate gland

Ask a doctor or pharmacist before use if you are taking tranquilizers or sedatives

When using this procuct
■ You may get drowsy   ■ Avoid alcoholic drinks
■ Alcohol, sedatives, and tranquilizers may increase drowsiness
■ Be careful when driving a motor vehicle or operating machinery
■ Excitability may occur, especially in children

If pregnant or breastfeeding, ask a health professional before use.
Keep out of reach of children. In case of overdose, get medical help or contact a Poison Control Center right away.

Directions

Adults and children 12 years and over	Take 2 tablets every 4 to 6 hours; not more than 12 tablets in 24 hours
Children 6 years to under 12 years	Take 1 tablet every 4 to 6 hours; not more than 6 tablets in 24 hours
Children under 6 years	Ask a doctor

Other information   Store at 20-25° C (68-77° F)
■ Protect from excessive moisture

Inactive ingredients D&C yellow no. 10, lactose, magnesium stearate, microcrystalline cellulose, pregelatinized starch

Environmental Health

The quality of the environment can affect women's health. Chemicals and other substances in the air, water, soil, and food may be toxic and cause health problems. The quality of the environment may have a greater impact on children than adults. This is because children are growing quickly and breathe more air, eat more food, and drink more water. Some toxins can be passed from mother to child during pregnancy or breastfeeding. If you are pregnant, nursing, or planning to become pregnant, talk to your doctor about environmental exposures you should avoid.

Outdoor air

There are many sources of pollution outdoors, such as emissions from cars and trucks, power plants that burn fossil fuels, factories, and forest fires.

Outdoor air pollution can irritate your eyes, nose, and throat. At high levels, some outdoor air pollutants may cause more serious health problems like cancer and lung damage. Children, the elderly, and people with heart or lung conditions are more likely to be affected by some types of outdoor air pollution.

The U.S. Environmental Protection Agency (EPA) protects the quality of the air throughout the country. However, some areas may have higher levels of outdoor air pollution than others. Find out about the air quality in your community. Check the daily Air Quality Index (AQI) in your local radio, television, or newspaper forecast. You can also

find your AQI online at the EPA's Web site.

You can reduce your exposure to air pollution by limiting outdoor activities when the AQI is high. By using less energy, you can help reduce the air pollution that comes from burning fossil fuels.

- Replace incandescent lightbulbs with compact fluorescent bulbs.
- Turn off lights and appliances when they're not in use.
- Reuse and recycle to conserve raw materials and energy.
- Buy ENERGY STAR appliances.
- Choose a vehicle with good fuel economy and low emissions.
- Drive less. Carpool, walk, bike, or use public transportation if you can.

Indoor air

Indoor air pollution can irritate your eyes, nose, and throat. It can cause headaches or make you feel dizzy or tired. These symptoms may seem similar to the symptoms of a cold or flu. But if your symptoms disappear when you are away from home, you may have an indoor air problem.

Indoor air pollution can also lead to serious health problems, such as heart and lung diseases and cancer. These problems may develop many years after exposure or after repeated exposures to indoor air pollutants.

Children, the elderly, and people with heart or lung conditions are more likely to be affected by indoor air pollution.

Some common sources of indoor air pollution include:

- gases from burning oil, gas, coal, wood used for heating and cooking
- smoke from tobacco products
- building materials, such as asbestos insulation and products made from pressed wood
- outdoor pollutants, such as radon, which can build up indoors
- chemicals used for cleaning, pest control, and painting
- personal care products such as hair spray and nail polish remover
- biological pollutants, such as bacteria, molds, mildew, and pet dander

You can improve the air quality in your home:

- Remove sources of pollution.
- Increase the ventilation (flow of air). Run exhaust and attic fans or open doors and windows. This is especially important when using household products that contain harmful chemicals.
- Use a home air cleaner to remove pollutants, if necessary.

Water quality

EPA sets standards for safe drinking water. Public water systems must meet these standards. Tap water, well water, and even bottled water may contain very small amounts of contaminants such as chemicals and bacteria. As long as levels are low enough to meet EPA's safety standards, your water is safe to drink.

You can take steps to make sure your water is safe to drink.

- People with weakened immune systems, infants, children, and the elderly may be more sensitive to some contaminants. Talk to your doctor about whether you need to take extra precautions.
- If your water comes from a private well, have your water tested at least once a year. Contact your local, county, or state health department for more information about water testing. Some health departments may help you with testing. If not, they can recommend a state-certified laboratory in your area.
- If your water comes from a public source, your water supplier is required to send you an annual water quality report.

Lead

Lead exposure can cause reproductive problems, high blood pressure, muscle and joint pain, and problems with memory or concentration. Lead can harm the developing brain and nervous system of children, infants, and unborn children.

Some common sources of lead exposure include:

- lead-based paint in houses built before 1978
- soil and household dust that may contain chips or dust from lead-based paints
- water from lead-lined pipes

You can reduce your exposure to lead.

- Have your home tested for lead.
- If you plan to remove or disturb lead-based paint, hire a contractor with special training. Leave the house until renovations are complete and the house is cleaned to remove any lead dust.
- Use only cold water to cook or to make baby formula.
- Run cold water for at least 1 minute before using it.
- Use a water filter certified by NSF (National Sanitation Foundation) International to remove lead.

Mercury

In both children and adults, high levels of mercury may affect the brain, heart, kidneys, lungs, and immune system. Children, infants, and unborn babies are most sensitive to mercury.

The most common source of exposure to mercury is fish and shellfish, which contain small amounts of mercury. Different kinds of fish contain different amounts. Women who may become pregnant, women who are pregnant or nursing, and young children should follow these guidelines:

- Don't eat shark, swordfish, king mackerel, or tilefish.
- Eat no more than 12 ounces (about 2 meals) of fish low in mercury each week. Low-mercury fish include shrimp, canned light tuna, salmon, pollock, and catfish.
- Eat no more than 6 ounces (about 1 meal) of albacore (white) tuna each week.
- Before eating fish caught in your area, check local fish safety advisories.

Mercury may also be found in thermometers, thermostats, and fluorescent lightbulbs. If these items break, people may be exposed to mercury. Do not use a vacuum to clean mercury spills. Contact

your local health department to find out how to properly clean and dispose of spilled mercury.

Pesticides

Chemicals used to kill pests such as insects, rodents, and mold can also affect human health. At high levels, pesticides may cause birth defects, nerve damage, and cancer.

Small amounts of pesticides may be found in air, water, and food. EPA limits pesticides used in farming to make sure your food is safe. Pesticides used in and around your home may contribute to indoor air pollution.

You can reduce your exposure to pesticides.

- Wash and scrub fruits and vegetables under running water, peel off skins, and trim outer leaves.

- Trim fat from your meat.

- Choose organic foods, grown without the use of synthetic pesticides.

- Eat a variety of foods to avoid high exposure to a single pesticide.

- If you use pesticides in your home, follow the instructions carefully. Keep pesticides out of reach of children. ■

Resources:

U.S. Environmental Protection Agency
Web site: www.epa.gov

Indoor Air Quality Information Clearinghouse: www.epa.gov/iaq
Phone number: (800) 438-4318

National Lead Information Center: www.epa.gov/lead
Phone number: (800) 424-5323

Safe water information where you live: www.epa.gov/safewater/ccr/whereyoulive.html

Food Safety Information Center, USDA
Web site: http://foodsafety.nal.usda.gov
Phone number: (301) 504-6835

National Center for Environmental Health, CDC

Web site: www.cdc.gov/nceh
Phone number: (800) 232-4636

National Institute of Environmental Health Sciences, NIH
Web site: www.niehs.nih.gov

National Poison Control Hotline
Web site: www.poison.org
Phone number: (800) 222-1222

Avian Flu

Avian influenza (flu) is not the same as pandemic flu. A pandemic flu is a global outbreak of a flu. A pandemic can happen when a new virus appears that people have little or no immunity against and for which there is no vaccine. (Having immunity means you are resistant to, or protected against, a disease.) A new virus can spread quickly from person to person around the world, causing severe illness and even death. Although it is hard to know when the next flu pandemic will happen or how dangerous it will be, you can be informed and take steps to prepare your family. Avian flu has received a lot of attention in recent years, raising many questions about the dangers of a flu pandemic.

What is avian flu?

Avian or "bird" flu is caused by influenza viruses that naturally affect birds. Wild birds carry these highly contagious viruses, but they generally do not become sick. Domesticated birds, though, are at great risk. Avian flu can cause serious illness and death for infected chickens, ducks, and turkeys.

Why are health officials concerned about avian flu for humans?

Although people are not usually at risk of getting avian flu viruses, a virus called H5N1 is one of the few strains that has crossed over to infect people. The H5N1 virus is powerful, having caused the deaths of more than half of the people infected. Experts think most of these cases have been caused by contact with infected birds. To date, there has been limited spread of the virus from person to person. The concern is that H5N1 will change into a virus that can pass from person to person more easily and more quickly. An increasing number of human cases have been found in Asian, European, and African countries. Health officials are watching the situation closely to prepare for the possibility that the virus may spread to other parts of the world.

Will getting a seasonal flu shot prevent me from getting avian flu?

No. The flu shot can help protect you only from seasonal flu. No vaccine is available to protect against the H5N1 virus that has been found in people, but researchers are working on making one.

What are the symptoms of avian flu?

Symptoms can include regular flu symptoms such as fever, cough, sore throat, and muscle aches. Other symptoms may include eye infections, pneumonia, and severe respiratory problems. There may be other symptoms that we do not yet know about.

Are there treatments available for avian flu?

The H5N1 virus is resistant to two medicines used to treat the flu: amantadine (uh-MAN-tuh-deen) and rimantadine (rih-MAN-tuh-deen). Two other flu medicines called oseltamivir (o-suhl-TAM-uh-vihr) and zanamivir (zuh-NAM-uh-vihr) may work to treat the flu caused by H5N1. More research is needed to test these medicines. Health researchers are also working on improving flu testing, to better detect which flu strain you have and where it came from. This will help government officials track dangerous flu viruses and help keep the public informed.

What can I do to help keep my family healthy?

You and members of your family can take steps to help limit the spread of germs.

- Wash your hands with soap and warm water often.

- Use an alcohol-based hand cleanser if you don't have soap handy.

- When coughing or sneezing, cover your mouth and nose with a tissue (or your upper sleeve if you don't have a tissue), throw used tissue away, and wash your hands afterward.

- If you are sick, stay home.

- It is also important to eat a balanced diet, drink plenty of water, get regular physical activity, and get enough rest.

What should I do to help my family prepare for a flu pandemic?

Visit www.pandemicflu.gov to learn how to prepare your family. This Web site provides preparation checklists for families and businesses, information for people who deal with poultry, and the latest information on how avian flu is affecting people around the world. If H5N1 does cause a pandemic flu, this Web site will offer important safety information. You can also call the Centers for Disease Control and Prevention Hotline at (800) CDC-INFO (800) 232-4636) or (888) 232-6348 (TDD) 24 hours a day, 7 days a week. ■

---

www.pandemicflu.gov
(800) CDC-INFO or
(888) 232-6348 (TDD)

Caregiver Stress

As the U.S. population ages, more people are faced with the responsibility of caring for elderly loved ones with Alzheimer's disease, cancer, or other health problems. Many parents are also raising children with severe disabilities at home. More often today, these caregivers are continuing to care for children with disabilities well into their adulthood.

The people needing care often need help with basic daily tasks. Caregivers help with a wide range of activities, including:

- cooking
- feeding
- giving medicine
- bathing
- running errands

People who do not get paid for providing care are known as informal caregivers or family caregivers. Most informal caregivers are women. Often, these women also have children to take care of and jobs outside the home.

Being an informal caregiver can have many rewards. It can give you a feeling of giving back to a loved one. It can make you feel needed and can lead to a stronger relationship with the person receiving care. However, caregiving can also take a toll on your mental and physical health.

What is caregiver stress?

Caregiver stress is the emotional strain of caregiving. It can take many forms. For instance, you may feel frustrated and angry taking care of someone with dementia (dih-MEN-chuh) who often wanders away or becomes easily upset. Or you may feel guilty because you think that you should be able to provide better care, despite all the other things that you have to do.

How can I tell if caregiving is putting too much stress on me?

Caregiving may be putting too much strain on you if you have any of the following symptoms:

- sleeping too much or too little
- gain or loss of a lot of weight
- feeling tired most of the time
- loss of interest in activities you used to enjoy
- becoming easily irritated or angered
- often feeling sad
- frequent headaches, bodily pain, or other physical problems
- abuse of alcohol or drugs, including prescription drugs

Talk to a counselor, psychologist, or other mental health professional right away if your stress leads you to physically or emotionally harm the person you are caring for.

How can caregiver stress affect my health?

Research shows that, compared with noncaregivers, caregivers:

- are more likely to have symptoms of depression or anxiety
- are more likely to have heart disease, cancer, diabetes, and arthritis

- have a weaker immune response, which can lead to frequent infections and increased risk of cancers
- have higher levels of obesity
- may be at higher risk of mental decline, including problems with memory and paying attention

What can I do to prevent or relieve stress?

First, never dismiss your feelings as "just stress." Caregiver stress can lead to serious health problems and you should take steps to reduce it as much as you can. Tips for reducing caregiver stress:

- Ask for and accept help.
- Say "no" to requests that are draining, such as hosting holiday meals.
- Stay in touch with family and friends.
- Join a caregiver support group.
- Attend a class to learn how to take care of someone with the disease that your loved one has.
- Prioritize, make lists, and establish a daily routine.
- Set realistic goals for each day.
- Get an annual medical checkup.
- Stay active, eat a healthy diet, and try to get enough sleep.

What caregiving services can I find in my community?

Caregiving services include:

- transportation
- meal delivery
- home health care services (such as nursing or physical therapy)
- nonmedical home care services (such as housekeeping or cooking)
- home modification (changes to the home that make it easier for your loved one to perform basic daily tasks, such as bathing, using the toilet, and moving around)
- legal and financial counseling

What can I do if I need a break?

Taking some time off from caregiving can reduce stress. "Respite care" provides substitute caregiving to give the regular caregiver a much-needed break. Respite care may be provided by:

- home health care workers
- adult day-care centers
- short-term nursing homes

How do I find out about caregiving services in my community?

Contact your local Area Agency on Aging (AAA) to learn about caregiving services where you live. AAAs are usually listed in the city or county government sections of the telephone directory under "Aging" or "Health and Human Services." The National Eldercare Locator, a service of the U.S. Administration on Aging, can also help you find your local AAA.

Resources:

Administration on Aging
www.aoa.gov
www.eldercare.gov
Eldercare Locator: (800) 677-1116

Family Caregiver Alliance
www.caregiver.org ∎

Understanding Genetics and Your Health

Humans have between 20,000 and 25,000 genes. Most genes are the same in all people. But small differences in these genes give you a one-of-a-kind look and contribute to your personality and talents. Genes also can affect your health. To understand how, it's helpful to learn what genes do.

Genes: Your body's blueprint

Genes, which are made up of DNA, contain the instructions your body's cells need to function. Genes are located on structures called chromosomes. Information from your genes is used to make proteins. Each cell contains thousands of proteins. Each protein has a specific job to do at a specific time for the cell to work properly.

Sometimes, a gene can have something wrong with it. This is called a gene mutation or a mutated gene. A mutation causes the gene to give the wrong instructions for making a protein, so that the protein works improperly or is missing. If the mutation affects a protein that plays an important role in the body, a medical problem could result. Most gene mutations have no effect on health or development.

Genetic disorders: The basics

The genes you are born with can affect your health in these ways:

- **Single gene disorders are caused by a mutation in one gene.** There is a pat-

How sickle cell anemia runs in families

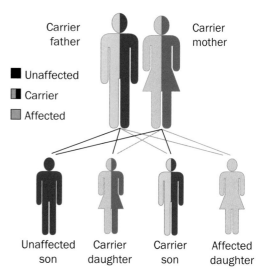

- ■ Unaffected
- ▣ Carrier
- ▨ Affected

Carrier father / Carrier mother

Unaffected son / Carrier daughter / Carrier son / Affected daughter

Two unaffected parents each carry one copy of a gene mutation for sickle cell anemia. They have one child with sickle cell anemia and three unaffected children. Two of the unaffected children inherit one copy of the gene mutation—as carriers, they can pass the sickle cell trait on to their children.

We are learning more and more about the role specific genes play in our health. For example, you may have heard about "breast cancer genes," called *BRCA* genes. All people have *BRCA* genes. But only women and men born with mutated *BRCA* genes are at higher risk of breast cancer. Still, some women born with mutated *BRCA* genes don't get breast cancer. And most women who get breast cancer are born with normal *BRCA* genes. Keep in mind that genes themselves do not cause disease, but that mutated genes may cause health problems.

tern to the way these genetic disorders show up in families. Even though the mutated gene is passed down from parent to child, not all family members are affected. Some members are "carriers" of the mutated gene. Examples of single-gene disorders are cystic fibrosis (SISS-tik-feye-BROH-suhss) and sickle cell anemia (uh-NEE-mee-uh).

- **Chromosome disorders occur when all or part of a chromosome is missing or extra, or if the structure of one or more chromosomes is not normal.** This can affect some of the genes. Most chromosome disorders involving whole chromosomes do not run in families. Genes can influence your risk of getting some diseases, such as breast cancer, heart disease, diabetes, and thyroid conditions. But other factors, such as lifestyle and environment, also play a role in developing these conditions. Rarely, single genes are responsible for these diseases; however, most of the time they are due to a combination of genes and environment. The role genes play in developing these conditions often is not known, but our understanding of this continues to grow through research.

Genetic counseling: What it is and who needs it

Genetic counseling gives information and support to people who have, or may be at risk of, genetic disorders. Some reasons a family might seek genetic counseling are:

- a family history of a genetic condition, birth defect, chromosomal disorder, or cancer

- two or more pregnancy losses, a stillbirth, or a baby who died

- a child with a known inherited disorder, birth defect, mental retardation, or developmental delay

- a woman who is pregnant or plans to become pregnant at 35 years or older

- test results that suggest a genetic condition is present

- increased risk of getting or passing on a genetic disorder because of one's ethnic background

- people related by blood who want to have children together

Your doctor can help you find a genetic professional if you might benefit from this service. During a consultation, the genetics professional meets with a person or family to discuss genetic risks or to diagnose, confirm, or rule out a genetic condition. Sometimes, a family chooses to have genetic testing. Most of the time, testing is used to find changes that are linked to genetic disorders. The results can confirm or rule out a condition. Tests also can help to know the chances that a person will get or pass on a genetic disorder. The genetics professional can help a family decide if genetic testing is the right choice for them. ■

Some companies offer genetic tests that you can do yourself through the mail. These tests may not provide true or meaningful information. These tests might even provide harmful information to consumers. Talk to your doctor before using this type of test.

Becoming a Research Volunteer

Today, women are living longer and healthier lives thanks, in part, to medical research. Because of research studies:

- We know what foods to eat to prevent heart disease.

- Doctors have better tools to detect health problems, such as mammograms for breast cancer.

- New drugs are available to treat diabetes, depression, and other diseases.

- We know that women respond differently than men to some drugs and medical treatments.

Important findings like these are not possible without the help of research volunteers. Many volunteers—and especially women—are needed for research studies. Whether to participate in a research study is a personal choice. Getting all the facts about the study will help you decide if volunteering is right for you.

Frequently asked questions about research studies

Are there different kinds of research studies?

Yes. Here are some examples.

- **Observational studies** follow one or more groups of the same people over a period of time to see how their health changes. A recent example is the Women's Health Initiative. This study tracked 93,676 postmenopausal women for about 8 years to learn more about risk factors for heart disease, cancer, and fractures.

- **Intervention studies** seek to improve people's health by finding ways to change behavior. An example would be a study to see whether teaching people how to read food labels leads to a healthier diet.

- **Clinical trials** are research studies that test new medical approaches in people. This includes new drugs and other treatments.

Where do research studies take place?

Research studies take place in doctors' offices, cancer centers, hospitals, and clinics in towns and cities across the United States and around the world. Some studies are held in a single location. Others involve hundreds of locations at the same time. Many types of organizations and individuals sponsor (fund) research studies. Many clinical trials are sponsored by government agencies or pharmaceutical companies. Some studies require you to travel, but sometimes a blood or other sample is all that is needed to participate.

What happens in a research study?

This depends on the type of study. For example, a study might ask you to keep track of how often you eat certain foods. Or a study might involve taking a drug and frequent visits to the doctor for tests. For all studies, you will work closely with the research team. The team will give you specific instructions according to the study's "protocol." The protocol is a carefully controlled study plan.

Who can participate in a research study?

The study's protocol sets guidelines about who can participate. Sometimes, a person who is willing to participate does not qualify. If this happens to you, don't take the rejection personally. Strict participation guidelines are in place to keep participants safe and to ensure that study results are reliable.

Will participation in a research study help me?

Research is not the same as treatment. Sometimes, participation in clinical trials gives you access to new treatments or drugs before they become widely available. These treatments may or may not help you. There also might be unpleasant, serious, or even life-threatening side effects. Or a study could involve not using a drug that can help you. Even if you are not helped personally, the study results could help many others in the future.

How will my safety be protected?

Researchers are required to care for your well-being just like the doctors who provide your regular medical care. Also, medical research studies that involve people have federally controlled safeguards, such as an "institutional review board," or IRB. The IRB is a group of people who make sure that a trial is ethical and the rights of participants are protected. Keep in mind that "protected" doesn't mean the study is risk free.

What is informed consent?

This is the process of learning the key facts about the research study before deciding whether to participate. The research team will explain all the study details to you. This includes the purpose of the study, how the trial might affect your daily life, how long the study will last, and the potential benefits and risks of participating. It's helpful to have a friend or family member with you during this discussion. If you agree to participate after learning all the facts, you will be asked to sign an informed consent form. This is not a contract. By signing the form, you are showing that you understand what is involved.

Who will pay for my medical care during the trial?

This depends on the study and your health insurance plan. Health plans do cover the costs that are part of your routine medical care. Often health plans do not cover the patient care costs related to clinical trials they deem to be "experimental." In many cases, the research team can help by talking with your plan provider. Also, many states require health plans to cover the costs for certain clinical trials, such as for new cancer treatments. There also are some government programs to help pay the costs of care. The research team can help you sort through any cost issues.

Can I quit after the study has begun?

Yes. You can leave a research study at any time. But be sure to tell the research team that you are withdrawing and your reasons why. ■

Where do I find out about research studies?

Talk to your doctor if you are interested in becoming a research volunteer. You also can find out about clinical trials at www.clinicaltrials.gov.

Important Screenings and Tests

Common Screening and Diagnostic Tests Explained

Test name	Definition
Angiography (an-jee-OG-ruh-fee)	Exam of your blood vessels using x-rays. The doctor inserts a small tube into the blood vessel and injects dye to see the vessels on the x-ray.
Barium enema	A lubricated enema tube is gently inserted into your rectum. Barium flows into your colon. An x-ray is taken of the large intestine.
Biopsy	A test that removes cells or tissues for examination by a pathologist to diagnose for disease. The tissue is examined under a microscope for cancer or other diseases.
Blood test	Blood is taken from a vein in the inside elbow or back of the hand to test for a health problem.
Bone mineral density (BMD) test	Special x-rays of your bones are used to test if you have osteoporosis, or a weakening of the bones.
Bronchoscopy (brong-KOSS-kuh-pee)	Exam of the lungs. A bronchoscope, or flexible tube, is put through the nose or mouth and into your trachea (windpipe).
Clinical breast exam (CBE)	A doctor, nurse, or other health professional uses his or her hands to examine your breasts and underarm areas to find lumps or other problems.
Chest x-ray	An x-ray of the chest, lungs, heart, large arteries, ribs, and diaphragm.
Colonoscopy (KOH-luhn-OSS-kuh-pee)	An examination of the inside of the colon using a colonoscope, inserted into the rectum. A colonoscope is a thin, tube-like instrument with a light and lens for viewing. It may also have a tool to remove tissue to be checked under a microscope for disease.
Computed tomography (tuh-MOG-ruh-fee) (CT or CAT) scan	The patient lies on a table and x-rays of the body are taken from different angles. Sometimes, a fluid is used to highlight parts of the body in the scan.
Echocardiography (ek-oh-kar-dee-OG-ruh-fee)	An instrument (that looks like a microphone) is placed on the chest. It uses sound waves to create a moving picture of the heart. A picture appears on a TV monitor, and the heart can be seen in different ways.
Electrocardiography (ih-lek-troh-kar-dee-OG-ruh-fee) (ECG or EKG)	A test that records the electrical activity of the heart, using electrodes placed on the arms, legs, and chest.
Electroencephalography (ih-lek-troh-en-sef-uhl-OG-ruh-fee) (EEG)	A test that measures the electrical activity of the brain, using electrodes that are put on the patient's scalp. Sometimes patients sleep during the test.
Exercise stress test	Electrodes are placed on the chest, arms, and legs to record the heart's activity. A blood pressure cuff is placed around the arm and is inflated every few minutes. Heart rate and blood pressure are taken before exercise starts. The patient walks on a treadmill or pedals a stationary bicycle. The pace of the treadmill is increased. The response of the heart is monitored. The test continues until target heart rate is reached. Monitoring continues after exercise for 10 to 15 minutes or until the heart rate returns to normal.
Fecal occult blood test (FOBT)	Detects hidden blood in a bowel movement. There are two types: the smear test and flushable reagent pads.

The Healthy Woman: A Complete Guide for All Ages

Common Screening and Diagnostic Tests Explained

Test name	Definition
Laparoscopy (lap-uh-ROSS-kuh-pee)	A small tube with a camera is inserted into the abdomen through a small cut in or just below the belly button to see inside the abdomen and pelvis. Other instruments can be inserted in the small cut as well. It is used for both diagnosing and treating problems inside the abdomen.
Magnetic resonance imaging (MRI)	A test that uses powerful magnets and radio waves to create a picture of the inside of your body without surgery. The patient lies on a table that slides into a large tunnel-like tube, which is surrounded by a scanner. Small coils may be placed around your head, arm, leg, or other areas.
Mammogram	X-rays of the breast taken by resting one breast at a time on a flat surface that contains an x-ray plate. A device presses firmly against the breast. An x-ray is taken to show a picture of the breast. Mammography is used to screen healthy women for signs of breast cancer. It can also be used to evaluate a woman who has symptoms of disease. It can, in some cases, detect breast cancers before you can feel them with your fingers.
Medical history	The doctor or nurse talks to the patient about current and past illnesses, surgeries, pregnancies, medications, allergies, use of alternative therapies, vitamins and supplements, diet, alcohol and drug use, physical activity, and family history of diseases.
Pap test	The nurse or doctor uses a small brush to take cells from the cervix (opening of the uterus) to look at under a microscope in a lab.
Pelvic exam	A doctor or nurse asks about the patient's health and looks at the vaginal area. The doctor or nurse checks the fallopian tubes, ovaries, and uterus by putting two gloved fingers inside the vagina. With the other hand, the doctor or nurse will feel from the outside for any lumps or tenderness.
Physical exam	The doctor or nurse will test for diseases, assess your risk of future medical problems, encourage a healthy lifestyle, and update your vaccinations.
Positron emission tomography (POZ-ih-tron ih-MISH-uhn tuh-MOG-ruh-fee) (PET) scan	The patient is injected with a radioactive substance, such as glucose. A scanner detects any cancerous areas in the body. Cancerous tissue absorbs more of the substance and looks brighter in images than normal tissue.
Sigmoidoscopy (SIG-moi-DOSS-kuh-pee)	The sigmoidoscope is a small camera attached to a flexible tube. This tube, about 20 inches long, is gently inserted into the colon. As the tube is slowly removed, the lining of the bowel is examined.
Spirometry (spuh-ROM-uh-tree)	The patient breathes into a mouthpiece that is connected to an instrument called a spirometer. The spirometer records the amount and the rate of air that is breathed in and out over a specified time. It measures how well the lungs exhale.
Ultrasound	A clear gel is put onto the skin over the area being examined. An instrument is then moved over that area. The machine sends out sound waves, which reflect off the body. A computer receives these waves and uses them to create pictures of the body.

Note: Anesthesia (medicine to block pain or sedate you) is given during some of these tests to keep you comfortable. Be sure to talk with your doctor or nurse about what to expect during and after tests, and how to prepare for tests.

General Screenings and Immunizations for Women

These charts are guidelines only. Your doctor will personalize the timing of each test and immunization to meet your health care needs.

Screening tests	Ages 18–39	Ages 40–49	Ages 50–64	Ages 65 and older
General health: Full checkup, including weight and height	Discuss with your doctor or nurse.	Discuss with your doctor or nurse.	Discuss with your doctor or nurse.	Discuss with your doctor or nurse.
Thyroid test (TSH)	Start at age 35, then every 5 years	Every 5 years	Every 5 years	Every 5 years
Heart health: Blood pressure test	At least every 2 years	At least every 2 years	At least every 2 years	At least every 2 years
Cholesterol test	Start at age 20, discuss with your doctor or nurse.	Discuss with your doctor or nurse.	Discuss with your doctor or nurse.	Discuss with your doctor or nurse.
Bone health: Bone mineral density test		Discuss with your doctor or nurse.	Discuss with your doctor or nurse.	Get a bone mineral density test at least once. Talk to your doctor or nurse about repeat testing.
Diabetes: Blood glucose test	Discuss with your doctor or nurse.	Start at age 45, then every 3 years	Every 3 years	Every 3 years
Breast health: Mammogram (x-ray of breast)		Every 1–2 years. Discuss with your doctor or nurse.	Every 1–2 years. Discuss with your doctor or nurse.	Every 1–2 years. Discuss with your doctor or nurse.
Reproductive health: Pap test and pelvic exam	Every 1–3 years if you have been sexually active or are older than 21	Every 1–3 years	Every 1–3 years	Discuss with your doctor or nurse.
Chlamydia test	Yearly until age 25 if sexually active. Older than age 25, get this test if you have new or multiple partners.	Get this test if you have new or multiple partners.	Get this test if you have new or multiple partners.	Get this test if you have new or multiple partners.
Sexually transmitted infection (STI) tests	Both partners should get tested for STIs, including HIV, before initiating sexual intercourse.	Both partners should get tested for STIs, including HIV, before initiating sexual intercourse.	Both partners should get tested for STIs, including HIV, before initiating sexual intercourse.	Both partners should get tested for STIs, including HIV, before initiating sexual intercourse.
Mental health screening	Discuss with your doctor or nurse.	Discuss with your doctor or nurse.	Discuss with your doctor or nurse.	Discuss with your doctor or nurse.
Colorectal health: Fecal occult blood test			Yearly	Yearly
Flexible sigmoidoscopy (with fecal occult blood test is preferred)			Every 5 years (if not having a colonoscopy)	Every 5 years (if not having a colonoscopy)

This chart lists recommended screenings and immunizations for women at average risk for most diseases. Citations for these recommendations can be found online at www.womenshealth.gov/screeningcharts/general/citations.cfm.

The Healthy Woman: A Complete Guide for All Ages

General Screenings and Immunizations for Women

These charts are guidelines only. Your doctor will personalize the timing of each test and immunization to meet your health care needs.

Screening tests	Ages 18–39	Ages 40–49	Ages 50–64	Ages 65 and older
Colorectal health (continued): Double contrast barium enema (DCBE)			Every 5–10 years (if not having a colonoscopy or sigmoidoscopy)	Every 5–10 years (if not having a colonoscopy or sigmoidoscopy)
Colonoscopy			Every 10 years	Every 10 years
Rectal exam	Discuss with your doctor or nurse.	Discuss with your doctor or nurse.	Every 5–10 years with each screening (sigmoidoscopy, colonoscopy, or DCBE)	Every 5–10 years with each screening (sigmoidoscopy, colonoscopy, or DCBE)
Eye and ear health: Complete eye exam	At least once between the ages 20 and 29 and at least twice between the ages 30 and 39, or any time you have a problem with your eye(s)	Every 2–4 years	Every 2–4 years	Every 1–2 years
Hearing test	Starting at age 18, then every 10 years	Every 10 years	Every 3 years	Every 3 years
Skin health: Mole exam	Monthly mole self-exam; by a doctor every 3 years, starting at age 20	Monthly mole self-exam; by a doctor every year	Monthly mole self-exam; by a doctor every year	Monthly mole self-exam; by a doctor every year
Oral health: Dental exam	One to two times every year	One to two times every year	One to two times every year	One to two times every year
Immunizations: Influenza vaccine	Discuss with your doctor or nurse.	Discuss with your doctor or nurse.	Yearly	Yearly
Pneumococcal vaccine				One time only
Tetanus-diphtheria booster vaccine	Every 10 years	Every 10 years	Every 10 years	Every 10 years
Human papillomavirus (HPV) vaccine	Up to age 26, discuss with your doctor or nurse.			
Meningococcal vaccine	Discuss with your doctor or nurse if attending college.			
Herpes zoster vaccine (to prevent shingles)			Starting at age 60, one time only. Ask your doctor if it is okay to get it.	Starting at age 60, one time only. Ask your doctor if it is okay to get it.

This chart lists recommended screenings and immunizations for women at average risk for most diseases. Citations for these recommendations can be found online at www.womenshealth.gov/screeningcharts/general/citations.cfm.

Recommended Screenings, Tests, and Immunizations for Women With High Risk Factors in the Family

✔ if it applies	Does your family history include?	Then ask your doctor or nurse if you need the following screenings, tests, exams, or vaccines more often or at a younger age:
	High blood pressure	Blood pressure test
	High cholesterol	Cholesterol test
	Heart disease, premature heart disease, or heart attack	Blood pressure test, cholesterol test, exercise stress test
	Diabetes	Blood glucose test
	Breast cancer	Mammogram, ovarian cancer tests
	Endometrial cancer	Colon screening
	Ovarian cancer	Pelvic exam, ovarian cancer tests, colon screening, clinical breast exam
	Osteoporosis, bone fracture in adulthood	Bone mineral density test
	Thyroid disease or thyroid cancer	Thyroid test and/or genetic counseling
	Gum (periodontal) disease	Oral exam
	Hearing problems, deafness	Hearing test
	Vision problems, eye disease, blindness	Vision exam
	Inflammatory bowel disease; colon polyps; colon, ovarian, or endometrial cancer	Colonoscopy, sigmoidoscopy, double contrast barium enema, rectal exam, fecal occult blood test, Pap test, pelvic exam, ovarian cancer tests
	Cancer, heart disease, or any illness at an unusually young age (50 or younger)	Genetic counseling, possible early screening tests
	Two relatives with the same kind of cancer	Genetic counseling, possible early screening tests
	Birth defects or genetic disorder (you or your partner)	Genetic counseling, possible early screening tests. If you want to become pregnant, genetic counseling for you and your partner.

This chart lists screenings, tests, or exams you might need more often or earlier because of having high risk factors or things in your life that increase your chances of developing a condition or disease. Citations for these recommendations can be found online at www.womenshealth.gov/screeningcharts/highrisk/citations.cfm.

Recommended Screenings, Tests, and Immunizations for Women With High Individual Risk Factors

✔ if it applies	Are you?	Then ask your doctor or nurse if you need the following screenings, tests, exams, or vaccines more often or at a younger age:
	African American	Blood pressure test, cholesterol test, blood glucose test, vision exam, colonoscopy, genetic counseling for sickle cell anemia
	Latina	Blood pressure test, cholesterol test, blood glucose test, colonoscopy
	Alaska Native or Pacific Islander	Blood glucose test, pneumococcal vaccine
	American Indian	Blood glucose test, pneumococcal vaccine
	Ashkenazi Jewish descent	Genetic counseling for Tay-Sachs disease, if you want to become pregnant
	Ashkenazi Jewish descent with family history of breast or ovarian cancer	Genetic counseling for possible *BRCA1/2* mutation
	Asian American	Blood glucose test
	Age 65 or older	Bone mineral density test, flu vaccine, pneumococcal vaccine
	Between the ages of 60 and 64, weigh less than 154 lbs, and not taking estrogen	Bone mineral density test
	College age	MMR vaccine, varicella vaccine, human papillomavirus (HPV) vaccine, meningococcal vaccine
	Postmenopausal	Bone mineral density test
	Pregnant	Blood pressure test, blood glucose test, urine test, HIV test, STI tests, MMR vaccine, hepatitis B antigen test
	A nonpregnant woman of childbearing age	MMR vaccine, varicella vaccine
	A smoker	Blood pressure test, cholesterol test, bone mineral density test, oral exam, vision exam
	Overweight	Blood pressure test, blood glucose test, weight
	Living in prison	Tuberculosis (TB) test, HIV test, STI tests, hepatitis A, B vaccines
	Living in long-term care	TB test, influenza vaccine, pneumococcal vaccine
	A health care worker	TB test, influenza vaccine, pneumococcal vaccine, MMR vaccine, varicella vaccine, HIV test, hepatitis test, hepatitis B vaccine if exposed to blood

This chart lists screenings, tests, or exams you might need more often or earlier because of having high risk factors or things in your life that increase your chances of developing a condition or disease. Citations for these recommendations can be found online at www.womenshealth.gov/screeningcharts/highrisk/citations.cfm.

MMR: measles, mumps, and rubella
STI: sexually transmitted infections

Recommended Screenings, Tests, and Immunizations for Women With High Individual Risk Factors

✔ if it applies	Do you have or have you had?	Then ask your doctor or nurse if you need the following screenings, tests, exams, or vaccines more often or at a younger age:
	High blood pressure	Blood pressure test, cholesterol test, blood glucose test
	High cholesterol	Blood pressure test, cholesterol test, blood glocose test
	Heart disease	Blood pressure test, cholesterol test, blood glucose test, influenza vaccine, pneumococcal vaccine
	Diabetes	Blood pressure test, cholesterol test, blood glucose test, vision exam, urine test
	Gestational diabetes (diabetes during pregnancy)	Blood glucose test
	A baby weighing more than 9 lbs	Blood glucose test
	Breast cancer	Mammogram, ovarian cancer tests
	Dense breast	Digital mammogram, clinical breast exam
	Cervical, uterine, endometrial, vaginal cancer	Pap test, pelvic exam, ovarian cancer tests, colon screening
	Ovarian cancer	Pelvic exam, ovarian cancer tests, mammogram, colon screening
	Previous abnormal Pap tests	Pap test, pelvic exam, human papillomavirus (HPV) vaccine
	Early menopause (natural or surgically induced); absent or infrequent menstrual periods; advanced age; a personal history of bone fracture in adulthood; lifelong low calcium intake; lifelong inactive lifestyle or little physical activity; low body weight (less than 154 lbs), or a history of an eating disorder such as anorexia nervosa	Bone mineral density test
	An autoimmune disease (including lupus, rheumatoid arthritis, scleroderma, multiple sclerosis, psoriasis)	Thyroid test, TB test, influenza shot, MMR vaccine, pneumococcal vaccine, autoimmune screening test, bone mineral density test

This chart lists screenings, tests, or exams you might need more often or earlier because of having high risk factors or things in your life that increase your chances of developing a condition or disease. Citations for these recommendations can be found online at www.womenshealth.gov/screeningcharts/highrisk/citations.cfm.

Recommended Screenings, Tests, and Immunizations for Women With High Individual Risk Factors

✔ if it applies	Do you have or have you had?	Then ask your doctor or nurse if you need the following screenings, tests, exams, or vaccines more often or at a younger age:
	Chronic lung disease	Influenza vaccine, pneumococcal vaccine
	Chronic liver disease	Hepatitis A and B vaccines
	Thyroid disease	Thyroid test, influenza vaccine, pneumococcal vaccine, bone mineral density test (if hyperthyroid)
	Gum (periodontal) disease	Oral exam
	Colon polyps; inflammatory bowel disease	Colonoscopy
	Colon cancer	Endometrial cancer screening, colon cancer screening tests
	A developmental delay	Vision exam, hearing test
	Eye injury or disease	Vision exam
	Ear injury or prolonged exposure to loud noise	Hearing test
	HIV/AIDS	Oral exam, vision exam, Pap test, pelvic exam, TB test, thyroid test, STI tests, influenza vaccine, pneumococcal vaccine, hepatitis screening, hepatitis A and B vaccines
	A blood transfusion or solid organ transplant before 1992	Hepatitis C test
	Received clotting factor concentrates made before 1987	Hepatitis C test
	A blood transfusion before 1985	HIV test
	Multiple sex partners (or a partner who has or had multiple sex partners)	STI tests, HIV test, hepatitis B vaccine, Pap test, pelvic exam, human papillomavirus (HPV) vaccine
	Alcoholism	Pneumococcal vaccine, TB test, psychological screening, liver tests
	Injection drug use (IDU) or addiction	Hepatitis A and B vaccines, hepatitis C test, TB test, STI tests, HIV test, psychological screening
	A sexually transmitted infection (STI)	STI tests, HIV test, Pap test, pelvic exam, hepatitis B vaccine, HPV vaccine
	Lived or worked with someone exposed to tuberculosis (TB)	TB test
	A serious injury (cut or laceration)	Tetanus-diphtheria booster vaccine
	A baby recently (within the past few weeks or months)	Postpartum depression screening

This chart lists screenings, tests, or exams you might need more often or earlier because of having high risk factors or things in your life that increase your chances of developing a condition or disease. Citations for these recommendations can be found online at www.womenshealth.gov/screeningcharts/highrisk/citations.cfm.

Health Resources for Women and Families

Health Resources for Women

General health

womenshealth.gov
200 Independence Ave SW, Room 712E
Washington, DC 20201
Web site: www.womenshealth.gov
Illnesses and Disabilities:
www.womenshealth.gov/wwd
Phone number: (800) 994-9662,
(888) 220-5446 TDD

**Agency for Healthcare Research and
Quality Clearinghouse**
PO Box 8547
Silver Spring, MD 20907
Web site: www.ahrq.gov/research/
womenix.htm
Phone number: (800) 358-9295,
(888) 586-6340 TDD

ClinicalTrials.gov
ClinicalTrials.gov is a registry of clinical
trials. The Web site gives you information
about a trial's purpose, who may participate, locations, and phone numbers for
more details.
Web site: www.clinicaltrials.gov

**Health Resources and Services
Administration Information Center**
PO Box 2910
Merrifield, VA 22116
Web site: www.hrsa.gov/WomensHealth
Phone number: (888) 275-4772,
(877) 489-4772 TTY

Indian Health Service
801 Thompson Ave, Suite 400
Rockville, MD 20852-1627
Web site: www.ihs.gov/MedicalPrograms/
MCH/W

MedlinePlus
MedlinePlus provides health information
from the National Institutes of Health and
other trusted sources. The Web site also
has a medical encyclopedia, information
on prescription and nonprescription drugs,
and the latest health news.
Web site: www.medlineplus.gov

National Institutes of Health
9000 Rockville Pike
Bethesda, MD 20892
Web site: www.nih.gov

**Office of Minority Health Resource
Center**
PO Box 37337
Washington, DC 20013-7337
Web site: www.omhrc.gov
Phone number: (800) 444-6472

**Office of Research on Women's Health,
NIH**
6707 Democracy Blvd, Suite 400
Bethesda, MD 20892-5484
Web site: http://orwh.od.nih.gov
Phone number: (301) 402-1770

Office of Women's Health, CDC
1600 Clifton Rd, MS E-89
Atlanta, GA 30333
Web site: www.cdc.gov/women
Phone number: (800) 232-4636, (888) 232-6348 TTY

Office of Women's Health, FDA
5600 Fishers Ln
Rockville, MD 20857
Web site: www.fda.gov/womens
Phone number: (888) 463-6332

American Academy of Family Physicians
PO Box 11210
Shawnee Mission, KS 66207-1210
Web site: www.familydoctor.org

American College of Obstetricians and Gynecologists
409 12th St SW, PO Box 96920
Washington, DC 20090-6920
Web site: www.acog.org
Phone number: (202) 863-2518
Resource Center

American Medical Women's Association
100 N 20th St, 4th Floor
Philadelphia, PA 19103
Web site: www.amwa-doc.org

Black Women's Health Imperative
1420 K St NW, Suite 1000
Washington, DC 20005
Web site: www.blackwomenshealth.org

National Alliance for Hispanic Health
1501 16th St NW
Washington, DC 20036
Web site: www.hispanichealth.org

National Asian Women's Health Organization
1 Embarcadero Center, Suite 500
San Francisco, CA 94111
Web site: www.nawho.org

National Women's Health Network
514 10th St NW, Suite 400
Washington, DC 20004
Web site: www.nwhn.org
Phone number: (202) 628-7814

National Women's Health Resource Center
157 Broad St, Suite 106
Red Bank, NJ 07701
Web site: www.healthywomen.org
Phone number: (877) 986-9472

Society for Women's Health Research
1025 Connecticut Ave NW, Suite 701
Washington, DC 20036
Web site: www.womenshealthresearch.org

Disease Risk Calculators

Heart Attack/Coronary Heart Disease risk assessment tool
On this Web site, find out if you are at risk of having a heart attack or dying of coronary heart disease in the next 10 years. You can also check to see if you may have a group of risk factors that increase your chances of developing heart disease, stroke, and diabetes.

Web site: www.americanheart.org/presenter.jhtml?identifier=3003499

Your disease risk
This Web site allows you to find out your risk of developing cancer, diabetes, heart disease, osteoporosis, and stroke. You can also get personalized tips for preventing these diseases.

Web site: www.yourdiseaserisk.wustl.edu

Assess your risk of periodontal disease
Find out on this Web site if you are at risk of developing periodontal, or gum, diseases.

Web site: www.perio.org/consumer/4a.html

Health Resources for Men

General health
Men's Health, womenshealth.gov
200 Independence Ave SW, Room 712E
Washington, DC 20201
Web site: www.womenshealth.gov/mens
Phone number: (800) 994-9662,
(888) 220-5446 TDD

U.S. Department of Health and Human Services
200 Independence Ave SW
Washington, DC 20201
Web site: www.hhs.gov/
specificpopulations

Divisions of HIV/AIDS Prevention, CDC
1600 Clifton Rd NE
Atlanta, GA 30333
Web site: www.cdc.gov/hiv
Phone number: (800) 232-4636,
(888) 232-6348 TTY

Healthfinder®
PO Box 1133
Washington, DC 20013-1133
Web site: www.healthfinder.gov/justforyou

MedlinePlus
8600 Rockville Pike
Bethesda, MD 20894
Web site: www.nlm.nih.gov/
medlineplus/men.html

Men's Health, CDC
1600 Clifton Rd NE
Atlanta, GA 30333
Web site: www.cdc.gov/men
Phone number: (800) 232-4636,
(888) 232-6348 TTY

Men's Health Program, AHRQ
PO Box 8547
Silver Spring, MD 2090
Web site: www.ahrq.gov/path/
menpath.htm
Phone number: (800) 358-9295,
(888) 586-6340 TDD

Promoting Responsible Fatherhood, HHS
200 Independence Ave SW
Washington, DC 20201
Web site: www.fatherhood.hhs.gov

Men's Health Network
PO Box 75972
Washington, DC 20013
Web site: www.menshealthnetwork.org

Heart health

National Heart, Lung, and Blood Institute Information Center, NIH
PO Box 30105
Bethesda, MD 20824-0105
Web site: www.nhlbi.nih.gov
Phone number: (301) 592-8573,
(240) 629-3255 TTY

American Heart Association
7272 Greenville Ave
Dallas, TX 75231
Web site: www.americanheart.org
Phone number: (800) 242-8721

Cancer

National Cancer Institute, NIH
6116 Executive Blvd, Room 3036A
Bethesda, MD 20892-8322
Web site: www.cancer.gov
Phone number: (800) 422-6237,
(800) 332-8615 TTY

American Cancer Society
250 Williams St
Atlanta, GA 30303
Web site: www.cancer.org
Phone number: (800) 227-2345,
(866) 228-4327 TTY

Mental health

National Clearinghouse for Alcohol and Drug Information, SAMHSA
1 Choke Cherry Rd
Rockville, MD 20857
Web site: www.ncadi.samhsa.gov
Phone number: (800) 729-6686,
(800) 487-4889 TDD

National Institute of Mental Health, NIH
6001 Executive Blvd, Room 8184,
MSC 9663
Bethesda, MD 20892-9663
Web site: www.nimh.nih.gov
Phone number: (866) 615-6464,
(866) 415-8051 TTY

National Mental Health Information Center, SAMHSA
PO Box 42557
Washington, DC 20015
Web site: http://mentalhealth.samhsa.gov
Phone number: (800) 789-2647,
(866) 889-2647 TDD

Urologic and reproductive health

National Kidney and Urologic Diseases Information Clearinghouse, NIH
3 Information Way
Bethesda, MD 20892-3580
Web site: www.kidney.niddk.nih.gov
Phone number: (800) 891-5390

Health Resources for Children

General health

girlshealth.gov
200 Independence Ave SW, Room 712E
Washington, DC 20201
Web site: www.girlshealth.gov
Phone number: (800) 994-9662,
(888) 220-5446 TDD

Building Blocks for a Healthy Future, SAMHSA
1 Choke Cherry Rd
Rockville, MD 20857
Web site: www.bblocks.samhsa.gov
Phone number: (800) 694–4747 ext.4820

Child and Adolescent Health, AHRQ
PO Box 8547
Silver Spring, MD 20907
Web site: www.ahrq.gov/child
Phone number: (800) 358-9295,
(888) 586-6340 TDD

U.S. Department of Health and Human Services
200 Independence Ave SW
Washington, DC 20201
Web site: www.hhs.gov/
specificpopulations

Family Guide to Keeping Youth Mentally Healthy and Drug Free, SAMHSA
1 Choke Cherry Rd
Rockville, MD 20857
Web site: www.family.samhsa.gov

Food and Drug Administration Kid's Page
5600 Fishers Ln
Rockville, MD 20857
Web site: www.fda.gov/oc/opacom/kids/
default.htm
Phone number: (888) 463-6332

Girl Power! Campaign
Web site: www.girlpower.gov
Phone number: (800) 729-6686

MedlinePlus
8600 Rockville Pike
Bethesda, MD 20894
Web site: www.nlm.nih.gov/
medlineplus/childrenandteenagers.html

My Bright Future: Physical Activity and Healthy Eating for Young Women, HRSA
PO Box 2910
Merrifield, VA 22116
Web site: www.hrsa.gov/womenshealth/
mybrightfuture/menu.html
Phone number: (888) 275-4772,
(877) 489-4772 TTY

Safe and Healthy Kids, CDC
1600 Clifton Rd, MS E-89
Atlanta, GA 30333
Web site: www.cdc.gov/women/kids
Phone number: (800) 232-4636,
(888) 232-6348 TTY

VERB™ It's What You Do, CDC
1600 Clifton Rd
Atlanta, GA 30333
Web site: www.verbnow.com
Phone number: (800) 232-4636,
(888) 232-6348 TTY

WISE EARS!®, NIH
1 Communication Ave
Bethesda, MD 20892-3456
Web site: www.nidcd.nih.gov/health/wise
Phone number: (800) 241-1044,
(800) 241-1055 TTY

American Academy of Pediatrics
141 Northwest Point Blvd
Elk Grove Village, IL 60007
Web site: www.aap.org

Kidshealth.org
Web site: www.kidshealth.org

Child abuse
Prevent Child Abuse America
500 N Michigan Ave, Suite 200
Chicago, IL 60611
Web site: www.preventchildabuse.org
Phone number: (800) 244-5373

Cancer
National Cancer Institute, NIH
6116 Executive Blvd, Room 3036A
Bethesda, MD 20892-8322
Web site: www.cancer.gov
Phone number: (800) 422-6237,
(800) 332-8615 TTY

Childhood asthma
American Lung Association
61 Broadway, 6th Floor
New York, NY 10006
Web site: www.lungusa.org
Phone number: (800) 548-8252

Childhood diabetes
**National Diabetes Information
Clearinghouse, NIH**
1 Information Way
Bethesda, MD 20892-3560
Web site: www.diabetes.niddk.nih.gov
Phone number: (800) 860-8747

American Woman Diabetes Association
1701 N Beauregard St
Alexandria, VA 22311
Web site: www.diabetes.org
Phone number: (800) 342-2383

Immunizations
**National Center for Immunization and
Respiratory Diseases, CDC**
1600 Clifton Rd NE, MS E-05
Atlanta, GA 30333
Web site: www.cdc.gov/vaccines
Phone number: (800) 232-4636,
(888) 232-6348 TTY

**Childhood Immunization Support
Program, AAP**
141 Northwest Point Blvd
Elk Grove Village, IL 60007
Web site: www.cispimmunize.org

Immunization Action Coalition
1573 Selby Ave, Suite 234
St Paul, MN 55104
Web site: www.immunize.org

    The Healthy Woman: A Complete Guide for All Ages

Child nutrition
Powerful Bones. Powerful Girls.
200 Independence Ave SW, Room 712E
Washington, DC 20201
Web site: www.girlshealth.gov/bones
Phone number: (800) 994-9662,
(888) 220-5446 TDD

School Meals, USDA
3101 Park Center Dr
Alexandria, VA 22302
Web site: www.fns.usda.gov/cnd

Safety and injury prevention
U.S. Consumer Product Safety Commission
4330 East West Highway
Bethesda, MD 20814
Web site: www.cpsc.gov
Phone number: (800) 638-2772, (800) 638-8270 TTY

National Center for Injury Prevention and Control, CDC
4770 Buford Highway NE, MS K-63
Atlanta, GA 30341-3717
Web site: www.cdc.gov/ncipc
Phone number: (800) 232-4636,
(888) 232-6348 TTY

National Highway Traffic Safety Administration
1200 New Jersey Ave SE, West Building
Washington, DC 20590
Web site: www.nhtsa.gov
Phone number: (888) 327-4236,
(800) 424-9153 TTY

Take A Stand. Lend A Hand. Stop Bullying Now!, HRSA
PO Box 2910
Merrifield, VA 22116
Web site: www.stopbullyingnow.hrsa.gov
Phone number: (888) 275-4772,
(877) 489-4772 TTY

Safe Kids Worldwide
1301 Pennsylvania Ave NW, Suite 1000
Washington DC 20004
Web site: www.safekids.org

Resources for Health Insurance

Each year, more American families find themselves without health insurance. In 2004, more than 45 million Americans didn't have health insurance. Sixteen million of them were women. These programs and resources may be able to help you and your family.

Government resources that can help

The Centers for Medicare and Medicaid Services (CMS), a federal government agency, administers health insurance programs such as Medicare, Medicaid, and the State Children's Health Insurance Program.

Medicare

Medicare is a health insurance program funded by the U.S. government. To qualify for these benefits, you must be 65 years old or older, or younger than 65 with certain disabilities, or a person of any age who has end-stage renal disease. (A person who has end-stage renal disease has permanent kidney failure that requires dialysis or a kidney transplant.)

Medicare has several parts. Your coverage depends on which parts of Medicare you have. Medicare Part A typically pays for your inpatient hospital expenses. Medicare Part B typically pays for your outpatient health care expenses, including doctor fees. You usually have to pay a monthly premium to be covered by Medicare Part B.

Beginning January 1, 2006, everyone who has Medicare is now eligible for

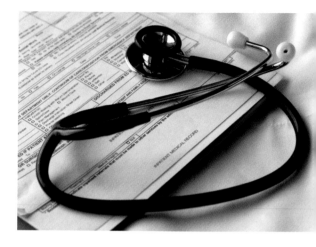

prescription drug coverage through the new Medicare Part D. This coverage is available regardless of your income and resources, your health status, or how much your prescriptions cost. It covers both brand-name and generic prescription drugs at participating pharmacies in your area. Medicare prescription drug coverage provides protection for people who have very high drug costs.

For general information, 24 hours a day, 7 days a week,

- Call toll free at (800) MEDICARE (800-633-4227) or TTY (877) 486-2048.

- Web site: www.cms.hhs.gov/home/medicare.asp

- Web site: The Official U.S. Government Site for People with Medicare: www.medicare.gov

If you have a limited income and resources, you may be eligible for extra help with your prescription drug costs. Almost 1 in 3 people with Medicare qualify for having almost all of their prescription drug costs paid for by the program. To find out if you are eligible for extra help, contact the Social Security Administration.

- Call the U.S. Social Security Administration toll free at (800) 772-1213 (TTY 800-325-0778).
- Web site: www.socialsecurity.gov

Medicaid

Medicaid is a health insurance program jointly funded by states, counties, and the U.S. government. Medicaid provides medical benefits to groups of low-income people that meet certain age, income, and resource requirements. People who have certain medical conditions such as blindness or who are pregnant may also qualify. Whether a person is eligible for Medicaid depends on the state where he or she lives.

In general, you should apply for Medicaid if your income is low and you or someone in your family needs health care. A qualified caseworker in your state can give you guidance about your situation. Your child may be eligible for coverage, even if you are not.

To find out more about Medicaid in your state,

- Call the toll free number for your state. A list of toll free numbers is on the CMS Web site at www.cms.hhs.gov/medicaid/consumer.asp.

State Children's Health Insurance Program (SCHIP)

Like Medicaid, the State Children's Health Insurance Program (SCHIP) is a partnership between the federal government and the states. SCHIP is designed to provide health insurance coverage to specific groups of low-income children. Families who earn too much money to be eligible for Medicaid but not enough money to purchase private health insurance may be eligible to get health insurance for their children.

Each state determines how its program is designed, who is eligible, what the benefits are, how costs are shared, and other features. For little or no cost, this insurance pays for children's doctor visits, immunizations, hospitalizations, and emergency room visits.

For more information about SCHIP, go to www.cms.hhs.gov/home/schip.asp.

To learn whom you should contact in your state or to read specific information about eligibility in your state, go to Insure Kids Now at www.insurekidsnow.gov.

Other government programs and benefits

To learn about the government benefits you may be entitled to,

- Call toll free (800) FED-INFO (800-333-4636). Calls are answered Monday through Friday, 8 AM to 8 PM, Eastern Standard Time.

- Web site: www.govbenefits.gov

Other public government and private resources that can help

For women who make too much money to qualify for these federal and state programs but who can't afford to pay for health insurance or costly health services, the choices are limited and difficult. Public and private resources may be able to help.

- **"Safety-net" facilities.** Community health centers, public hospitals, school-based centers, public housing primary care, and special-need facilities. Contact your local or state health department for more information or go to ask.hrsa.gov/pc.

- **Free clinics.** Free clinics provide health care services for the uninsured.

- **Prescription drug assistance.** Some states provide prescription drug assistance to women who cannot get Medicaid. Many drug companies will work with your doctor to provide free medicines to those in need. A list of resources can be found at www.disabilityresources.org/RX.html.

- **Women with cancer.** Women with cancer can find help through a variety of government-sponsored and volunteer organizations. For accurate, up-to-date information on cancer and resources for people dealing with cancer, go to the Web site of the National Cancer Institute (www.cancer.gov). You can also visit the Cancer Information Service of the National Cancer Institute on the Internet (http://cis.nci.nih.gov). To get answers to specific questions about cancer, call (800) 4-CANCER (800-422-6237), Monday through Friday, 9:00 AM to 4:30 PM to speak with a cancer information specialist. Deaf and hard-of-hearing callers with TTY equipment can call (800) 332-8615.

- **Women with HIV.** The federal Ryan White CARE Act funds health care services for women with HIV/AIDS who do not have health insurance or the financial resources to pay for care. To locate a CARE provider, contact your local or state health department or call (800) 994-9662.

- **Group health insurance.** Some states and localities, labor unions, professional clubs, associations, and organizations offer low-cost group health insurance to their members. These plans usually cost less than individual insurance and can be worth considering.

- **Temporary insurance.** Some individuals who have been denied health insurance because of a medical condition may be able to obtain coverage through their state's "risk pools." More than 30 states provide this temporary insurance assistance. For more information, go to the Web site of the Health Insurance Resource Center at www.healthinsurance.org/risk_pools.

Protect your health insurance coverage

If you have health insurance, you should know how to protect that insurance coverage. If you are losing your health insurance because you have lost your job, have reduced hours at work, have gotten a divorce, or have had your spouse die, you have certain rights and protections. These rights are described in the Health Insurance Portability and Accountability Act of 1996, or HIPAA.

Tips: What to do

- Obtain proof that you had previous health insurance coverage from your employer.

- Apply for COBRA, which stands for the Consolidated Omnibus Budget Reconciliation Act of 1985. COBRA requires most employers that have 20 or more employees to allow you to continue your health insurance for 18 months, but you must pay the full premium cost of the insurance. Ask your employer's human resources office about when and how you should apply for these benefits.

- Consider your health insurance situation carefully before agreeing to certain terms and conditions. It is especially important to think about your health care needs when you are separated from your spouse, divorced, or are a retiree with annuities.

- In a legal separation or divorce proceeding, you can get a court order to provide your children with health insurance under the health plan of the noncustodial parent. This act is called a qualified medical child support order.

- Act quickly to get the right information to protect you and your family. File any required forms promptly. Strict time limits often apply.

For more information about HIPAA,

- Call (866) 627-7748

- Web site: www.cms.hhs.gov/ HIPAAGenInfo

For more information on health insurance choices, go to the Web site of the Agency for Healthcare Research and Quality at www.ahrq.gov/consumer. ■

Glossary

ACE inhibitor(s): angiotensin converting enzyme inhibitor. A drug that is used to lower blood pressure.

acidic: produces acid, a sour substance.

acupuncture: the technique of inserting thin needles through the skin at specific points on the body to control pain and other symptoms. It is a type of complementary and alternative medicine.

addiction: uncontrollable craving, seeking, and use of a substance such as a drug or alcohol.

Addison's disease: an endocrine or hormonal disorder that occurs when the adrenal glands do not produce enough of the hormone cortisol and, in some cases, the hormone aldosterone. The disease is characterized by weight loss, muscle weakness, fatigue, low blood pressure, and sometimes darkening of the skin.

advance directive(s): a legal document that states the treatment or care a person wishes to receive or not receive if he or she becomes unable to make medical decisions; for example, as a result of being unconscious. Some types of advance directives are living wills and do-not-resuscitate (DNR) orders.

AIDS: see HIV/AIDS.

Alzheimer's disease: a brain disease that cripples the brain's nerve cells over time and destroys memory and learning. It usually starts in late middle age or old age and gets worse over time. Symptoms include loss of memory, confusion, problems in thinking, and changes in language, behavior, and personality.

amniotic fluid: clear, slightly yellowish liquid that surrounds the unborn baby or fetus during pregnancy.

anemia: when the amount of red blood cells, or hemoglobin, which is the substance in the blood that carries oxygen to organs, is below normal. Anemia can cause severe fatigue.

anesthesia: drugs or substances that cause loss of feeling or awareness. Local anesthetics cause loss of feeling in a part of a person's body. General anesthetics put a person to sleep.

angiotensin converting enzymes: substances in the body that cause the blood vessels to narrow and blood pressure to increase. Angiotensin converting enzyme (ACE) inhibitors are drugs that help relax blood vessels, which decreases blood pressure.

angiotensin II receptor blockers (ARBs): drugs that decrease blood pressure by blocking the effects of angiotensin II, a hormone that causes blood vessels to narrow.

antibodies: blood proteins made by certain white blood cells called B cells in response to germs or other foreign substances that enter the body. Antibodies help the body fight illness and disease by attaching to germs and marking them for destruction.

antibody rheumatoid factor (RF or rheumatoid factor): a marker in the blood that shows a person has rheumatoid arthritis, a type of arthritis in which a person's own body triggers inflammation or other responses in the joints, nerves, lungs, or skin.

antidepressant(s): drug(s) used to treat depression.

antigens: germs or other foreign substances that enter the body and cause the immune system to make a specific immune response, such as fever or inflammation.

antimicrobial drugs: drugs that kill microorganisms, such as bacteria or mold, or stop them from growing and causing disease.

antiphospholipid antibody syndrome: an autoimmune disorder in which the body's own immune system mistakenly produces antibodies that attack normal components of the blood, causing clots.

antiretroviral drugs: drugs that inhibit the ability of HIV or other types of retroviruses to multiply in the body.

anxiety disorder: a serious medical illness that fills people's lives with anxiety and fear. Some anxiety disorders include panic disorder, obsessive-compulsive disorder, posttraumatic stress disorder, social phobia or social anxiety disorder, specific phobias, and generalized anxiety disorder.

artery: a blood vessel that carries oxygen and blood from the heart to tissues and organs in the body.

arthritis: swelling, redness, warmth, and pain of the joints, the places where two bones meet, such as the elbow or knee. There are more than 100 types of arthritis.

artificial insemination: a process of introducing semen into the female reproductive tract by ways other than sexual intercourse. A woman or a couple experiencing infertility may go to a doctor for artificial insemination to increase the likelihood of pregnancy.

assisted reproductive technology (ART): a term used to describe several methods used to help infertile couples conceive. ART involves removing eggs from a woman's body, mixing them with sperm in the laboratory, and putting the embryos back into a woman's body. In vitro fertilization is one type.

asthma: a chronic disease of the lungs. Symptoms include cough, wheezing, a tight feeling in the chest and trouble breathing.

atopic dermatitis: dry and itchy skin, caused by certain diseases, irritating substances, allergies, or a person's genetic makeup.

attention-deficit/hyperactivity disorder (ADHD): a condition that starts in childhood that causes problems with hyperactivity, impulsivity, controlling behavior, and/or paying attention.

autoantibodies: blood proteins produced by the body's immune system that are meant to neutralize and destroy germs or other foreign substances, but instead attack healthy cells of the body.

autoimmune disease or disorder: a condition in which the body's immune system recognizes its own healthy tissues as foreign and directs an immune response or attack against them.

bacteria: microorganisms that exist all around us. Most bacteria are not harmful, and some protect us from harmful agents. Some bacteria can cause illness.

behavioral therapy: also called cognitive-behavioral therapy, a type of psychotherapy that helps people change the way they behave and react to certain situations.

benzene: a chemical that is used widely by the chemical industry and is also found in tobacco smoke, vehicle emissions, and gasoline fumes. Exposure to benzene may increase the risk of developing leukemia.

beta blockers: a type of medication that reduces nerve impulses to the heart and blood vessels, which makes the heart beat slower and with less force.

bile acid resins: drugs that help lower cholesterol levels in the blood by binding in the intestines with cholesterol-containing bile acids, which are then eliminated in the stool.

biopsy: the removal of body tissues for examination under a microscope or for other tests on the tissue.

bipolar disorder: a brain disorder that causes unusual, severe shifts in a person's mood, energy, and ability to function. It causes dramatic mood swings—from overly "high" and/or irritable to sad and hopeless, and then back again, often with periods of normal mood in between.

birth control pill: see oral contraceptive.

birth defect: a problem that happens while a baby is developing in the mother's body. Most birth defects happen during the first 3 months of pregnancy and may affect how the baby's body looks, works, or both. They can range from mild to severe.

bladder: the organ in the human body that stores urine. It is found in the lower part of the abdomen.

blood clot: a mass of blood that forms when blood platelets, proteins, and cells stick together. When a blood clot is attached to the wall of a blood vessel, it is called a thrombus. When it moves through the bloodstream and blocks the flow of blood in another part of the body, it is called an embolus.

blood glucose level: also called blood sugar level, it is the amount of glucose, or sugar, in the blood. Too much glucose in the blood for a long time can cause diabetes and damage many parts of the body, such as the heart, blood vessels, eyes, and kidneys.

blood pressure: the force of circulating blood on the walls of the arteries. Blood pressure is taken using two measurements: systolic (measured when the heart beats, when blood pressure is at its highest) and diastolic (measured between heartbeats, when blood pressure is at its lowest). Blood pressure is written with the systolic blood pressure first, followed by the diastolic blood pressure, such as 120/80.

blood sugar level: see blood glucose level.

blood vessel: a tube through which the blood circulates in the body. Blood vessels include a network of arteries, arterioles, capillaries, venules, and veins.

bone density test: a test to measure the bone density, or thickness of bone. This test is used to diagnose and monitor osteoporosis, a disease in which bones become thin and can easily break.

bone marrow disease or disorder: a problem with the bone marrow, or the soft, sponge-like tissue in the center of some bones that contains immature cells called stem cells. The stem cells can develop into the red blood cells that carry oxygen through your body, the white blood cells that fight infections, and the platelets that help with blood clotting.

bone marrow transplant: a method that takes bone marrow from a suitable donor and transfers it into another person to replace bone marrow that is diseased or that has been destroyed. Bone marrow is a soft tissue containing young blood cells and platelets, the source of various blood cells, found in the hollow center of bones.

calcium channel blockers: drugs that decrease the heart's pumping strength and relax blood vessels, decreasing blood pressure.

cancer: a term for diseases in which abnormal cells in the body divide without control. Cancer cells can invade nearby tissues and can spread to other parts of the body through the blood and lymphatic system, which is a network of tissues that clears infections and keeps body fluids in balance.

carbon monoxide: a poisonous gas that has no color or odor. It is given off by burning fuel, such as from exhaust from cars or household heaters and tobacco products. Carbon monoxide prevents red blood cells in the body from carrying enough oxygen for cells and tissues to live.

carcinogen: any substance that causes cancer.

cardiovascular disease (CVD): a class of diseases that affect the heart, or blood vessels, or both.

celiac disease: a digestive disease that damages the small intestine and interferes with absorption of nutrients from food. When people with celiac disease eat foods containing gluten, their immune system responds by damaging the small intestine.

cervix: the lower, narrow part of the uterus or womb. The cervix forms a canal that opens into the vagina, which leads to the outside of the body.

cesarean section or C-section: a surgery by which a baby is delivered through an abdominal incision in the mother.

chemotherapy: treatment with anticancer drugs.

chicken pox: a disease caused by the varicella-zoster virus, which results in a blister-like rash, itching, tiredness, and fever.

cholesterol: a waxy, fat-like substance made in the liver and found in the blood and in all cells of the body. It is important for good health and is needed for making cell walls, tissues, hormones, vitamin D, and bile acid. Cholesterol also comes from eating foods taken from animals, such as egg yolks, meat, and whole-milk dairy products. Too much cholesterol in the blood may build up in blood vessel walls, block blood flow to tissues and organs, and increase the risk of developing heart disease and stroke. In the blood, cholesterol is bound to chemicals called lipoproteins.

cholesterol absorption inhibitors: medicines that help lower blood cholesterol by reducing the amount of cholesterol absorbed by the intestines.

chronic disease or illness: a disease or condition that persists or progresses over a long period of time.

chronic kidney failure: a condition in which the kidneys slowly lose their ability to function properly, and excess fluids and waste accumulate in the blood. Chronic kidney failure worsens slowly and can be caused by health problems such as high blood pressure and diabetes.

chronic liver disease: a class of diseases, such as hepatitis C, liver cancer, and cirrhosis, that slowly destroy liver tissue over time.

chronic pain syndrome: a syndrome that affects a person's ability to function normally every day from a complex relation between body and mind influencing the level of pain felt by someone with chronic pain. The frustrating nature of the pain may cause emotional stress, psychological issues such as anxiety or depression, and addiction to pain-relieving medications.

chronic pancreatitis: a persistent inflammation of the pancreas, the organ that makes enzymes used for digestion and insulin, which regulates the use of blood glucose throughout the body. With this condition, digestive enzymes attack and destroy the pancreas and nearby tissues, causing scarring and pain.

cirrhosis: a type of chronic, progressive liver disease in which liver cells are replaced by scar tissue.

citrate: a substance in the urine that helps prevent the formation of calcium crystals. A patient with low urine citrate levels is at a higher risk of developing kidney stones.

citrulline antibodies test (CCP test): a test that detects the presence of citrulline antibodies in the blood, which are usually present in patients with rheumatoid arthritis. The CCP test has been shown to detect rheumatoid arthritis earlier than the rheumatoid factor test.

cleft lip or palate: abnormalities present at birth that affect the upper lip and the hard and soft palates of the mouth. Features range from a small notch in the lip to a complete fissure, or groove, extending into the roof of the mouth and nose. These features may occur separately or together.

clitoris: an external female sex organ located near the top of the inner labia of the vagina. The clitoris is very sensitive to the touch, and for most women it is a center of sexual pleasure.

colorectal cancer screening: tests to check for cancer, precancerous growths, or other abnormal conditions of the colon and rectum.

computed tomography (CT) scan: also called CAT scan. A series of detailed pictures of areas inside the body taken from different angles; the pictures are created by a computer linked to an x-ray machine.

connective tissue: supporting tissue that surrounds other tissues and organs. Specialized connective tissue includes bone, cartilage, blood, and fat.

contractions: when a woman's uterus, or womb, tightens, or contracts, during the birthing process.

conventional medicine: a system in which medical doctors and other health care professionals (such as nurses, pharmacists, and therapists) treat symptoms and diseases using drugs, radiation therapy, or surgery. Also called Western medicine, mainstream medicine, orthodox medicine, biomedicine, and allopathic medicine.

coronary angiography: a test that uses dye and special x-rays to show the inside of the coronary arteries, which supply blood and oxygen to the heart.

coronary artery disease (CAD): the most common type of heart disease that results from atherosclerosis—the gradual buildup of plaque in the coronary arteries, the blood vessels that bring blood to the muscles of the heart.

creatinine: a substance that is made by the body, found in the muscles, and used to store energy.

Cushing's syndrome: a hormonal disorder caused by prolonged exposure of the body's tissues to high levels of the hormone cortisol.

cyst: a sac or capsule in the body. It may be filled with fluid or other material.

cystic fibrosis (CF): one of the most common serious genetic, or inherited, diseases. CF causes the body to make abnormal secretions. This leads to mucus buildup, which impairs organs such as the pancreas, the intestine, and the lungs.

cytomegalovirus (CMV): a virus that may be carried in an inactive state for life by healthy persons. But it can cause severe pneumonia in people with suppressed immune systems and lifelong disabilities in babies.

dehydration: an excessive loss of body water that is necessary to carry on normal functions at an optimal level. Signs include increasing thirst, dry mouth, weakness or light-headedness (particularly if worse on standing), and a darkening of the urine or a decrease in urination.

depression: also called major depressive disorder or clinical depression, it is a serious medical illness that involves the brain in which feelings of sadness and the "blues" do not go away. Symptoms include sadness, loss of interest or pleasure in activities once enjoyed, change in weight, problems sleeping or oversleeping, energy loss, feelings of worthlessness, and thoughts of death or suicide. There are effective treatments—most people do best with both talk therapy and medicines.

dermatitis: see atopic dermatitis.

diabetes: a disease in which blood glucose or blood sugar levels are above normal. Type 2 diabetes, once known as adult-onset or noninsulin-dependent diabetes mellitus (NIDDM), is the most common form of diabetes. This form of diabetes usually begins with insulin resistance, a condition in which fat, muscle, and liver cells do not use insulin, a hormone that allows glucose to enter body cells for energy, properly. At first, the pancreas keeps up with the added demand by producing more insulin. In time, though, it loses the ability to secrete enough insulin in response to meals. Being overweight and inactive increases the chances of developing type 2 diabetes. Type 1 diabetes, once called juvenile or insulin-dependent diabetes, is a lifelong disease that occurs when the pancreas does not produce enough insulin to properly control blood glucose levels.

diaphragm: a birth control device consisting of a thin flexible disk, usually made of rubber, that is designed to cover the cervix to prevent the entry of sperm during sexual intercourse.

dietitian or registered dietitian: a food and nutrition expert who can help a person choose healthy foods and plan menus.

disability: a physical or mental impairment that interferes with or prevents "normal" achievement in a particular function.

discrimination: treating a person or group of people unfairly because of prejudice or a bias toward a certain racial group, ethnic group, or sex.

diuretic: a type of medication sometimes called a "water pill" because it works in the kidney and flushes excess water and sodium from the body.

DNA: deoxyribonucleic acid. The molecules inside the body's cells that carry genetic information and pass it from one generation to the next.

DNA test: a lab test on a small blood sample of a person to diagnose a genetic disorder, to find out if a person or his or her relatives are carriers of the mutated gene for a genetic disorder, or to find out if an unborn baby has inherited a genetic disorder.

douches: see douching.

douching: using water or a medicated solution to clean the vagina and cervix.

Down syndrome: the most frequent genetic cause for mild to moderate mental retardation and related medical problems. It is caused by a chromosomal abnormality. For an unknown reason, a change in cell growth results in 47 instead of the usual 46 chromosomes. This extra chromosome changes the orderly development of the body and brain.

eating disorder: a disorder that involves serious problems with normal eating behaviors, such as feelings of distress and concern about body shape or weight, severe overeating, or starving oneself. Anorexia nervosa, bulimia nervosa, and binge-eating disorder are types of eating disorders.

ectopic pregnancy: a pregnancy that does not occur in the uterus. It happens when a fertilized egg settles and grows in a place other than the inner lining of the uterus. Most ectopic pregnancies happen in the fallopian tube, but can happen in the ovary, cervix, or abdominal cavity.

eczema: a group of conditions in which the skin becomes inflamed, forms blisters, and becomes crusty, thick, and scaly. Eczema causes burning and itching and may occur over a long period of time. Atopic dermatitis is the most common type of eczema.

emergency contraception: emergency birth control, used to help keep a woman from getting pregnant after she has had sex without using birth control.

endometrial cancer: cancer that develops from the endometrium, or the inner lining of the uterus or womb.

endometriosis: a condition in which tissue that normally lines the uterus grows in other areas of the body, usually inside the abdominal cavity, but acts as if it were inside the uterus. Blood shed monthly from the misplaced tissue has no place to go, and tissues surrounding the area of endometriosis may become inflamed or swollen. This can produce scar tissue. Symptoms can include painful menstrual cramps that can be felt in the abdomen or lower back, pain during or after sexual activity, irregular bleeding, and infertility.

endometrium: the layer of tissue that lines the uterus.

epidural: a type of anesthesia in which a needle is inserted into the epidural space at the end of the spine to numb the lower body and reduce pain.

epilepsy: a physical disorder that involves recurrent seizures. It is caused by sudden changes in how the brain works.

esophagus: the muscular tube through which food passes from the throat to the stomach.

estrogen: a group of female hormones that are responsible for the development of breasts and other secondary sex characteristics in women. Estrogen is produced by the ovaries and other body tissues. Estrogen, along with the hormone progesterone, is important in preparing a woman's body for pregnancy.

exploitation: an act that victimizes someone, or the personal gain from the resources or labors of others for selfish reasons.

fibrates: cholesterol-lowering drugs that are primarily effective in lowering triglycerides and, to a lesser extent, in increasing HDL cholesterol levels.

fibroids: see uterine fibroids.

fibromyalgia (FM): a disorder that causes aches and pain all over the body, and involves "tender points" on specific places on the neck, shoulders, back, hips, arms, and legs that hurt when pressure is put on them.

folate: a B vitamin found naturally in some foods. It is used in the body to make new cells. See folic acid.

folic acid: a man-made form of folate found in supplements and added to fortified foods. It is a B vitamin used in the body to make new cells. If a woman has enough folic acid in her body before she is pregnant, it can help lower the risk of major birth defects of her baby's brain and spine.

Fragile X syndrome: a genetic condition in which there is a change, or mutation, in a single gene called the Fragile X Mental Retardation 1 (*FMR1*) gene. This gene normally makes a protein the body needs for the brain to develop. But when there is a change in this gene, the body makes only a little bit or none of the protein, which can cause the symptoms of Fragile X. It is the most common cause of inherited mental retardation.

fungal infection: an overgrowth of fungus, a plant-like organism. Some examples of fungus that grow in the body are yeast and molds.

gallstone: solid material that forms in the gallbladder or common bile duct. Gallstones are made of cholesterol or other substances found in the gallbladder. They may occur as one large stone or as many small ones and vary from the size of a grain of sand to a golf ball.

gastroesophageal reflux (GER): also called acid reflux, a condition in which the contents of the stomach come back up into the esophagus or food pipe, causing discomfort.

gastrointestinal tract: the stomach and intestines. The gastrointestinal tract is part of the digestive system, which also includes the salivary glands, mouth, esophagus, liver, pancreas, gallbladder, and rectum.

gene: the functional and physical unit of heredity composed of DNA, which has a specific function and is passed from parent to offspring.

gene therapy: a new treatment for replacing defective or missing genes to restore normal function.

generalized anxiety disorder (GAD): a condition marked by excessive worry and feelings of fear, dread, and uneasiness that lasts 6 months or longer. Other symptoms include being restless, being tired or irritable, muscle tension, not being able to concentrate or sleep well, shortness of breath, fast heartbeat, sweating, and dizziness.

genetic counseling: a communication process between a specially trained health professional and a person concerned about the genetic risk of disease. The person's family and personal medical history may be discussed, and counseling may lead to genetic testing.

genetic testing: analyzing DNA to look for a genetic alteration or mutation that may show an increased risk of developing a specific disease or disorder.

genital mutilation: the partial or total cutting away of the external genitalia or other injury to the genitals, for cultural or other nontherapeutic reasons.

gestational diabetes: diabetes that occurs during pregnancy.

glucose challenge screening: a standard test for pregnant women in the early part of the third trimester that measures how effectively the body processes glucose, and helps diagnose gestational diabetes.

growth hormone: also called somatotropin. A protein made by the pituitary gland that helps control body growth and the use of glucose and fat in the body.

gum disease: an infection of the tissues that hold a person's teeth in place.

harassment: to disturb or bother someone continually. It can be of a sexual, physical, racial, or other nature.

HDL cholesterol: high-density lipoprotein cholesterol, also sometimes called the "good" cholesterol because it is the cholesterol in the blood that carries cholesterol from other parts of the body back to the liver, which leads to its removal from the body and prevents its buildup in the walls of the arteries.

heart attack: occurs when blood flow to a section of heart muscle becomes blocked. If the flow of blood is not restored quickly, the section of heart muscle becomes damaged from the lack of oxygen and begins to die.

heart disease: a number of abnormal conditions affecting the heart and the blood vessels in the heart. The most common type of heart disease is coronary artery disease, which is the gradual buildup of plaque in the coronary arteries, the blood vessels that bring blood to the heart. This disease develops slowly and silently, over decades. It can go virtually unnoticed until it produces a heart attack.

heart failure: a condition in which the heart cannot pump all the blood it receives. This leads to buildup of fluids in the body tissues. It does not mean that the heart has stopped or is about to stop working. However, it is a serious condition that requires medical care.

hepatitis B: a serious disease caused by the hepatitis B virus (HBV) that attacks the liver. Infection is lifelong and can cause cirrhosis or scarring of the liver, liver cancer, liver failure, and death.

herbicides: chemicals that kill plants.

hereditary nonpolypsis colon cancer (HNPCC): an inherited disorder in which affected people have a higher-than-normal chance of developing colorectal cancer and certain other types of cancer, often before the age of 50.

herpes simplex virus (HSV): a virus that causes blisters and sores mainly around the mouth and genitals. There are two types. Type 1 is the most common and causes sores around the mouth, or cold sores. It is transmitted by infected saliva. Type 2 causes sores mainly on the genitals and is transmitted sexually.

high blood pressure: see hypertension.

HIV/AIDS: human immunodeficiency virus (HIV) is the virus that infects and destroys the body's immune cells and causes a disease called AIDS, or Acquired Immunodeficiency Syndrome. AIDS occurs in the most advanced stage of HIV infection, when a person's T-cell count goes below 200 and he or she becomes ill with one of the health problems common in people with AIDS. HIV/AIDS infection is lifelong—there is no cure, but there are many medicines to fight both HIV infection and the infections and cancers that come with it.

hives: red and sometimes itchy bumps on the skin, usually caused by an allergic reaction to a drug or a food.

hormone: a substance produced by one tissue and conveyed by the bloodstream to another tissue to affect a function of the body, such as growth or metabolism.

hormone therapy: the use of hormone drugs to treat a disease or condition. When used to treat the symptoms of menopause it is called menopausal hormone therapy.

hot flash: a sudden, temporary onset of body warmth, flushing, and sweating, often related to menopause.

HPV vaccine: a vaccine to help prevent infection with the human papillomavirus (HPV).

human papillomavirus (HPV): a member of a family of viruses that can cause abnormal tissue growth, such as genital warts, and other changes to cells. Infection with certain types of HPV increases the risk of developing cervical cancer.

human T-cell lymphotropic virus type 1 or type 2 (HTLV 1-2): viruses that infect T cells, a type of white blood cell, and can cause leukemia and lymphoma. HTLV 1-2 is spread by sharing syringes or needles, through blood transfusions or sexual contact, and from mother to child during birth or breastfeeding.

human trafficking: a form of modern-day slavery in which victims are subjected to force, fraud, or coercion, for the purpose of sexual exploitation or forced labor.

hyperemesis gravidarum: extreme, persistent nausea and vomiting during pregnancy that may lead to dehydration.

hypertension: also called high blood pressure, it is having blood pressure greater than 140 over 90 mmHg (millimeters of mercury). Long-term high blood pressure can damage blood vessels and organs, including the heart, kidneys, eyes, and brain.

hysterectomy: surgery to remove the uterus and, sometimes, the cervix. When the uterus and part or all of the cervix are removed, it is called a total hysterectomy. When only the uterus is removed, it is called a partial hysterectomy.

immune system: a complex system in the body that recognizes and responds to foreign and potentially harmful substances, such as infections, to protect the body.

immunization: also called vaccination, a shot that contains germs that have been killed or weakened. When given to a healthy person, it triggers the immune system to respond and build immunity to a disease.

incontinence: the inability to control the flow of urine from the bladder, called urinary incontinence, or the escape of stool from the rectum, called fecal incontinence.

infertility: a condition in which a couple has problems conceiving, or getting pregnant, after 1 year of regular sexual intercourse without using any birth control methods. If a woman keeps having miscarriages, it's also called infertility. Infertility can be caused by a problem with the man or the woman, or both.

inflammatory bowel disease (IBD): long-lasting health problems that cause inflammation, swelling, and ulcers in the digestive tract. Symptoms can include cramping, abdominal pain, and severe bloody diarrhea. The two main types are ulcerative colitis and Crohn's disease.

inherited genetic mutation: a change in the DNA sequence that parents pass on to their children.

insulin: a hormone that helps glucose, a type of sugar from the food a person eats, get into cells for energy. In people with diabetes, the body does not make enough insulin.

intestines: the long, tube-shaped organ in the abdomen that completes the process of digestion. The intestine has two parts, the small intestine and the large intestine, also called the colon or bowel.

intimate partner violence (IPV): abuse that occurs between two people in a close relationship, including current and former spouses and dating partners.

intrauterine device (IUD): a small device that is placed inside a woman's uterus by a health care provider, which prevents pregnancy by not allowing the sperm to fertilize the egg. There are two types of IUDs—a copper IUD and a hormonal IUD. IUDs do not protect a woman from HIV/AIDS or other sexually transmitted infections.

iodine: an element that is necessary for the body to make thyroid hormone. It is found in shellfish and iodized salt.

ionizing radiation: a type of radiation made or given off by x-rays, radioactive substances, rays that enter the Earth's atmosphere from outer space, and other sources. At high doses ionizing radiation increases chemical activity inside cells and can lead to health risks, including cancer.

irritable bowel syndrome (IBS): a disorder characterized most commonly by cramping, abdominal pain, bloating, constipation, and diarrhea. It causes a great deal of discomfort and distress, but it does not permanently harm the intestines and does not lead to a serious disease, such as cancer.

ischemic stroke: a blockage of blood vessels supplying blood to the brain, causing a decrease in blood supply. See stroke.

jaundice: a yellowing of the skin and the whites of the eyes, caused by too much bilirubin in the blood. Bilirubin is a yellowish fluid in bile, a fluid made by the liver. Although not a disease, jaundice can signal a liver or gallbladder problem. Newborns can develop jaundice, which is only temporary and goes away.

Kegel exercises: exercises to strengthen the pelvic floor muscles, which support the body's uterus, bladder, and bowel. If a person's pelvic floor muscles are toned, he or she may reduce the risk of incontinence and similar problems.

labia: the lip-like structures that surround the vulva and protect the female genitals. The outer set of labia are called the labia majora and the inner set are the labia minora.

lactase: an enzyme that breaks down lactose, a type of sugar found in milk and milk products.

lactational amenorrhea method (LAM): a method of birth control that is based on the natural infertility that happens after birth when a woman is breastfeeding and is not having her period, or is amenorrheic. The baby suckling at the breast suppresses the hormones in the mother's body that make ovulation take place. This method is 98 percent effective if a woman is exclusively or almost exclusively breastfeeding (using very little or no infant formula for her baby), has not had a menstrual period since giving birth, and the baby is less than 6 months old. It is most effective if a mother breastfeeds often and on the baby's request, both day and night, without long intervals of time passing without a feeding; does not use pacifiers; and does not supplement with formula. This method is easy to use, begins right after birth, and has no side effects. It does not offer protection against STIs or HIV.

lactose intolerance: a digestive disorder in which the body cannot digest or absorb lactose, a type of sugar found in milk and other dairy products.

LDL cholesterol: low-density lipoprotein cholesterol, also known as the "bad" cholesterol because it is the type of cholesterol in the blood that is the main source of damaging buildup and blockage in the arteries. The higher a person's LDL cholesterol level, the greater the risk of developing heart disease.

legumes: a class of vegetables that are high in protein, including beans, peas, and lentils.

leukemia: cancer that starts in blood-forming tissue, such as the bone marrow, and causes large numbers of blood cells to be produced and enter the bloodstream.

lipoproteins: substances in the blood that carry cholesterol to and from the liver.

low birth weight: having a weight at birth that is less than 2500 grams, or 5 pounds, 8 ounces.

lupus: also called systemic lupus erythematosus and SLE, it is a chronic, inflammatory, connective tissue disease that can affect the joints and many organs, including the skin, heart, lungs, kidneys, and nervous system. It can cause many different symptoms; however, not everyone with lupus has all the symptoms.

lymph node: a rounded mass of lymphatic tissue that is surrounded by a capsule of connective tissue. Lymph nodes filter lymph (lymphatic fluid), and they store white blood cells called lymphocytes.

major depressive disorder: see depression.

malaria: a mosquito-borne disease caused by a parasite. People with malaria often experience fever, chills, and flu-like illness. Left untreated, they may develop severe complications and die.

malnourished: lacking the proper nutrition or being unable to absorb nutrients from food.

mammogram: an x-ray of the breast.

measles: a highly contagious disease marked by fever, cough, and raised red spots on the skin. It is caused by a virus that usually affects children and is spread by coughing or contact with fluid from the nose or mouth of someone who has been infected.

melanoma: a disease in which cancer cells form in the skin cells called melanocytes, or the cells that color the skin. It is the most serious type of skin cancer, and it can occur anywhere on the body. Possible signs of melanoma include a change in the appearance of a mole or pigmented area of skin.

menopausal hormone therapy (MHT): replaces the hormones that a woman's ovaries stop making at the time of menopause, easing symptoms like hot flashes and vaginal dryness. It involves using man-made estrogen alone or estrogen with a progestin, often in the form of a pill or skin patch. MHT used to be called hormone replacement therapy, or HRT. [A recent, large study found that use of MHT poses some serious risks, such as increasing some women's risk of breast cancer, heart disease, stroke, and pulmonary embolism (blood clot in the lung). Women who choose to use MHT should use the lowest dose that helps for the shortest time needed. Talk with your doctor to find out if MHT is right for you and discuss other ways to relieve menopausal symptoms.]

menopausal symptoms: symptoms that a women can experience during menopause, which can include changes in menstruation, hot flashes, night sweats, problems sleeping, vaginal dryness and infections, mood changes, decreased sex drive, and more.

menopause: the normal change in a woman's life when her period stops. Menopause is often referred to as "the change of life" or "the change." During menopause a woman's body slowly produces less of the hormones estrogen and progesterone. This often happens between the ages of 45 and 55. A woman has reached menopause when she has not had a period for 12 months in a row.

menstruation: the blood flow from the uterus that happens about every 4 weeks in a woman. From puberty until menopause, menstruation occurs about every 28 days when a woman is not pregnant.

metabolic syndrome: a group of conditions that put a patient at risk of heart disease and diabetes. These conditions include high blood pressure, high blood glucose levels, high levels of triglycerides, low levels of HDL cholesterol, and having too much body fat around the waist.

methadone: a morphine-like drug used to treat severe pain and to prevent withdrawal symptoms in patients who are addicted to heroin or to other opiates. It may also be used to treat severe coughing in patients with lung cancer.

miscarriage: also called a spontaneous abortion, it is an unplanned loss of a pregnancy before 20 weeks.

miscarry: see miscarriage.

mole: a benign growth on the skin that is formed by a cluster of melanocytes, or cells that make the pigment melanin. Moles are usually dark in color and may be raised from the skin.

monoclonal gammopathy of undetermined significance (MGUS): a benign condition in which there is a higher-than-normal level of a protein called M protein in the blood. Patients with this condition are at an increased risk of developing cancer.

mons pubis: the soft mound of flesh protecting the pubic bone.

MSG: monosodium glutamate. A flavor enhancer used in some foods. Its use has become controversial in the past 30 years because of reports of adverse reactions in people who have eaten foods that contain MSG.

mutated gene: a gene that has changed, because of mistakes in cell division or exposure to DNA-damaging agents in the environment. Mutations can be harmful, beneficial, or have no effect. If they occur in cells that make eggs or sperm, they can be inherited; if mutations occur in other types of cells, they are not inherited. Certain mutations may lead to cancer or other diseases.

narcotic: an agent or drug that causes insensibility or stupor and can relieve pain.

natural family planning: a birth control method that involves not having sexual intercourse at the time in a woman's menstrual cycle when she is most likely to become pregnant (usually around the time of ovulation).

nitrates: medications that relax blood vessels and relieve chest pain caused by coronary artery disease.

nonsteroidal anti-inflammatory drugs (NSAIDs): pain relievers such as aspirin, ibuprofen, and naproxen. These medicines are safe and effective when taken as directed, but they can cause stomach bleeding or kidney problems in some people.

obsessive-compulsive disorder (OCD): an anxiety disorder in which a person has obsessive thoughts and compulsive actions, such as cleaning, checking, counting, or hoarding. The person becomes trapped in a pattern of repetitive thoughts and behaviors that are senseless and distressing but very hard to stop. OCD can be mild or severe, but if severe and left untreated can stop a person from being able to function at work, at school, or even in the home.

oral contraceptive: also called the birth control pill or "the pill," it is a medication that contains the hormones estrogen and progestin, or progestin only, and is taken to prevent pregnancy. The pill is 95 to 99.9 percent effective at preventing pregnancy, but it does not protect against HIV and other sexually transmitted infections. Some birth control pills are used to treat acne or premenstrual dysphoric disorder, the physical and emotional symptoms that occur before the menstrual period each month.

organ failure: when an organ, such as the heart or other part of the body that performs a specific function, stops functioning properly.

osteoarthritis: a joint disease that mostly affects cartilage, the slippery tissue that covers the ends of bones in a joint. The top layer of cartilage breaks down and wears away. This allows bones under the cartilage to rub together, which causes pain, swelling, and loss of motion of the joint.

osteoporosis: a bone disease that is characterized by progressive loss of bone density and thinning of bone tissue, causing bones to break easily.

overactive thyroid: also called hyperthyroidism, it is a condition in which the thyroid gland makes and releases too much thyroid hormone in the body. Symptoms can include weight loss, chest pain, cramps, diarrhea, and nervousness.

ovulation: the release from a follicle of a single egg that developed in the ovary, which is then pushed down the fallopian tube and is ready to be fertilized. It usually occurs regularly, around day 14 of a 28-day menstrual cycle.

oxalate: a chemical found in many foods that can be irritating to people with pain conditions, such as vulvodynia, fibromyalgia, and irritable bowel syndrome. Foods high in oxalate may also cause kidney stones in someone prone to forming calcium oxalate stones.

pancreas: a glandular organ located in the abdomen. It makes pancreatic juices, which contain enzymes that aid in digestion, and it produces several hormones, including insulin. The pancreas is surrounded by the stomach, intestines, and other organs.

panic attack: sudden feeling of terror for no reason that may also occur with physical symptoms such as fast heartbeat, chest pain, problems breathing, and dizziness.

panic disorder: an anxiety disorder in which a person has sudden attacks of fear and panic. The attacks may occur without a known reason, but many times they are triggered by events or thoughts that produce fear in the person, such as taking an elevator or driving. Symptoms of the attacks can include rapid heartbeat, chest sensations, shortness of breath, dizziness, tingling, and feeling anxious.

Pap test: a test that finds changes in the cells of the cervix. The test can find cancer or cells that can turn into cancer. To perform a Pap test, a health care provider uses a small brush to gently scrape cells from the cervix for examination under a microscope.

parasite: an organism that lives on or in a host organism and gets its food from or at the expense of its host.

parasitic infection: when a parasite invades the body and causes disease.

parvovirus B19: a virus that causes an illness called fifth disease, a mild rash illness that occurs most often in children. Fifth disease causes a "slapped-cheek" rash on the face and a lacy red rash on the trunk and limbs that may itch, but resolves within 7 to 10 days. An adult who has not been infected

with parvovirus B19 in the past can be infected and become ill.

pelvic inflammatory disease (PID): an infection of the female reproductive organs that are above the cervix, such as the fallopian tubes and ovaries. It is the most common and serious problem caused by sexually transmitted infections (STIs). PID can cause ectopic pregnancies, infertility, chronic pelvic pain, and other serious problems. Symptoms can include fever, foul-smelling vaginal discharge, extreme pain, and vaginal bleeding.

phenylketonuria (PKU): an inherited disorder in which the body cannot process a portion of the protein called phenylalanine (Phe), which is in almost all foods. If the Phe level gets too high, the brain can become damaged. All babies born in the United States are now tested for PKU soon after birth, making it easier to diagnose the disease and to treat it early.

phobia: an anxiety disorder in which a person has an unusual amount of fear of a certain activity or situation.

physical therapist: a health professional who teaches exercises and physical activities that help condition muscles and restore strength and movement.

physical therapy: therapy aimed to restore movement, balance, and coordination.

phytoestrogens: an estrogen-like substance found in some plants and plant products, such as herbs, grains, and fruits, which may have anticancer effects.

pill, "the pill": see oral contraceptive.

placenta: a temporary organ that joins the mother and fetus during pregnancy. The placenta transfers oxygen and nutrients from the mother to the fetus and permits the release of carbon dioxide and waste products from the fetus. It is then expelled from the mother's body during the birth process with the fetal membranes.

plaque: a buildup of fat, cholesterol, and other substances that accumulate in the walls of the arteries.

pneumonia: a severe inflammation of the lungs in which the alveoli, or tiny air sacs in the lungs, are filled with fluid. This may cause a decrease in the amount of oxygen that the blood can absorb from air breathed into the lung. Pneumonia is usually caused by infection but may also be caused by radiation treatment, allergy, or irritation of lung tissue by inhaled substances. It may involve part or all of the lungs.

polycystic kidney disease (PKD): a kidney disorder passed down through families in which multiple cysts form on the kidneys, causing them to become enlarged.

polycystic ovary syndrome (PCOS): a health problem that can affect a woman's menstrual cycle, ability to have children, hormones, heart, blood vessels, and appearance. With PCOS, women typically have high levels of androgens or male hormones, missed or irregular periods, and many small cysts in their ovaries.

postmenopausal: after menopause.

postpartum depression: a serious condition that requires treatment from a health care provider. With this condition, feelings of the "baby blues," such as feeling sad, anxious, afraid, or confused after having a baby, do not go away and may worsen.

posttraumatic stress disorder (PTSD): a psychological condition that can happen when a person sees or experiences something traumatic, such as rape, murder, torture, or wartime combat. A person can have many symptoms, including flashbacks or reliving the event, nightmares, fatigue, anxiety, and forgetfulness and may withdraw from family and friends.

preeclampsia: also known as toxemia, it is a syndrome occurring in a pregnant woman after her 20th week of pregnancy that causes high blood pressure and problems with the kidneys and other organs. Symptoms include sudden increase in blood pressure, too much protein in the urine, swelling in a woman's face and hands, headache, blurred vision, and abdominal pain.

premature birth: see preterm birth.

premenstrual syndrome (PMS): a group of symptoms linked to the menstrual cycle that occur in the week or 2 weeks before menstruation. The symptoms usually go away after menstruation begins and can include acne, breast swelling and tenderness, feeling tired, having trouble sleeping, upset stomach, bloating, constipation or diarrhea, headache or backache, appetite changes or food cravings, joint or muscle pain, trouble concentrating or remembering, tension, irritability, mood swings or crying spells, and anxiety or depression.

preterm birth: also called premature birth, it is a birth that occurs before the 37th week of pregnancy.

primary biliary cirrhosis: a disease that slowly destroys the liver's bile ducts. Bile is a substance produced in the liver that helps digest fat in the small intestine and remove toxins from the body. When the ducts are damaged, bile builds up in the liver and damages liver tissue. Biliary cirrhosis can develop over time and may cause the liver to stop working. The cause is unknown.

progesterone: a female hormone produced by the ovaries. Progesterone, along with estrogen, prepares the uterus (womb) for a possible pregnancy each month and supports the fertilized egg if conception occurs. Progesterone also helps prepare the breasts for milk production and breastfeeding.

progestin: an artificial or man-made hormone that works by causing changes in the uterus. When taken with the hormone estrogen, progestin works to prevent thickening of the lining of the uterus. This is helpful for women who are in menopause and are taking estrogen for their menopausal symptoms. Progestins also are prescribed to regulate the menstrual cycle, treat unusual stopping of the menstrual periods, help a pregnancy occur or maintain a pregnancy, or

treat unusual or heavy bleeding of the uterus. They also can be used to prevent pregnancy; help treat cancer of the breast, kidney, or uterus; and help treat loss of appetite and severe weight or muscle loss.

protein deficiency: a condition in the body caused by not having enough protein in the diet, which can lead to malnutrition. Early symptoms of any type of malnutrition are general and include fatigue, irritability, and lethargy. As protein deficiency continues, growth failure, loss of muscle mass, generalized swelling, and decreased immunity can occur.

proteins: large molecules that contain primarily carbon, hydrogen, oxygen, and nitrogen. Proteins are essential to the structure and function of all living cells. Examples of proteins in the body include enzymes, antibodies, and some hormones.

psoriasis: a chronic or long-lasting skin disease that causes patches of thick, red, or inflamed skin covered with silvery scales. These patches usually itch or feel sore and most often occur on the elbows, knees, other parts of the legs, scalp, lower back, face, palms, and soles of the feet, but they can occur on skin anywhere on the body. Psoriasis mostly affects adults.

psychological therapy: also called psychotherapy, it is counseling or "talk" therapy with a qualified health care provider in which a person can explore difficult, and often painful, emotions and experiences, such as feelings of anxiety, depression, or trauma. It is a process that aims to help the patient become better at making positive choices in his or her life and to become more self-sufficient. Psychotherapy can be given for an individual or in a group setting.

psychologist: a clinical psychologist is a professional who treats mental illness, emotional disturbance, and behavior problems. He or she uses talk therapy as treatment and cannot prescribe medication. A clinical psychologist will have a master's degree (MA) or doctorate (PhD) in psychology and possibly more training in a specific type of therapy.

qi energy: in traditional Chinese medicine, vital energy or life force.

racism: the belief that one race is better than another.

radiation treatment: also called radiation therapy, it is the use of high-energy radiation from x-rays, gamma rays, neutrons, protons, and other sources to kill cancer cells and shrink tumors. Radiation may come from a machine outside the body, or it may come from radioactive material placed in the body near cancer cells. Systemic radiation therapy uses a radioactive substance that travels in the blood to tissues throughout the body.

regulatory T cells: immune cells that help orchestrate the elaborate immune system and assist other cells to make antibodies. Helper T cells are essential for activating the body's defenses against foreign substances. Another subset of regulatory T cells prevent immune responses to self.

Without them autoimmune disease would flourish.

renal disease: also called kidney disease, it is any disease or disorder that affects the function of the kidneys.

renal tubular acidosis: a disease that occurs when the kidneys fail to excrete acids into the urine, which causes a person's blood to remain too acidic.

reproductive tract: the system of organs in males or females that act together to perform reproduction.

restless leg syndrome (RLS): a neurologic disorder that causes unpleasant sensations in the legs and an uncontrollable urge to move them for relief. Persons affected with the disorder describe the sensations as burning, creeping, tugging, or feelings like insects crawling inside the legs.

saturated fat: fat such as butter, solid shortening, lard, and fatback. It is recommended that people avoid saturated fat in their diets.

seizures: uncontrollable contractions of muscles that can result in sudden movement or loss of control, also known as convulsions.

self-esteem: how you feel about yourself, such as how you feel about who you are, the way you act, and how you look. When a person does not think too highly of himself or herself, he or she is said to have low self-esteem.

semen: the fluid that contains sperm that a male releases from his penis when he becomes sexually aroused or has an orgasm.

sexual assault: any form of sexual activity that you do not agree to, including inappropriate touching and vaginal, anal, or oral penetration. It includes rape, attempted rape, and child molestation. Sexual assault can be verbal, visual, or anything that forces a person to join in unwanted sexual contact or attention.

sexually transmitted infections (STIs): diseases that are spread by sexual activity. Also called sexually transmitted diseases (STDs).

sickle cell anemia: a serious, inherited condition in which the red blood cells can become sickle shaped, or "C" shaped, keeping them from moving easily through blood and to become stiff, sticky, form clumps, and get stuck in blood vessels, which can cause pain, infections, and organ damage.

sleep apnea: a disorder involving brief interruptions of breathing during sleep.

social anxiety disorder: an anxiety disorder in which a person feels overwhelming anxiety and excessive self-consciousness in everyday social situations. It can be limited to only one type of situation—such as a fear of speaking in formal or informal situations, or eating or drinking in front of others—or, in its most severe form, a person has symptoms almost anytime he or she is around other people.

spermicide: chemical jelly, foam, cream, or suppository inserted into the vagina before sexual intercourse that kills sperm to prevent pregnancy.

spina bifida: the most common disabling birth defect in the United States. Its name means "cleft spine," or failure of a fetal spine to close the right way when it is developing before birth. It occurs very early in pregnancy, roughly 3 to 4 weeks after conception, before most women know that they are pregnant.

spinal cord injury: includes any kind of physical trauma that crushes and compresses the vertebrae in the neck, which can cause injury at the cervical level of the spinal cord and below; injuries that penetrate the spinal cord; injuries that fracture or dislocate the vertebrae, which causes pieces of vertebrae to tear into cord tissue or press down on the nerve parts of the cord that carry signals between the brain and the rest of the body.

spleen: an organ above the stomach and under the ribs on the left side of the body. It is part of the lymphatic system, which fights infection and keeps body fluids in balance. It contains white blood cells that fight germs. It also helps control the amount of blood in the body and destroys old and damaged cells.

stalking: repeated harassing or threatening behavior by a person, such as following another person, appearing at that person's home or place of business, making harassing phone calls, leaving written messages or objects, or vandalizing his or her property. Almost any unwanted contact between two people that directly or indirectly communicates a threat or places the victim in fear can be considered stalking.

statins: the most commonly prescribed drugs for people who need a cholesterol-lowering medicine. Statins lower LDL cholesterol levels more than other types of drugs. They also moderately lower triglycerides and raise HDL cholesterol.

STDs: see sexually transmitted infections (STIs).

stillbirth: when a fetus dies during birth, or when the fetus dies during the late stages of pregnancy when it would have been otherwise expected to survive.

stimulus (plural, stimuli): anything that can trigger a physical or behavioral change, such as irritants, sights, sounds, heat, cold, smells, or other sensations.

stroke: stoppage of blood flow to an area of the brain, causing permanent damage to nerve cells in that region. A stroke can occur either because an artery is clogged by a blood clot (called ischemic stroke) or an artery tears and bleeds into the brain. A stroke can cause symptoms such as loss of consciousness, problems with movement, and loss of speech.

sudden infant death syndrome (SIDS): the diagnosis given for the sudden death of an infant younger than 1 year that remains unexplained after a complete investigation. Because most cases of SIDS occur when a baby is sleeping in a crib, SIDS is also commonly known as crib death.

systemic lupus erythematosus (SLE): see lupus.

tai chi: sometimes called "moving meditation," a mind-body practice that originated in China as a martial art. A person doing tai chi moves his or her body slowly and gently, while breathing deeply and meditating.

tension headache: the most common type of headache, caused by tight muscles in a person's shoulders, neck, scalp, and jaw. It is often related to stress, depression, or anxiety. A person is more likely to get tension headaches if he or she works too much, does not get enough sleep, misses meals, or uses alcohol.

thymus: a gland that lies in the upper chest area beneath the breastbone and plays an important role in the development of the immune system in early life. Its cells form a part of the body's normal immune system. The gland is somewhat large in infants, grows gradually until puberty, and then gets smaller and is replaced by fat with age.

thyroid: a small gland in the neck that makes and stores hormones that help regulate heart rate, blood pressure, body temperature, and the rate at which food is converted into energy.

thyroid disease: a disease of the thyroid gland that causes the body to use energy more slowly or quickly than it should. There are four main types of thyroid disease hyperthyroidism—too much thyroid hormone, hypothyroidism—too little thyroid hormone, benign (noncancerous) thyroid disease, and thyroid cancer.

tongue-tied: when the frenulum, the cord of tissue underneath the tongue, is too tight and inhibits feeding and speech in infants.

toxic shock syndrome: a severe disease that involves fever, shock, and problems with the function of several body organs. It is caused by a toxin produced by certain types of staphylococcus bacteria.

toxins: substances created by plants and animals that are poisonous to humans. Most toxins that cause problems in humans are released by microorganisms such as bacteria and viruses.

trans **fat:** a type of unsaturated fat. Most *trans* fats are chemically produced by food manufacturers to prolong the shelf life of processed food. Some *trans* fats occur naturally in meat and dairy products from animals such as cattle, goats, and sheep. Eating *trans* fats increases the risk of certain long-term illnesses, such as coronary artery disease. *Trans* fats can be monounsaturated or polyunsaturated.

tremor: unintentional trembling or shaking movements in one or more parts of the body.

triglyceride: a type of fat in the bloodstream and fat tissue. Normal triglyceride levels are below 150. Levels above 200 are considered high. High triglyceride levels can contribute to the hardening and narrowing of the arteries. This puts a person at a higher risk of having a heart attack or stroke. Diseases such as diabetes, obesity, kidney failure, or alcoholism can cause high triglycerides.

tuberculosis (TB): a disease caused by bacteria that usually affects the lungs. TB bacteria are spread through the air from one person to another. If someone with TB of the lungs or throat coughs or sneezes, people nearby who breathe in the bacteria can get TB. If the body cannot stop the bacteria from growing, a person will develop TB disease.

type 1 diabetes: see diabetes.

type 2 diabetes: see diabetes.

ulcer: also called peptic ulcer. It is a sore on the lining of the stomach or beginning of the small intestine. Peptic ulcers are common—1 in 10 Americans develops an ulcer at some time in his or her life. One cause of peptic ulcers is bacterial infection. But some ulcers are caused by long-term use of nonsteroidal anti-inflammatory drugs (NSAIDs). In a few cases, cancerous tumors in the stomach or pancreas can cause ulcers. Peptic ulcers are not caused by stress or eating spicy food.

ultrasound: also called sonography, it is a painless, harmless test that uses sound waves to produce images of the organs and structures of the body on a screen.

underactive thyroid: also called hypothyroidism, it is a condition in which the thyroid gland does not make enough thyroid hormone. Symptoms can include weight gain, constipation, dry skin, and sensitivity to the cold.

urinary tract infection (UTI): an infection anywhere in the urinary tract, or organs that collect and store urine and release it from your body (the kidneys, ureters, bladder, and urethra). An infection occurs when microorganisms, usually bacteria from the digestive tract, cling to the urethra (opening to the urinary tract) and begin to multiply.

uterine fibroids: common, benign, or noncancerous tumors that grow in the muscle of the uterus, or womb. Fibroids often cause no symptoms and need no treatment, and they usually shrink after menopause. But sometimes fibroids cause heavy bleeding or pain and require treatment.

uterus: a woman's womb, or the hollow, pear-shaped organ located in a woman's lower abdomen between the bladder and the rectum.

vaccines: see immunization.

vaginal fluid: fluid or liquid made by glands in a woman's vagina and cervix. The fluid flows out of the vagina and keeps it healthy and clean. The color and thickness of the discharge change with the menstrual cycle.

vaginal yeast infection: a common infection in women caused by an overgrowth of the fungus candida. It is normal to have some yeast in the vagina, but sometimes it can overgrow because of hormonal changes in the body, such as those that occur because of pregnancy, or from taking certain medications, such as antibiotics. Symptoms can include itching, burning, and irritation of the vagina; pain when urinating or with sexual intercourse; and vaginal discharge that looks like cottage cheese.

virus: a microorganism that can infect cells and cause disease.

vitiligo: a skin condition in which there is loss of pigment or color from areas of skin, resulting in irregular white patches that feel like normal skin.

voyeurism: the practice of watching private sexual acts.

womb: see uterus.

yeast infection: see vaginal yeast infection.

yoga: a mind-body exercise that combines stretching and controlled breathing to achieve relaxation and a stable mood. ■

Bibliography

HEART DISEASE

Oliver-McNeil S, Artinian NT. Women's perceptions of personal cardiovascular risk and their risk-reducing behaviors. *Am J Crit Care*. 2002;11(3):221-228. http://ajcc.aacnjournals.org/cgi/reprint/11/3/221. Published May 2002. Accessed May 15, 2007.

Sandmaier M. *The Healthy Heart Handbook for Women*. Bethesda, MD: National Heart, Lung, and Blood Institute, US Dept of Health and Human Services; 2007. NIH publication 07-2720. http://www.nhlbi.nih.gov/health/public/heart/other/hhw/hdbk_wmn.pdf. Revised March 2007. Accessed May 15, 2007.

How many women get breast cancer? American Cancer Society Web site. http://www.cancer.org/docroot/CRI/content/CRI_2_2_1X_How_many_people_get_breast_cancer_5.asp?sitearea=. Revised September 26, 2007. Accessed October 23, 2007.

Miracle VA. Coronary artery disease in women: the myth still exists. *Dimens Crit Care Nurs*. 2006;25(5):209-215.

Schulman KA, Berlin JA, Harless W, et al. The effect of race and sex on physicians' recommendations for cardiac catheterization. *N Engl J Med*. 1999;340(8):618-626. http://content.nejm.org/cgi/reprint/340/8/618.pdf. Published February 25, 1999. Accessed May 15, 2007.

Mosca L, Linfante AH, Benjamin EJ, et al. National study of physician awareness and adherence to cardiovascular disease prevention guidelines. *Circulation*. 2005;111(4):499-510. http://circ.ahajournals.org/cgi/reprint/111/4/499. Published February 1, 2005. Accessed May 15, 2007.

Blauwet LA, Hayes SN, McManus D, Redberg RF, Walsh MN. Low rate of sex-specific result reporting in cardiovascular trials. *Mayo Clin Proc*. 2007;82(2):166-170.

Duvall WL. Cardiovascular disease in women. *Mt Sinai J Med*. 2003;70(5):293-305.

Heart attack warning signs. National Heart, Lung, and Blood Institute Web site. http://www.nhlbi.nih.gov/actintime/haws/haws.htm. Accessed April 4, 2007.

Maruccio E, Loving N, Bennett SK, Hayes SN. A survey of attitudes and experiences of women with heart disease. *Womens Health Issues*. 2003;13(1):23-31.

Dollemore D. *Aging Hearts and Arteries: A Scientific Quest*. Bethesda, MD: National Institute on Aging, US Dept of Health and Human Services; 2005. NIH publication 05-3738. http://www.nia.nih.gov/NR/rdonlyres/0BBF820F-27D0-48EA-9820-736B7E9F08BB/0/Aging_Hearts_And_Arteries.pdf. Published April 2005. Accessed May 15, 2007.

Your Guide to Lowering Your Cholesterol With TLC: Therapeutic Lifestyle Changes. Bethesda, MD: National Heart, Lung, and Blood Institute, US Dept of Health and Human Services; 2005. NIH publication 06-235. http://www.nhlbi.nih.gov/health/public/heart/chol/chol_tlc.pdf. Published December 2005. Accessed April 2, 2007.

Writing Group of the American Heart Association Statistics Committee and Stroke Statistics Subcommittee. Heart disease and stroke statistics—2007 update. A report from the American Heart Association Statistics Committee and Stroke Statistics Subcommittee. *Circulation*. 2007;115(5):e69-171. http://circ.ahajournals.org/cgi/reprint/115/5/e69. Published February 6, 2007. Accessed May 15, 2007.

Cholesterol. In: Carlson KJ, Eisenstat SA, Ziporyn T, eds. *The New Harvard Guide to Women's Health*. Cambridge, MA: Harvard University Press; 2004:141-145.

Meagher EA. Addressing cardiovascular disease in women: focus on dyslipidemia. *J Am Board Fam Pract*. 2004;17(6):424-437. http://www.jabfm.org/cgi/reprint/17/6/424. Published November-December 2004. Accessed May 15, 2007.

Mosca L, Banka CL, Benjamin EJ, et al. Evidence-based guidelines for cardiovascular disease prevention in women: 2007 update. *Circulation*. 2007;115(11):1481-1501. http://circ.ahajournals.org/cgi/reprint/115/11/1481. Published March 20, 2007. Accessed May 15, 2007.

Albright C, Thompson DL. The effectiveness of walking in preventing cardiovascular disease in women: a review of the current literature. *J Womens Health (Larchmt)*. 2006;15(3):271-280.

Hyperlipoproteinemia. In: Beers MH, ed. *The Merck Manual of Medical Information—Second Home Edition*. http://www.merck.com/mmhe/sec12/ch157/ch157b.html?qt=hyperlipidemia&alt=sh. Revised February 2003. Accessed April 20, 2007.

Incidence and Prevalence: 2006 Chart Book on Cardiovascular and Lung Diseases. Bethesda, MD: National Heart, Lung, and Blood Institute, US Dept of Health and Human Services; 2007. http://www.nhlbi.nih.gov/resources/docs/06a_ip_chtbk.pdf. Accessed October 23, 2007.

Conen D, Ridker PM, Mora S, Buring JE, Glynn RJ. Blood pressure and risk of developing type 2 diabetes mellitus: The Women's Health Study [Published online ahead of print Oct 9, 2007]. *Eur Heart J*. doi:10.1093/eurheartj/ehm400.

Patient information sheet: angiotensin-converting enzyme inhibitor drugs (ACE inhibitors). US Food and Drug Administration Web site. http://www.fda.gov/cder/drug/InfoSheets/patient/ACEIPIS.htm. Published June 7, 2006. Accessed April 9, 2007.

Angiotensin II receptor blockers (ARBs). US Food and Drug Administration Web site. http://www.fda.gov/hearthealth/treatments/medications/arbs.html. Updated March 12, 2004. Accessed April 9, 2007.

Zoler ML. Dual-drug HT regimens first line for blacks. (new guidelines). *Family Practice News*. 2003;33(8):16. http://findarticles.com/p/articles/mi_m0CYD/is_8_38/ai_101495988. Published April 15, 2003. Accessed October 23, 2007.

Coronary artery disease. In: Carlson KJ, Eisenstat SA, Ziporyn T, eds. *The*

New Harvard Guide to Women's Health. Cambridge, MA: Harvard University Press; 2004:166-175.

Beckles GLA, Thompson-Reid PE, eds. *Diabetes and Women's Health Across the Life Stages: A Public Health Perspective*. Atlanta, GA: Centers for Disease Control and Prevention, US Dept of Health and Human Services; 2001. http://www.cdc.gov/diabetes/pubs/pdf/women.pdf. Accessed May 15, 2007.

Cersosimo E, DeFronzo RA. Insulin resistance and endothelial dysfunction: the road map to cardiovascular diseases. *Diabetes Metab Res Rev*. 2006;22(6):423-436.

Body mass index table. National Heart, Lung, and Blood Institute Web site. http://www.nhlbi.nih.gov/guidelines/obesity/bmi_tbl.htm. Accessed March 30, 2007.

Flier JS, Maratos-Flier E. Obesity. In: Kasper DL, Braunwald E, Fauci AS, Hauser SL, Longo DL, Jameson JL, eds. *Harrison's Principles of Internal Medicine*. 16th ed. New York, NY: McGraw-Hill; 2005:422-429.

Manson JE, Colditz GA, Stampfer MJ, et al. A prospective study of obesity and risk of coronary heart disease in women. *N Engl J Med*. 1990;322(13):882-889.

What is coronary artery disease? National Heart, Lung, and Blood Institute Web site. http://www.nhlbi.nih.gov/health/dci/Diseases/Cad/CAD_WhatIs.html. Published July 2006. Accessed January 30, 2007.

Strike PC, Steptoe A. Psychosocial factors in the development of coronary artery disease. *Prog Cardiovasc Dis*. 2004;46(4):337-347.

Lee S, Colditz GA, Berkman LF, Kawachi I. Caregiving and risk of coronary heart disease in U.S. women: a prospective study. *Am J Prev Med*. 2003;24(2):113-119.

Orth-Gomer K, Leineweber C. Multiple stressors and coronary disease in women. The Stockholm Female Coronary Risk Study. *Biol Psychol*. 2005;69(1):57-66.

Shuckit MA. Alcohol and alcoholism. In: Kasper DL, Braunwald E, Fauci AS, Hauser SL, Longo DL, Jameson JL, eds. *Harrison's Principles of Internal Medicine*. 16th ed. New York, NY: McGraw-Hill; 2005:2562-2566.

da Luz PL, Coimbra SR. Wine, alcohol and atherosclerosis: clinical evidences and mechanisms. *Braz J Med Biol Res*. 2004;37(9):1275-1295. http://www.scielo.br/pdf/bjmbr/v37n9/5502.pdf. Published September 2004. Accessed May 15, 2007.

Bliss RM. How are you fixed for flavonoids? US Department of Agriculture Web site. http://www.ars.usda.gov/is/pr/2007/070110.htm. Published January 10, 2007. Accessed April 9, 2007.

McBride J. Finessing the flavonoids. *Agricultural Research Magazine*. 2001;49(2):18-19. http://www.ars.usda.gov/is/AR/archive/feb01/flav0201.pdf. Published February 2001. Accessed April 9, 2007.

National Cancer Institute. Alcohol consumption. In: *Cancer Trends Progress Report-2005 Update*. Bethesda, MD: National Cancer Institute, US Dept of Health and Human Services; 2005. http://progressreport.cancer.gov/doc_detail.asp?pid=1&did=2005&chid=21&coid=206&mid=. Reviewed December 21, 2005. Accessed April 9, 2007.

Patel MJ, de Lemos JA, Philips B, et al. Implications of family history of myocardial infarction in young women. *Am Heart J*. 2007;154(3):454-460.

Lawlor DA, Smith GD, Ebrahim S. Association between childhood socioeconomic status and coronary heart disease risk among postmenopausal women: findings from the British Women's Heart and Health Study. *Am J Public Health*. 2004;94(8):1386-1392. http://www.ajph.org/cgi/reprint/94/8/1386. Published August 2004. Accessed May 15, 2007.

Beebe-Dimmer J, Lynch JW, Turrell G, Lustgarten S, Raghunathan T, Kaplan GA. Childhood and adult socioeconomic conditions and 31-year mortality risk in women. *Am J Epidemiol*. 2004;159(5):481-490. http://aje.oxfordjournals.org/cgi/reprint/159/5/481. Published March 1, 2004. Accessed May 15, 2007.

Gliksman MD, Kawachi I, Hunter D, et al. Childhood socioeconomic status and risk of cardiovascular disease in middle aged US women: a prospective study. *J Epidemiol Community Health*. 1995;49(1):10-15.

Lynch J, Davey Smith G, Harper S, Bainbridge K. Explaining the social gradient in coronary heart disease: comparing relative and absolute risk approaches. *J Epidemiol Community Health*. 2006;60(5):436-441. http://jech.bmj.com/cgi/reprint/60/5/maxtoshow=&HITS=10&hits=10&RESULTFORMAT=&andorexactfulltext=and&searchid=1&FIRSTINDEX=0&sortspec=relevance&volume=60&firstpage=436&resourcetype=HWCIT. Published May 2006. Accessed May 15, 2007.

Rutledge T, Reis SE, Olson M, et al. Socioeconomic status variables predict cardiovascular disease risk factors and prospective mortality risk among women with chest pain: the WISE study. *Behav Modif*. 2003;27(1):54-67.

Centers for Disease Control and Prevention. Cigarette Smoking Among Adults—United States, 2002. *MMWR*. 2004;53(20):427-431. http://www.cdc.gov/mmwr/preview/mmwrhtml/mm5320a2.htm. Published May 28, 2004. Accessed May 15, 2007.

Phillipson EA. Sleep apnea. In: Kasper DL, Braunwald E, Fauci AS, Hauser SL, Longo DL, Jameson JL, eds. *Harrison's Principles of Internal Medicine*. 16th ed. New York, NY: McGraw-Hill; 2005:1574.

How much sleep do we really need? National Sleep Foundation Web site. http://www.sleepfoundation.org/site/c.huIXKjM0IxF/b.2464493/apps/nl/content3.asp?content_id={E87FBE34-71FC-4892-A5D0-40FD978BEEBB}&notoc=1. Accessed April 2, 2007.

Summary of findings: 2005 sleep in America poll. National Sleep Foundation Web site. http://www.sleepfoundation.org/atf/cf/%7BF6BF2668-A1B4-4FE8-8D1A-A5D39340D9CB%7D/2005_summary_of_findings.pdf. Published March 29, 2005. Accessed February 9, 2007.

Healthy sleep tips. National Sleep Foundation Web site. http://www.sleepfoundation.org/site/c.huIXKjM0IxF/b.2419247/k.BCB0/Healthy_Sleep_Tips.htm. Copyright 2007. Accessed September 25, 2007.

Gangwisch JE, Heymsfield SB, Boden-Albala B, et al. Short sleep duration as a risk factor for hypertension: analyses of the first National Health and Nutrition Examination Survey. *Hypertension*. 2006;47(5):833-839. http://hyper.ahajournals.org/cgi/

reprint/47/5/833. Published May 2006. Accessed May 15, 2007.

Sharma A, Bordowitz R. Emphasizing the connection between diet, obesity, and cardiovascular disease through health screenings at the East New York Food Co-op. Talk presented at: American Public Health Association 2007 Annual Meeting and Expo; November 3-7, 2007; Washington, DC. http://apha.confex.com/apha/135am/techprogram/paper_150092.htm. Accessed December 14, 2007.

Price S, Sephton J. Health promotion. It's all at the shopping co-op. Interview by Cath Jackson. *Health Visit*. 1992;65(10):372-373.

Harralson TL, Emig JC, Polansky M, Walker RE, Cruz JO, Garcia-Leeds C. Un Corazón Saludable: factors influencing outcomes of an exercise program designed to impact cardiac and metabolic risks among urban Latinas. *J Community Health*. 2007;32(6):401-412.

Rimmer JH, Nicola T, Riley B, Creviston T. Exercise training for African Americans with disabilities residing in difficult social environments. *Am J Prev Med*. 2002;23(4):290-295.

Newest version of "the pill" confers same stroke risk as old pill. American Heart Association Web site. http://www.americanheart.org/presenter.jhtml?identifier=3000741. Published February 13, 2002. Accessed May 15, 2007.

Grodstein F, Manson JE, Stampfer MJ. Hormone therapy and coronary heart disease: the role of time since menopause and age at hormone initiation. *J Womens Health (Larchmt)*. 2006;15(1):35-44.

Facts About Menopausal Hormone Therapy. Bethesda, MD: National Heart, Lung, and Blood Institute, US Dept of Health and Human Services; 2005. NIH publication 05-5200. http://www.nhlbi.nih.gov/health/women/pht_facts.pdf. Revised June 2005. Accessed April 11, 2007.

Manson JE, Hsia J, Johnson KC, et al. Estrogen plus progestin and the risk of coronary heart disease. *N Engl J Med*. 2003;349(6):523-534. http://content.nejm.org/cgi/reprint/349/6/523.pdf. Published August 7, 2003. Accessed May 15, 2007.

Klaiber EL, Vogel W, Rako S. A critique of the Women's Health Initiative hormone therapy study. *Fertil Steril*. 2005;84:1589-1601.

Menopause. In: Carlson KJ, Eisenstat SA, Ziporyn T, eds. *The New Harvard Guide to Women's Health*. Cambridge, MA: Harvard University Press; 2004:374-377.

Dietary supplement fact sheet: folate. Office of Dietary Supplements Web site. http://ods.od.nih.gov/factsheets/folate.asp. Updated August 22, 2005. Accessed April 5, 2007.

Mosca L, Appel LJ, Benjamin EJ, et al. Evidence-based guidelines for cardiovascular disease prevention in women. *Circulation*. 2004;109(5):672-693. http://circ.ahajournals.org/cgi/reprint/109/5/672. Published February 10, 2004. Accessed May 15, 2007.

Ridker PM, Buring JE, Rifai N, Cook NR. Development and validation of improved algorithms for the assessment of global cardiovascular risk in women: the Reynolds Risk Score. *JAMA*. 2007;297(6):611-619. http://jama.ama-assn.org/cgi/reprint/297/6/611. Published February 14, 2007. Accessed May 15, 2007.

Mieres JH, Shaw LJ, Arai A, et al. Role of noninvasive testing in the clinical evaluation of women with suspected coronary artery disease: consensus statement from the Cardiac Imaging Committee, Council on Clinical Cardiology, and the Cardiovascular Imaging and Intervention Committee, Council on Cardiovascular Radiology and Intervention, American Heart Association. *Circulation*. 2005;111:682-696. http://circ.ahajournals.org/cgi/reprint/111/5/682. Published February 8, 2005. Accessed May 15, 2007.

Achenbach S. Computed tomography coronary angiography. *J Am Coll Cardiol*. 2006;48(10):1919-1928.

Paul AK, Nabi HA. Gated myocardial perfusion SPECT: basic principles, technical aspects, and clinical applications. *J Nucl Med Technol*. 2004;32(4):179-187. http://tech.snmjournals.org/cgi/reprint/32/4/179. Published December 2004. Accessed May 15, 2007.

How the heart works. National Heart,

Lung, and Blood Institute Web site. http://www.nhlbi.nih.gov/health/dci/Diseases/Hf/HF_HowHeartWorks.html. Accessed April 16, 2007.

What is heart failure? National Heart, Lung, and Blood Institute Web site. http://www.nhlbi.nih.gov/health/dci/Diseases/Hf/HF_WhatIs.html. Published June 2007. Accessed October 24, 2007.

Congestive heart failure. In: Carlson KJ, Eisenstat SA, Ziporyn T, eds. *The New Harvard Guide to Women's Health*. Cambridge, MA: Harvard University Press; 2004:161-162.

Hunt SA. Cardiac transplantation and prolonged assisted circulation. In: Kasper DL, Braunwald E, Fauci AS, Hauser SL, Longo DL, Jameson JL, eds. *Harrison's Principles of Internal Medicine*. 16th ed. New York, NY: McGraw-Hill; 2005:1378-1380.

What is an arrhythmia? National Heart, Lung, and Blood Institute Web site. http://www.nhlbi.nih.gov/health/dci/Diseases/arr/arr_whatis.html. Published May 2007. Accessed October 24, 2007.

Arrhythmia. In: Carlson KJ, Eisenstat SA, Ziporyn T, eds. *The New Harvard Guide to Women's Health*. Cambridge, MA: Harvard University Press; 2004:57-59.

Sudden cardiac arrest. National Heart, Lung, and Blood Institute Web site. http://www.nhlbi.nih.gov/health/dci/Diseases/scda/scda_whatis.html. Published August 2006. Accessed April 17, 2007.

Myerburg RI, Castellanos A. Cardiovascular collapse, cardiac arrest, and sudden cardiac death. In: Kasper DL, Braunwald E, Fauci AS, Hauser SL, Longo DL, Jameson JL, eds. *Harrison's Principles of Internal Medicine*. 16th ed. New York, NY: McGraw-Hill; 2005:1618-1624.

Sirois BC, Burg MM. Negative emotion and coronary heart disease: a review. *Behav Modif*. 2003;27(1):83-102.

Taylor, CB, Youngblood ME, Catellier D, et al. Effects of antidepressant medication on morbidity and mortality in depressed patients after myocardial infarction. *Arch Gen Psychiatry*. 2005;62(7):792-798. http://archpsyc.ama-assn.org/cgi/reprint/62/7/792. Published July 2005. Accessed May 15, 2007.

Glassman AH, Bigger JT Jr.

Antidepressants in coronary heart disease: SSRIs reduce depression, but do they save lives? *JAMA.* 2007;297(4):411-412.

Mosca L, Mochari H, Christian A, et al. National study of women's awareness, preventive action, and barriers to cardiovascular health. *Circulation.* 2006;113(4):525-534. http://circ.ahajournals.org/cgi/reprint/113/4/525. Published January 31, 2006. Accessed May 15, 2007.

Heart disease deaths in American women decline: 17,000 fewer women died of heart disease; awareness continues to climb. National Institutes of Health Web site. http://www.nih.gov/news/pr/feb2007/nhlbi-01.htm. Published February 1, 2007. Accessed February 5, 2007.

STROKE

Meadows M. Brain attack: a look at stroke prevention and treatment. *FDA Consumer.* 2005;39(2):20-27. http://www.fda.gov/fdac/features/2005/205_stroke.html. Published March-April 2005. Accessed June 12, 2007.

Smith WS, Johnston SC, Easton JD. Cerebrovascular diseases. In: Kasper DL, Braunwald E, Fauci AS, Hauser SL, Longo DL, Jameson JL, eds. *Harrison's Principles of Internal Medicine.* 16th ed. New York, NY: McGraw-Hill; 2005:2372-2393.

National Institute of Neurological Disorders and Stroke. *Stroke: Hope Through Research.* Bethesda, MD: National Institute of Neurological Disorders and Stroke, US Dept of Health and Human Services; 2007. NIH publication 99-2222. http://www.ninds.nih.gov/disorders/stroke/detail_stroke.htm#90111105. Updated October 19, 2007. Accessed October 25, 2007.

National Institute of Neurological Disorders and Stroke. *Brain Basics: Preventing Stroke.* Bethesda, MD: National Institute of Neurological Disorders and Stroke, US Dept of Health and Human Services; 2007. NIH publication 04-3440b. http://www.ninds.nih.gov/disorders/stroke/preventing_stroke.htm#Risk%20Factors. Updated October 11, 2007. Accessed October 25, 2007.

Adams HP Jr, del Zoppo G, Alberts MJ, et al. Guidelines for the early management of adults with ischemic stroke: a guideline from the American Heart Association/American Stroke Association Stroke Council, Clinical Cardiology Council, Cardiovascular Radiology and Intervention Council, and the Atherosclerotic Peripheral Vascular Disease and Quality of Care Outcomes in Research Interdisciplinary Working Groups: the American Academy of Neurology affirms the value of this guideline as an educational tool for neurologists. *Stroke.* 2007;38(5):1655-1711. http://stroke.ahajournals.org/cgi/reprint/38/5/1655. Published May 2007. Accessed June 12, 2007.

Johnston SC, Nguyen-Huynh MN, Schwarz ME, et al. National Stroke Association guidelines for the management of transient ischemic attacks. *Ann Neurol.* 2006;60(3):301-313. http://www3.interscience.wiley.com/cgi-bin/fulltext/112750592/PDFSTART. Published September 2006. Accessed June 12, 2007.

Public stroke prevention guidelines. National Stroke Association Web site. http://www.stroke.org/site/PageServer?pagename=PREVENT. Accessed June 14, 2007.

Towfighi A, Saver JL, Engelhardt R, Ovbiagele B. A midlife stroke surge among women in the United States. *Neurology.* 2007;69(20):1898-1904.

Menopause. American Heart Association Web site. http://www.americanheart.org/presenter.jhtml?identifier=4658. Published 2007. Accessed June 22, 2007.

Pines A, Bornstein NM, Shapira I. Menopause and ischaemic stroke: basic, clinical and epidemiological considerations. The role of hormone replacement. *Hum Reprod Update.* 2002;8(2):161-168. http://humupd.oxfordjournals.org/cgi/reprint/8/2/161. Published March-April 2002. Accessed June 22, 2007.

Pleis JR, Lethbridge-Çejku M. Summary health statistics for U.S. adults: National Health Interview Survey, 2005. National Center for Health Statistics. *Vital Health Stat* 2006; 10(232):17-18. http://www.cdc.gov/nchs/data/series/sr_10/sr10_232.pdf. Published December 2006. Accessed June 22, 2007.

National Stroke Association. *Women in Your Life.* Centennial, CO: National Stroke Association. http://www.stroke.org/site/DocServer/women05.pdf?docID=881. Accessed June 14, 2007.

Herning RI, Better WE, Tate K, Cadet JL. Marijuana abusers are at increased risk for stroke. Preliminary evidence from cerebrovascular perfusion data. *Ann NY Acad Sci.* 2001;939:413-415.

Stroke. In: Carlson KJ, Eisenstat SA, Ziporyn T, eds. *The New Harvard Guide to Women's Health.* Cambridge, MA: Harvard University Press; 2004:576-579.

Chan WS, Ray J, Wai EK, Ginsburg S, Hannah ME, Corey PN, Ginsberg JS. Risk of stroke in women exposed to low-dose oral contraceptives: a critical evaluation of the evidence. *Arch Intern Med.* 2004;164(7):741-747. http://archinte.ama-assn.org/cgi/reprint/164/7/741. Published April 12, 2004. Accessed June 22, 2007.

Roederer MW, Blackwell JC. FPIN's clinical inquiries. Risks and benefits of combination contraceptives. *Am Fam Physician.* 2006;74(11):1915-1916. http://www.aafp.org/afp/20061201/fpin.html. Published December 1, 2006. Accessed June 22, 2007.

Ortho Evra: important safety information. Ortho Evra Web site. http://www.orthoevra.com/html/pevr/safety.jsp;jsessionid=IAJYO4EEQ0VXKCQPCCEDC0YKB2IIWNSC. Updated May 2007. Accessed July 26, 2007.

National Heart, Lung, and Blood Institute. *Facts About Menopausal Hormone Therapy.* Bethesda, MD: National Heart, Lung, and Blood Institute, US Dept of Health and Human Services; 2005. NIH publication 05-5200. http://www.nhlbi.nih.gov/health/women/pht_facts.pdf. Revised June 2005. Accessed April 11, 2007.

National Institute of Neurological Disorders and Stroke. *Cerebral Aneurysm Fact Sheet.* Bethesda, MD: National Institute of Neurological Disorders and Stroke, US Dept of Health and Human Services; 2007. NIH publication 05-5505. http://www.ninds.nih.gov/disorders/cerebral_aneurysm/detail_cerebral_aneurysm.htm. Updated August 3, 2007. Accessed October 25, 2007.

US National Library of Medicine, National Institutes of Health. Stroke. MedlinePlus Medical Encyclopedia Web site. http://www.nlm.nih.gov/medlineplus/ency/imagepages/17133.

htm. Updated March 15, 2007. Accessed July 27, 2007.

Lloyd-Jones DM, Leip EP, Larson MG, et al. Prediction of lifetime risk for cardiovascular disease by risk factor burden at 50 years of age. *Circulation.* 2006;113(6):791-798. http://circ.ahajournals.org/cgi/reprint/113/6/791. Published February 14, 2006. Accessed July 27, 2007.

Ridker PM, Cook NR, Lee IM, et al. A randomized trial of low-dose aspirin in the primary prevention of cardiovascular disease in women. *N Engl J Med.* 2005;352(13):1293-1304. http://content.nejm.org/cgi/reprint/352/13/1293.pdf. Published March 31, 2005. Accessed July 27, 2007.

Chan AT, Manson JE, Feskanich D, Stampfer MJ, Colditz GA, Fuchs CS. Long-term aspirin use and mortality in women. *Arch Intern Med.* 2007;167(6):562-572.

Smith WS. Safety of mechanical thrombectomy and intravenous tissue plasminogen activator in acute ischemic stroke. Results of the multi Mechanical Embolus Removal in Cerebral Ischemia (MERCI) trial, part I. *AJNR Am J Neuroradiol.* 2006;27(6):1177-1182. http://www.ajnr.org/cgi/reprint/27/6/1177. Published June-July 2006. Accessed July 27, 2007.

Broderick J, Connolly S, Feldmann E, et al. Guidelines for the management of spontaneous intracerebral hemorrhage in adults: 2007 update: a guideline from the American Heart Association/American Stroke Association Stroke Council, High Blood Pressure Research Council, and the Quality of Care and Outcomes in Research Interdisciplinary Working Group. *Stroke.* 2007;38(6):2001-2023. http://stroke.ahajournals.org/cgi/reprint/38/6/2001. Published June 2007. Accessed July 27, 2007.

National Institute of Neurological Disorders and Stroke. *Post-Stroke Rehabilitation Fact Sheet.* Bethesda, MD: National Institute of Neurological Disorders and Stroke, US Dept of Health and Human Services; 2007. NIH publication 02-4846. http://www.ninds.nih.gov/disorders/stroke/poststrokerehab.htm. Updated October 19, 2007. Accessed October 25, 2007.

Recovery after stroke: coping with emotions. National Stroke Association Web site. http://www.stroke.org/site/DocServer/NSAFactSheet_Emotions.pdf?docID=990. Published 2006. Accessed June 27, 2007.

Involuntary emotional expression disorder (IEED): explaining unpredictable emotional episodes. National Stroke Association Web site. http://www.stroke.org/site/PageServer?pagename=IEED. Updated October 30, 2006. Accessed June 21, 2007.

Teasell RW, Kalra L. What's new in stroke rehabilitation: back to basics. *Stroke.* 2005;36(2):215-217. http://stroke.ahajournals.org/cgi/reprint/36/2/215. Published February 2005. Accessed June 27, 2007.

Stroke myths. National Stroke Association Web site. http://www.stroke.org/site/PageServer?pagename=MYTH. Accessed June 21, 2007.

Stein J, Narendran K, McBean J, Krebs K, Hughes R. Electromyography-controlled exoskeletal upper-limb-powered orthosis for exercise training after stroke. *Am J Phys Med Rehabil.* 2007;86(4):255-261.

Rehabilitation therapy: robots and stroke. National Stroke Association Web site. http://www.stroke.org/site/PageServer?pagename=Robot. Accessed June 28, 2007.

CANCER

Leading causes of death in females, United States, 2004. Centers for Disease Control and Prevention Web site. http://www.cdc.gov/women/lcod.htm. Accessed October 15, 2007.

American Cancer Society. *Cancer Facts and Figures 2007.* Atlanta, GA: American Cancer Society; 2007. http://www.cancer.org/docroot/STT/content/STT_1x_Cancer_Facts__Figures_2007.asp. Accessed July 3, 2007.

Tumor. Dictionary of cancer terms. National Cancer Institute Web site. http://www.cancer.gov/Templates/db_alpha.aspx?CdrID=46634. Accessed August 6, 2007.

What you need to know about™ cancer: an overview. National Cancer Institute Web site. http://www.cancer.gov/cancertopics/wyntk/overview. October 4, 2006. Accessed August 6, 2007.

Frenkel EP. Overview of cancer. In: Porter RS, Kaplan JL, eds. *The*

Merck Manuals Online Medical Library: Home Edition for Patients and Caregivers. Online edition. Whitehouse Station, NJ: Merck Research Laboratories; 2007. http://www.merck.com/mmhe/print/sec15/ch180/ch180a.html. Revised February 2003. Accessed August 6, 2007.

Lymphoma. Dictionary of cancer terms. National Cancer Institute Web site. http://www.cancer.gov/Templates/db_alpha.aspx?print=1&cdrid=45368. Accessed August 6, 2007.

Mutation. Dictionary of cancer terms. National Cancer Institute Web site. http://www.cancer.gov/Templates/db_alpha.aspx?print=1&cdrid=46063. Accessed August 30, 2007.

Collins FS, Trent JM. Cancer genetics. In: Fauci AS, Braunwald E, Isselbacher KJ, Wilson JD, Martin JB, Kasper DL, Hauser SL, Longo DL, eds. *Harrison's Principles of Internal Medicine.* 14th ed. New York: NY: McGraw-Hill; 1998:514.

Genetics of breast and ovarian cancer (PDQ®). Health professional version. National Cancer Institute Web site. http://www.cancer.gov/cancertopics/pdq/genetics/breast-and-ovarian/healthprofessional. August 9, 2007. Accessed August 23, 2007.

American Cancer Society. *Breast Cancer Facts and Figures 2005-2006.* Atlanta, GA: American Cancer Society; 2007. http://www.cancer.org/docroot/STT/content/STT_1x_Breast_Cancer_Facts__Figures_2005-2006.asp. Accessed July 6, 2007.

American Cancer Society. *Cancer Prevention and Early Detection Facts and Figures 2007.* Atlanta, GA: American Cancer Society; 2007. http://www.cancer.org/docroot/STT/content/STT_1x_Cancer_Prevention_and_Early_Detection_Facts__Figures_2007.asp. Accessed July 3, 2007.

US Department of Health and Human Services. Chapter 7: cancer among adults from exposure to secondhand smoke. In: *The Health Consequences of Smoking: a Report of the Surgeon General.* Washington, DC: US Department of Health and Human Services, Centers for Disease Control and Prevention, National Center for Chronic Disease Prevention and Health Promotion, Office on Smoking and Health; 2006: 421-506. http://www.cdc.gov/tobacco/data_

statistics/sgr/sgr_2006/index.htm. Accessed August 9, 2007.

International Agency for Research on Cancer. *IARC Monographs on the Evaluation of Carcinogenic Risks to Humans. Volume 83: Tobacco Smoke and Involuntary Smoking.* Lyon, France: IARC Press; 2004:3-6. http://monographs.iarc.fr/ENG/Monographs/index.php. Accessed August 9, 2007.

US Department of Health and Human Services. Chapter 4: smoking cessation and respiratory cancers. Chapter 5: smoking cessation and nonrespiratory cancers. In: *The Health Benefits of Smoking Cessation: a Report of the Surgeon General.* Washington, DC: US Department of Health and Human Services, Centers for Disease Control and Prevention, National Center for Chronic Disease Prevention and Health Promotion, Office on Smoking and Health; 1990:103-186. http://profiles.nlm.nih.gov/NN/B/B/C/T/. Accessed August 28, 2007.

Corrao G, Bagnardi V, Zambon A, La Vecchia C. A meta-analysis of alcohol consumption and the risk of 15 diseases. *Prev Med.* 2004;38(5): 613-619. doi:10.1016/j.ypmed.2003.11.027. Accessed August 10, 2007.

Bagnardi V, Blangiardo M, La Vecchia C, Corrao G. A meta-analysis of alcohol drinking and cancer risk. *Br Jo Cancer* [serial online]. 2001; 85(11):1700-1705. Available from: Ebsco Academic Search Premier. Accessed August 10, 2007.

US Department of Health and Human Services and US Department of Agriculture. Chapter 9: alcoholic beverages. *Dietary Guidelines for All Americans, 2005.* 6th ed. Washington, DC: US Government Printing Office, 2005. http://www.health.gov/dietaryguidelines/dga2005/document/html/chapter9.htm. Accessed August 9, 2007.

Skin cancer: protect yourself from the sun. Centers for Disease Control and Prevention Web site. http://www.cdc.gov/cancer/skin/basic_info/howto.htm. Accessed August 10, 2007.

Menopausal hormone use and cancer: question and answers. National Cancer Institute Web site. http://www.cancer.gov/cancertopics/factsheet/Risk/menopausal-hormones.

October 4, 2006. Accessed August 10, 2007.

Menopausal hormone replacement therapy and cancer risk. American Cancer Society Web site. http://www.cancer.org/docroot/CRI/content/CRI_2_6x_Menopausal_Hormone_Replacement_Therapy_and_Cancer_Risk.asp. September 20, 2006. Accessed August 10, 2007.

Oral contraceptives and cancer risk: questions and answers. National Cancer Institute Web site. http://www.cancer.gov/cancertopics/factsheet/Risk/oral-contraceptives. May 4, 2006. Accessed August 10, 2007.

National Institutes of Health, National Cancer Institute, and National Institute of Environmental Health Sciences. *Cancer and the Environment.* Washington, DC: National Cancer Institute; 2003. http://www.cancer.gov/images/Documents/5d17e03e-b39f-4b40-a214-e9e9099c4220/Cancer%20and%20the%20Environment.pdf. Accessed August 13, 2007.

Harvard Center for Cancer Prevention. Volume I: human causes of cancer. Harvard Reports on Cancer Prevention Web site. http://www.hsph.harvard.edu/cancer/resources_materials/reports/HCCPreport_1prescription.htm. November 1996. Accessed August 10, 2007.

American Cancer Society. Special section: environmental pollutants and cancer. *Cancer Facts and Figures 2006.* Atlanta, GA: American Cancer Society; 2006:22-31. http://www.cancer.org/docroot/STT/content/STT_1x_Cancer_Facts__Figures_2006.asp. Accessed July 6, 2007.

American Cancer Society. Special section: cancers linked to infectious diseases. *Cancer Facts and Figures 2005.* Atlanta, GA: American Cancer Society; 2005:22-35. http://www.cancer.org/docroot/STT/content/STT_1x_Cancer_Facts__Figures_2005.asp. Accessed July 6, 2007.

Ries LAG, Melbert D, Krapcho M, et al, eds. *SEER Cancer Statistics Review, 1975-2004.* Bethesda, MD: National Cancer Institute; 2007. http://seer.cancer.gov/csr/1975_2004. Accessed August 8, 2007.

What you need to know about™ brain tumors. National Cancer Institute Web site. http://www.cancer.gov/

cancertopics/wyntk/brain. March 31, 2003. Accessed August 23, 2007.

What you need to know about™ liver cancer. National Cancer Institute Web site. http://www.cancer.gov/cancertopics/wyntk/liver. February 8, 2002. Updated September 16, 2002. Accessed August 23, 2007.

What you need to know about™ multiple myeloma. National Cancer Institute Web site. http://www.cancer.gov/cancertopics/wyntk/myeloma. March 18, 2005. Accessed August 23, 2007.

Symptoms of ovarian cancer. Ovarian Cancer National Alliance Web site. http://www.ovariancancer.org/index.cfm?fuseaction=Page.viewPage&pageId=521&parentID=473&nodeID=1. June 13, 2007. Accessed October 17, 2007.

What you need to know about™ thyroid cancer. National Cancer Institute Web site. http://www.cancer.gov/cancertopics/wyntk/thyroid. Accessed August 23, 2007.

Morris GJ, Naidu S, Topham AK, et al. Differences in breast carcinoma characteristics in newly diagnosed African-American and Caucasian patients: a single-institution compilation compared with the National Cancer Institute's Surveillance, Epidemiology, and End Results database [abstract]. *Cancer.* 2007;110(4):876-884. http://www.ncbi.nlm.nih.gov/sites/entrez?Db=pubmed&Cmd=ShowDetailView&TermToSearch=17620276&ordinalpos=11&itool=EntrezSystem2.PEntrez.Pubmed.Pubmed_ResultsPanel.Pubmed_RVDocSum. Accessed August 25, 2007.

Aliff T, Fury MG, Pfister DG. Symptoms and diagnosis of cancer. In: Porter RS, Kaplan JL, eds. *The Merck Manuals Online Medical Library: Home Edition for Patients and Caregivers.* Online edition. Whitehouse Station, NJ: Merck Research Laboratories; 2007. http://www.merck.com/mmhe/sec15/ch181/ch181a.html. Revised October 2006. Accessed August 13, 2007.

The Pap test: questions and answers. National Cancer Institute Web site. http://www.cancer.gov/cancertopics/factsheet/Detection/Pap-test. March 2007. Accessed October 18, 2007.

Colorectal cancer: health professionals' facts on screening. Centers for

Disease Control and Prevention Web site. http://www.cdc.gov/cancer/colorectal/basic_info/screening/guidelines.htm. July 2000. Accessed August 14, 2007.

How is colorectal cancer found? American Cancer Society Web site. http://www.cancer.org/docroot/CRI/content/CRI_2_2_3X_How_is_colorectal_cancer_found.asp. April 18, 2007. Accessed October 15, 2007.

Stage. Dictionary of cancer terms. National Cancer Institute Web site. http://www.cancer.gov/Templates/db_alpha.aspx?CdrID=45885. Accessed August 6, 2007.

Chabner BA, Thompson EC. Prevention and treatment of cancer. In: Porter RS, Kaplan JL, eds. *The Merck Manuals Online Medical Library: Home Edition for Patients and Caregivers*. Online edition. Whitehouse Station, NJ: Merck Research Laboratories; 2007. http://www.merck.com/mmhe/sec15/ch182/ch182a.html. Revised August 2007. Accessed August 28, 2007.

Questions and answers about chemotherapy. *Chemotherapy and You: Support for People with Cancer*. National Cancer Institute Web site. http://www.cancer.gov/cancertopics/chemotherapy-and-you/page2. June 29, 2007. Accessed August 14, 2007.

Radiation therapy for cancer: questions and answers. National Cancer Institute Web site. http://www.cancer.gov/cancertopics/factsheet/Therapy/radiation. August 25, 2004. Accessed August 14, 2007.

Biological therapy. National Cancer Institute Web site. http://www.cancer.gov/cancertopics/biologicaltherapy. January 14, 2004. Accessed August 14, 2007.

Hormone therapy: cancer treatment for certain hormone-sensitive cancers. Mayo Clinic Web site. http://www.mayoclinic.com/health/cancer-treatment/CA00039. March 6, 2006. Accessed October 15, 2007.

Understanding CAM. National Cancer Institute, Office of Cancer Complementary and Alternative Medicine Web site. http://www.cancer.gov/CAM/health_understanding.html. October 18, 2005. Accessed August 26, 2007.

Thinking about complementary and alternative medicine: a guide for people with cancer. National Center for Complementary and Alternative Medicine Web site. http://www.cancer.gov/cancertopics/thinking-about-CAM. April 2005. Accessed August 14, 2007.

Developing effective and efficient treatments. *The Nation's Investment in Cancer Research: A Plan and Budget Proposal for Fiscal Year 2008*. National Cancer Institute Web site. http://plan.cancer.gov/strategicobjectives5.shtml. Accessed August 30, 2007.

Coping with physical and emotional changes: how does cancer treatment affect fertility? American Cancer Society Web site. http://www.cancer.org/docroot/MBC/content/MBC_2_3X_How_Can_I_Preserve_My_Fertility_Before_or_During_Cancer_Treatment.asp?sitearea=MBChttp://www.cancer.org/docroot/MBC/content/MBC_2_3X_How_Does_Cancer_Treatment_Affect_Fertility.asp?sitearea=MBC. Accessed August 20, 2007.

Coping with physical and emotional changes: how can I preserve my fertility before or during cancer treatment? American Cancer Society Web site. http://www.cancer.org/docroot/MBC/content/MBC_2_3X_How_Can_I_Preserve_My_Fertility_Before_or_During_Cancer_Treatment.asp?sitearea=MBC. Accessed August 20, 2007.

Coping with physical and emotional changes: other frequently asked questions. American Cancer Society Web site. http://www.cancer.org/docroot/MBC/content/MBC_2_3X_Other_Frequently_Asked_Questions.asp?sitearea=MBC. Accessed August 20, 2007.

Coping with physical and emotional changes: is pregnancy safe after cancer? American Cancer Society Web site. http://www.cancer.org/docroot/MBC/content/MBC_2_3X_Is_Pregnancy_Safe_After_Cancer.asp?sitearea=MBC. Accessed August 20, 2007.

Fatigue (PDQ®): patient version. National Cancer Society Web site. http://www.cancer.gov/cancertopics/pdq/supportivecare/fatigue/patient. July 16, 2007. Accessed August 20, 2007.

Pain (PDQ®): Health Professional Version. National Cancer Institute Web site http://www.cancer.gov/cancertopics/pdq/supportivecare/pain/healthprofessional. July 19, 2007. Accessed August 20, 2007.

Pain control: a guide for people with cancer and their families. American Cancer Society Web site. http://www.cancer.org/docroot/MIT/content/MIT_7_2x_Pain_Control_A_Guide_for_People_with_Cancer_and_Their_Families.asp. Accessed August 21, 2007.

Meisler JG. Toward optimal health: the experts discuss the routine care of women with cancer. *J Women Health* [serial online]. 2003;12(4):315-320. Available from: Ebsco Academic Search Premier. Accessed August 16, 2007.

The emotional impact of a cancer diagnosis. American Cancer Society Web site. http://www.cancer.org/docroot/MBC/content/MBC_4_1X_The_Emotional_Impact_of_A_Cancer_Diagnosis.asp?sitearea=MBC. March 15, 2007. Accessed August 21, 2007.

Facing forward: life after cancer treatment. National Cancer Institute Web site. http://www.cancer.gov/cancertopics/life-after-treatment. September 1, 2006. Accessed August 26, 2007.

TYPE 2 DIABETES

National Institute of Diabetes and Digestive and Kidney Diseases. National Diabetes Statistics fact sheet: general information and national estimates on diabetes in the United States, 2005. Bethesda, MD: US Dept of Health and Human Services, National Institutes of Health, 2005. NIH Publication 06-3892. http://diabetes.niddk.nih.gov/dm/pubs/statistics/index.htm. Accessed September 1, 2007.

American Diabetes Association. Standards of medical care in diabetes—2008. *Diabetes Care*. 2008;31(suppl 1):12S-54S.

National Institute of Diabetes and Digestive and Kidney Diseases. *Diabetes Overview*. Bethesda, MD: US Dept of Health and Human Services, National Institutes of Health, 2006. NIH Publication 06-3873. http://diabetes.niddk.nih.gov/dm/pubs/overview/index.htm. Accessed September 1, 2007.

Department of Health and Human Services. *National Agenda for Public Health Action: The National Public Health Initiative on Diabetes and Women's Health*. Atlanta, GA: Department of Health and Human Services, Centers for Disease Control and Prevention; 2003.

National Institute of Diabetes and Digestive and Kidney Diseases. *Am I at Risk for Type 2 Diabetes?* Bethesda, MD: US Dept of Health and Human Services, National Institutes of Health, 2006. NIH Publication 07-4805. http://diabetes.niddk.nih.gov/dm/pubs/riskfortype2/index.htm. Accessed September 1, 2007.

National Diabetes Education Program. *Small Steps, Big Rewards. Your Game Plan to Prevent Type 2 Diabetes.* NIH Publication 06-5334. http://www.ndep.nih.gov/campaigns/SmallSteps/SmallSteps_yourgameplan.htm. Revised October 2006. Accessed September 1, 2007.

Metabolic syndrome. National Heart, Lung, and Blood Institute Web site. http://www.nhlbi.nih.gov/health/dci/Diseases/ms/ms_whatis.html. April 2007. Accessed September 1, 2007.

National Institute of Diabetes and Digestive and Kidney Diseases. *Your Guide to Diabetes: Type 1 and Type 2.* Bethesda, MD: US Dept of Health and Human Services, National Institutes of Health, 2006. NIH Publication 08-4016. http://diabetes.niddk.nih.gov/dm/pubs/type1and2/index.htm. Accessed September 1, 2007.

National Institute of Diabetes and Digestive and Kidney Diseases. *Diagnosis of Diabetes.* Bethesda, MD: US Dept of Health and Human Services, National Institutes of Health, January 2005. NIH Publication 05-4642. http://diabetes.niddk.nih.gov/dm/pubs/diagnosis/index.htm. Accessed September 1, 2007.

American Diabetes Association. Diagnosis and classification of diabetes mellitus. *Diabetes Care.* 2007;30(suppl 1):42S-47S.

Glucose. Lab Tests Online® Web site. http://www.labtestsonline.org/understanding/analytes/glucose/test.html. Reviewed March 2005. Accessed September 1, 2007.

Brown JS, Wessells J, Chancellor MB, et al. Urologic complications of diabetes. *Diabetes Care.* 2005;28(1):177-185.

Harmel AP, Mathur R. *Davidson's Diabetes Mellitus: Diagnosis and Treatment.* 5th ed. Philadelphia, PA: Saunders; 2004.

Poirier LM, Coburn KM. *Women and Diabetes: Staying Healthy in Body, Mind, and Spirit.* 2nd ed. Alexandria, VA: American Diabetes Association; 2000.

American Diabetes Association. Preconception care of women with diabetes. *Diabetes Care.* 2004;27(suppl 1):76S-78S.

National Diabetes Education Program. *4 Steps to Control Your Diabetes. For Life.* http://www.ndep.nih.gov/diabetes/control/4Steps.htm. NIH Publication 06-5492. Published October 2006. Accessed September 1, 2007.

American Diabetes Association. Nutrition recommendations and interventions for diabetes. *Diabetes Care.* 2007;30(suppl 1):48S-65S.

Diabetes medications. In: Centers for Disease Control and Prevention. *Working Together to Manage Diabetes: A Guide for Pharmacy, Podiatry, Optometry, and Dental Professionals.* Atlanta, GA: U.S. Department of Health and Human Services, Public Health Service, Centers for Disease Control and Prevention, National Center for Chronic Disease Prevention and Health Promotion, 2007. http://www.ndep.nih.gov/diabetes/WTMD/index.htm. Accessed September 2, 2007.

All about your blood glucose for people with type 2 diabetes (Diabetes and cardiovascular disease toolkit No. 4). American Diabetes Association Web site. http://www.diabetes.org/uedocuments/04-Blood-Sugar.pdf. March 2004. Accessed September 1, 2007.

National Diabetes Education Program. *The Power to Control Diabetes Is in Your Hands.* NIH Publication 00-4849. http://www.ndep.nih.gov/campaigns/Power/control_diabetes.htm. Revised September 2005. Accessed September 1, 2007.

National Institute of Diabetes and Digestive and Kidney Diseases. *Hypoglycemia.* Bethesda, MD: US Dept of Health and Human Services, National Institutes of Health, 2003. NIH Publication 03-3926. http://diabetes.niddk.nih.gov/dm/pubs/hypoglycemia/index.htm. Accessed September 1, 2007.

National Institute of Diabetes and Digestive and Kidney Diseases. *Prevent Diabetes Problems: Keep Your Diabetes Under Control.* Bethesda, MD: US Dept of Health and Human Services, National Institutes of Health, 2007. NIH Publication 07-4349. http://diabetes.niddk.nih.

gov/dm/pubs/complications_control/index.htm. Accessed September 1, 2007.

Recognizing and handling depression for people with diabetes (Diabetes and cardiovascular disease toolkit No. 15). American Diabetes Association Web site. http://www.diabetes.org/uedocuments/15-Depression.pdf. March 2004. Accessed September 2, 2007.

Nichols GA, Brown JB. Unadjusted and adjusted prevalence of diagnosed depression in type 2 diabetes. *Diabetes Care.* 2003;26(3):744-749.

AUTOIMMUNE DISEASES

The Autoimmune Diseases Coordinating Committee. *Progress in Autoimmune Diseases Research.* Bethesda, MD: National Institutes of Health, US Dept of Health and Human Services; 2005. NIH publication 05-5140. http://www.niaid.nih.gov/dait/pdf/ADCC_Final.pdf. Published March 2005. Accessed February 23, 2007.

National Institute of Arthritis and Musculoskeletal and Skin Diseases. *Questions and Answers about Autoimmunity.* Bethesda, MD: National Institute of Arthritis and Musculoskeletal and Skin Diseases, US Dept of Health and Human Services; 2002.

Perkel J. Scientists spot key autoimmune disease genes [news release]. Norwalk, CT: HealthDay; January 22, 2007. http://www.healthday.com/Article.asp?AID=601164. Accessed February 23, 2007.

National Cancer Institute, National Institute of Allergy and Infectious Diseases. *Understanding the Immune System: How It Works.* Bethesda, MD: National Institutes of Health, US Dept of Health and Human Services; 2003. NIH publication 03-5423. http://www.niaid.nih.gov/publications/immune/the_immune_system.pdf. Published September 2003. Accessed February 23, 2007.

American Association for Clinical Chemistry. Autoantibodies. Lab Tests Online Web site. http://www.labtestsonline.org/understanding/analytes/autoantibodies/glance.html. Reviewed April 17, 2007. Accessed November 16, 2007.

Autoimmune diseases in women: the facts. American Autoimmune Related

Diseases Association Web site. http://www.aarda.org/women.php. Accessed February 23, 2007.

US National Library of Medicine and National Institutes of Health. Autoimmune disorders. MedlinePlus Medical Encyclopedia Web site. http://www.nlm.nih.gov/medlineplus/ency/article/000816.htm. Updated May 27, 2007. Accessed November 16, 2007.

Fairweather D, Rose NR. Women and autoimmune diseases. *Emerg Infect Dis.* 2004;10(11):2005-2011. http://www.cdc.gov/ncidod/EID/vol10no11/pdfs/04-0367.pdf. Published November 2004. Accessed February 23, 2007.

American Association for Clinical Chemistry. Autoimmune disorders. Lab Tests Online Web site. http://www.labtestsonline.org/understanding/conditions/autoimmune.html. Reviewed March 11, 2007. Accessed November 20, 2007.

Walsh SJ, Rau LM. Autoimmune diseases: a leading cause of death among young and middle-aged women in the United States. *Am J Public Health.* 2000;90(9):1463-1466. http://www.ajph.org/cgi/reprint/90/9/1463. Published September 2000. Accessed February 23, 2007.

Part V. The immune system in health and disease. In: Janeway CA, Travers P, Walport M, Shlomchik MJ. *Immunobiology.* 5th ed. New York, NY: Garland Publishing; 2001. http://www.ncbi.nlm.nih.gov/books/bv.fcgi?rid=imm.part.1478. Published 2001. Accessed February 23, 2007.

Maharshak N, Brenner S. Gender differences in vesiculobullous autoimmune skin diseases. *SKINmed.* 2002;1(1):25-30. http://www.medscape.com/viewarticle/446352. Published January-February 2002. Accessed February 23, 2007.

Luborsky J. Endocrine autoimmunity. *InFocus.* 1998;6(1). American Autoimmune Related Diseases Association Web site. http://www.aarda.org/infocus_article.php?ID=20. Published 1998. Accessed March 1, 2007.

Criswell LA, Pfeiffer KA, Lum RF, et al. Analysis of families in the multiple autoimmune disease genetics consortium (MADGC) collection: the PTPN22 620W allele associates with multiple autoimmune phenotypes. *Am J Hum Genet.* 2005;76(4):561-571. http://www.pubmedcentral.nih.gov/picrender.fcgi?artid=1199294&blobtype=pdf. Published April 2005. Accessed March 1, 2007.

Scleroderma (systemic sclerosis). American College of Rheumatology Web site. http://www.rheumatology.org/public/factsheets/scler_new.asp? Updated June 2005. Accessed March 14, 2007.

Rose NR, Rasooly L, Saboori AM, Burek CL. Linking iodine with autoimmune thyroiditis. *Environ Health Perspect.* 1999;107(suppl 5):749-752. http://www.pubmedcentral.nih.gov/picrender.fcgi?artid=1566262&blobtype=pdf. Published October 1999. Accessed February 7, 2007.

Lupus. National Institutes of Health Web site. http://www.nih.gov/about/researchresultsforthepublic/Lupus.pdf. Accessed March 1, 2007.

Gershwin ME, Selmi C, Worman HJ, et al. Risk factors and comorbidities in primary biliary cirrhosis: a controlled interview-based study of 1032 patients. *Hepatology.* 2005;42(5):1194-1202. http://www3.interscience.wiley.com/cgi-bin/fulltext/112136238/PDFSTART. Published November 2005. Accessed March 1, 2007.

Smoking and the risk of rheumatoid arthritis: study shows significantly higher risk for the disease among current smokers with a classic genetic risk factor [press release]. American College of Rheumatology Web site. http://www.rheumatology.org/press/2004/rasmoke1004.asp?aud=prs. Published September 9, 2004. Accessed March 1, 2007.

National Institute of Arthritis and Musculoskeletal and Skin Diseases. *The Many Shades of Lupus: Information for Multicultural Communities.* Bethesda, MD: National Institute of Arthritis and Musculoskeletal and Skin Diseases, US Dept of Health and Human Services; 2001. NIH publication 01-4958. http://www.niams.nih.gov/Health_Info/Lupus/shades_of_lupus.pdf. Published August 2001. Accessed March 1, 2007.

Reveille JD. Ethnicity and race and systemic sclerosis: how it affects susceptibility, severity, antibody genetics, and clinical manifestations. *Curr Rheumatol Rep.* 2003;5(2):160-167.

Mayes MD. Race, scleroderma, and survival: why is there a difference? *J Rheumatol.* 2005;32(10):1873-1874. http://www.jrheum.com/subscribers/05/10/1873.html. Published October 2005. Accessed March 1, 2007.

NINDS antiphospholipid syndrome information page. National Institute of Neurological Disorders and Stroke Web site. http://www.ninds.nih.gov/disorders/antiphospholipid.htm. Updated November 22, 2006. Accessed March 1, 2007.

US National Library of Medicine and National Institutes of Health. Autoimmune hepatitis. MedlinePlus Medical Encyclopedia Web site. http://www.nlm.nih.gov/medlineplus/ency/article/000245.htm. Updated July 25, 2006. Accessed February 23, 2007.

National Institute of Diabetes and Digestive and Kidney Diseases. *Crohn's Disease.* Bethesda, MD: National Institute of Diabetes and Digestive and Kidney Diseases, US Dept of Health and Human Services; 2005. NIH publication 06-3410. http://digestive.niddk.nih.gov/ddiseases/pubs/crohns/index.htm#symp. Published February 2006. Accessed May 2, 2007.

Scully C, Shotts R. ABC of oral health: mouth ulcers and other causes of orofacial soreness and pain. *BMJ.* 2000;321(7254):162-165. http://www.bmj.com/cgi/reprint/321/7254/162. Published July 15, 2000. Accessed May 2, 2007.

US National Library of Medicine and National Institutes of Health. Graves' disease. MedlinePlus Medical Encyclopedia Web site. http://www.nlm.nih.gov/medlineplus/ency/article/000358.htm. Updated August 8, 2006. Accessed February 23, 2007.

US National Library of Medicine and National Institutes of Health. Chronic thyroiditis (Hashimoto's disease). MedlinePlus Medical Encyclopedia Web site. http://www.nlm.nih.gov/medlineplus/ency/article/000371.htm. Updated May 12, 2006. Accessed February 23, 2007.

US National Library of Medicine and National Institutes of Health.

Multiple sclerosis. MedlinePlus Medical Encyclopedia Web site. http://www.nlm.nih.gov/medlineplus/ency/article/000737.htm. Updated August 6, 2007. Accessed November 27, 2007.

National Institute of Neurological Disorders and Stroke. *Myasthenia Gravis Fact Sheet*. Bethesda, MD: National Institute of Neurological Disorders and Stroke, US Dept of Health and Human Services; 2005. NIH publication 99-768. http://www.ninds.nih.gov/disorders/myasthenia_gravis/detail_myasthenia_gravis.htm#83993153. Updated November 19, 2007. Accessed November 27, 2007.

US National Library of Medicine and National Institutes of Health. Primary biliary cirrhosis. MedlinePlus Medical Encyclopedia Web site. http://www.nlm.nih.gov/medlineplus/ency/article/000282.htm. Updated May 4, 2006. Accessed March 14, 2007.

Osteoporosis and arthritis: two common but different conditions. National Institutes of Health Osteoporosis and Related Bone Diseases—National Resource Center Web site. http://www.niams.nih.gov/Health_Info/Bone/Osteoporosis/Conditions_Behaviors/osteoporosis_arthritis.pdf. Revised May 2006. Accessed March 7, 2007.

US National Library of Medicine and National Institutes of Health. Rheumatoid arthritis. MedlinePlus Medical Encyclopedia Web site. http://www.nlm.nih.gov/medlineplus/ency/article/000431.htm. Updated July 27, 2007. Accessed November 27, 2007.

Bathon J. Anti-TNF Therapy for the treatment of rheumatoid arthritis. The Johns Hopkins Arthritis Center Web site. http://www.hopkins-arthritis.som.jhmi.edu/rheumatoid/tnf.html. Accessed February 23, 2007.

US National Library of Medicine and National Institutes of Health. Scleroderma. MedlinePlus Medical Encyclopedia Web site. http://www.nlm.nih.gov/medlineplus/ency/article/000429.htm. Updated April 26, 2007. Accessed November 27, 2007.

US National Library of Medicine and National Institutes of Health. Sjogren syndrome. MedlinePlus Medical Encyclopedia Web site. http://www.nlm.nih.gov/medlineplus/ency/article/000456.htm. Updated May 27, 2007. Accessed November 27, 2007.

Marrack P, Kappler J, Kotzin BL. Autoimmune disease: why and where it occurs. *Nat Med*. 2001;7(8):899-905. http://www.nature.com/nm/journal/v7/n8/pdf/nm0801_899.pdf. Published August 1, 2001. Accessed February 23, 2007.

National Institute of Arthritis and Musculoskeletal and Skin Diseases. *Handout on Health: Systemic Lupus Erythematosus*. Bethesda, MD: National Institute of Arthritis and Musculoskeletal and Skin Diseases, US Dept of Health and Human Services; 2003. NIH publication 03-4178. http://www.niams.nih.gov/Health_Info/Lupus/systemic_lupus_erythematosus_hoh.pdf. Revised August 2003. Accessed May 2, 2007.

US National Library of Medicine and the National Institutes of Health. Ulcerative colitis. MedlinePlus Medical Encyclopedia Web site. http://www.nlm.nih.gov/medlineplus/ency/article/000250.htm. Updated October 13, 2006. Accessed March 1, 2007.

American Association for Clinical Chemistry. ANA. Lab Tests Online Web site. http://labtestsonline.org/understanding/analytes/ana/glance.html. Reviewed August 12, 2007. Accessed November 28, 2007.

American Association for Clinical Chemistry. Rheumatoid factor. Lab Tests Online Web site. http://labtestsonline.org/understanding/analytes/rheumatoid/sample.html. Reviewed September 30, 2006. Accessed March 7, 2007.

American Association for Clinical Chemistry. C-reactive protein. Lab Tests Online Web site. http://labtestsonline.org/understanding/analytes/crp/glance.html. Reviewed September 3, 2004. Accessed March 7, 2007.

American Association for Clinical Chemistry. ESR. Lab Tests Online Web site. http://labtestsonline.org/understanding/analytes/esr/glance.html. Reviewed May 3, 2006. Accessed March 7, 2007.

American Association for Clinical Chemistry. CCP. Lab Tests Online Web site. http://labtestsonline.org/understanding/analytes/ccp/glance.html. Reviewed January 15, 2005. Accessed May 2, 2007.

Tips for getting a proper diagnosis of an autoimmune disease. *InFocus*. 2002;10(2). American Autoimmune Related Diseases Association Web site. http://www.aarda.org/infocus_article.php?ID=15. Published June 2002. Accessed January 13, 2007.

Gordon C. Pregnancy and autoimmune diseases. *Best Pract Res Clin Rheumatol*. 2004;18(3):359-379.

Myasthenia gravis. UAB Health System Web site. http://www.health.uab.edu/15401/. Accessed March 12, 2007.

Definition. Society for Maternal-Fetal Medicine Web site. http://www.smfm.org/index.cfm?zone=info&nav=definition. Accessed May 3, 2007.

Antiphospholipid syndrome (aPL). UAB Health System Web site. http://www.health.uab.edu/15400. Accessed March 12, 2007.

What causes hypothyroidism? University of Maryland Medical Center Web site. http://www.umm.edu/patiented/articles/what_causes_hypothyroidism_000038_2.htm. Reviewed March 20, 2007. Accessed March 16, 2007.

Thyroiditis. New York Thyroid Center Web site. http://cpmcnet.columbia.edu/dept/thyroid/thyroiditis.html. Accessed March 16, 2007.

Pregnancy and rheumatic disease. American College of Rheumatology Web site. http://www.rheumatology.org/public/factsheets/pregnancy.asp. Published July 2006. Accessed March 16, 2007.

Ostensen M, Khamashta M, Lockshin M, et al. Anti-inflammatory and imunosuppressive drugs and reproduction. *Arthritis Res Ther*. 2006;8(3):209. http://arthritis-research.com/content/pdf/ar1957.pdf. Accessed November 28, 2007.

Pregnancy and lupus. Lupus Foundation of America Web site. http://www.lupus.org/education/brochures/pregnancy.html. Accessed May 2, 2007.

Megan EB, Magder LS, Petri M. Impact of the intensity and timing of lupus activity on pregnancy outcomes. Paper presented at: American College of Rheumatology 2003 Annual Scientific Meeting;

October 23-26, 2003; Orlando, FL. http://www.abstractsonline.com/viewer/viewAbstractPrintFriendly. asp?CKey={245E12AD-2A85-403D-A3CF-CF212AE4C43E}&SKey= {F980C599-8E5E-4ACC-AED1-11289B33DED0}&MKey={323AC1 9D-B4A8-4A76-8BAD-18A67410 BF79}&AKey={AA45DD66-F113-4CDD-8E62-01A05F613C0D}. Accessed November 28, 2007.

Hyperthyroidism and pregnancy. UAB Health Systems Web site. http://www.health.uab.edu/15452/. Accessed March 16, 2007.

Dunkin MA. Doctor says newly diagnosed scleroderma patients should avoid pregnancy for three years. Scleroderma Foundation Web site. http://www.scleroderma.org/medical/other_articles/Dunkin_2006. shtm. Updated November 21, 2007. Accessed November 28, 2007.

Multiple sclerosis and pregnancy. UAB Health Systems Web site. http://www.health.uab.edu/15430/. Accessed March 16, 2007.

Myasthenia gravis. UAB Health Systems Web site. http://www.health.uab.edu/15401/. Accessed March 12, 2007.

Willems JJ. Obstetric and gynecologic considerations of Sjogren's syndrome. Sjogren's Syndrome Foundation Web site. http://sjogrens.org/pdf/sjo_obgyn.pdf. Accessed March 16, 2007.

Czaja AJ. Autoimmune liver disease and rheumatic manifestations. *Curr Opin Rheumatol.* 2007;19(1):74-80. http://www.medscape.com/viewarticle/551531_1. Published January 2007. Accessed March 1, 2007.

Botoman VA, Bonner GF, Botoman DA. Management of inflammatory bowel disease. *Am Fam Physician.* 1998;57(1):57-68, 71-72. http://www.aafp.org/afp/980101ap/botoman. html. Published January 1, 1998. Accessed March 1, 2007.

Infertility in women. University of Maryland Medical Center Web site. http://www.umm.edu/patiented/articles/what_causes_female_infertility_000022_4.htm. Reviewed October 19, 2006. Accessed March 13, 2007.

Cihakova D. Autoimmune oophoritis. Johns Hopkins Medical Institutions Web site. http://autoimmune.pathology.jhmi.edu/diseases.cfm?sys temID=3&DiseaseID=19. Modified September 10, 2001. Accessed March 13, 2007.

How rheumatologists use chemotherapy. The Cleveland Clinic Web site. http://www.clevelandclinic.org/arthritis/treat/facts/chemo.htm. Published February 13, 2006. Accessed January 13, 2007.

Luborsky JL, Shatavi SV. Autoimmune ovarian failure. *InFocus.* 2004;12(3). American Autoimmune Related Diseases Association Web site. http://www.aarda.org/infocus_article. php?ID=25. Published September 2004. Accessed March 12, 2007.

Perspectives on the headlines: oral contraceptives in lupus. Lupus Research Institute Web site. http://www.lupusresearchinstitute.org/print. php?id=press/perspectives. Accessed March 14, 2007.

US National Library of Medicine and National Institutes of Health. Fibromyalgia. MedlinePlus Medical Encyclopedia Web site. http://www.nlm.nih.gov/medlineplus/ency/article/000427.htm. Updated May 3, 2006. Accessed March 1, 2007.

Krumholz HM. Lupus: atherosclerosis risk factor. Journal Watch Web site. http://cardiology.jwatch.org/cgi/content/full/2004/305/1. Published March 5, 2004. Accessed March 1, 2007.

What people with lupus need to know about osteoporosis. National Institutes of Health Osteoporosis and Related Bone Diseases—National Resource Center Web site. http://www.niams.nih.gov/Health_Info/Bone/Osteoporosis/Conditions_Behaviors/osteoporosis_lupus.pdf. Revised November 2006. Accessed March 1, 2007.

What is atherosclerosis? National Heart, Lung, and Blood Institute Web site. http://www.nhlbi.nih.gov/health/dci/Diseases/Atherosclerosis/Atherosclerosis_WhatIs.html. Published November 2007. Accessed November 28, 2007.

What is bone? National Institutes of Health Osteoporosis and Related Bone Diseases—National Resource Center Web site. http://www.niams. nih.gov/Health_Info/Bone/Bone_Health/what_is_bone.pdf. Revised August 2005. Accessed March 1, 2007.

What is autoimmunity? Johns Hopkins Medical Institutions Web site. http://autoimmune.pathology.jhmi.edu/ whatisautoimmunity.cfm. Modified July 10, 2006. Accessed March 1, 2007.

National Institute of Arthritis and Musculoskeletal and Skin Diseases. *Do I Have Lupus?* Bethesda, MD: National Institute of Arthritis and Musculoskeletal and Skin Diseases, US Dept of Health and Human Services; 2003. NIH publication 03-5321. http://www.niams.nih.gov/Portal_En_Espanol/Informacion_de_Salud/Lupus/tengo_lupus_espanol. pdf. Published March 2003. Accessed March 1, 2007.

National Institute of Arthritis and Musculoskeletal and Skin Diseases. *Questions and Answers about Vitiligo.* Bethesda, MD: National Institute of Arthritis and Musculoskeletal and Skin Diseases, US Dept of Health and Human Services; 2006. NIH publication 07-4909. http://www. niams.nih.gov/Health_Info/Vitiligo/vitiligo_qa.pdf. Revised October 2006. Accessed March 1, 2007.

Ladd V. Coping with autoimmunity. American Autoimmune Related Diseases Association Web site. http://www.aarda.org/coping_art.html. Published 2001. Accessed March 1, 2007.

BLOOD DISORDERS

What is blood? America's Blood Centers Web site. http://www. americasblood.org/go.cfm?do=Page. View&pid=11. Accessed September 14, 2007.

Frenkel EP. Biology of blood. In: Porter RS, Kaplan JL, eds. *The Merck Manuals Online Medical Library: Home Edition for Patients and Caregivers.* Online edition. Whitehouse Station, NJ: Merck Research Laboratories; 2007. http://www.merck.com/mmhe/sec14/ch169/ch169a.html. Revised August 2006. Accessed July 16, 2007.

Blood plasma. Medical Dictionary. Medline Plus Web site. http://www2. merriam-webster.com/cgi-bin/mwmednlm?book=Medical&va= blood%20plasma. Accessed September 21, 2007.

Bone marrow diseases. Medline Plus Web site. http://www.nlm.nih.gov/medlineplus/bonemarrowdiseases. html. October 22, 2007. Accessed November 8, 2007.

Ruscetti FW, Keller JR, Longo DL. Hematopoiesis. In: Fauci AS,

Braunwald E, Isselbacher KJ, Wilson JD, Martin JB, Kasper DL, Hauser SL, Longo DL, eds. *Harrison's Principles of Internal Medicine*. 14th ed. New York: NY: McGraw-Hill; 1998:634.

Kroft SH. Symptoms and diagnosis of blood disorders. In: Porter RS, Kaplan JL, eds. *The Merck Manuals Online Medical Library: Home Edition for Patients and Caregivers*. Online edition. Whitehouse Station, NJ: Merck Research Laboratories; 2007. http://www.merck.com/mmhe/sec14/ch170/ch170a.html Revised May 2006. Accessed July 16, 2007.

Acute. Medical Dictionary. Medline Plus Web site. http://www2.merriam-webster.com/cgi-bin/mwmednlm?book=Medical&va=acute. Accessed September 21, 2007.

Chronic. Medical Dictionary. Medline Plus Web site. http://www2.merriam-webster.com/cgi-bin/mwmednlm?book=Medical&va=chronic. Accessed September 21, 2007.

Moake, JL. Bleeding and clotting disorders. In: Porter RS, Kaplan JL, eds. *The Merck Manuals Online Medical Library: Home Edition for Patients and Caregivers*. Online edition. Whitehouse Station, NJ: Merck Research Laboratories; 2007. http://www.merck.com/mmhe/sec14/ch173/ch173a.html. Revised May 2006. Accessed July 16, 2007.

Paper R. Gynaecological complications in women with bleeding disorders. *Haemophilia* [serial online]. 2000;6(suppl 1):28-33. Available from: Ebsco Academic Search Premier. Accessed July 19, 2007.

James AH, Ragni MV, Picozzi VJ. ASH special educational symposium: bleeding disorders in premenopausal women: (another) public health crisis for hematology? *Hematology*. 2006: 474-485. http://asheducationbook.hematologylibrary.org/cgi/content/full/2006/1/474. Accessed July 17, 2007.

Handin, RI. Disorders of coagulation and thrombosis. In: Fauci AS, Braunwald E, Isselbacher KJ, Wilson JD, Martin JB, Kasper DL, Hauser SL, Longo DL, eds. *Harrison's Principles of Internal Medicine*. 14th ed. New York: NY: McGraw-Hill; 1998:739.

Hayward CPM. Diagnosis and management of mild bleeding disorders. *Hematology*. 2005:423-428. http://asheducationbook.hematologylibrary.org/content/vol2005/issue1. Accessed July 17, 2007.

James AH. More than menorrhagia: a review of the obstetric and gynaecological manifestations of bleeding disorders. *Haemophilia* [serial online]. 2005;11: 295-307. Available from: Ebsco Academic Search Premier. Accessed July 19, 2007.

What is a bleeding disorder? National Hemophilia Foundation Web site. http://www.hemophilia.org/NHFWeb/MainPgs/MainNHF.aspx?menuid=26&contentid=5&rptname=bleeding. 2006. Accessed October 24, 2007.

Medical and Scientific Advisory Council (MASAC) recommendation #172: MASAC recommendations regarding women with inherited bleeding disorders. National Hemophilia Foundation Web site. http://www.hemophilia.org/NHFWeb/MainPgs/MainNHF.aspx?menuid=57&contentid=688. Updated 2006. Accessed July 18, 2007.

Menstrual periods—heavy, prolonged, or irregular. Medline Plus Medical Encyclopedia. http://www.nlm.nih.gov/medlineplus/ency/article/003263.htm. August 17, 2007. Accessed November 2, 2007.

Von Willebrand Disease. National Heart, Lung, and Blood Institute Diseases and Conditions Index Web site. http://www.nhlbi.nih.gov/health/dci/Diseases/vWD/vWD_All.html. September 2007. Accessed November 2, 2007.

Lee CA. Women and von Willebrand disease. *Haemophilia* [serial online]. 1999;5(suppl 2):38-45. Available from: Ebsco Academic Search Premier. Accessed July 19, 2007.

Handin, RI. Disorders of the platelet and vessel wall. In: Fauci AS, Braunwald E, Isselbacher KJ, Wilson JD, Martin JB, Kasper DL, Hauser SL, Longo DL, eds. *Harrison's Principles of Internal Medicine*. 14th ed. New York: NY: McGraw-Hill; 1998:733.

Ragni MV, Bontempo FA, Hassett AC. von Willebrand disease and bleeding in women. Haemophilia [serial online]. 1999;5:313-317. Available from: Ebsco Academic Search Premier. Accessed July 19, 2007.

Medical and Scientific Advisory Council (MASAC) recommendation #173: MASAC recommendations regarding the treatment of von Willebrand disease. National Hemophilia Foundation Web site. http://www.hemophilia.org/NHFWeb/MainPgs/MainNHF.aspx?menuid=57&contentid=689. Updated 2006. Accessed July 18, 2007.

Smith N. Testing options for women: finding out. *Hémaware*. 2003;8(1):60-62. Project Red Flag Web site. http://www.projectredflag.org. Accessed July 18, 2007.

Smith N. Carrier issues and giving birth. *Hémaware*. 2003;8(3):88-90. Project Red Flag Web site. http://www.projectredflag.org. Accessed July 18, 2007.

Hemophilia. National Heart, Lung, and Blood Institute Diseases and Conditions Index Web site. http://www.nhlbi.nih.gov/health/dci/Diseases/hemophilia/hemophilia_all.html. June 2007. Accessed September 21, 2007.

National Hemophilia Foundation. An overview of thrombophilia: a q & a with Amy D. Shapiro, M.D. *Hémaware*. 2001;6(5):13-16. National Alliance for Thrombosis and Thrombophilia Web site. http://www.nattinfo.org/learn-thrombophilia.htm. Accessed September 5, 2007.

Freedman ML, Sutin D. Blood disorders. In: Beers MH, Jones TV, eds. *The Merck Manual of Health and Aging*. Online edition. Whitehouse Station, NJ: Merck Research Laboratories; 2005. http://www.merck.com/pubs/mmanual_ha/sec3/ch49/ch49a.html. Accessed September 4, 2007.

Coulam CB, Jeyendran RS, Fishel LA, Roussev R. Multiple thrombophilic gene mutations rather than specific gene mutations are risk factors for recurrent miscarriage. *Am J Reprod Immunol* [serial online]. 2006;55:360-368. Available from: Ebsco Academic Search Premier. Accessed September 5, 2007.

Martínez F, Avecilla A. Combined hormonal contraception and venous thromboembolism. *Euro J Contracept and Reprod Health Care* [serial online]. 2007;12(2):97-106. Available from: Ebsco Academic Search Premier. Accessed September 5, 2007.

Kujovich JL. Hormones and pregnancy:

thromboembolic risks for women. *Br J Haematol* [serial online]. 2004;126:443-454. Available from: Ebsco Academic Search Premier. Accessed September 5, 2007.

Deep vein thrombosis. National Heart, Lung, and Blood Institute Diseases and Conditions Index Web site. http://www.nhlbi.nih.gov/health/dci/Diseases/Dvt/DVT_WhatIs.html. May 2007. Accessed July 25, 2007.

Alexander JK. Pulmonary embolism. In: Porter RS, Kaplan JL, eds. *The Merck Manuals Online Medical Library: Home Edition for Patients and Caregivers*. Online edition. Whitehouse Station, NJ: Merck Research Laboratories; 2007. http://www.merck.com/mmhe/sec04/ch046/ch046a.html. Reviewed February 2003. Accessed July 25, 2007.

The thrombophilias and pregnancy. March of Dimes Web site. http://www.marchofdimes.com/professionals/14332_9264.asp. October 2006. Accessed September 5, 2007.

Thrombophilia/clotting disorders. Centers for Disease Control and Prevention Web site. http://www.cdc.gov/ncbddd/hbd/clotting.htm. November 21, 2005. Accessed September 21, 2007.

Becker R. Hypercoagulability and anticoagulation. In: Beers MH, Jones TV, eds. *The Merck Manuals Online Medical Library: The Merck Manual of Geriatrics*. Online edition. Whitehouse Station, NJ: Merck Research Laboratories; 2000-2006. http://www.merck.com/mkgr/mmg/sec9/ch70/ch70a.jsp. Accessed November 2, 2007.

Toh CH, Dennis M. Disseminated intravascular coagulation: old disease, new hope. *BMJ*. 2003;327(7421):974-977. http://www.bmj.com/cgi/content/full/327/7421/974.

Anemia. National Heart, Lung, and Blood Institute Diseases and Conditions Index Web site. http://www.nhlbi.nih.gov/health/dci/Diseases/anemia/anemia_all.html. May 2006. Accessed September 6, 2007.

Frenkel EP. Anemia. In: Porter RS, Kaplan JL, eds. *The Merck Manuals Online Medical Library: Home Edition for Patients and Caregivers*. Online edition. Whitehouse Station, NJ: Merck Research Laboratories; 2007. http://www.merck.com/mmhe/

sec14/ch172/ch172a.html. Reviewed February 2003. Accessed September 6, 2007.

Thalassemia. National Heart, Lung, and Blood Institute Diseases and Conditions Index Web site. http://www.nhlbi.nih.gov/health/dci/Diseases/Thalassemia/Thalassemia_All.html. May 2006. Accessed September 13, 2007.

Sickle cell anemia. National Heart, Lung, and Blood Institute Diseases and Conditions Index Web site. http://www.nhlbi.nih.gov/health/dci/Diseases/Sca/SCA_All.html. May 2007. Accessed September 13, 2007.

Creary M, Williamson D, Kulkarni R. Sickle cell disease: current activities, public health implications, and future directions. Report from the CDC. *J Women Health* [serial online]. 2007;16(5):575-582. Available from: Ebsco Academic Search Premier. Accessed September 13, 2007.

Iron-deficiency anemia. National Heart, Lung, and Blood Institute Diseases and Conditions Index Web site. http://www.nhlbi.nih.gov/health/dci/Diseases/ida/ida_all.html. May 2006. Accessed September 6, 2007.

US Preventive Services Task Force. Screening for iron deficiency anemia, including iron supplementations for children and pregnant women: recommendation statement. *Am Fam Physician*. 2006;74(3):461-464. American Family Physician Web site. http://www.aafp.org/afp. Accessed September 6, 2007.

about thalassemia. Cooley's Anemia Foundation Web site. http://www.cooleysanemia.org/sections.php?sec=1. 2001. Accessed September 6, 2007.

Fruchtman, SM. Myeloproliferative disorders. In: Porter RS, Kaplan JL, eds. *The Merck Manuals Online Medical Library: Home Edition for Patients and Caregivers*. Online edition. Whitehouse Station, NJ: Merck Research Laboratories; 2007. http://www.merck.com/mmhe/sec14/ch178/ch178a.html. Reviewed February 2003. Accessed September 7, 2007.

Schiffer CA. Leukemias. In: Porter RS, Kaplan JL, eds. *The Merck Manuals Online Medical Library: Home Edition for Patients and Caregivers*. Online edition. Whitehouse Station, NJ: Merck Research Laboratories; 2007. http://www.merck.com/mmhe/

sec14/ch176/ch176a.html. Reviewed February 2003. Accessed September 7, 2007.

SEXUALLY TRANSMITTED INFECTIONS

STD communications database general public focus group findings. Centers for Disease Control and Prevention Web site. http://www.cdc.gov/std/HealthComm/stdcom-db-focus.htm. Published February 2004. Accessed May 7, 2007.

Centers for Disease Control and Prevention. Sexually transmitted disease surveillance, 2005. http://www.cdc.gov/std/stats/toc2005.htm. Published November 2006. Accessed May 2, 2007.

Soler H, Quadagno D, Sly D, Riehman K, Eberstein I, Harrison D. Relationship dynamic, ethnicity and condom use among low-income women. *Fam Plann Perspect*. 2000;32(2):82-88 and 101.

Harvey SM, Bird ST, Galavotti C, Duncan EA, Greenberg D. Relationship power, sexual decision making and condom use among women at risk for HIV/STDs. *Women Health*. 2002;36(4):69-83.

Eng TR, Butler WT, eds. *The Hidden Epidemic: Confronting Sexually Transmitted Diseases*. Washington, DC: National Academy Press; 1997.

Bacterial vaginosis fact sheet. Centers for Disease Control and Prevention Web site. http://www.cdc.gov/std/bv/STDFact-Bacterial-Vaginosis.htm. Reviewed May 2004. Accessed April 5, 2007.

Chlamydia fact sheet. Centers for Disease Control and Prevention Web site. http://www.cdc.gov/std/chlamydia/STDFact-Chlamydia.htm. Reviewed April 2006. Accessed April 5, 2007.

Genital herpes fact sheet. Centers for Disease Control and Prevention Web site. http://www.cdc.gov/std/Herpes/STDFact-Herpes.htm. Reviewed May 2004. Accessed May 4, 2007.

Learn about herpes: questions and answers. American Social Health Association Web site. http://www.ashastd.org/herpes/herpes_learn_questions.cfm#3. Accessed May 4, 2007.

Centers for Disease Control and Prevention. Sexually transmitted diseases treatment guidelines, 2006. *MMWR* 2006;55(RR-11):1-94.

http://www.cdc.gov/STD/treatment. Accessed May 7, 2007.

Gonorrhea fact sheet. Centers for Disease Control and Prevention Web site. http://www.cdc.gov/std/Gonorrhea/STDFact-gonorrhea.htm. Reviewed April 2006. Accessed April 5, 2007.

Hepatitis B fact sheet. Centers for Disease Control and Prevention Web site. http://www.cdc.gov/std/hepatitis/STDFact-Hepatitis-B.htm. Reviewed September 2006. Accessed April 5, 2007.

Genital HPV infection fact sheet. Centers for Disease Control and Prevention Web site. http://www.cdc.gov/std/HPV/STDFact-HPV.htm. Reviewed May 2004. Accessed April 5, 2007.

Pubic lice infestation fact sheet. Centers for Disease Control and Prevention Web site. http://www.cdc.gov/ncidod/dpd/parasites/lice/factsht_pubic_lice.htm. Reviewed October 2004. Accessed May 4, 2007.

Syphilis fact sheet. Centers for Disease Control and Prevention Web site. http://www.cdc.gov/std/syphilis/STDFact-Syphilis.htm. Reviewed May 2004. Accessed April 5, 2007.

Trichomoniasis fact sheet. Centers for Disease Control and Prevention Web site. http://www.cdc.gov/std/trichomonas/STDFact-Trichomoniasis.htm. Reviewed May 2004. Accessed April 5, 2007.

Pelvic inflammatory disease fact sheet. Centers for Disease Control and Prevention Web site. http://www.cdc.gov/std/PID/STDFact-PID.htm. Reviewed May 2004. Accessed May 7, 2007.

STDs and pregnancy fact sheet. Centers for Disease Control and Prevention Web site. http://www.cdc.gov/std/STDFact-STDs&Pregnancy.htm#affect. Reviewed May 2004. Accessed April 5, 2007.

Centers for Disease Control and Prevention. A comprehensive immunization strategy to eliminate transmission of hepatitis B virus infection in the United States. *MMWR* 2005;54(RR-16):1-23. http://www.cdc.gov/MMWR/preview/mmwrhtml/rr5416a1.htm. Accessed April 5, 2007.

Male latex condoms and sexually transmitted diseases. Centers for Disease Control and Prevention Web site. http://www.cdc.gov/condomeffectiveness/latex.htm Reviewed December 31, 2005. Accessed May 18, 2007.

STD/STI prevention tips. American Social Health Association Web site. http://www.ashastd.org/learn/learn_prevention.cfm. Accessed April 12, 2007.

Galvao LW, Oliveira LC, Diaz J, et al. Effectiveness of female and male condoms in preventing exposure to semen during vaginal intercourse: a randomized trial. *Contraception*. 2005;71:130-136.

How to use a condom American Social Health Association Web site. http://www.ashastd.org/condom/condom_overview.cfm. Accessed April 12, 2007.

Working with FC female condom®. The Female Health Company Web site. http://www.femalehealth.com/resources_PDFs/miniguide.pdf. Modified December 15, 2005. Accessed May 23, 2007.

Cushman L, Romero D, Kalmuss D, Davidson A, Heartwell S, Rulin M. Condom use among women choosing long-term hormonal contraception. *Fam Plann Perspect*. 1998;30(5):240-243.

Thierry J, Marrazzo J, LaMarre M. Barriers to infectious disease prevention among women. *Emerg Infec Dis* [serial on the Internet]. 2004 Nov. http://www.cdc.gov/ncidod/EID/vol10no11/04-0622_08.htm. Accessed December 21, 2007.

Substance Abuse and Mental Health Services Administration, Office of Applied Studies. The NSDUH report: sexually transmitted diseases and substance use. http://www.oas.samhsa.gov/2k7/STD/STD.cfm. Published March 30, 2007. Accessed May 2, 2007.

Fraley SS. Psychosocial outcomes in individuals living with genital herpes. *J Obstet Gynecol Neonatal Nurs*. 2002;31(5):508-513.

Horvath MA, Brown J. The role of drugs and alcohol in rape. *Med Sci Law*. 2006;46(3):219-228.

HPV and HPV vaccine: information for healthcare providers. Centers for Disease Control and Prevention Web site. http://www.cdc.gov/std/HPV/STDFact-HPV-vaccine-hcp.htm. Revised August 2006. Accessed May 4, 2007.

HPV vaccine questions and answers. Centers for Disease Control and Prevention Web site. http://www.cdc.gov/nip/vaccine/hpv/hpv-faqs.htm. Revised August 2006. Accessed May 4, 2007.

Centers for Disease Control and Prevention. Expedited partner therapy in the management of sexually transmitted diseases: review and guidance. http://www.cdc.gov/std/treatment/EPTFinalReport2006.pdf. Published February 2, 2006. Accessed April 9, 2007.

Holgate H, Longman C. Some people's psychological experiences of attending a sexual health clinic and having a sexually transmitted infection. *J R Soc Health*. 1998;118(2):94-96.

Fortenberry JD. The effects of stigma on genital herpes care-seeking behaviours. *Herpes*. 2004;11(1):8-11.

HIV/AIDS

How HIV causes AIDS. National Institute of Allergy and Infectious Diseases Web site. http://www.niaid.nih.gov/factsheets/howhiv.htm. Updated March 6, 2006. Accessed August 17, 2007.

Fauci AS, Lane HC. Human immunodeficiency virus disease: AIDS and related disorders. In: Kasper DL, Braunwald E, Fauci AS, Hauser SL, Longo DL, Jameson JL, eds. *Harrison's Principles of Internal Medicine*. 16th ed. New York, NY: McGraw-Hill; 2005:1076-1139.

Hessol NA, Gandhi M, Greenblatt RM. I. Epidemiology and natural history of HIV infection in women. In: Anderson JR, ed. *A Guide to the Clinical Care of Women with HIV*. Rockville, MD: Health Resources and Services Administration, US Dept of Health and Human Services; 2005:1-34. ftp://ftp.hrsa.gov/hab/WG05chap1.pdf. Published 2005. Accessed August 17, 2007.

National Center for Health Statistics. *Health, United States, 2006 With Chartbook on Trends in the Health of Americans*. Hyattsville, MD: National Center for Health Statistics, US Dept of Health and Human Services; 2006:242-243. DHHS publication 2006-1232. http://www.cdc.gov/nchs/data/hus/hus06.pdf. Published November 2006. Accessed August 17, 2007.

HIV/AIDS among women. Centers for Disease Control and Prevention Web site. http://www.cdc.gov/hiv/topics/women/resources/factsheets/pdf/women.pdf. Revised June 2007.

Accessed August 20, 2007.

Centers for Disease Control and Prevention. *HIV/AIDS Surveillance Report, 2005*. Vol. 17. Rev. ed. Atlanta, GA: Centers for Disease Control and Prevention, US Dept of Health and Human Services; 2007:36. http://www.cdc.gov/hiv/topics/surveillance/resources/reports/2005report/table17.htm. Updated June 28, 2007. Accessed August 27, 2007.

Dental dams. Brown University Health Education Web site. http://www.brown.edu/Student_Services/Health_Services/Health_Education/sexual_health/ssc/dams.htm. Updated February 9, 2007. Accessed August 27, 2007.

Baeten JM, Wang C, Celum C. III. Prevention of HIV. In: Anderson JR, ed. *A Guide to the Clinical Care of Women with HIV*. Rockville, MD: Health Resources and Services Administration, US Dept of Health and Human Services; 2005:47-90. ftp://ftp.hrsa.gov/hab/WG05chap3.pdf. Published 2005. Accessed August 22, 2007.

In the meantime...what can women do today? Global Campaign for Microbicides Web site. http://www.global-campaign.org/meantime.htm. Accessed August 27, 2007.

HIV/AIDS and women: what women can do. Centers for Disease Control and Prevention Web site. http://www.cdc.gov/hiv/topics/women/protection.htm. Updated April 5, 2007. Accessed August 28, 2007.

Padian NS, van der Straten A, Ramjee G, et al. Diaphragm and lubricant gel for prevention of HIV acquisition in southern African women: a randomised controlled trial. *Lancet*. 2007;370(9583):251-261.

Pregnancy and HIV disease: issues that positive women may face when they're pregnant. Project Inform Web site. http://www.projinf.org/pdf/pregnancy.pdf. Published August 2005. Accessed August 27, 2007.

HIV during pregnancy, labor and delivery, and after birth: health information for HIV positive pregnant women. AIDSinfo Web site. http://aidsinfo.nih.gov/contentfiles/Perinatal_FS_en.pdf. Published August 2006. Accessed August 27, 2007.

HIV/AIDS during pregnancy. American Pregnancy Association Web site. http://www.americanpregnancy.org/pregnancycomplications/hivaids.html. Updated April 2007. Accessed August 27, 2007.

HIV infection and AIDS: an overview. National Institute of Allergy and Infectious Diseases Web site. http://www.niaid.nih.gov/factsheets/hivinf.htm. Updated October 8, 2007. Accessed October 26, 2007.

Smith DK, Grohskopf LA, Black RJ, et al. Antiretroviral postexposure prophylaxis after sexual, injection-drug use, or other nonoccupational exposure to HIV in the United States: recommendations from the US Department of Health and Human Services. *MMWR Recomm Rep*. 2005;54(RR-2):1-20. http://www.cdc.gov/mmwr/preview/mmwrhtml/rr5402a1.htm. Published January 21, 2005. Accessed August 27, 2007.

HIV/AIDS statistics and surveillance: basic statistics. Centers for Disease Control and Prevention Web site. http://www.cdc.gov/hiv/topics/surveillance/basic.htm. Updated June 28, 2007. Accessed August 28, 2007.

Greenwald JL, Burstein GR, Pincus J, Branson B. A rapid review of rapid HIV antibody tests. *Curr Infect Dis Rep*. 2006;8(2):125-131.

Marks G, Crepaz N, Janssen RS. Estimating sexual transmission of HIV from persons aware and unaware that they are infected with the virus in the USA. *AIDS*. 2006;20(10):1447-1450.

Feinberg J, Maenza J. IV. Primary medical care. In: Anderson JR, ed. *A Guide to the Clinical Care of Women with HIV*. Rockville, MD: Health Resources and Services Administration, Department of Health and Human Services; 2005:91-166. ftp://ftp.hrsa.gov/hab/WG05chap4.pdf. Published 2005. Accessed August 28, 2007.

How do HIV tests work? Centers for Disease Control and Prevention Web site. http://www.cdc.gov/hiv/topics/testing/resources/qa/tests_work.htm. Updated January 22, 2007. Accessed October 3, 2007.

Testing yourself for HIV-1, the virus that causes AIDS. U.S. Food and Drug Administration Web site. http://www.fda.gov/cber/infosheets/hiv-home2.htm. Updated April 4, 2006. Accessed August 28, 2007.

Branson BM, Handsfield HH, Lampe MA, et al. Revised recommendations for HIV testing of adults, adolescents, and pregnant women in health-care settings. *MMWR Recomm Rep*. 2006;55(RR-14):1-17. http://www.cdc.gov/mmwr/preview/mmwrhtml/rr5514a1.htm. Published September 22, 2006. Accessed August 28, 2007.

Hessol NA, Gandhi M, Greenblatt RM. I. Epidemiology and natural history of HIV infection in women. In: Anderson JR, ed. *A Guide to the Clinical Care of Women with HIV*. Rockville, MD: Health Resources and Services Administration, US Dept of Health and Human Services; 2005:1-34. ftp://ftp.hrsa.gov/hab/WG05chap1.pdf. Published 2005. Accessed August 29, 2007.

Candidiasis. Harvard Medical School, InteliHealth Web site. http://www.intelihealth.com/IH/ihtIH/WSIHW000/9339/31092.html. Updated August 20, 2005. Accessed August 29, 2007.

Toxoplasmosis. Centers for Disease Control and Prevention Web site. http://www.cdc.gov/ncidod/dpd/parasites/toxoplasmosis/factsht_toxoplasmosis.htm#prevent. Revised February 2007. Accessed August 29, 2007.

You can prevent toxo. Centers for Disease Control and Prevention Web site. http://www.cdc.gov/hiv/pubs/brochure/oi_toxo.htm. Updated June 21, 2007. Accessed October 3, 2007.

You can prevent CMV. Centers for Disease Control and Prevention Web site. http://www.cdc.gov/hiv/pubs/brochure/Oi_cmv.htm. Updated June 21, 2007. Accessed August 29, 2007.

Tuberculosis: a guide for adults and adolescents with HIV. Centers for Disease Control and Prevention Web site. http://www.cdc.gov/hiv/resources/brochures/tb.htm. Updated June 21, 2007. Accessed August 29, 2007.

HIV and AIDS: medicines to help you. U.S. Food and Drug Administration Web site. http://www.fda.gov/womens/medicinecharts/hiv.html. Published 2007. Accessed August 29, 2007.

Treatment of HIV infection. National Institute of Allergy and Infectious Diseases Web site. http://www.niaid.nih.gov/factsheets/treat-hiv.htm. Updated August 18, 2006. Accessed August 29, 2007.

Side effects of anti-HIV medications. AIDSinfo Web site. http://

aidsinfo.nih.gov/contentfiles/ SideEffectAnitHIVMeds_cbrochure_ en.pdf. Published October 2005. Accessed August 29, 2007.

Cheever LW. V. Adherence to HIV therapies. In: Anderson JR, ed. *A Guide to the Clinical Care of Women with HIV*. Rockville, MD: Health Resources and Services Administration, US Dept of Health and Human Services; 2005:167-175. ftp://ftp.hrsa.gov/hab/WG05chap5.pdf. Published 2005. Accessed August 29, 2007.

Recommended immunizations for HIV positive adults. AIDSinfo Web site. http://aidsinfo.nih.gov/contentfiles/ Recommended_Immunizations_ FS_en.pdf. Published January 2007. Accessed August 29, 2007.

Living with HIV/AIDS. Centers for Disease Control and Prevention Web site. http://www.cdc.gov/hiv/ pubs/brochure/LivingwithHIV.pdf. Updated June 21, 2007. Accessed October 3, 2007.

Kobayashi JS. Psychiatric issues. In: Anderson JR, ed. *A Guide to the Clinical Care of Women with HIV*. Rockville, MD: Health Resources and Services Administration, US Dept of Health and Human Services; 2005:347-376. ftp://ftp.hrsa.gov/hab/ WG05chap9.pdf. Published 2005. Accessed August 30, 2007.

Buseh AG, Stevens PE. Constrained but not determined by stigma: resistance by African American women living with HIV. *Women Health*. 2006;44(3):1-18.

REPRODUCTIVE HEALTH

Manassiev N, Keating F. The female reproductive system—anatomy and physiology. In: Manassiev N, Whitehead M, eds. *Female Reproductive Health*. New York, NY: Parthenon Publishing; 2004:1-12.

Vulvar problems. American College of Obstetricians and Gynecologists Web site. http://www.acog.org/ publications/patient_education/ bp088.cfm. Published February 2007. Accessed June 12, 2007.

Cottrell BH. Discussing the health risks of douching. *AWHONN Lifelines*. 2006;10(2):130-136.

Baird DD, Weinberg CR, Voigt LF, Daling JR. Vaginal douching and reduced fertility. *Am J Public Health*. 1996;86(6):844-850.

Centers for Disease Control and Prevention. Sexually Transmitted Diseases Treatment Guidelines, 2006. *MMWR*. 2007;55(No. RR-11).

Menstruation and the menstrual cycle. National Institute of Child Health and Human Development Web site. http://www.nichd.nih. gov/health/topics/menstruation_and_ the_menstrual_cycle.cfm. Updated September 10, 2006. Accessed August 10, 2007.

O'Herlihy C, Robinson HP, de Crespigny LJ. Mittelschmerz is a preovulatory symptom. *Br Med J*. 1980;280(6219):986.

Amenorrhea. National Institute of Child Health and Human Development Web site. http:// www.nichd.nih.gov/health/topics/ amenorrhea.cfm. Updated May 14, 2007. Accessed June 13, 2007.

Apgar BS, Kaufman AH, George-Nwogu U, Kittendorf A. Treatment of menorrhagia. *Am Fam Physician*. 2007;75(12):1813-1819.

Fazio SB, Ship AN. Abnormal uterine bleeding. *South Med J*. 2007;100(4):376-382.

American Academy of Pediatrics Committee on Adolescence, American College of Obstetricians and Gynecologists Committee on Adolescent Health Care. Menstruation in girls and adolescents: using the menstrual cycle as a vital sign. *Pediatrics*. 2006;118(5):2245-2250.

Master-Hunter T, Heiman DL. Amenorrhea: evaluation and treatment. *Am Fam Physician*. 2006;73(8):1375-1382.

Goodman LR, Warren MP. The female athlete and menstrual function. *Curr Opin Obstet Gynecol*. 2005;17(5):466-470.

Menstrual irregularities. National Institute of Child Health and Human Development Web site. http://www.nichd.nih.gov/health/ topics/Menstrual_Irregularities.cfm. Updated May 24, 2007. Accessed August 10, 2007.

Dysmenorrhea. American College of Obstetricians and Gynecologists Web site. http://www.acog.org/ publications/patient_education/ bp046.cfm. Published December 2006. Accessed June 12, 2007.

National Institute of Child Health and Human Development, National Institutes of Health. *Do I Have Premature Ovarian Failure?* Washington, DC: US Dept of Health and Human Services; 2003.

Nelson LM. Menstrual cycles, the FMR1 premutation, and "primary ovarian insufficiency." *Natl Fragile X Foundation Q*. 2007;26:22-23.

Abrams L. What does it mean to be a carrier? National Fragile X Foundation Web site. http://www. fragilex.org/html/carriers.htm. Updated November 2006. Accessed August 20, 2007.

Early Menopause Guidebook, 6th ed. Cleveland, OH: North American Menopause Society; 2006.

Endometrial hyperplasia. American College of Obstetricians and Gynecologists Web site. http://www. acog.org/publications/patient_ education/bp147.cfm. Published April 2001. Accessed June 12, 2007.

National Institute of Child Health and Human, National Institutes of Health. *Endometriosis*. Washington, DC: US Dept of Health and Human Services; 2002.

Ovarian cyst. American Academy of Family Physicians Web site. http:// familydoctor.org/online/famdocen/ home/women/reproductive/ gynecologic/279.html. Updated October 2005. Accessed August 29, 2007.

Heim LJ. Evaluation and differential diagnosis of dyspareunia. *Am Fam Physician*. 2001;63(8):1535-1544.

Pelvic floor disorders. National Institute of Child Health and Human Development Web site. http://www. nichd.nih.gov/health/topics/Pelvic_ Floor_Disorders.cfm. Updated January 10, 2007. Accessed August 22, 2007.

Pelvic support problems. American College of Obstetricians and Gynecologists Web site. http://www. acog.org/publications/patient_ education/bp012.cfm. Published April 2004. Accessed June 12, 2007.

Pelvic pain. American College of Obstetricians and Gynecologists Web site. http://www.acog.org/ publications/patient_education/ bp099.cfm. Published January 2006. Accessed June 12, 2007.

Polycystic ovarian syndrome. National Institute of Child Health and Human Development Web site. http://www.nichd.nih.gov/health/ topics/Polycystic_Ovary_Syndrome.

cfm. Updated May 25, 2007. Accessed August 22, 2007.

Wise LA, Palmer JR, Stewart EA, Rosenberg L. Polycystic ovary syndrome and risk of uterine leiomyomata. *Fertil Steril.* 2007;87(5):1108-1115.

Hollinrake E, Abreu A, Maifeld M, Van Voorhis BJ, Dokras A. Increased risk of depressive disorders in women with polycystic ovary syndrome. *Fertil Steril.* 2007;87(6):1369-1376.

Uterine fibroids. National Institute of Child Health and Human Development Web site. http://www.nichd.nih.gov/health/topics/uterine_fibroids.cfm. Updated February 19, 2007. Accessed June 12, 2007.

National Institute of Child Health and Human Development, National Institutes of Health. *Uterine Fibroids.* Washington, DC: US Dept of Health and Human Services; 2005.

Vaginitis. National Institute of Child Health and Human Development Web site. http://www.nichd.nih.gov/health/topics/vaginitis.cfm. Updated February 19, 2007. Accessed August 23, 2007.

Vaginitis. American College of Obstetricians and Gynecologists Web site. http://www.acog.org/publications/patient_educaiton/bp028.cfm Published July 2005. Accessed June 12, 2007.

About vulvodynia. National Vulvodynia Web site. http://www.nva.org/about_vulvodynia/what_is_vulvodynia/hml. Updated March 7, 2007. Accessed June 13, 2007.

Leppert P, Turner M, eds. *Vulvodynia: Toward Understanding a Pain Syndrome.* National Institutes of Health, US Dept of Health and Human Services; 2003.

Bachmann GA, Rosen R, Pinn VW, et al. Vulvodynia: a state-of-the-art consensus on definitions, diagnosis and management. *J Reprod Med.* 2006;51(6):447-456.

Keschavarz H, Hillis SD, Kieke BA, Marchbanks PA. Hysterectomy surveillance: United States, 1994-1999. *MMWR CDC Surveillance Summary.* 2002;51(SS05):1-8.

Bren L. Alternatives to hysterectomy: new technologies, more options. US Food and Drug Administration Web site. http://www.fda.gov/fdac/features/2001.601_tech.html. Published November/December 2001. Accessed August 30, 2007.

Understanding breast changes: a health guide for women. National Cancer Institute Web site. http://www.cancer.gov/cancertopics/understanding-breast-changes. Accessed June 12, 2007.

Screening mammograms: questions and answers. National Cancer Institute Web site. http://www.cancer.gov/cancertopics/factsheet/detection/screening-mammograms. Reviewed May 23, 2006. Accessed August 24, 2007.

Finer LF, Henshaw SK. Disparities in rates of unintended pregnancy in the United States, 1994 and 2001. *Perspect Sex Reprod Health.* 2006;38(2):90-96.

Burnhill M. Contraceptive use: the U.S. perspective. *Int J Gynecol Obstet.* 1998;629(suppl 1):S17-S23.

Birth control guide (chart). US Food and Drug Administration Web site. http://www.fda.gov/womens/healthinformation/Birth%20Control%20Chart.pdf. 2007. Accessed November 21, 2007.

Birth control guide. FDA Web site. http://www.fda.gov/womens/healthinformation/birthcontrolguide.html. Accessed November 21, 2007.

Edleman AB, Gallo MF, Jensen JT, Nichols MD, Schulz KF, Grimes DA. Continuous or extended cycle vs. cyclic use of combined oral contraceptives for contraception. *Cochrain Database Syst Rev.* 2005;(3):CD004695.

Holt VL, Scholes D, Wicklund KG, Cushing-Haugen KL, Daling JR. Body mass index, weight, and oral contraceptive failure risk. *Obstet Gynecol.* 2005;105:46-52.

Trussell J. Contraceptive efficacy. In: Hatcher RA, Trussell J, Nelson AL, Cates W, Stewart FH, Kowal D. *Contraceptive Technology.* 19th rev ed. New York, NY: Ardent Media; 2007. http://www.contraceptivetechnology.org/table.htm. Accessed November 21, 2007.

Wilcox AJ, Dunson D, Baird DD. The timing of the "fertile window" in the menstrual cycle: day specific estimates from a prospective study. *BMJ.* 2000;321:1259-1262.

Centers for Disease Control and Prevention. Sexually transmitted diseases treatment guidelines 2006. *MMWR.* 2006;55(No. RR-11):4.

HPV and HPV vaccine: information for healthcare providers. Centers for Disease Control and Prevention

Web site. http://www.cdc.gov/std/HPV/STDFact-HPV-vaccine-hcp.htm#provhpvrec. Revised August 2006. Accessed August 24, 2007.

The pap test: questions and answers. National Cancer Institute Web site. http://www.cancer.gov/cancertopics/factsheet/Detection/Pap-test Reviewed March 29, 2007. Accessed August 24, 2007.

Centers for Disease Control and Prevention. Sexually transmitted diseases treatment guidelines 2006. *MMWR.* 2006;55(No. RR-11):3-4.

PREGNANCY

Centers for Disease Control and Prevention. Preconception health and care, 2006. http://www.cdc.gov/ncbddd/preconception/documents/At-a-glance-4-11-06.pdf. Revised March 2007. Accessed December 7, 2007.

Stoppard M. *Conception, Pregnancy and Birth.* Rev ed. New York, NY: DK Publishing; 2005.

Regan L. *I'm Pregnant: A Week-by-Week Guide from Conception to Birth.* New York, NY: DK Publishing; 2005.

Age and fertility: a guide for patients [patient brochure]. Birmingham, AL: American Society of Reproductive Medicine; 2003. http://www.asrm.org/Patients/patientbooklets/agefertility.pdf. Accessed November 6, 2007.

Preconception care. National Institute of Child Health and Human Development Web site. http://www.nichd.nih.gov/health/topics/preconception_care.cfm. Updated May 25, 2007. Accessed October 24, 2007.

Birth defects: having a healthy pregnancy. Centers for Disease Control and Prevention Web site. http://www.cdc.gov/ncbddd/bd/abc.htm. October 5, 2005. Accessed October 8, 2007.

Johnson K, Posner SF, Beirmann J, Cordero JF, Atrash HK, Parker CS, Boulet S, Curtis MG; CDC/ATSDR Preconception Care Work Group; Select Panel on Preconception Care. Recommendations to improve preconception health and health Care—United States. *MMWR.* 2006;55(RR-6):1-23. http://www.cdc.gov/mmwr/preview/mmwrhtml/rr5506a1.htm. Accessed October 24, 2007.

Getting healthy before pregnancy. March of Dimes Web site. http://

www.marchofdimes.com/pnhec/173_17483.asp. March 2007. Accessed February 1, 2008.

Preconception care questions and answers. Centers for Disease Control and Prevention Web site. http://www.cdc.gov/ncbddd/preconception/QandA.htm. April 12, 2006. Accessed January 23, 2008.

Exercise during pregnancy [patient brochure]. American College of Obstetricians and Gynecologists Web site. http://www.acog.org/publications/patient_education/bp119.cfm. Published June 2003. Accessed October 24, 2007.

Fit for two: tips for pregnancy. National Institute of Diabetes and Digestive and Kidney Diseases Weight-control Information Network Web site. http://win.niddk.nih.gov/publications/two.htm. Updated September 2006. Accessed October 9, 2007.

Environmental risk and pregnancy. March of Dimes Web site. October 2007. http://www.marchofdimes.com/professionals/14332_9146.asp. Accessed February 8, 2008.

Callahan TL and Caughey AB. *BluePrints: Obstetrics and Gynecology*. 4th ed. Baltimore, MD: Lippincott Williams and Wilkins; 2007.

Understanding ovulation. American Pregnancy Association Web site. http://americanpregnancy.org/gettingpregnant/understandingovulation.html. Updated August 2006. Accessed October 25, 2007.

Home-use tests—pregnancy. US Food and Drug Administration Web site. http://www.fda.gov/cdrh/oivd/homeuse-pregnancy.html. Updated February 1, 2003. Accessed November 1, 2007.

Infertility. US Food and Drug Administration Web site. http://www.fda.gov/womens/getthefacts/infertility.html. August 2005. Accessed December 10, 2007.

Infertility/fertility. National Institute of Child Health and Human Development Web site. http://www.nichd.nih.gov/health/topics/infertility_fertility.cfm. Updated October 30, 2006. Accessed October 10, 2007.

You and your baby [patient brochure]. American College of Obstetricians and Gynecologists Web site. http://www.acog.org/publications/patient_education/ab005.cfm. Published January 2007. Accessed October 25, 2007.

Tenore J. Ectopic pregnancy: problem oriented diagnosis. *Am Fam Physician*. 2000;61(4):1080-1088. http://www.aafp.org/afp/20000215/1080.html. Accessed October 10, 2007.

Ectopic pregnancy [patient brochure]. American College of Obstetrician and Gynecologists Web site. http://www.acog.org/publications/patient_education/bp155.cfm. Published April 2002. Accessed January 2, 2008.

Prenatal care. March of Dimes Web Site. http://www.marchofdimes.com/pnhec/159_513.asp. 2007. Accessed October 25, 2007.

Pregnancy: taking care of you and your baby. American Academy of Family Physicians Web site. http://familydoctor.org/online/famdocen/home/women/pregnancy/basics/053.html. Updated July 2005. Accessed October 25, 2007.

Pregnancy FAQ: early pregnancy. American Pregnancy Association Web site. http://americanpregnancy.org/gettingpregnant/pregnancyfaq.htm. Updated November 2004. Accessed October 8, 2007.

Routine tests in pregnancy [patient brochure]. American College of Obstetricians and Gynecologists Web site. http://www.acog.com/publications/patient_education/bp133.cfm. Published January 2007. Accessed December 5, 2007.

Chorionic villus sampling: CVS. American Pregnancy Association Web site. http://americanpregnancy.org/prenataltesting/cvs.html. Updated April 2006. Accessed October 9, 2007.

First trimester screen. American Pregnancy Association Web site. http://americanpregnancy.org/prenataltesting/firstscreen.html. Updated February 2006. Accessed October 9, 2007.

Amniocentesis. American Pregnancy Association Web site. http://americanpregnancy.org/prenataltesting/amniocentesis.html. Updated April 2006. Accessed October 9, 2007.

Glucose challenge screening and glucose tolerance test. American Pregnancy Association Web site. http://americanpregnancy.org/prenataltesting/glucosetest.html. Updated August 2007. Accessed October 9, 2007.

Biophysical profile. American Pregnancy Association Web site. http://americanpregnancy.org/prenataltesting/biophysicalprofile.html. Updated August 2006. Accessed October 15, 2007.

High-risk pregnancy. National Institute of Child Health and Human Development Web site. http://www.nichd.nih.gov/health/topics/high_risk_pregnancy.cfm. Updated December 4, 2006. Accessed October 10, 2007.

My pyramid plan for moms. US Dept of Agriculture Web site. http://www.mypyramid.gov/mypyramidmoms/index.html. Accessed November 1, 2007.

Nutrition and lifestyle for a healthy pregnancy outcome [American Dietetic Association position statement]. *J Am Diet Assoc.* 2002;102(10):1479-1490. http://www.eatright.org/cps/rde/xchg/ada/hs.xsl/advocacy_3773_ENU_HTML.htm. Accessed October 26, 2007.

Caffeine. National Toxicology Center for the Evaluation of Risks to Human Reproduction Web site. http://cerhr.niehs.nih.gov/common/caffeine.html#Caffeine%20and%20Pregnancy. Updated December 21, 2005. Accessed December 13, 2007.

Caffeine. March of Dimes Web site. http://www.marchofdimes.com/pnhec/159_816.asp. Updated January 2008. Accessed February 1, 2008.

Pregnancy and pica: nonfood cravings. American Pregnancy Association Web site. http://www.americanpregnancy.org/pregnancyhealth/unusualcravingspica.html. Updated March 2007. Accessed December 13, 2007.

Your guide to diabetes: type 1 and type 2. National Diabetes Information Clearinghouse Web site. http://diabetes.niddk.nih.gov/dm/pubs/type1and2/index.htm. Updated April 2006. Accessed October 11, 2007.

Phenylketonuria (PKU). National Institute of Child Health and Human Development Web site. http://www.nichd.nih.gov/health/topics/phenylketonuria.cfm. Updated

August 25, 2006. Accessed December 12, 2007.

Food safety for pregnant and breastfeeding women. US Dept of Agriculture Web site. http://www.mypyramid.gov/mypyramidmoms/food_safety.html. Accessed November 2, 2007.

Protect your baby and yourself from listeriosis. US Dept of Agriculture Web site. http://www.fsis.usda.gov/PDF/Protect_Your_Baby.pdf. Revised April 2006. Accessed December 11, 2007.

Toxoplasma: frequently asked questions. US Food and Drug Administration Center for Food Safety and Applied Nutrition Web site. http://www.cfsan.fda.gov/~pregnant/whiltoxo.html. August 24, 2005. Accessed December 11, 2007.

Pregnancy: should I use a seat belt? American Academy of Physicians Web site. http://familydoctor.org/online/famdocen/home/women/pregnancy/basics/824.html. Updated July 2005. Accessed December 6, 2007.

Sex. March of Dimes Web site. http://www.marchofdimes.com/pnhec/159_516.asp. Accessed December 28, 2007.

Constipation. National Institutes of Diabetes and Digestive and Kidney Disorders Web site. http://digestive.niddk.nih.gov/ddiseases/pubs/constipation/index.htm. Updated July 2007. Accessed October 13, 2007.

Hemorrhoids. National Institutes of Diabetes and Digestive and Kidney Disorders Web site. http://digestive.niddk.nih.gov/ddiseases/pubs/hemorrhoids/index.htm. Updated November 2004. Accessed October 13, 2007.

Pregnancy and dizziness. American Pregnancy Association Web site. http://www.americanpregnancy.org/pregnancyhealth/dizziness.html. Updated March 2007. Accessed January 2, 2008.

Wrist pain. National Library of Medicine Web site. http://www.nlm.nih.gov/medlineplus/ency/article/003175.htm. Updated May 6, 2007. Accessed January 2, 2008.

Melasma. National Library of Medicine Web site. http://www.nlm.nih.gov/medlineplus/ency/article/000836.htm. Updated December 25, 2006. Accessed January 2, 2008.

Multiple pregnancies: twins, triplets and more. American Pregnancy Association Web site. http://americanpregnancy.org/multiples/multiples.html. Updated May 2007. Accessed October 8, 2007.

Dennis CL, Hodnett E. Psychosocial and psychological interventions for treating postpartum depression. *Cochrane Database Syst Rev*. 2007;(4):CD006116.

Intrauterine growth restriction: when your baby stops growing before birth. American Academy of Family Physicians Web site. http://familydoctor.org/online/famdocen/home/women/pregnancy/fetal/313.html. Updated October 2005. Accessed December 5, 2007.

Congenital heart defects. American Pregnancy Association. http://americanpregnancy.org/birthdefects/congenitalheart.html. Updated February 2007. Accessed January 5, 2008.

Birth defects [patient brochure]. American College of Obstetricians and Gynecologists Web site. http://www.acog.org/publications/patient_education/bp146.cfm. Published 2005. Accessed January 5, 2008.

Fibroids. US Food and Drug Administration Web site. http://www.fda.gov/womens/getthefacts/fibroids.html. August 2005. Accessed October 13, 2007.

Uterine fibroids [patient brochure]. American College of Obstetricians and Gynecologists Web site. http://www.acog.org/publications/patient_education/bp074.cfm. Published February 2005. Accessed October 18, 2007.

Am I at risk for gestational diabetes? National Diabetes Information Clearinghouse Web site. http://diabetes.niddk.nih.gov/dm/pubs/riskfortype2. December 2006. Accessed October 12, 2007.

Pregnancy and hepatitis B: frequently asked questions. Centers for Disease Control and Prevention Web site. http://www.cdc.gov/ncidod/diseases/hepatitis/b/faqb-pregnancy.htm. Reviewed December 8, 2006. Accessed January 4, 2008.

High blood pressure during pregnancy. American Academy of Family Physicians familydoctor Web site. http://familydoctor.org/online/famdocen/home/women/pregnancy/complications/695.html. Reviewed September 2005. Accessed January 5, 2008.

Zamorski MA, Green LA. NHBPEP report on high blood pressure in pregnancy: a summary for family physicians. *Am Fam Physician*. 2001;64(2):263-270. http://www.aafp.org/afp/20010715/263.html. Accessed February 5, 2008.

Hyperemesis gravidarum. American Pregnancy Association Web site. http://www.americanpregnancy.org/pregnancyhealth/hyperemesisgravidarum.html. Updated July 2006. Accessed January 5, 2008.

Miscarriage. National Institute of Child Health and Human Development Web site. http://www.nichd.nih.gov/health/topics/Miscarriage.cfm. Updated May 24, 2007. Accessed February 6, 2008.

Bleeding during pregnancy [patient brochure]. American College of Obstetricians and Gynecologists Web site. http://www.acog.org/publications/patient_education/bp038.cfm. Published April 1999. Accessed February 6, 2008.

What is "fifth disease"? Centers for Disease Control and Prevention Web site. http://www.cdc.gov/ncidod/dvrd/revb/respiratory/parvo_b19.htm. Reviewed January 21, 2005. Accessed October 15, 2007.

Grant D. Clinical presentations of parvovirus B19 infection. *Am Fam Physician*. 2007;75(3):373-376.

Preeclampsia and eclampsia. National Institute of Child Health and Human Development Web site. http://www.nichd.nih.gov/health/topics/Preeclampsia_and_Eclampsia.cfm. Updated September 10, 2006. Accessed January 5, 2008.

About prematurity. March of Dimes Web site. http://www.marchofdimes.com/prematurity/21191_5804.asp. May 2007. Accessed November 2, 2007.

Delzell JE, Lefevre ML. Urinary tract infections during pregnancy. *Am Fam Physician*. 2000;61(3):713-721. http://www.aafp.org/afp/20000201/713.html. Accessed October 15, 2007.

Managing gestational diabetes: a patient's guide to a healthy pregnancy. National Institute of Child Health and Human Development Web site. http://www.nichd.nih.gov/publications/pubs/gest_diabetes/. Updated September 11, 2006. Accessed February 1, 2008.

Preterm labor. March of Dimes Web site. http://www.marchofdimes.com/

pnhec/188_1080.asp. March 2006. Accessed December 13, 2007.

More babies born prematurely, new report shows [press release]. White Plains, NY: March of Dimes; December 5, 2007. http://www.marchofdimes.com/aboutus/22663_27994.asp. Accessed December 13, 2007.

March of Dimes thanks President Bush for signing bill calling for public-private effort to prevent preterm births [press release]. White Plains, NY: March of Dimes; December 22, 2006. http://www.marchofdimes.com/aboutus/22663_22620.asp. Accessed December 13, 2007.

Childbirth education classes. American Pregnancy Association Web site. http://americanpregnancy.org/labornbirth/childbirtheducation.html. Updated July 2007. Accessed October 8, 2007.

Epidural anesthesia. American Pregnancy Association Web site. http://www.americanpregnancy.org/labornbirth/epidural.htm. Updated August 2007. Accessed October 9, 2007.

Packing for the hospital or birth center. American Pregnancy Association Web site. http://americanpregnancy.org/planningandpreparing/packinglist.htm. Updated July 2007. Accessed October 8, 2007.

Stages of childbirth: stage I. American Pregnancy Association Web site. http://americanpregnancy.org/labornbirth/firststage.html. Updated May 2007. Accessed October 8, 2007.

Stages of childbirth: stage II. American Pregnancy Association Web site. http://americanpregnancy.org/labornbirth/secondstage.html. Updated August 2007. Accessed October 8, 2007.

Stages of childbirth: stage III. American Pregnancy Association Web site. http://americanpregnancy.org/labornbirth/thirdstage.html. Updated December 2006. Accessed October 8, 2007.

Braxton Hicks contractions. American Pregnancy Association Web site. http://americanpregnancy.org/labornbirth/braxtonhicks.html. Updated November 2006. Accessed October 8, 2007.

You and your baby: prenatal care, labor and delivery, and postpartum care [patient pamphlet]. American College Obstetricians and Gynecologists

Web site. http://www.acog.org/publications/patient_education/ab005.cfm. Published January 2007. Accessed January 7, 2008.

Cesarean section. National Library of Medicine MedlinePlus Web site. http://www.nlm.nih.gov/medlineplus/cesareansection.html. Reviewed September 10, 2007. Accessed January 7, 2008.

Inducing labor. American Pregnancy Association Web site. http://americanpregnancy.org/labornbirth/inducinglabor.html. Updated January 2007. Accessed October 8, 2007.

Assisted delivery. American Pregnancy Association Web site. Accessed October 8, 2007.

Breech births. American Pregnancy Association Web site. http://americanpregnancy.org/labornbirth/breechpresentation.html. Updated May 2007. Accessed October 8, 2007.

How much do newborns weigh? Nemours Foundation Web site. http://www.kidshealth.org/parent/growth/growth/grownewborn.html. Reviewed August 2005. Accessed October 28, 2007.

Newborn testing. American Pregnancy Association Web site. http://americanpregnancy.org/labornbirth/newborntesting.html. Updated May 2007. Accessed October 8, 2007.

Centers for Disease Control and Prevention. 2007 Recommended immunizations for babies. Centers for Disease Control and Prevention Web site. http://www.cdc.gov/vaccines/spec-grps/infants/downloads/rec-iz-babies.pdf. 2007. Accessed October 27, 2007.

Recovering from delivery. Nemours Foundation Web site. http://www.kidshealth.org/parent/pregnancy/birth/recovering_delivery.html. Reviewed May 2005. Accessed October 25, 2007.

BREASTFEEDING

American Academy of Pediatrics. Breastfeeding and the use of human milk [policy statement]. *Pediatrics.* 2005;115(2):496-506.

US Department of Health and Human Services, Office on Women's Health. *HHS Blueprint for Action on Breastfeeding.* 2000.

Ip S, Chung M, Raman G, et al. *Breastfeeding and Maternal and Infant Health Outcomes in Developed Countries.* Evidence Report/Technology Assessment No. 153

(Prepared by Tufts-New England Medical Center Evidence-based Practice Center, under Contract No. 290-02-0022). AHRQ Publication No. 07-E007. Rockville, MD: Agency for Healthcare Research and Quality; April 2007.

Should I breastfeed my baby? American Academy of Pediatrics Web site. http://www.aap.org/publiced/BR_BFBenefits.htm. Published March 2007. Accessed November 7, 2007.

Mohrbacher N, Stock J. Breast anatomy. In: *La Leche League International, The Breastfeeding Answer Book.* 3rd ed. Schaumburg, IL: La Leche League International; 2003:6-17.

Meyer B, Arnold J, Pascali-Bonaro D. Social support by doulas during labor and the early postpartum period. *Hosp Physician.* 2001:37(9):57-65.

Taylor J. Caregiver support for women during childbirth: does the presence of a labor-support person affect maternal-child outcomes? *Am Fam Physician.* 2002;66(7):1205-1206.

Shealy KR, Li R, Benton-Davis S. Grummer-Strawn LM. *The CDC Guide to Breastfeeding Interventions.* Atlanta, GA: US Department of Health and Human Services, Centers for Disease Control and Prevention; 2005.

Page D. Breastfeeding: learning the dance of latching. *J Hum Lact.* 2007;23(1):111-112.

Thorley V. Mothers' behavior that undermines breastfeeding latch: The fear response. *J Hum Lact.* 2005;21(3):243-244.

Wiessinger D. The world of latch-on: one leader's journey. *LEAVEN.* 2004;40(1):3-6.

Newman J, Pitman T. What is a good latch? In: *The Ultimate Breastfeeding Book of Answers.* New York, NY: Three Rivers Press; 2000:60-63.

Smillie C. Baby-led latching: A neurobehavioral model for how infants learn to latch [slide presentation]. Stratford, CT; 2005.

First food first. World Health Organization Web site. http://www.who.int/nutrition/topics/world_breastfeeding_week/en. Accessed September 23, 2007.

Mohrbacher N, Stock J. Positioning, latch-on, and the baby's suck. In: *La Leche League International, The Breastfeeding Answer Book.* 3rd ed. Schaumburg, IL: La Leche League International; 2003:72-81.

International Lactation Consultant Association. *Clinical Guidelines for the Establishment of Exclusive Breastfeeding*. Raleigh, NC: International Lactation Consultant Association; June 2005.

Eastman A. The mother-baby dance: positioning and latch-on. *LEAVEN*. 2000;36(4):63-68.

How do I position my baby to breastfeed? La Leche League International Web site. http://www.llli.org/FAQ/positioning.html. Updated February 21, 2007. Accessed October 2, 2007.

I'm breastfeeding my baby. How can I tell if she's getting enough milk? American Academy of Pediatrics Web site. http://www.aap.org/publiced/BR_BFGettingEnough.htm. Published March 2007. Accessed November 7, 2007.

Mohrbacher N, Stock J. Health problems—baby. The baby with a chronic illness or physical limitation. In: *La Leche League International, The Breastfeeding Answer Book*. 3rd ed. Schaumburg, IL: La Leche League International; 2003:327-369.

Frequently asked questions. Human Milk Banking Association of North America Web site. http://www.hmbana.org/index.php?mode=faq. Published 2005. Accessed October, 25 2007.

Mohrbacher N, Stock J. Expression and storage of human milk. In: *La Leche League International, The Breastfeeding Answer Book*. 3rd ed. Schaumburg, IL: La Leche League International; 2003:210-215.

Neifert M. Supporting breastfeeding mothers as they return to work. *Am Acad Pediatrics Newslet*. 2000.

Shealy KR, Li R, Benton-Davis S, Grummer-Strawn LM. *The CDC Guide to Breastfeeding Interventions*. Atlanta, GA: US Department of Health and Human Services, Centers for Disease Control and Prevention, 2005.

Bar-Yam N. Breastfeeding and human rights: is there a right to breastfeed? *J Hum Lact*. 2003;19(4):357-361.

Travel recommendations for the nursing mother. Centers for Disease Control and Prevention Web site. http://www.cdc.gov/breastfeeding/recommendations/travel_recommen. Published May 22, 2007. Accessed October 9, 2007.

Mohrbacher N, Stock J. The breast and how it works. In: *La Leche League*

International, The Breastfeeding Answer Book. 3rd ed. Schaumburg, IL: La Leche League International; 2003:21.

Mohrbacher N, Stock J. Health problems—baby. Breastfeeding after breast surgery or injury. In: *La Leche League International, The Breastfeeding Answer Book*. 3rd ed. Schaumburg, IL: La Leche League International; 2003:517-518.

Mohrbacher N, Stock J. Health problems—mother. When mother is ill. In: *La Leche League International, The Breastfeeding Answer Book*. 3rd ed. Schaumburg, IL: La Leche League International; 2003:530-575.

American Academy of Pediatrics. The transfer of drugs and other chemicals into human milk [policy statement]. *Pediatrics*. 2001;108(3):776-789.

FDA warning on codeine use by nursing mothers [news release]. Rockville, MD: US Food and Drug Administration Press Office, August 17, 2007.

Mohrbacher N, Stock J. The vegetarian mother. In: *La Leche League International, The Breastfeeding Answer Book*. 3rd ed. Schaumburg, IL: La Leche League International; 2003:444-445.

Mohrbacher N, Stock J. Basics of milk expression. In: *La Leche League International, The Breastfeeding Answer Book*. 3rd ed. Schaumburg, IL: La Leche League International; 2003:212.

Mohrbacher N, Stock J. Sensitivity or allergy. In: *La Leche League International, The Breastfeeding Answer Book*. 3rd ed. Schaumburg, IL: La Leche League International; 2003:129-133.

Su D, Zhao Y, Binns C, Scott J, Oddy W. Breastfeeding mothers can exercise: results of cohort study. *Public Health Nutr*. 2007;10(10):1089-1093.

Will my milk supply be affected if I exercise? La Leche League International Web site. http://www.llli.org/FAQ/exercise.html. Updated August 29, 2006. Accessed September 23, 2007.

Lovelady CA, Hunter CP, Geigerman C. Effect of exercise on immunologic factors in breast milk. *Pediatrics*. 2003;111(2):e148-e152.

Jordan P, Wall V. Supporting the father when an infant is breastfed. *J Hum Lact*. 1993;9(1):31-34.

Mohrbacher N, Stock J. Breastfeeding and sexuality. The baby with a chronic illness or physical limitation. In:

La Leche League International, *The Breastfeeding Answer Book*. 3rd ed. Schaumburg, IL: La Leche League International; 2003:327-369.

The Academy of Breastfeeding Medicine. ABM Clinical Protocol #13. Contraception during breastfeeding. February 1, 2005.

Safe food: crucial for child development [poster]. World Health Organization Web site. http://www.who.int/ceh/publications/en/poster15new.pdf. Accessed October 7, 2007.

Nickerson K. Environmental contaminants in breast milk. *J Midwifery Womens Health*. 2006;51(1):26-34.

Boersma ER, Lanting Cl. Environmental exposure to polychlorinated biphenyls (PCBs) and dioxins: consequences for longterm neurological and cognitive development of the child lactation. In: Koletzko B, Michaelson KF, Hernell O, eds. *Short and Long Term Effects of Breastfeeding on Child Health*. New York, NY: Kluwer Academic/Plenum Publishers, 2000:271-287. Advances in Experimental Medicine and Biology; vol 478.

Rabas-Fito N, Grimalt JO, Marco E, Sala M, Maon C, Sunyer J. Breastfeeding and concentrations of HCB and p,p-DDE at the age of 1 year. *Environ Res*. 2005;98(1):8-13.

International Lactation Consultant Association. *Position on Breastfeeding, Breast Milk, and Environmental Contaminants*, October 2001.

Bartmess J. The risk of polychlorinated dibenzodioxins in human milk. *J Hum Lact*. 1998;4:105.

LaKind JS, Wilkins Amina A, Berlin CM Jr. Environmental chemicals in human milk: a review of levels, infant exposures and health, and guidance for future research. *Toxicol Appl Pharmacol*. 2004;198(2):184-208.

Schreiber JS. Parents worried about milk contamination. What is best for baby? *Pediatr Clin North Am*. 2001;48(5):1113-1127, vii.

Ribas-Fito N, Cardo E, Sala M, et al. Breastfeeding, exposure to organochlorine compounds, and neurodevelopment in infants. *Pediatrics*. 2003;111(5 Pt 1):e580-e585.

van Esterik P. Towards healthy environments for children. Frequently asked questions (FAQ) about breastfeeding in a contaminated environment. World Alliance for

Breastfeeding Action Web site. http://www.waba.org.my/environment. Published October 22, 2003. Accessed September 27, 2007.

Exposure to environmental toxins. Centers for Disease Control and Prevention Web site. http://www.cdc.gov/breastfeeding/disease/environmental_toxins.htm. Updated May 22, 2007. Accessed October 9, 2007.

Hollis BW, Wagner CL. Vitamin D requirements during lactation: high-dose maternal supplementation as therapy to prevent hypovitaminosis D for both the mother and the nursing infant. *Am J Clin Nutr.* 2004;80(6):1752S-1758S.

Vitamin D deficiency clinical report: patient FAQs. American Academy of Pediatrics Web site. http://www.aap.org/family/vitdpatients.htm. Accessed October 9, 2007.

Gartner LM, Greer FR, American Academy of Pediatrics Section on Breastfeeding and Committee on Nurtrition. Prevention of rickets and vitamin D deficiency: new guidelines for vitamin D intake. *Pediatrics.* 2003;111(4):908-910.

Vaccinations and precautions for breastfeeding. Centers for Disease Control and Prevention Web site. www.cdc.gov/breastfeeding/recommendations/vaccinations.htm. Updated May 22, 2007. Accessed October 9, 2007.

Mohrbacher N, Stock J. Teething and biting. In: *La Leche League International, The Breastfeeding Answer Book.* 3rd ed. Schaumburg, IL: La Leche League International; 2003:478-480.

Mohrbacher N, Stock J. Breastfeeding during pregnancy. In: *La Leche League International, The Breastfeeding Answer Book.* 3rd ed. Schaumburg, IL: La Leche League International; 2003:406-408.

MENTAL HEALTH

US Department of Health and Human Services. The fundamentals of mental health and mental illness. In: *Mental Health: A Report of the Surgeon General.* http://www.surgeongeneral.gov/library/mentalhealth/chapter2/sec3.html. Published 1999. Accessed July 25, 2007.

Mental health. Medline Plus Web site. http://www.nlm.nih.gov/medlineplus/mentalhealth.html. Updated May 31, 2007. Accessed June 1, 2007.

US Department of Health and Human Services. Introduction and themes. In: *Mental Health: A Report of the Surgeon General.* http://www.surgeongeneral.gov/library/mentalhealth/chapter1/sec1.html. Published 1999. Accessed July 25, 2007.

Introduction. In: Slater L, Daniel JH, Banks AE, eds. *The Complete Guide to Mental Health for Women.* Boston, MA: Beacon Press; 2003:vii-ix.

Ray O. How the mind hurts and heals the body. *Am Psychol.* 2004;59(1):29-40.

Holmes TH, Rahe RH. The social readjustment rating scale. *J Psychosom Res.* 1967;11(2):213-218.

Wyche KF. Poverty and women's mental health. In: Slater L, Daniel JH, Banks AE, eds. *The Complete Guide to Mental Health for Women.* Boston, MA: Beacon Press; 2003:185-189.

Greene B. Racism and mental health. In: Slater L, Daniel JH, Banks AE, eds. *The Complete Guide to Mental Health for Women.* Boston, MA: Beacon Press; 2003:190-193.

Pavalko EK, Mossakowski KN, Hamilton VJ. Does perceived discrimination affect health? longitudinal relationships between work discrimination and women's physical and emotional health. *J Health Soc Behav.* 2003;43:18-33.

Gutek BA, Done, RS. Sexual harassment. In: Unger R, ed. *Handbook of Psychology of Women and Gender.* New York, NY: John Wiley & Sons; 2001:367-387.

Anxiety disorders. National Institute of Mental Health Web site. http://www.nimh.nih.gov/publicat/anxiety.cfm. Updated February 7, 2007. Accessed June 5, 2007.

Bonomi AE, Thompson R, Anderson M, Reid R, Carrell D, Dimer J, Rivara F. Intimate partner violence and women's physical, mental, and social functioning. *Am J Prev Med.* 2006;30(56):458-466.

Anda RF, Whitfield CL, Felitti V, et al. Adverse childhood experiences, alcoholic parents, and later risk of alcoholism and depression. *Psychiatr Serv.* 2002;53(8):1001-1009.

Felitti VJ, Anda RF, Nordenberg D, et al. Relationship of childhood abuse and household dysfunction to many of the leading causes of death in adults: the adverse childhood experiences (ACE) study. *Am J Prev Med.* 1998;14(4):245-258.

Eisendrath SJ, Prakken SD. The mind and somatic illness: psychological factors affecting physical illness. In: Goldman H, ed. *Review of General Psychiatry.* 5th ed. New York, NY: McGraw-Hill; 2000:13-20.

Garrett-Akinsanya B. Stress management for women. In: Slater L, Daniel JH, Banks AE, eds. *The Complete Guide to Mental Health for Women.* Boston, MA: Beacon Press; 2003:369-374.

Goodwin R. Association between physical activity and mental disorders among adults in the United States. *Prev Med.* 2003;36:698-703.

Chan CS. The importance of exercise and physical activity for women. In: Slater L, Daniel JH, Banks AE, eds. *The Complete Guide to Mental Health for Women.* Boston, MA: Beacon Press; 2003:363-368.

Shrier D. Psychosocial aspects of women's lives: work, family, and life cycle issues. *Psychiatr Clin N Am.* 2003;26:741-757.

Burt VK, Stein K. Epidemiology of depression throughout the female life cycle. *J Clin Psychiatry.* 2002;63(suppl 7):9-15.

Fink G. Estrogen-serotonin link: effects on mood, mental state, and memory [abstract S47]. *Arch Womens Ment Health.* 2001;3(suppl 2):10.

Depression: what every woman should know. National Institute of Mental Health Web site. http://www.nimh.nih.gov/publicat/depwomenknows.cfm. Updated February 16, 2006. Accessed June 5, 2007.

Mann M, Hosman CMH, Schaalma HP, de Vries NK. Self-esteem in a broad-spectrum approach for mental health promotion. *Health Educ Res.* 2004;19(4):357-372.

Seligman M. *Learned Optimism: How to Change Your Mind and Your Life.* New York, NY: Alfred A. Knopf; 1998.

Sheldom KM, Ryan RM, Deci EL, Kasser T. The independent effects of goal contents and motives on well-being: it's both what you pursue and why you pursue it. *Pers Soc Psychol Bull.* 2004;30(4):475-486.

Hong RY. Worry and rumination: differential associations with anxious and depressive symptoms and coping behavior. *Behav Res Ther.* 2007;45(2):277-290.

Jordan J, Banks AE, Walker M. Growth in connection. In: Slater L, Daniel JH, Banks AE, eds. *The Complete Guide to Mental Health for Women.* Boston, MA: Beacon Press; 2003:92-99.

Greene B. Women of color and relationships. In: Slater L, Daniel JH, Banks AE, eds. *The Complete Guide to Mental Health for Women.* Boston, MA: Beacon Press; 2003:100-103.

US Department of Health and Human Services. Alcohol: a woman's health issue. http://pubs.niaaa.nih.gov/publications/brochurewomen/women.htm. Revised January 2005. Accessed July 25, 2007.

The numbers count: mental disorders in America. National Institute of Mental Health Web site. http://www.nimh.nih.gov/publicat/numbers.cfm. Updated December 26, 2006. Accessed May 31, 2007.

Eliminate disparities in mental health. Centers for Disease Control and Prevention Web site. http://www.cdc.gov/omh/AMH/factsheets/mental.htm. Updated May 11, 2007. Accessed May 31, 2007.

Co-occurring disorders and depression. Mental Health America Web site. http://www.nmha.org/go/information/get-info/depression/co-occurring-disorders-and-depression. Updated November 8, 2006. Accessed September 4, 2007.

Depression and thyroid illness. The Thyroid Foundation of America Web site. http://www.allthyroid.org/disorders/related/depression.html. Published 2004. Accessed August 2, 2007.

National Center for Health Statistics. *Health, United States, 2006.* Hyatttsville, MD: National Center for Health Statistics; 2006:262.

US Department of Health and Human Services. *Mental Health: Culture, Race, and Ethnicity—Executive Summary.* http://www.surgeongeneral.gov/library/mentalhealth/cre/execsummary-1.html. Published 2001. Accessed June 4, 2007.

Biederman J, Mick E, Faraone SV, et al. Influence of gender on attention deficit hyperactivity disorder in children referred to a psychiatric clinic. *Am J Psychiatry.* 2002;159(1):36-42.

Kessler RC, Wai TC, Demler O, Merikangas K, Walters E. Prevalence, severity, comorbidity of 12-month *DSM-IV* disorders in the National Comorbidity Survey Replication. *Arch Gen Psychiatry.* 2005;62:617-627.

Depression. National Institute of Mental Health Web site. http://www.nimh.nih.gov/publicat/depression.cfm. Updated September 13, 2006. Accessed June 5, 2007.

Bipolar disorder. National Institute of Mental Health Web site. http://www.nimh.nih.gov/publicat/bipolar.cfm. Updated January 24, 2007. Accessed June 5, 2007.

Eating disorders: facts about eating disorders and the search for solutions. National Institute of Mental Health Web site. http://www.nimh.nih.gov/publicat/eatingdisorders.cfm. Updated February 17, 2006. Accessed June 5, 2007.

Phillips K. *The Broken Mirror: Understanding and Treating Body Dysmorphic Disorder.* New York, NY: Oxford University Press; 1996:32.

Davis K. Women and addictions. In: Slater L, Daniel JH, Banks AE, eds. *The Complete Guide to Mental Health for Women.* Boston, MA: Beacon Press; 2003:238-249.

Schizophrenia. National Institute of Mental Health Web site. http://www.nimh.nih.gov/publicat/schizophrenia.cfm. Reviewed 2006. Accessed June 5, 2007.

Personality disorders. Medline Plus Web site. http://www.nlm.nih.gov/medlineplus/print/personalitydisorders.html.Upated April 13, 2007. Accessed August 2, 2007.

Borderline personality disorder. National Institute of Mental Health Web site. http://www.nimh.nih.gov/publicat/bpd.cfm. Updated February 17, 2006. Accessed June 5, 2007.

Misri S. Depression during pregnancy. Paper presented at: 1st World Congress on Women's Mental Health; March 27-31 2001; Berlin, Germany. http://www.medscape.com/viewprogram/843_pnt. Accessed June 5, 2007.

Riecher-Rössler A. Postpartum disorders. Paper presented at: 1st World Congress on Women's Mental Health; March 27-31 2001; Berlin, Germany. http://www.medscape.com/viewprogram/843_pnt. Accessed June 5, 2007.

Murray L, Fiori-Cowley A, Hooper R, Cooper P. The impact of postnatal depression and associated adversity on early mother-infant interactions and later infant outcome. *Child Dev.* 1996;67(5):2512-2526.

Postpartum depression. American College of Obstetrician and Gynecologists Web site. http://www.acog.org/publications/patient_education/bp091.cfm. Published 2007. Accessed September 4, 2007.

What is mental illness: mental illness facts. National Alliance on Mental Illness Web site. http://www.nami.org/Content/NavigationMenu/Inform_Yourself/About_Mental_Illness/About_Mental_Illness.htm. Updated 2007. Accessed May 31, 2007.

Link BG, Phelan JC, Bresnahan M, Stueve A, Pescosolido BA. Public conceptions of mental illness: labels, causes, dangerousness, and social distance. *Am J Pub Health.* 1999;89(9):1329-1332.

What a difference a friend makes: social acceptance is key to mental health recovery. Substance Abuse and Mental Health Services Administration Web site. http://mentalhealth.samhsa.gov/publications/allpubs/SMA07-4257/default.asp. Updated March 2007. Accessed May 31, 2007.

Mental illness and the family: finding the right mental health care for you. Mental Health America Web site. http://www.mentalhealthamerica.net/farcry/go/information/get-info/mi-and-the-family/finding-the-right-mental-health-care-for-you/mental-illness-and-the-family-finding-the-right-mental-health-care-for-you. Updated March 12, 2007. Accessed May 31, 2007.

Kessler RC, Berglund P, Demler O, Jin R, Merikangas K, Walters E. Lifetime prevalence and age-of-onset distributions of DSM-IV disorders in the National Comorbidity Survey Replication. *Arch Gen Psychiatry.* 2005;62:593-602.

HEALTHY AGING

Physiologic clues. In: *Aging Under the Microscope.* Bethesda, MD: National Institute on Aging; September 2002. NIH publication

02-2756. http://www.nia.nih.gov/HealthInformation/Publications/AgingUndertheMicroscope. Updated May 16, 2007. Accessed September 10, 2007.

Centers for Disease Control and Prevention and the Merck Company Foundation. *The State of Aging and Health in America 2007*. http://www.cdc.gov/aging/saha.htm. Reviewed March 28, 2007. Accessed September 10, 2007.

He W, Sengupta M, Velkoff VA, DeBarros KA, US Census Bureau. *65+ in the United States: 2005*. http://www.census.gov/prod/2006pubs/p23-209.pdf. Issued December 2005. Accessed October 5, 2007.

Inside the human brain. In: *Unraveling the Mystery*. Bethesda, MD: National Institute on Aging; December 2003. NIH publication 02-3782. http://www.nia.nih.gov/Alzheimers/Publications/UnravelingTheMystery/. Updated August 29, 2006. Accessed October 11, 2007.

North American Menopause Society. *Menopause Guidebook: Helping Women Make Informed Healthcare Decisions Around Menopause and Beyond*. Cleveland, OH: North American Menopause Society, October 2006. http://www.menopause.org/edumaterials/guidebook/mgtoc.htm. Accessed October 12, 2007.

Biochemistry and aging. In: *Aging Under the Microscope*. Bethesda, MD: National Institute on Aging; September 2002. NIH publication 02-2756. http://www.nia.nih.gov/HealthInformation/Publications/AgingUndertheMicroscope. Updated May 16, 2007. Accessed September 10, 2007.

Menopause. National Institute of Aging Web site. http://www.niapublications.org/agepages/menopause.asp. Updated May 2005. Accessed October 12, 2007.

Osteoporosis. National Institutes of Health Senior Health Web site. http://nihseniorhealth.gov/osteoporosis. Reviewed January 3, 2006. Accessed October 15, 2007.

Osteoporosis. National Institute of Arthritis and Muscoloskeletal and Skin Disease Web site. http://www.niams.nih.gov/Health_Info/Bone/Osteoporosis/default.asp. Updated

November 2006. Accessed November 7, 2007.

US Dept of Health and Human Services. *Bone Health and Osteoporosis: A Report of the Surgeon General*. Rockville, MD: US Dept of Health and Human Services, Office of the Surgeon General; October 2004. http://www.surgeongeneral.gov/library/bonehealth. Accessed October 11, 2007.

US Preventive Services Task Force. *Screening for Osteoporosis in Postmenopausal Women: Recommendations and Rationale*. Rockville, MD: Agency for Healthcare Research and Quality; September 2002. http://www.ahrq.gov/clinic/3rduspstf/osteoporosis/osteorr.htm. Accessed October 16, 2007.

National Osteoporosis Foundation. *Physician's Guide to Prevention and Treatment of Osteoporosis*. Washington, DC: National Osteoporosis Foundation; 2003. http://www.nof.org/physguide/index.asp. Accessed October 16, 2007.

Wong PK, Christie JJ, Wark JD. The effects of smoking on bone health. *Clin Sci (Lond)*. 2007;113(5):233-241.

Stevenson JS. Alcohol use, misuse, abuse, and dependence in later adulthood. *Annu Rev Nurs Res*. 2005;23:245-280.

National Osteoporosis Foundation. Pharmacologic options. In: *Physician's Guide to Prevention and Treatment of Osteoporosis*. Washington, DC: National Osteoporosis Foundation; 2003. http://www.nof.org/physguide/index.asp. Section updated 2005. Accessed October 16, 2007.

Phytoestrogens and bone health. National Institute of Arthritis and Musculoskeletal and Skin Diseases Web site. http://www.niams.nih.gov/Health_Info/Bone/Osteoporosis/Menopause/bone_phyto.asp. Updated August 2005. Accessed October 16, 2007.

Rao SS. Prevention of falls in older adults. *Am Fam Physician*. 2005;72(1):81-88. http://www.aafp.org/afp/20050701/81.html. Accessed September 10, 2007.

Falls among older adults: an overview. Centers for Disease Control and Prevention Web site. http://www.cdc.

gov/ncipc/factsheets/adultfalls.htm. Modified June 27, 2007. Accessed October 16, 2007.

What you can do to prevent falls. Centers for Disease Control and Prevention Web site. http://www.cdc.gov/ncipc/pub-res/toolkit/WhatYouCanDoToPreventFalls.htm Updated September 7, 2006. Accessed October 16, 2007.

The American Academy of Ophthalmology. Policy statement: frequency of ocular examinations; 2006. http://www.aao.org/education/statements/loader.cfm?url=/commonspot/security/getfile.cfm&PageID=19545. Revised August 2006. Accessed October 25, 2006.

American Society of Aging, MetLife Foundation. *Attitudes and Awareness of Brain Health Poll*. San Francisco, CA: American Society of Aging, 2006. http://www.asaging.org/asav2/mindalert/brainhealthpoll.cfm. Accessed October 17, 2007.

National Council on the Aging. *American Perceptions of the Aging in the 21st Century: 2002 Update*. Washington, DC: National Council on the Aging; 2002. http://www.ncoa.org/attachments/AmericanAgingPerceptions.pdf. Accessed October 17, 2007.

Understanding the aging mind. In: National Research Council Committee on Future Directions for Cognitive Research, Stern PC, Carstensen LL, eds. *The Aging Mind: Opportunities in Cognitive Research*. Washington, DC: National Academy Press; 2000:7-13. http://www.nap.edu/openbook.php?isbn=0309069408. Accessed October 18, 2007.

Kukull WA, Higdon R, Bowen JD, et al. Dementia and Alzheimer's disease incidence: a prospective cohort study. *Arch Neurol*. 2002;59:1737-1746.

Petersen R. Mild cognitive impairment. *J Intern Med*. 2004;256(3):183-194.

Albert MS, Blacker D. Mild cognitive impairment and dementia. *Annu Rev Clini Psychol*. 2006;2:379-388.

Bäckman L, Jones S, Berger A, Laukka EJ, Small BJ. Cognitive impairment in preclinical Alzheimer's disease: a meta-analysis. *Neuropsychology*. 2005;19(4):520-531.

New techniques help in diagnosing AD. In: *Unraveling the Mystery*.

Bethesda, MD: National Institute on Aging; December 2003. NIH publication 02-3782. http://www.nia.nih.gov/Alzheimers/Publications/UnravelingTheMystery/. Updated August 29, 2006. Accessed October 18, 2007.

Dementia information page. National Institute of Neurological Disorders and Stroke Web site. http://www.ninds.nih.gov/disorders/dementias/dementia.htm. Updated October 16, 2007. Accessed October 17, 2007.

Alzheimer's Association. Alzheimer's disease facts and figures 2007. http://www.alz.org/alzheimers_disease_alzheimer_statistics.asp. Published 2007. Accessed October 18, 2007.

Arias EA. United States life tables, 2003. *National Vital Statistics Reports.* 2006;54(14):1-6. http://www.cdc.gov/nchs/data/nvsr/nvsr54/nvsr54_14.pdf. Revised March 28, 2007. Accessed October 18, 2007.

Waldstein SR. Health effects on cognitive aging. In: National Research Council Committee on Future Directions for Cognitive Research, Stern PC, Carstensen LL, eds. *The Aging Mind: Opportunities in Cognitive Research.* Washington, DC: National Academy Press; 2000:189-217. http://www.nap.edu/openbook.php?isbn=0309069408. Accessed October 18, 2007.

Arvanitakis Z, Wilson RS, Bienias JL, Evans DA, Bennett DA. Diabetes mellitus and risk of Alzheimer disease and decline in cognitive function. *Arch Neurol.* 2004;61:661-666.

Albert MS, Brown DR, Buchner D. The healthy brain and our aging population: translating science to public health practice. *Alzheimers Dement* 2007;3(suppl 1):s3-s5.

Health information for older adults. Centers for Disease Control and Prevention Web site. http://www.cdc.gov/aging/info.htm. Reviewed April 9, 2007. Accessed September 6, 2007.

Hendrie HC, Albert MS, Butters MA, et al. Report from the Critical Evaluation Study Committee of the Cognitive and Emotional Health Project. *Alzheimers Dement.* 2006;2:12-32.

Genes, lifestyles, and crossword puzzles: can Alzheimer's disease be prevented? National Institute on Aging Web site. http://www.nia.nih.gov/Alzheimers/Publications/ADPrevented. Updated

July 28, 2007. Accessed September 10, 2007.

Asthma and older people. American Lung Association Web site. http://www.lungusa.org/site/pp.asp?c=dvLUK9O0E&b=22598. Updated August 2006. Accessed September 10, 2007.

US Cancer Statistics Working Group. *United States Cancer Statistics, 2003 Incidence and Mortality.* Atlanta, GA: US Dept of Health and Human Services, Centers for Disease Control and Prevention and National Cancer Institute; 2006. http://www.cdc.gov/cancer/npcr/npcrpdfs/US_Cancer_Statistics_2003_Incidence_and_Mortality.pdf. Accessed October 24, 2007.

COPD. NIH Senior Health Web site. http://nihseniorhealth.gov/copd/toc.html. Reviewed January 6, 2006. Accessed October 22, 2007.

Depression: what every woman should know. National Institute of Mental Health Web site. http://www.nimh.nih.gov/health/publications/depression-what-every-woman-should-know/complete-publication.shtml. Reviewed October 23, 2007. Accessed October 25, 2007.

Diabetes and women's health across the life stages: a public health perspective. Centers for Disease Control and Prevention Web site. http://www.cdc.gov/diabetes/pubs/women. Reviewed February 3, 2006. Accessed October 25, 2007.

Seniors and seizures. Epilepsy Foundation Web site. http://www.epilepsyfoundation.org/living/seniors/. Updated 2006. Accessed October 23, 2007.

Oral health for older Americans. Centers for Disease Control and Prevention Web site. http://www.cdc.gov/OralHealth/factsheets/adult-older.htm. Updated December 21, 2006. Accessed October 29, 2007.

Åkesson A, Weismayer C, Newby PK, Wolk A. Combined effect of low-risk dietary and lifestyle behaviors in primary prevention of myocardial infarction in women. *Arch Intern Med.* 2007;167(19):2122-2127.

A special message for women. American Heart Association Web site. http://www.americanheart.org/presenter.jhtml?identifier=2123. Reviewed July 7, 2007. Accessed October 25, 2007.

HIV, AIDS, and older people. National Institute on Aging Web site. http://

www.nia.nih.gov/HealthInformation/Publications/hiv-aids.htm. Reviewed October 16, 2007. Accessed October 25, 2007.

Facts and statistics. National Association for Continence. http://www.nafc.org/statistics/index.htm. Updated December 4, 2006. Accessed October 25, 2007.

Treatment options for urinary incontinence. National Association for Continence. http://www.nafc.org/about_incontinence/treatment.htm. Accessed October 25, 2007.

Davis MP, Srivastava M. Demographics, assessment and management of pain in the elderly. *Drugs Aging.* 2003;20(1):23-57.

Zhu K, Devine A, Dick IM, Prince RL. Association of back pain frequency with mortality, coronary heart events, mobility, and quality of life in elderly women. *Spine.* 2007;32(18):2012-2018.

Stroke causes special problems for women. National Stroke Association Web site. http://www.stroke.org/site/PageServer?pagename=WOMCOMP. Accessed October 26, 2007.

Arthritis. NIH Senior Health Web site. http://nihseniorhealth.gov/arthritis/toc.html. Reviewed August 15, 2006. Accessed October 22, 2007.

Arthritis advice. National Institute on Aging Web site. http://www.nia.nih.gov/HealthInformation/Publications/arthritis.htm. Updated October 16, 2007. Accessed October 24, 2007.

Balance problems. NIH Senior Health Web site. http://nihseniorhealth.gov/balanceproblems/toc.html. Reviewed January 26, 2007. Accessed October 22, 2007.

Balance, dizziness, and you. National Institute on Deafness and Other Communication Disorders Web site. http://www.nidcd.nih.gov/health/balance/baldizz.asp. Updated September 25, 2007. Accessed October 24, 2007.

Skin care and aging. National Institute on Aging Web site. http://www.niapublications.org/agepages/skin.asp. Updated December 29, 2005. Accessed October 23, 2007.

Aging and your eyes. National Institute on Aging Web site. http://www.nia.nih.gov/HealthInformation/Publications/eyes.htm. Updated June 15, 2007. Accessed September 10, 2007.

Bibliography

Flu-get the shot. National Institute on Aging Web site. http://www.nia.nih.gov/HealthInformation/Publications/flu.htm. Updated October 16, 2007. Accessed October 23, 2007.

Key facts about seasonal flu vaccine. Centers for Disease Control and Prevention Web site. http://www.cdc.gov/flu/protect/keyfacts.htm. Updated September 19, 2007. Accessed October 23, 2007.

Good health habits for prevention. Centers for Disease Control and Prevention Web site. http://www.cdc.gov/flu/protect/habits.htm. Updated October 6, 2006. Accessed October 24, 2007.

Centers for Disease Control and Prevention. Recommended Adult Immunization Schedule—United States, October 2007—September 2008. *MMWR.* 2007;56(41):Q1-Q4.

Hearing loss. NIH Senior Health Web site. http://nihseniorhealth.gov/hearingloss/toc.html. Reviewed March 13, 2007. Accessed October 22, 2007.

Hearing screening. American Speech-Language Association Web site. http://www.asha.org/public/hearing/testing. Updated . Accessed October 25, 2007.

Medication effects on hearing. American Speech-Language Association Web site. http://www.asha.org/public/hearing/disorders/med_effects.htm Accessed October 25, 2007.

Self-test. American Speech-Language Association Web site. http://www.asha.org/public/hearing/disorders/Self-Test.htm. Accessed October 25, 2007.

How do I know if I have a hearing loss? American Speech-Language Association Web site. http://www.asha.org/public/hearing/disorders/how_know.htm. Accessed October 25, 2007.

Shingles. National Institute of Allergy and Infectious Diseases Web site. http://www3.niaid.nih.gov/healthscience/healthtopics/shingles. Updated September 27, 2006. Accessed October 22, 2007.

Lindau ST, Schumm P, Laumann EO, et al. A study of sexuality and health among older adults in the United States. *N Eng J Med.* 2007;357:762-774.

Sexuality in later life. National Institute on Aging Web site. http://www.

niapublications.org/agepages/sexuality.asp. Updated December 20, 2005. Accessed October 26, 2007.

A good night's sleep. National Institute on Aging Web site. http://www.niapublications.org/agepages/sleep.asp. Updated June 25, 2007. Accessed September 10, 2007.

Wolkove N, Elkholy O, Baltzan M, Palayew M. Sleep and aging: 1. Sleep disorders commonly found in older people. *CMAJ* 2007;176(9):1299-1304.

Nielsen-Bohlman L, Panzer AM, Kindig DA, Eds. *Health Literacy: A Prescription to End Confusion.* Washington, DC: National Academies Press; 2004:63. http://www.nap.edu/openbook.php?isbn=0309091179. Accessed December 12, 2007.

Health quackery: spotting health scams. National Institute on Aging Web site. http://www.niapublications.org/agepages/healthqy.asp. Updated June 26, 2006. Accessed September 10, 2007.

Healthy aging, preserving function, and improving quality of life among older Americans: at a glance 2007. Centers for Disease Control and Prevention Web site. http://www.cdc.gov/nccdphp/publications/aag/aging.htm. Reviewed May 24, 2007. Accessed September 6, 2007.

Torpy JM. Frailty in older adults. JAMA. 2006;296(18):2280. http://jama.ama-assn.org/cgi/content/full/296/18/maxtoshow=&HITS=10&hits=10&RESULTFORMAT=&fulltext=frailty&searchid=1&FIRSTINDEX=0&resourcetype=HWCIT. Accessed October 11, 2007.

US Dept of Health and Human Services. *Physical Activity and Health: A Report of the Surgeon General.* Atlanta, GA: US Dept of Health and Human Services, Centers for Disease Control and Prevention, National Center for Chronic Disease Prevention and Health Promotion, 1996. http://www.cdc.gov/nccdphp/sgr/sgr.htm. Accessed October 11, 2007.

Taylor AH, Cable NT, Faulkner G, Hillsdon M, Narici M Van Der Bij AK. Physical activity and older adults: a review of health benefits and the effectiveness of interventions. *J Sports Sci.* 2004;22(8):703-725.

Exercise. National Institute on Aging Web site. http://www.nia.nih.

gov/healthinformation/publications/exercise.htm. Updated August 14, 2007. Accessed September 6, 2007.

Good nutrition: it's a way of life. National Institute on Aging Web site. http://www.niapublications.org/agepages/nutrition.asp. Updated December 29, 2005. Accessed October 23, 2007.

US Dept of Health and Human Services. *The Health Benefits of Smoking Cessation: A Report of the Surgeon General.* Atlanta, GA: US Dept of Health and Human Services, Public Health Service, Centers for Disease Control, Center for Chronic Disease Prevention and Health Promotion, Office on Smoking and Health, 1990. http://profiles.nlm.nih.gov/NN/B/B/C/T/. Accessed October 11, 2007.

Alcohol use and abuse. National Institutes on Aging Web site. http://www.nia.nih.gov/HealthInformation/Publications/alcohol.htm. Updated October 16, 2007. Accessed October 23, 2007.

Getting your affairs in order. National Institute on Aging Web site. http://www.nia.nih.gov/HealthInformation/Publications/Affairs.htm. Updated May 16, 2007. Accessed September 10, 2007.

VIOLENCE AGAINST WOMEN

Violence against women fact sheet. United National Population Fund Web site. http://www.unfpa.org/swp/2005/presskit/factsheets/facts_vaw.htm. Published 2005. Accessed September 1, 2007.

Domestic violence is a serious, widespread social problem in America: the facts. Family Violence Prevention Fund Web site. http://endabuse.org/resources/facts. Published 2007. Accessed August 31, 2007.

Collins KS, Schoen C, Joseph S, et al. Health concerns across a woman's lifespan: 1998 survey of women's health. The Commonwealth Fund Web site. http://www.commonwealthfund.org/publications/publications_show.htm?doc_id=221554#areaCitation. Published May 5, 1999. Accessed September 3, 2007.

Violence against women in the United States. National Organization for Women Web site. http://www.now.org/issues/violence/stats.html. Accessed September 13, 2007.

Rennison CM, Welchans S. Intimate partner violence. *Bureau of Justice Statistics Special Report*. May 2000.

Teen dating violence statistics. Bureau of Justice Web site. http://www.safenetwork.org/date_rape_statistics.html. Published May 2000. Accessed September 4, 2007.

Intimate partner violence: overview. Centers for Disease Control and Prevention Web site. http://www.cdc.gov/ncipc/factsheets/ipvfacts.htm. Updated August 26, 2006. Accessed September 1, 2007.

Survey of recent statistics. American Bar Association Web site. http://www.abanet.org/domviol/statistics.html. Accessed October 22, 2007.

Rice M. Domestic violence. National Center for PTSD, US Department of Veterans Affairs Web site. http://www.ncptsd.va.gov/ncmain/ncdocs/fact_shts/fs_domestic_violence.html. Updated May 22, 2007. Accessed September 13, 2007.

Violence against women. World Health Organization Web site. http://www.who.int/mediacentre/factsheets/fs239/en/print.html. Updated June 2000. Accessed September 1, 2007.

Interpersonal violence: economic impact of violence. Disease Control Priorities Project Web site. http://www.dcp2.org/pubs/DCP/40/Section/5678. Published 2006. Accessed September 2, 2007.

The facts on preventing violence against women and children. Family Violence Prevention Fund Web site. http://www.endabuse.org. Accessed September 13, 2007.

Tjaden P, Toennes N. Extent, nature, and consequences of intimate partner violence against women: findings from the national violence against women survey. The National Institute of Justice and the Centers for Disease Control and Prevention Web site. http://www.ncjrs.gov/txtfiles1/nij/181867.txt. Published July 2000. Accessed September 1, 2007.

Coker AL, Smith PH, Bethea L, King MR, McKeown RE. Physical health consequences of physical and psychological intimate partner violence. *Arch Fam Med*. 2000;9:451-457.

Edleson JL. Mothers and children: understanding the links between woman battering and child abuse. Minnesota Center Against Violence and Abuse Web site. http://www.mincava.umn.edu/documents/nij/nij.html. Published 1995. Accessed September 13, 2007.

Child abuse and domestic violence. Family Violence Prevention Fund Web site. http://endabuse.org/programs/printable/display.php3?NewsFlashID=284. Published October 18, 2001. Accessed September 13, 2007.

Parker M, Bergmark RE, Attridge M, Miller-Burke J. Domestic violence and its effect on children. Optum Research Web site. http://www.optumanswers.com/research/articles/domestic/shtml. Published December 2000. Accessed September 12, 2007.

About domestic violence. Office on Violence Against Women Web site. http://www.usdoj.gov/ovw/domviolence.htm. Accessed August 28, 2007.

Dating violence. Alabama Coalition Against Domestic Violence Web site. http://www.acadv.org/dating.html. Accessed August 28, 2007.

Dating violence. The National Center for Victims of Crime Web site. http://www.ncvc.org/ncvc/main.aspx?dbid=db_DVRCTipSheets750. Published 2007. Accessed September 10, 2007.

Teen dating abuse fact sheet. Centers for Disease Control and Prevention Web site. http://www.cdc.gov/ncipc/dvp/datingviolence.htm. Published 2006. Accessed August 27, 2007.

What you need to know about dating violence: a teen's handbook. Liz Claiborne Women's Work Web site. http://www.loveisrespect.org/resources/teen_handbook.pdf. Published 2000. Accessed September 10, 2007.

Warning signs of dating violence. My Sistahs: A Project from Advocates for Youth Web site. http://www.mysistahs.org/features/datingviolence/warningsigns.htm. Accessed September 13, 2007.

Understanding intimate partner violence. Centers for Disease Control and Prevention Web site. http://www.cdc.gov/ncicp/dvp/ipv_factsheet.pdf. Published 2006. Accessed October 22, 2007.

Safety planning. WomensLaw.org Web site. http://www.womenslaw.org/safety5.htm. Updated July 13, 2005. Accessed October 4, 2007.

Heise L, Ellsberg M, Gottemoeller M. Ending violence against women. Issues in World Health, Series L, Number 11. *Population Reports*. Baltimore, MD: Population Information Program, The Johns Hopkins University School of Public Health. XXVII(4):1999.

Domestic violence. The American College of Obstetricians and Gynecologists Web site. http://www.acog.org/publications/patient_education/bp083.cfm. Published May 2002. Accessed September 3, 2007.

Relationships and dating. Teen Health Connection Web site. http://www.teenhealthconnection.org/relationships.htm. Accessed November 1, 2007.

Get the facts: what's a healthy relationship? Centers for Disease Control and Prevention Injury Center's ChooseRespect.org Web site. http://www.chooserespect.org/scripts/teens/healthy.asp. Accessed November 1, 2007.

Healthy vs. unhealthy relationships. Texas Woman's University Web site. http://www.twu.edu/o-sl/counseling/SelfHelp023.html. Updated August 1, 2007. Accessed November 1, 2007.

Characteristics of healthy and unhealthy relationships. Avalon Sexual Assault Centre Web site. http://www.avaloncentre.ca. Accessed November 1, 2007.

Healthy and unhealthy relationships: what's the difference? Jewish Women International Web site. http://www.jwi.org/site/c.okLWJ3MPKtH/b.2448601/k.9799/healthy_and_unhealthy_relationships_whats_the_difference.htm. Published 2006. Accessed November 1, 2007.

Healthy vs. unhealthy relationships. Advocates for Youth Web site. http://www.advocatesforyouth.org/youth/health/relationships/healthy.htm. Accessed October 30, 2007.

Domestic violence warning signs. Turning Point Services Web site. http://www.turningpointservices.org/Domestic%20Violence%20-%20Warning%20Signs.htm. Accessed September 13, 2007.

Let's talk about domestic violence. American Psychiatric Association Web site. http://www.healthyminds.org/multimedia/domesticviolence.pdf. Published 2005. Accessed September 7, 2007.

Meichenbaum D. Family violence: treatment of perpetrators and victims. The Melissa Institute for Violence

Prevention and Treatment Web site. http://www.melissainstitute.org/documents/treating_perpetrators.pdf. Accessed October 12, 2007.

Stith SM, Smith DB, Penn CE, Ward DB, Tritt D. Intimate partner physical abuse perpetration and victimization risk factors: a meta-analytic review. *Aggress Violent Behav.* 2004;10:65-98.

Chapter 4: violence by intimate partners. In: Krug EG, Dahlberg LL, Mercy JA, Zwi AB, Lozano R, eds. *World Report on Violence and Health.* Geneva, Switzerland:World Health Organization. 2002:87-121.

Intimate partner violence. Help for Domestic Violence Web site. http://www.helpfordomesticviolence.com/intimate%20partner%20violence%20abuse.htm. Accessed October 24, 2007.

Violence against women: identifying risk factors. National Institute of Justice. Office of Justice Programs, US Department of Justice Web site. http://www.ojp.usdoj.gov/nij/pubs-sum/197019.htm. Published November 2004. Accessed September 1, 2007.

O'Keefe M. Teen dating violence: a review of risk factors and prevention efforts. National Online Resource Center on Violence Against Women Web site. http://new.vawnet.org/category/documents.php?docid=409&category_id=695. Published April 2005. Accessed September 7, 2007.

Varia S. Dating violence among adolescents. Advocates for Youth Web site. http://www.advocatesforyouth.org/publications/factsheet/fsdating.htm. Published November 2006. Accessed September 9, 2007.

Finkel EJ. Impelling and inhibiting forces in the perpetration of intimate partner violence. *Rev Gen Psychol.* 2007;11(2): 193-207.

Domestic violence safety plan. American Bar Association Web site. http://www.abanet.org/tips/dvsafety.html. Accessed September 13, 2007.

Safety plan. National Coalition Against Domestic Violence Web site. http://www.ncadv.org/protectyourself/SafetyPlan_130.html. Published 2005. Accessed September 10, 2007.

Having a crisis: violence? Crisis Intervention of Houston Web site. http://www.crisishotline.org/having_violence_1.html. Accessed October 14, 2007.

Domestic violence and abuse: help, treatment, intervention, and prevention. HelpGuide.org Web site. http://www.helpguide.org/mental/domestic_violence_abuse_help_treatment_prevention.htm. Updated September 4, 2007. Accessed September 14, 2007.

Personal safety planning. Domestic Abuse Project Web site. http://www.domesticabuseproject.org/safetyplanning.asp. Published 2004. September 14, 2007.

Safety planning. Domestic Violence Forum Web site. http://www.dvforum.co.uk/safety_planning. Accessed September 14, 2007.

Cycle of violence. Crisis Support Network Web site. http://crisis-support.org/cycle.htm. Accessed September 6, 2007.

Cycle of violence. Eastside Domestic Violence Program Web site. http://www.edvp.org/aboutdv/cycle.htm. Accessed September 6, 2007.

Breaking free from domestic violence. Florida International University Web site. http://www.fiu.edu/~oea/InsightsFall2004/online_library/articles/breaking%20free%20from%20domestic%20violence.htm. Published 2003. Accessed December 11, 2007.

Teen dating violence. National Youth Violence Prevention Resource Center Web site. http://www.safeyouth.org/scripts/teens/dating.asp. Accessed September 9, 2007.

Elder abuse. MedlinePlus Web site. http://www.nlm.nih.gov/medlineplus/elderabuse.html. Updated October 24, 2007. Accessed November 20, 2007.

The national elder abuse incidence study. The National Center on Elder Abuse at The American Public Human Services Association in collaboration with Westat, Inc. Administration on Aging Website. http://www.aoa.gov/eldfam/elder_rights/elder_abuse/abusereport_full.pdf. Published September 1998. Accessed November 19, 2007.

Wolf RS. The nature and scope of elder abuse. American Society on Aging Web site. http://www.asaging.org/generations/gen-24-2/intro.html. Accessed December 17, 2007.

Frequently asked questions. National Center on Elder Abuse Web site. http://www.elderabusecenter.org/default.cfm?p=faqs.cfm. Published 2007. Accessed November 20, 2007.

What should I do if someone I know is being abused. National Committee for the Prevention of Elder Abuse Web site. http://www.preventelderabuse.org/help/should_ido.html. Updated March 2003. Accessed November 20, 2007.

Sexual assault. The National Center for Victims of Crime Web site. http://www.ncvc.org/ncvc/main.aspx?dbname=documentviewer&documentid=32369. Accessed September 4, 2007.

Sexual assault. Minnesota Department of Public Safety, Office of Justice Programs Web site. http://www.ojp.state.mn.us/cj/publications/FS-2003-001_Sexual_%20Assault.pdf. Published December 2003. Accessed September 5, 2007.

Crime characteristics. US Department of Justice, Office of Justice Programs, Bureau of Justice Web site. http://www.ojp.usdoj.gov/bjs/cvict_c.htm. Updated August 9, 2007. Accessed September 5, 2007.

Sexual violence: fact sheet. Centers for Disease Control and Prevention Web site. http://www.cdc.gov/ncipc/factsheets/svfacts.htm. Updated April 10, 2007. Accessed September 13, 2007.

Preventing sexual harassment: a fact sheet for employees. US Department of Transportation Web site. http://www.dotcr.ost.dot.gov/Documents/complaint/Preventing_Sexual_Harassment.htm. Published 2001. Accessed September 13, 2007.

Sexual harassment. The US Equal Employment Opportunity Commission Web site. http://www.eeoc.gov/types/sexual_harassment.html. Updated May 17, 2007. Accessed September 13, 2007.

What to do if you are raped or sexually assaulted. Center for Substance Abuse Prevention Web site. http://pathwayscourses.samhsa.gov/vawc/vawc_8_pg1.htm. Updated June 15, 2004. Accessed September 5, 2007.

Preventing sexual assaults. Center for Substance Abuse Prevention Web site. http://pathwayscourses.samhsa.gov/vawc/vawc_fs_07.htm. Updated June 15, 2004. Accessed September 4, 2007.

Preventing sexual assault. Crime and Violence Prevention Center. California Department of Justice Web site. http://www.sfgov.org/site/uploadedfiles/police/information/sexualassualt.pdf. Accessed September 13, 2007.

Stalking fact sheet. The National Center for Victims of Crime Web site. http://www.ncvc.org/src/agp.net/components/documentviewer/download.aspxnz?documentid=40616. Updated October 2005. Accessed September 8, 2007.

Tjaden P, Thoennes N. Stalking in America: findings from the national violence against women survey. US Department of Justice, National Criminal Justice Reference Service Web site. http://www.ncjrs.org/pdffiles/169592.pdf. Published April 1998. Accessed September 10, 2007.

10 things you need to know about stalking. The National Center for Victims of Crime Web site. http://www.ncvc.org. Accessed September 10, 2007.

Southworth C, Dawson S, Fraser C, Tucker S. A high-tech twist on abuse: technology, intimate partner stalking, and advocacy. Violence Against Women Online Resources Web site. http://www.mincava.umn.edu/documents/commissioned/stalkingandtech/stalkingandtech.html. Published June 2005. Accessed September 7, 2007.

Stalking. The National Center for Victims of Crime Web site. http://www.ncvc.org/src/agp.net/components/documentviewer/download.aspxnz?documentid=40616. Accessed September 10, 2007.

Gregorie TM. Cyberstalking: dangers on the information superhighway. Stalking Resource Center, The National Center for Victims of Crime Web site. http://www.ncvc.org/src/main.aspx?dbid=db_cyberstalking814. Accessed September 12, 2007.

Are you being stalked? The National Center for Victims of Crime Web site. http://www.ncvc.org/src/agp.net/components/documentviewer/download.aspxnz?documentid=37408. Accessed September 6, 2007.

Stalking victimization. Office for Victims of Crime Web site. http://www.ojp.usdoj.gov/ovc/publications/infores/help_series/pdftxt/stalkingvictimization.pdf. Accessed September 3, 2007.

Brody JE. Do's and don'ts for thwarting stalkers. Crisis Support Network Web site. http://crisis-support.org/news.htm. Published August 25, 1998. Accessed September 10, 2007.

1999 report on cyberstalking: a new challenge for law enforcement and industry. US Department of Justice

Web site. http://www.usdoj.gov/criminal/cybercrime/cyberstalking.htm. Published August 1999. Accessed October 22, 2007.

Cyberstalking/harassment. CyberAngels Web site. http://www.cyberangels.org/security/stalking.html. Published 2007. Accessed October 22, 2007.

Cyberstalking. The National Center for Victims of Crime Web site. http://www.ncvc.org/ncvc/main.aspx?dbname=documentviewer&documentid=32458#4. Published 2003. Accessed October 22, 2007.

UROLOGIC AND KIDNEY HEALTH

Your urinary system and how it works. National Institute of Diabetes and Digestive and Kidney Diseases Web site. http://kidney.niddk.nih.gov/kudiseases/pubs/yoururinary/index.htm. Updated October 2006. Accessed August 3, 2007.

What I need to know about urinary tract infections. National Institute of Diabetes and Digestive and Kidney Diseases Web site. http://kidney.niddk.nih.gov/kudiseases/pubs/uti_ez/index.htm. Updated August 2007. Accessed August 30, 2007.

Urinary incontinence in women. National Institute of Diabetes and Digestive and Kidney Diseases Web site. http://kidney.niddk.nih.gov/kudiseases/pubs/uiwomen/index.htm. Updated October 2007. Accessed August 6, 2007.

What I need to know about kidney stones. National Institute of Diabetes and Digestive and Kidney Diseases Web site. http://kidney.niddk.nih.gov/kudiseases/pubs/stones_ez/index.htm. Updated April 2007. Accessed August 13, 2007.

Talking to your health care team about bladder control. National Institute of Diabetes and Digestive and Kidney Diseases Web site. http://kidney.niddk.nih.gov/kudiseases/pubs/talk_ez/index.htm. Published August 2003. Accessed August 3, 2007.

Your daily bladder diary. National Institute of Diabetes and Digestive and Kidney Diseases Web site. http://kidney.niddk.nih.gov/kudiseases/pubs/diary/pages/page1.htm. Accessed Aug 7, 2007.

Litwan MS, Saigal CS, eds. Urologic Diseases in America. US Department of Health and Human Services, Public Health Service, National Institutes of Health, National Institute of Diabetes and Digestive

and Kidney Diseases. Washington, DC: US Government Printing Office; 2007. NIH Publication 07-5512.

Interstitial cystitis/painful bladder syndrome. National Institute of Diabetes and Digestive and Kidney Diseases Web site. http://kidney.niddk.nih.gov/kudiseases/pubs/interstitialcystitis/index.htm. Published June 2005. Accessed August 13, 2007.

Urinary tract infections in adults. American Urological Association Web site. http://www.urologyhealth.org/search/index.cfm?topic=147&search=urinary%20AND%20tract%20AND%20infections&searchtype=and. Accessed August 8, 2007.

Urinary tract infections. National Kidney Foundation Web site. http://www.kidney.org/atoz/atozItem.cfm?id=116. May 2005. Accessed August 3, 2007.

Stewart EG, Spencer P. The V Book: A Doctor's Guide to Complete Vulvovaginal Health. New York, NY: Bantam Books; 2002:347-358.

Causes and natural history of bladder control problems. American Urological Association Web site. http://www.urologyhealth.org/search/index.cfm?topic=172&search=bladder%20AND%20control&searchtype=and. Accessed August 8, 2007.

Culligan P, Heit M. Urinary incontinence in women: evaluation and management. Am Fam Physician. The American Academy of Family Physicians Web site. http://www.aafp.org/afp/20001201/2433.html. Published December 1, 2000. Accessed December 13, 2007.

Bren L. Controlling urinary incontinence. FDA Consumer. http://www.fda.gov/fdac/features/2005/505_incontinence.html. Published September-October 2005. Accessed August 7, 2007.

Urinary incontinence. National Kidney Foundation Web site. http://www.kidney.org/atoz/atozItem.cfm?id=79. Published May 2004. Accessed August 8, 2007.

Urinary incontinence. The American College of Obstetricians and Gynecologists Web site. http://www.acog.org/publications/patient_education/bp081.cfm. Published November 2005. Accessed August 9, 2007.

Nerve disease and bladder control. National Institute of Diabetes and

Digestive and Kidney Diseases Web site. http://kidney.niddk.nih.gov/kudiseases/pubs/nervedisease/index.htm. Published January 2005. Accessed August 4, 2007.

Treatments for urinary incontinence in women. National Institute of Diabetes and Digestive and Kidney Diseases Web site. http://kidney.niddk.nih.gov/kudiseases/pubs/treatmentsuiwomen/index.htm. Published June 2003. Accessed August 9, 2007.

Brubaker, L. Postpartum urinary incontinence. *BMJ.* 2002;324:1227-1228.

Menopause and bladder control. National Institute of Diabetes and Digestive and Kidney Diseases Web site. http://kidney.niddk.nih.gov/kudiseases/pubs/menopause_ez/index.htm. Published April 2004. Accessed August 13, 2007.

Bladder prolapse (cystocele). American Urological Association Web site. http://www.urologyhealth.org/adult/index.cfm?cat=03&topic=590. Published December 2005. Accessed August 12, 2007.

Cystocele (fallen bladder). National Institute of Diabetes and Digestive and Kidney Diseases Web site. http://kidney.niddk.nih.gov/kudiseases/pubs/cystocele/index.htm. Published November 2004. Accessed August 13, 2007.

Angello A. Cystocele. University of Michigan Health System Web site. http://www.med.umich.edu/1libr/wha/wha_cystocel_crs.htm. Published November 2004. Accessed Aug 2, 2007.

Hendrix SL, Clark A, Nygaard I, Aragaki A, Barnabei V, McTiernan, A. Pelvic organ prolapse in the women's health initiative: gravity and gravidity. *Am J Obstet Gynecol.* 2002;186(6):1160-1166.

Rortveit G, Brown JS, Thom DH, Van Den Eeden SK, Creasman JM, Subak LL. Symptomatic pelvic organ prolapse: prevalence and risk factors in a population-based, racially diverse cohort. *Obstet Gynecol.* 2007;109(6):1396-1403.

Interstitial cystitis. American Urological Association Web site. http://www.urologyhealth.org/search/index.cfm?topic=210&search=interstitial&searchtype=and. Published January 2004. Accessed August 12, 2007.

MacDiarmid SA, Sand PK. Diagnosis of interstitial cystitis/painful bladder syndrome in patients with overactive bladder symptoms. *Rev Urol.* 2007;9(1):9-16.

An introduction to interstitial cystitis. Interstitial Cystitis Association Web site. http://www.ichelp.org/PatientInformation/AnIntroductiontoInterstitialCystitis/tabid/80/Default.aspx. Accessed August 4, 2007.

Interstitial cystitis: what is interstitial cystitis? National Kidney Foundation Web site. http://www.kidney.org/atoz/atozitem.cfm?id=81. Updated April 27, 2004. Accessed August 5, 2007.

ICA and ARHP Host Washington DC Consensus Meeting on Interstitial Cystitis/Painful Bladder Syndrome. *ICA Physicians' Resources.* Interstitial Cystitis Association Web site. http://www.ichelp.org/PhysiciansResources/ProfessionalPerspectivesSpring2007.htm. Published Spring 2007. Accessed August 12, 2007.

What I need to know about interstitial cystitis/painful bladder syndrome. National Institute of Diabetes and Digestive and Kidney Diseases Web site. http://kidney.niddk.nih.gov/kudiseases/pubs/interstitialcystitis_ez/. Updated October 2007. Accessed December 13, 2007.

Diagnosis: cystoscopy with hydrodistention. Interstitial Cystitis Association Web site. http://www.ichelp.org/treatmentandselfhelp/cystoscopyandhydrodistention.html. Published 2002. Accessed August 7, 2007.

Oral medications for IC: an expanded treatment arsenal. *ICA Update.* Interstitial Cystitis Association Web site. http://www.ichelp.org/treatmentandselfhelp/oralmedsforic.html. Published May/June 2002. Accessed August 4, 2007.

Have you thought about trying these medications? *ICA Update.* Interstitial Cystitis Association Web site. http://www.ichelp.org/treatmentandselfhelp/haveyouthoughtabouttryingthesemeds.html. Published December 2003/January 2004. Accessed August 5, 2007.

Daily living with IC: over-the-counter products that can help you. *ICA Update.* Interstitial Cystitis Association Web site. http://www.ichelp.org/treatmentandselfhelp/dailylivingwithicotcproducts.html. Published November 2005. Accessed August 5, 2007.

Alternative strategies in the treatment of IC: over-the-counter help for your symptoms. *ICA Update.* Interstitial Cystitis Association Web site. http://www.ichelp.org/treatmentandselfhelp/altstrategiesinictreatment.html. Published November 2005. Accessed August 3, 2007.

Surgical procedures. Interstitial Cystitis Association Web site. http://www.ichelp.org/treatmentandselfhelp/surgery.html. Published November 2005. Accessed August 5, 2007.

ICA Professional Perspectives. Interstitial Cystitis Association Web site. http://www.ichelp.org/physiciansresources/professionalperspectivesspring2006.html. Published spring 2006. Accessed August 5, 2007.

Medical management of stone disease. American Urological Association Web site. http://www.urologyhealth.org/search/index.cfm?topic=102&search=stone%20AND%20disease&searchtype=and. Published September 2003. Accessed August 13, 2007.

Kidney stones. National Kidney Foundation Web site. http://www.kidney.org/atoz/atozItem.cfm?id=84. Published May 2004. Accessed August 13, 2007.

What I need to know about kidney stones. National Institute of Diabetes and Digestive and Kidney Diseases Web site. http://kidney.niddk.nih.gov/kudiseases/pubs/stones_ez/index.htm. Updated April 2007. Accessed August 13, 2007.

Kidney stones. Medline Plus Web site. http://www.nlm.nih.gov/medlineplus/kidneystones.html. Updated August 14, 2007. Accessed October 5, 2007.

Kidney stones in adults. National Institute of Diabetes and Digestive and Kidney Diseases Web site. http://kidney.niddk.nih.gov/kudiseases/pubs/stonesadults/index.htm. Published December 2004. Accessed October 3, 2007.

Chronic kidney disease: a family affair. National Institute of Diabetes and Digestive and Kidney Diseases Web site. http://kidney.niddk.nih.gov/kudiseases/pubs/chronickidneydiseases/index.htm. Published March 2005. Accessed August 11, 2007.

Coresh J, Selvin E, Stevens L, et al. Prevalence of chronic kidney disease in the United States. *JAMA.* 2007;298(17):2038-2047.

Your kidneys and how they work. National Institute of Diabetes and

Digestive and Kidney Diseases Web site. http://kidney.niddk.nih.gov/kudiseases/pubs/yourkidneys/index.htm#rate. Published November 2005. Accessed August 19, 2007.

Chronic kidney disease (CKD). National Kidney Foundation Web site. http://www.kidney.org/kidneydisease/ckd/index.cfm. Accessed August 7, 2007.

Chronic renal failure. MedlinePlus Web site. http://www.nlm.nih.gov/medlineplus/ency/article/000471.htm. Published September 2005. Accessed August 13, 2007.

Kidney disease of diabetes. National Institute of Diabetes and Digestive and Kidney Diseases Web site. http://kidney.niddk.nih.gov/kudiseases/pubs/kdd/index.htm. Updated October 2006. Accessed August 11, 2007.

Sexuality and chronic kidney disease. National Kidney Foundation Web site. http://www.kidney.org/atoz/atozItem.cfm?id=108. Published May 2004. Accessed August 13, 2007.

IC and sexuality. Interstitial Cystitis Association Web site. http://www.ichelp.org/PatientInformation/TreatmentOptions/Brochures/ICandSexuality/tabid/249/Default.aspx. Published 2007. Accessed December 13, 2007.

Exercising your pelvic muscles. National Institute of Diabetes and Digestive and Kidney Diseases Web site. http://kidney.niddk.nih.gov/kudiseases/pubs/exercise_ez/index.htm. April 2002. Published April 2002. Accessed August 3, 2007.

DIGESTIVE HEALTH

Your digestive system and how it works. National Institute of Diabetes and Digestive and Kidney Diseases Web site. http://digestive.niddk.nih.gov/ddiseases/pubs/yrdd/index.htm. Published May 2004. Accessed September 12, 2007.

Ovarian Cancer Symptoms Consensus Statement. Women's Cancer Network Web site. http://www.wcn.org/ov_cancer_cons.html. Published 2007. Accessed September 10, 2007.

Weber AM, Belinson JL. Inflammatory bowel disease—a complicating factor in gynecologic disorders? *Medscape Gen Med*. 1999;1(2):408847. http://www.medscape.com/viewarticle/408847_print. February 1997. Accessed November 5, 2007.

Celiac disease. National Institute of Diabetes and Digestive and Kidney Diseases Web site. http://digestive.niddk.nih.gov/ddiseases/pubs/celiac/index.htm. Published August 2007. Accessed September 14, 2007.

Heartburn, gastroesophageal reflux (GER), and gastroesophageal reflux disease (GERD). National Institute of Diabetes and Digestive and Kidney Diseases Web site. http://digestive.niddk.nih.gov/ddiseases/pubs/gerd/index.htm. Published May 2007. Accessed September 14, 2007.

Morning sickness. The American College of Obstetricians and Gynecologists Web site. http://www.acog.org/publications/patient_education/bp126.cfm. Published September 2005. Accessed October 9, 2007.

Pregnancy symptoms: what to expect during the second trimester. Mayo Clinic Web site. http://mayoclinic.com/print/pregnancy/PR00018/METHOD=print. Published June 2007. Accessed October 9, 2007.

Pregnancy symptoms: what to expect during the third trimester. Mayo Clinic Web site. http://mayoclinic.com/print/pregnancy/PR00009/METHOD=print. Published June 2007. Accessed October 9, 2007.

Irritable bowel syndrome. National Institute of Diabetes and Digestive and Kidney Diseases Web site. http://digestive.niddk.nih.gov/ddiseases/pubs/ibs/index.htm. Published September 2007. Accessed September 14, 2007.

Karlstadt RG. What everyone should know about gastrointestinal disorders in women. American College of Gastroenterology Web site. http://www.acg.gi.org/patients/gihealth/women.asp. Updated April 2007. Accessed July 31, 2007.

Chang L, Toner BB, Fukudo S, et al. Gender, age, society, culture, and the patient's perspective in the functional gastrointestinal disorders. *Gastroenterology*. 2006;130:1435-1446.

Foxx-Orenstein A. IBS—review and what's new. *MedGenMed*. 2006;8(3):20.

Frissora CL. Nuances in treating irritable bowel syndrome. *Rev Gastroenterol Disord*. 2007;7(2):89-96.

Coping with IBS. WebMD Web site. http://www.webmd.com/ibs/guide/coping-with-ibs. Published May 2004. Accessed August 31, 2007.

Gallstones. National Institute of Diabetes and Digestive and Kidney Diseases Web site. http://digestive.niddk.nih.gov/ddiseases/pubs/gallstones/index.htm. Published July 2007. Accessed September 12, 2007. Published July 2007. Accessed September 12, 2007.

Lactose intolerance. National Institute of Diabetes and Digestive and Kidney Diseases Web site. http://digestive.niddk.nih.gov/ddiseases/pubs/lactoseintolerance/index.htm. Published March 2006. Accessed September 14, 2007.

GERD. Mayo Clinic Web site. http://mayoclinic.com/print/gerd/DS00967/DSECTION=all&METHOD=print. Published May 25, 2007. Accessed September 15, 2007.

Viral hepatitis: A through E and beyond. National Institute of Diabetes and Digestive and Kidney Diseases Web site. http://digestive.niddk.nih.gov/ddiseases/pubs/viralhepatitis/index.htm. Published May 2003. Accessed November 8, 2007.

Crohn's disease. National Institute of Diabetes and Digestive and Kidney Diseases Web site. http://digestive.niddk.nih.gov/ddiseases/pubs/crohns/index.htm. Published February 2006. Accessed September 14, 2007.

Ulcerative colitis. National Institute of Diabetes and Digestive and Kidney Diseases Web site. http://digestive.niddk.nih.gov/ddiseases/pubs/colitis/index.htm. Published February 2006. Accessed September 14, 2007.

American Gastroenterological Association Institute. American Gastroenterological Association Institute medical position statement on the use of gastrointestinal medications in pregnancy. *Gastroenterology*. 2006;131:278-282.

Mahadevan U. Fertility and pregnancy in the patient with inflammatory bowel disease. *Gut*. 2006;55:1198-1206.

The intimate relationship of sex and IBD. Crohn's and Colitis Foundation of America Web site. http://www.ccfa.org/media/pdf/ibdsexuality.pdf. Accessed October 9, 2007.

Summers RW. Novel and future medical management of inflammatory bowel disease. *Surg Clin North Am*. 2007;87(3):727-741.

Autoimmune hepatitis. National Institute of Diabetes and Digestive and Kidney Diseases Web site. http://

digestive.niddk.nih.gov/ddiseases/
pubs/autoimmunehep/index.htm.
Published March 2004. Accessed
September 15, 2007.

Primary biliary cirrhosis. National
Institute of Diabetes and Digestive
and Kidney Diseases Web site. http://
digestive.niddk.nih.gov/ddiseases/
pubs/primarybiliarycirrhosis/index.
htm. Published April 2007. Accessed
September 15, 2007.

Gass J, Bethune MT, Siegel M, Spencer
A, Khosla C. Combination enzyme
therapy for gastric digestion of dietary
gluten in patients with celiac sprue.
Gastroenterology. 2007;133:472-480.

RESPIRATORY HEALTH

Lung diseases. Medline Plus Web site.
http://www.nlm.nih.gov/medlineplus/
lungdiseases.html. October 15, 2007.
Accessed July 24, 2007.

Respiratory diseases. US Department
of Health and Human Services
Healthy People Web site. http://www.
healthypeople.gov/data/2010prog/
focus24/default.htm. June 29, 2004.
Accessed July 6, 2007.

Breathing problems. American
Geriatrics Society Web site.
http://www.healthinaging.org/
agingintheknow/chapters_ch_trial.
asp?ch=45. August 5, 2005. Accessed
July 25, 2007.

Pulmonary function tests. Medical
Encyclopedia. Medline Plus Web site.
http://www.nlm.nih.gov/medlineplus/
ency/article/003853.htm. February 27,
2006. Accessed September 4, 2007.

Blood gases. American Association
for Clinical Chemistry Web site.
http://www.labtestsonline.org/
understanding/analytes/blood_gases/
test.html. April 25, 2005. Accessed
July 26, 2007.

Bronchoscopy. Medline Plus Web site.
Medical Encyclopedia. http://www.
nlm.nih.gov/medlineplus/ency/
article/003857.htm. March 2, 2006.
Accessed August 27, 2007.

Chest x-ray. Radiological Society of
North America Web site. http://
www.radiologyinfo.org/en/info.
cfm?pg=chestrad&bhcp=1. August 15,
2006. Accessed July 25, 2007.

Thoracic CT. Medical Encyclopedia.
Medline Plus Web site. http://www.
nlm.nih.gov/medlineplus/ency/
article/003788.htm. July 18, 2007.
Accessed August 27, 2007.

ECG. Medical Encyclopedia. Medline
Plus Web site. http://www.nlm.nih.
gov/medlineplus/ency/article/003868.

htm. July 17, 2006. Accessed August
27, 2007.

The lung center. Cedars-Sinai Web site.
http://www.cedars- sinai.edu/2243.
html?wt.srch=1&cpid=msn&kw=chr
onic+lung+disease. Accessed October
18, 2007.

LAM. National Heart, Lung, and Blood
Institute Web site. http://www.nhlbi.
nih.gov/health/dci/Diseases/lam/
lam_all.html. July 2006. Accessed
December 3, 2007.

Sarcoidosis. National Heart, Lung, and
Blood Institute Web site. http://www.
nhlbi.nih.gov/health/dci/Diseases/
sarc/sar_all.html. June 2006. Accessed
December 3, 2007.

Cystic fibrosis. National Heart, Lung,
and Blood Institute Web site.
http://www.nhlbi.nih.gov/health/dci/
Diseases/cf/cf_all.html. August 2007.
Accessed December 3, 2007.

Pulmonary arterial hypertension.
National Heart, Lung, and Blood
Institute Web site. http://www.nhlbi.
nih.gov/health/dci/Diseases/pah/
pah_all.html. August 2006. Accessed
December 3, 2007.

Asthma. US Food and Drug
Administration Office of Women's
Health Web site. http://www.fda.
gov/womens/getthefacts/asthma.html.
October 2003. Accessed August 17,
2007.

Exercise-induced asthma. National
Jewish Medical and Research Center
Web site. http://www.njc.org/disease-
info/diseases/asthma/living/healthy/
exercise.aspx. July 2002. Accessed
August 10, 2007.

Asthma. National Heart, Lung, and
Blood Institute Web site. http://www.
nhlbi.nih.gov/health/dci/Diseases/
Asthma/Asthma_WhatIs.html. May
2006. Accessed July 24, 2007.

Summary health statistics for US adults:
national health interview survey, 2005.
US Centers for Disease Control and
Prevention Web site. http://www.cdc.
gov/nchs/data/series/sr_10/sr10_232.
pdf. December 2006. Accessed July
26, 2007.

Cydulka RK, Emerman CL, Rowe BH,
et al. Differences between men and
women in reporting of symptoms
during an asthma exacerbation. *Ann
Emerg Med*. 2001;38(2):123-128.

Graham Barr R, Wentowski CC,
Grodstein F, et al. Prospective study
of postmenopausal hormone use and
newly diagnosed asthma and chronic
obstructive pulmonary disease. *Arch
Intern Med*. 2004;164(4):379-386.

NINDS sleep apnea information page.
National Institute of Neurological
Disorders and Stroke Web site.
http://www.ninds.nih.gov/disorders/
sleep_apnea/sleep_apnea.htm. June
22, 2007. Accessed July 26, 2007.

New treatment guidelines for pregnant
women with asthma--monitoring
and managing asthma important for
healthy mother and baby. National
Institutes of Health Web site. http://
www.nhlbi.nih.gov/new/press/05-01-
11.htm. January 11, 2005. Accessed
August 24, 2007.

Asthma: a growing problem for women.
American Academy of Allergy,
Asthma, and Immunology Web
site. http://www.aaaai.org/patients/
advocate/2003/spring/women.stm.
Spring 2003. Accessed August 24,
2007.

Flu season resources. Pregnancy and the
flu. Palo Alto Medical Foundation
Web site. http://www.pamf.org/flu/
preg.html. August 2007. Accessed
October 18, 2007.

COPD. National Heart, Lung, and
Blood Institute Web site. http//www.
nhlbi.nih.gov/health/dci/Diseases/
Copd/Copd_All.html. July 2007.
Accessed July 24, 2007.

Mannino DM, Homa DM, Akinbami
LJ, et al. Chronic Obstructive
pulmonary disease surveillance-
-United States, 1971-2000.
Surveillance Summaries. *MMER*.
2002;51(No. SS-6): 1-16.

Martinez FJ, Curtis JL, Sciurba F, et al.
Sex differences in severe pulmonary
emphysema. *Am J Respira Crit Care
Med*. 2007;176:243-252.

Pulmonary rehabilitation. A team
approach to improving quality of
life. American College of Chest
Physicians Web site. http://www.
chestnet.org/patients/guides/
pulmonary/p2.php. Accessed October
9, 2007.

Women and lung cancer. American
Society of Clinical Oncology Web
site. http://www.plwc.org/portal/site/
PLWC/menuitem. 169f5d85214941
ccfd748f68ee37a01d/vgnextoid=c3b4
41eca8daa010VgnVCM100000ed73
0ad1RCRD. Updated September 16,
2005. Accessed October 18, 2007.

Lung cancer. US Centers for Disease
Control and Prevention Web site.
http://www.cdc.gov/cancer/lung/
statistics. June 25, 2007. Accessed July
26, 2007.

Facts about lung cancer. American Lung
Association Web site. http://www.

lungusa.org/site/pp.asp?c=dvLUK 9O0E&b=35427. November 2006. Accessed October 18, 2007.

Loganathan RS, Stover DE, Shi W, Venkatraman E. Prevalence of COPD in women compared to men around the time of diagnosis of primary lung cancer. *Chest.* 2006;129:1305-1312.

What you need to know about lung cancer. National Cancer Institute Web site. http://www.cancer.gov/cancertopics/wyntk/lung/page6. Updated July 26, 2007. Accessed October 18, 2007.

Sleep apnea. National Heart, Lung, and Blood Institute Web site. http://www.nhlbi.nih.gov/health/dci/Diseases/SleepApnea/SleepApnea_WhatIs.html. Updated February 2006. Accessed December 3, 2007.

Quitting smoking. Why to quit and how to get help. National Cancer Institute Web site. http://www.cancer.gov/cancertopics/factsheet/tobacco/cessation. Updated August 17, 2007. Accessed October 18, 2007.

Healthy living: coping with indoor air pollution. American Association for Respiratory Care Web site. http://www.yourlunghealth.org/healthy_living/pollution/indoor/coping.cfm. Updated May 26, 2005. Accessed October 18, 2007.

Tips to remember: exercise-induced asthma. American Academy of Allergy, Asthma, and Immunology Web site. http://www.aaaai.org/patients/publicedmat/tips/exerciseinducedasthma.stm. Published 2006. Accessed August 28, 2007.

Exercise-induced asthma. Asthma and Allergy Foundation of America Web site. http://www.aafa.org/display.cfm?id=8&sub=17&cont=168. Updated 2005. Accessed August 28, 2007.

ORAL HEALTH

Prevent diabetes problems: keep your teeth and gums healthy. National Institute of Diabetes and Digestive and Kidney Diseases Web site. http://diabetes.niddk.nih.gov/dm/pubs/complications_teeth. Updated January 2007. Accessed December 13, 2007.

Tooth eruption charts. American Dental Association Web site. http://www.ada.org/public/topics/tooth_eruption.asp. Updated March 14, 2007. Accessed December 9, 2007.

What causes a cavity? The Nova Scotia Dental Association Web site. http://www.healthyteeth.org/cavities.cavities.html. Accessed December 8, 2007.

Dental cavities. US National Library of Medicine, MedlinePlus Web site. http:// www.nlm.nih.gov/medlineplus/ency/article/001055.htm. Updated August 8, 2007. Accessed December 13, 2007.

Fluoride facts. American Dental Hygienists' Association Web site. http://www.adha.org/oralhealth/fluoride_facts.htm. Published 2005. Accessed December 11, 2007.

Fluoride. American Academy of Pediatric Dentistry Web site. http://www.aapd.org/publications/brochures/floride.asp. Published 2002. Accessed December 8, 2007.

Fluoride and fluoridation. American Dental Association Web site. http://www.ada.org/public/topics/fluoride/fluoride_article01.asp. Updated March 14, 2005. Accessed December 11, 2007.

Recommendations for using fluoride to prevent and control dental caries in the United States. Centers for Disease Control and Prevention Web site. http://www.cdc.gov/mmwr/preview/mmwrhtml/rr5014a1.htm. Published August 17, 2001. Accessed December 11, 2007.

Clinical guideline on fluoride therapy. National Guideline Clearinghouse Web site. http://www.guideline.gov/summary/summary.aspx?ss=15&doc_id=6272&nbr=4027. Published April 18, 2005. Accessed December 11. 2007.

Skip the fluoride: semiannual treatments pointless for many kids. HealthScout Web site. http://fluoridealert.org/media/2000a.html. Published May 24, 2000. Accessed December 11, 2007.

Sealants. American Dental Association Web site. http://www.ada.org/public/topics/sealants_faq.asp. Updated March 14, 2005. Accessed December 9, 2007.

Dental sealants: frequently asked questions. Centers for Disease Control and Prevention Web site. http://www.cdc.gov/OralHealth/factsheets/sealants-faq.htm. Updated October 4, 2004. Accessed December 9, 2007.

Dental filling options. American Dental Association Web site. http://www.ada.org/public/topics/fillings.asp. Updated March 14, 2005. Accessed February 11, 2008.

Amalgam (silver-colored) fillings: frequently asked questions. American Dental Association Web site. http://www.ada.org/public/topics/fillings_

faq.asp. Updated March 14, 2005. Accessed December 9, 2007.

Questions and answers on dental amalgam. US Food and Drug Administration Web site. http://www.fda.gov/cdrh/consumer/amalgams.html. Updated October 31, 2006. Accessed December 19, 2007.

Studies evaluate health effects of dental amalgam fillings in children. National Institute of Dental and Craniofacial Research Web site. http://www.nidcr.nih.gov/newsandreports/newsreleases/newrelease04182006.htm. Published April 18, 2006. Accessed December 10, 2007.

Periodontal (gum) diseases. American Academy of Periodontology. http://www.perio.org/consumer/2a.html. Updated November 10, 2006. Accessed December 13, 2007.

What you need to know about oral cancer. National Cancer Institute Web site. http://www.cancer.gov/cancertopics/wyntk/oral. Accessed December 13, 2007.

Tobacco and healthy teeth don't mix. Healthy Teeth Web site. http://www.healthyteeth.org/tobacco/index.html. Accessed December 12, 2007.

Oral health: halitosis (bad breath). University of Maryland Medical Center Web site. http://www.umm.edu/oralhealth/halito.htm. Published 2007. Accessed December 11, 2007.

Halitosis (bad breath). Familydoctor.org Web site. http://familydoctor.org/online/famdocen/home/articles/169.printerview.html. Updated June 2007. Accessed December 11, 2007.

Bad breath (halitosis). American Dental Association Web site. http://www.ada.org/public/topics/bad_breath.asp. Published 2002. Accessed December 11, 2007.

Cold sores (mouth herpes). Herpes-Coldsores.com Web site. http://herpes-coldsores.com/cold_sores.htm. Published 2007. Accessed December 13, 2007.

Maddin S. The facts about cold sores. Skin Care Guide Web site. http://www.coldsores.ca/articles/facts_cold_sores.html. Updated August 1, 2007. Accessed December 13, 2007.

Canker sores. US National Library of Medicine, MedlinePlus Web site. http://www.nlm.nih.gov/medlineplus/ency/article/000998.htm. Updated December 18, 2006. Accessed December 13, 2007.

Fever blisters and canker sores. Federal Citizen Information Center Web site.

http://www.pueblo.gsa.gov/cic_text/ health/fever-blister/fever-canker.html. Updated July 1992. Accessed January 31, 2008.

Oropharyngeal candidiasis (OPC, thrush). Centers for Disease Control and Prevention Web site. http://www. cdc.gov/ncidod/dbmd/diseaseinfo/ candidiasis_opc_g.htm. Published October 6, 2005. Accessed December 10, 2007.

Thrush. National Library of Medicine MedlinePlus Web site. http://www. nlm.nih.gov/medlineplus/ency/ article/000626.htm. Updated July 25, 2007. Accessed December 13, 2007.

Dry mouth. National Institute of Dental and Craniofacial Research Web site. http://www.nidcr. nih.gov/HealthInformation/ DiseasesAndConditions/ DryMouthXerostomia/DryMouth. htm. Updated November 15, 2007. Accessed December 11, 2007.

Treating the cause(s) of oral dryness. Drymouth.info Web site. http:// www.drymouth.info/consumer/ TreatmentForDm.asp. Accessed December 11, 2007.

Burning mouth syndrome. National Institute of Dental and Craniofacial Research Web site. http://www. nidcr.nih.gov/HealthInformation/ DiseasesAndConditions/ BurningMouth.htm. Published October 2007. Accessed December 15, 2007.

Taste and smell disorders. US National Library of Medicine, MedlinePlus Web site. http://www. nlm.nih.gov/medlineplus/print/ tasteandsmelldisorders.html. Updated October 25, 2007. Accessed December 11, 2007.

Smell and taste disorders. Massachusetts Eye and Ear Infirmary Web site. http://www.meei.harvard.edu/ patient/tasteandsmell.php. Updated September 16, 2005. Accessed December 11, 2007.

Bromley SM. Smell and taste disorders: A primary care approach. *Am Fam Physician*. American Academy of Family Physicians Web site. http:// www.aafp.org/afp/20000115/427. html. Published January 15, 2000. Accessed December 11, 2007.

Taste disorders. National Institute on Deafness and Other Communication Disorders Web site. http://www. nidcd.nih.gov/health/smelltaste/taste. asp. Updated March 2002. Accessed December 12, 2007.

Smell and taste. American Academy of Otolaryngology—Head and Neck Surgery Web site. http://www.entnet. org/healthinfo/topics/smell_taste.cfm. Published 2007. Accessed December 12, 2007.

Osteonecrosis of the jaw. American Dental Association Web site. http:// www.ada.org/prof/resources/topics/ osteonecrosis.asp. Updated March 14, 2005. Accessed December 11, 2007.

Chemotherapy and your mouth. National Institute of Dental and Craniofacial Research Web site. http://www.nidcr. nih.gov/HealthInformation/ DiseasesAndConditions/ CancerTreatmentAndOralHealth/ ChemotherapyandYourMouth.htm. Updated November 9, 2007. Accessed December 13, 2007.

Oral health and HIV disease. Health Resources and Services Administration Web site. http://hab. hrsa.gov/publications/april2002. htm. Updated April 2002. Accessed December 11, 2007.

Mouth problems and HIV. National Institute of Dental and Craniofacial Research Web site. http://www. nidcr.nih.gov/HealthInformation/ DiseasesAndConditions/HivAids/ MouthProblemsAndHIV.htm. Updated November 9, 2007. Accessed December 13, 2007.

Research presented today provides further evidence on the importance of good oral health in pregnant women. American Academy of Periodontology Web site. http://www. perio.org/consumer/women_risk.htm. Updated March 18, 2005. Accessed December 13, 2007.

Baby steps to a healthy pregnancy and on-time delivery. American Academy of Periodontology Web site. http:// www.perio.org/consumer/pregnancy. htm. Update March 17, 2005. Accessed December 13, 2007.

Pregnancy: frequently asked questions. American Dental Association Web site. http://www.ada.org/public/ topics/pregnancy_faq.asp. Updated March 14, 2005. Accessed December 13, 2007.

X-rays (radiographs). American Dental Association Web site. http://www. ada.org/public/topics/xrays_faq.asp. Updated March 14, 2007. Accessed December 12, 2007.

Pregnancy and x-rays: good or bad? American Pregnancy Association Web site. http://

www.americanpregnancy.org/ pregnancyhealth/xrays.html. Published 2000. Accessed December 11, 2007.

X-rays, pregnancy, and you. US Food and Drug Administration Web site. http://www.fda.gov/cdrh/consumer/ xraypreg.html. Updated May 11, 2001. Accessed December 12, 2007.

Radiation exposure in x-ray examinations. RadiologyInfo Web site. http://www.radiologyinfo. org/en/safety/index.cfm?pg=sfty_ xray&bhcp=1. Published February 2007. Accessed December 12, 2007.

Bobetsis YA, Barros SP, Offenbacher S. Exploring the relationship between periodontal disease and pregnancy complications. *J Am Dent Assoc*. 2006;137(2):7S-13S. http://jada.ada. org/cgi/content/full/137/suppl_2/7S. Accessed January 31, 2008.

Offenbacher S, Boggess KA, Murtha AP, et al. Progressive periodontal disease and risk of very preterm delivery. *Obstet Gynecol*. 2006;107:27-36. http://www.greenjournal.org/ cgi/content/full/107/1/29. Accessed January 31, 2008.

Study finds periodontal care not linked to low birthweight babies. National Institute of Dental and Craniofacial Research Web site. http://www.nidcr.nih.gov/ newsandreports/sciencenewsinbrief/ PeriodontalCareLowBirthWeight Babies.htm. Published February 16, 2006. Accessed January 31, 2008.

Cleaning your teeth and gums (oral hygiene). American Dental Association Web site. http://www. ada.org/public/topics/cleaning.asp. Updated March 14, 2007. Accessed December 12, 2007.

Plaque: what it is and how to get rid of it. National Institute of Dental and Craniofacial Research. http:// www.nidcr.nih.gov/NR/rdonlyres/ DB2E21FD-E8CD-4C1D-B50F-775AC01EF11F/0/Plaque_brochure. pdf. Updated July 1999. Accessed December 14, 2007.

Smoking and sleep top the list of lifestyle factors impacting oral health. American Academy of Periodontology Web site. http:// www.perio.org/consumer/lifestyle-factors.htm. May 15, 2007. Accessed December 13, 2007.

ADA weighs in on school vending machines. American Dental Association Web site. http://www. ada.org/public/media/releases/0202_ release02.asp. Published February 2003. Accessed January 31, 2008.

Dental checkup. The Cleveland Clinic Web site. http://www.clevelandclinic.org/health/health-info/docs/3200/3237.asp?index=11187&src=news. Updated August 4, 2003. Accessed December 13, 2007.

Dental x-rays. US National Library of Medicine, MedlinePlus Web site. http://www.nlm.nih.gov/medlineplus/ency/article/003801.htm. Updated August 8, 2007. Accessed December 12, 2007.

The Pocket Guide to Good Health for Adults. Agency for Healthcare Research and Quality Web site. http://www.ahrq.gov/ppip/adguide/adguide.pdf. Published May 2003. Accessed December 14, 2007.

Antibiotics and your heart. American Dental Association Web site. http://www.ada.org/public/topics/antibiotics.asp. Updated 2007. Accessed December 12, 2007.

Wilson W, Taubert KA, Gewitz M, et al. Prevention of infective endocarditis: Guidelines from the American Heart Association. *J Am Dent Assoc.* 2007; 138:739-760.

Braces and orthodontics. American Dental Association Web site. http://www.ada.org/public/topics/braces_faq.asp. Updated March 14, 2005. Accessed December 12, 2007.

Dental implants: teeth that look and feel like your own. American Academy of Periodontology Web site. http://www.perio.org/consumer/2m.htm. Updated June 11, 2004. Accessed December 12, 2007.

Dental implants. American Association of Oral and Maxillofacial Surgeons Web site. http://www.aaoms.org/dental_impants.php. Published 2005. Accessed December 12, 2007.

Dentures: frequently asked questions. American Dental Association Web site. http://www.ada.org/public/topics/dentures_faq.asp. Updated March 14, 2005. Accessed December 12, 2007.

Tooth whitening treatments. American Dental Association Web site. http://www.ada.org/public/topics/whitening_faq.asp. Updated March 14, 2005. Accessed December 13, 2007.

A fatal fad? Tongue studs cause more problems than chipped teeth. Academy of General Dentistry Web site. http://www.agd.org/public/

oralhealth/defualt.asp?IsssID=321&Topic=O&ArtID=1297. Updated February 2007. Accessed December 12, 2007.

Finding low-cost dental care. National Institute of Dental and Craniofacial Research Web site. http://www.nidcr.nih.gov/HealthInformation/FindingDentalCare/FactSheet.htm. Updated November 19, 2007. Accessed December 12, 2007.

SKIN AND HAIR HEALTH

Skin conditions. US National Library of Medicine Web site. http://www.nlm.nih.gov/medlineplus/skinconditions.html. Reviewed July 27, 2007. Accessed October 24, 2007.

Hair follicle anatomy. US National Library of Medicine. http://www.nlm.nih.gov/medlineplus/ency/imagepages/9703.htm. Updated November 13, 2006. Accessed November 15, 2007.

Casper KA, Mehta BH. Healthy skin for women: a review of common conditions and therapies. *J Am Pharm Assoc.* 2002;42(2):206-215.

Shapiro J. Hair loss in women. *N Engl J Med.* 2007;357:1620-1630.

Peacock L. *Good Hair: Health, Care and Beauty Solutions.* London, England: New Holland Publishers; 2005:12-13;14-19;20-21.

Wood I. *Good Skin: Health, Care and Beauty Solutions.* London, England: New Holland Publishers; 2005:18-22.

Taking care of your skin starts from within. American Academy of Dermatology Web site. http://www.aad.org/media/background/news/skinconditions_2007_11_08_within.html. Posted November 8, 2007. Accessed November 30, 2007.

Taking care of your skin. Nemours Foundation Kidshealth Web site. http://www.kidshealth.org/kid/stay_healthy/body/skin_care.html. Reviewed September 2007. Accessed November 28, 2007.

Skin and aging. National Institute on Aging Web site. http://www.niapublications.org/agepages/skin.asp. Updated December 29, 2005. Accessed October 24, 2007.

What you need to know about skin cancer. National Cancer Institute Web site. http://www.cancer.gov/cancertopics/wyntk/skin. August 1, 2005. Accessed November 15, 2007.

Protect yourself from the sun. Centers for Disease Control and Prevention

Web site. http://www.cdc.gov/cancer/skin/basic_info/howto.htm. Updated May 17, 2007. Accessed December 21, 2007.

Bruise. US National Library of Medicine Web site. http://www.nlm.nih.gov/medlineplus/ency/article/007213.htm. Updated May 17, 2007. Accessed November 15, 2007.

Skin cancer prevention and early detection. American Cancer Society Web site. http://www.cancer.org/docroot/PED/content/ped_7_1_Skin_Cancer_Detection_What_You_Can_Do.asp. Updated June 29, 2007. Accessed November 2, 2007.

Vitamin B6. US National Library of Medicine Web site. http://www.nlm.nih.gov/medlineplus/druginfo/natural/patient-b6.html. Updated September 1 2006. Accessed November 3, 2007.

Skin rashes and other changes. American Academy of Family Physicians Web site. http://familydoctor.org/online/famdocen/home/tools/symptom/545.pinterview.html. Updated 2006. Accessed November 1, 2007.

Tips to remember: allergic skin conditions. American Academy of Allergy, Asthma, and Immunology Web site. http://www.aaaai.org/patients/publicedmat/tips/allergicskinconditions.stm. 2007. Accessed November 30, 2007.

Hair loss and its cause. American Academy of Family Physicians Web site. http://familydoctor.org/online/famdocen/home/men/general/081.html. Updated December 2006. Accessed October 24, 2007.

Waardenburg syndrome. National Institutes on Deafness and Other Communication Disorders Web site. http://www.nidcd.nih.gov/health/hearing/waard.asp. Updated March 1999. Accessed October 23, 2007.

Frequently asked questions about aging skin. American Academy of Dermatology AgingSkinNet Web site. http://www.skincarephysicians.com/agingskinnet/FAQs.html#liver. Accessed December 6, 2007.

Nail diseases. US National Library of Medicine Web site. http://www.nlm.nih.gov/medlineplus/naildiseases.html. Reviewed September 24, 2007. Accessed October 24, 2007.

Kurtzweil P. Fingernails: looking good while playing safe. *FDA Consumer.* 1995;29(10). http://www.fda.gov/

fdac/features/095_nail.html. Accessed
November 16, 2007.

Nail fungus and nail health. American
Academy of Dermatology Web
site. http://www.aad.org/public/
Publications/pamphlets/NailHealth.
htm. 2006. Accessed November 28,
2007.

More than skin deep: unique care
and treatment of skin of color.
American Academy of Dermatology
Web site. http://www.aad.
org/public/News/NewsReleases/
Press+Release+Archives/
Skin+Conditions/Skin+of+Color.htm.
Updated November 2, 2005. Accessed
November 24, 2007.

Kligman AM, Sadiq I, Zhen Y, Crosby
M. Experimental studies on the
nature of sensitive skin. *Skin Res
Technol.* 2006;12(4):217-222.

What is acne? National Institute of
Arthritis and Musculoskeletal and
Skin Diseases Web site. http://www.
niams.nih.gov/Health_Info/Acne/
acne_ff.asp. Reviewed August 2006.
Accessed October 23, 2007.

Isotretinoin (marketed as Accutane)
capsule information. US Food and
Drug Administration Web site.
http://www.fda.gov/cder/drug/
infopage/accutane. Updated October
26, 1007. Accessed October 26, 2007.

Wesley NO, Maibach HI. Racial
(ethnic) differences in skin properties:
the objective data. *Am J Clin Dermatol.*
2003;4(12):843-860.

Cellulite. US National Library of
Medicine Web site. http://www.
nlm.nih.gov/medlineplus/ency/
article/002033.htm. Updated October
13, 2006. Accessed October 4, 2007.

2006 quick facts: cosmetic and
reconstructive plastic surgery trends.
American Society of Plastic Surgeons
Web site. http://www.plasticsurgery.
org/media/statistics/loader.cfm?url=/
commonspot/security/getfile.cfm&
PageID=23625. 2007. Accessed
December 1. 2007.

Striae. US National Library of Medicine
Web site. http://www.nlm.nih.gov/
medlineplus/ency/article/003287.htm.
Updated April 16, 2007. Accessed
October 24, 2007.

Athlete's foot. US National Library of
Medicine Web site. http://www.nlm.
nih.gov/medlineplus/athletesfoot.
html. Reviewed November 11, 2007.
Accessed December 6, 2007.

Burns. US National Library of
Medicine Web site. http://www.
nlm.nih.gov/medlineplus/burns.
html. Reviewed September 15, 2007.
Accessed December 6, 2007.

Cellulitis. US National Library of
Medicine Web site. http://www.
nlm.nih.gov/medlineplus/cellulitis.
html. Reviewed December 5, 2007.
Updated December 6, 2007.

Herpes simplex. American Academy
of Dermatology Web site. http://
www.aad.org/public/Publications/
pamphlets/HerpesSimplex.htm.
Revised 2003. Accessed December
6, 2007.

Corns and calluses. US National Library
of Medicine Web site. http://www.
nlm.nih.gov/medlineplus/ency/
article/001232.htm. Updated May 6,
2007. Accessed December 6, 2007.

Schwartz RA, Janusz CA, Janniger CK.
Seborrheic dermatitis: an overview.
Am Fam Physician. 2006;74(1):125-
130. http://www.aafp.org/
afp/20060701/125.html. Accessed
November 30, 2007.

Nowicki R. [Modern management
of dandruff] [abstract] *Pol Merkur
Lekarski.* 2006;20(115):121-124.

Selenium sulfide. US National Library
of Medicine Web site. http://www.
nlm.nih.gov/medlineplus/druginfo/
medmaster/a682258.html. Revised
April 1, 2000. Accessed October 24,
2007.

What is atopic dermatitis? National
Institute of Arthritis and
Musculoskeletal and Skin Diseases
Web site. http://www.niams.nih.
gov/Health_Info/Atopic_Dermatitis/
atopic_dermatitis_ff.asp. Published
August 2005. Accessed October 23,
2007.

Head lice infestation. Centers for
Disease Control and Prevention Web
site. http://www.cdc.gov/ncidod/dpd/
parasites/lice/factsht_head_lice.htm.
Updated August 19, 2005. Accessed
October 24, 2007.

Impetigo. US National Library of
Medicine Web site. http://www.
nlm.nih.gov/medlineplus/impetigo.
html. Updated November 29, 2007.
Accessed December 6, 2007.

Skin pigmentation disorders.
US National Library of
Medicine Web site. http://www.
nlm.nih.gov/medlineplus/
skinpigmentationdisorders.html.

Reviewed August 6, 2007. Accessed
December 6, 2007.

Questions and answers about psoriasis.
National Institute of Arthritis and
Musculoskeletal and Skin Diseases
Web site. http://www.niams.nih.
gov/Health_Info/Psoriasis/default.
asp. Published May 2003. Accessed
October 23, 2007.

What is rosacea? National Institute of
Arthritis and Musculoskeletal and
Skin Diseases Web site. http://www.
niams.nih.gov/Health_Info/Rosacea/
default.asp. Published March 2005.
Accessed October 23, 2007.

Scabies. US National Library of
Medicine Web site. http://www.nlm.
nih.gov/medlineplus/scabies.html.
Reviewed October 4, 2007. Accessed
December 6, 2007.

Shingles. US National Library of
Medicine Web site. http://www.
nlm.nih.gov/medlineplus/shingles.
html. Reviewed December 5, 2007.
Accessed December 6, 2007.

Centers for Disease Control and
Prevention. Recommended Adult
Immunization Schedule—United
States, October 2007-September
2008. *MMWR.* 2007;56(41):Q1-Q4.

What is vitiligo? National Institute of
Arthritis and Musculoskeletal and
Skin Diseases Web site. http://www.
niams.nih.gov/Health_Info/Vitiligo/
vitiligo_ff.asp. Revised March 2007.
Accessed October 23, 2007.

Haggerty M. Healthy hair is
always in style. *Dermatol Insights.*
2001;2(2):29. http://www.aad.org/
public/conditions/_doc/DIfall01.pdf.
Accessed December 3, 2007.

Hair dye and hair relaxers. US Food
and Drug Administration Web
site. http://www.fda.gov/womens/
getthefacts/hairdye.html. 2005.
Accessed October 24, 2007.

Hair diseases and hair loss. US National
Library of Medicine Web site.
http://www.nlm.nih.gov/medlineplus/
hairdiseasesandhairloss.html.
Reviewed October 4, 2007. Accessed
November 20, 2007.

What is alopecia areata? National
Institute of Arthritis and
Musculoskeletal and Skin Diseases
Web site. http://www.niams.nih.
gov/Health_Info/Alopecia_Areata/
alopecia_areata_ff.pdf. Published July
2005. Accessed October 23, 2007.

Alopecia. National Library of Medicine

Web site. http://www.nlm.nih. gov/medlineplus/tutorials/alopecia/ dm029102.pdf. 2004. Accessed December 2, 2007.

Female pattern baldness. US National Library of Medicine Web site. http:// www.nlm.nih.gov/medlineplus/ency/ article/001173.htm. Updated May 3, 2006. Accessed October 23, 2007.

Hirsutism (excess hair). Academy of Family Physicians Web site. http:// familydoctor.org/online/famdocen/ home/common/hormone/210. html. Updated May 2007. Accessed October 23, 2007.

Polycystic ovary syndrome (PCOS). National Institute of Child Health and Human Development Web site. http://www.nichd.nih.gov/health/ topics/Polycystic_Ovary_Syndrome. cfm. Updated May 25, 2007. Accessed October 25, 2007.

Trichotillomania. US National Library of Medicine Web site. http://www. nlm.nih.gov/medlineplus/ency/ article/001517.htm. Updated May 17, 2006. Accessed October 24, 2007.

Trichotillomania. Mental Health America Web site. http://www. nmha.org/go/information/get-info/ trichotillomania. Updated November 8, 2006. Accessed December 2, 2007.

Cosmetics. US Food and Drug Administration Web site. http:// www.fda.gov/womens/getthefacts/ cosmetics.html. 2006. Accessed October 24, 2007.

Tattoos and permanent makeup. US Food and Drug Administration Web site. http://www.fda.gov/womens/ getthefacts/tattoos.html. August 2005. Accessed October 24, 2007.

Temporary tattoos and henna/mehndi. US Food and Drug Administration Web site. http://www.cfsan.fda. gov/~dms/cos-tatt.html. Updated September 18, 2006. Accessed December 20, 2007.

Removing hair safely. US Food and Drug Administration Web site. http://www.fda.gov/consumer/ updates/hair062707.html. Posted June 27, 2007. Accessed October 24, 2007.

Body piercing. Nemours Foundation Web site. http://www.kidshealth. org/teen/your_body/skin_stuff/body_ piercing_safe.html. Updated May 2006. Accessed October 24, 2007.

NUTRITION

A healthier you. Office of Disease Prevention and Health Promotion, US Department of Health and Human Services Web site. http:// www.health.gov/dietaryguidelines/ dga2005/healthieryou/contents.htm. October 2005. Accessed September 17, 2007.

My pyramid—getting started. Center for Nutrition Policy and Promotion, US Department of Agriculture Web site. http://www.mypyramid.gov/ professionals/index.html. April 2005. Accessed September 20, 2007.

Lactose intolerance. National Institute of Diabetes and Digestive and Kidney Diseases Web site. http://digestive. niddk.nih.gov/ddiseases/pubs/ lactoseintolerance. March 2006. Accessed September 28, 2007.

Learning how to change habits (toolkit no. 14). American Diabetes Association, Diabetes and Cardiovascular Disease Toolkit Web site. http://www.diabetes.org/for-health-professionals-and-scientists/ CVD.jsp. March 2004. Accessed September 23, 2007.

Vitamin and mineral supplement fact sheets. Office of Dietary Supplements, National Institutes of Health. http:// dietary-supplements.info.nih.gov/ Health_Information/Vitamin_and_ Mineral_Supplement_Fact_Sheets. aspx. Updated August 5, 2005. Accessed September 28, 2007.

Health information Web site. Office of Dietary Supplements, National Institutes of Health Web Site. http://www.ods.od.nih.gov/health_ information/health_information.aspx. Accessed September 29, 2007.

Finding your way to a healthier you: based on the dietary guidelines for Americans. US Department of Health and Human Services, US Department of Agriculture Web site. http://www. healthierus.gov/dietaryguidelines. 2005. Accessed September 23, 2007.

How to understand and use the nutrition facts label. US Food and Drug Administration Web site. http://www.cfsan.fda.gov/~dms/ foodlab.html. November 2004. Accessed September 23, 2007.

How much do you eat? Food and Nutrition Service, US Department of Agriculture Web site. http://www. fns.usda.gov/tn/Resources/howmuch. html. November 2006. Accessed December 4, 2007.

Your personal path to health: steps to a healthier you! International Food Information Council Web site. Food Marketing Institute, US Department of Agriculture Center for Nutrition Policy and Promotion. http://www. ific.org/publications/brochures/ pyramidbroch.cfm. June 2006. Accessed September 27, 2007.

Low-calorie, lower-fat alternative foods. National Heart, Lung, and Blood Institute Web site. http://www.nhlbi. nih.gov/health/public/heart/obesity/ lose_wt/lcal_fat.htm. Accessed September 27, 2007.

ClinicalTrials.gov Web Site. National Library of Medicine, National Institutes of Health Web site. http:// clinicaltrials.gov. Accessed October 4, 2007.

FITNESS

U.S. physical activity statistics: state summary data. Centers for Disease Control and Prevention Web site. http://apps.nccd.cdc.gov/ PASurveillance/StateSumResultV.asp. Reviewed March 2, 2007. Accessed September 17, 2007.

Physical activity. In: US Dept of Health and Human Services and US Dept of Agriculture. *Dietary Guidelines for Americans, 2005.* 6th ed. Washington, DC: US Government Printing Office; 2005:19-22. http://www.health.gov/ dietaryguidelines/dga2005/document/ pdf/Chapter4.pdf. Published January 2005. Accessed November 20, 2007.

World Health Organization, International Agency for Research on Cancer. *Weight Control and Physical Activity.* Albany, NY: WHO Press; 2002. *IARC Handbooks of Cancer Prevention*; vol 6.

How active do adults need to be to gain some benefit? Centers for Disease Control and Prevention Web site. http://www.cdc.gov/nccdphp/dnpa/ physical/recommendations/adults. htm. Updated May 22, 2007. Accessed November 20, 2007.

Physical activity terms. Centers for Disease Control and Prevention Web site. http://www.cdc.gov/nccdphp/ dnpa/physical/terms. Updated May 22, 2007. Accessed November 20, 2007.

General physical activities defined by level of intensity. Centers for Disease Control and Prevention Web site. http://www.cdc.gov/nccdphp/dnpa/

physical/pdf/PA_Intensity_table_2_1.pdf. Updated May 22, 2007. Accessed November 21, 2007.

Exercise and physical activity: getting fit for life. National Institute on Aging Web site. http://www.nia.nih.gov/HealthInformation/Publications/exercise.htm. Updated October 16, 2007. Accessed November 23, 2007.

Exercise: a Guide from the National Institute on Aging. Bethesda, MD: National Institute on Aging, US Dept of Health and Human Services. NIH publication 01-4258. http://www.nia.nih.gov/NR/rdonlyres/8E3B798C-237E-469B-A508-94CA4E537D4C/0/NIA_Exercise_Guide407.pdf. Reprinted September 2007. Accessed December 20, 2007.

Wellman N, Weddle D, Sanchez NK, Rosenzweig L. *Eat Better and Move More: A Guidebook for Community Programs.* Administration on Aging Web site. http://www.aoa.gov/youcan/Partners/Documents/07.2YouCanGuidebook_HR.pdf. Published July 2004. Accessed December 4, 2007.

Nelson ME, Rejeski WJ, Blair SN, et al. Physical activity and public health in older adults: recommendation from the American College of Sports Medicine and the American Heart Association. *Circulation.* 2007;116(9):1094-1105. http://circ.ahajournals.org/cgi/reprint/116/9/1094. Published August 28, 2007. Accessed September 22, 2007.

Haskell WL, Lee IM, Pate RR, et al. Physical activity and public health: updated recommendation for adults from the American College of Sports Medicine and the American Heart Association. *Circulation.* 2007;116(9):1081-1093. http://circ.ahajournals.org/cgi/reprint/116/9/1081. Published August 28, 2007. Accessed September 19, 2007.

Faststats: women's health. Centers for Disease Control and Prevention Web site. http://www.cdc.gov/nchs/fastats/womens_health.htm. Reviewed November 20, 2007. Accessed December 20, 2007.

Overweight and obesity. Centers for Disease Control and Prevention Web site. http://www.cdc.gov/nccdphp/dnpa/obesity. Updated May 2007. Accessed September 17, 2007.

Obesity and cancer: questions and answers. National Cancer Institute Web site. http://www.cancer.gov/images/Documents/0ed3af8f-0d8d-41aa-8613-acf53a1070f3/fs3_70.pdf. Reviewed March 16, 2004. Accessed November 29, 2007.

Irwin ML, Yasui Y, Ulrich CM, et al. Effect of exercise on total and intra-abdominal body fat in postmenopausal women: a randomized controlled trial. *JAMA.* 2003;289(3):323-330. http://jama.ama-assn.org/cgi/reprint/289/3/323. Published January 15, 2003. Accessed September 19, 2007.

Your Guide to Lowering Your Cholesterol With TLC. Bethesda, MD: National Heart, Lung, and Blood Institute, US Dept of Health and Human Services. NIH publication 06-5235. http://www.nhlbi.nih.gov/health/public/heart/chol/chol_tlc.pdf. Published December 2005. Accessed April 2, 2007.

Sutton-Tyrrell K, Kuller LH, Edmundowicz D, et al. Usefulness of electron beam tomography to detect progression of coronary and aortic calcium in middle-aged women. *Am J Cardiol.* 2001;87(5):560-564.

Stroke. In: Carlson KJ, Eisenstat SA, Ziporyn T, eds. *The New Harvard Guide to Women's Health.* Cambridge, MA: Harvard University Press; 2004:576-579.

Hu FB, Stampfer MJ, Colditz GA, et al. Physical activity and risk of stroke in women. *JAMA.* 2000;283(22):2961-2967. http://jama.ama-assn.org/cgi/reprint/283/22/2961. Published June 14, 2000. Accessed September 19, 2007.

Gillies CL, Abrams KR, Lambert PC, et al. Pharmacological and lifestyle interventions to prevent or delay type 2 diabetes in people with impaired glucose tolerance: systematic review and meta-analysis. *BMJ.* 2007;334(7588):299. http://www.bmj.com/cgi/reprint/334/7588/299. Published February 10, 2007. Accessed September 19, 2007.

Sigal RJ, Kenny GP, Boulé NG, et al. Effects of aerobic training, resistance training, or both on glycemic control in type 2 diabetes: a randomized trial. *Ann Intern Med.* 2007;147(6):357-369.

Kushi LH, Byers T, Doyle C, et al. American Cancer Society Guidelines on Nutrition and Physical Activity for cancer prevention: reducing the risk of cancer with healthy food choices and physical activity. *CA Cancer J Clin.* 2006;56(5):254-281. http://caonline.amcancersoc.org/cgi/reprint/56/5/254. Published September-October 2006. Accessed September 20, 2007.

McTiernan A, Kooperberg C, White E, et al. Recreational physical activity and the risk of breast cancer in postmenopausal women: the Women's Health Initiative Cohort Study. *JAMA.* 2003;290(10):1331-1336. http://jama.ama-assn.org/cgi/reprint/290/10/1331. Published September 10, 2003. Accessed September 20, 2007.

McTiernan A, Wu L, Chen C, et al. Relation of BMI and physical activity to sex hormones in postmenopausal women. *Obesity (Silver Spring).* 2006;14(9):1662-1677. http://www.obesityresearch.org/cgi/reprint/14/9/1662. Published September 2006. Accessed September 20, 2007.

Doyle C, Kushi LH, Byers T, et al. Nutrition and physical activity during and after cancer treatment: an American Cancer Society guide for informed choices. *CA Cancer J Clin.* 2006;56(6):323-353. http://caonline.amcancersoc.org/cgi/reprint/56/6/323. Published November-December 2006. Accessed September 20, 2007.

Alfano CM, Smith AW, Irwin ML, et al. Physical activity, long-term symptoms, and physical health-related quality of life among breast cancer survivors: a prospective analysis. *J Cancer Survivorship.* 1(2):116-128.

Hutnick NA, Williams NI, Kraemer WJ, et al. Exercise and lymphocyte activation following chemotherapy for breast cancer. *Med Sci Sports Exerc.* 2005;37(11):1827-1835.

Demark-Wahnefried W, Peterson BL, Winer EP, et al. Changes in weight, body composition, and factors influencing energy balance among premenopausal breast cancer patients receiving adjuvant chemotherapy. *J Clin Oncol.* 2001;19(9):2381-2389. http://jco.ascopubs.org/cgi/reprint/19/9/2381. Published May 1, 2001. Accessed September 20, 2007.

Holmes MD, Chen WY, Feskanich D, Kroenke CH, Colditz GA.

Physical activity and survival after breast cancer diagnosis. *JAMA*. 2005;293(20):2479-2486. http://jama.ama-assn.org/cgi/reprint/293/20/2479. Published May 25, 2005. Accessed September 20, 2007.

Meyerhardt JA, Giovannucci EL, Holmes MD, et al. Physical activity and survival after colorectal cancer diagnosis. *J Clin Oncol*. 2006;24(22):3527-3534. http://jco.ascopubs.org/cgi/reprint/24/22/3527. Published August 1, 2006. Accessed September 20, 2007.

Meyerhardt JA, Heseltine D, Niedzwiecki D, et al. Impact of physical activity on cancer recurrence and survival in patients with stage III colon cancer: findings from CALGB 89803. *J Clin Oncol*. 2006;24(22):3535-3541. http://jco.ascopubs.org/cgi/reprint/24/22/3535. Published August 1, 2006. Accessed September 20, 2007.

Stewart KJ, Deregis JR, Turner KL, et al. Fitness, fatness and activity as predictors of bone mineral density in older persons. *J Intern Med*. 2002;252(5):381-388.

Cussler EC, Going SB, Houtkooper LB, et al. Exercise frequency and calcium intake predict 4-year bone changes in postmenopausal women. *Osteoporos Int*. 2005;16(12):2129-2141.

Snow CM, Shaw JM, Winters KM, Witzke KA. Long-term exercise using weighted vests prevents hip bone loss in postmenopausal women. *J Gerontol A Biol Sci Med Sci*. 2000;55(9):M489-491.

Sinaki M, Itoi E, Wahner HW, Wollan P, et al. Stronger back muscles reduce the incidence of vertebral fractures: a prospective 10 year follow-up of postmenopausal women. *Bone*. 2002;30(6):836-841.

Exercise: a healthy habit to start and keep. Familydoctor.org Web site. http://familydoctor.org/online/famdocen/home/healthy/physical/basics/059.html. Updated April 2005. Accessed November 26, 2007.

Manninen P, Riihimaki H, Heliovaara M, Suomalainen O. Physical exercise and risk of severe knee osteoarthritis requiring arthroplasty. *Rheumatology*. 2001;40(4):432-437. http://rheumatology.oxfordjournals.org/cgi/reprint/40/4/432. Published April 2001. Accessed September 20, 2007.

The effects of physical activity on health and disease. In: US Dept of Health and Human Services. Public Health Service. Office of the Surgeon General. *Physical Activity and Health: A Report of the Surgeon General*. Atlanta, GA: Centers for Disease Control and Prevention, US Dept of Health and Human Services; 1996:85-172. http://www.cdc.gov/nccdphp/sgr/pdf/chap4.pdf. Accessed September 28, 2007.

Freeman MP, Helgason C, Hill RA. Selected integrative medicine treatments for depression: considerations for women. *J Am Med Womens Assoc*. 2004;59(3):216-224.

Jorm AF, Christensen H, Griffiths KM, Rodgers B. Effectiveness of complementary and self-help treatments for depression. *Med J Aust*. 2002;176 (suppl):S84-96.

Blumenthal JA, Babyak MA, Doraiswamy PM, et al. Exercise and pharmacotherapy in the treatment of major depressive disorder. *Psychosom Med*. 2007;69(7):587-596.

Blumenthal JA, Babyak MA, Moore KA, et al. Effects of exercise training on older patients with major depression. *Arch Intern Med*. 1999;159(19):2349-2356.

Derby CA, Lasater TM, Vass K, Gonzalez S, Carleton RA. Characteristics of smokers who attempt to quit and of those who recently succeeded. *Am J Prev Med*. 1994;10(6):327-334.

Marcus BH, Albrecht AE, King TK, et al. The efficacy of exercise as an aid for smoking cessation in women: a randomized controlled trial. *Arch Intern Med*. 1999;159(11):1229-1234. http://archinte.ama-assn.org/cgi/reprint/159/11/1229. Published June 14, 1999. Accessed September 21, 2007.

Colcombe S, Kramer AF. Fitness effects on the cognitive function of older adults: a meta-analytic study. *Psychol Sci*. 2003;14(2):125-130.

Kramer AF, Hahn S, Cohen NJ, et al. Ageing, fitness and neurocognitive function. *Nature*. 1999;400(6743):418-419. doi:10.1038/22682.

Weuve J, Kang JH, Manson JE, Breteler MM, Ware JH, Grodstein F. Physical activity, including walking, and cognitive function in older women. *JAMA*. 2004;292(12):1454-1461. http://jama.ama-assn.org/cgi/reprint/292/12/1454. Published

September 22, 2004. Accessed September 21, 2007.

Pereira AC, Huddleston DE, Brickman AM, et al. An in vivo correlate of exercise-induced neurogenesis in the adult dentate gyrus. *Proc Natl Acad Sci U S A*. 2007;104(13):5638-5643. http://www.pnas.org/cgi/reprint/104/13/5638. Published March 27, 2007. Accessed December 20, 2007.

American College of Obstetricians and Gynecologists. *You and Your Baby: Prenatal Care, Labor and Delivery, and Postpartum Care*. Washington, DC: American College of Obstetricians and Gynecologists; 2007. http://www.acog.org/publications/patient_education/ab005.cfm. Published January 2007. Accessed November 29, 2007.

Having a healthy pregnancy. Centers for Disease Control and Prevention Web site. http://www.cdc.gov/ncbddd/bd/abc.htm. Published October 5, 2005. Accessed November 29, 2007.

Yeo S, Steele NM, Chang MC, Leclaire SM, Ronis DL, Hayashi R. Effect of exercise on blood pressure in pregnant women with a high risk of gestational hypertensive disorders. *J Reprod Med*. 2000;45(4):293-298.

Haas JS, Jackson RA, Fuentes-Afflick E, et al. Changes in the health status of women during and after pregnancy. *J Gen Intern Med*. 2005;20(1):45-51. http://www.blackwell-synergy.com/doi/pdf/10.1111/j.1525-1497.2004.40097.x. Published January 2005. Accessed September 21, 2007.

Rooney BL, Schauberger CW. Excess pregnancy weight gain and long-term obesity: one decade later. *Obstet Gynecol*. 2002;100(2):245-252. http://www.greenjournal.org/cgi/reprint/100/2/245. Published August 2002. Accessed September 21, 2007.

American Academy of Family Physicians. Information from your family doctor. Pregnancy: keeping yourself and your baby healthy. *Am Fam Physician*. 2005;71(7):1321-1322. http://www.aafp.org/afp/20050401/1321ph.html. Published April 1, 2005. Accessed September 21, 2007.

Exercise. In: Carlson KJ, Eisenstat SA, Ziporyn T, eds. *The New Harvard Guide to Women's Health*. Cambridge, MA: Harvard University Press; 2004:228-233.

Pregnancy and exercise: what you can do

for a healthy pregnancy. Familydoctor. org Web site. http://familydoctor. org/online/famdocen/home/women/ pregnancy/basics/305.html. Updated October 2005. Accessed September 27, 2007.

Exercise guidelines during pregnancy. American Pregnancy Association Web site. http:// www.americanpregnancy.org/ pregnancyhealth/exerciseguidelines. html. Updated July 2006. Accessed September 27, 2007.

Greendale GA, Gold EB. Lifestyle factors: are they related to vasomotor symptoms and do they modify the effectiveness or side effects of hormone therapy? *Am J Med.* 2005;118 (suppl 12B):148-154.

Tworoger SS, Yasui Y, Vitiello MV, et al. Effects of a yearlong moderate-intensity exercise and a stretching intervention on sleep quality in postmenopausal women. *Sleep.* 2003;26(7):830-836.

Ueda M. A 12-week structured education and exercise program improved climacteric symptoms in middle-aged women. *J Physiol Anthropol Appl Human Sci.* 2004;23(5):143-148. http://www. jstage.jst.go.jp/article/jpa/23/5/143/_ pdf. Published September 2004. Accessed September 21, 2007.

Asbury EA, Chandrruangphen P, Collins P. The importance of continued exercise participation in quality of life and psychological well-being in previously inactive postmenopausal women: a pilot study. *Menopause.* 2006;13(4):561-567.

PAIN

Calderon KL. The influence of gender on the frequency of pain and sedative medicine administered to postoperative patients. *Sex Roles.* 1990;23(11-12):713-725.

Hoffman DE, Tarzian AJ. The girl who cried pain: a bias against women in the treatment of pain. *J Law Med Ethics.* 2001;29(1):13-27.

Holdcroft A, Berkley KJ. Sex and gender differences in pain and its relief. In: McMahon SB, Koltzenburg M, eds. *Wall and Melzack's Textbook of Pain.* 5th ed. Philadelphia, PA: Elsevier/Churchill Livingstone; 2006:1181-1197.

Pain management. In: Carlson KJ, Eisenstat SA, Ziporyn T, eds. *The New Harvard Guide to Women's Health.* Cambridge, MA: Harvard University Press; 2004:441-443.

NIH Guide: New Directions in Pain Research I. National Institutes of Health Web site. http://grants.nih. gov/grants/guide/pa-files/PA-98-102. html. Released September 4, 1998. Accessed May 1, 2007.

CME Module 7: Pain management. Assessing and treating persistent nonmalignant pain: an overview. American Medical Association Web site. http://www.ama-cmeonline. com/pain_mgmt/printversion/ ama_painmgmt_m7.pdf. Published September 2007. Accessed October 22, 2007.

Pain intensity instruments. National Institutes of Health Pain Consortium Web site. http://painconsortium.nih. gov/pain_scales/NumericRatingScale. pdf. Published July 2003. Accessed April 25, 2007.

Bieri D, Reeve RA, Champion GD, Addicoat L, Ziegler JB. The Faces Pain Scale for the self-assessment of the severity of pain experienced by children: development, initial validation, and preliminary investigation for ratio scale properties. *Pain.* 1990;41(2):139-150.

Herr KA, Spratt K, Mobily PR, Richardson G. Pain intensity assessment in older adults: use of experimental pain to compare psychometric properties and usability of selected pain scales with younger adults. *Clin J Pain.* 2004;20(4):207-219.

Vossen HG, van Os J, Hermens H, Lousberg R. Evidence that trait-anxiety and trait-depression differentially moderate cortical processing of pain. *Clin J Pain.* 2006;22(8):725-729.

Pain and depression. The National Pain Foundation Web site. http:// www.nationalpainfoundation. org/MyTreatment/News_ PainAndDepression.asp. Updated August 19, 2005. Accessed May 1, 2007.

Boyles S. Study links depression and pain: pain severity predicts treatment outcome. WebMD Web site. http://www.webmd.com/depression/ news/20040826/study-links-depression-pain. Published August 26, 2004. Accessed May 1, 2007.

Seeman MV, Gordon AS. A pain consultation clinic for women. *CMAJ.* 1998;159(4):382-384. http://www. cmaj.ca/cgi/reprint/159/4/382.

Published August 25, 1998. Accessed May 1, 2007.

Fields HL, Martin JB. Pain: pathophysiology and management. In: Kasper DL, Braunwald E, Fauci AS, Hauser SL, Longo DL, Jameson JL, eds. *Harrison's Principles of Internal Medicine.* 16th ed. New York, NY: McGraw-Hill; 2005:71-76.

Antman EM, Bennett JS, Daugherty A, Furberg C, Roberts H, Taubert KA; American Heart Association. Use of nonsteroidal antiinflammatory drugs: an update for clinicians: a scientific statement from the American Heart Association. *Circulation.* 2007;115(12):1634-1642. http://circ.ahajournals.org/ cgi/reprint/115/12/1634. Published March 27, 2007. Accessed May 1, 2007.

Krantz MJ, Lewkowiez L, Hays H, Woodroffe MA, Robertson AD, Mehler PS. Torsade de pointes associated with very-high-dose methadone. *Ann Intern Med.* 2002;137(6):501-504. http://www. annals.org/cgi/reprint/137/6/501. pdf. Published September 17, 2002. Accessed May 1, 2007.

Summaries for patients. Very high doses of methadone may cause abnormal heart rhythm. *Ann Intern Med.* 2002;137(6):I42. http://www. annals.org/cgi/reprint/137/6/I-42.pdf. Published September 17, 2002. Accessed May 1, 2007.

Bessette M, Jacobson S. Torsade de pointes. Emedicine from WebMD Web site. 2006. http://www. emedicine.com/EMERG/topic596. htm. Updated May 11, 2006. Accessed April 30, 2007.

Ventricular tachycardia. MedlinePlus Medical Encyclopedia Web site. http://www.nlm.nih.gov/medlineplus/ ency/article/000187.htm. Updated May 31, 2006. Accessed April 30, 2007.

Opiate withdrawal. MedlinePlus Medical Encyclopedia Web site. http://www.nlm.nih.gov/medlineplus/ ency/article/000949.htm. Updated May 17, 2006. Accessed April 30, 2007.

Gear RW, Gordon NC, Heller PH, Paul S, Miaskowski C, Levine JD. Gender difference in analgesic response to the kappa-opioid pentazocine. *Neurosci Lett.* 1996;205(3):207-209.

Gear RW, Miaskowski C, Gordon NC, Paul SM, Heller PH, Levine JD.

Kappa-opioids produce significantly greater analgesia in women than in men. *Nat Med.* 1996;2(11):1248-1250.

Gear RW, Miaskowski C, Gordon NC, Paul SM, Heller PH, Levine JD. The kappa opioid nalbuphine produces gender- and dose-dependent analgesia and antianalgesia in patients with postoperative pain. *Pain.* 1999;83(2):339-345.

Baranowski A, Holdcroft A. Gender and pain. In: Holdcroft A, Jaggar SI, eds. *Core Topics in Pain.* Cambridge; New York, NY: Cambridge University Press; 2005:195-200.

Ananthan S. Opioid ligands with mixed mu/delta opioid receptor interactions: an emerging approach to novel analgesics. *AAPS J.* 2006;8(1):E118-125. http://www.aapsj.org/articles/aapsj0801/aapsj080114/aapsj080114.pdf. Published March 10, 2006. Accessed May 1, 2007.

Jensen IB, Bergstrom G, Ljungquist T, Bodin L, Nygren AL. A randomized controlled component analysis of a behavioral medicine rehabilitation program for chronic spinal pain: are the effects dependent on gender? *Pain.* 2001;91(1-2):65-78.

Dahlin L, Lund I, Lundeberg T, Molander C. Vibratory stimulation increase the electro-cutaneous sensory detection and pain thresholds in women but not in men. *BMC Complement Altern Med.* 2006;6:20. http://www.biomedcentral.com/content/pdf/1472-6882-6-20.pdf. Published May 23, 2006. Accessed May 1, 2007.

Marchand S, Arsenault P. Odors modulate pain perception: a gender-specific effect. *Physiol Behav.* 2002;76(2):251-256.

Rehabilitation. In: Beers MH, ed. *The Merck Manual of Medical Information—Second Home Edition, Online Version.* http://www.merck.com/mmhe/sec01/ch007/ch007a.html. Revised July 2007. Accessed October 22, 2007.

Types of alternative medicine. In: Beers MH, ed. *The Merck Manual of Medical Information—Second Home Edition, Online Version.* http://www.merck.com/mmhe/sec25/ch302/ch302c.html?qt=massage&alt=sh. Revised February 2003. Accessed April 27, 2007.

Keefe FJ. Cognitive behavioral therapy for managing pain. *Clin Psychologist.* 1996;49(3):4-5. http://www.apa.org/divisions/div12/rev_est/cbt_pain.html. Accessed May 1, 2007.

The relationship between pain, depression, and mood: an interview with Rollin Gallagher, MD, MPH. The National Pain Foundation Web site. http://www.nationalpainfoundation.org/MyTreatment/News_PainAndDepression_GallagherInterview.asp. Updated November 8, 2006. Accessed May 1, 2007.

Depression and pain: hurting bodies and suffering minds often require the same treatment. *Harvard Mental Health Letter.* http://www.health.harvard.edu/newsweek/Depression_and_pain.htm. Published September 2004. Accessed May 1, 2007.

Pain. Society for Women's Health Research Web site. http://www.womenshealthresearch.org/site/PageServer?pagename=hs_consumerfacts_pain. Updated August 2004. Accessed March 12, 2007.

National Institute of Neurological Disorders and Stroke. *Headache: Hope Through Research.* Bethesda, MD: National Institute of Neurological Disorders and Stroke, US Dept of Health and Human Services; 2007. NIH publication 02-158. http://www.ninds.nih.gov/disorders/headache/detail_headache.htm. Updated October 16, 2007. Accessed October 22, 2007.

Diamond S. Depression and headaches. National Headache Foundation Web site. http://www.headaches.org/consumer/topicsheets/depression.html. Published 2005. Accessed May 1, 2007.

Raskin NH. Headache. In: Kasper DL, Braunwald E, Fauci AS, Hauser SL, Longo DL, Jameson JL, eds. *Harrison's Principles of Internal Medicine.* 16th ed. New York, NY: McGraw-Hill; 2005:85-94.

Migraines. In: Beers MH, ed. *The Merck Manual of Medical Information—Second Home Edition, Online Version.* http://www.merck.com/mmhe/sec06/ch079/ch079c.html?qt=migraines&alt=sh. Revised February 2003. Accessed March 13, 2007.

Dao TT, LeResche L. Gender differences in pain. *J Orofac Pain.* 2000;14(3):169-184.

Bren L. Managing migraines. *FDA Consumer.* http://www.fda.gov/fdac/features/2006/206_migraines.html. Published March-April 2006. Accessed May 2, 2007.

Silberstein SD. Practice parameter: Evidence-based guidelines for migraine headache (an evidence-based review): Report of the Quality Standards Subcommittee of the American Academy of Neurology. *Neurology.* 2000;55(6):754-762. http://www.neurology.org/cgi/content/full/55/6/754. Current as of October 31, 2007. Accessed October 31, 2007.

Hack JB. Oral sumatriptan-induced myocardial infarction. *J Toxicol Clin Toxicol.* 2004;42(3):309-311.

Dodick D, Lipton RB, Martin V, et al; Triptan Cardiovascular Safety Expert Panel. Consensus statement: cardiovascular safety profile of triptans (5-HT agonists) in the acute treatment of migraine. *Headache.* 2004;44(5):414-425.

Treating migraine headaches—the triptans. *Consumer Reports.* http://www.crbestbuydrugs.org/drugreport_DR_triptans.shtml. Updated February 2006. Accessed May 2, 2007.

Beal MF, Hauser SL. Trigeminal neuralgia, Bell's palsy, and other cranial nerve disorders. In: Kasper DL, Braunwald E, Fauci AS, Hauser SL, Longo DL, Jameson JL, eds. *Harrison's Principles of Internal Medicine.* 16th ed. New York, NY: McGraw-Hill; 2005:2434-2435.

Occipital neuralgia information page. National Institute of Neurological Disorders and Stroke Web site. http://www.ninds.nih.gov/disorders/occipitalneuralgia/occipitalneuralgia.htm. Updated March 5, 2007. Accessed March 13, 2007.

Durso SC. Oral manifestations of disease. In: Kasper DL, Braunwald E, Fauci AS, Hauser SL, Longo DL, Jameson JL, eds. *Harrison's Principles of Internal Medicine.* 16th ed. New York, NY: McGraw-Hill; 2005:195.

TMJ disorders. National Institute of Dental and Craniofacial Research Web site. http://www.nidcr.nih.gov/HealthInformation/DiseasesAndConditions/TMDTMJ/TmjDisorders.htm. Revised June 2006. Accessed October 31, 2007.

National Institute of Arthritis and Musculoskeletal and Skin Diseases. *Questions and Answers About Polymyalgia Rheumatica and Giant Cell Arteritis.* Bethesda, MD:

National Institute of Arthritis and Musculoskeletal and Skin Diseases, US Dept of Health and Human Services; 2006. NIH publication 07-4908. http://www.niams.nih.gov/Health_Info/Polymyalgia/default.asp. Revised December 2006. Accessed March 13, 2007.

Psychosomatic disorders. In: Carlson KJ, Eisenstat SA, Ziporyn T, eds. *The New Harvard Guide to Women's Health*. Cambridge, MA: Harvard University Press; 2004:505-506.

Gilliland BC. Fibromyalgia, arthritis associated with systemic disease, and other arthritides. In: Kasper DL, Braunwald E, Fauci AS, Hauser SL, Longo DL, Jameson JL, eds. *Harrison's Principles of Internal Medicine*. 16th ed. New York, NY: McGraw-Hill; 2005:2055-2057.

Fibromyalgia. In: Carlson KJ, Eisenstat SA, Ziporyn T, eds. *The New Harvard Guide to Women's Health*. Cambridge, MA: Harvard University Press; 2004:237-238.

FDA Approves First Drug for Treating Fibromyalgia [press release]. U.S. Food and Drug Administration Web site. http://www.fda.gov/bbs/topics/NEWS/2007/NEW01656.html. Published June 21, 2007. Accessed December 18, 2007.

Straus SE. Chronic fatigue syndrome. In: Kasper DL, Braunwald E, Fauci AS, Hauser SL, Longo DL, Jameson JL, eds. *Harrison's Principles of Internal Medicine*. 16th ed. New York, NY: McGraw-Hill; 2005:2545-2547.

Brandt KD. Osteoarthritis. In: Kasper DL, Braunwald E, Fauci AS, Hauser SL, Longo DL, Jameson JL, eds. *Harrison's Principles of Internal Medicine*. 16th ed. New York, NY: McGraw-Hill; 2005:2036-2045.

Osteoarthritis. MedlinePlus Medical Encyclopedia Web site. http://www.nlm.nih.gov/medlineplus/ency/article/000423.htm. Updated August 6, 2007. Accessed October 23, 2007.

Carpal tunnel syndrome. MedlinePlus Medical Encyclopedia Web site. http://www.nlm.nih.gov/medlineplus/ency/article/000433.htm. Updated September 26, 2006. Accessed April 30, 2007.

Liu CW, Chen TW, Wang MC, Chen CH, Lee CL, Huang MH. Relationship between carpal tunnel syndrome and wrist angle in computer workers. *Kaohsiung J Med Sci*. 2003;19(12):617-623. http://health.elsevier.com/ajws_archive/2003121912A92.pdf. Published December 2003. Accessed May 1, 2007.

National Institute of Neurological Disorders and Stroke. *Carpal Tunnel Syndrome Fact Sheet*. Bethesda, MD: National Institute of Neurological Disorders and Stroke, US Dept of Health and Human Services; 2007. NIH publication 03-4898. http://www.ninds.nih.gov/disorders/carpal_tunnel/detail_carpal_tunnel.htm. Updated February 12, 2007. Accessed March 14, 2007.

Ferry S, Hannaford P, Warskyj M, Lewis M, Croft P. Carpal tunnel syndrome: a nested case-control study of risk factors in women. *Am J Epidemiol*. 2000;151(6):566-574. http://aje.oxfordjournals.org/cgi/reprint/151/6/566. Published Mar 15, 2000. Accessed May 1, 2007.

Solomon DH, Katz JN, Bohn R, Mogun H, Avorn J. Nonoccupational risk factors for carpal tunnel syndrome. *J Gen Intern Med*. 1999;14(5):310-314. http://www.blackwell-synergy.com/doi/pdf/10.1046/j.1525-1497.1999.00340.x. Published May 1999. Accessed May 1, 2007.

Guinsburg R, de Araujo Peres C, Branco de Almeida MF, et al. Differences in pain expression between male and female newborn infants. *Pain*. 2000;85(1-2):127-133.

Mylius V, Kunz M, Schepelmann K, Lautenbacher S. Sex differences in nociceptive withdrawal reflex and pain perception. *Somatosens Mot Res*. 2005;22(3):207-211.

Sarlani E, Greenspan JD. Why look in the brain for answers to temporomandibular disorder pain? *Cells Tissues Organs*. 2005;180(1):69-75.

Rollman GB, Abdel-Shaheed J, Gillespie JM, Jones KS. Does past pain influence current pain: biological and psychosocial models of sex differences. *Eur J Pain*. 2004;8(5):427-433.

LeResche L. Gender, cultural, and environmental aspects of pain. In: Loeser JD, ed. *Bonica's Management of Pain*. 3rd ed. Philadelphia, PA: Lippincott Williams & Wilkins; 2001:191-195.

COMPLEMENTARY AND ALTERNATIVE MEDICINE

Barnes P, Powell-Griner E, McFann K, Nahin R. Complementary and alternative medicine use among adults: United States, 2002. *Adv Data*. 2004;(343):1-20. http://www.cdc.gov/nchs/data/ad/ad343.pdf. Published May 27, 2004. Accessed July 23, 2007.

National Center for Complementary and Alternative Medicine. *What Is CAM?* Bethesda, MD: National Center for Complementary and Alternative Medicine, US Dept of Health and Human Services; 2007. NCCAM publication D347. http://nccam.nih.gov/health/whatiscam. Updated February 2007. Accessed July 10, 2007.

The use of complementary and alternative medicine in the United States. National Center for Complementary and Alternative Medicine Web site. http://nccam.nih.gov/news/camsurvey_fs1.htm. Updated May 2007. Accessed July 10, 2007.

Straus SE. Complementary and alternative medicine. In: Kasper DL, Braunwald E, Fauci AS, Hauser SL, Longo DL, Jameson JL, eds. *Harrison's Principles of Internal Medicine*. 16th ed. New York, NY: McGraw-Hill; 2005:66-70.

Ephedra. National Center for Complementary and Alternative Medicine Web site. http://nccam.nih.gov/health/alerts/ephedra/consumeradvisory.htm. Updated October 2004. Accessed July 10, 2007.

National Center for Complementary and Alternative Medicine. *St. John's Wort*. Bethesda, MD: National Center for Complementary and Alternative Medicine, US Dept of Health and Human Services; 2005. NCCAM publication D269. http://nccam.nih.gov/health/stjohnswort/. Published July 2005. Accessed July 10, 2007.

Hall SD, Wang Z, Huang SM, et al. The interaction between St John's wort and an oral contraceptive. *Clin Pharmacol Ther*. 2003;74(6):525-535.

Natural herbs and vitamins during pregnancy. American Pregnancy Association Web site. http://www.americanpregnancy.org/pregnancyhealth/naturalherbsvitamins.html. Updated March 2007. Accessed July 24, 2007.

Alternative therapies. In: Carlson KJ, Eisenstat SA, Ziporyn T, eds. *The New Harvard Guide to Women's Health*. Cambridge, MA: Harvard University Press; 2004:24-29.

Mahdi JG, Mahdi AJ, Mahdi AJ, Bowen ID. The historical analysis of aspirin discovery, its relation to the willow tree and antiproliferative and anticancer potential. *Cell Prolif.* 2006;39(2):147-155.

National Center for Complementary and Alternative Medicine. *What's in the Bottle? An Introduction to Dietary Supplements*. Bethesda, MD: National Center for Complementary and Alternative Medicine, US Dept of Health and Human Services; 2007. NCCAM publication D191. http://nccam.nih.gov/health/bottle. Updated February 2007. Accessed July 11, 2007.

National Center for Complementary and Alternative Medicine. *Herbal Supplements: Consider Safety, Too*. Bethesda, MD: National Center for Complementary and Alternative Medicine, US Dept of Health and Human Services; 2006. NCCAM publication D190. http://nccam.nih.gov/health/supplement-safety. Updated December 2006. Accessed July 11, 2007.

FDA Issues Dietary Supplements Final Rule. US Food and Drug Administration Web site. http://www.fda.gov/bbs/topics/NEWS/2007/NEW01657.html. Published June 22, 2007. Accessed September 6, 2007.

National Center for Complementary and Alternative Medicine. *Black Cohosh*. Bethesda, MD: National Center for Complementary and Alternative Medicine, US Dept of Health and Human Services; 2005. NCCAM publication D268. http://nccam.nih.gov/health/blackcohosh. Published July 2005. Accessed July 11, 2007.

Natural Standard Research Collaboration. Black cohosh (*Cimicifuga racemosa* [L.] Nutt.). Natural Standard Database Web site. http://www.naturalstandard.com. Published 2007. Accessed June 27, 2007.

Newton KM, Reed SD, LaCroix AZ, Grothaus LC, Ehrlich K, Guiltinan J. Treatment of vasomotor symptoms of menopause with black cohosh, multibotanicals, soy, hormone therapy, or placebo: a randomized trial. *Ann Intern Med.* 2006;145(12):869-

879. http://www.annals.org/cgi/reprint/145/12/869.pdf. Published December 19, 2006. Accessed June 27, 2007.

Uebelhack R, Blohmer JU, Graubaum HJ, Busch R, Gruenwald J, Wernecke KD. Black cohosh and St. John's wort for climacteric complaints: a randomized trial. *Obstet Gynecol.* 2006;107(2 Pt 1):247-255. http://www.greenjournal.org/cgi/reprint/107/2/247. Published February 2006. Accessed June 27, 2007.

Questions and answers about black cohosh and the symptoms of menopause. Office of Dietary Supplements Web site. http://ods.od.nih.gov/factsheets/blackcohosh.asp#h11. Updated June 18, 2006. Accessed September 5, 2007.

National Center for Complementary and Alternative Medicine. *Do CAM Therapies Help Menopausal Symptoms?* Bethesda, MD: National Center for Complementary and Alternative Medicine, US Dept of Health and Human Services; 2005. NCCAM publication D297. http://nccam.nih.gov/health/menopauseandcam. Published November 2005. Accessed July 23, 2007.

Natural medicines in the clinical management of menopausal symptoms. Natural Medicines Comprehensive Database Web site. http://www.naturaldatabase.com/(S(ze4xx42wbf1xwq455iudlzyk))/ce/ceCourse.aspx?s=ND&cs=&st=0&li=0&pc=06%2D30&cec=1&pm=5. Updated October 25, 2007. Accessed October 26, 2007.

Unfer V, Casini ML, Costabile L, Mignosa M, Gerli S, Di Renzo GC. Endometrial effects of long-term treatment with phytoestrogens: a randomized, double-blind, placebo-controlled study. *Fertil Steril.* 2004;82(1):145-148.

The American College of Obstetricians and Gynecologists. Endometrial hyperplasia. Medem Web site. http://www.medem.com/MedLB/article_detaillb.cfm?article_ID=ZZZ7Z2GWQMC&sub_cat=9. Published April 2001. Accessed July 24, 2007.

Jepson RG, Mihaljevic L, Craig J. Cranberries for preventing urinary tract infections. *Cochrane Database Syst Rev.* 2004;(2):CD001321. doi:10.1002/14651858.CD001321.pub3.

Turner RB, Bauer R, Woelkart K, Hulsey TC, Gangemi JD. An evaluation of echinacea angustifolia in experimental rhinovirus infections. *N Engl J Med.* 2005;353(4):341-348. http://content.nejm.org/cgi/reprint/353/4/341.pdf. Published July 28, 2005. Accessed July 24, 2007.

Yale SH, Liu K. Echinacea purpurea therapy for the treatment of the common cold: a randomized, double-blind, placebo-controlled clinical trial. *Arch Intern Med.* 2004;164(11):1237-1241. http://archinte.ama-assn.org/cgi/reprint/164/11/1237. Published June 14, 2004. Accessed July 24, 2007.

Weber W, Taylor JA, Stoep AV, Weiss NS, Standish LJ, Calabrese C. Echinacea purpurea for prevention of upper respiratory tract infections in children. *J Altern Complement Med.* 2005;11(6):1021-1026.

National Center for Complementary and Alternative Medicine. *Ginger*. Bethesda, MD: National Center for Complementary and Alternative Medicine, US Dept of Health and Human Services; 2006. NCCAM publication D320. http://nccam.nih.gov/health/ginger/index.htm. Published May 2006. Accessed July 23, 2007.

Natural Standard Research Collaboration. Ginger (Zingiber officinale Roscoe). MedlinePlus Web site. http://www.nlm.nih.gov/medlineplus/druginfo/natural/patient-ginger.html. Published November 2006. Accessed July 23, 2007.

Vutyavanich T, Kraisarin T, Ruangsri R. Ginger for nausea and vomiting in pregnancy: randomized, double-masked, placebo-controlled trial. *Obstet Gynecol.* 2001;97(4):577-582. http://www.greenjournal.org/cgi/reprint/97/4/577. Published April 2001. Accessed July 23, 2007.

Smith C, Crowther C, Willson K, Hotham N, McMillian V. A randomized controlled trial of ginger to treat nausea and vomiting in pregnancy. *Obstet Gynecol.* 2004;103(4):639-645. http://www.greenjournal.org/cgi/reprint/103/4/639. Published April 2004. Accessed July 23, 2007.

Natural Standard Research Collaboration. Magnet therapy. Natural Standard Database Web site. http://www.naturalstandard.com. Published 2007. Accessed June 27, 2007.

Eccles NK. A randomized, double-blinded, placebo-controlled pilot study to investigate the effectiveness of a static magnet to relieve dysmenorrhea. *J Altern Complement Med.* 2005;11(4):681-687.

National Center for Complementary and Alternative Medicine. *Questions and Answers About Using Magnets to Treat Pain.* Bethesda, MD: National Center for Complementary and Alternative Medicine, US Dept of Health and Human Services; 2004. NCCAM publication D208. http://nccam.nih.gov/health/magnet/magnet.htm. Published May 2004. Accessed July 13, 2007.

Harlow T, Greaves C, White A, Brown L, Hart A, Ernst E. Randomised controlled trial of magnetic bracelets for relieving pain in osteoarthritis of the hip and knee. *BMJ.* 2004;329(7480):1450-1454. http://www.bmj.com/cgi/reprint/329/7480/1450. Published December 18, 2004. Accessed July 13, 2007.

DiNucci EM. Energy healing: a complementary treatment for orthopaedic and other conditions. *Orthop Nurs.* 2005;24(4):259-269.

National Center for Complementary and Alternative Medicine. *Energy Medicine: An Overview.* Bethesda, MD: National Center for Complementary and Alternative Medicine, US Dept of Health and Human Services; 2007. NCCAM publication D235. http://nccam.nih.gov/health/backgrounds/energymed.htm. Updated March 2007. Accessed September 6, 2007.

Weze C, Leathard HL, Stevens G. Evaluation of healing by gentle touch for the treatment of musculoskeletal disorders. *Am J Public Health.* 2004;94(1):50-52. http://www.ajph.org/cgi/reprint/94/1/50. Published January 2004. Accessed July 13, 2007.

Cook CA, Guerrerio JF, Slater VE. Healing touch and quality of life in women receiving radiation treatment for cancer: a randomized controlled trial. *Altern Ther Health Med.* 2004;10(3):34-41.

Gillespie EA, Gillespie BW, Stevens MJ. Painful diabetic neuropathy: impact of an alternative approach. *Diabetes Care.* 2007;30(4):999-1001. http://care.diabetesjournals.org/cgi/reprint/30/4/999. Published April 2007. Accessed July 13, 2007.

Shiflett SC, Nayak S, Bid C, Miles P, Agostinelli S. Effect of Reiki treatments on functional recovery in patients in poststroke rehabilitation: a pilot study. *J Altern Complement Med.* 2002;8(6):755-763.

National Center for Complementary and Alternative Medicine. *About Chiropractic and Its Use in Treating Low-Back Pain.* Bethesda, MD: National Center for Complementary and Alternative Medicine, US Dept of Health and Human Services; 2003. NCCAM publication D196. http://nccam.nih.gov/health/chiropractic/. Published November 2003. Accessed July 16, 2007.

Natural Standard Research Collaboration. Chiropractic. Natural Standard Database Web site. http://www.naturalstandard.com/. Published 2007. Accessed June 27, 2007.

Hoiriis KT, Pfleger B, McDuffie FC, Cotsonis G, Elsangak O, Hinson R, Verzosa GT. A randomized clinical trial comparing chiropractic adjustments to muscle relaxants for subacute low back pain. *J Manipulative Physiol Ther.* 2004;27(6):388-398.

Giles LG, Muller R. Chronic spinal pain syndromes: a clinical pilot trial comparing acupuncture, a nonsteroidal anti-inflammatory drug, and spinal manipulation. *J Manipulative Physiol Ther.* 1999;22(6):376-381.

Ernst E. Chiropractors' use of X-rays. *Br J Radiol.* 1998;71(843):249-251. http://bjr.birjournals.org/cgi/reprint/71/843/249. Published March 1998. Accessed July 16, 2007.

Ammendolia C, Bombardier C, Hogg-Johnson S, Glazier R. Views on radiography use for patients with acute low back pain among chiropractors in an Ontario community. *J Manipulative Physiol Ther.* 2002;25(8):511-520.

Aroua A, Decka I, Robert J, Vader JP, Valley JF. Chiropractor's use of radiography in Switzerland. *J Manipulative Physiol Ther.* 2003;26(1):9-16.

Degenhardt BF. Osteopathic manipulative medicine: optimizing patient-focused health care. American Association of Colleges of Osteopathic Medicine Web site. http://www.aacom.org/om/omm-degenhardt.html. Published December 2000. Accessed September 11, 2007.

Glossary of Osteopathic Terminology Usage Guide. American Association of Colleges of Osteopathic Medicine Web site. http://www.aacom.org/om/Glossary.pdf. Published July 2006. Accessed September 11, 2007.

Natural Standard Research Collaboration. Osteopathy. Natural Standard Database Web site. http://www.naturalstandard.com. Published 2007. Accessed June 27, 2007.

National Center for Complementary and Alternative Medicine. *Massage Therapy as CAM.* Bethesda, MD: National Center for Complementary and Alternative Medicine, US Dept of Health and Human Services; 2006. NCCAM publication D327. http://nccam.nih.gov/health/massage. Published September 2006. Accessed July 17, 2007.

Massage. In: Bauer B, ed. *Mayo Clinic Book of Alternative Medicine: The New Approach to Using the Best of Natural Therapies and Conventional Medicine.* New York, NY: Time Inc. Home Entertainment; 2007:117.

Field T, Diego M, Cullen C, Hernandez-Reif M, Sunshine W, Douglas S. Fibromyalgia pain and substance P decrease and sleep improves after massage therapy. *J Clin Rheumatol.* 2002;8(2):72-76.

Perlman AI, Sabina A, Williams AL, Njike VY, Katz DL. Massage therapy for osteoarthritis of the knee: a randomized controlled trial. *Arch Intern Med.* 2006;166(22):2533-2538.

Field T, Morrow C, Valdeon C, Larson S, Kuhn C, Schanberg S. Massage reduces anxiety in child and adolescent psychiatric patients. *J Am Acad Child Adolesc Psychiatry.* 1992;31(1):125-131.

Field T, Diego MA, Hernandez-Reif M, Deeds O, Figuereido B. Moderate versus light pressure massage therapy leads to greater weight gain in preterm infants. *Infant Behav Dev.* 2006;29(4):574-578.

Hernandez-Reif M, Diego M, Field T. Preterm infants show reduced stress behaviors and activity after 5 days of massage therapy. *Infant Behav Dev.* 2007;30(4):557-561.

Cohen S, Doyle WJ, Turner RB, Alper CM, Skoner DP. Emotional style and susceptibility to the common cold. *Psychosom Med*. 2003;65(4):652-657. http://www.psychosomaticmedicine.org/cgi/reprint/65/4/652. Published July-August 2003. Accessed July 18, 2007.

National Center for Complementary and Alternative Medicine. *Mind-Body Medicine: An Overview*. Bethesda, MD: National Center for Complementary and Alternative Medicine, US Dept of Health and Human Services; 2007. NCCAM publication D239. http://nccam.nih.gov/health/backgrounds/mindbody.htm. Updated May 2007. Accessed July 18, 2007.

Smith A, Nicholson K. Psychosocial factors, respiratory viruses and exacerbation of asthma. *Psychoneuroendocrinology*. 2001;26(4):411-420.

Natural Standard Research Collaboration. Biofeedback. Natural Standard Database Web site. http://www.naturalstandard.com/. Published 2007. Accessed June 27, 2007.

Natural Standard Research Collaboration. Hypnotherapy, hypnosis. Natural Standard Database Web site. http://www.naturalstandard.com/. Published 2007. Accessed June 27, 2007.

Nash MR. The truth and hype of hypnosis. *Sci Am*. 2001;285(1):46-49, 52-55. http://www.sciam.com/article.cfm?chanID=sa006&colID=1&articleID=0008D31F-BD5B-1C6F-84A9809EC588EF21. Published July 2001. Accessed July 18, 2007.

National Center for Complementary and Alternative Medicine. *Whole Medical Systems: An Overview*. Bethesda, MD: National Center for Complementary and Alternative Medicine, US Dept of Health and Human Services; 2007. NCCAM publication D236. http://nccam.nih.gov/health/backgrounds/wholemed.htm. Updated March 2007. Accessed July 19, 2007.

National Center for Complementary and Alternative Medicine. *Acupuncture*. Bethesda, MD: National Center for Complementary and Alternative Medicine, US Dept of Health and Human Services; 2004. NCCAM publication D003. http://nccam.nih.gov/health/acupuncture.

Revised December 2004. Accessed July 19, 2007.

Natural Standard Research Collaboration. Acupuncture. Natural Standard Database Web site. http://www.naturalstandard.com. Published 2007. Accessed June 27, 2007.

Carlsson CP, Axemo P, Bodin A, et al. Manual acupuncture reduces hyperemesis gravidarum: a placebo-controlled, randomized, single-blind, crossover study. *J Pain Symptom Manage*. 2000;20(4):273-279.

Smith CA, Collins CT, Cyna AM, Crowther CA. Complementary and alternative therapies for pain management in labour. *Cochrane Database Syst Rev*. 2006;(4):CD003521. doi:10.1002/14651858.CD003521.pub2.

Bjordal JM, Johnson MI, Lopes-Martins RA, Bogen B, Chow R, Ljunggren AE. Short-term efficacy of physical interventions in osteoarthritic knee pain. A systematic review and meta-analysis of randomised placebo-controlled trials. *BMC Musculoskelet Disord*. 2007;8:51. doi:10.1186/1471-2474-8-51. Published June 22, 2007. Accessed July 19, 2007.

Neri I, Airola G, Contu G, Allais G, Facchinetti F, Benedetto C. Acupuncture plus moxibustion to resolve breech presentation: a randomized controlled study. *J Matern Fetal Neonatal Med*. 2004;15(4):247-252.

Natural Standard Research Collaboration. Traditional Chinese medicine. Natural Standard Database Web site. http://www.naturalstandard.com. Published 2007. Accessed June 27, 2007.

Klayman DL. Qinghaosu (artemisinin): an antimalarial drug from China. *Science*. 1985;228(4703):1049-1055.

Import alert IA6610. U.S. Food and Drug Administration Web site. http://www.fda.gov/ora/fiars/ora_import_ia6610.html. Updated August 16, 2005. Accessed September 5, 2007.

Natural Standard Research Collaboration. Ayurveda. Natural Standard Database Web site. http://www.naturalstandard.com. Published 2007. Accessed June 27, 2007.

Fiala M, Liu PT, Espinosa-Jeffrey A, et al. Innate immunity and transcription of MGAT-III and Toll-like receptors in Alzheimer's disease patients are

improved by bisdemethoxycurcumin. *Proc Natl Acad Sci U S A*. 2007;104(31):12849-12854.

Saper RB, Kales SN, Paquin J, et al. Heavy metal content of ayurvedic herbal medicine products. *JAMA*. 2004;292(23):2868-2873. http://jama.ama-assn.org/cgi/reprint/292/23/2868. Published December 15, 2004. Accessed June 27, 2007.

National Center for Complementary and Alternative Medicine. *Questions and Answers About Homeopathy*. Bethesda, MD: National Center for Complementary and Alternative Medicine, US Dept of Health and Human Services; 2003. NCCAM publication D183. http://nccam.nih.gov/health/homeopathy. Published April 2003. Accessed July 20, 2007.

Natural Standard Research Collaboration. Homeopathy. Natural Standard Database Web site. http://www.naturalstandard.com. Published 2007. Accessed June 27, 2007.

National Center for Complementary and Alternative Medicine. *Selecting a CAM Practitioner*. Bethesda, MD: National Center for Complementary and Alternative Medicine, US Dept of Health and Human Services; 2007. NCCAM publication D346. http://nccam.nih.gov/health/practitioner/index.htm. Updated February 2007. Accessed July 20, 2007. ■

Index